41: *Afro-American Poets Since 1955,* edited by Trudier Harris and Thadious M. Davis (1985)

42: *American Writers for Children Before 1900,* edited by Glenn E. Estes (1985)

43: *American Newspaper Journalists, 1690-1872,* edited by Perry J. Ashley (1986)

44: *American Screenwriters,* Second Series, edited by Randall Clark, Robert E. Morsberger, and Stephen O. Lesser (1986)

45: *American Poets, 1880-1945,* First Series, edited by Peter Quartermain (1986)

46: *American Literary Publishing Houses, 1900-1980: Trade and Paperback,* edited by Peter Dzwonkoski (1986)

47: *American Historians, 1866-1912,* edited by Clyde N. Wilson (1986)

48: *American Poets, 1880-1945,* Second Series, edited by Peter Quartermain (1986)

49: *American Literary Publishing Houses, 1638-1899,* 2 parts, edited by Peter Dzwonkoski (1986)

50: *Afro-American Writers Before the Harlem Renaissance,* edited by Trudier Harris (1986)

51: *Afro-American Writers from the Harlem Renaissance to 1940,* edited by Trudier Harris (1987)

52: *American Writers for Children Since 1960: Fiction,* edited by Glenn E. Estes (1986)

53: *Canadian Writers Since 1960,* First Series, edited by W. H. New (1986)

54: *American Poets, 1880-1945,* Third Series, 2 parts, edited by Peter Quartermain (1987)

55: *Victorian Prose Writers Before 1867,* edited by William B. Thesing (1987)

56: *German Fiction Writers, 1914-1945,* edited by James Hardin (1987)

57: *Victorian Prose Writers After 1867,* edited by William B. Thesing (1987)

58: *Jacobean and Caroline Dramatists,* edited by Fredson Bowers (1987)

59: *American Literary Critics and Scholars, 1800-1850,* edited by John W. Rathbun and Monica M. Grecu (1987)

60: *Canadian Writers Since 1960,* Second Series, edited by W. H. New (1987)

61: *American Writers for Children Since 1960: Poets, Illustrators, and Nonfiction Authors,* edited by Glenn E. Estes (1987)

62: *Elizabethan Dramatists,* edited by Fredson Bowers (1987)

63: *Modern American Critics, 1920-1955,* edited by Gregory S. Jay (1988)

64: *American Literary Critics and Scholars, 1850-1880,* edited by John W. Rathbun and Monica M. Grecu (1988)

65: *French Novelists, 1900-1930,* edited by Catharine Savage Brosman (1988)

66: *German Fiction Writers, 1885-1913,* 2 parts, edited by James Hardin (1988)

67: *Modern American Critics Since 1955,* edited by Gregory S. Jay (1988)

68: *Canadian Writers, 1920-1959,* First Series, edited by W. H. New (1988)

69: *Contemporary German Fiction Writers,* First Series, edited by Wolfgang D. Elfe and James Hardin (1988)

70: *British Mystery Writers, 1860-1919,* edited by Bernard Benstock and Thomas F. Staley (1988)

71: *American Literary Critics and Scholars, 1880-1900,* edited by John W. Rathbun and Monica M. Grecu (1988)

72: *French Novelists, 1930-1960,* edited by Catharine Savage Brosman (1988)

73: *American Magazine Journalists, 1741-1850,* edited by Sam G. Riley (1988)

74: *American Short-Story Writers Before 1880,* edited by Bobby Ellen Kimbel, with the assistance of William E. Grant (1988)

75: *Contemporary German Fiction Writers,* Second Series, edited by Wolfgang D. Elfe and James Hardin (1988)

76: *Afro-American Writers, 1940-1955,* edited by Trudier Harris (1988)

77: *British Mystery Writers, 1920-1939,* edited by Bernard Benstock and Thomas F. Staley (1988)

78: *American Short-Story Writers, 1880-1910,* edited by Bobby Ellen Kimbel, with the assistance of William E. Grant (1988)

79: *American Magazine Journalists, 1850-1900,* edited by Sam G. Riley (1988)

(Continued on back endsheets)

Dictionary of Literary Biography • Volume One Hundred Thirteen

Modern Latin-American Fiction Writers
First Series

Dictionary of Literary Biography • Volume One Hundred Thirteen

Modern Latin-American Fiction Writers
First Series

Edited by
William Luis
Vanderbilt University

A Bruccoli Clark Layman Book
Gale Research Inc.
Detroit, London

Advisory Board for
DICTIONARY OF LITERARY BIOGRAPHY

John Baker
William Cagle
Jane Christensen
Patrick O'Connor
Peter S. Prescott

Matthew J. Bruccoli and Richard Layman, *Editorial Directors*
C. E. Frazer Clark, Jr., *Managing Editor*

Printed in the United States of America

Published simultaneously in the United Kingdom
by Gale Research International Limited
(An affiliated company of Gale Research Inc.)

The paper used in this publication meets the minimum requirements
of American National Standard for Information Sciences—Permanence
Paper for Printed Library Materials, ANSI Z39.48-1984.

Copyright © 1992
Gale Research Inc.
835 Penobscot Bldg.
Detroit, MI 48226-4094

Library of Congress Catalog Card Number 92-43479
ISBN 0-8103-7590-7

For our children, Gabriel, Stephanie, Tammy, Christopher, Amanda, Esmeralda, Sterling, Skye, and Neelam

Contents

Plan of the Series..ix
Foreword..xi
Acknowledgments...xvii
Ciro Alegría (1909-1967)...3
   Antonio Cornejo-Polar
Jorge Amado (1912-)..9
   Bobby J. Chamberlain
José María Arguedas (1911-1969).......................18
   Sara Castro-Klaren
Juan José Arreola (1918-)..................................29
   Sara Poot-Herrera
Miguel Angel Asturias (1899-1974)....................37
   Diane E. Marting
Mario Benedetti (1920-)....................................48
   María Rosa Olivera-Williams
Adolfo Bioy Casares (1914-)..............................55
   Suzanne Jill Levine
Jorge Luis Borges (1899-1986).............................67
   Alberto Julián Pérez
Guillermo Cabrera Infante (1929-)...................82
   Ardis L. Nelson
Alejo Carpentier (1904-1980)..............................96
   Roberto Gonzalez-Echevarría
Rosario Castellanos (1925-1974)........................110
   Willy O. Muñoz
Julio Cortázar (1914-1984)..................................119
   Steven Boldy
José Donoso (1924-)..134
   Ricardo Gutiérrez Mouat
Carlos Fuentes (1928-).....................................150
   Lanin A. Gyurko
Gabriel García Marquez (1928-)......................168
   Alicia Borinsky

José Lezama Lima (1910-1976).........................183
   J. C. Ulloa and L. A. de Ulloa
Clarice Lispector (1925-1977)............................197
   Earl E. Fitz
René Marqués (1919-1979)................................205
   Aníbal González
Manuel Mejía Vallejo (1923-)..........................214
   Raymond Leslie Williams
Juan Carlos Onetti (1909-)..............................221
   Zunilda Gertel
Elena Poniatowska (1933-)..............................228
   María-Inés Lagos
Manuel Puig (1932-1990)...................................235
   Lucille Kerr
Augusto Roa Bastos (1917-)............................248
   Randolph D. Pope
João Guimarães Rosa (1908-1967)....................256
   Jon S. Vincent
Juan Rulfo (1918-1986).......................................270
   Luis Leal
Severo Sarduy (1937-)......................................278
   Julia A. Kushigian
Lygia Fagundes Telles (1924-).......................287
   Fábio Lucas
Arturo Uslar Pietri (1906-)..............................293
   Jorge Marbán
Luisa Valenzuela (1938-)..................................303
   Leticia Reyes-Tatinclaux
Manuel Zapata Olivella (1920-)......................313
   Antonio Olliz Boyd
Checklist of Further Readings..........................323
Contributors...329
Cumulative Index..333

Plan of the Series

...Almost the most prodigious asset of a country, and perhaps its most precious possession, is its native literary product—when that product is fine and noble and enduring.

Mark Twain*

The advisory board, the editors, and the publisher of the *Dictionary of Literary Biography* are joined in endorsing Mark Twain's declaration. The literature of a nation provides an inexhaustible resource of permanent worth. We intend to make literature and its creators better understood and more accessible to students and the reading public, while satisfying the standards of teachers and scholars.

To meet these requirements, *literary biography* has been construed in terms of the author's achievement. The most important thing about a writer is his writing. Accordingly, the entries in *DLB* are career biographies, tracing the development of the author's canon and the evolution of his reputation.

The purpose of *DLB* is not only to provide reliable information in a convenient format but also to place the figures in the larger perspective of literary history and to offer appraisals of their accomplishments by qualified scholars.

The publication plan for *DLB* resulted from two years of preparation. The project was proposed to Bruccoli Clark by Frederick G. Ruffner, president of the Gale Research Company, in November 1975. After specimen entries were prepared and typeset, an advisory board was formed to refine the entry format and develop the series rationale. In meetings held during 1976, the publisher, series editors, and advisory board approved the scheme for a comprehensive biographical dictionary of persons who contributed to North American literature. Editorial work on the first volume began in January 1977, and it was published in 1978. In order to make *DLB* more than a reference tool and to compile volumes that individually have claim to status as literary history, it was decided to organize volumes by topic, period, or genre. Each of these freestanding volumes provides a biographical-bibliographical guide and overview for a particular area of literature. We are convinced that this organization—as opposed to a single alphabet method—constitutes a valuable innovation in the presentation of reference material. The volume plan necessarily requires many decisions for the placement and treatment of authors who might properly be included in two or three volumes. In some instances a major figure will be included in separate volumes, but with different entries emphasizing the aspect of his career appropriate to each volume. Ernest Hemingway, for example, is represented in *American Writers in Paris, 1920-1939* by an entry focusing on his expatriate apprenticeship; he is also in *American Novelists, 1910-1945* with an entry surveying his entire career. Each volume includes a cumulative index of subject authors and articles. Comprehensive indexes to the entire series are planned.

With volume ten in 1982 it was decided to enlarge the scope of *DLB*. By the end of 1986 twenty-one volumes treating British literature had been published, and volumes for Commonwealth and Modern European literature were in progress. The series has been further augmented by the *DLB Yearbooks* (since 1981) which update published entries and add new entries to keep the *DLB* current with contemporary activity. There have also been *DLB Documentary Series* volumes which provide biographical and critical source materials for figures whose work is judged to have particular interest for students. One of these companion volumes is entirely devoted to Tennessee Williams.

We define literature as the *intellectual commerce of a nation:* not merely as belles lettres but as that ample and complex process by which ideas are generated, shaped, and transmitted. *DLB* entries are not limited to "creative writers" but extend to other figures who in their time and in their way influenced the mind of a people. Thus the series encompasses historians, journalists, publishers, and screenwriters. By this means readers of *DLB* may be aided to perceive litera-

---

*From an unpublished section of Mark Twain's autobiography, copyright © by the Mark Twain Company.

Plan of the Series

ture not as cult scripture in the keeping of intellectual high priests but firmly positioned at the center of a nation's life.

DLB includes the major writers appropriate to each volume and those standing in the ranks immediately behind them. Scholarly and critical counsel has been sought in deciding which minor figures to include and how full their entries should be. Wherever possible, useful references are made to figures who do not warrant separate entries.

Each *DLB* volume has a volume editor responsible for planning the volume, selecting the figures for inclusion, and assigning the entries. Volume editors are also responsible for preparing, where appropriate, appendices surveying the major periodicals and literary and intellectual movements for their volumes, as well as lists of further readings. Work on the series as a whole is coordinated at the Bruccoli Clark Layman editorial center in Columbia, South Carolina, where the editorial staff is responsible for accuracy of the published volumes.

One feature that distinguishes *DLB* is the illustration policy—its concern with the iconography of literature. Just as an author is influenced by his surroundings, so is the reader's understanding of the author enhanced by a knowledge of his environment. Therefore *DLB* volumes include not only drawings, paintings, and photographs of authors, often depicting them at various stages in their careers, but also illustrations of their families and places where they lived. Title pages are regularly reproduced in facsimile along with dust jackets for modern authors. The dust jackets are a special feature of *DLB* because they often document better than anything else the way in which an author's work was perceived in its own time. Specimens of the writers' manuscripts are included when feasible.

Samuel Johnson rightly decreed that "The chief glory of every people arises from its authors." The purpose of the *Dictionary of Literary Biography* is to compile literary history in the surest way available to us—by accurate and comprehensive treatment of the lives and work of those who contributed to it.

The *DLB* Advisory Board

Foreword

The so-called Boom period of the 1960s and the publication of novels such as Carlos Fuentes's *La muerte de Artemio Cruz* (1962; translated as *The Death of Artemio Cruz*, 1964), Julio Cortázar's *Rayuela* (1963; translated as *Hopscotch*, 1966), Mario Vargas Llosa's *La casa verde* (1966; translated as *The Green House*, 1968), Guillermo Cabrera Infante's *Tres tristes tigres* (1967; translated as *Three Trapped Tigers*, 1971), and Gabriel García Márquez's *Cien años de soledad* (1967; translated as *One Hundred Years of Solitude*, 1970) gave Latin-American literature instant recognition worldwide. These works reflect the local conditions of Mexico, Argentina, Peru, Cuba, and Colombia, respectively, but also narrate themes which transcend the concerns of any one country and appeal to a broader audience. The literary and commercial explosion of the 1960s produced works which were exciting, creative, innovative, imaginative, and proposed theoretical issues which pertained to reading, writing, spoken language, translation, history, and fiction. Many of these works contained their own criticism and even suggested to the reader how they should be read. In some cases these works attempted to question the boundaries between the canny and the uncanny, the real and the magic, reality and dreams, and to reveal that knowledge is not a given but is subject to interpretation.

Works such as *Cien años de soledad* and *Rayuela*, but also Alejo Carpentier's *El siglo de las luces* (1962; translated as *Explosion in a Cathedral*, 1963), Jorge Luis Borges's *Ficciones* (1944; translated as *Fictions*, 1965), and João Guimarães Rosa's *Grande Sertão: Veredas* (1956; translated as *The Devil to Pay in the Backlands*, 1963) have received international recognition and have been widely read outside of the authors' country of origin. However, these works come from an earlier Latin-American literary tradition which can be traced to the moment Europeans began to write about the New World and, more precisely, when the inhabitants of the New World began to document their own experiences. In Spanish-American narrative the trend may have begun in the early nineteenth century, when authors set the groundwork for a truly modern literature. For example, in Cuba the antislavery narrative focused on the plight of the slaves who worked in sugar plantations, and it described the coming together of the white and black races. In Argentina literary works took the form of a protest against Juan Manuel Rosas, the governor and dictator of the province of Buenos Aires.

Some may argue that Spanish-American literature began toward the end of the nineteenth century with Rubén Darío and *modernismo*, a literary current of and for a minority concerned with beauty and elegance; or perhaps some decades later with the regionist novel, a narrative about rural themes which attempted to define national identity. In Brazil the trend may have been initiated with modernism, corresponding to the avant-garde of Spanish-American literature and adapting European ideas to a Brazilian context. Although the origin may be in dispute, there is no doubt but that these and other literary movements gave Latin-American literature a character of its own. Modern Latin-American fiction can be traced to the 1940s and the end of World War II, a period which showed a dramatic increase in the number of foundational writers and works.

World War II had a strong influence in Latin America, where political leaders and writers were struggling with the question of national identity. Indeed, the war is associated with a moment of liminality and linked to a series of events which signaled the beginning of a new order that stimulated the development of Latin-American literature. Some years before the war, Spain had experienced a civil war which turned the country into an international battleground. The success of Gen. Francisco Franco's army over the Republicans forced many Spanish intellectuals into exile, many to Spanish America, where they continued their literary production and contributed to an increasing dialogue among writers living in Spanish-speaking countries. In the prewar years Franklin Delano Roosevelt's Good Neighbor Policy helped to improve relations between Latin America and the United States and created a mechanism of political and economic support. By 1942 nine countries had declared war on the Axis nations and nine others had severed relations with them; by 1945 the declaration of war was unanimous. As a result of World War II the Allied forces established their predominance in the West and looked to Latin America to spread and strengthen their influence, continuing a trend which dates to the early nineteenth century and the U.S. proclamation of the Monroe Doctrine. During the war period, Latin America experienced an unprecedented period of growth, contributing foodstuffs and strategic materials to the Allied victory. The revenues created by the increased industrial production had a marked effect on the development of literature and culture in Latin America. In addition, the war forced North American and European countries to recognize the existence of other countries and cultures, including those of Latin America, as independent nations but also subject to external influences, in some cases compromising the sovereignty of nations such as Haiti, the Dominican Republic, and Guatemala.

A rediscovery of Latin America began after Fidel Castro's Rebel Army marched into Havana in January 1959, and during the Cuban Missile Crisis three years later. Events related to Castro placed Cuba and Latin America in the middle of a major international confrontation between the United States and the Soviet Union which many feared would launch the third and final world war. The Cuban threat of the 1960s, and the Nicaraguan one of the 1980s, to establish a Communist stronghold and spread revolutions throughout Latin America, continued to focus world attention on countries south of the U.S. border. With Cuba the Soviet Union had finally obtained a sphere of influence ninety miles from the U.S. mainland. As a reaction to the popularity of the Castro government, President John F. Kennedy initiated his Alliance for Progress, an economic aid program to support culture and education in Latin America and prevent the spread of Communism. This program also contributed to the development of contemporary Latin-American literature generally, and the Boom novel specifically.

In the postwar period Latin-American literature underwent significant development. In 1945 the Chilean poet Gabriela Mistral became the first Latin-American writer to receive the Nobel Prize for Literature, thus bringing international recognition to her and her regional counterparts. The World War II period also marked the Brazilian postmodernist Generation of 1945, when, as a result of the war, authors returned to writing about international issues. But in Spanish America, modern fiction is a reaction to the regionalist novel, which included works such as José Eustasio Rivera's *La vorágine* (1924; translated as *The Vortex*, 1935), Rómulo Gallegos's *Doña Bárbara* (1929; translated 1931), Alejo Carpentier's *¡Ecue Yamba-O!* (1933; Praised Be the Lord!), and Ricardo Güiraldes's *Don Segundo Sombra* (1926; translated as *Don Segundo Sombra: Shadow on the Pampas*, 1935). These novels described the countryside, a symbol of the nation, and local scenes, characters, and traditions. The emergence of contemporary narrative was accompanied by a thematic shift from the country to the city, which soon became the center of national identity.

After Mistral other Latin-American writers have received the highest international acclaim. Recipients of the Nobel Prize for Literature include the Guatemalan Miguel Angel Asturias in 1967, the Chilean Pablo Neruda in 1971, the Colombian Gabriel García Márquez in 1982, and the Mexican Octavio Paz in 1990. In the contemporary period, master writers such as Jorge Luis Borges, Alejo Carpentier, and João Guimarães Rosa, to name three of the most influential, have been strong contenders for the same prize and have received numerous awards. The number of distinguished narrators has increased in the 1960s with writers of the Boom and in the 1970s with those of the post-Boom. Some critics even argue that with the works of the younger writers we are on the threshold of a new style of Latin-American narrative.

The 1930s and, in particular, the 1940s and the postwar period became the training ground for the master Latin-American writers, including Jorge Amado, Alejo Carpentier, José María Arguedas, Juan Rulfo, and João Guimarães Rosa, but they went on to produce even more important works in the 1950s and 1960s. A sample of the publication history of some of these writers will help to illustrate this idea. For example, Carpentier published his first novel *¡Ecue Yamba-O!* in 1933, but he wrote his best short stories in the 1940s. He published "Oficio de tinieblas" (Morning Office) and "Viaje a la semilla" (translated as "Journey Back to the Source") in 1944 and "Los fugitivos" (The Fugitives) in 1946. He later gathered "Viaje a la semilla" and other stories in *Guerra del tiempo* (1958; translated as *War of Time*, 1970) in 1958. Like Carpentier, Rulfo published his first short stories—"La vida no es muy seria sus cosas" (Life

Is Not Very Serious About Things), "Nos han dado la tierra" (translated as "They Gave Us the Land," 1965), and "Macario" (translated 1959) —in 1945. The latter two were included in *El llano en llamas* (translated as *The Burning Plain and Other Stories*, 1967) in 1953. Unlike the previous two writers, Guimarães Rosa wrote his first collection of stories, *Sagarana* (translated as *Sagarana: A Cycle of Stories*, 1966) in 1937, but he rewrote it five years later and, like Carpentier and Rulfo with their stories, published it in the same decade, in 1946; it was received with tremendous enthusiasm. Arguedas wrote and published his initial collection of short stories, *Agua* (Water), in 1935, but it was *Yawar fiesta* (translated as *Yawar Fiesta*, 1985) published in 1941 which confirmed his importance as a writer.

Although these and other writers began to produce foundational works in the decade of the 1940s, it was in the 1950s that they wrote and published narratives that heavily contributed to their national and international reputation. Carpentier and Rulfo wrote important novels in the 1950s: Carpentier published *Los pasos perdidos* (translated as *The Lost Steps*, 1956), in 1953, and *El acoso* (translated as *Manhunt*, 1959), in 1956, and Rulfo his *Pedro Páramo* (translated 1959), in 1955. Other writers followed a similar pattern: Guimarães Rosa with *Grande Sertão: Veredas* in 1956, and Arguedas with *Los ríos profundos* (translated as *Deep Rivers*, 1978) in 1958.

Still other writers had established themselves in the 1940s, including Clarice Lispector who published her first novel *Perto do Coração Selvagem* (Close to the Savage Heart) in 1944, followed by *Lustre* (The Chandelier) in 1946, and *A Cidade Sitiada* (The Besieged City) in 1949; Adolfo Bioy Casares did the same with his novels *La invención de Morel* (translated as *The Invention of Morel and Other Stories*, 1965) in 1940 and *Plan de evasión* (translated as *A Plan for Escape*, 1975) in 1945, and the collection of stories *La trama celeste* (The Celestial Plot) in 1948; Juan José Arreola published his collection *Varia invención* (Various Inventions) in 1949; and Lygia Fagundes Telles presented her stories in *Praia Viva* (Living Beach) in 1944 and *O Cacto Vermelho* (The Red Cactus) in 1949.

Many of the foundational writers received their literary training in Europe, where they witnessed and participated in new literary and artistic trends. For example, in Paris writers such as Alejo Carpentier, Miguel Angel Asturias, and Arturo Uslar Pietri had the opportunity to meet intellectuals including André Breton, Paul Valéry, Salvador Dalí, and many others. Upon the return to their native country, these Spanish American authors brought back current literary trends as illustrated by the books they read and the works they wrote.

With the rise of the United States as a military power, the North American continent became the subject of world attention. The war increased contact between the United States and Latin America and writers south of the Rio Grande became familiar with and were influenced by their North American counterparts in general and John Dos Passos, Ernest Hemingway, and William Faulkner, in particular. Latin-American writers read these and other writers in the original and in translation; some even translated the works themselves. This was the case of Lino Novás Calvo, who wrote articles about Faulkner and Hemingway and translated the latter's *The Old Man and the Sea* in the Cuban magazine *Bohemia* in 1955. Novás Calvo's translation of Hemingway's novel is a subject of discussion between Silvestre and Arcenio Cué, two characters in Cabrera Infante's *Tres tristes tigres*, who feel that the translation is not a good one, pointing out that Novás Calvo made three serious mistakes on the first page and turned African lions into marine lions on the last one. These characters are more complimentary about how Novás Calvo adopted the writing styles associated with Faulkner and Hemingway to Cuban Spanish. Dos Passos's name also appears in Cabrera Infante's novel.

The Cuban Revolution also contributed to the contact between European and Latin-American writers, and most importantly among Latin-American writers themselves. Early in the revolution intellectuals throughout the world, and in particular Latin America, identified with the goals of the Fidel Castro government. They were invited to visit Cuba by the newspaper *Revolución*, edited by Carlos Franqui, and by its weekly literary supplement, *Lunes de Revolución*, edited by Cabrera Infante. After the closing of *Lunes*, in November 1961, Casa de las Américas with its journal of the same name, became the center of culture in Latin America. Writers such as Carlos Fuentes, José Donoso, Gabriel García Márquez, and Julio Cortázar, among many others, traveled to Cuba, met other Latin-American writers and read each others' works.

Since Latin-American literature is an expansive subject which covers various genres and literary and historical periods, from its inception in the fifteenth century to the present, and in order to differentiate this work from other anthologies compiled on the same subject, I chose to focus the project on the narrative of the contemporary period: Modern Latin-American fiction has opened the door to all of Latin-American literature. Although no one will dispute the talents of Pablo Neruda and Octavio Paz, to name two of the most important poets, it was the novel which became an instant literary success. In addition, the contemporary novel has inspired critics to rediscover other writers, genres, and periods.

Even though the time frame used for the volume is 1945, the end of World War II, and gathers writers whose major narrative production flourished after that period, I have also broken with it in order to include writers like Borges, a monumental figure in Latin-American literature. Borges's early contribution falls outside of our time frame since *Historia universal de la infamia* (translated as *A Universal History of Infamy*, 1972) and *Ficciones* were published in 1935 and 1944, respectively; but he and his narrative have had a profound and lasting effect on subsequent generations of Latin-American writers. Modern Latin-American literature and criticism is not possible without the presence of Borges.

Modern Latin-American Fiction Writers gathers major figures in Latin-American narrative; giants such as Jorge Luis Borges, Alejo Carpentier, José Lezama Lima, and João Guimarães Rosa; and popular writers, such as Julio Cortázar, Carlos Fuentes, Gabriel García Márquez, and Lygia Faguntes Telles. Some are controversial, like Jorge Amado; others are prolific like Mario Benedetti; and still others have left their mark with one or two works, like Juan Rulfo. Even though *Modern Latin-American Fiction Writers* is dedicated to the prose works of the authors contained herein, many of them have not limited their literary production to the novel and the short story. Some have also distinguished themselves in the essay, theater, and poetry; for example, the works of Cortázar and Benedetti, in the essay, René Marqués in the theater, and Borges and Lezama Lima, in poetry, are well known. Therefore, references about the authors' work in other genres have been included.

Modern Latin-American Fiction Writers consists of two series. This first one contains entries on important early authors, many of whom set the foundation for Latin-American narrative. The second will emphasize younger writers, those who are leaving or will leave a lasting mark in literature. The essay on Mario Vargas Llosa, which was to appear in volume one, will be included in volume two, along with essays about authors such as Luis Rafael Sánchez, Miguel Barnet, Elena Garro, Osman Lins, Isabel Allende, Lino Novás Calvo, Claribel Alegría, and Nélida Piñón. With additional time and resources we could have added other renowned figures which already have earned a permanent place in Latin-American criticism, such as Antonio Benítez-Rojo, Dalton Trevesars, and Antonio Ferreira Filho.

Linguistically and geographically speaking, Latin-American literature should gather works and authors from the Francophone and Anglophone Caribbean, the Netherland Antilles, and Creole areas. However, in these two volumes, Latin-American literature reflects the Latin-American component of academic departments in the United States as represented by departments of Foreign Languages, Modern Languages, Romance Languages, and Spanish and Portuguese. In this study, Latin-American literature is defined by the Spanish-speaking Caribbean, Central, and South America, and Portuguese-speaking Brazil.

Modern Latin-American fiction is rich and varied. Some themes transcend national boundaries, while others are prevalent in one particular country. Of the former, literature of the fantastic is found in the works of Borges and Bioy Casares; magical or marvelous realism in those of García Márquez and Carpentier; the testimonial or documentary in those of Elena Poniatowska; history in Fuentes, García Márquez, Uslar Pietri, and Carpentier; the erotic in Amado, Manuel Puig, and Lezama Lima; homosexuality in Lezama Lima and Puig; blacks and their concerns in Carpentier, Amado, and Manuel Zapata Olivella; Amerindian issues in Arguedas, Ciro Alegría, Rosario Castellanos, and Asturias; revolutions in Carpentier and Fuentes; tyranny in Carpentier, Uslar Pietri, García Márquez, Augusto Roa Bastos, and Asturias; social criticism in Asturias, Amado, and Benedetti; the bourgeoisie in Donoso and Puig; rural concerns in Manuel Mejía Vallejo, Guimarães Rosa, and Rulfo; themes related to music in Carpentier; autobiography in Lispector and Cabrera Infante; women's issues in Luisa Valenzuela, Castellanos, Lispector, and Poniatowska; the use of language in Cabrera Infante, Lispector, and Guimarães Rosa; and concern for structure in Cabrera Infante, Cortázar, and García Márquez. The themes associated mainly with one country include the Cuban neobaroque in Carpentier, Lezama Lima, and Severo Sarduy; Peruvian Amerindians issues in Arguedas and Alegría; the Mexican Revolution in Fuentes and Poniatowska; Amerindians in Mexican society in Castellanos and Poniatowaska; colonialism in Puerto Rico in Marqués; social criticism in Uruguay in Benedetti; and Brazilian rural concerns in Guimarães Rosa and Amado.

Contemporary literary concerns and events have influenced the selection of authors for these *DLB* volumes. With the breakthrough of the literature of the post-Boom period, which has profited from the publicity attained by the writers of the Boom, much needed attention has been brought to women and black writers and themes. The presence of women and black authors in Latin-American literature is not new. Women have been represented by writers such as Sor Juana Inés de la Cruz in the eighteenth century, the Condesa de Merlín in the nineteenth, and María Luisa Bombal in the twentieth; black writers such as Juan Francisco Manzano and Martín Morúa Delgado wrote in the nineteenth century, and Adalberto Ortiz and Nelson Estupiñán Bass in the twentieth. However, black and women writers were generally excluded from any commentary about the Boom period, but they have become more prevalent in recent decades and are receiving recognition which has been long overdue. With these concerns in mind, we have selected a representative sample of women and black writers and critics. As younger writers continue to establish themselves, I am certain that future volumes will gather entries on authors such as Ana Lydia Vega and Carlos Guillermo Wilson. In the not-so-distant future I also expect to see more importance given to Latin-American writers living, writing, and publishing in the United States and writing in Spanish or English or in both languages. I am referring to Chicano, Nuyorican, and Cuban American writers to name three of the most prominent national minorities.

I would like to thank Professors Roberto González Echevarría, Raúl Bueno, Diane E. Marting, Jon S. Vincent, and Ana Luisa de Andrade for providing valuable suggestions regarding the writers contained herein and to Jack Turner, in-house editor for the *DLB*, for making editing this project an enjoyable task.

—*William Luis*

Acknowledgments

This book was produced by Bruccoli Clark Layman, Inc. Karen L. Rood is senior editor for the *Dictionary of Literary Biography* series. Jack Turner was the in-house editor.

Production coordinator is James W. Hipp. Projects manager is Charles D. Brower. Photography editors are Edward Scott and Timothy C. Lundy. Layout and graphics supervisor is Penney L. Haughton. Copyediting supervisor is Bill Adams. Typesetting supervisor is Kathleen M. Flanagan. Systems manager is George F. Dodge. The production staff includes Rowena Betts, Teresa Chaney, Patricia Coate, Gail Crouch, Margaret McGinty Cureton, Bonita Dingle, Mary Scott Dye, Sarah A. Estes, Robert Fowler, Cynthia Hallman, Ellen McCracken, Kathy Lawler Merlette, John Myrick, Pamela D. Norton, Jean W. Ross, Laurrè Sinckler-Reeder, Thomasina Singleton, Maxine K. Smalls, and Betsy L. Weinberg.

Walter W. Ross and Henry Cuningham did library research. They were assisted by the following librarians at the Thomas Cooper Library of the University of South Carolina: Jens Holley and the interlibrary-loan staff; reference librarians Gwen Baxter, Daniel Boice, Faye Chadwell, Jo Cottingham, Cathy Eckman, Rhonda Felder, Gary Geer, Jackie Kinder, Laurie Preston, Jean Rhyne, Carol Tobin, Virginia Weathers, and Connie Widney; circulation-department head Thomas Marcil; and acquisitions-searching supervisor David Haggard.

Dictionary of Literary Biography • Volume One Hundred Thirteen

Modern Latin-American Fiction Writers
First Series

Dictionary of Literary Biography

Ciro Alegría
(4 November 1909 - 17 February 1967)

Antonio Cornejo-Polar
University of Pittsburgh
(Translated by Virginia Lawreck)

BOOKS: *La serpiente de oro* (Santiago, Chile: Nascimento, 1935); translated by Harriet de Onís as *The Golden Serpent* (New York & Toronto: Farrar & Rinehart, 1943);
Los perros hambrientos (Santiago, Chile: Zig-zag, 1939; revised, 1942);
El mundo es ancho y ajeno (Santiago, Chile: Ercilla, 1941); translated by de Onís as *Broad and Alien Is the World* (New York: Farrar & Rinehart, 1941; London: Merlin, 1941);
Duelo de caballeros (Lima: Populibros Peruanos, 1963);
Gabriela Mistral íntima, edited by Dora Varona (Lima: Universo, 1968);
La ofrenda de piedra (Lima: Universo, 1968);
Panki y el guerrero (Lima: Colección Infantil, 1968);
Sueño y verdad de América (Lima: Universo, 1969);
Lázaro (Buenos Aires: Losada, 1973);
La revolución cubana: Un testimonio personal (Lima: Peisa, 1973);
Mucha suerte con harto palo: Memorias, edited by Varona (Buenos Aires: Losada, 1976);
7 cuentos quirománticos (Lima: Varona, 1978);
El dilema de Krause: Penitenciaría de Lima (Lima: Varona, 1979);
El sol de los jaguares (Lima: Varona, 1979);
Fábulas y leyendas americanas (Madrid: Espasa-Calpe, 1982);
Relatos (Madrid: Alianza, 1983).
Collection: *Novelas completas* (Madrid: Aguilar, 1959).

Ciro Alegría is unanimously considered Peru's first classic novelist, but he is much more. Writing during the decline of the regionalist novel, he consistently transformed and enriched the tradition of this literary movement in Spanish America while maintaining a sense of realism. He tried his best to ascertain and express the true identity of the peasant classes in his novels, short stories, and fables.

Ciro Alegría Bazan was born on 4 November 1909 at the Quilca hacienda in Sartimbaba, a remote district of Huamachuco, a province located in the northern mountains of Peru. His family belonged to the old-world, Andean landed class, which includes precisely the exploitive caciques whom the so-called indigenist novelists, including Alegría, never tire of censuring. Yet, according to him, his grandfather and father distinguished themselves from other landowners by managing their haciendas in a kindly, patriarchal fashion—a marked contrast to their neighbors, who did indeed exploit inhumanely the Indian and mestizo peasants. Alegría lived nearly all of his childhood and part of his adolescence at Quilca, on other family haciendas (mostly in Marcabal Grande), or in small pueblos (like Cajabamba) in the same region. These experiences marked Alegría's life and work.

In 1917, while living and studying in Trujillo, Alegría had the fortune to be a student of the great poet César Vallejo. In 1924 Alegría began his studies for his *bachillerato*, and in 1930, degree in hand, he entered the Universidad Nacional. In this same year, he joined the Aprista party, a Marxist movement, and founded the first Aprista group in Trujillo. Although by this time Alegría had published a few poems and numerous newspaper articles, these were primarily years of political rather than literary activity.

In 1931 the leaders of the Aprista party gave Alegría the responsibility of organizing a revolutionary movement in Cajamarca. This rebellion failed, and the future novelist was jailed and tortured. In 1932 Alegría was freed by Aprista revolutionaries and actively participated in the development of another rebellion. The repression that followed resulted in Alegría's incarceration in the Panóptico in Lima. In 1933 Alegría was again freed, this time by an amnesty decree by the Oscar Benavides government. Within a year, Alegría was conspiring in yet other subversive acts, for which he was deported to Chile, where he resided from 1934 to 1941 and where he wrote the best of his work: the novels *La serpiente de oro* (1935; translated as *The Golden Serpent*, 1943), *Los perros hambrientos* (The Hungry Dogs, 1939), and *El mundo es ancho y ajeno* (1941; translated as *Broad and Alien Is the World*, 1941).

These three novels represent the culmination of the Indianist movement. The central paradox of Indianism consists of an individual foreign to the indigenous culture who attempts to interpret that world and to restore indigenous rights through literature. The use of the classic European genre, the novel, often resulted in inflammatory, libelous tales and offensive parables abounding in archetypes of the noble savage. This, however, is not the case with Alegría, who, because of his own provincial background, was more than a mere witness of this world. Alegría remembered the limitless admiration with which he listened to the stories and happenings told to him by the Indian and mestizo farmers who worked on his family's haciendas. It is from them he claims that he learned the art of narration.

During his years in exile in Chile, Alegría transformed the world of his childhood into the subject of his three novels, and he broke with the traditional limits of the genre. In fact *La serpiente de oro*, which received first prize in the Chilean publishing house Nascimento's literary contest, has neither the setting nor the characters typical of the Indianist novel. Calemar, a remote pueblo on the banks of the Marañón River, becomes the epicenter in which the *cholos* ("civilized" natives) of the Marañón reach epic status in the novel, not as standard bearers that move the reader to pity or protest but rather as simple, steadfast inhabitants of an unusual, harsh world. Despite these variants, *La serpiente de oro* is organized according to the specifications of the Indianist novel: the banks of the Marañón are equally unfamiliar as the peaks of the sierra, and the culture of those who dwell in the region, though somewhat more civilized, is just as different from the modern, urban world as that of the Quechua. Alegría explains the origin of his novel: "[While I was] dedicated to the search of a theme, the memory of a *cholo* named Manuel Baca came to me, and the dramatic occurrence that he related one night ... [while] chewing coconut [and] sitting in the foyer of the cabana where we took a break from our farmwork."

Alegría does not appear to give much importance to the distinction between direct access to reality, by means of his own experience, and indirect access to reality, by means of the previous experience of others. In the end each constitutes a single, individual experience. In order to elaborate his tales, Alegría relies to a great extent on what he knew, not personally, but vicariously, through popular stories and legends.

It is important to note the function of this original literary influence, most certainly transformed in his novels, since it is there that one finds indications of the concrete nature of the relationship between the author and the world his literature aims to reveal. If, on the one hand, the popular sources, with their own particular cultural codification, mediate between the world they represent and the narrator, then, as folklore, which expresses the conscience of the men who inhabit that world, they give the narrator the option of assuming, in varying degrees, that interior perspective, and they draw him nearer to his point of reference. This dual and unstable condition of distancing and rapprochement of the novelist to the world he narrates is the central contradiction of the Indianist novel, and it defines the dilemma this literary tendency raises.

At first Alegría tried to resolve this dilemma through the use of an undefined "we" in the narrative; however, it was soon clear that this was an artificial perspective, and he opted for situating himself behind, or within, the psychology of one of his characters. This approach also soon proved artificial, and Alegría finally settled on the traditional third-person-omniscient narrator for *Los perros hambrientos* and his later novels. Of course, his indecision was a result of the inexperience of a writer who had only recently begun his literary work; however, it is above all an expression of the conflicts in the literature itself, which is caught between the archaism of its frame of reference and the modernity of its creator and the context in which he acts.

In the strictest of terms *La serpiente de oro* lacks plot. The novel is not organized in a sequence of related events that leads to a narrative climax but rather is built upon a series of relatively independent "frames," some of which could be considered short stories unto themselves. The ultimate goal of the combination of these scenes is the creation of a prism through which the reader can experience the world being represented.

In *La serpiente de oro*, as in many other works of the period, the most important theme is that which examines the relationship of man and nature. However, contrary to the usual problem presented in this type of novel, Alegría attempts to invert the old Latin-American theme of nature as an overwhelming force and emphasizes the heroism of those who confront this power and conquer it. Along these lines Alegría's first novel represents a transformation of the bases of regionalist literature. Nature is represented by the Marañón river, which is as much an agent of destruction and death as it is the giver of life and happiness. Man appears symbolized by the ferrymen of the Marañón, who have the daily task of confronting the river and triumphing over its violence. In this fight is the typical tragic background: the river is the face of destiny, and man, as he challenges her, is asserting his free will. Perhaps for this reason the humble *cholos* acquire a heroic dimension that goes beyond simple courage: their story becomes universal.

Faced with this unique world, Alegría does not hide his admiration. In this place distanced from civilization he finds values and forms of social relationships more honorable than those of modern society. One might say that, while distressed in his exile, by attempting to forge an image of a lost nation, Alegría regained his faith and was able to question the unjust and powerful social order that had expelled him.

Los perros hambrientos, a novel situated in the inhospitable high plateau of Peru, is Alegría's second major work. Alegría again takes up the theme of the ties between humankind and nature; however, the terms of the relationship differ. More than the bravery and daring admired in *La serpiente de oro*, the stoicism and solidarity with which the natives confront nature's hostile challenge, in order to make more bearable their misfortune, are the focus. In contrast, *Los perros hambrientos* is a less optimistic portrayal of the struggle with nature.

Although organized in the conventional manner (it is narrated in the third person and recounts a sequence of events), this novel continues to maintain the partially fragmented system seen in *La serpiente de oro*, relying on the presentation of various autonomous scenes. Therefore, as in the first novel, some chapters can be read as independent anecdotes that relate popular legends and myths. In this sense the most significant episode of the novel is the one that has as its protagonists the Celedonians—an episode that occupies nearly three chapters. It is somewhat surprising that such emphasis is given to this group of bandits, who have apparently no connection to the tale as a whole.

Los perros hambrientos is centered on a natural occurrence that frequently plagues the An-

Dust jacket for Alegría's 1941 novel, which exposes the barbarity of the modern world while demonstrating the truly civilized nature of the native Quechua culture

dean Sierra: a drought. Initially the tale evokes a picture of bucolic, country life in normal times; however, beginning with the second chapter, the panorama changes dramatically. The drought begins to affect each of the components of this modest but happy world. The vegetation disappears, the animals get thin, and an atrocious hunger weakens the Indians. Some try to move to the cities, where they find even more misfortune; others stubbornly try to maintain their ties to the now-infertile land; and many, most of all the children, die of hunger. With this tragic plot, Alegría constructs an opposition between a cruel reality and a painful affirmation of life.

In this second novel, he observes how collective misfortune destroys customs and institutions that are in one way or another superficial and unjust. In this way, for example, the relationship between the natives and the landowners enters a period of crisis, then shows its exploitative roots, and eventually deteriorates. In the same way, on another level, certain religious behaviors are destroyed, and the natives lose their faith in supernatural powers, which once strongly influenced their way of life. As an antithesis to this process of deterioration, the novel affirms the preservation of the most elemental social values: love, pity, and solidarity among sufferers.

On the level of plot, the narrator emphasizes the most characteristic indigenist theme: the Franciscan relationship between humans and animals. The natives of the Sierra love their animals with unsurpassable tenderness. The novel examines with subtlety and lyricism this fraternal bond between the natives and their animals, especially their dogs. As a result the identification between man and beast that underlies the title of the novel is in no way a form of humiliation, for it is not the animalization of man that prevails but rather the humanization of the animal, expressed in an almost magical context. It is not until the last chapter that the rains return and the Andean world is resuscitated with a shudder of new life. What has been told in lineal succession adopts a temporary circularity, which reflects the indigenous concept of time: history begins again; only now the survivors have confirmed the efficacy of those values essential to their culture, above all their fraternal solidarity, which enables them to preserve their dignity and conquer death.

El mundo es ancho y ajeno is Alegría's most ambitious and successful novel, in the eyes of both the critics and the public. This work, which maintains several of the thematic and formal elements of his former works, demonstrates the creative skill developed by the author throughout his career as a novelist. There is evidence in this novel of a new narrative style and a new conception of the world that he wishes to portray. The most notable of the changes stems from the emergence of a new sense of history. In the earlier books, the narrator essentially develops an interpretation of time as the reiteration of a primordial act, such as the intersection of free will and destiny in the first novel, or the circular movement of time in the second. In contrast, Alegría's third book presents a more rationalistic concept of historic flux, with its chain of causes and effects, and favors a linear presentation of the sequence of events.

The incorporation of this concept of history is linked to the obvious growth in social constraints. In fact the history traced is that of the social process of the indigenous community and its relationship to the Andean landowners as well as the dominant groups of the national society. The perspective cannot avoid underscoring the injustice faced by the indigenous population nor the exploitive nature of their oppressors, who stripped them of their fertile lands and, in the end, tried to annihilate them. In all of indigenous thought, the community is the representative symbol of perfect social organization, which some interpret as the last trace of primitive communism and others imagine as the native seed of a future socialist society. Alegría, no doubt, held the latter opinion.

From this point of view, *El mundo es ancho y ajeno* should be read as fervent praise of community life. Tomás G. Escajadillo has demonstrated that this novel is structured around a reiterated affirmation: that the community is the only sociocultural arena in which the indigenous peasant can live with dignity. This may be undeniably true, but the significance of Alegría's novel transcends this specific reference and affirms that the community system is intrinsically superior to any other form of social organization: episodes tell of the difficult life of the *comuneros* who find themselves forced to abandon their community and who find only humiliation and exploitation on the haciendas, the jungle plantations, or in the cities. The novel proposes, although indirectly, an axiological comparison between distinct ways of life, and in all of these cases the community holds the most distinguished values.

Paradoxically *El mundo es ancho y ajeno* narrates the history of the crisis and the final destruction of Rumi, a community of emblematic character. First the community loses its best lands because of a fraudulent court decision that gives the landowner confidence that he can rely on the complicity of the central and regional powers. When the inhabitants of Rumi later violently oppose a second pillage, which would mean the destruction of the community, they are bloodily defeated by the repressive forces of the state.

In the beginning an old man, Rosendo Maqui, a personification of the ancestral wisdom of the Quechua (and one of the great figures in the Latin-American novel) is the community's leader. Later, when Maqui fails in his attempt to defend the community and dies, he is replaced by Benito Castro, a young mestizo who represents a modernizing opposition and proposes armed resistance against the abuses of the caciques. In the final battle Castro dies with many other *comuneros*. With this plot, Alegría examines the conflict between the preservation of the old in-

Alegría in Havana, 1953 (photograph by Sueiro)

digenous values, incarnate in Maqui, and the new ideal, represented by Castro. In the end, the narrator chooses, not without difficulty, the second option. If it wants to survive, the indigenous community will have to change. This change, however, as Alegría proposes it, does not imply a cancellation of the community's most profound cultural identity.

The modern alternative also fails, although it is implied that Rumi could have triumphed if it had organized its resistance and promoted a general indigenous subversion. Nonetheless in the final conflict the community has only precarious allies and defeat is inevitable. As a result Rumi disappears. From this vantage point the novel is a painful eulogy that bids a nostalgic farewell to a humane way of life, at the same time angrily recognizing that personal interests and the interests of those in power have taken over Peru. One cannot help but note a sense of pessimism in the tragic history of Rumi: with the disappearance of the exemplary community there cannot be another exactly like it. "This is the reality," Alegría implies.

With regard to the social process of the indigenous communities, Alegría's commentary is accurate. In 1941 the communities were in decline and many were about to disappear or had disintegrated completely. In addition the novel not only reveals and denounces a real situation but also postulates something of an exercise in social consciousness for a nation. The eulogy for a disappearing social order is transformed into a violent opposition of the dominant social system and an appeal for the old values. Within this context Alegría is the first Indianist novelist to defend consistently the indigenous community, not only with regard to political, social, and economic factors but also, in an often more intense way, with his attention to ethnic and cultural viewpoints. *El mundo es ancho y ajeno* expresses again and again a fervent and sustained admiration for the Quechua culture. Alegría makes explicit his admiration by contrasting "the wisdom of the ignorant" with the crudeness and egotism of the dominant classes. Hence this novel produces a significant inversion of the old stereotype created by Domingo Faustino Sarmiento, which interprets the Spanish-American saga as a conflict between civilization and barbarism, a theme that prevails in many regionalist novels, such as Romulo Gallegos's *Doña Bárbara* (1929). Although Alegría does not break with the traditional structure of the regionalist novel, he modifies the underlying meaning of its terms: the true civilization, with respect to man and nature, is that of the native, while barbarism corresponds to the false emissaries of a Western culture degraded by self-interest and incapable of comprehending the legitimacy and greatness of other forms of conscience.

From 1941 to 1949 Alegría lived in New York, where he worked for the Prensa news agency and taught literature at Columbia University. In 1949 he moved to Puerto Rico to become a professor at the national university. After 1953 he lived in Havana and wrote full time, though he traveled widely to give lectures and readings.

In addition to his three novels, Alegría published *Duelo de caballeros* (Duel of Gentlemen, 1963), a collection of nine short pieces, seven of which the author refers to as stories, with two less-fictional pieces that he calls accounts. Although some of the stories and the title account are laudable, *Duelo de caballeros* adds little to Alegría's literary merits overall.

After his death from a cerebral hemorrhage on 17 February 1967, Alegría's widow, Dora Varona, undertook the task of publishing her late husband's previously unpublished texts and of compiling these and some already-known works in new collections. Among these works the incomplete novel *Lázaro* (1973) is worth noting. What would have been, when finished, a novelistic chronicle of the 1932 Aprista revolution in Trujillo only tells of the buildup to the rebellion. The sixteen fragments as published seem to constitute scarcely the beginning of a much more substantial work. *Mucha suerte con harto palo* (Much Luck with a Full Tree, 1976) is another of the works put together by Varona. It is a collage of Alegría's autobiographical texts, the equivalent of his memoirs. All of Alegría's brief narrations have been gathered into a single volume titled *Relatos* (Stories, 1983).

Ciro Alegría produced literary transformations of considerable significance. As do all great authors, he took on a tradition that suited him and then changed and superseded it within the limits of the awareness possible in his time.

References:

Fernando Alegría, *Nueva historia de la novela hispanoamericana* (Hanover, N.H.: Ediciones del Norte, 1986);

Hans Bunte, *Ciro Alegría y su obra* (Lima: Mejía Baca, 1961);

Jorge Cornejo-Polar, *La novela peruana* (Lima: Horizonte, 1989);

Cornejo-Polar, comp., *La obra de Ciro Alegría* (Arequipa, Peru: Universidad de San Agustín, 1976);

Tomás G. Escajadillo, *Ciro Alegría y "El mundo es ancho y ajeno"* (Lima: Universidad de San Marcos, 1983);

João Francisco Férreira, *O Indio no Romance de Ciro Alegría* (Porto Alegre, Brazil: Imprensa Universitária, 1957);

Emir Rodríguez Monegal, *Narradores de esta América* (Montevideo: Alfa, 1969);

Goran Tocilovac, *La comunidad indígena y Ciro Alegría* (Lima: Biblioteca Universitaria, 1972);

Dora Varona, comp., *Ciro Alegría: Trayectoria y mensaje* (Lima: Plenitud, 1972);

Matilde Villariño de Olivieri, *Las novelas de Ciro Alegría* (Santander, Spain: Hnos Bedía, 1956); revised and enlarged as *La novelística de Ciro Alegría* (Río Piedras, P.R., 1980).

Jorge Amado
(10 August 1912 -   )

Bobby J. Chamberlain
University of Pittsburgh

BOOKS: *Lenita*, by Amado, Dias da Costa, and Edison Carneiro (Rio de Janeiro: Coelho Branco Filho, 1930);

O paiz do carnaval (Rio de Janeiro: Schmidt, 1931);

Cacau (Rio de Janeiro: Ariel, 1933);

Suor (Rio de Janeiro: Ariel, 1934);

Jubiabá (Rio de Janeiro: Olympio, 1935); translated by Margaret Neves (New York: Avon, 1984);

Mar morto (Rio de Janeiro: Olympio, 1936); translated by Gregory Rabassa as *Sea of Death* (New York: Avon, 1984);

Capitães da areia (Rio de Janeiro: Olympio, 1937); translated by Rabassa as *Captains of the Sands* (New York: Avon, 1988);

A estrada do mar (Estância, Brazil: Popular, 1938);

ABC de Castro Alves (São Paulo: Martins, 1941);

Vida de Luiz Carlos Prestes, el caballero de la esperanza (Buenos Aires: Claridad, 1942);

Brandão entre o mar e o amor, by Amado and others (São Paulo: Martins, 1942);

Terras do sem fim (São Paulo: Martins, 1943); translated by Samuel Putnam as *The Violent Land* (New York: Knopf, 1945);

São Jorge dos Ilhéus (São Paulo: Martins, 1944);

Bahia de Todos os Santos (São Paulo: Martins, 1945);

Homens e coisas do Partido Comunista (Rio de Janeiro: Horizonte, 1946);

Seara vermelha (São Paulo: Martins, 1946);

O amor de Castro Alves (Rio de Janeiro: Povo, 1947); republished as *O amor do soldado* (São Paulo: Martins, 1958);

O mundo da paz (Rio de Janeiro: Vitória, 1950);

Os subterrâneos da liberdade, 3 volumes (São Paulo: Martins, 1954);

Gabriela, cravo e canela (São Paulo: Martins, 1958); translated by James L. Taylor and William L. Grossman as *Gabriela, Clove and Cinnamon* (New York: Knopf, 1962; London: Chatto & Windus, 1963);

Os velhos marinheiros ["A morte e a morte de Quincas Berro D'Agua" and "A completa ver-

Jorge Amado, circa 1986 (photograph © Jerry Bauer)

dade sobre as discutidas aventuras do Comandante Vasco Moscoso de Aragão"] (São Paulo: Martins, 1961); first story translated by Barbara Shelby as *The Two Deaths of Quincas Wateryell* (New York: Knopf, 1965); second story translated by Harriet de Onís as *Home Is the Sailor* (New York: Knopf, 1964);

Os pastores da noite (São Paulo: Martins, 1964); translated by de Onís as *Shepherds of the Night* (New York: Knopf, 1967);

Dona Flor e seus dois maridos, história moral e de amor (São Paulo: Martins, 1966); translated by de Onís as *Dona Flor and Her Two Husbands* (New York: Knopf, 1969; London: Weidenfeld & Nicolson, 1969);

Tenda dos milagres (São Paulo: Martins, 1969); translated by Shelby as *Tent of Miracles* (New York: Knopf, 1971);

Tereza Batista cansada de guerra (São Paulo: Martins, 1972); translated by Shelby as *Tereza Batista: Home from the Wars* (New York: Knopf, 1975);

O gato malhado e a andorinha Sinhá (Rio de Janeiro: Record, 1976); translated by Barbara Shelby Merello as *The Swallow and the Tomcat* (New York: Delacorte/Friede, 1982);

Tieta do Agreste: Pastora de cabras (Rio de Janeiro: Record, 1977); translated by Shelby Merello as *Tieta the Goat Girl* (New York: Knopf, 1979);

Farda, fardão, camisola de dormir (Rio de Janeiro: Record, 1979); translated by Helen R. Lane as *Pen, Sword, Camisole* (Boston: Godine, 1985);

O menino grapiúna (Rio de Janeiro: Record, 1981);

A bola e o goleiro (Rio de Janeiro: Record, 1984);

Tocaia Grande (Rio de Janeiro: Record, 1984); translated by Rabassa as *Showdown* (New York & Toronto: Bantam, 1988);

O sumiço da santa (Rio de Janeiro: Record, 1988);

Chapada Diamantina (Rio de Janeiro: AC & M, 1989).

Collection: *Obras*, 17 volumes (São Paulo: Martins, 1944-1967).

Over the last sixty years Jorge Amado has become the most widely published and translated of Brazilian writers. To date he has written more than thirty books, including fiction, poetry, biography, theater, memoirs, children's stories, and travel literature. Several of his works have been turned into motion pictures or *telenovelas* (television serial dramas). It is as a prose fictionist, however, that he has made his greatest contribution to literature. His twenty novels, many of them best-sellers, have been reprinted many times, and most have been translated into one or more of forty foreign languages. Blending social criticism with liberal doses of Afro-Brazilian and Luso-Brazilian folk culture, lyricism, humor, ribaldry, and politics, his fiction has evolved from an early proletarian or socialist-realist cast (from the 1930s to the early 1950s) to a later social-satirical modality (from the late 1950s to the present). In the process, Amado has gone from being considered a political pamphleteer, pornographer, and his country's best-known Communist writer to being hailed by some as a national treasure and reviled by others as a bourgeois literary hack.

He was born on 10 August 1912 to João and Eulália (Leal) Amado de Faria on their cacao farm in the interior of southern Bahia, a Brazilian frontier region plagued by land wars and rampant boomtown violence. Before his first birthday, Jorge Amado had already survived an assassination attempt directed at his father, and he was to undergo a string of hardships—floods, poverty, a smallpox epidemic, and the death of a younger brother—before reaching the age of ten. By then the family had begun to prosper and he was sent to a boarding school in the Bahian state capital, Salvador. There he first came into contact with the works of the Portuguese romantics and with those of Jonathan Swift, Sir Walter Scott, and Charles Dickens, who has remained a favorite of his.

In 1924 Amado ran away from school and made his way to the home of his paternal grandfather, José Amado, in the neighboring state of Sergipe. After two months he was returned to Salvador and enrolled in another boarding school, where he discovered the works of Honoré de Balzac and Guy de Maupassant, of several Spanish-American authors, and of the Brazilian modernists. Modernism had begun to spread by the mid 1920s from its hub in São Paulo and Rio de Janeiro to the provincial capitals, and Amado, a young adolescent, was drawn to the iconoclasm of the new aesthetics. He joined a circle of young bohemian writers and began to produce short stories, poetry, and essays for literary magazines. In 1927 he left the *colégio* to work as a reporter for a local newspaper, *Diário da Bahia*, and the following year he moved into the Pelourinho district of downtown Salvador, where he set about writing a short novel, *Suor* (Sweat, 1934), dealing with the vices and exploitation of slum tenants. Not until six years later would he be able to finish and publish the project.

By then Amado had moved to Rio to enter law school and had married his first wife, Matilde Garcia Rosa (in 1933). He had also published two other short novels, *O paiz do carnaval* (The Land of Carnival, 1931) and *Cacau* (Cacao, 1933), both of which had won him some acclaim. The former centered on the lives of a group of young writers much like the one to which he had belonged in Salvador. In it he depicted his own search for values and that of his generation. By contrast, the latter decried the social injustices associated with the traditional Brazilian landholding system and affirmed the value of class consciousness. Amado had found his niche and begun to establish himself as a champion of social causes and leftist politics, a trend that would be further accentuated with the publication of *Suor*.

His first child, Lila, was born in 1935. *Jubiabá* was published the same year. Unlike the preceding three novelettes, which were little more than brief sketches, it affords a rich tapestry of Bahian life, weaving Afro-Brazilian religious elements with those of the earlier works into a more structurally complex whole. Like *Suor* it depicts the lives of the urban masses; like *Cacau* it portrays the lot of farm workers and planters. It mixes melodrama with realism, lyricism with crudity, and local color with political commitment. The text is interspersed with calling cards, circus posters, and the like. Luso-Brazilian folk culture also pervades the work. Yet it is first and foremost the story of Antônio Balduíno, a poor black youth brought up on the streets of Salvador, from his boyhood of picaresque adventures to adulthood and political militancy. The work ends with a victorious dockworkers' strike led by the erstwhile ne'er-do-well protagonist, a fact that has caused many critics to question its plausibility and regard it as a flawed masterpiece.

In 1935 Amado also finished law school but refused to pick up his diploma. The following year he was jailed briefly by the Getúlio Vargas regime (which had seized power in 1930) for his alleged support of an abortive rebellion in Natal the previous November. *Mar morto* (translated in 1984 as *Sea of Death*) was published in 1936. Like *Jubiabá* it portrays Afro-Bahian customs and religion centering on the lives of the urban poor. It tells the story of Guma, the owner of a small transport boat, and his wife, Lívia, and recounts the daily hardships and violence to which they are subjected. It also features several strong female characters. As in *Jubiabá*, too, there is a heavy dose of popular culture. Yet, much more than the previous works, *Mar morto* is suffused with lyricism, particularly in its descriptions of the sea. Some saw in this an attenuation of the political advocacy that had marked Amado's fiction for the last several years.

Capitães da areia (1937; translated as *Captains of the Sands*, 1988) continues in the manner of *Jubiabá* and *Mar morto*. It, too, treats the downtrodden of Salvador, depicting the lives of a gang of street waifs of the 1930s. Fictional newspaper headlines, stories, and letters to the editor supplement the prose narration. More vehement than its predecessors in its denunciation of social ills, the novel blames the authorities and a brutal correctional system for much of the city's juvenile crime problem.

The novelist had traveled around South America and to Mexico and the United States before the publication of *Capitães da areia*, meeting such figures as Diego Rivera, David Alfaro Siqueiros, José Orozco, Paul Robeson, and Michael Gold. Gold's *Jews Without Money* (1930) had influenced Amado's *Suor*, and later the two would become fast friends. Amado was again imprisoned upon his return to Brazil in October 1937, and his books were banned, culminating in public book burnings in Salvador and São Paulo, in which many copies of his works were destroyed. Shortly thereafter Vargas proclaimed his Estado Novo (New State) dictatorship.

After Amado's release in January 1938 he spent several months in São Paulo and Sergipe. He returned to Rio the following year, upon the outbreak of World War II, to continue his writing but decided to quit Brazil for Argentina two years later (in 1941) due to the oppressive political climate of the Estado Novo. While in exile he wrote several books, among them a biography of Luiz Carlos Prestes, the Brazilian Communist leader. In 1942 he returned to Brazil and was arrested, then released on the condition that he remain in Salvador. He spent the next two years working as a journalist for the newspaper *O Imparcial* and campaigning for the return of democracy.

The year 1943 saw the publication of *Terras do sem fim* (translated as *The Violent Land*, 1945), which Amado had written and copyrighted the year before while living for a while in Montevideo, Uruguay. Set in the cacao-growing region of southern Bahia during the land wars of 1911 and 1912, the work drew heavily on the novelist's childhood experiences and on the tales of relatives and frontier storytellers. It was to become the high point of the first phase of his career, and there are still many critics who regard it as his masterpiece. In it he fashions a deeper and much broader picture of Bahian society than he had before, even in *Jubiabá*. Characters are treated with greater detachment, but their thoughts and feelings are probed more deftly. Rather than offering the largely Manichaean portrayals of his earlier novels, Amado sets before the reader a gallery of human types—planters, gunslingers, gamblers, adventurers, laborers, and prostitutes—all of whom he regards as victims of the cacao juggernaut. Lyric descriptions of the

Amado, Pablo Neruda, and Jan Orba at Dobris Castle in Czechoslovakia, 1951

dark tropical forests are juxtaposed with episodes of frontier violence and crudity. Humor assumes a greater role. Popular speech patterns and vocabulary, long a hallmark of his works, are used, along with fictitious newspaper accounts and the tales of backwoods poets, to evoke the flavor of the region.

In 1944 Amado was legally separated from Matilde, and the following year he married Zélia Gattai (on 8 July). They were to have a son, João Jorge, and a daughter, Paloma. A sequel to *Terras do sem fim*, titled *São Jorge dos Ilhéus* (St. George of Ilhéus), was published in 1944, but it lacks the accomplishment and grandeur of its predecessor and did not fare as well with the critics. In 1946 he published *Seara vermelha* (Red Harvest), which tells of the hardships experienced by a migrant family escaping from a drought. It is also a strongly political work and became a best-seller in Brazil and several of the Eastern-bloc countries.

During these years, Amado's political activities were at their height. He became a friend of the Chilean poet Pablo Neruda in 1945 and joined him and Prestes on the podium in São Paulo at the political rally commemorating the latter's release from prison. With the end of World War II the Vargas dictatorship was overthrown; political parties were again legalized; and Amado, running on the Communist party ticket, was elected as a national deputy from São Paulo state. His son, João Jorge, was born in Rio in 1947. But the next year the party was again outlawed, and Amado went into voluntary exile in France. While living in Paris, he befriended Jean-Paul Sartre, Simone de Beauvoir, Pablo Picasso, and Louis Aragon; in Poland, where he traveled as vice-president of the World Congress of Writers and Artists for Peace, he came into contact with Ilya Grigoryevich Ehrenburg, Julian Huxley, and other European intellectuals. In 1948 and 1949 he visited many of the countries of Eastern and Western Europe. In December 1949 his daughter Lila died suddenly in Rio de Janeiro.

The following year Amado took his family to live in Czechoslovakia. In 1950 he had published *O mundo da paz* (The World of Peace), a book about his Eastern European travels, which was declared subversive in Brazil and confiscated. In 1951 he received the Stalin Peace Prize in

Moscow and, the next year, returned to Brazil after journeying to China and Mongolia. *Os subterrâneos da liberdade* (The Freedom Underground), a trilogy chronicling the activities of the Communist party during the Vargas dictatorship, was published in 1954. It was by far the novelist's most ambitious work and surpassed even *Seara vermelha* in its political tendentiousness. Some of the characters and episodes are based on real people and events, though the former are often disguised with fictitious names. The dominant tone of the novel is that of the epic, but humor and caricature are sometimes employed for sardonic effect.

Following the death of Joseph Stalin in 1953 and Nikita Khrushchev's subsequent de-Stalinization campaign in the Soviet Union, Brazilian Communists, Amado among them, began to call into question many of the precepts of socialist realism. Frustrated by the party's attempts to thwart open discussion and outraged by the Soviet invasion of Hungary in 1956, some Brazilian intellectuals renounced their party membership altogether. Amado reportedly denounced the invasion and even returned his Stalin prize in protest. But many of the details of his break with the party have remained a mystery.

What is certain is that *Gabriela, cravo e canela* (1958; translated as *Gabriela, Clove and Cinnamon*, 1962) marked a pronounced shift in Amado's aesthetics and has come to be regarded as a watershed in his literary production. The work's appearance led many longtime admirers, particularly dogmatic party members, to brand the author as an ideological heretic. They saw in its greater infusion of humor, irony, and social satire a wholesale abandonment of his leftist worldview and an avowed partiality for picaresque and bourgeois fiction. Many objected to the seeming frivolity of his characters and plot. Yet even more critics of both right and left hailed the work as proof of Amado's forsaking of prescriptive Marxist aesthetics and of his increased literary maturity. They welcomed this new direction as a change of tactics, rather than of strategy or underlying ideological beliefs, and asserted that, in large measure, *Gabriela* was but an intensification of long-standing Amadian literary practices.

Comic exaggeration and caricature had long been mainstays of his writing. So, too, had such devices as crude humor, class satire, parody, and appropriation of popular culture. But what had usually remained in the background in earlier novels had come to the fore. Humor in the broad sense was all-pervasive. Starting with the lengthy, archaic chapter and section titles and continuing with the many tongue-in-cheek catalogues, antiphrases, zeugmatic constructions, and incongruous juxtapositions, the cultivation of satirical humor in *Gabriela* reveals a strong preference for carnivalization of social injustice and struggle, as opposed to the earlier denunciatory practices. The novel garnered five major prizes and sold one hundred thousand copies in the first year alone. Within four months it had gone through six printings.

The story revolves around the 1925 arrival in Ilhéus of Gabriela, an impoverished and attractive young mulatto woman fleeing the droughts of the northeastern interior. A talented cook, she is promptly hired by Syrian-born Nacib Saad, a bar owner, to do his cooking chores. Within a short time they are lovers, but Nacib insists on marriage; thus the problems begin. Although the bar owner does everything in his power to shape his bride into a "proper" middle-class lady, Gabriela resists being stripped of her cherished freedom and is eventually caught in flagrante delicto with a friend of her husband's. Nacib beats her but breaks with the local custom of wife-killing and is thus proclaimed the town's most civilized citizen. Months later, feeling incomplete without Gabriela, he once again hires her as a cook, and, within a short time, the two resume their amorous relationship.

Although Gabriela herself is undeniably a sensuous *mulata* stereotype, the book makes a serious attempt to address the need for women's emancipation. Each of the novel's four parts treats a separate female character, ranging from a fabled colonial maiden to a kept mistress, a defiant daughter, and the protagonist herself, all of whom strive for greater control over their own destinies. Furthermore, the story is set against a recent episode involving the slaying of an unfaithful local churchwoman by her irate husband, and a political subplot embodies the transition from a waning feudal order to incipient capitalism. More than mere ornaments, the women characters are primary indicators of an evolving social system, and in the end it is they, as much as the planters, merchants, and politicians, who effect the social changes requisite for greater material and cultural progress.

In 1959 Amado was made a lay dignitary in a prominent Salvador *candomblé* (Afro-Brazilian religious) congregation, and in 1961 he was elected unanimously to the Brazilian Academy of Letters.

Os velhos marinheiros (The Old Sailors, 1961) comprises two novelettes that confirmed his aesthetic, if not also his ideological, conversion. As in *Gabriela* satirical humor is omnipresent; but, unlike *Gabriela*, the *Os velhos marinheiros* stories satirize the society of the Bahian capital, particularly the *bas-fonds* and the lower middle classes. Less encumbered by digressions than *Gabriela* but no less leisurely in their narration, both novelettes thematize the relativity of truth and narrative discourse.

The first, translated in 1965 as *The Two Deaths of Quincas Wateryell*, is the story of a middle-aged petit bourgeois who renounces his family and respectability to consort with harlots and thieves. When he dies years later amidst the filth and depravity of the city's skid-row tenements, his family is only too happy to lay him to rest with as little publicity and expense as possible in order to avoid further embarrassment. But, at the behest of his vagrant friends, a wake is hastily organized, and, following the departure of his relatives, Quincas is said by his inebriated companions to have come back to life and accompanied them to the waterfront for a seafood dinner. During the revelry, which occurs on a boat, a storm arises, and Quincas is reported to have dived of his own free will into the surf of the bay. The reality of his actions and utterances is rendered ambiguous by the novelist. And it is not always possible to ascertain the veracity of the events.

The case of Vasco Moscoso de Aragão, the protagonist of the other novelette (translated as *Home Is the Sailor*, 1964), is similarly puzzling. Double perspective is again employed to characterize the hero, but this time the controversy does not involve the inconsistencies of successive periods of his life or the circumstances of his death but rather the truth or falsehood of his proclaimed identity. By his account he is a retired sea captain, but according to one mean-spirited soul he is an imposter. Amado sets a bumbling dramatized narrator to untangle the conundrum. The initial narration of events is contradicted by a second narration, each version seemingly precluding the other. Or so it appears, at least, until one day Vasco is called upon to take command of a ship that has lost its captain. Ironically, throughout this "initiation ordeal," the two realities are meshed as though they constituted a seamless whole. Upon reaching Belém, the port of destination, Vasco, despite clear weather, orders all the ship's moorings fastened, and it appears that he has thus exposed himself as a fraud. But during

Dust jacket for the 1988 translation of Amado's Tocaia Grande *(1984), set at the turn of the century in the interior of southern Bahia, the region of Brazil where Amado spent his childhood*

the night the city is ravaged by a fierce, unexpected storm, destroying all but Vasco's vessel, thus again lending credence to his version of the truth. As with the first story, in the end there is a stalemate, a blockage, and it is the reader who must ultimately "write" the story. Little wonder, then, that the two novelettes have long been favorites of many Amadian critics.

Not so the sequel *Os pastores da noite* (1964; translated as *Shepherds of the Night*, 1967). Amado, after traveling to Cuba and Mexico in 1962—following his father's death—established permanent residence in Salvador the following year. He published *Os pastores da noite* just three months after the military overthrow of the João Goulart government. A triptych plagued by its uneven development, the work portrays several of the same characters as *A morte e a morte*, treating them in a similar, carnivalized fashion. It opens with the story of Cabo Martim's ill-fated marriage. This is followed by a rather esoteric episode in which an ingenious solution to a baptismal problem is concocted by Exu, the trickster god of *candomblé*. The final episode narrates a violent confrontation between police and squatters in which the latter ultimately prevail by their cunning. Critical reaction to *Os pastores da noite* was not as enthusiastic as it had been for the two preceding books, many critics taking exception to what they considered the excessive romanticization of the "noble poor."

Dona Flor e seus dois maridos (1966; translated as *Dona Flor and Her Two Husbands*, 1969) is the story of Florípedes Paiva, a lower-middle-class cooking instructor in the Salvador of the 1920s and 1930s, whose marriage to a profligate, wife-beating charmer named Vadinho Guimarães ends abruptly during carnival time with his premature death. Running close to five hundred pages, the book is chock-full of gossipy episodes, supplemented by recipes and menus. Almost half of the more than three hundred characters in the novel were taken from real life, most of them Amado's friends and acquaintances, many retaining their actual names. Although Flor is devastated by Vadinho's passing—he had been the source of both her joy and suffering—she eventually remarries, in the process attaining the respectability he had denied her. Teodoro, her second mate, is in every way Vadinho's opposite, from his moral virtue and work ethic to his fastidious eating and lovemaking habits. Much of the novel's humor derives from these oppositions and from Vadinho's ghostly return to reclaim his place in the marriage bed. The ultimate solution to Flor's dilemma is her deliberate refusal to choose between the two husbands, and it involves the magical intervention of the Yoruban supernatural, resembling what occurs in the middle section of *Os pastores da noite*.

Yet behind the levity there is much more to *Dona Flor*. The fact that it was published barely two years after the imposition of a brutal military regime and that Amado had only recently forsaken Marxist orthodoxy is in itself ample cause for suspicion. The two husbands could be metaphors for contradictory class ethics or political ideologies. The heroine's magical synthesis of the two and the developments leading up to it could be interpreted in a similar fashion.

In 1969 Amado published *Tenda dos milagres* (translated as *Tent of Miracles*, 1971), an indictment in novel form of the racism and violence to which Brazilian blacks have long been victim. The work centers on the life of Pedro Archanjo, a mulatto university beadle and self-taught researcher of Bahian folklore and racial history, who published several monographs at the turn of the century. Long consigned to obscurity in Brazil, Archanjo and his books are discovered by a visiting American scholar and promptly become the focus of intense national attention. Accounts of Archanjo's struggle against racial discrimination alternate with scenes of the 1969 preparations for the centenary of his birth, producing an ironic contrapuntal structure and exposing the continuing bigotry and hypocrisy of rich white Brazilians who are motivated more by profits, fads, and xenophilia than social justice or historical veracity. Amado's use of an inept narrator endows the text with a measure of irony and humor. Yet in the final analysis *Tenda dos milagres* is a much more somber work than any of Amado's other books written since 1958, its satire succumbing in large part to an overarching polemicism.

Amado traveled to Europe, Canada, and the United States in 1971, spending several months as writer in residence at Pennsylvania State University. The following year he published *Tereza Batista cansada de guerra* (translated as *Tereza Batista: Home from the Wars*, 1975), which recounts the tribulations of a Bahian prostitute in the style of the high-flown folk verse known as *literatura de cordel* ("string literature," for the sellers' custom of displaying the leaflets on a piece of twine). Among the *cordel* characteristics that the novel stylizes are the introductory woodcuts (by artist Calasans Neto), the enumerative section titles, and the ABC form used to narrate one of the episodes. *Tereza Batista* also contains a great deal of hyperbole, which, along with a recourse to the supernatural, farce, and traditional plot formulas, is reminiscent of folk literature.

The story is pieced together from the accounts of more than a dozen secondary narrators, most of them based on living or historical figures. Sold into bondage at the age of thirteen, Tereza is subjected to all manner of physical abuse and sexual humiliations by her sadistic captor. Only by killing him is she finally able to escape. Later she is the mistress of a married man. After his death she becomes a prostitute, leads an army of harlots in fighting a backlands smallpox epidemic, and finally spearheads a prostitutes' strike in the Bahian capital before marrying and settling down. The book was published with great fanfare, and Amado, though receiving the usual kudos for his performance, was also criticized both for his portrayal of the prostitute heroine, which some regarded as a carnivalized trivialization, and for his cultivation of timeworn narrative formulas.

Tieta do Agreste, pastora de cabras (1977; translated as *Tieta the Goat Girl*, 1979) also tells of the life of a prostitute, one who has had a successful career as a madam in São Paulo and seeks retirement in her hometown in the rural Northeast. As with *Dona Flor* the book draws much of its impetus and humor from the conflict between permissiveness and traditional mores, but underneath its veneer of frivolity it also attempts to deal with more serious issues, such as environmental pollution, the celibacy of priests, and internal colonialism.

The 1979 publication of *Farda, fardão, camisola de dormir* (translated as *Pen, Sword, Camisole*, 1985) marked the first time since 1954 that Amado had written a novel unfolding entirely outside of Bahia. Set in Rio during the Vargas dictatorship, the work relates the story of a clever campaign to deny a seat in the Brazilian Academy of Letters to a profascist colonel. Although it displays most of the same characteristics of other recent Amadian fiction, *Farda* was panned by many critics. Meanwhile Amado traveled to Senegal as a guest of President Léopold Senghor and visited Angola at the invitation of Agostinho Neto, the country's first president.

With *Tocaia Grande* (1984; translated as *Showdown*, 1988) Amado returns to the cacao region of southern Bahia and the frontier violence of his boyhood. The novel tells the story of the founding of a backwoods town at the turn of the century and contains much of the adventure, crudity, picaresque humor, and memorable character types of *Terras do sem fim*. Moreover it represents an attempt to deprecate the official versions of history, which have so often ignored the signal role played by the common people, to their detriment and to that of historical accuracy.

The year 1985 saw the arrival of the New Republic and with it the beginnings of democratic government in Brazil. During the succession of military regimes that had ruled the country for the past twenty-one years, Amado had been one of the staunchest opponents of censorship, having been one of the few literary figures whose vast popularity was usually sufficient to exempt him from persecution. In 1987 the Jorge Amado Cultural Foundation was opened in the Pelourinho district of Salvador, which had served as the setting of *Suor* a half century earlier, and in 1988 he published the novel *O sumiço da santa* (The Disappearance of the Saint).

Amado in Paris, 1987 (photograph courtesy of Zélia Gattai and the Fundacão Casa de Jorge Amado)

In recent years Amado has done much of his writing outside of Salvador, in Paris or London, or while staying at the *fazendas* (estates) of friends in the interior of Brazil. His residence in Rio Vermelho, outside the Bahian capital, has become a tourist attraction and has ceased to afford him the privacy so requisite for his craft. Since the early 1960s he has surrounded himself with a large circle of Brazilian and émigré writers and artists, who have made Salvador an important Brazilian cultural center. With his storyteller narration, penchant for excess, and what some have termed his asymmetric baroque style, Amado has seemed to be a superb interpreter of an exuberant tropical reality. He has indeed come to be regarded by a large segment of Brazilians as a national monument of sorts. To others he has become in recent decades a caricature of his earlier self, trading social commitment and the moral high ground for a neo-Romantic comic populism that caters to the mediocrity and prurient interests of the marketplace. Detractors often compare his works to television soap operas and other products of the "culture industry."

A confirmed materialist who has lost faith in the ability of religious and political ideologies to supply viable solutions to human problems, Amado has indeed abandoned many of the easy formulas of his earlier works. Stark portrayals of social injustice and heroic popular uprisings have given way in most cases to the "magic realism" and circuslike atmosphere of the deus ex machina, wrought by a pantheon of Afro-Brazilian deities whose very existence is regarded as more metaphorical than real. But there is no denying that he has at the same time clung to other pat formulas, some of them outmoded, in the later works: excessive discursiveness, racial and sexual stereotyping, populism, trite plot motifs, and a marked preference for closed narrative models. Theurgical intervention is in itself a formula with little room for variation. Yet it is fair to say that many of these same devices have also long constituted his strengths as a writer, one who is uncomfortable with the experimentation, vulgar psychologism, and language games of many of his contemporaries.

While Amado's most ardent admirers have often tended to overlook his excesses and to deny some of the contradictions that underlie his later works, many of his detractors have taken the long-windedness and trite narrative formulas at face value, failing to detect their inherent polysemy. They see in his imitation of popular literature an attempt at mystification, but they are often blind to his demystifying subtext. Behind the veil of simplicity that cloaks many of these works, then, there is a great deal of sophistication of the kind that only the perspicacious reader will appreciate. Amado is, indeed, one of the masters of Brazilian fiction—not in the sense that he is on the cutting edge of aesthetic innovation, nor in the sense that he is a crafter of tight-knit plots or a metaphysician in novelist's clothing, but rather because he has consistently been able to capture the reader's heart and fancy with his incomparable genius for characterization, his flair for broad humor, folk culture, and popular speech, and his superb ability to involve readers in the lives of his humble characters.

Biography:

Miécio Táti, *Jorge Amado: Vida e obra* (Belo Horizonte, Brazil: Itatiaia, 1960).

References:

Alfredo Wagner Berno de Almeida, *Jorge Amado: Política e literatura* (Rio de Janeiro: Campus, 1979);

Juarez da Gama Batista, *O barroco e o maravilhoso no romance de Jorge Amado* (João Pessoa, Brazil: Chaves, 1973);

Bobby J. Chamberlain, *Jorge Amado* (Boston: Twayne, 1990);

Mark J. Curran, *Jorge Amado e a literatura de cordel* (Salvador, Brazil: Fundação Cultural do Estado da Bahia, 1981);

Fred P. Ellison, *Brazil's New Novel* (Berkeley: University of California Press, 1954), pp. 83-108;

Walnice Nogueira Galvão, *Saco de gatos* (São Paulo: Duas Cidades, 1976), pp. 13-22;

Jorge Amado: Documentos (Lisban: Europa América, 1964);

Jorge Amado: Ensaios sobre o escritor (Salvador: Universidade Federal da Bahia, 1982);

Luis Costa Lima, "Jorge Amado," in *A literatura no Brasil*, 6 volumes, edited by Afrânio Coutinho, second edition, revised (Rio de Janeiro: Sul Americana, 1970), V: 304-326;

Alvaro Salema, *Jorge Amado: O homem e a obra* (Lisbon: Europa-América, 1982);

Malcolm Silverman, *Moderna ficção brasileira*, translated into Portuguese by J. G. Linke (Rio de Janeiro: Civilização Brasileira, 1978), pp. 137-157;

Paulo Tavares, *Criaturas de Jorge Amado*, second edition, revised (Rio de Janeiro: Record, 1985);

Tavares, *O baiano Jorge Amado e sua obra* (Rio de Janeiro: Record, 1980);

Tempo Brasileiro 74: Jorge Amado, Km 70 (July-September 1983);

Jon S. Vincent, "Jorge Amado," in *Latin American Writers*, 3 volumes, edited by C. A. Solé and M. I. Abreu (New York: Scribners, 1989), III: 1153-1162;

Vincent, "Jorge Amado, Jorge Desprezado," *Luso-Brazilian Review*, supplementary issue, 15 (Summer 1978): 11-17.

José María Arguedas
(18 January 1911 - 28 November 1969)

Sara Castro-Klarén
Johns Hopkins University

BOOKS: *Agua. Los escoleros. Warma kukay* (Lima: Impresiones & Publicidad, 1935); enlarged as *Agua* (Lima: Nuevo Mundo, 1961; enlarged again, Lima: Millà Batres, 1974);

Runa yupay (Lima: Comisión Central del Censo, 1939);

Yawar fiesta (Lima: Mejía Baca/CIP, 1941);

Diamantes y pedernales. Agua (Lima: Mejía Baca & Villanueva, 1954);

Los ríos profundos (Buenos Aires: Losada, 1958); translated by Frances Barraclough as *Deep Rivers* (Austin: University of Texas Press, 1978); enlarged as *Los ríos profundos y selección de cuentos* (Caracas: Ayacucho, 1978);

Bibliografía del folklore peruano (Mexico City: Instituto Panamericano, 1960);

El sexto (Lima: Mejía Baca, 1961);

La agonía de "Rasu Niti" (Lima: Talleres Gráficos Icaro/Camino del Hombre, 1962);

Túpac Amaru Kamaq taytanchisman; Haylli-taki. A nuestro padre creador Túpac Amaru; Himno-canción (Lima: Salqantay, 1962);

Todas las sangres (Buenos Aires: Losada, 1964);

El sueño del pongo (Lima: Salqantay, 1965);

La amante de la culebra (Paris: Lettres modernes, 1966);

Amor mundo y otros relatos (Montevideo: Arca, 1967); enlarged as *Amor mundo y todos los cuentos de José María Arguedas* (Lima: Moncloa, 1967);

Las comunidades de España y del Peru (Lima: Universidad Nacional Mayor de San Marcos, 1968);

El zorro de arriba y el zorro de abajo (Buenos Aires: Losada, 1971);

El forastero y otros cuentos (Montevideo: Sandino, 1972);

Páginas escogidas (Lima: Universo, 1972);

Cuentos olvidados, edited by José Luis Rouillón (Lima: Imágenes & Letras, 1973);

Relatos completos, edited by Jorge Lafforgue (Buenos Aires: Losada, 1974);

Formación de una cultura nacional indoamericana, edited by Angel Rama (Mexico City: Siglo Veintiuno, 1975);

José María Arguedas (photograph by Abraham Guillen)

Señores e indios, edited by Rama (Buenos Aires: Arca, 1976);

Dos estudios sobre Huancayo (Huancayo, Peru: Universidad Nacional del Centro del Perú, 1978);

Obras completas, 5 volumes, edited by Sybila Arredondo de Arguedas and others (Lima: Horizonte, 1983);

Indios, mestizos y señores (Lima: Horizonte, 1985).

OTHER: *Dioses y hombres de Huarochirí*, translated from Quechua into Spanish by Arguedas (Lima: Museo Nacional de Historia, 1966).

José María Arguedas's original intent as a writer was not to create highly crafted fiction but to understand the nature of the society in which he lived. This is partly why he chose to pursue anthropology. In it he found a discipline and a logic capable of understanding living societies. Arguedas repeatedly criticized Hispanist and Indianist historians, as well as the social scientists studying Peru, for not linking the experience of Indians and mestizo cultures living today with the Chavin, Nazca, Chimú, and Inca civilizations of the past. When Arguedas began to write fiction, he did so because he was convinced that the world of his childhood had never been captured in any text he had read thus far. His short stories and novels would bring forth an unprecedented universe in which human relations, feeling, and a sense of the relationship of men to the gods were infused with a theretofore unwritten sense of life in the Andes.

Arguedas was born on 18 January 1911 in the province of Andahuaylas in the southern Peruvian Andes. His full biography is yet to be written; thus little reliable information is available on his life, in spite of the fact that he spent most of his life engaged in academic and intellectual circles in Lima. Much of what is known about him is taken either from interviews he gave or from public records. He was the son of Victor Manuel Arguedas Arellano, a lawyer, and Victoria Altamirano Navarro, from a well-known family in San Pedro. By his own account Arguedas moved from Andahuaylas to Lima around 1930 because his father had decided that he and his older brother should enter the Universidad Nacional Mayor de San Marcos. At that time the Arguedas family was miserably poor, and the young Arguedas brothers, after spending a few days in a little hotel by the railroad station in downtown Lima, found themselves living in the streets. An old friend of their father eventually helped José María to find a menial job at the Lima post office.

Although as a university student he often interrupted his studies because of financial need, he basically remained tied to the academic and intellectual circles interested in change and social justice in Peru. His often marginal, but important, association with the emerging political-left parties landed him in jail in 1937 during the dictatorship of Gen. Oscar Raimundo Benavides. Due to the efforts of Arguedas's future wife, Celia Bustamante Vernal (whom he married in 1939), and a dedicated core of friends, he and many other innocent people were freed, after periods of six to eighteen months of incarceration. Arguedas soon became a full-time anthropologist, field researcher, and novelist. Eventually (from 1963 until 1969) he would hold one of the most important teaching positions in Peru at the prestigious Universidad Nacional Agraria in La Molina. In 1963 he would also become director of the Casa de la Cultura, Peru's major institution for the organization and promotion of artistic and intellectual activity. With the publication of his second novel, the classic *Los ríos profundos* (1958; translated as *Deep Rivers*, 1978), Arguedas became a preeminent figure, not only in Peruvian life but also among the international scholars who study Peru's ancient and contemporary civilizations.

Arguedas shortly before he became a professor at the Universidad Nacional Agraria of Peru and director of the Casa de la Cultura

The anthropologist and the novelist in Arguedas continually nurtured each other, enriching the quality of Arguedas's discourse on Andean society. But his change in residence from the Andean world and rural Indian communities to the world of the modern, yet colonial, crowded and chaotic city of Lima precipitated a fracture in his life that never quite healed. Arguedas often experienced, for periods of weeks and even months, intense and even crippling depression. In 1966, late in his life and soon after his divorce from his first wife, Arguedas attempted suicide. Supported and encouraged by his many friends, he tried psychotherapy. In 1967 his second marriage, to Sybila Arredondo, a young and beautiful Chilean woman, was a positive experience in his tumultuous inner life. He has written that his second marriage gave him great happiness. Even so, as Arguedas indicated in the diaries included in his unfinished novel *El zorro de arriba y el zorro de abajo* (The Fox from Above and the Fox from Below, 1971), his increasing withdrawal from life, the life he so passionately loved, grew to an unremitting, unbearably painful point. The reasons for such despair and alienation lay deeply buried in his highly sensitive mind. In 1969, in a bathroom near his office at La Molina, he committed suicide, thus ending the life of one of Latin America's most singular and important writers.

Arguedas's first book was *Agua. Los escoleros. Warma kukay* (Water. The Students. Puppy Love, 1935), usually referred to as *Agua*, which brings together three short stories. In 1941 he published his first novel, *Yawar fiesta* (Blood Fiesta). *Diamantes y pedernales. Agua* (Diamonds and Flintstones. Water, 1954) includes the contents of *Agua*, with a biobibliographic prologue, and introduces his first and only novella, *Diamantes y pedernales*. His major novel, *Los ríos profundos*, was published four years later. The transparency of the autobiographical *Los ríos profundos* was followed by the wrenching world of *El sexto* (The Sixth, 1961), a novel about the confinement of political prisoners in the most dreaded of Peruvian prisons, El Sexto. This hallucinatory novel was followed by the pristine story of Rasu Niti, the master scissor dancer in *La agonía de "Rasu Niti"* (Rasu Niti's Agony, 1962). That same year, Arguedas published his unusual hymn *Túpac Amaru Kamaq taytanchisman; Haylli-taki. A nuestro padre creador Túpac Amaru; Himno-canción* (To Our Lord the Father-Creator Túpac Amaru; Hymn and Song).

His most ambitious novel, *Todas las sangres* (All Bloods), was published in 1964. Like *Los ríos profundos*, this novel was published in Buenos Aires, and publication by one of Buenos Aires's major editorial houses is generally taken in Latin America as an indication of success and recognition. Beginning with *Los ríos profundos* Arguedas's work earned international regard in Spanish-speaking countries. At his many friends' behest, Arguedas gathered those he considered his best short stories, together with several unpublished texts, and published *Amor mundo y otros relatos* (Love World and Other Stories, 1967), enlarged that same year as *Amor mundo y todos los cuentos* (Love World and All the Short Stories). *El zorro de arriba y el zorro de abajo* was published almost two years after Arguedas's death. Since then there have been several new editions of his works, and also new collections of his short stories and anthropological writings. His widow, Sybila, with others, has edited and published his *Obras completas* (Complete Works, five volumes, 1983).

The year 1935 in Peru witnessed the publication of two important narratives: *La serpiente de oro* (translated as *The Golden Serpent*, 1943) by Ciro Alegría—who in 1941 would publish the prizewinning *El mundo es ancho y ajeno* (translated as *Broad and Alien Is the World*, 1941)—and *Agua. Los escoleros. Warma kukay* by Arguedas. Almost no one, with the exception of a few friends of Arguedas, saw the promise of a major talent in the "odd" style of the *Agua* collection or the neo-indigenist quality of its plots. Arguedas was seen by most as one more unknown young writer destined to increase the rank and file of the many one-book storytellers. Today, however, a cursory reading of the three short stories in *Agua* immediately reveals the power in Arguedas's fictional world.

The *Agua* stories, like *La serpiente de oro*, deal with the economically exploited Indian communities. Arguedas's book portrays the life of landless Indian peasants caught in a silent, never-ending struggle against their oppressive masters. But in *Agua* the silence turns out to be simply a delusion in the eye of the outside observer. *Agua* makes *indigenismo* reverberate with proud self-regard, doubt, fear, and love in the face of conflict. Above all, *Agua* portrays a social world attuned to and happy with the workings of nature.

In his prologue to *Diamantes y pedernales. Agua*, Arguedas states that he wrote the tales in *Agua* when he had just begun as a student at San Marcos in Lima. At that time he felt himself to be not only a man from the highlands but a Quechua man, a person from a different culture, and, especially, a man whose mother tongue was not Spanish. In contrast, he believes that his novella *Diamantes y pedernales*, written after twenty-three years of exhausting work, hard city living, a bit of traveling, and some reading, represents another point in his long journey of discovery within two cultures and two languages.

His birth and childhood in Andahuaylas were important to the world he created in fiction and informed his historical sense of Andean peoples. Access to Andahuaylas still remains difficult. Its capital city, Abancay, located on the low eastern slopes of the Andes' western chain, was then and remains today oriented toward Cuzco, the ancient center of the Incan empire. After his mother died, Arguedas, son of a *criollo* (Creole) itinerant lawyer, grew up as a virtual servant in his stepmother's hacienda. There, although he was white, the child grew up within the economic, political, familial, linguistic, and religious structures of what is generally called the Indian world. More accurately speaking, the "Indian world" is the culture of the Quechua or Aymara-speaking peoples residing in the Andes. Andeans are heirs to a very ancient and coherent cultural tradition. The ecological and human territory where Arguedas grew up has been historically marked by the stubborn and lively permanence of Andean social formations in a constant give-and-take with invading Spanish-American cultural patterns. For all practical purposes, Arguedas grew up not only within the Indian culture of the house servants and field workers in the hacienda, but also as a monolingual Quechua speaker. Only after he turned fourteen years old, when his father impressed upon him the need to do his schooling in Spanish, did Arguedas begin a serious and painful acquisition of this second language as a literary and intellectual vehicle of expression. But his acquisition of Spanish was never intended to entail the discarding of Quechua, his nurturing mother tongue. Throughout his life Arguedas continued to write in Quechua—alongside his production in Spanish—in an effort to convert it into a modern literary language.

Arguedas's creative enterprise was not caught in or destroyed by his bilingualism. On the contrary, the cornerstone of his achievement rests on the fact that he managed to translate and express qualities and characteristics of one language and culture into the other.

Yet this happy consciousness of mutual empowerment was not always Arguedas's own state of mind. Conscious of the tremendous difficulties before him, in his early years Arguedas often perceived more structural and cultural abysses between the two languages than possible fields of coincidence. His initial attempts to write short fiction were in Quechua. At that time he felt that only in Quechua could he find the appropriate expression of feeling for the lived experiences and memories of the village life he wanted to inscribe. The memory of those events appeared to be sealed in Quechua, and the language itself was one with the experience or the sight he wanted to transpose from memory into writing. His friends pointed out the unavoidable truth: Quechua as a language in print, as a "literary" language, did not for all practical purposes, exist. If he persisted in writing in Quechua, his friends counseled, he would be a writer without readers, for even his fellow Quechua speakers would be unable to read him, since they were for the most part illiterate. Spanish thus became his only available tool. Mastering the secrets of this old and complex instrument, a tool associated with the harsh rule of masters in a world divided between Indians and lords was not an easy or welcome task.

Early on in his career as an anthropologist and novelist, Arguedas spoke about the painful task of creating an imaginary world that was based on his hatred of the world order created by the *señores* (masters) in order to oppress the Indians. Thirteen years after the publication of *Agua*, he said he wrote it in a fit of rage (*arrebato*).

Such a confrontational opposition became the core of Arguedas's plot structures. As Antonio Cornejo-Polar has shown in *Los universos narrativos de José María Arguedas* (1973), Arguedas's entire fictional corpus is anchored on a coherent play of oppositions, which develops a series of variations of ever-richer colorations and complexity. In *Agua* the point of view of the stories coincides with the consciousness of a child living the dramas enacted in the village by the grown-ups. *Yawar fiesta* is set in a provincial capital, Puquio. The point of view in the story, narrated in the third person, is of one of the mestizo youths returning for the local celebration of the Yawar fiesta, an Andean version of the Spanish bullfight.

Arguedas's geographic and social scope widens significantly with *Los ríos profundos*. The main character, an adolescent named Ernesto, ranges widely throughout the southern Peruvian Andes. With his father, an itinerant lawyer, Ernesto travels from town to town, visits Cuzco, and spends a few months in Abancay.

It is widely agreed that *Los ríos profundos* is Arguedas's masterpiece. In it he manages to pull together the two strands he had earlier developed with *Agua* and *Yawar fiesta*. In *Los ríos profundos* Ernesto again appears torn between two separate worlds. The novel starts out on a note of intense intimacy when he begins his recollection of the humiliating yet glorious night he and his father spent in Cuzco. This first chapter opens yet another retrospective of a time when the boy was his father's companion as they traveled in search of litigants who could not find relief in the oppressive system of "justice" in the Andes. Visions of tiny, flowering towns nestled in the pockets of the highest peaks or the lowest valleys of the Andes star the novel's narration. However, this quick deployment through the Andes comes to an abrupt stop in Abancay, where the boy is left in boarding school. In this hot town, named after the intensely red flower of the "awankay," Ernesto and his father part. The adolescent, a fiery yet naive boy, is left in a religious school while the father continues his traveling and work.

One of Ernesto's immediate discoveries is that in the school, too, social tension between dominant and oppressed peoples is the order of the day. The boys abuse each other in all sorts of ways right under the vigilant eyes of the priests. One of the rituals of abuse and self-deprecation involves Opa, a retarded young woman brought into the convent as a servant but in fact used by many of the boys and even the priests as a sexual object. As in several of Arguedas's other books, including *Todas las sangres*, sex, for the boy, appears connected to the desire for large or deformed half-witted women. Although driven by her beastly and irrepressible desire, Opa knows the sexual encounter to be a sin. The twin discovery of sexual and social violence torments Ernesto, who sees himself as the next victim of the older boys' violence. Saturated by anxiety and terrified at the prospect of forced sex with Opa or beatings by older boys, Ernesto runs away in search of fields of corn, the uncontaminated beauty of a cliff, the pure language of rivers, and the company of Indians. Expecting to find proud and defiant *ayllu* Indians, like the K'ayaus in *Yawar fiesta*, Ernesto enters the Patibamba hacienda. Here the Indians are serfs of the lord of Patibamba. The misery,

Dust jacket for Arguedas's 1964 novel, which focuses on the struggles of two powerful landowners and the Indian farmers as Peru becomes increasingly modernized

filth, and fear in which these serfs live shocks Ernesto. Although these serfs are almost speechless and recoil in animal-like gestures of self-defense when he approaches them, Ernesto manages to understand that they are restless. As it turns out, the government has decided to confiscate the allotment of salt for the town and thus for the serfs. There are rumors that there is also a typhus epidemic afoot.

On his way back to school, depressed and aimless, Ernesto stops by a *chichería*, a local Indian and mestizo pub. There he makes contact once again with free Indians, their inspiring music, and the fearless *chicheras*, mestizo women who own these restaurants and pubs. Reinvigorated after a return to nature, to freedom, and especially to music—invariably good in Arguedas's world—Ernesto finds that the seedling of solidarity amongst the humble, small, and oppressed boys at his school has grown into a full rebellion.

Having identified and chosen a leader, the small boys challenge the system of violence and corruption established by the older boys. As the solidarity of the weak erupts within the school walls, in the city the *chicheras*, too, have rebelled against the denial of salt distribution. Inside the school, Ernesto hears the clamor of the mutiny. He learns that the serfs also have rebelled, not against their masters but against the idea that they should be left to suffer the typhus epidemic without religious or magical assistance to stop it. As the old order begins to crumble, the army steps in.

Because Opa is believed to have come down with typhus, the schoolboys are all sent home. Just before leaving, Ernesto goes to visit the retarded woman. He believes that she has suffered much and that she will be forgiven for her sins. After his farewell to Opa, Ernesto, the orphan boy of *Agua*, must once again confront his solitude. For him, there is no home to which he can return. In spite of a deep mutual love between father and son, the father is unable to take care of the boy. Ernesto walks on a path leading out of the valley, filling his mind with memories of the happy days when he lived as an Indian boy.

Perhaps it is in *Los ríos profundos* where Andean music and singing play the most important and integral part in Arguedas's fiction. He was one of the first anthropologists to demonstrate the ample range, role, and significance of poetic composition for the singing and complex arrangements. Arguedas himself composed many short ballads and lyrics in Quechua. But perhaps his greatest poetic composition in Quechua is his *Túpac Amaru Kamaq taytanchisman; Haylli-taki. A nuestro padre creador Túpac Amaru; Himno-canción.*

In short poetical compositions designed to commemorate all sorts of ritualized routine, as well as unusual events in the life of individuals and the community as a whole, singing functions as a record of an informal oral history. When Ernesto visits the pub, he walks in hoping to find musicians, eager to find pleasure and solace in old and new *huaynos* (songs). This single occasion in the novel provides the opportunity for a crisp and knowledgeable review of the *huayno* repertoire of the southern Andes. For the clientele of the pub each *huayno* is special and distinct depending on its regional origin; the subject of the composition; the execution by each famous harpist, violinist, or *charanguero*; or the ritual feast with which it is associated. Ernesto, the fan, upon hearing the harpists' music, enters into a trancelike state. A similar state of ecstasy has been experienced by him earlier in Cuzco while standing before the Incan wall, hearing the golden bells of Cuzco. Ernesto's lyrical sense of the ineffable also finds a metaphor in his vision of light on the flowering, blue potato fields or in the music of the deep rivers. Music, light, nature, and the heritage of a great past become in Arguedas the points of contact with depthless happiness. For Ernesto the call to heroic action, which he sees for himself, the other boys, the *chicheras*, and the serfs as their immediate destiny, is adumbrated in the rhythm of the *huaynos*.

The thematic and technical risks Arguedas was willing to take increased with the publication of each of his narratives. His scenario changed from the Andean villages of *Los ríos profundos*—set in the early 1920s before roads, cars, and trucks made communication easier among the many isolated areas of the Andean territory—to a deteriorating and partially abandoned provincial capital in *Todas las sangres*. As the title of the novel indicates, the plot attempts to bring together the many races (or bloods) that constitute a fragmented and varied society caught in the corrosive process of becoming a nation. The original oppositional forces of *señores* and Indians, and their respective irreconcilable worldviews, again constitute the main axis for conflict in *Todas las sangres*. But in this novel each image or force is deployed in a double or triple set of valences. Indians and *señores* no longer appear or behave as parts of solid, unbreachable, economic, ideological blocks. Bringing to bear his mature powers of observation and understanding, Arguedas displays his characters and their actions realistically. His psychological penetration blends with social analysis. A scientific attitude is mixed with a deeply personal and reflective mood. Political and ethical matters appear inseparable from the presence of the magical.

In *Todas las sangres* the two Arango brothers, Don Fermín and Don Bruno, who are powerful *señores*, fight for the privilege, or damnation, of shaping a future for the emerging new order. These two men, who see each other as an enemy, must in turn deal with other people, whom they see as either allies or enemies. Thus Don Fermín appears as the evil brother who has made a Faustian pact with the commercial and industrializing forces from Lima. These forces care little for the welfare of Indians, *señores*, smaller Andean landholders, or for the preservation of the environment. Don Fermín and his technical engineers see only profit and power. His brother, the blond, lecherous, carnal, and eroticized Don Bruno, is the other evil brother, who opposes all forces of change. Don Bruno, a reluctant heir to the world of his father, the great *señor* who publicly takes his own life in protest over the decay of the old social order, swears to keep "his" Indians "pure" by continuing his totalitarian tutelage over their lives. The two "evil" brothers are, however, being watched and assessed by a new and unsuspected force: Rendón, an Indian who was greatly humiliated by the brothers' father when, as a child, he had wanted to go to school. Rendón immigrated to Lima. There, amidst the garbage heaps, he claims to have learned what Peru was really about. Rendón has a plan for the forging of the new nation which includes the liberation of his fellow Indians. Lima, in *Todas las sangres*, represents both new and old forces of moral decay, places in which each human being is his brother's own enemy. Rendón—the new Indian—rejects this alienated world and struggles to find ways of modernizing the Indian world without losing its most precious asset: human solidarity. Rendón is eventually accused of communist activity and shot by government soldiers, his former fellow Indians.

In a way, *Todas las sangres* spells out the beginning of the end of the world of *Agua*. Arguedas saw that ending with more terror than relief, for the Andean culture he had so passionately depicted the Andean culture whose achievements and beauty he had so dexterously portrayed in *Amor mundo*, in his bilingual *El sueño del pongo* (The Pongo's Dream, 1965), and in *La agonía de "Rasu Ñiti,"* that pristine world of love and hatred, of immeasurable beauty and light—could no longer aspire to continue untouched if at the same time the Indians were to liberate themselves from domination. In *El zorro de arriba y el zorro de abajo* Arguedas attempts to come to grips with the new world wrought in Peru by the forces of hunger, improved communications, the fast influx of foreign capital, and the contending ideologies of the time.

Aware of the need for a new departure, for a form capable of presenting the complexity demanded by his project, Arguedas hit a dry spell in his narrative production. Arguedas's search for a novelistic form empowered to bridge his own personal turbulence, the speed and puzzlement of social change around him, and his sense of the continuity of Andean cultural formations is, however, tentatively met in *El Zorro*. He achieves this by setting up a system of alternation between two different series. One series of chapters corresponds to a diary, and the other narrates the chapters of a novel centered in the town of Chimbote.

The chronology of events in Chimbote develops over a much shorter time than in either *Los ríos profundos* or *Todas las sangres*. But the historical and personal time that Arguedas attempts to plumb reaches much further into both the past and the future.

While Arguedas's fictional world is keenly attuned to the most minimal economy in nature as a system of crucial and wondrous minutiae, the same world often seems to be embedded in myth and religious belief. Arguedas's work as an anthropologist had led him back to the Andean villages of Peru. There, asking as both a man in love with the world of his childhood and as an anthropologist doing strict fieldwork, he collected folktales, songs, and myths. Arguedas thus lived deeply aware of the Andean literary legacy in the form of legend, myth, or humor. When the sixteenth-century manuscript of myths and stories of the valley of Huarochirí was found, Arguedas was one of the first scholars to recognize the importance of the manuscript and to certify its Andean authenticity.

Arguedas held the post of director of the Museo Nacional de Historia from 1964 to 1969, and he undertook the translation—from Quechua into Spanish—of the myths of Huarochirí. This work on the translation of the Huarochirí myths coincided with the dry period of his output of fiction, the years when he struggled to find a form for his new novel. *Dioses y hombres de Huarochirí* (Gods and Men of Huarochirí) was finally completed in 1966. It is a bilingual edition of the myths that had been collected by Francisco de Avila, a priest in charge of the parish of San Damián in the valley of Huarochirí. In these stories, which relate the feats of the cultural heroes of Huarochirí, the fox often appears as a character or as the anthropomorphic shape adopted by the hero facing an impossible task or challenge.

In *El zorro* Arguedas reinscribes these figures in an ongoing dialogue or dispute between the men and culture of the highlands and the people from the lowlands, who after having remained separate for so many centuries must, in the Chimbote of the 1960s, come together. In a way the Huarochirí myths become a metaphor for the cultural problem that Arguedas faced

Page from the first draft for an unfinished novel, "Se muda el sol" (The Sun Itself Changes), published in Arguedas's Obras completas, *volume 2 (by permission of the Estate of José María Arguedas)*

throughout his life in an attempt to understand and portray the world of the Andean peoples. The kernel of the problem contains two often contradictory and yet inevitable forces: the continuity of the authentically Andean cultural forms; and the adaptation of European cultural formations, or transculturation.

In his search for solutions to his problem of authenticity, he searched for the means by which Spanish as a literary system would not betray the essence or the difference of what he wanted to inscribe: the Indian and his world as seen by himself. In the writing of *Agua*, he had redoubled his contact with the indigenist novel in Peru. He found these texts to offer a deeply false and negative view of the Indian world. Arguedas found the Indian inner self, the meaning of his world and actions, terribly distorted. Arguedas felt that these indigenist novels, including the mother of the genre, *Aves sin nido* (Birds Without a Nest, 1918) by Clorinda Matto de Turner, in their teary but uninformed portrayal of Indian characters and life patterns had perpetuated a great fraud. Arguedas's objective in writing fiction as well as his final choice of writing in Spanish was thus in part driven by the passion to correct a falsehood and the need to portray exactly the world of his childhood.

Quickly Arguedas found that the styles and strategies required—namely realism—for the portrayal of a world "exactly as it is," were not only beyond his experience of oral storytelling but also complex and elusive. Arguedas faced a triple task: how to transform the contents of his memory and passion into readable stories; how to avoid falling into the trap of being inauthentic in the process of appropriating established conventions for storytelling; and how to infuse into the cardboard, dry, formulaic, sentimental Spanish of the indigenist novel the necessary deviations to make it a trustworthy messenger of a theretofore unwritten sense of the world.

For Arguedas there was not only a struggle between his inner self and Spanish as an obstacle to the expression of that self, but also between the beauty of the land and a language that is not Quechua. Some students of Arguedas's work have argued that Arguedas's creation of a "castellano indio," or an Indian Spanish, for the use of his Indian characters represents a solution to the problem. But Arguedas himself did not, of course, write in this "castellano indio." The fact is that, like any other Latin-American writer, Arguedas struggled with a Spanish encased in a lit-

Arguedas in 1968, the year before he committed suicide (photograph by Olga Luna)

erary system and therefore in a worldview that was not originally his own. His struggle entails the appropriation of Spanish as a linguistic, literary, and cultural system capable of "speaking" (coding, encoding, and decoding) Arguedas's deeply lived and memorialized world of his Indian childhood. This enterprise of writing as a painful and conscious process of recoding a series of symbolic systems already given has been characterized by Alejo Carpentier as the search for an Adamic language on the part of the Latin-American writer. Nevertheless, Arguedas did write in Spanish, and the recognition of his artistic achievement is in part due to the style he created and introduced, as well as to the efficacy of his prose in conveying the authenticity of his fictional world.

Arguedas wrote *El zorro de arriba y el zorro de abajo* in the midst of the horror of having to witness the disappearance of the world he so fiercely loved. While Arguedas managed to avoid the false Indians of the novels and essays of López Albújar and Ventura García Calderón, he still needed to find a satisfactory narrative strategy to relate what he called the epic nature of the events (*gestas*) lived by and recorded in the oral memory of Andean societies. Arguedas's reading of the works of Leo Tolstoy and Fyodor Dostoyevski opened windows for the portrayal of the oppressed and the suffering. Arguedas seems to have seen a way in which to render the myriad suffering and exploitation of the Andean people.

Arguedas's challenge was to reinscribe the glory and beauty of Andean nature and the limitless suffering of Indians into a new style and understanding of the Andean world and the human species. The epic character of his stories constitutes a revision of the regionalist and indigenist desolate landscape of unmitigated pain and humiliation. Arguedas sounds the key of joy and solidarity in the black hole of despair. A very personal existentialism, a deep faith in the goodness of those who suffer together, informs Arguedas's rebellious hope. Until the writing of *El zorro* Arguedas apparently believed that social justice in Peru was just around the corner.

In *El zorro* Arguedas's childhood world is gone forever. Chimbote is a makeshift boomtown filled with unplugged refrigerators sitting on the mud floors of one-room "houses." Thousands of people arrive every day in search of work in this large fishing port. The town is basically full of transient people. Chimbote turns out to be a place in nowhere, a sort of inverted utopia, where existential man faces both the greatest opportunity to discover being anew or to plunge into the hell of nonbeing.

In *Cultura popular andina y forma novelesca* (1982), a book entirely dedicated to the exploration of this unfinished novel, Martin Lienhard attempts to show how the two parallel series of stories upon which the novel revolves can be integrated into a single coherent reading of the whole text. Because the novel contains a series of "Diarios" with another series more overtly fictional, some readers have seen a compelling, confessional, autobiographical text in the diaries, next to, but not really connected to, the story of Chimbote. There is no question that *El zorro* tests the limits of the novelistic form because of the decidedly confessional, wrenching tone and content of the diaries. The autobiographical reading of the diaries is justified if one takes into account that the subject called "I" or "Arguedas" in the diaries is writing after a failed attempt to commit suicide and upon the counsel of his therapist, who argues that if Arguedas writes, suicide can be held in abeyance. The diaries thus become the taut line between life and death.

Ironically it is in *El zorro* that Arguedas's keen sense of humor and the grotesque can perhaps be best discovered. Together with the comical appears the deadly serious question of sex and prostitution. In *Amor mundo*, sex appears as the tarrying discovery of a desired but sinful act on the part of an adolescent boy. In general, until *El zorro* women as sexual beings/objects appear in Arguedas's work under the contradictory tenets of Marianism or the cult of the Virgin-and-Mother.

El zorro becomes Arguedas's last and closing novel, not only because of his death but also because in it, the oppositions with which he had built his fictional universe reach the point of exhaustion. With the variants of the oppositions historically spent by the Peruvian society of the 1920s, Arguedas's contrasts turn into irreconcilable contradictions that cannot be muffled either by the nostalgia of memory or by the utopia of language. *El zorro de arriba y el zorro de abajo* is thus to be read as the answer to the ambiguous ending of *Todas las sangres* and as a novel deeply embedded in both its verbal reality and the historical web in which it forges its meaning.

Bibliography:
Mildred E. Merino de Zela, Bibliography, in "Vida y obra de José María Arguedas," *Revista Peruana de Cultura*, 13-14 (December 1970): 127-178.

Biography:
Mildred E. Merino de Zela, "Vida y obra de José María Arguedas," *Revista Peruana de Cultura*, 13-14 (December 1970): 127-178.

References:
"Arguedas: el narrador y el antropólogo frente al lenguaje," *Revista Iberoamericana*, 49 (January-March 1983): 97-109;

Damián Arguedas, E. Murrugarra, and H. Blanco, *José María Arguedas Testimonios* (Lima: Instituto Cultural José María Arguedas, 1980);

Moisés Arroyo Posadas, *La multitud y el paisaje peruano en los relatos de José María Arguedas* (Lima: Impresiones & Publicidad, 1939);

Edmundo Bendezú Aibar, " 'Yawar fiesta: Espejo quechua,' de José María Arguedas," *Insula*, 29 (July-August 1974): 9, 23;

Sara Castro-Klarén, "Crimen y castigo: Sexualidad en J. M. Arguedas," *Revista Iberoamericana*, 122 (January-March 1983): 55-65;

Castro-Klarén, *El mundo mágico de José María Arguedas* (Lima: Instituto de Estudios Peruanos, 1973);

Castro-Klarén, "Mundo y palabra: Hacia una problemática del bilingüismo en Arguedas," *Runa*, 6 (November-December 1979): 8-10, 39;

Castro-Klarén, "Testimonio sobre preguntas de José María Arguedas," *Hispamérica*, 4, no. 10 (1975): 45-54;

Antonio Cornejo Polar, "El sentido de la narrativa de Arguedas," *Revista Peruana de Cultura*, 13-14 (December 1970): 17-48;

Cornejo Polar, *Los universos narrativos de José María Arguedas* (Buenos Aires: Losada, 1973);

George Robert Coulthard, "Un problema de estilo," *Mundo Nuevo*, 19 (January 1968): 73-77;

Juan Carlos Curuchet, "José María Arguedas: Peruano universal," *Cuadernos Hispanoamericanos*, 228 (December 1968): 749-755;

Tomás G. Escajadillo, "Meditación preliminar acerca de José María Arguedas y el indigenismo," *Revista Peruana de Cultura*, 13-14 (December 1970): 82-126;

Alberto Escobar, "Relectura de Arguedas: Dos proposiciónes," *Ultima Hora* (11 January 1976): 11;

Escobar and others, *Giornata di studio su José María Arguedas* (Rome: Instituto Italo Latino Americano, 1981?);

Eve-Marie Fell, "José María Arguedas et le problème du métissage," in *Travaux de l'Institut d'Etudes Hispaniques et Portugaises de l'Université de Tours* (Tours: Université de Tours, 1979), pp. 89-102;

Peter Gold, "The *indigenista* fiction of José María Arguedas," *Bulletin of Hispanic Studies*, 50 (January 1973): 56-70;

Regina Harrison, "José María Arguedas: el substrato quechua," *Revista Iberoamericana*, 49 (January-March 1983): 111-132;

Juan Larco, Prologue to his *Recopilación de textos sobre José María Arguedas* (Havana: Casa de las Américas, 1976), pp. 7-20;

César Lévano, *Arguedas un sentimiento trágico de la vida* (Lima: Gráfica Labor, 1969);

Martin Lienhard, *Cultura popular andina y forma novelesca: Zorros y danzantes en la última novela de Arguedas* (Lima: Latinoamericana Editores-Tarea, 1982);

Naomi Lindstron, "*El zorro de arriba y el zorro de abajo:* Una marginación al nivel del discurso," *Revista Iberoamericana*, 49 (January-March 1983): 211-218;

Alejandro Losada, "La obra de José María Arguedas y la sociedad andina: Interpretación de su creación como praxis social," *Eco*, 162 (April 1974): 592-620;

Yerko Moretic, "Tras las huellas del indigenismo literario en el Perú," *Atenea*, 156 (October-December 1964): 205-216;

John V. Murra, Introduction to Arguedas's *Deep Rivers*, translated by Frances H. Barraclough (Austin: University of Texas Press, 1978), pp. ix-xv;

Julio Ortega, "Sobre la última novela de Arguedas," in his *La imaginación crítica: Ensayos sobre la modernidad en el Perú* (Lima: Peisa, 1974), pp. 189-198;

Ortega, *Texto, comunicación y cultura*, Los ríos profundos *de José María Arguedas* (Lima: CEDEP, 1982);

Angel Rama, Introduction to Arguedas's *Formación de una cultura nacional indoamericana*, edited by Rama (Mexico City: Siglo Veintiuno, 1975), pp. ix-xxiv;

Rama, "José María Arguedas, transculturador," prologue to Arguedas's *Señores e indios*, edited by Rama (Buenos Aires: Arca, 1976), pp. 7-38;

Julio Ramón Ribeyro, "José María Arguedas o la destrucción de la Arcadia," in his *La caza sutil* (Lima: Milla Batres, 1976), pp. 85-93;

Julio Rodríguez-Luis, *Hermenéutica y praxis del indigenismo* (Mexico City: Tierra Firme/FCE, 1980);

María Rostworowski de Diez Canseco, *Estructuras andinas del poder: Ideología religiosa y política* (Lima: Instituto de Estudios Peruanos, 1983);

José Luis Rouillon, "José María Arguedas y la Religión," *Páginas*, 2, no. 15 (1978): 11-30;

Rouillon, "Presentación y notas criticas a la obra de José María Arguedas," in Arguedas's *Cuentos olvidados*, edited by Rouillon (Lima: Imágenes & Letras, 1973);

William Rowe, *Mito e ideología en la obra de José María Arguedas* (Lima: Instituto Nacional de Cultura, 1979);

Rowe, "Mito, lenguaje e ideología en *Los ríos pro-

fundos," Textual, 7 (1973): 2-12;
Pedro Trigo, *Arguedas: Mito, historia y religión* (Lima: Centro de Estudios & Publicaciones, 1982);

Mario Vargas Llosa, "Tres notas sobre Arguedas," in his *Nueva novela latinoamericana* (Buenos Aires: Paidós, 1972), pp. 30-54.

Juan José Arreola

(21 September 1918 -)

Sara Poot-Herrera
University of California, Santa Barbara

BOOKS: *Gunther Stapenhorst* (Mexico City: Lunes, 1946);
Varia invención (Mexico City: Tezontle, 1949);
Cinco Cuentos (Mexico City: Los Presentes, 1951);
Confabulario (Mexico City: Cultura Económica, 1952); enlarged as *Confabulario y Varia invención* (Mexico City: Cultura Económica, 1955); enlarged again as *Confabulario total* (Mexico City: Cultura Económica, 1962); translated by George G. Schade as *Confabulario and Other Inventions* (Austin: University of Texas Press, 1964);
La hora de todos (Mexico City: Los Presentes, 1954);
Bestiario: Punta de plata (Mexico City: Universidad Nacional Autónoma de México, 1958; revised edition, Mexico City: Mortiz, 1981);
La feria (Mexico City: Mortiz, 1963); translated by John Upton as *The Fair* (Austin: University of Texas Press, 1977);
Cuentos (Havana: Casa de las Américas, 1969);
Palindroma (Mexico City: Mortiz, 1971);
La palabra educación, edited by Jorge Arturo Ojeda (Mexico City: Secretaría de Educación Pública, 1973);
Y ahora, la mujer, edited by Ojeda (Mexico City: Secretaría de Educación Pública, 1975);
Inventario (Mexico City: Grijalbo, 1976);
Ramón López Velarde: Una lectura parcial de Juan José Arreola (Mexico City: Cultural Bancen, 1988).

Editions and Collections: *Antología de Juan José Arreola*, edited by Jorge Arturo Ojeda (Mexico City: Oasis, 1969);

Mujeres, animales y fantasías mecánicas, edited by Ojeda (Barcelona: Tusquets, 1972);
Confabulario antológico (Madrid: Círculo de Lectores, 1973);
Mi confabulario (Mexico City: Promexa, 1979);
Confabulario personal (Barcelona: Bruguera, 1980);
Imagen y obra escogida (Mexico City: Universidad Nacional Autónoma de México, 1984);
Estas páginas mías (Mexico City: Cultura Económica, 1985);
Confabulario, special edition (Mexico City: Cultura Económica, 1985);
Confabulario definitivo, edited by Carmen de Mora (Madrid: Cátedra, 1986).

OTHER: *Cuadernos del Unicornio*, 5 volumes, edited by Arreola (Mexico City, 1958-1960);
Lectura en voz alta, edited by Arreola (Mexico City: Porrúa, 1968);
"La implantación del espíritu," in *Imagen y realidad de la mujer*, edited by Elena Urrutia (Mexico City: Secretaría de Educación Pública, 1975), pp. 44-61.

Juan José Arreola's literary creations are the result of the enjoyable and playful activity of the artisan. His concept of literature and his works have served as a canon in the training of new writers, a task to which Arreola has dedicated a great part of his career. His creative diversity is based on his unusual artistic abilities and an emphasis on the use of and play with language. Added to Arreola's literary capacity are his mimetic ability, a good ear, and an extraordinary memory, which enable him to capture phrases, fragments, entire

Juan José Arreola circa 1959 (photograph by Hans Beacham)

texts, and different styles; these he reproduces and transforms in his works. His love of literature, his concern with writing, the appreciation of words—both spoken and written—the pleasure of acting, and his appraisal of different skills and occupations have created an oeuvre characterized by its briefness while maintaining diversity and a capacity for innumerable developments.

Arreola's body of work is composed mostly of short stories, a genre he promotes in Mexican literature and by which he is best known. Some of his texts are best described as exercises of style and syntax, as well as aphorisms, maxims, and reflections. Many of his first short stories were compiled in *Varia invención* (Various Inventions, 1949), in *Cinco Cuentos* (Five Tales, 1951), and in the first *Confabulario* (1952).

In his "De memoria y olvido" (Of Memory and Forgetting), a miniscule autobiography, Arreola speaks of his birthplace: "Yo, señores, soy de Zapotlán el Grande. Un pueblo que de tan grande nos lo hicieron Ciudad Guzmán hace cien años. Pero nosotros seguimos siendo tan pueblo que todavía le decimos Zapotlán" (I, gentlemen, am from Zapotlán el Grande. A town that because it grew so large was renamed Ciudad Guzmán a hundred years ago. But we are in essence still a small town, so we continue calling it Zapotlán). The fourth of fourteen children, Arreola was born on 21 September 1918 to Felipe Arreola Mendoza and the former Victoria Zuñiga. Of his parents, he says: "soy herrero por parte de mi madre y carpintero a título paterno. De allí mi pasión por el lenguaje" (I am a blacksmith on my mother's side and a carpenter from my father's. Thus my passion for the craft of language). Juan José Arreola eventually married Sara Sánchez Torres.

Arreola is mostly self-taught. He went from diverse jobs held during his youth to a series of activities related to literature: as writer, editor, teacher, translator, and actor. As an actor he participated in Xavier Villaurrutia and Rodolfo

Usigli's drama group; in 1945 he studied in Paris, where he played small roles in the Comédie Française; and in Mexico he was a founding member and actor of Poesía en Voz Alta, a group of artists, writers, and playwrights. Arreola has also played an important cultural role in Mexican television, including his televised literary dialogues with Jorge Luis Borges in 1978, when the poetry of Luis de Góngora and Francisco de Quevedo was discussed.

The short story that truly represents the beginning of Arreola's important fiction oeuvre is "Hizo el bien mientras vivió" (He Did Good While He Lived; collected in *Varia invención*), written in 1941 and first published in 1943 in *Eos*. Arreola's editorial participation was vital in both *Eos* and *Pan*, two literary journals from Guadalajara, and he went on to establish the literary series of *Los Presentes*, *Libros*, and *Cuadernos del Unicornio*. In these publications Arreola introduced several major figures of the literary generation of the 1950s, including Elena Poniatowska, Carlos Fuentes, José Emilio Pacheco, and Fernando del Paso. His support for the young emerging writers was also important at the Centro Mexicano de Escritores. In addition Arreola was one of the founders of literary workshops in Mexico: Mester (meaning craft or trade), one of his workshops, began in the 1960s along with a publication of the same name, in which some young writers published their works; for example, José Agustín's first novel, *La tumba* (The Grave, 1964), first appeared there.

After the publication of his first short-story collections, Arreola began to branch out into other genres more, publishing the play *La hora de todos* (Everybody's Time, 1954), which was awarded a prize by the Instituto Nacional de Bellas Artes; *Bestiario: Punta de plata* (Bestiary: Silver Tip, 1958), a book of satires; and *La feria* (1963; translated as *The Fair*, 1977), his only novel, for which he shared the Xavier Villaurrutia prize with Elena Garro, author of *Los recuerdos del porvenir* (Remembrances of Things to Come). Eight years after the publication of *La feria*, Arreola published *Palindroma*, which, as its name indicates, contains verbal and intellectual games.

Arreola published some works before *Varia invención*, including a small book comprising the short story *Gunther Stapenhorst* (1946); other works, such as *Inventario* (1976) and a book about Ramón López Velarde (1988), were published after *Palindroma*. However, Arreola's major writing is in *Varia invención*, *La feria*, *Bestiario*, *Palindroma*, and the various editions of *Confabulario*.

Confabulario total contains five sections that comprise his works written up until that moment. "Prosodia" (from which some texts appeared in the 1952 and in the 1955 editions of *Confabulario*) is the first part of *Confabulario total*; *Bestiario* is second (with the same texts from the original edition); in the middle stands the first *Confabulario*; *La hora de todos*, which Arreola calls "juguete cómico en un acto" (a funny toy in one act), is the fourth section; and last is *Varia invención*.

The short stories of *Varia invención* belong to the first stage of Arreola's writing and illustrate some of the purified and synthetized elements characteristic of his style. From the first to the latest of his short stories—from "Hizo el bien mientras vivió" of *Varia invención* to "Tres días y un cenicero" (Three Days and an Ashtray) of *Palindroma*—Arreola often utilizes the diary form. The first story recapitulates everyday actions and thus reveals the internalized space of the one who writes the diary, who in this case is a small-town lawyer. This character—like many of Arreola's—writes and is conscious of his writing.

Another short story in *Varia invención*, "La vida privada" (Private Life), deals with the problems of a love triangle. Arreola explores this theme repeatedly with multiple variants in different stories. For instance, in "La vida privada" the narrator of the story is the husband, while in "El faro" (The Lighthouse) the lover presents his perspective. A love triangle is also found in "Apuntes de un rencoroso" (Notes Full of Rancor), where the third party, forgotten and resentful, speaks one of those poetic and accurate Arreolan phrases: "giro en la espiral del insomnio" (I spin in the spiral of insomnia).

The thematic weaving of Arreola's first story collection contains other fundamental aspects. In "La vida privada," for example, there is a connection between the characters' lives and a play that is performed in the story. The relation between life and literature is also characteristic of Arreola's oeuvre, reflecting his experience, as he has many times converted life into literature, and vice versa. The text focuses on the essence and actions of particular characters, who are usually lonely and tend to reveal their intimacy during some sort of confession.

The appraisal of skills and occupations is important for Arreola, and this is best displayed in "Carta a un zapatero" (Letter to a Shoemaker).

Dust jacket for the 1964 translation of Arreola's 1952 book, a collection of short stories and brief exercises in wordplay

This short story—an extraordinary sample of Arreola's letter writing—is a tribute to professions and art crafts. This characteristic of Arreola is also manifested in the main character of "El fraude" (The Fraud), a stove salesman who recognizes that he could have been "un juglar, un mendigo, un narrador de cuentos" (a minstrel, a beggar, a teller of stories). These words announce Arreola's interest in entertainment as well as in popular and street culture, an interest present throughout his literary production (for example, in *La feria*).

Varia invención also includes "El cuervero" (The Crow Catcher), set in a rural area and related in theme and language to some passages of *La feria*. Both the story and the novel, as well as other works by Arreola, have ties with Juan Rulfo's writings. The first half of the 1940s was important for the literary training of these two writers. Both were good friends of Antonio Alatorre, with whom Arreola founded the literary journal *Pan*. The personal and literary relationship between Arreola and Rulfo included waiting for the arrival of foreign books at bookstores, sharing readings, walking through the streets of Guadalajara, and being committed to *Pan*, where Rulfo published two short stories before being put in charge of the journal. Efrén Hernández was a short-story writer of great influence on the two of them: they published some of their first stories in the literary journal *América*, which Hernández directed. Just as elements of world literature appear in Arreola's oeuvre from the start—which was not very common in Mexican literature at the time—so do aspects of the lives of peasants and Indians, to whom *La feria* is dedicated.

La hora de todos takes its title from a play by Quevedo. Both *culteranismo* and *conceptismo* are evident in Arreola's style; he assimilates and modifies these literary trends in his works.

La hora de todos and *Varia invención* introduced the strong intertextual net that was to be seen throughout the entire body of his work. This net is embroidered with obvious signs and elaborate clues, in the titles, the epigraphs, the beginning lines, and in between the lines, in the organization, themes, characters, and speeches. The transformation of these elements is part of the relationship that Arreola maintains with the culture and literature that appear in his productions. Arreola himself has spoken about his debt to other writers, which has also been pointed out by critics: readers see signs of Giovanni Papini, Marcel Schwob, Franz Kafka, and Borges, among others.

Confabulario, Arreola's third short-story collection, is the nucleus of all his writings. The word *confabulario*, invented by Arreola, refers to his entire literary creation. Furthermore, the book called *Confabulario* contains most of the stories that have made Arreola well known.

"El guardagujas" (The Switchman), for example, shows the wild imagination of Arreola through the words of the switchman who narrates most of the tale. During a dialogue between the switchman and a foreigner, the latter speaks of his need to get to a particular place, and the switchman tells him of the impossibility of his reaching it. The stories about trains told by the switchman amount to a social criticism of the train system of a certain country. The switchman's stories end when the train arrives, and surprisingly the foreigner creates an absurd situation by changing the initial *T* of the town he was seeking to *X*. The story concludes with ambiguity, created by the foreigner's words, and the disappearance of the switchman, who runs to meet the train. The technique and the art of Arreola's storytelling make "El guardagujas" one of the best short stories in Mexican fiction, and among all of Arreola's stories, it is the one that has captured the most critical attention.

The grace and tenderness of the switchman are the same qualities that Arreola projects onto other texts and characters. It is the grace with which "Pueblerina" (Village Maiden), for instance, presents a palpable Kafkaesque feeling. In this short story Kafka's influence is not in the use of a letter to identify places, but in the absurd situations, as in the case of the character who grows horns overnight.

The absurdity in Arreola's short stories appears with different modifications. In "Una reputación" (A Reputation) everyday life is depicted, but the story is nonetheless set on a bus where the protagonist sees himself as the hero and savior of the women who ride the bus. "Parábola del trueque" (Parable of the Exchange) presents another situation with absurd elements: a merchant arrives in a certain town to trade old wives for new ones. The character that narrates the story does not trade his, and thus he is not a victim of the deception suffered by the husbands who are dazzled by the mirage of the promised exchange.

An important aspect of "Parábola del trueque," and throughout Arreola's oeuvre, is his portrayal of female characters. In this story a representative female is the element of exchange and merchandise as well as the instrument of justice and morality. She is granted privileged status at the end of the story after her husband decides not to trade her for a new wife.

Men's attitudes toward women are contradictory throughout Arreola's canon, as is the case in "Una mujer amaestrada" (A Tamed Woman). A woman's inhuman status as the object of a street show ends at the conclusion of the story when the narrator values and honors her. The strong feminine characters can never be subjugated, as illustrated in "La migala" (The Bird Spider), which prefigures *Bestiario* with its treatment of the animal/human being relationship. "La migala" is distinctly a horror story, told by a narrator who is, or at least feels, caught between life and death. The anguish of being trapped by a spider reminds him of the feeling he previously experienced with a woman, with whom he was also unable to live. Absurdity is again present: the main character has bought the spider and taken it home. Arreola's prose creates a poetic vision out of a situation where horror is established from the very first lines.

Arreola's work also contains dialogues with God, as seen in "El silencio de Dios" and "Pablo" (both in *Varia invención*); in the latter the mystic main character feels chosen as he prepares himself for a different existence in another world. Angels and demons appear in "Sinesio de Rodas" (in *Confabulario*) and "Un pacto con el diablo" (A Pact with the Devil; in *Varia invención*), the latter story taking place during the main character's dreams, film watching, and real life. The process of creation that occurs in "Parturient montes" (Divided Mountains; in *Confabulario*) is also present in these texts. Arreola presents biblical beliefs mixed with scientific experiments, such as the theme of the camel that goes through the eye of a needle in "Verdad os digo" (I'm Telling You the Truth); there are also classic characters and themes, as in "El prodigioso miligramo" (The Prodigious Milligram) and "Los alimentos terrestres" (The Earthly Fruit), which is a Gongorian text (all three collected in *Confabulario*).

In *Confabulario* one also finds the presence of female voices that narrate their experiences. For example, there is a woman character who talks about living with an ex-husband and compares him to an animal in "El rinoceronte" (The Rhinoceros"); there is also the female character of "Epitalamio" (Epithalamium), who is the victim of abuse and reflects with remorse and skepticism on her rape.

In many of his stories Arreola uses irony and humor, as in "De balística" (On Ballistics; in *Confabulario*) and "Corrido" (Street Ballad; from *Varia invención*), where his ability to imitate and transform is evident. The latter example recreates the theme of the wanton woman of some Mexican *corridos* and, although written in prose, maintains the rhythm of *corridos*. Arreola's stylistic games are repeatedly evident throughout his works; for instance, in *Confabulario* he imitates the "literary" writing style in "Dulcinea" and the commercial style in "Baby H. P." and "Anuncio" (Announcement).

An important part of Arreola's work is *Bestiario*, which is part of a tradition. It is a legacy of and also pays tribute to the medieval and Renaissance bestiaries as well as to *modernista* literature. In *Bestiario* there are mythological, prehistoric, and legendary animals—for example, the owl, the bison, and the axolotl—creatures from the sea, the jungle, the desert, and the bog; and domestic animals.

Arreola gathers and describes poetically and philosophically a varied bestiary, where animals act as reflectors of human qualities and vices, "y la fealdad del sapo aparece ante nosotros con una abrumadora cualidad de espejo" (and the ugliness of the toad appears before us with the overwhelming quality of a mirror). As in almost all Arreola's works, from beginning to end there are in *Bestiario* comparisons between animals and people, as intensified in some lines from "Aves acuáticas" (Aquatic Birds): "Pueblo multicolor y palabrero donde todos graznan y nadie se entiende" (Multicolored and talkative town where everybody cackles and no one understands).

The briefness and variety of Arreola's texts are also found in *La feria*, his only novel. Many stories are told with diverse voices, and there is a great variety of characters and settings. The stories unfold in a discontinuous way, separated by blank spaces and by a series of vignettes that allude directly or indirectly to the stories. The novel reflects the history and everyday life of Zapotlán, to which Arreola pays homage. The different stories include tales of the repossession of the land by the native Indians over the course of the centuries; an earthquake that makes everybody go to confession; the patron saint of Zapotlán, the icon behind the traditional festivity celebrated every year; the founding and the events of the red zone; the meetings of the town's Ateneo Literario (literary group); the adolescent who goes to confession and writes about his love experiences in the confessional; the shoemaker who becomes a failed farm worker and also writes about his experiences; the town's rich and poor; and the home and work life of the chandler, whose story intertwines with other important narratives in the novel.

La feria is made up of different discourses, in which the voices of characters and the writing of notes and documents predominate. The novel's epigraph announces its relationship with other texts, especially the Bible, which also is acknowledged by the characters.

Arreola's next book, *Palindroma*, responds to the question of how to construct and deconstruct a text, and how to read a text inside and out. This book, characterized by intellectual games, is divided into three sections: "Palindroma," "Variaciones sintácticas," and the play "Tercera llamada ¡tercera! o Empezamos sin usted" (Last Call, Last Call! or We'll Start Without You"). The first two sections illustrate a purified language in

Juan José Arreola

its minimal expression. "Tercera llamada" reintroduces the drama genre to his works. However, the characters and scenes of his narrative often have dramatic features, too.

Inventario, a series of reflections on culture, was published in 1976; years later a literary study followed—*Ramón López Velarde: Una lectura parcial de Juan José Arreola* (1988). With this book Arreola pays homage to a poet he recognizes as an important presence in his works: "Mis búsquedas, mis disparates y mis fortunas surgen de López Velarde" (My search, my nonsense and my fortune come from López Velarde). Mexican literature has two major figures in these two provincial writers: López Velarde in poetry and Arreola in prose. Both have also written prose poems, a genre they share with Gutiérrez Nájera, Alfonso Reyes, and Julio Torri. The artistry of Arreola's works; his respectful yet irreverent assault on other literatures, which converge and undergo a transformation in his work; the variety of his styles; the effect of spoken language captured in prose; and his work as a teacher and guide of various generations of writers make Juan José Arreola one of the most important figures in contemporary Mexican and Latin-American literature.

Interviews:
Emmanuel Carballo, "Juan José Arreola," in his

Diecinueve protagonistas de la literatura mexicana del siglo xx (Mexico City: Empresas, 1968), pp. 359-407;

Mauricio de la Selva, "Autovivisección de Juan José Arreola," *Cuadernos Americanos*, 29 (July-August 1970): 69-118;

Federico Campbell, "Juan José Arreola," in his *Conversaciones con escritores* (Mexico City: Secretaría de Educación Pública, 1972), pp. 37-57;

Máximo Simpson, "Sólo sirve la página viva, la que se queda parada en la mesa," *Crisis*, 18 (1974): 41-47;

Ambra Polidori, "La palabra puede ser un espectáculo," *Sábado*, Saturday supplement of *Uno más uno*, 11 February 1978;

Javier Molina, "El que pueda que se haga una estatua en mámol; el que no, aunque sea una fotografía amplificada," *Uno más uno*, 26 March 1979;

Cristina Peri Rossi, "Yo señores soy de Zapotlán el Grande," *Quimera*, 1 (1980): 23-27;

Molina, "El taller *Mester* fue el último grupo con una voluntad literaria verdadera," *Uno más uno*, 14 August 1982;

Vicente Leñero, "Cuarenta años de amistad. ¿Te acuerdas de Rulfo, Juan José Arreola?," *Proceso*, 482 (1986): 45-51.

Bibliographies:

Arthur and Fern L. Ramírez, "Hacia una bibliografía de y sobre Juan José Arreola," *Revista Iberoamericana*, 45 (July-December 1979): 651-667;

David William Foster, "Juan José Arreola," in his *Mexican Literature: A Bibliography of Secondary Sources* (Metuchen, N.J.: Scarecrow Press, 1981), pp. 91-95.

References:

Bertie Acker, *El cuento mexicano contemporáneo. Rulfo, Arreola y Fuentes: Temas y cosmovisión* (Madrid: Playor, 1984);

José Agustín, "Arreola influenció a todos los de Mester," *Uno más uno*, 26 June 1985;

Antonio Alatorre, "Para la historia de la cultura provinciana," *Vuelta*, 104 (July 1985): 48-54;

Alatorre, "Presentation," written introduction to the recorded anthology *Juan José Arreola: Voz viva de México* (Mexico City: Universidad Nacional Autónoma de México, 1961), pp. 1-3;

Helena Araujo, "Arreola, machista y feminista," *Ideología y sociedad*, 21 (1975): 41-46;

Ana María Barrenechea, "Elaboración de la 'circunstancia mejicana' en tres cuentos de Arreola," in her *Textos hispanoamericanos: De Sarmiento a Sarduy* (Caracas: Monte Avila, 1979), pp. 235-246;

Jorge Benítez, "J. J. Arreola: Las experiencias del paciente," *Mundo Nuevo*, 1, no. 7 (1974): 27-37;

Thomas O. Bente, "'El guardagujas' de Juan José Arreola: ¿sátira política o indagación metafísica?," *Cuadernos Americanos*, 31 (November-December 1972): 205-212;

John P. Boyd, "Imágenes de animales y la batalla entre los sexos en dos obras de Juan José Arreola," *Nueva Narrativa Hispanoamericana*, 1 (September 1971): 73-77;

Rosa Cabrera, "*La feria* de Juan José Arreola: la picaresca como manifestación colectiva," in *Actas del Sexto Congreso Internacional de Hispanistas*, edited by G. Alan and Evelynn Rugg (Toronto: University of Toronto Press, 1980), pp. 136-138;

Emmanuel Carballo, "Arreola y Rulfo, cuentistas," *Revista de la Universidad de México*, 8, no. 7 (1954): 28-29, 32;

Rosario Castellanos, "Vitalidad de la novela mexicana," *Mundo de los Libros*, 1 (1964): 8-9;

Centro de Investigaciones Lingüístico-Literarias de la Universidad Veracruzana, "*La feria*: México sagrado y profano," *Texto Crítico*, 5 (September-December 1976): 23-52;

Raúl Chávarri, "Arreola en su varia creación," *Cuadernos Hispanoamericanos*, 242 (February 1970): 418-425;

Leonard A. Cheever, "The Little Girl and the Cat: 'Kafkaesque' Elements in Arreola's 'The Switchman,'" *American Hispanist*, 4 (March-April 1979): 3-4;

Manuel Durán, "El Premio Villaurrutia y la novela mexicana contemporánea," *La Torre*, 13, no. 49 (1965): 233-238;

Evelio Echevarría, "'El guardagujas': Ideario vital y existencial de Juan José Arreola," *Nueva Narrativa Hispanoamericana*, 4 (January-September 1974): 221-226;

Read G. Gilgen, "Absurdist Techniques in the Short Stories of J. J. Arreola," *Journal of Spanish Studies: Twentieth Century*, 8, no. 1 (1980): 67-77;

Margo Glantz, "Juan José Arreola y los bestiarios," in her *Repeticiones: Ensayos sobre litera-

tura mexicana (Veracruz: Universidad Veracruzana, 1979), pp. 47-54;

Angel González-Araúzo, "Ida y vuelta al *Confabulario*," *Revista Iberoamericana*, 34 (January-April 1968): 103-107;

Theda M. Herz, "Las fuentes ocultas de la sátira del *Confabulario*," *Hispanófila*, 72 (May 1981): 31-49;

Paula R. Heusinkveld, "Juan José Arreola: Allegorist in an Age of Uncertainty," *Chasqui*, 13 (February-May 1984): 33-43;

Didier T. Jaén, "Transformación y literatura fantástica: 'El guardagujas' de Arreola," *Texto Crítico*, 26-27 (January-December 1983): 159-167;

"Juan José Arreola," in *Los narradores ante el público*, volume 1 (Mexico City: Mortiz, 1966), pp. 27-48;

Bettina Knapp, "Arreola's 'The Switchman': The Train and the Desert Experience Confluencia," *Revista Hispánica de Cultura y Literatura*, 3, no. 1 (1987): 85-94;

Dolores M. Koch, "El micro-relato en México: Torri, Arreola, Monterroso y Avilés Fabila," *Hispamérica*, 30 (December 1981): 123-130;

David Lagmanovich, "Estructura y efecto en 'La migala,' de Juan José Arreola," *Cuadernos Hispanoamericanos*, 320-321 (February-March 1977): 419-428;

Ross Larson, "La visión realista de Juan José Arreola," *Cuadernos Americanos*, 29 (July-August 1970): 226-232;

Luis Leal, "Un cuento de Juan José Arreola," *Rehilete*, 29 (1969): 46-48;

Leal, "*La feria* de Juan José Arreola," *Nueva Narrativa Hispanoamericana*, 1 (January 1971): 41-48;

Javier Martínez Palacio, "La maestría de Juan José Arreola," *Insula*, 240 (1966): 1, 15;

George R. McMurray, "Albert Camus' Concept of the Absurd and Juan José Arreola's 'The Switchman,'" *Latin American Literary Review*, 6 (Fall-Winter 1977): 31-35;

Seymour Menton, *Juan José Arreola*, translated by Carlos Valdés and Rogelio Llopis (Havana: Casa de las Américas, 1964);

Menton, "Juan José Arreola and the Twentieth Century Short Story," *Hispania*, 42, no. 3 (1959): 295-308;

Floyd Merrell, "*Los de abajo*, *La feria*, and the Notion of Space-Time Categories in the Narrative Text," *Hispanófila*, 27 (September 1983): 77-91;

Jerry Newgord, "Dos cuentos de Juan José Arreola," *Cuadernos Hispanoamericanos*, 336 (June 1978): 527-533;

José Ortega, "Etica y estética en algunos cuentos de *Confabulario*," *Sin Nombre*, 13, no. 3 (1983): 52-59;

Julio Ortega, "*La feria*," in his *La contemplación y la fiesta* (Caracas: Monte Avila, 1969), pp. 51-56;

Mauricio Ostria, "Valor estructural del fragmento en *La feria* de Juan José Arreola," *Estudios Filológicos*, 6 (1970): 177-225;

José Otero, "Religión, moral y existencia en tres cuentos de Juan José Arreola," *Cuadernos Americanos*, 234, no. 1 (1981): 222-231;

Thomas J. Tomanek, "The Estranged Man: Kafka's Influence on Arreola," *Revue des Langues Vivantes*, 37 (1971): 305-308;

Juan Valencia, "La estructura del *Confabulario*," in *Variaciones interpretativas en torno a la nueva novela hispanoamericana*, edited by Donald W. Bleznick (Santiago, Chile: Universitaria, 1972), pp. 101-111;

Yulan M. Washburn, *Juan José Arreola* (Boston: Twayne, 1983);

Ramón Xirau, "*Inventario* de Juan José Arreola," *Vuelta*, 5 (1977): 38-39.

Miguel Angel Asturias

(19 October 1899 - 9 June 1974)

Diane E. Marting
Columbia University

BOOKS: *Sociología guatemalteca: El problema social del indio* (Guatemala City: Sánchez & de Guise, 1923); translated by Maureen Ahern as *Guatemalan Sociology* (Tempe: Arizona State University, 1977);

Rayito de estrella (Paris, 1929);

Leyendas de Guatemala (Madrid: Oriente, 1930; enlarged edition, Buenos Aires: Pleamar, 1948);

El señor Presidente (Mexico City: Costa-Amic, 1946); translated by Frances Partridge as *The President* (London: Gollancz, 1963; New York: Atheneum, 1969);

Hombres de maíz (Buenos Aires: Losada, 1949); translated by Gerald Martin as *Men of Maize* (New York: Delacorte, 1975);

Poesía, sien de alondra (Buenos Aires: Argos, 1949);

Viento fuerte (Guatemala City: Ministerio de Educación Pública, 1950); translated by Darwin Flakoll and Claribel Alegría as *Cyclone* (London: Owen, 1967); translated by Gregory Rabassa as *Strong Wind* (New York: Delacorte, 1968);

El Papa Verde (Buenos Aires: Losada, 1954); translated by Rabassa as *The Green Pope* (New York: Delacorte, 1971);

Soluna: Comedia prodigiosa en dos jornadas y un final (Buenos Aires: Losange, 1955);

Week-end en Guatemala (Buenos Aires: Goyanarte, 1956);

La audiencia de los confines (Buenos Aires: Ariadna, 1957);

Nombre custodio, e Imagen pasajera (Havana: Laura, 1959);

Los ojos de los enterrados (Buenos Aires: Losada, 1960); translated by Rabassa as *The Eyes of the Interred* (New York: Delacorte, 1973; London: Cape, 1974);

El Alhajadito (Buenos Aires: Goyanarte, 1961); translated by Martin Shuttleworth as *The Bejeweled Boy* (Garden City, N.Y.: Doubleday, 1971);

Mulata de Tal (Buenos Aires: Losada, 1963); translated by Rabassa as *Mulata* (New York: Delacorte, 1967);

Teatro (Buenos Aires: Losada, 1964);

Rumania, su nueva imagen (Xalapa: Universidad Veracruzana, 1964);

Clarivigilia primaveral (Buenos Aires: Losada, 1965);

El espejo de Lida Sal (Mexico City: Siglo Veintiuno, 1967);
Torotumbo (Barcelona: Plaza & Janes, 1967);
Latinoamérica y otros ensayos (Madrid: Guadiana, 1968);
Maladrón (Buenos Aires: Losada, 1969);
Comiendo en Hungría, by Asturias and Pablo Neruda (Barcelona: Lumen, 1969); translated by Barna Balogh and Mary Arias as *Sentimental Journey around the Hungarian Cuisine* (Budapest: Corvina, 1969);
Novelas y cuentos de juventud, edited by Claude Couffon (Paris: Institut d'Etudes Hispaniques, 1971);
Amanecer en el delta del Parana e altre poesie (Milan: M'Arte, 1972);
Viernes de dolores (Buenos Aires: Losada, 1972);
Juárez (Mexico City: Comisión Nacional, 1972);
América, edited by Richard Callan (Caracas: Monte Avila, 1972);
Incontro con Miguel Angel Asturias (Rome: IILA, 1973);
Dos veces bastardo (Buenos Aires: Losada, 1974);
Tres de cuatro soles, edited by Dorita Nouhaud (Madrid: Closas-Orcoyen, 1977);
Sinceridades, edited by Epaminondas Quintana (Guatemala City: Académica Centroamericana, 1980);
El hombre que lo tenía todo, todo, todo (Barcelona: Bruguera, 1981);
Paris, 1924-1933, edited by Amos Segala (Madrid: C.S.I.C., 1988).

Collections: *Obras escogidas,* 2 volumes (Madrid: Aguilar, 1955, 1961; enlarged, 3 volumes, 1964-1968);
Obras completas (Madrid: Aguilar, 1967; enlarged, 3 volumes, 1969; critical edition, Madrid: Fondo de Cultura Económica, 1977-1978);
Antología, edited by Pablo Palomino (Mexico City: Costa-Amic, 1968);
Mi mejor obra: Autoantología (Mexico City: Novaro, 1973);
Tres obras, edited by Giuseppe Bellini (Caracas: Ayacucho, 1977);
Viajes, ensayos y fantasías (Buenos Aires: Losada, 1981).

Edition in English: *The Talking Machine,* translated by Jacqueline Duhéme (Garden City, N.Y.: Doubleday, 1971).

TRANSLATION: Georges Raynaud, *Los dioses, los héroes, y los hombres de Guatemala antigua: El Popol Vuh o El libro del consejo de los indios quichés,* translated by Asturias and J. M. González de Mendoza (Paris: Paris-America, 1927).

Through his imaginative writing, Miguel Angel Asturias bridged the gap between myth and social commitment, and he relied on his love for language, for freedom, for Guatemala, and for the many different peoples and cultures of Central America to save him from the dangers of pedantic representations or social-realist distortions. Asturias fought for the rights of contemporary Indians, for the autonomy of Latin-American countries from intervention—especially from the United States—and for a more just distribution of wealth. His literary work unites this fight with an avant-garde, oneiric poetics; a contemporary scholarly understanding of ancient Quiché religion and culture; and his direct childhood experiences of rural Indian life in Guatemala. The ever-popular works of Asturias have undergone a critical reevaluation in the light of recent theories of literature and semiotics, and taking into consideration the directions in which Latin-American fiction has developed since his death in 1974. New scrutiny will result in a different vision of his contribution to world literature, but it is also clear that his place among the most important Latin-American novelists of this century is assured. Asturias earned both the Lenin Peace Prize (1966) and the Nobel Prize for Literature (1967). Many of his works have since been successful in translation. Better known as a novelist, Asturias was also an accomplished short-story writer, poet, dramatist, editor, translator, and a mentor for younger writers who sought him out for help and support. His mature prose is full of neologisms and the written representation of oral language, especially regional and individual speech effects.

Asturias was born to Ernesto Asturias, a lawyer, and María Rosales de Asturias, a teacher, on 19 October 1899 in Guatemala City and educated there. His experience of the pain and suffering during the 1917 Guatemala earthquakes first showed the young Asturias that writing of such sorrow was to be his vocation, and social concerns were to characterize his works. Asturias's thesis for graduation from law school, *Sociología guatemalteca: El problema social del indio* (1923; translated as *Guatemalan Sociology,* 1977), won a prize for its animated prose and was immediately published. Asturias's activities in a leftist movement while in school and afterward, during the presidency of José María Orellana, led to his brief incarceration and his travel to London and Paris in 1924 as a precaution against further trouble. The feelings expressed by the unnamed student in Asturias's *El señor Presidente* (1946; translated as *The President*, 1963) are often considered autobiographical for this reason. During this first period abroad Asturias lived on money sent by his family and funds earned from his contributions to newspapers and magazines.

While in Paris, Asturias came to know surrealism, Dada, and other intellectual and artistic fashions of many writers and painters who lived in or passed through the city. His social and bohemian nature can be seen in the quantity and quality of the acquaintances and friendships he made during his visits to Paris. Each had a varying impact on him as a developing writer; he met Ramón del Valle-Inclán, Miguel de Unamuno, James Joyce, André Breton, Pablo Picasso, Tristan Tzara, Alejo Carpentier, Alfonso Reyes, Arturo Uslar Pietri, Pablo Neruda, Robert Desnos, and Louis Aragon, among others. Furthermore, while there Asturias began his studies of ancient Mayan culture and comparative religions with Professor Georges Raynaud at the Sorbonne. He studied not only classic pre-Columbian culture but also other myths and religions such as the Greek, the Babylonian, and the early Christian, during this and other times in his life, and these other cultures also had a discernible effect on his writing. The main change in Asturias's writing, as a result of his Paris experiences, can be described as a movement toward experimentation, the avant-garde, and automatic writing, and away from modernism, in the Latin-American sense of the term (a Parnassian or symbolist mode of expression.

Asturias conceived his first novel during these early years in Paris. He wanted to write a panoramic vision of Guatemala, beginning before the conquest and including both history and myth in a single dreamlike unity. According to Jimena Sáenz, Asturias's proposed epic novel was to have been called "Tohil," after the Mayan god of war. Due to the obvious difficulties of such a large project, however, Asturias decided to publish several long pieces as individual books. *Leyendas de Guatemala* (Legends of Guatemala), published in Madrid in 1930, parts of *El señor Presidente*, written between 1922 and 1945, and sections of other novels were originally intended to be included in a single work. "Guatemala," the first chapter of *Leyendas*, situates the country within a specific historical and geographical context, whereas *El señor Presidente* presents an urban political nightmare: dictatorship, corruption, incarceration, and torture. The process of planning a huge literary project later to be divided into separate books would repeat itself several times in Asturias's career, principally because of his tendency to rewrite and to polish pieces of works over a period of years. *El Alhajadito* (1961; translated as *The Bejeweled Boy*, 1971), a series of interconnected stories for or about children, is the most extreme instance of this process in that sections of it were written as early as 1928. In addition, early in his native country, Asturias became confirmed in the practice of reading aloud his writing to friends at soirees and *tertulias* (literary meetings); in later years he would read aloud to himself in order to achieve maximum sonority and music, whether in fiction or poetry.

In Asturias's first major book, *Leyendas de Guatemala*, he invented a new kind of short story; his legends show the young Asturias at his most magical and most modernist, searching for beauty through images of nature and through unusual stylization. Some of his legends were inspired by his studies of Maya-Quiché texts, like the play "Cuculcán"; some by Hispanic stories, such as "El Cadejo"; and others mix the two main sources. Never is the original source left untouched, however, and the language is always poetic and musical. Soon after the Spanish original appeared, Paul Valéry wrote a highly laudatory letter to Francis Miomandre, Asturias's friend and French translator, about the *Leyendas* collection in French, which appeared soon after the Spanish original. The innate quality of *Leyendas*, Valéry's letter (often included in later editions), and the prize won by the French translation all helped Asturias's reputation abroad, while he was still relatively young, and greatly eased his acceptance into important international literary circles.

Upon his return to Guatemala in 1933, he was a recognized author and became a journalist and professor until his exile in Mexico (1944-1946), after which he entered government service. Only with the successful publication of his first novel, *El señor Presidente*, however, would Asturias begin to have financial independence from his family. Even when he was a diplomat in future years (for example, the ambassador to France from 1966 to 1970), he kept up his constant literary and journalistic production.

Asturias had married Clemencia Amado in 1939, and they had two sons before being di-

Asturias with his wife, Clemencia Amado de Asturias, and their sons, Miguel and Rodrigo, during a 1945 visit to Mexico City

vorced in 1947. In 1950 Asturias married Blanca Mora y Arauja, an Argentinian.

El señor Presidente has often been considered his best novel and is his most popular. At one time intended as a short story called "Los mendigos políticos" (The Political Beggars), then expanded and extensively rewritten over a period of twenty-four years, the novel contains passages of great musicality and sociopsychological penetration. As often occurs in Asturias's works, the novel's focus is very broad: it paints a situation rather than tracing an individual drama. As a result the plot is more diffuse than in a traditional novel, and at times interesting characters come and go with little warning. In *El señor Presidente* this technique adds to the general climate of confusion, fear, and paranoia, which is one of the novel's many accomplishments.

El señor Presidente begins in the middle of a night with the not-so-accidental killing of Col. Parrales Sonriente by Pelele, a semiretarded, starved beggar, in front of the Portal del Señor, a plaza that existed in Guatemala City before the 1917 earthquake, but with a typical name so that it could conceivably be located in almost any Spanish-American city. The president takes advantage of this event to round up several military leaders of whom he is suspicious, and then he accuses them of the crime. Soon other innocents are affected by the arrests of the generals and thus trapped in the growing net of accusations and imprisonments. The few references to a countryside of idyllic calm, beauty, and safety serve as contrasts to the chaos, ugliness, and danger of the urban center. In a similar way women represent goodness, fertility, and innocence in contrast to the evil, sterility, and guilt that impinge on the men in the political arena.

Against a background of an urban, nocturnal environment with touches of Xibalbá, the Quiché version of the underworld/hell, the beggars featured in the first part of the novel play a major role as a chorus to the common tragedy. Individually the beggars are described grotesquely and naturalistically but with dignity. For example, the most mutilated and the most ridiculous of the beggars who are tortured for having been in the plaza on the night of the murder, El Mosco (The Fly), is also the bravest and the only one to die never affirming the lie asked of him. Asturias's description of the poor and the handicapped here has much in common with his later use of the grotesque in other works, a form employed for both political and mythical reasons.

The president's right-hand man, Miguel Cara de Angel, whose name means "Michael

Angel Face," falls in love with the daughter of one of the framed generals and swiftly loses his foothold in the encroaching turmoil. Cara de Angel becomes yet another victim of the president's machinations, which by this point have continued beyond even his diabolical intentions: the president's former favorite is tortured by the prison guards mentally and physically more than the other prisoners; he is punished for having been the closest of all to the devilish figure at the center of power. The central role of the president places *El señor Presidente* in the subgenre of the dictator novel, with such important works as José Marmol's *Amalia* (1851), and with Alejo Carpentier's *El recurso del método* (1974; translated as *Reasons of State*, 1976), Augusto Roa Bastos's *Yo, el supremo* (1974; translated as *I, the Supreme*, 1987), and Gabriel García Márquez's *El otoño del patriarca* (1975; translated as *The Autumn of the Patriarch*, 1976).

Hombres de maíz (1949; translated as *Men of Maize*, 1975) competes with *El señor Presidente* for the title of Asturias's most studied work. In this second novel the countryside replaces the city as context, and cultural conflict replaces political injustice as the theme. The plot is even more diffuse than *El señor Presidente*, and the book has been mistaken for a short-story collection. Ancient Indian texts and contemporary Indian beliefs provide connections among the episodes as well as among elements of plot and even certain aspects of character. Divided into six parts, each named for the main character of the section, plus an epilogue, the novel audaciously and agilely fuses a denunciation of the repression of Indians and Indian culture with the creation of a magical/mythical world new to fiction. *Nahualismo*, for example, the belief in an animal double that at times houses a human soul, lies at the center of the chapter "Correo-Coyote," in which a rural postman ritually enters his coyote *nahual*. *Nahualismo* also provides the surprising ending of "Venado de siete-rozas," in which the killing of the *nahual*, the *venado* (male deer), simultaneously kills the shaman of the title. Thus the border between the animal and the human disappears for the reader because the narrative point of view has rejected the absolute separation of the two as a conception that blinds its believers to their common source with animals in nature. In this novel Asturias develops a new way of writing that never disappears from his style, even when he is at his most realistic in the three novels of the so-called banana cycle; it is a manner of telling a story that borders on the creation of myth.

The title of *Hombres de maíz* refers to the men of maize who were opposed to the men of wood and the men of mud in the cosmogonic vision of the *Popol Vuh*, the sacred text of the Quiché Indians written down at the time of the conquest. According to the *Popol Vuh*, the gods created and destroyed humanity in several attempts to form beings who would praise their creators with their voices. In Asturias's novel the men of maize have the Indian conception of nature, crops, and food as part of an essentially religious and continuous cycle, whereas the aim in cultivation for the Hispanized Indians and the mestizos is profit from sales. The whites and the mixed races burn off more land than they need for corn to eat; the Indians farm only the essential and respect rather than destroy the rest. The Indian leader Gaspar Ilóm's death, structurally comparable to the death of Parrales Sonriente in *El señor Presidente*, provokes in the following chapters the revenge of the "brujos de las luciérnagas" (firefly sorcerers). The individual and collective search for revenge and for survival for those left behind by Ilóm becomes increasingly difficult in the rapid transition of the rural community from its traditional beliefs to Western ones imposed by modernization, commercialization, and miscegenation.

Asturias wrote and spoke extensively about his process of creation in articles and interviews. According to him words carry magic power and change reality. His novels, poems, stories, and plays do not merely entertain; they interpret nature in a magical and therefore essentially human form. *El señor Presidente* was an attempt to change politics; *Hombres de maíz* deals out fictional retribution for the injustices suffered by the Indian population. The power of words, in Asturias's rendering of an Indian conception, approximates that described by Asturias's friend André Breton, whose first manifestos of surrealism appeared in 1924. Asturias also shared the ideological dedication to leftist politics to be found in the late surrealist texts, as his works in the 1950s and 1960s show. Yet he later agreed with the Cuban novelist Alejo Carpentier that European surrealism is forced and artificial in comparison to the authentic magic of reality in the Americas.

The first novel of the banana trilogy, *Viento fuerte* (1950; translated as *Cyclone*, 1967), explores the harsh exploitation by an American-owned

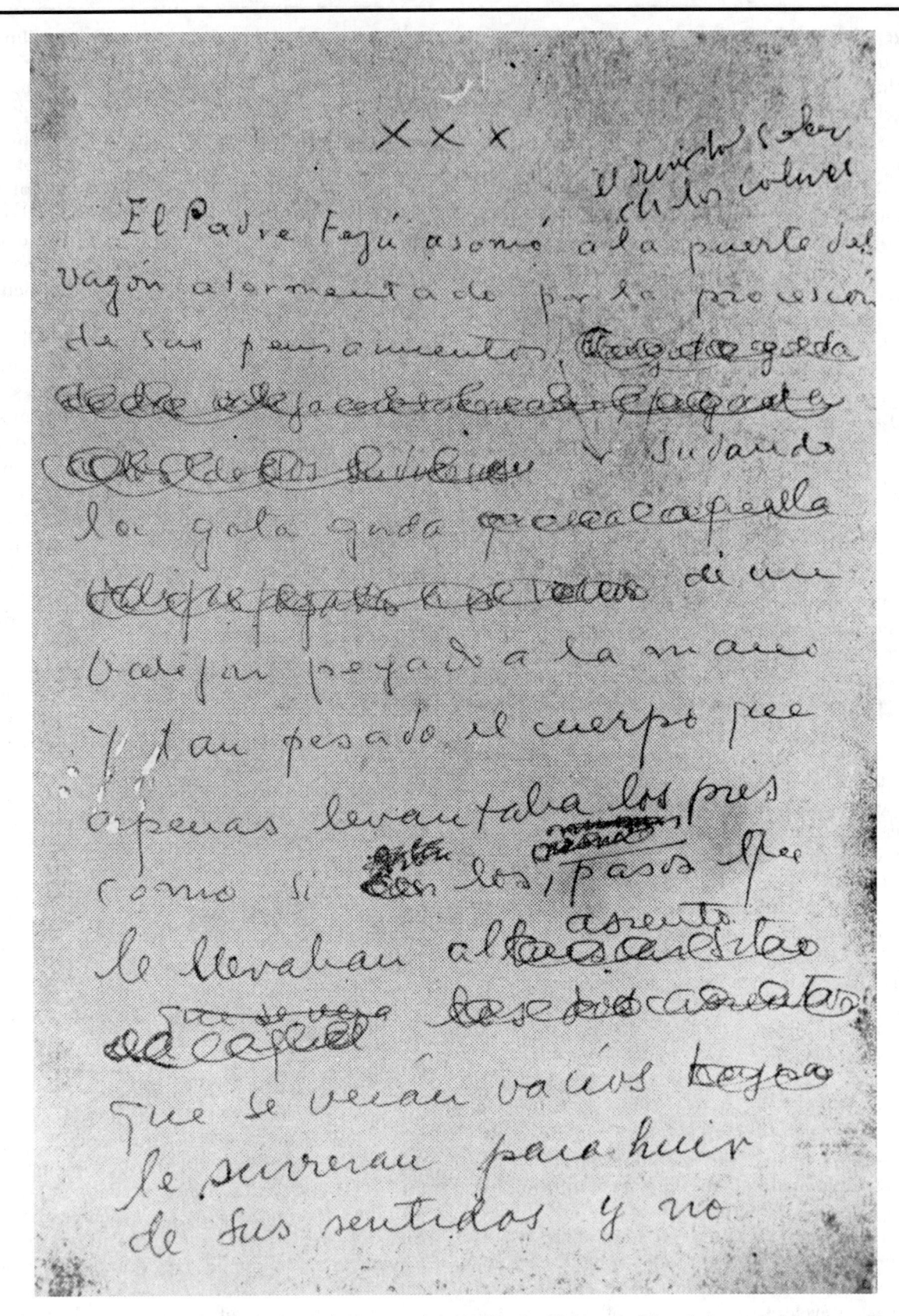

Page from the manuscript for Los ojos de los enterrados *(1960), the third novel of Asturias's so-called banana trilogy (from Jimena Sáenz,* Genio y figura de Miguel Angel Asturias, *1974)*

fruit company of the resources and the people of the coasts of an unnamed Central American country. The possibility of earning better wages than the return from subsistence farming in the highlands attracts several poor farmers and their families to the coast. In the hot, tropical coastland the newcomers often find disease and death, but sometimes they merely find hard work and a chance to earn enough pay at great sacrifice to buy a little land. Several of these families, particularly the Lucero family, befriend Cosi—also known as Lester Mead and Lester Stoner in other circumstances—a half-crazy American who sells needles and thread for pennies in the vicinity. The gringo is a bored millionaire and a major stockholder in the banana company that controls the area, traveling incognito in Central America to study the success of his investments. The novel ends with a holocaust, the strong wind of the title, which wipes away many of the company's holdings and kills many Americans, including Cosi and his beautiful blond wife, Leland. The strong wind is a magical revenge occasioned by a cruelly exploited peon, willing to be killed in order to have revenge done by the gods Cabracán (Earthquake) and Huracán (Wind).

The improbability of much of the story has led to an underevaluation of *Viento fuerte* among Asturias's works. The harsh working conditions and the political and economic concessions given to American companies are real enough; Asturias admitted to Luis Harss and Barbara Dohmann in an interview that several of the episodes of injustice are based on nonfiction sources, such as Charles David Kepner's *The Banana Empire: A Case Study in Economic Imperialism* (1935), and Asturias's criticism of American-Central American relations is not unique to him. But his way of combining naturalistic descriptions that evoke pathos with myth, magic, and fantasy has been more felicitous in other works. Certainly *Viento fuerte* is a brief novel that is easy to read, requiring much less of readers than is common in Asturias's other works.

El Papa Verde (1954; translated as *The Green Pope*, 1971), the second novel in Asturias's banana series, features an American robber baron as its protagonist. The so-called Green Pope (the nickname based on his venality), Geo Maker Thompson, occupies the stage for much, but not all, of the drama. A blond giant whose name reminds one of an earth/creation god, Geo Maker is willing to kill, burn, or steal in order to acquire land, workers, money, and power for the fruit company and for himself. In this novel Cosi's poverty-stricken friends from *Viento fuerte* have inherited his financial legacy. As the attention of the company and of its Green Pope focuses on converting the newly rich families into allies, they soon begin to fight among themselves. Cosi's project of a worker's cooperative is lost in the families' struggles to maintain their new wealth and power in the midst of international border disputes, the rivalry between the two fruit companies in the region, and the tense world political situation in the late 1920s, events that are as much the themes of this novel as the portrait of the Green Pope or the destruction of the families' integrity.

When the American government sent troops to Guatemala in 1954, overthrowing the government of Jacobo Arbenz Guzmán and imposing the military dictatorship of Carlos Castillo Armas, Asturias had already completed a draft of his next novel, the third of the banana trilogy, *Los ojos de los enterrados* (1960; translated as *The Eyes of the Interred*, 1973). Like his friend Pablo Neruda and other politically committed intellectuals and writers, Asturias mourned the 1954 events in Guatemala in his writings. He was forced to begin a period of exile in Argentina after many years abroad as a student and a diplomat. He set aside his novel and only published a revised version six years later, turning instead to the short-story genre. The result was *Week-end en Guatemala*, published in 1956, a collection of long narratives about the American participation in the coup d'état of 1954. "¡Americanos Tudos!" is the story most explicitly related to the tourism implied in the book's title, and it is one of Asturias's most interesting political treatments of his favorite themes: mixed loyalties, mixed cultures, and mixed races. These themes also are important in *Hombres de maíz* and pivotal in the character of Juambo in *Los ojos de los enterrados*. In the story, a Guatemalan tourist guide and American citizen, Emilio Milocho, witnesses at close range the death and destruction caused by the 1954 weekend attack by the U.S. military. Tortured by his memory and unintentionally goaded by his insensitive American girlfriend, Milocho takes his revenge by running his bus full of American tourists off the side of one of the beautiful mountains that he had previously taken such pleasure and pride in showing.

In *Los ojos de los enterrados* Asturias creates a wide panorama of Guatemalan places and people, but this time the events revolve around the

Asturias receiving the 1967 Nobel Prize for Literature

theme of a general strike among both the banana workers and the middle-class employees in the capital. The revolutionary and amorous activities of Tabío San (also called Octavio Sansur and Juan Pablo Mondragón) in the capital, on the Southern Pacific coast, and in a small rural town, Cerropóm, provide the thread that unites the vast novel. Many characters or children of characters from *Viento fuerte* and *El Papa Verde* reappear here, yet some are "the buried ones," *los enterrados*, whose eyes cannot close, that is, who cannot rest in peace, until justice is accomplished. The children of the buried bear the responsibility for righting the wrongs done to their parents. This emotional and metaphysical burden falls most heavily on Juambo and his family, who carry the theme to the end of the novel, paralleling and at times meshing with the sociopolitical drama. The adult grandson of Geo Maker, Boby, still innocent of crime, is also "responsible" for the unjust actions of his predecessors. He is mistaken for another man and brutally murdered by his own lover Clara María, who believed herself the victim of witchcraft. Simultaneously, the country's president is forced to resign as a result of the political pressure by the workers. Thus *Los ojos de los enterrados* ends with the termination of the Maker family line and the beginning of political change for the country.

In 1959 Asturias was permitted to visit Guatemala, but he maintained his residence in Argentina until 1962. In that year he began a few years of traveling, receiving literary prizes, and giving lectures.

Asturias's political fiction and his historical works differ from his mythical works in that the political/historical structure places the text's magic and myth within the characters, such as Clara María, rather than as a fact of the narrative universe. In *Mulata de Tal* (1963; translated as *Mulata*, 1967), Asturias's next novel, one finds the mythical extreme, in which the novel is structured and executed within a magical conception, in its rambling Dionysian story line, its picaresque narrational voice, and its flat Apollinian characterization. Paradoxically, *Mulata de Tal* is one of Asturias's most delightful and most difficult works, because it follows a Rabelaisian, nonrational, noncausal logic all its own. In interviews Asturias asserted that he made Tazol, the Mulata de Tal, a *mulata*, a mixture of black and white races, rather than a mestiza, a mixture of Indian and white, for two reasons: first, because he believed that *mulata* women are more beautiful, sensual, and seductive than mestiza women; and second, because of the sound of the word *mulata* itself, which he found particularly delightful. If the book had pretensions to realism or to representational accuracy, Tazol's being a *mulata* would contradict her position as Indian corn goddess, but in fact the *mulata* is not a particular woman at all. She represents an ever-changing metaphor for devils, forces of nature, and evil: she is a seductive country girl at a local fair, a shrewish and sadistic wife, an erupting volcano, and a witch dismembered by her enemies. Even in the banana series Asturias felt free to modify dates, places, and people to suit his fiction. What is new in *Mulata de Tal* is the preponderance of parody, myth, and comedy, successfully mixed with a piquant streak of social criticism, which differs from the tragic vision of his previous works.

Mulata de Tal is one of the few Asturias works in which the female characters are almost as important as the male ones, although even here the male narrative perspective prevails, and the male protagonist, El Brujo Bragueta (the Fly

Wizard), occupies with Tazol the central narrative attention. Asturias's other female characters are either idealistically angelic (Camila in *El señor Presidente;* Malena Tabay in *Los ojos de los enterrados*), absent (María Tecún in *Hombres de maíz;* Ninica in *Soluna,* 1955), or a type such as a local bar woman. Most frequently Asturias's women are important because of the male protagonists' love for them. Moreover, sexuality appears as a major theme in *Mulata de Tal,* whereas it is rarely treated to any great extent in Asturias's other works. The novel begins when El Brujo Bragueta appears during a mass; later he sells his wife in order to gain riches. The Mulata herself has her sexuality stolen and thus loses her power and strength. In this respect Asturias's oeuvre differs from the Latin-American writers of the so-called boom and postboom eras and remains closer to that of his contemporaries Jorge Luis Borges and Carpentier, in whose works sexuality appears as an incidental fact of personality rather than a social, psychological, and artistic theme to be explored in fiction. In *Mulata de Tal,* however, sexuality contributes in a necessary way to the grotesque aspects of mythic storytelling and to the surrealistic flow of linguistic associations.

In 1964 Asturias published *Teatro* (Theater), his first collection of plays, two of which had been previously published. "Cuculcán," a short play included in *Leyendas de Guatemala* thirty years before, was his first published attempt in this genre, although biographers insist that he often wrote plays for the amusement of friends in private performances. *La audiencia de los confines* (The Audience of the Prison; published separately in 1957) has been the most widely read and performed of Asturias's plays, and it is also his most traditional. It treats an episode in Fray Bartolomé de las Casas's struggles to free Indian slaves in the Spanish colonies. He is shown as contrite for his suggestion to substitute African slaves for Indian ones, who were dying at an alarming rate from disease, malnutrition, and overwork, but he is victorious in his efforts on behalf of the Indian. *Soluna* (published separately in 1955), a light comedy, is Asturias's play that has been best received by theater critics. The educated, farm-owning protagonist, Mauro, wants to believe in the nahualistic transformation of humans into their animal form and other magical events, in order to win back his wife who has left him. Soluna, a shaman whose name is formed from *sol* (sun) and *luna* (moon), provides Mauro

Dust jacket for Asturias's last novel, which focuses on the Spanish conquest of the Americas

with a magical object capable of making time pass rapidly and imperceptibly, and the events end happily. *Chantaje* (Blackmail) and *Dique seco* (Dry Dock), the previously unpublished plays in the collection, while of respectable artistic quality, are untypical of Asturias's production in general and are not as successful dramatically as *Soluna. Chantaje* deserves note for the opening street scenes that feature music and urban noise in experimental ways that Asturias had not attempted previously in his fiction—striving for cacophony itself rather than for a written representation or oral effects. *Dique seco* is set in the rooms of an aging nobleman who is so in debt that his last pieces of furniture will soon be confiscated. The play ridicules the noble pretensions of the protagonist, who, in a humorous way, uses trickery and disloyalty to friends to postpone the inevitable.

The main character in the title story of Asturias's 1967 short-story collection, *El espejo de Lida Sal* (The Mirror of Lida Sal), is a poor young girl who works washing dishes. Lida has fallen in love with Felipito, the brash son of a nearby farm owner. There is a local belief that if a young woman sleeps for seven nights in the fancy clothes her beloved will wear in a certain popular religious festival, and then sees herself full-length in a mirror, then the loved one will be forced to reciprocate the young woman's love, as a victim of the magic of her body, of the Virgin, and of love itself. Magic is seen as part of the world, not a matter of private and perhaps mistaken belief. Felipito's mother, for instance, bewitched her husband just as Lida wishes to bewitch Felipito. Afflicted by her love, Lida has managed everything except to see herself in a mirror from head to toe—she cannot afford such a large mirror. The night before the festival, Lida's last chance to complete the ritual, she goes to a nearby lake, where, in the moonlight, she hopes to see her complete image. With difficulty she climbs the high rocks surrounding the lake, but she slips and drowns in the heavy costume, a tragic victim of her pursuit of love.

In 1966 Asturias had returned to Guatemala and was named ambassador to France. He returned to Central American history when he placed the events of his last novel, *Maladrón* (1969), during the time of the conquest of the Americas. Some Spanish explorers search for a river connecting the Atlantic and the Pacific Oceans, while others seek to convert the Indians and other Spaniards to the belief in the Mal Ladrón (Bad Thief), Gestas, the thief who died on the cross to the left of Christ. The church of Maladrón teaches materialism, the belief that the soul does not exist and that there is no life after death. The Mal Ladrón also appears in several of Asturias's earlier works. Asturias's brief novel portrays the marvelous and the grotesque in personal religious beliefs, in the savagery of nature in the Americas, and in established religions, be they indigenous, Christian, or anti-Christian. His surrealistic/magic-realistic treatment of visions and religious events enhances the novella's meshing of reality, history, and the human psyche in a style that has become Asturias's trademark and his main contribution to Latin-American literature.

Asturias continued writing and speaking until his health no longer permitted them. In 1973 he planned to visit his close friend Pablo Neruda in Chile but was never able to go. Asturias died on 9 June 1974 in Madrid and was buried in Paris.

Interviews:

Luis Harss and Barbara Dohmann, "Miguel Angel Asturias, or the Land Where the Flowers Bloom," in their *Into the Mainstream, Conversations with Latin American Writers* (New York: Harper & Row, 1967), pp. 68-101;

Luis López Alvarez, *Conversaciones con Miguel Angel Asturias* (Madrid: Magisterio Español, 1974).

Bibliographies:

Pedro F. de Andrea, "Miguel Angel Asturias: Anticipo bibliográfico," *Revista Iberoamericana*, 35, no. 67 (1969): 133-270;

Richard Moore, "Miguel Angel Asturias: A Bio-Bibliography," *Bulletin of Bibliography*, 27, no. 4 (1970): 85-90, 107-111.

Biographies:

Atilio Jorge Castelpoggi, *Miguel Angel Asturias* (Buenos Aires: La Mandrágora, 1961);

Claude Couffon, *Miguel Angel Asturias* (Paris: Seghers, 1970);

Carlos Meneses, *Miguel Angel Asturias* (Madrid: Jícar, 1975).

References:

Giuseppe Bellini, *La narrativa de Miguel Angel Asturias*, translated from Italian to Spanish by Ignacio Soriano (Buenos Aires: Losada, 1969);

Elizabeth A. Benedict, "Surrealism in the Novels of Miguel Angel Asturias," Ph.D. dissertation, University of North Carolina, 1977;

Gordon Brotherston, "The Presence of Mayan Literature in *Hombres de maíz* and Other Works by Miguel Angel Asturias," *Hispania*, 58 (March 1975): 68-74;

Richard Callan, *Miguel Angel Asturias* (New York: Twayne, 1970);

Sister Mary A. Connolly, "The Narrative Prose of Miguel Angel Asturias," Ph.D. dissertation, Yale University, 1970;

Nancy Gray Díaz, "Metamorphosis as Integration in Miguel Angel Asturias' *Hombres de maíz*," *Revista Canadiense de Estudios Hispánicos*, 12 (Winter 1988): 235-252;

Jaime Díaz Rozzotto, "*El Popol Vuh:* Fuente estética del realismo mágico de Miguel Angel Asturias," *Cuadernos Americanos,* 201 (July-August 1975): 85-92;

Europe, special Asturias double issue, 553-554 (May-June 1975);

Emilia García, *"Hombres de maíz," unidad y sentido a través de sus símbolos mitológicos* (Miami: Universal, 1978);

Paul Alexandru Georgescu, "Casualidad natural y conexión mágica en la obra de Miguel Angel Asturias," *Ibero-Romania* (Munich), new series 2 (1975): 157-175;

Helmy F. Giacoman, ed., *Homenaje a Miguel Angel Asturias* (New York: Las Américas, 1971);

Luis González del Valle and Vicente Cabrera, *La nueva ficción hispanoamericana a través de Miguel Angel Asturias y Gabriel García Márquez* (New York: Torres, 1972);

Eladia León Hill, *Miguel Angel Asturias: Lo ancestral en su obra literaria* (New York: Torres, 1972);

Jack Himelblau, "The Sociopolitical Views of Miguel Angel Asturias: 1920-1930," *Hispanófila,* 61 (September 1977): 61-80;

Luis Leal, "Myth and Social Realism in Miguel Angel Asturias," *Comparative Literature Studies,* 5 (1968): 237-247;

Vera Popov Maligec, "Telluric Forces and Literary Creativity in Miguel Angel Asturias," Ph.D. dissertation, Columbia University, 1976;

Carlos E. Martin, "Los recursos retóricos como instrumento para la denuncia social en las novelas de Miguel Angel Asturias," Ph.D. dissertation, Northwestern University, 1972;

Gerald Martin, "*Mulata de Tal:* The Novel as Animated Cartoon," *Hispanic Review,* 41 (1973): 397-415;

Teresa McKenna, "The Politics of Metaphor: Dialectics of Oppression in Miguel Angel Asturias and Elsa Morante," Ph.D. dissertation, University of California at Los Angeles, 1980;

Seymour Menton, "Miguel Angel Asturias: Realidad y Fantasía," *Historia crítica de la novela guatemalteca* (Guatemala City: Editorial Universitaria, 1960), pp. 195-241;

Marta Pilón, *Miguel Angel Asturias: Semblanza para el estudio de su vida y obra* (Guatemala City: Cultural Centroamericana, 1968);

Oralia Muñoz Preble, "The Poetic Expression of Miguel Angel Asturias," Ph.D. dissertation, University of North Carolina, 1977;

René Prieto, "El papel de la fauna y de los símbolos precolombinos en la obra de Miguel Angel Asturias y de José María Arguedas," *Discurso Literario,* 4, no. 2 (1987): 401-414;

Prieto, "A Semiotic Analysis of *Hombres de maíz* by Miguel Angel Asturias," Ph.D. dissertation, Stanford University, 1980;

Emir Rodríguez Monegal, "Los dos Asturias," *Revista Iberoamericana,* 35 (January-April 1969): 13-20;

Jimena Sáenz, *Genio y figura de Miguel Angel Asturias* (Buenos Aires: Universitaria de Buenos Aires, 1974);

Aurora Sierra Franco, *Miguel Angel Asturias en la literatura,* edited by Melinton Salazar (Guatemala City: Istmo, 1969);

Joseph Sommers, "The Indian-Oriented Novel in Latin America," *Journal of Inter-American Studies* (Gainesville), 6 (April 1964): 249-266;

Ray Angelo Verazsconi, "Magical Realism and the Literary World of Miguel Angel Asturias," Ph.D. dissertation, University of Washington, 1965;

Iber Verdugo, *El carácter de la literatura hispanoamericana y la novelística de Miguel Angel Asturias* (Guatemala City: Universitaria, 1968).

Mario Benedetti
(14 September 1920 -   )

María Rosa Olivera-Williams
University of Notre Dame

BOOKS: *La víspera indeleble* (Montevideo: Prometeo, 1945);
Peripecia y novela (Montevideo: Prometeo, 1948);
Esta mañana (Montevideo: Prometeo, 1949); enlarged as *Esta mañana y otros cuentos* (Montevideo: Arca, 1967);
Sólo mientras tanto (Montevideo: Número, 1950);
El último viaje y otros cuentos (Montevideo: Número, 1951);
Marcel Proust y otros ensayos (Montevideo: Número, 1951);
Quién de nosotros (Montevideo: Número, 1953);
Ustedes, por ejemplo (Montevideo: Número, 1953);
Poemas de la oficina (Montevideo: Número, 1956); enlarged as *Poemas de la oficina y otros expedientes* (Montevideo: Reunidos Arca, 1969);
El reportaje (Montevideo: Marcha, 1958);
Montevideanos (Montevideo: Alfa, 1959; enlarged, 1961);
La tregua (Montevideo: Alfa, 1960); translated by Benjamin Graham as *The Truce* (New York: Harper & Row, 1969);
El país de la cola de paja (Montevideo: Asir, 1960);
Mejor es Meneallo (Montevideo: Alfa, 1961);
Poemas del hoyporhoy (Montevideo: Alfa, 1961);
Ida y vuelta (Buenos Aires: Talía, 1963);
Inventario (Montevideo: Alfa, 1963);
Literatura uruguaya siglo XX (Montevideo: Alfa, 1963; enlarged, 1969);
Gracias por el fuego (Montevideo: Alfa, 1965);
Contra los puentes levadizos (Montevideo: Alfa, 1966);
Genio y figura de José Enrique Rodó (Buenos Aires: EUDEBA, 1966);
Letras del continente mestizo (Montevideo: Arca, 1967);
Antología natural (Montevideo: Alfa, 1967);
A ras de sueño (Montevideo: Alfa, 1967);
Datos para el viudo (Buenos Aires: Galerna, 1967);
La muerte y otras sorpresas (Mexico City: Siglo XXI, 1968);
Sobre artes y oficios: ensayo (Montevideo: Alfa, 1968);
Cuaderno cubano (Montevideo: Arca, 1969);

Mario Benedetti

Cuentos completos (Santiago, Chile: Universitaria, 1970);
Crítica cómplice (Havana: Instituto Cubano del Libro, 1971);
El cumpleaños de Juan Angel (Mexico City: Siglo XXI, 1971); translated by David Arthur McMurray as *Juan Angel's Birthday* (Amherst, Mass., 1974);
Los poetas comunicantes (Montevideo: Marcha, 1972);
Crónicas del 71 (Montevideo: Arca, 1972);
Terremoto y después (Montevideo: Arca, 1973);
Letras de emergencia (Buenos Aires: Alfa, 1973);

Daniel Viglietti (Madrid: Júcar, 1974);
Poemas de otros (Buenos Aires: Alfa, 1974);
El recurso del supremo patriarca (Buenos Aires: Alfa, 1974);
El escritor latinoamericano y la revolución posible (Buenos Aires: Alfa, 1974);
Hasta aquí (Buenos Aires: Linea, 1974);
La casa y el ladrillo (Mexico City: Siglo XXI, 1976);
Con y sin nostalgia (Mexico City: Siglo XXI, 1977);
Cotidianas (Mexico City: Siglo XXI, 1979);
Notres sobre algunas formas subsidiarias de la penetración cultural (Mexico City: Tierra Adentro, 1979);
Pedro y el capitán (Mexico City: Nueva Imagen, 1979);
El ejercicio del criterio (Mexico City: Nueva Imagen, 1981);
Viento del exilio (Mexico City: Nueva Imagen, 1981);
Primavera con una esquina rota (Mexico City: Nueva Imagen, 1982);
Panorama histórico-literario de nuestra América (Havana: Casa de las Américas / New York: Vitral, 1982);
Geografías (Mexico City: Nueva Imagen, 1984);
El desexilio y otras conjeturas (Madrid: El País, 1984);
La cultura, ese blanco móvil (Montevideo: Universidad de la República, 1985);
Escritos políticos (Montevideo: Arca, 1985);
Noción de patria (Madrid: Visor, 1985);
Cultura entre dos fuegos (Montevideo: Universidad de la República, 1986);
Preguntas al azar (Madrid: Visor, 1986);
Yesterday y mañana (Montevideo: Arca, 1987);
Recuerdos olvidados (Montevideo: Trilce, 1988);
Despistes y franquezas (Montevideo: Arca/Nueva Imagen, 1989).

PLAY PRODUCTION: *Pedro y el capitán*, Mexico City, El Galpón Theater, 28 March 1979.

RECORDING: *Mario Benedetti: Poemas y cuentos*, Havana, Casa de las Américas, LD-CA-2.

Mario Benedetti is one of Uruguay's most prolific writers. He excels in all literary genres: novels, short stories, poems, plays, essays, political articles, and polemical songs. Benedetti's seemingly inexhaustible creative power parallels his constant activity to improve the sociopolitical situation of his country and, by extension, all of Latin America. His writing reflects the idiosyncrasies of the Uruguayan middle class, the group that has been shaping the nation. The close relationship between his literature and exterior reality, or contemporary history, could be viewed as weakening the poetic value of his work. Some critics might classify Benedetti's oeuvre as "committed" or "engagé" literature. But Benedetti's literary works, even those of the 1970s, which clearly show his political preoccupations, are not merely representative or primarily didactic in intent. Benedetti transforms into literature the middle-class myths and reactions to contemporary history, becoming the sagacious and sympathetic contemporary analyst of the Uruguayan mind. This attitude toward literature has converted him to the most representative author of the "Generation of 1945" or "the critical generation." These terms, unanimously accepted by critics, denominate a group of writers who by 1945 were using literature as one of the ways to show the inherent contradictions of reality. Literature by them, especially the narrative form, came to be written in an objective and realistic mode.

Benedetti was born on 14 September 1920 in Paso de los Toros, a small rural city in Tacuarembó, Uruguay. His parents were Breno Benedetti—the son of an established Italian viniculturist and chemist—who had come to Uruguay and developed the best vineyards in Piriapolis, a fashionable seaside resort on the Atlantic Ocean in the early 1920s; and Matilde Farrugia Benedetti, the daughter of a Spaniard and a Frenchwoman. The family moved to the capital, Montevideo, when Mario was four years old. This city, with its European style and aspirations, inspired Benedetti and shaped his writing. Benedetti defined himself as a *Montevideano*, and his literary work is essentially urban. In a country where half of the population lives in a single city, it is difficult not to be urban. Nevertheless, until the end of the 1930s Uruguayan literature had been primarily rural. The prestige of gaucho and, later on, Creole literature, in which gauchos and rural men were observed with nostalgia, had kept the national literature and subject matter essentially rural in character. In 1939 Juan Carlos Onetti, the greatest Uruguayan novelist of the twentieth century, complained that Montevideo did not exist, because writers did not re-create the city in their works.

Benedetti's literary work shows a critical and realistic portrait of Uruguayans in Montevideo and their diaspora, which occurred as the result of the dictatorial military regime that governed Uruguay from 1973 until 1985. From a localist literature, which reflected the dreams, deceptions, frustration, and mediocrity of the Uruguayan middle class, Benedetti's literary works moved parallel with Uruguayan history and showed that the suffering of his countrymen was also the suffering of the rest of the Latin-American countries.

His first book, published in 1945, was a collection of poems, *La víspera indeleble* (The Ineffaceable Eve), a product of a young writer learning his profession. Benedetti regretted its publication, and in 1963, when collecting his poetry in *Inventario* (Inventory), he did not include any of its poems. Benedetti continued his development by publishing in many literary magazines, some of which he directed: *Marginalia* (1948), *Número* (1943-1955 and 1966), and the literary section of *Marcha* (1954 and 1960). In 1946 he married Luz Lopez Alegre. In 1948 he published a book of essays, *Peripecia y novela* (Incident and Novel); in 1949, short stories, *Esta mañana* (This Morning); in 1950, poetry, *Sólo mientras tanto* (Only in the Meanwhile); and in 1951, *El último viaje y otros cuentos* (The Last Trip and Other Short Stories). All these books that formed the period of literary initiation of Benedetti were later revised and published in new editions.

The short stories of *Esta mañana* show Benedetti's literary preferences: William Faulkner, Marcel Proust (whom he admired especially), James Joyce, Virginia Woolf, and Onetti. Onetti had already adopted and reformed the narrative strategies of the masters of Western literature, and his work became influential among the young writers of the Generation of 1945. Stream of consciousness and the interior monologue are the predominant narrative techniques in *Esta mañana*. The young Benedetti sought to surprise, to astonish his readers with his short narrations. But the complex structure of the short stories of his first collection weakens the impact. Nevertheless, in this early book are the themes that, a few years later, would make Benedetti a writer of bestsellers: the office world—with its ho-hum characters who dream of a salary raise that never arrives, and with the worthlessness of bureaucracy, which traps public employees in its maze of papers and endless meetings—appears in "El presupuesto" (The Budget); "Esta mañana" shows Montevideo as the realm of the middle class, where people are divided into two groups—bosses, and subordinates who envy and loathe their bosses but want to become them; the negative effect of a routine life is seen in "Como siempre" (Like Always) and "Idilio" (Idyl); and the topics of love—its deterioration and destruction owing to the tedious lives of the characters—fate, death, and time (as a powerful force human beings cannot hope to overcome) are all present in this first book.

In 1953 Benedetti published his first novel, *Quién de nosotros* (Who of Us), a short novel about a love triangle where all the relationships end in frustration. Benedetti continued his mastering of the narrative techniques of Faulkner, Woolf, and Joyce: the novel is narrated according to the different perspectives of its characters. Even though these books represent Benedetti's apprenticeship, the gray tones of his literary world and the mediocrity of his characters did not correspond to the myth of Uruguay as the "Switzerland of South America." Benedetti, as well as Onetti, foresaw the problems of the proud Uruguayan society. The economic structure of the country reached its financial crisis in 1955. But signs of the weakening system appeared in the late 1930s; Benedetti paid attention to those signs and portrayed them in the weaknesses of his characters.

In 1956 Benedetti published *Poemas de la oficina* (Office Poems), and with this book Uruguayan poetry changed. Benedetti introduced a new theme to poetry: life, or lack of life, in an office. This topic had been considered antipoetic since there was nothing interesting in the monotonous routine of an office. Nevertheless, numbers, balances, inventories, accounts, salaries, budgets, ink stains, calendars, and telephone calls became the new language of poetry. And this book was a success. Like his early narratives, it interpreted the bureaucratic middle class, which almost completely constituted Montevideo. Benedetti himself had been an employee of that bureaucratic system (in spite of his solid education in the German School, one of the most prestigious schools in the country, where he learned foreign languages); he knew intimately the feelings of those people who were intelligent and educated but whose lives deteriorated in an office job without a future. Furthermore, the style of his poetry is direct and colloquial, which makes it very easy to read. However, this kind of poetry (which would become successful years later) was not popular in Latin America in 1956. Even so, the novelty and themes of *Poemas de la oficina* assured its success.

The book initiated Benedetti's period of literary maturity, and those works that soon followed—*Montevideanos* (short stories, 1959), *La tregua*

(1960; translated as *The Truce*, 1969), and *El país de la cola de paja* (The Country with the Straw Tail, essays, 1960)—made him the most read Uruguayan author in the country and abroad. Benedetti had found the topic he knew best: the world of the middle class to which he belonged. His characters are common people whose stories are, or may be, everybody's stories—although they take unexpected turns—and the style of his narrative and poetry is simple and clear. Benedetti's readings and literary preferences dissolved in a style coherent with his theme. His works became mature literature.

In *Montevideanos* he enlarged the social sector of his characters from the bureaucracy to the entire middle class—in all its economic and social levels. Benedetti succeeded in interpreting and representing the Uruguayan urban sector through an increasing understanding of his people and a strong command of narrative techniques. In all his mature books there is a moral and humane criticism of individuals who are motivated by mediocre goals, by envy, by inertia, or by tediousness. Benedetti showed empathy for his characters, but at the same time he separated himself from them. He understood his characters' idiosyncrasies, but he worried for the future of a country whose inhabitants had been anesthetized by old myths that did not work any longer. In "Retrato de Elisa" (Portrait of Elisa) the title character has fallen from her middle-class status into poverty, and she struggles until the end of her life (she is dying of cancer) to differentiate her extreme poverty from that of the rest of the populace. She cannot do anything to stop her decline; her only preoccupation is to save the illusory nobility of her class. Benedetti felt that another sort of cancer, unlike the one that attacked Elisa Montes, was torturing and destroying the country. Nevertheless, there is no overt political or social criticism in these stories. The alienation of the Uruguayan is re-created in the psychology of Benedetti's characters.

La tregua and *El país de la cola de paja* are transitional works. In the novel, as well as in the book of essays, there are traces of political preoccupations, even though these books are not primarily political. In *La tregua* the character Santomé is about to turn fifty years old, and his only expectation is his retirement; Avellaneda is the young woman who for a short time has given Santomé love, life, and hope. They start thinking of the problem of their flattened and grayish country; they have progressive attitudes and search for authenticity in a country of appearances. Hence, Avellaneda is not the woman-trophy in the office, the one wanted by the employees because she is the property of the boss, as women are sometimes portrayed in Benedetti's previous works—for example, in "Familia Iriarte" (Iriarte Family) from *Montevideanos*. Avellaneda is just another employee, but she is Santomé's companion, friend, partner, and lover.

By the end of the 1950s more Uruguayans were becoming aware of the illness of their country, but in 1957, the time in *La tregua*, it was too early to show changes. This novel won the Premio Municipal de Literatura and years later was adapted for the theater and cinema. The positive literary criticism this novel received was backed by a strong popular reception for all its versions.

El país de la cola de paja has the identical function of *La tregua*: to show the moral crisis Uruguay was suffering. In the novel, Benedetti did not develop the political crisis, but, in the essays, he wrote directly about the corruption of the political parties. However, Benedetti did not pretend to assume the role of a political scientist or sociologist. In the prologue to the first edition, he acknowledged his limitations. Critics reacted negatively to the essays, but other Uruguayans found in them an expression of their feelings and thoughts, and this book became another bestseller.

A very important year for Benedetti was 1959. Two events made him more deeply interested in the political dimension of Uruguay, as well as of the rest of Latin America: the Cuban Revolution and his trip to the United States with a drama fellowship from the American Council of Education. The revolution showed him that Uruguay was not isolated from the rest of Latin America and that revolution was a new possibility for the solution of Uruguayan problems. The trip to the United States, besides allowing him to study great American theater, showed him poverty, social injustice, racism, and solitude. His American experience is reflected in the poem "Cumpleaños en Manhattan" (Birthday in Manhattan), in *Poemas del hoyporhoy* (Day to Day Poems, 1961)—written in New York, where Benedetti turned thirty-nine years old—and in the short story "El resto es selva" (The Rest is Jungle), in *Montevideanos*. Both works show the solitude of the protagonist, but his solitude is not alienation. In the powerful United States, where different races and nationalities meet, the protagonist feels part of the marginalized Latin Americans.

Benedetti's third novel, *Gracias por el fuego* (Thank You for the Light, 1965), also re-creates some experiences in the United States. The novel opens with a group of Uruguayan tourists and Uruguayan residents of the United States who meet at a Hispanic restaurant in New York. The restaurant is in the Spanish section, and Benedetti comments on the poverty, dirtiness, and inhuman conditions in which Hispanics live. Nevertheless, the Uruguayans who are away from their country do not dwell on the misery that surrounds them, and they admire the greatness and excellence of the United States. After the economic crisis of 1955 many Uruguayans lost faith in their country and saw it as a crippling place where no one wanted to work. The Uruguayan privileged class tried to blame the working class for the crisis of the country. Although some critics thought that this U.S. chapter did not add much to the main story of the novel, which mostly takes place in Montevideo, it is important that the protagonist, Ramón Budiño, is one of the Uruguayans at the Tequila Restaurant. After he returns home from the United States, Ramón examines his guilt, a central problem in the story of his family. Ramón's drama—his frustrating struggle against Edmundo Budiño, his father, who is a powerful politician and businessman—which ends in Ramón's suicide, cannot be a local, existential story. The sociopolitical conditions of Uruguay that also force Ramón to act are related to the rest of Latin America.

Ramón Budiño realizes that others—the hegemonic sector, his father—dictate principles and morality. Ramón belongs to the generation who knew the apparently paradisiacal Uruguay in their childhood, and he has admired his father as one of its creators. But at the same time Ramón is aware that the creators of the old myth are the destroyers of the country. He both loves and hates his father. These feelings should not be read as an Oedipus complex but as the frustrations of a social sector that does not know how to fight against the demanding system that makes possible its well-being. Thus, Ramón's death is—in a way—a positive act. Even when he cannot destroy the system or kill his father, he can stop supporting them. The younger generation, including Ramón's son, Gustavo, will have to try to change the corruption.

Benedetti finished *Gracias por el fuego* in 1963 and entered it in the literary competition of

Benedetti circa 1969 (photograph by M. C. Orive, Paris)

Seix Barral, the prestigious Spanish publishing house in Barcelona. Even though his novel was one of the finalists in the competition, Spanish censorship did not allow its publication there. The localism of some early works of Benedetti had vanished, and although he was and is one of the most conscientious Uruguayan writers in regard to his country, his literature reflects many, if not all, contemporary Hispanic societies. Two years later *Gracias por el fuego* was published in Uruguay.

During the 1960s Benedetti traveled extensively. In 1966, 1967, and 1968 he stayed in Cuba for long periods, and he reflected in his literature the social experience of the Cuban Revolution—not the abstract concept of the revolution, but the time he had worked there. In the 1960s Benedetti published several books, including the collection of short stories *La muerte y otras sorpresas* (Death and Other Surprises, 1968), where he looks for new ways to express his themes, which have become more universal.

In the 1970s Benedetti began a more intense political and literary life. By the end of the 1960s Uruguay was in a state of unrest, ending in the coup d'état of 27 June 1973. In 1971

Benedetti became the leader of a movement that united the left-leaning parties. His political speeches and articles that had been published in the journal *Marcha* were compiled in *Crónicas del 71* (Chronicles of '71), published in 1972. Benedetti not only opposed the government (which was becoming more and more repressive) with his writing—like other progressive intellectuals—but he participated directly in Uruguayan political life.

In 1971 Benedetti published *El cumpleaños de Juan Angel* (translated as *Juan Angel's Birthday*, 1974). This work has been defined by Benedetti as "a novel written in verse." *Juan Angel* is his literary answer to the sociopolitical process of Uruguay, an extremely fast process in which the long Uruguayan tradition of peace, order, and content was disrupted in a few years. Once Uruguayans awoke from the lethargic myth of Uruguay as the "Switzerland of South America," the country experienced in a very short time several different historical periods. Hence Benedetti synthesized in one day the entire life of a character as a symbol of that rapid process. In one day, which starts at 7:50 in the morning and ends at midnight, Osvaldo Puente (who later changes his name to Juan Angel) lives twenty-seven years. On the morning of 27 August he turns eight years old. During the course of the day he grows as a member of the Uruguayan middle-class: he studies; obtains a bureaucratic position; gets married; and has two children. But at 8:40 at night, when Osvaldo turns thirty-three years old, he becomes Juan Angel, a member of the Tupamaro guerrilla movement. The biblical allusion, with the symbolic death of Osvaldo at thirty-three and his rebirth as a revolutionary, is not gratuitous. Like Jesus, Juan is going to offer his life in order to serve his people. At twelve o'clock at night he becomes a thirty-five-year-old revolutionary penetrating the underworld.

Each birthday, each period of the life of Osvaldo Puente/Juan Angel is in the present time, on top of which another present time is superimposed: the narrator-protagonist, already converted into a revolutionary, comments critically on his past. The unity and integrity of this novel is reinforced by its poetic conception (the narrative is in verse). Poetry can transform the past into a continued present and show Juan Angel in a continuous state of change and growth.

After the coup d'état of 1973, censorship, torture, death, exile, and *desaparecidos* (missing persons—unexplained disappearances) were the most powerful weapons the military regime used in order to attack those who opposed its ideology. Thus Benedetti joined the diaspora of Uruguayan intellectuals, and his work and name were banished from the country. Benedetti lived in Argentina, Peru, Cuba for some time, and then in Spain. Benedetti subverted the punishment of exile by writing and publishing constantly, and his old works reached new readers when the earlier books were almost all republished in Mexico. Benedetti's work could not be read in Uruguay, but Uruguayan literature, thanks to Benedetti, among other important writers in exile, was being read in other parts of the continent as well as in Europe and North America.

Benedetti's writing in exile had the important function of informing the rest of the world of what was happening in his country, a painful personal and collective experience. Living in Spain offered Benedetti the advantage of being able to publish articles in *El País*, the most important Spanish newspaper, soon after his arrival. This material was compiled in *El desexilio y otras conjeturas* (The "Unexile" and Other Conjectures, 1984). But Benedetti did not write only testimonial articles. The historical, personal, and collective events were transformed into literature. He increased his amount of work in almost all genres, even theater, a genre almost abandoned by Benedetti since 1955. In 1979 the play *Pedro y el capitán* was published, and on the same day of the book's official presentation, 28 March 1979, the Uruguayan theater company in exile in Mexico, known as "El Galpón" (The Shed), staged it. This play is the first work by Benedetti that deals directly with the theme of the Uruguayan military horror.

Benedetti's work in exile is characterized by its hybrid nature: testimonial writing is linked with fiction—as in the novel *Primavera con una esquina rota* (Spring With a Broken Corner, 1982); poetry and prose are strongly united—as seen in *Geografías* (Diverse Geography, 1984), in which the fourteen sections are made up of a poem and a short story each. The poems have the function of long epigraphs. They contain the essence of the stories that follow them. Contemporary literature is characterized by the dissolution of the traditional generic borders, and Benedetti's later works show that not only the topic of exile but the experience itself are such complex realities that their transformation into literature overflows the traditional divisions of genres.

Currently living in Madrid for six months, then in Montevideo for the other half of each year, Benedetti has succeeded in showing the world a new, more complex and contemporary image of Latin America, and Uruguay in particular. Through his literary work, as well as through the works of other Latin-American writers formerly or now in exile, Spaniards especially feel a growing interest in Latin America and in the problems of the Southern Cone countries. Benedetti is aware of the importance of keeping alive this interest. He continues to strengthen the literary and cultural link between Uruguay and Spain.

Bibliography:
Ambrosio Fornet, ed., *Recopilación de textos sobre Mario Benedetti* (Havana: Casa de las Américas, 1976).

References:
Germán D. Carrillo, "La biopsia como técnica literaria de Mario Benedetti en *Gracias por el fuego*," *Cuadernos Americanos*, 30 (July-August 1971): 217-233;

Rubén Cotelo, *Narradores uruguayos* (Caracas: Monte Avila, 1969), pp. 201-202, 203-211;

Juan Carlos Curutchet, "Los montevideanos de Mario Benedetti," *Cuadernos Hispanoamericanos*, 232 (April 1969): 141-148;

John E. Englekirk and Margaret M. Ramos, *La narrativa uruguaya* (Berkeley & Los Angeles, 1967), pp. 21, 121-123;

Ambrosio Fornet, "Mario Benedetti y la revolución posible," *Revista de Crítica Literari la Latinoamericana*, 1, no. 2 (1975): 63-72;

Rose Lee Hayden, *An Existential Focus on Some Novels of the River Plate* (East Lansing, Mich.: Latin-American Studies Center, 1973);

Ricardo Latcham, "*Montevideanos*, por Mario Benedetti" and "*La tregua*, por Mario Benedetti," in his *Carnet crítico: Ensayos* (Montevideo: Alfa, 1962), pp. 141-147, 148-152;

Dante Liano, "Album de familia: La pequeña burguesía en la narrativa de Mario Benedetti," *Studi di Letteratura Ispano-Americana*, 13-14 (1983): 199-212;

Gioconda Marún, "Análisis literario de *El cumpleaños de Juan Angel*, de Mario Benedetti," *Texto Crítico*, 3 (January-April 1977): 161-177;

Joseph V. Ricapito, "Sobre *La tregua* de Mario Benedetti," *Cuadernos Hispanoamericanos*, 331 (January 1978): 143-151;

Emir Rodríguez Monegal, "Las ficciones de un testigo implicado: Mario Benedetti," in his *Narradores de esta América* (Montevideo: Arca, 1961), pp. 209-255;

Jorge Ruffinelli, ed., "Mario Benedetti: Perfil literario," *Studi di Letteratura Ispano-americana*, 13-14 (1983): 103-111;

Ruffinelli, ed., *Mario Benedetti: Variaciones críticas* (Montevideo: Astillero, 1973);

Mario Spitaleri, "*Gracias por el fuego*: Estudios de variabbles temáticas," *Chasqui: Revista de Literatura Hispanoamericana*, 2, no. 1 (1972): 31-44;

Eileen M. Zeitz, "Entrevista a Mario Benedetti," *Hispania*, 63 (May 1980): 417-419;

Zeitz, "Los personajes de Benedetti: En busca de identidad y existencia," *Cuadernos Hispanoamericanos*, 297 (March 1975): 635-644.

Adolfo Bioy Casares

(15 September 1914 -)

Suzanne Jill Levine
University of California, Santa Barbara

BOOKS: *Prólogo* (Buenos Aires: Biblos, 1929);
17 disparos contra lo porvenir, as Martín Sacastru (Buenos Aires: Tor, 1933);
Caos (Buenos Aires: Viau & Zona, 1934);
La nueva tormenta; o, La vida múltiple de Juan Ruteno (Buenos Aires: Colombo, 1935);
La estatua casera (Buenos Aires: Jacaranda, 1936);
Luis Greve, muerto (Buenos Aires: Destiempo, 1937);
La invención de Morel (Buenos Aires: Losada, 1940); translated by Ruth L. C. Simms in her *The Invention of Morel and Other Stories* (Austin: University of Texas Press, 1964);
Seis problemas para Don Isidro Parodi, by Bioy Casares and Jorge Luis Borges, as H. Bustos Domecq (Buenos Aires: Sur, 1942); translated by Norman Thomas di Giovanni as *Six Problems for Don Isidro Parodi* (New York: Dutton, 1981);
El perjurio de la nieve (Buenos Aires: Emecé, 1944); translated by Simms as *The Perjury of the Snow* (New York: Vanishing Rotating Triangle, 1964);
Plan de evasión (Buenos Aires: Emecé, 1945); translated by Suzanne Jill Levine as *A Plan for Escape* (New York: Dutton, 1975);
Los que aman, odian, by Bioy Casares and Silvina Ocampo (Buenos Aires: Emecé, 1946);
Dos fantasías memorables, by Bioy Casares and Borges, as Bustos Domecq (Buenos Aires: Oportet, 1946);
Un modelo para la muerte, by Bioy Casares and Borges, as B. Suárez Lynch (Buenos Aires: Oportet & Haereses, 1946);
La trama celeste (Buenos Aires: Sur, 1948);
Homenaje a Francisco Almeyra (Buenos Aires: Destiempo, 1954);
El sueño de los heroes (Buenos Aires: Losada, 1954); translated by Diana Thorold as *The Dream of Heroes* (London: Quartet, 1987; New York: Dutton, 1988);
Los orilleros; El paraíso de los creyentes, by Bioy Casares and Borges (Buenos Aires: Losada, 1955);

Historia prodigiosa (Mexico City: Obregón, 1956; enlarged edition, Buenos Aires: Emecé, 1961);
Guirnalda con amores (Buenos Aires: Emecé, 1959);
El lado de la sombra (Buenos Aires: Emecé, 1962);
La tarde de un fauno (Madrid: Cuadernos Hispanoamericanos, 1964);
Crónicas de Bustos Domecq, by Bioy Casares and Borges (Buenos Aires: Losada, 1967); translated by di Giovanni as *Chronicles of Bustos Domecq* (New York: Dutton, 1976; London: Lane, 1982);
El gran serafín (Buenos Aires: Emecé, 1967);
La otra aventura (Buenos Aires: Galerna, 1968);
Diario de la guerra del cerdo (Buenos Aires: Emecé, 1969); translated by Gregory Woodruff and Donald A. Yates as *Diary of the War of the Pig* (New York: McGraw-Hill, 1972);
Adversos milagros, edited by Enrique Pezzoni (Caracas: Monte Avila, 1969);
Memoria sobre la pampa y los gauchos (Buenos Aires: Sur, 1970);
Breve diccionario del argentino exquisito, as Javier Miranda (Buenos Aires: Barros Merino, 1971);
Historias de amor (Buenos Aires: Emecé, 1972);
Historias fantásticas (Buenos Aires: Emecé, 1972);
Dormir al sol (Buenos Aires: Emecé, 1973); translated by Levine as *Asleep in the Sun* (New York: Persea, 1978);
Nuevos cuentos de Bustos Domecq, by Bioy Casares and Borges (Buenos Aires: Libería La Ciudad, 1977);
El héroe de las mujeres (Buenos Aires: Emecé, 1978);
Páginas (Buenos Aires: Celtia, 1985);
La aventura de un fotógrafo en La Plata (Buenos Aires: Emecé, 1985); translated by Levine as *The Adventures of a Photographer in La Plata* (New York: Dutton, 1989);
Obras escogidas, 2 volumes (Buenos Aires: Emecé/Círculo de Lectores, 1986);
Historias desaforadas (Buenos Aires: Emecé, 1987);
Una muñeca rusa (Buenos Aires: Tusquets, 1991).

Adolfo Bioy Casares and Jorge Luis Borges. They met in 1931 and started the magazine Destiempo *five years later.*

MOTION PICTURES: *Invasión*, screenplay by Bioy Casares, Jorge Luis Borges, and Hugo Santiago, Buenos Aires, 1969;

Les Autres, screenplay by Bioy Casares, Borges, and Santiago, Paris, Bourgois, 1974.

OTHER: *Antología de la literatura fantástica*, edited by Bioy Casares, Silvina Ocampo, and Jorge Luis Borges (Buenos Aires: Sudamericana, 1940; enlarged, 1965);

Antología poética argentina, edited by Bioy Casares, Ocampo, and Borges (Buenos Aires: Sudamericana, 1941);

Los mejores cuentos policiales, 2 volumes, edited by Bioy Casares and Borges (Buenos Aires: Emecé, 1943, 1951);

Fernando de Rojas, *La Celestina*, prologue by Bioy Casares (Buenos Aires: Estrada, 1949);

Cuentos breves y extraordinarios, edited by Bioy Casares and Borges (Buenos Aires: Raigal, 1955); translated by Anthony Kerrigan as *Extraordinary Tales* (New York: Herder & Herder, 1971);

Poesía gauchesca, edited by Bioy Casares and Borges (Mexico City: Fondo de Cultura Economica, 1955);

Francisco de Quevedo, *Prosa y verso*, selected by Bioy Casares and Borges (Buenos Aires: Emecé, 1960).

SELECTED PERIODICAL PUBLICATIONS—
UNCOLLECTED: "Rudyard Kipling, la litera fantástica," *Sur*, 95 (August 1942): 80-81;

"El hijo de su amigo," by Bioy Casares and Borges, *Número*, 19 (April-June 1952): 101-119;

"La fiesta del Monstruo," by Bioy Casares and Jorge Luis Borges, *Marcha* (30 September 1955): 20-23;

"Un nuevo surco," *Crisis*, 9 (January 1974): 44-47;

"Chronology," *Review 75* (Fall 1975).

The Argentine Adolfo Bioy Casares, popularly known as an author of "fantastic literature," has inspired generations of Latin-American readers and writers with his elegant humor and prophetic imagination. Bioy (as he is often referred to) began writing as the young colleague of the metaphysical fabulist Jorge Luis Borges, within the cosmopolitan sphere of *Sur* magazine—founded by the influential woman of letters Victoria Ocampo—in Buenos Aires in the early 1930s. Borges prefaced Bioy's best-known work, *La invención de Morel* (1940; translated as *The Invention of Morel*, 1964), with a virtual manifesto of fantastic literature, reacting against what he believed to be the impoverished artifice of realism. Citing *La invención de Morel* as a perfect contemporary model of the genre, he placed the twenty-six-year-old writer's first successful novella in the company of Henry James's *The Turn of the Screw* (1898) and Franz Kafka's *The Trial* (first published as *Der Prozess*, 1925). The fantastic or "magic" emanates from premodern modes of thought; fantastic narrative, as defined by Borges, involves the irruption of a lucid magical system of causation upon what we know to be natural causation, making the reader question the normal boundaries between fantasy and reality.

Rather than classify Bioy as a fantasist, Mexican poet and essayist Octavio Paz, in *Alternating Current* (1973), has described the Argentine's principal thematics as: "not cosmic but rather metaphysical: the body is imaginary, and we bow to the tyranny of a phantom. Love is a privileged perception, the most total and lucid not only of the unreality of the world but of our own unreality: not only do we traverse a realm of shadows; we ourselves are shadows." From *La invención de Morel* to *Guirnalda con amores* (Garland With Love, 1959)—a miscellany of stories and aphorisms on love—to *La aventura de un fotógrafo en La Plata* (1985; translated as *The Adventures of a Photographer in La Plata*, 1989), the perception of desire serves to make protagonist and reader painfully aware of solitude, of the tragicomic ways in which lovers lose one another, and of the impossibility of being the heroic master of one's destiny.

Adolfo Bioy Casares was born in Buenos Aires on 15 September 1914, the only child of wealthy parents. His father, Adolfo Bioy, descendant of a French family from Béarn (the southwestern region of France often in the background of his son's stories), was the author of two volumes of memoirs. He married Marta Casares, considered a great beauty in her day, who came from a well-established family, owners of the largest dairy chain in the La Martona region of Argentina. It was through her friendship with the Ocampo family that her son, at seventeen, would meet his wife-to-be—Victoria Ocampo's sister the writer Silvina Ocampo—and his literary mentor Borges. Rincón Viejo, the Bioy family ranch in Pardo in the province of Buenos Aires, was to give Bioy and Borges their first pretext to write in collaboration, as Bioy explains in the 1937 entry of his "Chronology," a jocular curriculum vitae published in *Review 75* (Fall 1975): "During the winter, Borges spends a week in the country with me. We write a pamphlet on curdled milk (our first joint effort). We plan a story we will never write, which is the germ of *Seis problemas para Don Isidro Parodi* (*Six Problems for Don Isidro Parodi*, 1942 [translated, 1981]), about a German philanthropist, Dr. Praetorius, who by hedonistic methods—music, ceaseless games—murders children." This tongue-in-cheek collaboration (inspired by Adolf Hitler's regime) led to many stories, translations, anthologies, and film scripts, and to the occasional invention of a third writer (with several pseudonyms) christened, by the Uruguayan critic Emir Rodríguez Monegal, "Biorges."

The familiar image of Bioy as disciple and collaborator of Borges placed him in the Latin-American canon under the shadow of the maestro. Even though Borges once called Bioy the secret master who led him out of his experimentation with baroque metaphors into classical prose, Borges's message was, as always, double: master in the sense that children teach their parents. It was Borges who told Bioy in an early conversation: "If you want to write, don't mess around with publishing companies or literary magazines. Just read and write." Despite this dictum, Borges and Bioy would initiate in 1936 a short-lived magazine and press called *Destiempo* (Out of Time), challenging in its nomenclature the historicist approach of traditional literary criticism. Borges's advice still reverberates in a recent story by Bioy, "Trio" (1986), where a friend advises the narrator: "When you spend too much time analyzing your projects, you don't do them. The best way to write is to write."

But more than mentor and disciple Borges and Bioy were lifelong friends, whose ingenious and impassioned discussions of literature were mutually nourishing. Bioy has said that, while Borges and he shared a similar and largely Victorian literary taste (for Robert Louis Stevenson, G. K. Chesterton, Edgar Allan Poe, H. G. Wells, Rudyard Kipling, and, of course, Kafka), each had different literary penchants: Borges favored the epic, as his enthusiasm for Walt Whitman and his admiration for *compadres* (local gangsters) testify, whereas Bioy tended toward the lyrical: Charles-Pierre Baudelaire, Arthur Rimbaud, and especially Paul Verlaine.

At age five Bioy discovered the bittersweet (and often comic) lyricism of love, as he describes in "Chronology": "I fall in love with a girl called

Nelida. Nelida's mother, a gentle, beautiful woman, appears one night, pursued by a drunken cook brandishing a knife. *Exeunt* all, including Nelida. I fall in love with a girl called Raquelita, who makes revelations to me in a laurel bower." Love was always to be an endangered and endangering obsession in Bioy: the sweet revelations in the laurel bower can bring catastrophe, whether that evil be banal stupidity or some divine (or diabolical) wrath.

Bioy was also acquainted with the Argentine classics, thanks to his father's nightly readings of José Hernández's gaucho epic *Martín Fierro* (1872) and Estanislao del Campo's *Fausto* (1874). Bioy would always feel close ties with the real as well as the literary world of the gauchos. In 1955 Bioy and Borges published an anthology of their favorite Gauchesque poetry, *Poesía gauchesca*, and in 1970 Bioy published an evocative memoir about the gauchos and the pampas. Furthermore, as with Borges, his love of Argentine poetry did not exclude its most popular form, tango lyrics.

Adolfo Bioy supported his son's literary progress until his death in 1962, and he encouraged Bioy to publish his first miscellany at age fifteen, called prophetically *Prólogo* (1929). Marta Casares, a reader of the works of Marcus Aurelius, taught the young Bioy stoic philosophy and the importance of willpower and discipline, lessons that served him well as a writer. Bioy later expanded his pragmatic and idealist philosophical repertoire, from the works of Bertrand Russell to those of Arthur Schopenhauer and William James. Bioy also remembers from childhood, "My mother tells me stories about animals who stray from the nest, are exposed to danger, and in the end, after many adventures, return to the security of the nest. The theme of the safe, or apparently safe, haven and of the dangers that lurk outside still appeals to me."

Bioy's life has been a gentler version of these fables. A shy yet witty, melancholy, and handsome man, he has traveled often, mainly to France—a second home and, as for many Latin-American intellectuals, a cultural mecca. Despite or because of his timidity, he has been a *héroe de las mujeres* (hero of women)—the title of his 1978 volume of stories. He has received literary prizes at home and abroad (including the 1969 Premio Nacional de Literatura), and films in Argentina and Europe have been based on his stories and novels—for example, the Italian Emidio Grecco directed *L'Invenzione di Morel* in 1974, and the Argentine Leopoldo Torress Nilsson directed *The War of the Pig* in 1975. But Bioy has lived a basically private life among friends and family in the same apartment in Buenos Aires for many years, in an elegant neighborhood near the Plaza de Francia. He writes every day in his studio there; or at Pardo, where he composed *La invención de Morel*, *El sueño de los heroes* (1954; translated as *The Dream of Heroes*, 1987), and *Dormir al sol* (1973; translated as *Asleep in the Sun*, 1978); or at his beach house "La Silvina" in Mar del Plata, where he wrote *Diario de la guerra del cerdo* (1969; translated as *Diary of the War of the Pig*, 1972). Even though he has fraternized with many famous writers and intellectuals, out of timidity or good manners he has remained virtually aloof from the world of literary politics. (When Octavio Paz and the novelist Elena Garro—Paz's first wife—introduced Bioy in the late 1950s to André Breton in Paris, the surrealist guru struck Bioy as a cross between "an army colonel and an infantile prankster," as Bioy said in private conversation.)

In his writing Bioy obsessively reenacts his early fascination with the ominous adventure. Time and again his hesitant protagonists are thrust headlong—out of some inevitable necessity—into situations they cannot comprehend and whose consequences may be disastrous. Wells's scientific romance *The Island of Dr. Moreau* (1896), in which a mad scientist turns beasts into men, becomes a kind of leitmotif throughout Bioy's novels, from *La invención de Morel* (the name an obvious allusion) and *Plan de evasión* (1945; translated as *A Plan for Escape*, 1975) to *Dormir al sol*. In the last, the animal metaphor for the human condition becomes literal when good-natured Lucio Bordenave suspects that a sinister doctor has transformed his wife (literally) into a canine bitch. Lucio's life is completely dissolved when *his* soul, too, is transferred into a dog's body.

Friends "explained" the supernatural to Bioy at any early age, as he recalls:

Through cracks that might open at any moment in the earth's crust, a devil might grab you by the foot and drag you down to hell. The supernatural as something terrifying and sad.
While we play at throwing a ball against the wall in back of the house, my friend Drago Mitre explains that heaven and hell are the lies of religion. I feel relieved. I would like to go inside a three-way mirror, where the images would re-

peat themselves clearly. The supernatural as something attractive.

Whereas for Borges the multiplication of oneself—of mankind "through mirrors and copulation" (the phrase attributed to a character named Bioy Casares in Borges's story "Tlön, Uqbar, Orbis Tertius," 1941 [in *Ficciones*, 1944])—produces the monstrous other and the horror of the uncanny, for Bioy the mirror may symbolize the other as an object desired, or an adventure both terrifying and fascinating.

In *Plan de evasión* the imaginative "evasion" invented by the mad scientist-governor of a penal colony (an apocryphal Devil's Island in 1914, when the historic Devil's Island had already ceased to function) involves cells lined with mirrors in which prisoners, their senses altered by a synesthetic operation, "see" visions of deserted paradise islands. The Victorian Sir Francis Galton's *Inquiries into Human Faculty* (1883) and the synesthetic experiments of French symbolist poetry provided the inspiration for Bioy's fusion of science and fiction. What is hell in Poe's story "The Pit and the Pendulum"—in which a prisoner of the Inquisition is exposed to the torture of burning, shining walls closing in on him—becomes in Bioy's blackly comic and allusive novella an ambiguous heaven. The mirror that reflects (but also threatens to supplant oneself) can be sinister or good, fearful or beautiful depending upon how it is perceived. In Bioy's paradoxical universe the symbol turns upon itself: his texts are filled with tantalizing allusions and symbols that are no longer keys but rather enigmatic ciphers.

Bioy wrote and published six books before 1940, but he considers (as do his critics) that his real literary production began with *La invención de Morel*. To entertain friends in later years he would often trot out one of the earlier attempts. He would claim it was written by some young writer, read a section that would be sure to produce mocking laughter, and then reveal that he was the author. In the 1937 entry of his "Chronology" he writes:

> I publish *Luis Greve, muerto* (Luis Greve, Deceased [1937]). As always when I publish, my friends look sad and don't know what to say to me.
> At Pardo I glimpse what will be the plot of *The Invention of Morel*. I understand that something is wrong with my way of writing and I tell myself it's time to do something about it. For reasons of caution, in writing the new novel, I don't strive to make a big hit, just to avoid errors.

Bioy's early writings "suffered," according to him, from the chaotic influence of surrealism and James Joyce's stream-of-consciousness technique. In Bioy and Borges's first conversation, a discussion between an apprentice writer and a known one, Borges responded to Bioy's enthusiasm for Joyce, emblem of the modern and total freedom, by suggesting—against the grain—that *Ulysses* (1922) was more a promise than an achieved masterpiece. Borges may have brought Bioy to the classical at this early stage, citing Horace and promoting the virtues of narrative rigor, such as to be found in the plots of Chesterton. Bioy embraced Borges's poetics of condensation and concision, which favored the speculative and the artistic over the novelist's expansive representation of human experience. By the mere fact of writing novels, however, Bioy would always be more concerned than Borges with re-creating the lived and the seen.

Although Bioy had still not discovered a comfortable mode in *Luis Greve, muerto*, Borges found in this book the seed of the writer to be, as he concluded in a December 1937 review in *Sur*: "Our literature is poor in fantastic narratives, preferring the formless *tranche de vie* or the episodic. Which makes Bioy Casares' work unusual. In *Caos* [Chaos, 1934] and *La nueva tormenta* [The New Storm, 1935] imagination predominates; in this book—in the best pages of this book—that imagination obeys an order. 'Nothing is so rare as order in the operations of the spirit,' said [François] Fénelon." In *Luis Greve, muerto* Bioy began to master games with time and space that attempt to impose another order—a literary one—upon an absurd universe. One of the stories in the volume, "Los novios en tarjetas postales" (The Couple in Postcards), about a young man who interpolates his image into the photograph of a girl he loves, anticipates *La invención de Morel*, in which *l'amour fou* (mad love) is carried to its ultimate consequences.

The plot of *La invención de Morel* transports this love into the realm of science fiction and away from Argentina to an unknown and supposedly deserted island—much as in his own life Bioy needed to remove himself from the subjectivity of his immediate Argentine reality to gain aesthetic distance. The protagonist, a fugitive from Venezuela who writes a diary, discovers strange inhabitants who turn out to be three-dimensional

Bioy Casares with his daughter, Marta, at his family's ranch, Rincón Viejo, near Buenos Aires, 1962 (photograph by Silvina Ocampo)

movie images. Like Villiers de l'Isle-Adam did in *L'Eve Future* (The Future Eve, 1888), Bioy intuitively foresees the future invention of the holograph. His typically bungling antihero (Bioy's creation of characters is inspired by a mixture of silent-movie comedy and Kafkaesque absurdity) falls madly in love with a woman named, allusively, Faustine. After learning how to activate the machine that has captured these images, he proceeds to interpolate himself near her, making it look as if a relationship exists between the two, though she is unaware of his existence. His actions are tragic since Faustine and now the narrator, like all who are photographed by Morel's machine, are dead.

The encounter between the "real-life" fugitive and the "magical" Faustine (and the supernatural machine that created her) makes Bioy's work paradigmatic of the fantastic. But allegorical interpretations are tempting. The novella has been interpreted as a parable of the relationship between reader and text: the nameless narrator-protagonist encounters the fictional characters invented by the mad scientist Morel and interpolates himself—his interpretation—upon them. Or, like Morel, the narrator is the artist who ultimately sacrifices his life for art. *La invención de Morel* can also be read as Bioy's homage to cinema and photography (he is an aficionado of both). Whatever the interpretation, the author has been dethroned in this paranoid narrative where the narrator may be—like Morel—a crazy inventor of the whole story. What remains is a text that speaks of other texts, from *The Island of Dr. Moreau* to a tradition of utopian literature going back to Plato's *Atlantis*.

Bioy's meticulously wrought novella of 120 pages was received with acclaim and brought him recognition beyond the borders of the *Sur* group; he was awarded the 1940 Buenos Aires municipal prize for literature. When translated into French in 1953, his narrative device of two lovers coexisting spatially in two different temporal dimensions would inspire Alain Robbe-Grillet's script for Alain Resnais's film *Last Year at Marienbad* (1961). Aside from several movie and television versions made in France, Italy, and Argentina, *La invención de Morel* has become a cult reference, as for example in the Argentine Hector Subiella's metaphysical film *Man Facing Southeast* (1985). At the same time, among the proponents of realism, the book caused Bioy to acquire the reputation of an intellectual enamored of his own mental constructions, or "bachelor machines." Lucio Bordenave, the bungling clockmaker in *Dormir al sol*, was perhaps a burlesque response to this misreading—but even Bioy himself felt that it was not until the story "The Idol" in *La trama celeste* (The Celestial Plot, 1948) that he had truly found his style.

Bioy's brief sentences reflect his tendency toward shorter, concise narrative forms (stories, novellas, and short novels). His style is terse and understated: his narrators tend to say little, inviting one to read ironic humor between the lines. Bioy's elliptical, matter-of-fact manner of communicating bewilderment makes the reader both laugh at and sympathize with these bunglers who do not quite have a grip on reality but are doing their best. Bioy could be considered a Kafka with a light touch, or a *porteño* (Buenos Aires) Woody Allen.

Beneath this mild-mannered surface Bioy's elegant textual machines, like the invention of the mad scientist Morel, are works of passion, expressing a desire for eternal love and a poignant failure to counter the dissolution wrought by mortality. Already in the early work of Bioy one can see a lucid irony that maintains distance between the passion with which he denounces the evils of the world and the curiosity with which he registers them. The futuristic machine as the pathetic or sinister vehicle of human hopes in this century of technology, emblematic of limitations, is both a comic and a terrifying motif throughout Bioy's work: he compares humankind to a mechanical monkey on a bicycle that gradually rusts away and wears down with use.

Both science fiction and detective genres, along with a metaphysical treatise, make up what Bioy was first to call the hybrid genre of the fantastic. In his May 1942 review (in *Sur*) of Borges's first volume of *ficciones* (*El jardín de senderos que se bifurcan* [The Garden of Forking Paths, 1942]) Bioy wrote: "Borges, like the philosophers of Tlön, has discovered the literary possibilities of metaphysics." Science fiction provides the fantastic invention or event; the detective genre contributes the intricate yet elegantly methodical plot. Science fiction—from its origins in the works of Plato and in Sir Thomas More's *Utopia* (1516) to Aldous Huxley's *Brave New World* (1932)—and detective stories, from Poe's "Purloined Letter" to Raymond Chandler's American Gothic exposés of corruption, have also served as modes of social and political satire.

Bioy and Borges's works in collaboration, beginning with *Seis problemas para Don Isidro Parodi*, written under their principal pseudonym, H. Bustos Domecq (Bustos, a family name from Borges's ancestors; Domecq from Bioy's grandmother), are vehicles of satire. A local Argentine version of Chesterton's rational priest, Father Brown, and of Poe's melancholy logician, Dupin, the barber Don Isidro is a grotesque parody: he mentally solves crime mysteries while doing time in prison. Bioy and Borges pay homage to the narrative art of Chesterton and Poe through the baroque excess of complicated plots, puns, and caricaturesque representations of local dialect. Throughout their hilarious collaborations (Silvina Ocampo once said that she could always tell when they were working together by the howls of laughter echoing through the apartment), Borges and Bioy would invent a secret language based on *lunfardo*, local Italianate slang, that neither used when writing on his own but which had repercussions on Bioy's later writing. Bioy and Ocampo (who married in 1940 and later had a child, Marta) also wrote together a parodic detective novel about a crime of passion: *Los que aman, odian* (Those Who Love, Also Hate, 1946).

Borges and Bioy invented a literary language, a secret code that served not so much to make fun of local types as to challenge language's conventional use as transparent communication, to expose its artifice. In 1946 they published longer detectivesque stories in *Dos fantasías memorables* (Two Memorable Fantasies) and *Un modelo para la muerte* (Death Kit; under the name of B. Suárez Lynch, the last name originating from the Irish side of Bioy's ancestry); the stories also satirized Argentine social mores.

Although politics may appear in the background of Bioy's fictions, a more metaphysical despair tends to overtake political concerns. "The Myth of Orpheus and Eurydice" in *Guirnalda con amores* was motivated by a Peronist injustice, the razing of the Jockey Club to punish its members. But the story turned into a version of the Orphic legend, the subterranean baths of the club becoming the netherworld where Silveira seeks hopelessly to recuperate his dead beloved, Virginia. The much-lamented death of Bioy's mother in 1952 was probably the more profound motivation of this somber story, as well as of "Homage a Francisco Almeyra," about which Bioy says, "My mother died during the Peron era. For the one who dies during a dictatorship, that dictatorship is forever." *Diario de la guerra del cerdo*, about a futuristic war against the old people in Buenos Aires, doubtlessly reflects political malaise in Argentina before the repressive 1970s, but its overriding concern is mortality, against which love wages war. *La aventura de un fotógrafo en La Plata* presents the mortality theme even more poignantly. Political circumstances—the protagonist's friend is a policeman who may be involved in the temporary disappearance of a young revolutionary—again provide a smokescreen for a more sinister plot. An old gentleman—Don Juan Lombardo—may be trying magically to usurp the body of Nicolasito Almanza, the young and naive protagonist, reminding one of Robert Louis Stevenson's "The Bodysnatchers."

In 1967 Bioy and Borges turned from humorously self-conscious critical fictions to fictional criticism in *Crónicas de Bustos Domecq* (translated as *Chronicles of Bustos Domecq*, 1976), a metacommentative work that makes fun of itself at the same time it mocks cultural subjects high and low, from the so-called geniuses of modernism—Pablo Picasso, Charles-Edouard Le Corbusier, and Joyce—to whom the book is jocularly dedicated, to thinly disguised local artists and writers.

Bioy and Borges shared a nihilistic spirit toward literature, but not even nihilism is sacred. In *Guirnalda con amores* Bioy personifies nihilism as "one of those tiresome people who always have to have something interesting to say." In 1939 the two friends came up with a list of everything to be avoided, including all the literary devices ever used, and not only injunctions against realism and naturalism but against "pretentious distortions of space and time: [William] Faulkner, Borges, Bioy Casares." Bioy later published this list—which was the seed of Borges's parable of reading-as-writing titled "Pierre Menard, autor del Quijote"—in a slim collection of reviews and prologues called appropriately *La otra aventura* (The Other Adventure), in 1968. In articles on various works, from Fernando de Rojas's fifteenth-century masterpiece *La Celestina* to Mary McCarthy's *A Charmed Life* (1955), Bioy reveals an eclectic and keen critical eye. He prefers Benjamin Constant's unsentimental treatment of love, and that of Julien Green, whose divided narrator in *Le Voyageur sur la terre* (Pilgrim on Earth, 1927) is a forerunner of Bioy's in *La invención de Morel*. The two volumes of *Los mejores cuentos policiales* (The Best Detective Stories, 1943, 1951) reveal Borges and Bioy's favorite detective writers, and *Cuentos breves y extraordinarios* (1955; translated as *Extraordinary Tales*, 1971) is a curious miscellany of epigrams and stories, attributed to a variety of authors including Bioy and Borges, in which authorship is playfully subverted.

Their most important anthology is probably the *Antología de la literatura fantástica* (Anthology of Fantastic Literature), compiled with Ocampo in 1940 and expanded in 1965, which introduced to Latin-American readers a group of talented young Argentine writers within a broad context of fiction from many different languages and eras. The local writers include Ocampo herself, Santiago Dabove, H. A. Murena, José Bianco, J. R. Wilcock, Macedonio Fernández (whose philosophical and literary experiments inspired other writers), and Julio Cortázar, as well as Bioy and Borges; the diverse list of foreign writers includes Kafka, Poe, Wells, de L'Isle-Adam, Alexandra David-Neel, Emanuel Swedenborg, and François Rabelais. The reader of this anthology can gain entrance to the literary and philosophical inspirations that form the allusive universe found in all of Bioy's novels and stories, but most explicitly so in his early works. De L'Isle-Adam's *L'Eve Future* (1886), like the Peruvian Ricardo Palma's *XYZ*, offers a preview of Morel's futuristic Faustine. Along with Bioy's many readings of Eastern fabulists (Lady Shikibu Murasaki, Sei Shonagon), Alexandra David-Neel's revelations about the fusion of reality and fantasy in the rituals practiced by Tibetan monks in *Magic and Mystery in Tibet* (1929) also added fuel to Bioy's inventions. The philosopher Emanuel Swedenborg's versions of death as a dream and of hell as an everyday room with barely perceptible differences were to haunt Bioy's worlds, where dream and vigil often merge.

The many allusions in Bioy's works, from a boat named Rimbaud to a character named Dreyfus in *Plan de evasión* are enigmas rather than keys. Dreyfus brings to mind, on his apocryphal Devil's Island, the historical Alfred Dreyfus, but he is no relation. *Plan de evasión*, like *La invención de Morel*, leads the reader into a labyrinth of texts in which the truth is always one step beyond. Perhaps his most effective device as a novelist is what has been termed by Maribel Tamargo a "discurso de paranoia." One of Cortázar's last stories, "Diario de un cuento" (Diary of a Story), pays homage to Bioy's uncanny ability to represent simultaneously a divided consciousness from within and at a distance.

Is the narrator of *La invención de Morel* hallucinating or awake? Neither he nor the reader can be sure; in footnotes an "editor" contradicts infor-

Dust jacket for the 1972 collection in which Bioy Casares included revised versions of "fantastic stories" from his 1956 book, Historia prodigiosa

mation given by the narrator. And Morel's explanation of his machine is clearly in the words of a lucid but mad scientist. In *Plan de evasión* the narrative voices are even more multiple. Henri Nevers, a young French officer posted at the infamous penal colony, writes dramatic letters to his Uncle Antoine, who often doubts his nephew's sanity (Henri has been sent into exile, away from his beloved Irene, because of some family scandal never specified, just as the fugitive's vaguely political reasons are never explained in *La invención de Morel*). But one also doubts Antoine's motivations, as well as those of Henri's cousin Javier Brissac, who will replace him on the island; Javier has apparently stolen Irene from Henri. And then there's an "editor" who makes contradictory notations. *Etc.* is the last word of this open-ended comic nightmare, in which readers never find out what happens to Henri.

Bioy achieved in his early novels what Borges set out to do with the short story, as the narrator in his "Tlön" comments: "compose a novel in the first person, whose narrator would omit or disfigure the facts and indulge in various contradictions that would permit a few readers . . . to perceive an atrocious or banal reality." By dethroning the author, and also the reader as reliable interpreter, Bioy has subverted writing and reading as privileged moments, producing a discourse of surfaces and disturbing effects of infinite uncertainty. Bioy continued to use unreliable or duplicitous narrators in his later novels, but he employed more realistic narrative strategies and everyday Argentine voices, which render the resulting ambiguity even more disturbing. His later novels carry forth his perception of unreality but in a more convincing way, revealing the fissure beneath the common word or cliché, where before he used the obscure allusion.

Between 1944 and 1967 Bioy published eight volumes of stories—including *Historia prodigiosa* (Prodigious Story, 1956), from which he selected and revised, in 1972, two volumes of stories: *Historias de amor* (Love Stories) and *Historias fantásticas* (Fantastic Stories). The love stories are ironic fables about human follies. The fantastic stories present futuristic machines or supernatural events. In "El gran Serafín" (The Great Seraphim), for example (later included in the book of that name), a Neptune-like creature emerges from the sea at a beach resort. But parody transcends both categories, as it does Bioy's manipulation of detective and science fiction genres. Bioy's stories, like his novels, are really fantastic comedies, as Peruvian critic José Miguel Oviedo aptly calls them, in which the void produces laughter (the other side of terror) and in which Bioy's men are often like reckless or fearful children, at the mercy of beloved women who are often abominable monsters.

For the volume titled *El lado de la sombra* (The Shady Side, 1962) Bioy was awarded the Secondo Premio Nacional in 1963; *El gran serafín* (1967) won for him in 1969 the Premio Nacional. Many of the stories are detectivesque intrigues whose resolutions are ambiguous because of supernatural consequences or a hallucinatory narrator; the formula of the fantastic again weds detective plot and science fantasy. A victimized woman is indestructible in several stories, such as *El perjurio de la nieve* (1944; translated as *The Perjury of the Snow*, 1964) and "Memoria de Paulina"—which, along with *La trama celeste*, are among Bioy's best-known stories.

One of Bioy's first ambiguous local heroes appears in *El sueño de los héroes*. Situated in the Bue-

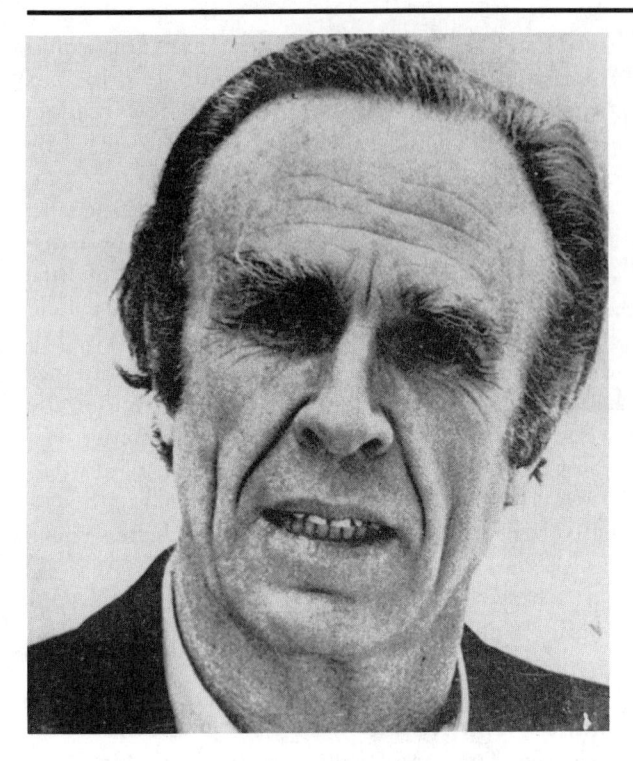

Bioy Casares circa 1978

nos Aires of the 1920s and 1930s, the novel is considered Bioy's most Borgesian work in its transfigurations of time and identity: protagonist Emilio Gauna has a chance to correct the past by literally reliving it. But the Nietzschean "eternal return" matters less here than the Oedipal drama in which a young man attempts to destroy a dominating father figure. A parricide turns against itself to become filicide: Bioy's novels seem obsessed with sons who are suicidal in their failure to supplant the father. Love is lost, too, since Gauna pursues a masked object of desire who, he fatally fails to realize, is his own loving wife.

Bioy placed his next two novels in lower-middle-class Buenos Aires and created a literary language—which would inspire Cortázar among others—out of the discourse of the lower and middle classes. The language spoken in his early narratives stylizes the speech of the cultivated. *El sueño de los heroes* contrasts the educated narrator's discourse with the picturesque speech of the *compadritos*, or local gangsters; but from the time of *Diario de la guerra del cerdo* on, Bioy's narrators are lower-middle-class characters. In 1971 Bioy compiled a playful *Breve diccionario del argentino exquisito* (Brief Dictionary of the Exquisite Argentine), which mocks the officialese used by bureaucrats and the euphemisms employed by the middle and upper classes. This "dictionary"—in the spirit of Gustave Flaubert's *Dictionnaire des idées reçues* (Dictionary of Received Ideas, 1951)—reveals once again Bioy's ability to manipulate spoken language and to insinuate the truths (or horrors) social discourse tries so hard to conceal.

The "war of the pig" occurs in the near future, a time when gangs of young people chase and eventually murder the old. Yet the novel ends optimistically, focusing on the magic of love—between an aging man and a young woman. Bioy's most recent novels, however, emphasize frustration and dissolution. *Dormir al sol* transcends the comic bleakness of *Plan de evasión*, where at least Nevers's letters remain. In *Dormir al sol* Lucio's tragicomic call for help, in the form of his letter—which constitutes the main body of the novel—is finally not heard since the receiver and reader of the letter, a distant friend named Félix Ramos, loses the document and is reluctant to investigate for fear that he, too, may lose his soul.

The misadventure of love, the artist's sacrifice of life (and love) for art in *La invención de Morel*, and the fear that people are merely Platonic shadows living in a Swedenborgian dream—these topoi again resurface in 1985 in *La aventura de un fotógrafo en La Plata*. The emphatically mundane title indicates a banal reality: a young small-town photographer comes to photograph the provincial city of La Plata, in his eyes the "big city" but in reality a rundown monument to a more prosperous past. Argentina, too, may be a dream (or nightmare), though the buildings, the photographs, and the ruins will remain.

Love is the sweetest dream from which, unlike death, people seem doomed to awake: the photographer Nicolasito ultimately falls from grace not by losing his body or soul to the devil (or to Don Juan) but by leaving Don Juan's daughter, Julia. Like Alfred Hitchcock's oneiric film *Vertigo* (1958), the novel ends with their abrupt parting at the bus station. Nicolasito escapes, or has no choice but to leave, the utopia of communion; freedom is an illusion. Bioy's young man is endearing but weak, a handsome, fading photograph, while the aging Don Juan looms relentlessly.

Recently Bioy has received long-overdue recognition: in 1991 he was awarded the Premio Cervantes—the most prestigious prize in the Hispanic literary world—in Spain, and the Premio Alfonso Reyes in Mexico. Aside from two recent volumes of stories, *Historias desaforadas* (Stories Out of Bounds, 1987) and *Una muñeca rusa* (A Russian Doll, 1991), Bioy has just finished a novel called "Un campeón desparejo" (An Uneven Champion). He is always writing narratives or thinking up plots—his desk drawers are filled with works in progress—and he keeps his anthologists busy, as in the latest edition of works new and old, *La invención y la trama*, and in a comprehensive collection of miscellany and unpublished texts titled in acronymic homage the "ABC of Adolfo Bioy Casares."

Interviews:
Luisa Futoransky, "Una conversación con Adolfo Bioy Casares," *Cuaderno Cultural*, 11 (1969): 91-96;

Marcelo Pichon Riviere, "Adolfo Bioy Casares: 'yo necesito la tormenta,' " *Crisis*, 1 (January 1974);

Martha Paley de Francescato, "Adolfo Bioy Casares," *Hispamérica*, 3, no. 9 (February 1975): 75-81;

Alicia Borinsky, "Entrevista con Adolfo Bioy Casares," *Modern Language Notes*, 91 (March 1976): 356-359;

Danubio Torres Fierro, "Las utopias pesimistas de Adolfo Bioy Casares," *Plural*, 55 (April 1976): 47-53.

Bibliographies:
Raquel Puig Zaldívar, "Bibliografía de y sobre Adolfo Bioy Casares," *Revista Iberoamericana*, 40 (January-March 1974): 173-178;

Rodolfo A. Borello, "Bibliografía sobre Adolfo Bioy Casares (Algunas nuevas fichas)," *Revista Iberoamericana*, 91 (April-June 1975): 367-368.

Biographies:
Ofelia Kovacci, Biography, in her *Adolfo Bioy Casares* (Buenos Aires: Culturales Argentinas, 1963);

Oscar Hermes Villordo, *Genio y Figura de Adolfo Bioy Casares* (Buenos Aires: Eudeba, 1983).

References:
María Luisa Bastos, "Desapego crítico y compromiso narrativo: El subtexto de 'El sueño de los heroes,' " *Texto/Contexto en la literatura iberoamericana*, edited by Keith McDuffie and Alfredo Roggiano (Madrid: Artes Gráficas Benzal, 1981);

Bastos, "Habla popular/Discurso unificador: *El sueño de los heroes* de Adolfo Bioy Casares," *Revista Iberoamericana*, 125 (October-December 1983): 753-766;

Jorge Luis Borges, "Adolfo Bioy Casares: El sueño de los heroes," *Sur*, 235 (July-August 1955): 88-89;

Borges, "La estatua casera," *Sur*, 18 (March 1936);

Alicia Borinsky, "*Plan de evasión* de Adolfo Bioy Casares: La representacion de la representacion," in *Otros mundos otros fuegos: Fantasía y realismo mágico en Iberoamerica*, edited by D. A. Yates (East Lansing: Michigan State University Press, 1975);

David P. Gallagher, "The Novels and Short Stories of Adolfo Bioy Casares," *Bulletin of Hispanic Studies*, 52 (July 1975): 247-266;

Juan Carlos Ghiano, "Dos cuentistas extraños: Bioy Casares y Gloria Alcorta," *Ficción*, 11 (January 1958): 163-166;

Jacques Goimard, "Bioy Casares: Entre Stevenson et Robbe-Grillet," *Le Monde* (9 August 1973), p. 9;

Suzanne Jill Levine, "Adolfo Bioy Casares y Jorge Luis Borges: La utopía como texto," *Revista Iberoamericana*, 43 (July-December 1977): 415-432;

Levine, "Ficción vs. Ciencia en *La isla del doctor Moreau* de H. G. Wells, *La invención de Morel* y *Plan de evasión* de Bioy Casares," in *Texto/Contexto en la literatura iberoamericana*; translated, *Latin American Literary Review*, 9 (Spring-Summer 1981): 17-26;

Levine, *Guía de Bioy Casares* (Madrid: Fundamentos, 1982);

Levine, "Parody Island: Two Novels by Adolfo Bioy Casares," *Hispanic Journal*, 4 (Spring 1983): 43-49;

Levine, "La tendencia pastoril en dos obras," *Eco*, 208 (February 1979): 377-402;

Alfred J. MacAdam, "The Lying Compass" and "Satire and Self-Portrait," in his *Modern Latin American Narratives: The Dreams of Reason* (Chicago: University of Chicago Press, 1977);

MacAdam, "The Mirror and the Lie: Two Stories by Jorge Luis Borges and Adolfo Bioy Casares," *Modern Fiction Studies*, 19 (Autumn 1973): 353-362;

David Maldavsky, "Las opciones y el azar en el universo narrativo de Bioy Casares: Un enfoque sintáctico," *Nueva Narrativa Hispanoamericana*, 2 (September 1972): 45-64;

Alberto Manguel, Introduction and notes to Bioy Casares's *Plan de evasión* (Buenos Aires: Kapelusz, 1974);

Julio Matas, "Bioy Casares o la aventura de narrar," *Nueva revista de filología hispánica*, 27, no. 1: 112-123;

Thomas Meehan, "Estructura y tema de *El sueño de los heroes*," *Kentucky Romance Quarterly*, 20, no. 1 (1973): 31-58;

Martin Muller, "Cuando los argentinos quieren ser exquisitos," *Revista La Nación* (30 April 1978);

José Miguel Oviedo, "Angeles abominables: Las mujeres en las historias fantásticas de Bioy Casares" and "Hipótesis del tigre," in his *Escrito al margen* (Bogota: Procultura, 1982);

Oviedo, "La aventura de un fotógrafo en La Plata," *Vuelta*, 120 (November 1986): 58-60;

Octavio Paz, *Alternating Current* (New York: Viking, 1973), pp. 43-44;

Jaime Rest, "Las invenciones de Bioy Casares," *Los Libros*, 2 (1969);

Alain Robbe-Grillet, "Adolfo Bioy Casares, *L'invention de Morel*," *Critique*, 69 (February 1953);

Emir Rodríguez Monegal, "Dos cuentistas argentinos," *Clinamen*, 3 (July-August 1947);

Rodríguez Monegal, "La invención de Bioy Casares," *Plural*, 3 (February 1974): 57-59; translated as "The Invention of Bioy Casares," *Review 75* (Fall 1975): 41-44;

Reina Roffé, "Adolfo Bioy Casares, sus laberintos y perjurios," *Revista Siete Días* (28 July 1977);

Graciela Scheines, "Los personajes de Bioy Casares: Criaturas entre dos mundos," *La Gaceta* (November 1981);

Ernesto Schoo, "Los infinitos mundos de Adolfo Bioy Casares," *Nacion* (21 June 1969);

Margaret L. Snook, "The Narrator as Creator and Critic in *The Invention of Morel*," *Latin American Literary Review*, 7 (Spring-Summer 1979): 45-51;

Maribel Tamargo, *La narrativa de Bioy Casares: El texto como escritura-lectura* (Madrid: Playor, 1983).

Jorge Luis Borges
(24 August 1899 - 14 June 1986)

Alberto Julián Pérez
Dartmouth College
(Translated by Virginia Lawreck)

BOOKS: *Fervor de Buenos Aires* (Buenos Aires: Privately printed, 1923; revised and enlarged edition, Buenos Aires: Emecé, 1969);
Luna de enfrente (Buenos Aires: Proa, 1925);
Inquisiciones (Buenos Aires: Proa, 1925);
El tamaño de mi esperanza (Buenos Aires: Proa, 1926);
El idioma de los argentinos (Buenos Aires: Gleizer, 1928);
Cuaderno de San Martín (Buenos Aires: Proa, 1929);
Evaristo Carriego (Buenos Aires: Gleizer, 1930); translated by Norman Thomas di Giovanni and Susan Ashe as *Evaristo Carriego: A Book About Old-Time Buenos Aires* (New York: Dutton, 1983);
Discusión (Buenos Aires: Gleizer, 1932; revised edition, Madrid: Alianza / Buenos Aires: Emecé, 1976);
Historia universal de la infamia (Buenos Aires: Tor, 1935; revised edition, Buenos Aires: Emecé, 1954); translated by di Giovanni as *A Universal History of Infamy* (New York: Dutton, 1972; London: Lane, 1973);
Historia de la eternidad (Buenos Aires: Viau & Zona, 1936; revised and enlarged edition, Buenos Aires: Emecé, 1953);
El jardín de senderos que se bifurcan (Buenos Aires: Sur, 1942);
Seis problemas para Don Isidro Parodi, by Borges and Adolfo Bioy Casares, as H. Bustos Domecq (Buenos Aires: Sur, 1942); translated by di Giovanni as *Six Problems for Don Isidro Parodi* (New York: Dutton, 1980);
Poemas (1922-1943) (Buenos Aires: Losada, 1943); revised and enlarged as *Poemas, 1923-1953* (Buenos Aires: Emecé, 1954); revised and enlarged again as *Poemas, 1923-1958* (Buenos Aires: Emecé, 1958);
Ficciones (1935-1944) (Buenos Aires: Sur, 1944); enlarged as *Ficciones* (Buenos Aires: Emecé, 1956); translated by Anthony Kerrigan and others, and edited by Kerrigan (London: Weidenfeld, 1962; New York: Grove, 1962);
El compadrito, su destino, sus barrios, su música, by Borges and Silvina Bullrich Palenque (Buenos Aires: Emecé, 1945; enlarged edition, Buenos Aires: General Fabril, 1968);
Dos fantasías memorables, by Borges and Bioy Casares, as Bustos Domecq (Buenos Aires: Oportet, 1946);

Jorge Luis Borges circa 1972 (photograph by Jesse A. Fernández)

Un modelo para la muerte, by Borges and Bioy Casares, as B. Suárez Lynch (Buenos Aires: Oportet & Haereses, 1946);

El Aleph (Buenos Aires: Losada, 1949; enlarged, 1952); translated and edited by Borges and di Giovanni as *The Aleph and Other Stories, 1933-1969, Together with Commentaries and an Autobiographical Essay* (New York: Dutton, 1970; London: Cape, 1971);

La muerte y la brújula (Buenos Aires: Emecé, 1951);

Otras inquisiciones (1937-1952) (Buenos Aires: Sur, 1952); translated by Ruth L. C. Simms as *Other Inquisitions, 1937-1952* (Austin: University of Texas Press, 1964; London: Souvenir, 1973);

El "Martín Fierro," by Borges and Margarita Guerrero (Buenos Aires: Columba, 1953);

La hermana de Eloísa, by Borges and L. M. Levinson (Buenos Aires: Ene, 1955);

Los orilleros, by Borges and Bioy Casares (Buenos Aires: Losada, 1955);

Leopoldo Lugones, by Borges and Betina Edelberg (Buenos Aires: Troquel, 1955);

Manual de zoología fantástica, by Borges and Guerrero (Mexico City & Buenos Aires: Fondo de Cultura Económica, 1957);

El hacedor (Buenos Aires: Emecé, 1960); translated by Mildred Boyer and Harold Morland as *Dreamtigers* (Austin: University of Texas Press, 1964; London: Souvenir, 1973);

Antología personal (Buenos Aires: Emecé, 1961); translated by Kerrigan and others, and edited by Kerrigan as *Personal Anthology* (New York: Grove, 1967; London: Cape, 1968);

Obra poética, 1923-1964 (Buenos Aires: Emecé, 1964); enlarged as *Obra poética, 1923-1966* (Buenos Aires: Emecé, 1966); enlarged again as *Obra poética, 1923-1967* (Buenos Aires: Emecé, 1967); enlarged again as *Obra poética, 1923-1969* (Buenos Aires: Emecé, 1972); enlarged again as *Obra poética, 1923-1976* (Buenos Aires: Emecé, 1977);

Para las seis cuerdas (Buenos Aires: Emecé, 1965);

Introducción a la literatura inglesa, by Borges and María Esther Vázquez (Buenos Aires: Columba, 1965); translated and edited by L. Clark Keating and Robert O. Evans as *An Introduction to English Literature* (Lexington: University Press of Kentucky, 1974);

Literaturas germánicas medievales, by Borges and Vázquez (Buenos Aires: Falbo Librero, 1966);

Crónicas de Bustos Domecq, by Borges and Bioy Casares (Buenos Aires: Losada, 1967); translated by di Giovanni as *Chronicles of Bustos Domecq* (New York: Dutton, 1976);

El libro de los seres imaginarios, by Borges and Guerrero (Buenos Aires: Kier, 1967); revised, enlarged, and translated by Borges and di Giovanni as *The Book of Imaginary Beings* (New York: Dutton, 1969; Harmondsworth, U.K.: Penguin, 1974);

Introducción a la literatura norteamericana, by Borges and Esther Zemborain de Torres (Buenos Aires: Columba, 1967); translated and edited by Keating and Evans as *An Introduction to American Literature* (New York: Schocken, 1973);

Nueva antología personal (Buenos Aires: Emecé, 1968);

Elogio de la sombra (Buenos Aires: Emecé, 1969); translated by di Giovanni as *In Praise of Darkness* (New York: Dutton, 1974; London: Lane, 1975);

El otro, el mismo (Buenos Aires: Emecé, 1969);

El informe de Brodie (Buenos Aires: Emecé, 1970); translated by Borges and di Giovanni as *Doctor Brodie's Report* (New York: Bantam, 1973; London: Lane, 1974);

El Congreso (Buenos Aires: Archibrazo, 1971); translated by Borges and di Giovanni as *The Congress* (London: Enitharmon, 1974);

El oro de los tigres (Buenos Aires: Emecé, 1972); translated, in part, by Alastair Reid in *The Gold of the Tigers: Selected Later Poems* (New York: Dutton, 1977);

Prólogos, con un prólogo de prólogos (Buenos Aires: Torres Agüero, 1975);

El libro de arena (Buenos Aires: Emecé, 1975); translated by di Giovanni as *The Book of Sand* (New York: Dutton, 1977; London: Lane, 1979);

La rosa profunda (Buenos Aires: Emecé, 1975); translated, in part, by Reid in *The Gold of the Tigers: Selected Later Poems*;

Diálogos, by Borges and Ernesto Sábato (Buenos Aires: Emecé, 1976);

Qué es el budismo, by Borges and Alicia Jurado (Buenos Aires: Columba, 1976);

La moneda de hierro (Buenos Aires: Emecé, 1976);

Historia de la noche (Buenos Aires: Emecé, 1977);

Nuevos cuentos de Bustos Domecq, by Borges and Bioy Casares (Buenos Aires: Librería La Ciudad, 1977);

Borges para millones (Buenos Aires: Corregidor, 1978);

Borges as a child in Buenos Aires (Sotheby's auction catalogue, sale number 5796, 19 December 1988)

Borges, oral (Buenos Aires: Emecé, 1979);
Siete noches (Mexico City & Buenos Aires: Fondo de Cultura Económica, 1980); translated by Eliot Weinberger as *Seven Nights* (New York: New Directions, 1984; London: Faber, 1984);
La Cifra (Buenos Aires: Emecé, 1981);
Nueve ensayos dantescos (Madrid: Espasa-Calpe, 1982);
Veinticinco Agosto 1983 y otros cuentos (Madrid: Siruela, 1983);
Atlas, by Borges and María Kodama (Buenos Aires: Sudamericana, 1984); translated by Kerrigan (New York: Dutton, 1985);
Los conjurados (Madrid: Alianza, 1985);
Textos Cautivos: Ensayos y reseñas en "El Hogar," edited by Enrique Sacerio Garí and Emir Rodríguez Monegal (Barcelona: Tusquets, 1986);
A/Z (Madrid: Siruela, 1988);
Biblioteca personal: Prólogos (Madrid: Alianza, 1988).

Collections: *Obras completas*, 9 volumes (Buenos Aires: Emecé, 1953-1960); revised edition, 1 volume, edited by Carlos V. Frías (Buenos Aires: Emecé, 1974);
Obras completas en colaboración, by Borges and others (Buenos Aires: Emecé, 1979);
Prosa completa, 2 volumes (Barcelona: Bruguera, 1980);
Antología poética, 1923-1977 (Madrid: Alianza, 1981).

Editions in English: *Labyrinths: Selected Stories & Other Writings*, edited by Donald A. Yates and James E. Irby (New York: New Directions, 1962);
Selected Poems, 1923-1967, translated and edited by Norman Thomas di Giovanni (London: Lane/Penguin, 1972; New York: Dell, 1973);
Borges: A Reader, edited by Emir Rodríguez Monegal and Alastair Reid (New York: Dutton, 1981).

The Argentine writer Jorge Luis Borges is one of the most prominent figures in contemporary world literature. Continuing the tradition of fantastic literature established by Edgar Allan Poe in the nineteenth century, he transformed the genre into an eclectic whole that allowed him to explore philosophical ideas and to pose relevant questions. After participating in and observing the development of the avant-garde during the first quarter of the century, Borges created his own type of post-avant-garde literature—which shows the process of critical self-examination that reveals the moment in which literature becomes a reflection of itself, distanced from life—in order to reveal the formal and intellectual density involved in writing. Borges's influence is seen, especially in Latin-American literature, in the use of intertextuality and parodic and satiric elements by various writers such as Julio Cortázar and Gabriel García Márquez, his confessed admirers.

Borges was born in downtown Buenos Aires on 24 August 1899 and was the son of Jorge Guillermo Borges, a lawyer, and Leonor Acevedo de Borges, who learned English from her husband and became a translator of works by Nathaniel Hawthorne, Katherine Mansfield, and William Saroyan. Her mother was related to the Argentine patriot Francisco Narciso de Laprida and to Col. Isidoro Suárez, who fought in the war of independence. Jorge Luis Borges's paternal grandfather was Col. Francisco Borges, who married an Englishwoman and died in 1874 fighting in the Argentine civil wars. In 1901 the Borges family moved to the Palermo area, on the outskirts of Buenos Aires. Even though Borges later said, "Lo cierto es que me crié en un jardín, detrás de una verja con lanzas y en una biblioteca de ilimitados libros ingleses" (The truth is that I grew up in a garden, behind a railroad spar and in an unlimited library of English books)—in the foreword to his *Evaristo Carriego* (1930; translated, 1983)—Palermo also provided him with a rich source of popular character types that he used in his writing. Borges's father was a cultured man and an amateur writer; he boasted an extensive library of English works, but also with many books in Spanish and French. Georgie, as the young Borges was affectionately called, learned Spanish and English simultaneously.

A sustained economic boom in Argentina allowed the Borges family to live in Europe from 1914 to 1921, and the two children, Georgie and his sister, Norah, went to school for four years at the Collège Calvin in Geneva; the education was in French, so Borges had to master his third language. A fourth language, Latin, became his chief subject. He also became familiar with French and German literature. In 1919 his family went to Spain and stayed in Palma de Mallorca for almost a year. They later lived in Seville and Madrid, and in the latter city the young Borges met the writer Rafael Cansinos Assens, became familiar with local avant-garde movements—including ultraism—and published his first poems in local literary magazines. By 1921 the family had returned to Buenos Aires, which caused Borges to rediscover the city, a predominant topic of his poetry. He soon met the writer Macedonio Fernández, a friend of his father's, who would become a strong literary influence. With other young writers, Borges founded a literary magazine, *Prisma*, in 1921 and the review *Proa* in 1922.

The respect for the literary world and for reading in the Borges household was the result of a fin de siècle, modernist environment. Reading, more than direct experience with the world, transformed itself into the impetus behind Borges's creations, distinguishing him in this aspect from other avant-garde writers who were less intellectually oriented than he. Borges's avidity as a reader and his curiosity were extraordinary. He did not limit himself to reading works of fiction; history, philosophy, and science all formed an integral part of his interests. The breadth of his intellectual appetite puts Borges in a special category of readers known as "savage readers." The savage reader is one who approaches the cultural creations of the world with a sense of irreverent freedom and an unlimited appetite, without consideration of genre or discipline. He is capable of developing a new norm, free of the restrictions imposed by genre and the determinations of the past. Poe and Walt Whitman, along with Domingo F. Sarmiento and Rubén Darío, belong to this category. One of the major advantages of the American savage reader, compared to the European reader, is his ability to see the diverse and conflictive European culture as a simultaneous and integral whole. Borges transformed this advantage into the central theme of his narrative, surprising his European readers, who marveled that a Latin-American author was capable of doing what their own contemporary writers could not: offering them a finalized and comic image of their culture. Despite the fact that Borges never manifested as great an appreciation for the French culture as he did for the English, it is not coincidental that France was the first country to recognize him. French intellectuals welcomed him as a much-needed, intellectual writer interested in metaphysical paradoxes and games.

During the second decade of the twentieth century, the literary scene—which had until then been dominated in Spanish America by the modernist (Parnassian-symbolist) movement—radically changed when the avant-garde movement developed innovative forms of artistic representation that modified the sensibilities of the reading public. The avant-garde poets rebelled against turn-of-the-century modernism, its versification system, its thematics, and the musical aspect of its verse, and they proposed instead a nonrepresentative poetics, in which the semantic and even the grammatical bases of the language gave way to an explosion of anarchic freedom. The specific characteristics of the avant-garde groups in the Hispanic world and their idiosyncratic features were a consequence of the particular way in which they strived to adapt to the problem of cultural and literary identity. The literary creations of the young Borges belong to this moment in literary history.

The most recognized contribution of Borges's poetry to the Hispanic avant-garde movement is an urban thematic, associated with metaphysical speculation, which depicts local symbols

Borges circa 1918, when he was a student in Geneva

such as a sunset on the suburbs and includes the description of streets and old neighborhoods of the city—as in *Fervor de Buenos Aires* (1923), *Luna de enfrente* (Opposite Moon, 1925), and *Cuaderno de San Martín* (San Martín Notebook, 1929). Having finished this initial poetic cycle, Borges strove to understand the literature of his period from a critical point of view and then transcend it. The result of this process can be seen in his collection of essays *Discusión* (1932). In "La supersticiosa ética del lector" (The "Superstitious Ethic of the Reader), "La postulación de la realidad" (The Postulation of Reality), and "El arte narrativo y la magia" (Narrative Art and Magic), Borges reflects upon the exaggerated idealization of style by many readers who consider it to be an absolute literary value, situated above the text, an end unto itself. He studies the effects of literary techniques used to suggest reality and unreality, and he affirms that magical causality is much more acceptable in the narrative than the linear representation of time and the serial representation of plot.

Borges meditated insistently on the possibilities of prose fiction. He preserves in his prose the tendency, begun in his poetry, toward the symbolic description of urban scenes and the philosophical meditation on traditional metaphysical problems, such as death, time, and identity. He also retains the approaches he elaborates in his first collections of essays and in his literary biography of the poet Evaristo Carriego. In these works Borges examines Hispanic and European writers, studies metaphysics, writes morphological-historical presentations, does biographical-literary analyses of authors, and reflects on the writing profession. In these essays, stylistic bases of his future narratives of ideas, there are elements inherited from the modernist essay that tend to reappear transformed: the tendency toward symbolization, the study of rare or exotic themes, the obsessive interest in art as a problem, and the multiple intertextual references.

From 16 September 1933, the date of publication in *Crítica* of "Hombre de las orillas" (Man of the Outskirts)—collected as "Hombre de la esquina rosada" (Streetcorner Man) in *Historia universal de la infamia* (1935; translated as *A Universal History of Infamy*, 1972)—to 1939, when "Pierre Menard, autor del Quijote" (collected in *Ficciones*, 1944) appeared in *Sur*, Borges searched for new means of expression and underwent a literary transition. It was a difficult time for him: his father, who was blind during the last years of his life, died in 1938. Borges, who until that moment had dedicated all his energies to his writing, was forced by financial constraints to take a boring and uninspiring job at a local municipal library—a position he kept until 1946, when pressure by the Juan Perón dictatorship caused him to resign. He attempted during this time of transition to find a narrative form capable of allowing him to manifest his interest in different branches of knowledge, his reflective and philosophical nature, and his passion for intense reading and brief writing. These demands caused him to discard the most popular narrative genres, such as the novel and the realist story—the novel because of the prolonged effort demanded of the writer (which Borges considered debilitating and difficult to control due to the vast quantity of narrative material), and the realist story because in it the principal weight of the action falls to the description of trivial circumstances surrounding the resolution of the anecdote, thus hindering the treatment of transcendent, intellectual problems. He searched for a solution, following Poe's example and experimenting with the possibilities opened to him by so-called fantastic literature.

"Hombre de la esquina rosada" was, according to Borges, a false step, as it led him toward realism and the overuse of local color. He maintains in this story the interest in themes and characters of the barrios, which he had displayed previously in his poetry and in *Evaristo Carriego*. The narrator tells the story of a duel between the strongmen of two barrios. Each gang has its own territory, one the North of the city, the other the South. Francisco Real, the leader of the northern gang, heads south to challenge Rosendo Juárez; the duel has no other motive than the desire to test one's mettle and to challenge one's rival. The narrator plays an ambiguous role but is the principal element in the climax: he changes from a secondary character and witness into the unsuspected hero of the story. Borges surrounds each strongman with mythical attributes of power; he presents them in the first part of the story as absolute and omnipotent. La Lujanera, Rosendo's mistress, functions as an exchange-object passed on to the hands of the most valiant, and predictably she ends up with the narrator. The action takes place at a local dance in a slum on the outskirts of Buenos Aires. This setting tempted Borges to overuse local color (the principal reason behind his self-criticism and his later rejection of the story); to experiment with a sensationalist narrative in which he exaggerates the dramatic description, imitating cinematographic close-ups (especially in the duel and dance scenes); and to reproduce popular, colloquial language, which is littered with traditional maxims and colorful idiomatic expressions. The story was well received because of its exaggerations and the inversion of the narrator's role, which provoke astonishment in the reader.

Borges did not return to the easily sensationalist type of story; sensationalism is not absent in his literature, but later it is not easily sensational—it is complex, intellectual, and erudite. This rebellion by Borges against his own success was a reaction against what he considered faults of his contemporaries: the misuse of description and the abuse of garish, popular figures—bad habits of a late-nationalistic modernism continued by some avant-garde writers such as Federico García Lorca, who based part of his literary success on the exaggeration of local color and the mythical presentation of one of the most ill-treated popular figures in literature, the Gypsy. Borges did not concur with Lorca and made the conscious de-

Drawing of Borges by his sister, Norah, 1926 (from Emir Rodríguez Monegal, Jorge Luis Borges: A Literary Biography, *1978)*

cision not to make his own literature colorful and commercial. In his rejection of the unrefined reader, Borges continues the elitist attitude of the turn-of-the-century modernists, who were the creators of a complex and erudite literary code that required of its reader a difficult process of initiation.

The "biographies" written in 1933 and 1934 and published in *Historia universal de la infamia* constitute the second stage in the development of Borges's narrative style. In a prologue written for the 1954 edition, Borges explains that the book has a baroque nature and that the baroque is the final stage of all art. For Borges, the baroque is not in itself an autonomous artistic movement but rather the stage in which art reflects upon itself and takes itself as an object of representation. It is art of a "second degree." This self-observation of the means of expression creates the dual point of view typical of irony. Borges's art in this period, as suggested by his prologue, has changed its character, moving beyond moderately avant-garde art and evolving into an art that questions the principles of composition held by the avant-garde.

Borges uses biography with a literary purpose, basing his so-called biographies on readings that he slants and distorts with the intention of parody, in order to create a comic commentary with respect to biography as a canon. He presents the lives of men who, far from being models of virtue as in the serious biography of an exemplary individual in society, are rather models of perversity and infamy. This use of a body of knowledge as a "scientific" base of information, with parodic intent, comically relativizes the "objectivity" of history and the process of inference that sociology uses. Compared to the techniques in "Hombre de la esquina rosada," this new approach gave Borges much more intellectual freedom to narrate in a different voice than that of his characters. In "El tintorero enmascarado Hákim de Merv" (The Masked Dyer, Hakim of Merv), a parodic biography of the Veiled Prophet of Khorassan, Borges introduces commentaries about his sources, a starting point for the technique he would later use extensively in his fiction: including literary analysis as an integral part of the narration.

In *Historia universal de la infamia* Borges abandons the realist approach to narration. He concentrates on the presentation of the strange, the exotic, trying to astonish his reader, scorning naturalist verisimilitude, and approaching the poetics of the prose in fantastic literature. He places great emphasis on the process of "rewriting" the stories that have more or less incidental sources, and he assumes a pseudopedagogical distance, convenient for the satirist, relating facts whose causal connection is unsuspected and giving them a mockingly "universal" value.

In his next collection of essays, *Historia de la eternidad* (History of Eternity, 1936), there are two exemplary texts: the title work and the pseudoliterary note "El acercamiento a Almotástim" (The Approach to al-Mu'tasim). In the title essay Borges tries to depict the different notions of the concept of eternity. He describes the opposite ideas "dreamed" by the realists and nominalists; the concept of eternity according to the interpretation of platonic archetypes; and the eternity imagined by the church, linked to the theory of the Trinity, and he shows the "life" that is in them, given their profound relation to human desire, suggesting that nostalgia was the cause responsible for the creation of these models. Borges considers the idea conceived by the church to be unbelievable, and he satirizes the theologians who exhausted the Hebrew scriptures "en pos de fraudulentas confirmaciones, donde parace que el Espíritu Santo dijo muy mal lo que dice bien el comentador" (in pursuit of fraudulent confirmations, in which it seemed that the Holy Spirit said very poorly what the commentator says so well). Borges shows that, underlying the metaphysical conceptions, there is a fantastic aspect, a discovery that would lead him to the use of these metaphysical conceptions, exaggerated with parodic intent, as a thematic base of his fantastic stories, for example, in "Tlön, Uqbar, Orbis Tertius" (in *Ficciones*).

In "El acercamiento a Almotástim" Borges creates one of his most transcendent literary models: the fictitious literary note or article. He comments on a novel of a hybrid nature, written by an imaginary author, which combines elements of the detective story with others derived from mythical-allegorical Persian poetry. Borges summarizes the plot in such a way that it appears framed by his commentary, and he links this invented story to real literature by mentioning the names of Farīd 'Attār, Wilkie Collins, James Joyce, Rudyard Kipling, and T. S. Eliot. In this manner he produces—like the most conventional authors of fiction who attempt to adhere to the constraints of their genre so as not to disappoint the reading public—a sense of verisimilitude and credibility, respecting the conventions of the literary note to the point that many readers failed to perceive the witticism and searched for the interesting novel he had analyzed.

"El acercamiento a Almotástim," written in 1935, is the last direct antecedent of Borges's *ficciones*, which he began to create in 1939, when he published "Pierre Menard, autor del Quijote." From that date until 1953 Borges published thirty-three short stories, which do not amount to more than two hundred printed pages; all are compiled in the enlarged editions of *Ficciones* and *El Aleph* (1949). Upon these works rests Borges's worldwide reputation as an innovator of contemporary literature. From a formal point of view, it is the fantastic story, as conceived by Poe, that is the generic source most evident in Borges's stories. But as much as Borges enriches the approaches to fantastic literature, it is for him (as it is for other writers and thinkers, such as Voltaire, Jonathan Swift, and Franz Kafka) not an end but rather a means to an end. Fundamental to Borges's style is the manner in which he uses these literary approaches to create a literature of ideas, capable of commenting on the questions and broodings of the cultural world.

The uses of these fantastic techniques did not hinder him in giving a role to topics and characters of Argentinian literature. He brings together themes and characters from gaucho literature and assigns them a symbolic function in which the particular acquires a wider meaning. In "El sur" (The South, in *Ficciones*), for example, Borges introduces in a contemporary setting an immemorial gaucho who symbolizes the mythical South that no longer exists. He throws his dagger at the feet of a convalescent librarian, who is thus obliged to accept a duel and feels that such a fatal destiny is more romantic and noble than the destiny his humiliating illness had previously mapped out for him. In "El fin" (The End, in *Ficciones*) and "Biografía de Tadeo Isidoro Cruz (1829-1874)" (in *El Aleph*) Borges creates two continuations of the ultimate example of gaucho literature, José Hernández's *Martín Fierro* (two volumes, 1872, 1879), choosing intertextuality as the adequate approach to uphold this literary tradition. Borges resolves a conflict over which his generation had toiled, preoccupied with the possibility of creating an authentically national literature; for him, as he states in "El escritor argentino y la tradición" (The Argentine Writer and Tradition, in the 1976 edition of *Discusión*), the Argentine writer should try out all themes without limiting himself to a local thematic and be open to a universal thematic, disregarding local color.

In his fiction Borges repeatedly utilizes two approaches that constitute his most permanent contributions to contemporary literature: the creation of stories whose principal objective is to deal with critical, literary, or aesthetic problems; and the development of plots that communicate elaborate and complex ideas that are transformed into the main thematic base of the story, provoking the action and relegating the characters—who appear as passive subjects in this inhuman, nightmarish world—to a secondary plane. John Sturrock, in his *Paper Tigers* (1977), has noted that Borges's stories function as literary criticism "at the same time as extending the possibilities of creative writing." Among the stories that present literary or aesthetic problems, "Pierre Menard, autor del Quijote" criticizes and satirizes symbolist writers, and "Examen de la obra de Herbert Quain" (An Examination of the Work of Herbert Quain, in *Ficciones*) satirizes a fictitious avant-garde author.

"Pierre Menard, autor del Quijote" is, like "El acercamiento a Almotástim," a literary note or review, but instead of referring to an imaginary author and book, Borges conceived in this case an imaginary author whose name has historic resonance (one can associate it with the symbolist Louis Menard) and who decides to "write" a pre-existing work—nothing less than Miguel de Cervantes' *Don Quixote* (two parts, 1605, 1615). Borges's "story" is intentionally exaggerated and farcically "exemplary." He introduces a virtuoso symbolist writer whose obsessive concern for style transforms him into the victim of his own literary asceticism and leads him to self-denial when he attempts an impossible undertaking destined to fail: the writing of the *Quixote*—itself a realist parody of the fantastic genre—whose literary conception was considerably distanced from that of the symbolists, devoted as they were to their stylistic mannerisms. Borges takes advantage of the situation in order to laugh at himself, inasmuch as his perfectionist way of writing and his love of quotations and intertextual references draw him sufficiently close to the meticulous, intellectual, and obsessive Menard. He divides Menard's work into two parts: the visible, represented by symbolist poems, monographs, philosophical and literary studies, and translations; and the secret, the "writing" of three chapters of the *Quixote*. In this second part, Borges makes perspicacious commentaries on the relevance of reading as an activity, and he poses the question of the change of emphasis on the classics, whose significance varies as the historical context and approach to reading change. Using the format of the literary note, Borges succeeds in satirizing the intellectual habit of the symbolist writers and their conception of the writer as an aesthete and a scholar.

In his "examination" of the work of Quain, Borges repeats the format of the previous piece: he begins with the indication that the author has died and proceeds to examine his literary work. In his story about Menard, Borges had directed all the desecrating power of satire to ridicule the type of writer that symbolism made possible; in the story about Quain he satirizes avant-garde writers by describing their extreme positions. Quain is characterized as an experimental writer, and his work, though inventive, does not pertain to art but rather to the mere history of art. In contrast with the symbolist, who patiently submits himself to the execution of slow, laborious works,

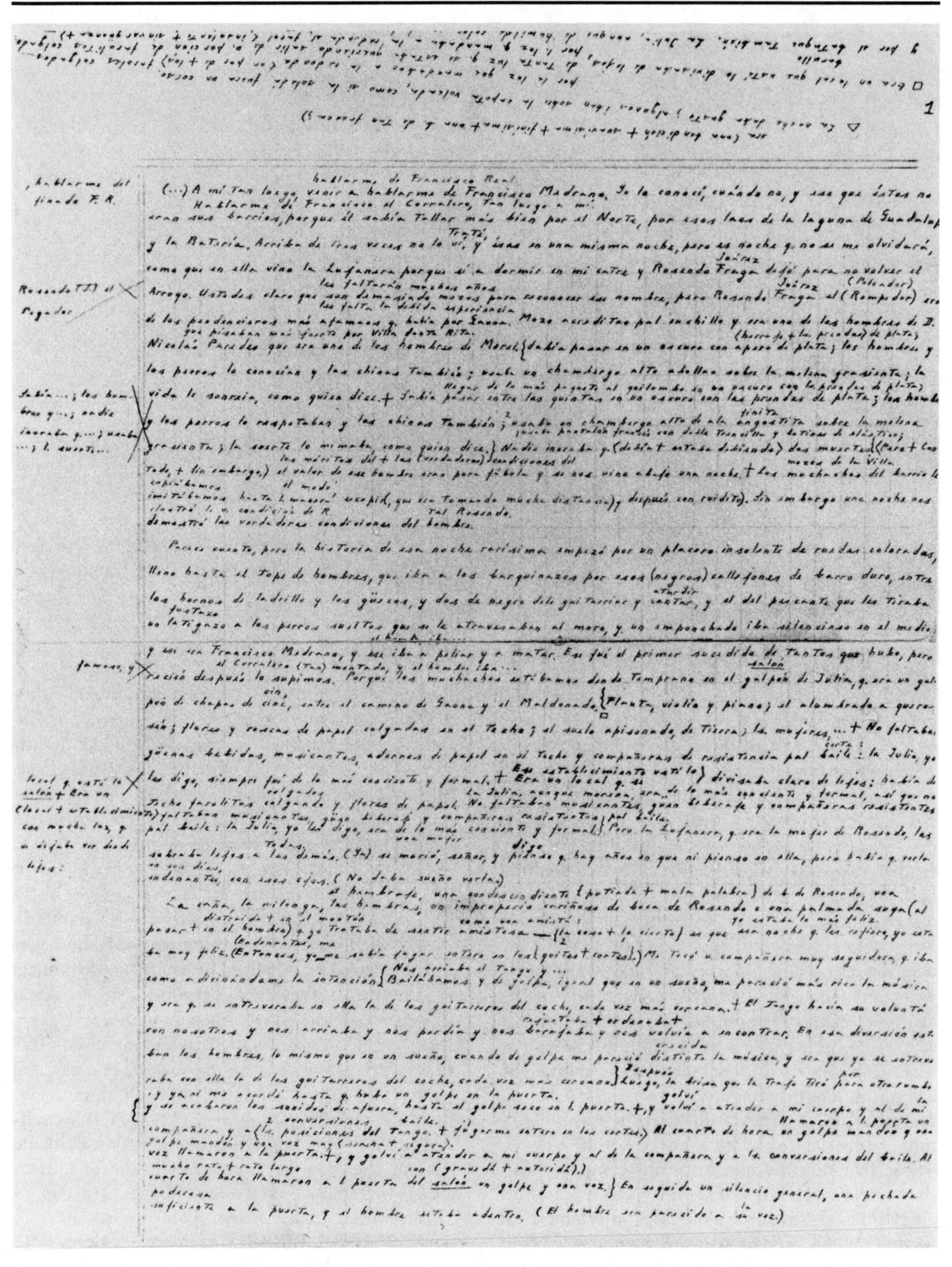

Page from the manuscript for "Hombre de la esquina rosada" (Streetcorner Man), collected in Historia universal de la infamia (Sotheby's auction catalogue, sale number 5563, 18 June 1987)

Jorge Luis Borges (photograph by Julio Mendez Ezcurra)

Quain was supposedly a man who believed that good literature could be easily created, if and only if the writer had the capacity for invention, a literary virtue fundamental to the avant-garde. The narrator comments that Quain created a special literary approach in order to make his readers feel as if they were inventing the plot as they read; unlike Menard, he underestimated reading and mourned the dependence of many writers on past works. Quain thought all Europeans were writers, whether potential or actual—extraordinary praise since, as an avant-garde writer, he believed in the generative power of the artist. In order to expound better upon the excesses of avant-garde imagination, Borges comments critically on the works he assigns to his character; the lengthy, outlandish novel *April March*, for example, a product of Quain's radical attitude, consists of nine novels-within-a-novel, whose structure the narrator-critic compares with the twelve Kantian categories, which sacrifice everything to "un furor simetrico" (a symmetrical furor). When imagining the symbolist writer Menard, Borges makes him French, France being the international center of the symbolist movement; the avant-garde writer is English, England being the place where Virginia Woolf and other avant-garde writers worked. Borges does not employ the note, or literary study, as the main discursive genre in other tales in *Ficciones* or *El Aleph*. However, he includes it as a secondary genre, combined with others, in almost all his stories in which he presents character-writers, as in "El milagro secreto" (The Secret Miracle, in *Ficciones*) and "El Aleph."

The other contribution by Borges to contemporary fiction is the development of thematics that provoke the action. The characters, reduced to subordinate figures, depend on a superior will that guides them, in what occurs between the creator and his creation in "Las ruinas circulares" (The Circular Ruins; in *Ficciones*); or they are victims of a cultural tradition imposed upon the individual, leading him in a search for self-destruction, a victim of his death wish—as in the case of the Nazi in "Deutsches Requiem" (in *El Aleph*); or characters are led, like the traveler in "El inmortal" (in *El Aleph*), from one situation to another as a result of coincidence. Along with the devalued human hero, Borges presents ideas as the center of the narrative action. He provides a detailed image of them, which demands of the reader an aptitude for abstraction, generalization, and comparison. Utilizing literary and extraliterary discursive genres, he considerably widens the zone of reading commonly considered proper in fiction. It is an inclusive mythologizing presentation, as if these ideas were a totality in themselves, which the reader can observe as independent external objects. Borges exaggerates characteristics, deforming them and provoking a comic response in the reader who identifies with the critical point of view of the satirist.

Borges describes the ideas of various philosophical schools, real or imaginary, utilizing metalinguistic approaches, similar to those evident in dictionaries, to define a term: he employs paraphrasing, explains and abstracts the concept, and gives other information. To represent these ideas, he diminishes or exalts them, or does both things simultaneously, parodying the idea; for example, in "Tlön, Uqbar, Orbis Tertius" he introduces a group of wise men who invent a world, taking to the extreme the idealist conception. Ideas in the world called Tlön have been deformed to the point that they become a parody of idealism. The philosophers do not search for truth, but rather "wonder," and they consider metaphysics a branch of fantastic literature. With permanent irony Borges presents ambivalent ideas that at a given moment in the narration can change their sign, revealing the relativity of values and the false universality of culture.

Borges draws his favorite techniques from the tradition of satire as well as from philosophy and the social sciences. He utilizes rhetorical figures such as hyperbole and enumeration, and he presents opposing ideas that aspire to destroy one another. Hyperbole is the main figure in "La biblioteca de Babel" (The Library of Babel, in *Ficciones*), where he describes an unlimited generic library, and, given that it is an allegory for infinity, he incorporates the mathematical notion of periodic repetition so that the reader is able to intuit the concept. In "La lotería en Babilonia" (The Babylon Lottery, in *Ficciones*) he methodically presents the concept of the lottery, making use of a "scientific" approach, relating each of the parts to the whole. He searches for a formula for the system, following rules of inference and establishing a list of statements that explain the whole and its aim. Borges's objective in this story is to satirize man's rational zeal for systematically organizing his surroundings in a useful way; Borges shows a world without aim, dominated by game and chance. In "Los teólogos" (The Theologians, in the 1952 edition of *El Aleph*) Borges uses an approach derived from polemics and rhetoric: he tells of an imaginary theological polemic in which the characters are finally defeated by a heretical idea that establishes its truth in spite of those who fought to disprove it. The medieval fable is transformed into a burlesque "morality," a modern narration about the problems of personal identity and the division of the self.

One of the most surprising techniques Borges uses to associate the representation of an idea with a character is that of "revelation." A revelation occurs when human understanding can relate itself with an infinite mind, or when the divinity can communicate with a chosen individual. The divine message, in turn, intrinsically transforms people by confronting them with revealed truth. It is a literary approach derived from religious texts, and fantastic literature made use of it, adapting it to its prose poetics. Borges employs this technique following the religious tradition of miracles and the popular magical tradition of folklore. In "El Aleph," "El Zahir," and "La escritura del Dios" (The Writing of the God)— all in *El Aleph*—he creates situations in which the characters have fleeting contact (which is materialized in some magical object: a small sphere, a coin, a wheel) with the divine. The sphere of "El Aleph," for example, according to the narrator of the story, contains the universe in its entirety and serves as a symbolic synthesis of space and time. The revelation profoundly alters the destiny of the character, uniting him with the mythical world and rendering meaningless the familiar.

In other cases, Borges creates a revelation leaving out the magical object, by confronting the character with his own personal, profound truth. This happens in "Biografía de Tadeo Isidoro Cruz (1829-1874)" when Sergeant Cruz sees a reflection of himself in the deserter Fierro and discovers that he, the pursuer, is in reality the pursued, and he joins Fierro in a battle against his own men. This is a moment of vital discovery in which the aggressor recognizes himself in his victim. Readers see this situation again in "Deutsches Requiem," when the Nazi, who tortures his innocent victim in order to destroy his own feeling of compassion, understands that what has led Germany to war was a wish for death and self-destruction, its unconscious desire to be transformed into the victim.

In his fiction Borges combines literary and extraliterary genres in order to create a dynamic, eclectic genre. Within the extraliterary genres he employs historical genres, such as the biography, the autobiography, and the chronicle, in some instances with a serious purpose, and, in others, with a satirical aim. In many of his stories, he creates a narrator, "Borges," introducing real autobiographical facts combined with other, imaginary ones. This narrator is unable to embrace himself in his totality. He provides an incomplete image of himself, and it is the reader who can grasp his identity by observing the situations the narrator-character confronts, as in "El Aleph" when "Borges" receives, without expecting it, the revelation of the universe in the basement of a house in Buenos Aires.

Within the rhetorical genres Borges includes in his stories, the report and the confession predominate. In the report, the narrator respectfully distances himself from the events he narrates, and explains the position from which he views the scene, establishing, in an imitation of an authentic report, his intention of being "objective." Readers tend to assume that the rapporteur enjoys a superior vision with respect to the facts of his report. In "La secta del Fénix" (The Phoenix Sect, in the 1956 edition of *Ficciones*) the rapporteur gradually describes the characteristics of the sect, transforming the tale into a type of riddle. In "El informe de Brodie" (Dr. Brodie's Report, in the book of that name, 1970) Brodie describes the missionary as a civilized informant and the culture of the Yahoos as primitive in order to suggest ironically, at the end of the story, that "superior Western culture" is as barbarian and sophisticated as that of the Yahoos, since there is an obvious similarity between their institutions and beliefs and those of the missionary.

In the confession, contrary to the report, the subjectivity of the narrator prevails: the confessor recognizes or declares, by force of reason or other motive, what he could not declare or recognize any other way. He creates an image of himself through the faults he confesses, and he pursues a persuasive end: to obtain acceptance or complicity. He makes public something intimate in a critical moment that has public justification. The confession of the Nazi Zur Linde in "Deutsches Requiem," for example, brings to light intimate aspects of his life that are symbols of the criminal arrogance that brought his people to destruction. In the confession, the confessor acquires an active role, and the rhetorical style of judicial discourse prevails: the accusation and the defense. In this genre there is always a fault the character committed and deserves to be punished for because it constitutes a violation of the social norm. This imminent punishment gives a pathetic air to the events of the story.

All of Borges's extraliterary genres, however, appear within a literary framework, dominated by the techniques of composition characteristic of fantastic literature. The narrator gives the reader less knowledge than he needs, assuring only a minimal coherence for his subjective and emphatic discourse. Borges's style of presentation is neither paraphrasable nor does it contain redundant information, and, further, it displays little of the psychology of the characters, incorporating ambiguous heroes whose reality is doubtful to the reader and plots that are not predictable and can potentially affect the integrity of the narrator. Borges uses metalanguages, quotations, intertextuality, parody, and imitation. The real being of characters and objects do not necessarily coincide with their appearance, and the world is, generally, indescribable, unnamable, and monstrous. Each story creates a particular narrative system, and the narrator delays the resolution of the posited conflict, holding back the revelation of the story's meaning until its end.

Starting in 1946, after his resignation from the library job, Borges made a living by teaching at the Instituto Superior de Cultura Inglesa and the Colegio Libre de Estudios Superiores. He had moved with his mother to an apartment in downtown Buenos Aires, where he lived for most of his life thereafter. When Perón fell from power in 1955, Borges was named the director of the Biblioteca Nacional by the new government, and he kept this position until his retirement in 1973. He also became a professor of German, English, and North American literatures at the Facultad de Filosofia y Letras.

After 1953 Borges, tired of his image as an author of fantastic stories, an image his own work had created, and obstructed in his writing by his failing vision, which was progressing slowly toward total blindness, stopped writing stories for almost twenty years. He collected his brief essays written between 1937 and 1952 in *Otras inquisiciones* (1952; translated as *Other Inquisitions*, 1964) and began to write, by dictation, short fables in prose, such as "Los espejos velados" (The Veiled Mirrors) and "El simulacro" (The Simulacrum), both in *El hacedor* (1960; translated as *Dreamtigers*, 1964). He returned to his old habit of writing poetry, with a new neoclassic approach

Page from the manuscript for "Kafka y sus precursores," collected in Otras inquisiciones *(by permission of the Estate of Jorge Luis Borges)* in which he tried to apply some of the principles used in his prose (intertextual reference, the articulation of the whole), availing himself of poetic elements discarded by the avant-garde poets, such as rhyme and meter, in order to initiate a more conservative style. He undertook the regular publication of works in collaboration, especially with his friend Adolfo Bioy Casares. *Crónicas de Bustos Domecq* (1967; translated as *Chronicles of Bustos Domecq*, 1976) stands out among these as an excellent collection of satires on contemporary artistic life. By giving up his singular authorial persona and sharing his growing international fame (in 1961, together with Samuel Beckett, he won the prestigious Formentor Prize), Borges made a conscious attempt to relativize his authorial image, since, for him, the idealization of the author was one of the great faults of contemporary literature and was a detriment to readers. Being a writer in the plenitude of his creative powers, Borges dedicated, with great modesty, long, patient years to the study of Old English and the literary works of others. Beyond that, he converted himself into a conversationalist and an oral teacher. *Borges, oral* (1979) and *Siete noches* (1980; translated as *Seven Nights*, 1984) are representative collections of his lectures.

After 1961 Borges traveled extensively throughout the world and received a great deal of recognition for his works, which had been translated into several languages. In September 1967 he married Elsa Astete Millán, and they visited the United States, where Borges taught at Harvard and lectured at various other universities. In 1968 they returned to Buenos Aires. Two years later they were divorced, and Borges again moved in with his mother.

At the end of the 1960s Borges returned to fiction to write realist or "direct" stories, which he collected in *El informe de Brodie*. In this book he recovers many of the favorite themes of his youth (the adventures of hoodlums and knife duels), but the author who mastered so well the poetics of the fantastic tale could not apply to his work the poetics of realism with equal success. The rules of realist composition are different, even opposite, to those of fantastic literature and involve many of the narrative "vices" that Borges had wanted to eradicate: redundance of content, predictability, and the commonplace. Tales such as "Juan Muraña" and "La señora mayor" (The Older Woman) display a simplicity hardly satisfactory for the reader who is accustomed to the literary exploits of Borges's fantastic narrations.

His most refined stories are those in which he resigns himself to his destiny as a fabulator: "El evangelio según Marcos" (The Gospel According to Mark) and "El informe de Brodie." In 1975, when Borges was over seventy-five years of age, he published *El libro de arena* (translated as *The Book of Sand*, 1977), a collection of fantastic stories equal to his best works of the 1940s, which, together with the tales published in 1983—*Veinticinco Agosto 1983 y otros cuentos* (August 1983 and Other Stories)—are the last short stories written by him. During the last years of his life, though totally blind, Borges spent much of his time writing (dictating) poetry and very short prose pieces and traveling. In 1980 he won Spain's Cervantes prize with fellow ultraist Gerardo Diego. When Borges discovered he was terminally ill with liver cancer, he moved to Geneva, where he had lived as a teenager. On 26 April 1986 he married his longtime secretary and collaborator María Kodama. He died in Geneva on 14 June of that same year.

Borges was essentially a writer of fantastic stories who belonged, because of the era in which he wrote his narratives and because of the aesthetic evolution of his work, to the post-avant-garde. However, his success as a raconteur is due less to his choice and synthesis of literary techniques than the way in which he used them in the creation of a literature of ideas. Given his approach to the world of letters, he belongs to a prestigious tradition of writers not easily imitable—the writer-philosophers, creators of a metaliterature that, feeding upon literature, stands above it and forges an art conscious of itself, relativizing culture by exposing its dogmatism and its unsolvable paradoxes. These writers have found in literature an adequate means to comment about their place in the world. Faced with the difficult task of being human, they have made use of comical-critical techniques, such as parody and satire, to express disappointment and disenchantment with their world. They may be humanists and professional philosophers, such as Erasmus, Voltaire, Friedrich Nietzsche, or Miguel de Unamuno, or writers fascinated by ideas, such as Swift, Kafka, and Borges—they all share an interest in studying and criticizing their culture or its literature. They have appropriated the generic canon in order to parody it and create a double vision, simultaneously directed toward the world represented in the work and toward the work itself, thus achieving the evolving process of reflecting the means of representation in the world being represented. Within this metaliterary tradition, Borges's work constitutes, through his extreme linguistic conscience and a formal synthesis capable of representing the most varied ideas, an instance of supreme development in and renovation of narrative techniques. With his exemplary literary advances and the reflective sharpness of his metaliterature, he has effectively influenced the destiny of literature.

Interviews:

Richard Burgin, *Conversations with Jorge Luis Borges* (New York: Holt, Rinehart & Winston, 1969);

Fernando Sorrentino, *Siete conversaciones con Jorge Luis Borges* (Buenos Aires: Casa Pardo, 1973); translated by Clark M. Zlotchew as *Seven Conversations with Jorge Luis Borges* (Troy, N.Y.: Whitston, 1982);

Willis Barnstone, *Borges at Eighty: Conversations* (Bloomington: Indiana University Press, 1982);

Antonio Carrizo, *Borges, el memorioso: Conversaciones de Jorge Luis Borges con Antonio Carrizo* (Mexico City & Buenos Aires: Fondo de Cultura Económica, 1982).

Bibliographies:

Horacio Jorge Becco, *Jorge Luis Borges: Bibliografía total, 1923-1973* (Buenos Aires: Casa Pardo, 1973);

David William Foster, *Jorge Luis Borges: An Annotated Primary and Secondary Bibliography* (New York & London: Garland, 1984).

Biographies:

Alicia Jurado, *Genio y figura de Jorge Luis Borges* (Buenos Aires: EUDEBA, 1964);

María Angélica Bosco, *Borges y los otros* (Buenos Aires: Fabril, 1967);

Marcos Ricardo Barnatán, *Borges* (Madrid: E.P.E.S.A., 1972);

Emir Rodríguez Monegal, *Jorge Luis Borges: A Literary Biography* (New York: Dutton, 1978);

Jorge Oscar Pickenhaym, *Borges: Algebra y fuego vida y obra del gran escritor argentino* (Buenos Aires: Belgrano, 1982).

References:

Jaime Alazraki, *La prosa narrativa de Jorge Luis Borges: Temas-Estilo* (Madrid: Gredos, 1968);

Alazraki, ed., *Critical Essays on Jorge Luis Borges* (Boston: G. K. Hall, 1987);

Alazraki, ed., *Jorge Luis Borges* (Madrid: Taurus, 1976);

Luis H. Antezana, *Algebra y fuego: Lectura de Borges* (Louvain, Belgium: Nauwelaerts, 1978);

Ana María Barrenechea, *La expresión de la irrealidad en la obra de Jorge Luis Borges* (Mexico City: Colegio de México, 1957); translated by Robert Lima as *Borges, the Labyrinth Maker* (New York: New York University Press, 1965);

Gene Bell-Villada, *Borges and His Fiction: A Guide to His Mind and Art* (Chapel Hill: University of North Carolina Press, 1981);

Ronald Christ, *The Narrow Act: Borges' Art of Allusion* (New York: New York University Press, 1969);

Lowell Dunham and Ivar Ivask, eds., *The Cardinal Points of Borges* (Norman: University of Oklahoma Press, 1971);

Arturo Echavarría, *Lengua y literatura en Borges* (Barcelona: Ariel, 1983);

Mary L. Friedman, *The Emperor's Kites: A Morphology of Borges' Tales* (Durham: Duke University Press, 1987);

Mary Kinzie, *Prose for Borges* (Evanston, Ill.: Northwestern University Press, 1974);

Sylvia Molloy, *Las letras de Borges* (Buenos Aires: Sudamericana, 1979);

Alberto Julián Pérez, *Poética de la prosa de Jorge Luis Borges* (Madrid: Gredos, 1986);

Martin Stabb, *Borges Revisited* (Boston: Twayne, 1991);

Stabb, *Jorge Luis Borges* (New York: Twayne, 1970);

John Sturrock, *Paper Tigers: The Ideal Fictions of Jorge Luis Borges* (Oxford: Clarendon Press, 1977);

Guillermo Sucre, *Borges el poeta* (Mexico City: U.N.A.M., 1967);

Carter Wheelock, *The Mythmaker: A Study of Motif and Symbol in the Short Stories of Jorge Luis Borges* (Austin: University of Texas Press, 1969).

Papers:

A Descriptive Catalogue of the Jorge Luis Borges Collection at the University of Virginia Library, by C. Jared Loewenstein (Charlottesville: University Press of Virginia, 1991), lists all the Borges material—much of which is unpublished—at that library, which holds the most extensive and complete collection.

Guillermo Cabrera Infante
(22 April 1929 -)

Ardis L. Nelson
Florida State University

BOOKS: *Así en la paz como en la guerra* (Havana: Ediciones R, 1960; revised edition, Montevideo: Alfa, 1968);

Un oficio del siglo XX, as G. Caín (Havana: Ediciones R, 1963); translated by Kenneth Hall and Cabrera Infante as *A Twentieth-Century Job* (London: Faber & Faber, 1991);

Tres tristes tigres (Barcelona: Seix Barral, 1967); translated by Donald Gardner, Suzanne Jill Levine, and Cabrera Infante as *Three Trapped Tigers* (New York: Harper & Row, 1971; London: Picador, 1980);

Vista del amanecer en el trópico (Barcelona: Seix Barral, 1974); translated by Levine as *View of Dawn in the Tropics* (New York: Harper & Row, 1978);

O (Barcelona: Seix Barral, 1975);

Exorcismos de esti(l)o (Barcelona: Seix Barral, 1976);

Arcadia todas las noches (Barcelona: Seix Barral, 1978);

La Habana para un Infante difunto (Barcelona: Seix Barral, 1979); translated by Levine and Cabrera Infante as *Infante's Inferno* (New York: Harper & Row, 1984; London: Faber & Faber, 1984);

Holy Smoke (New York: Harper & Row, 1985; London: Faber & Faber, 1985).

MOTION PICTURES: *Wonderwall*, screenplay by Cabrera Infante, London, Alen Clore Productions, 1968;

Vanishing Point, screenplay by Cabrera Infante, Hollywood, 20th Century-Fox, 1970;

Under the Volcano, screenplay by Cabrera Infante, Hollywood, Universal, 1972.

OTHER: "Salsa para una ensalada," in *Literatures in Transition: The Many Voices of the Caribbean*, edited by Rose S. Minc (Gaithersburg, Md.: Hispamérica, 1982), pp. 21-36;

"Meta-final/Meta-End," translated by Roberto González Echevarría, in *The Voice of the Masters: Writing and Authority in Modern Latin American Literature*, edited by Echevarría (Austin: University of Texas Press, 1985), pp. 137-168;

"Bad Babs," in *Diablesas y diosas*, edited by Joaquim Romaguera Ramió and Eduardo Suárez (Barcelona: Laertes, 1990), pp. 9-15.

SELECTED PERIODICAL PUBLICATIONS—
UNCOLLECTED: "Delito por bailar el chachachá," *Mundo Nuevo*, 25 (July 1968): 59-71;

Guillermo Cabrera Infante circa 1971

"La confundida lengua del poeta," *Primera Plana* (Buenos Aires), 316 (14 January 1969): 64-65;

"(C)ave Attemptor! A Chronology of GCI (After Laurence Sterne's)," *Review*, 72 (Winter 1971 - Spring 1972): 5-9;

"Epilogue for Late(nt) Readers," *Review*, 72 (Winter 1971 - Spring 1972): 23-32;

"Encuentros y recuerdos con José Lezama Lima," *Vuelta*, 1 (February 1977): 46-48;

"Todo está escrito con espejos," *Vuelta*, 1 (May 1977): 7-8;

"El amor que (no) se atreve a decir su nombre," *Vuelta*, 2 (December 1977): 49-50;

"Mi personaje inolvidable," *Escandalar*, 2, no. 3 (1979): 8-24;

"Vidas para leerlas," *Vuelta*, 4 (April 1980): 4-16;

"El actor como político y el político como actor," *Vuelta*, 5 (August 1981): 14-17;

"Quién mató a Calvert Casey?," *Quimera*, 26 (December 1982): 42-53;

"El exilio invisible," *Vuelta*, 7 (August 1983): 47-49;

"Cuba's Shadow," *Film Comment*, 21 (May-June 1985): 43-45;

"Lives of a Hero," translated by Peggy Boyers, *Salmagundi*, 67 (Summer 1985): 13-33;

"Talent of 2wo Cities," *Review*, 35 (July-December 1985): 17-18;

"Piñera's Virgil," *Review*, 35 (July-December 1985): 19;

"Brief Encounters in Havana," *World Literature Today*, 61 (Autumn 1987): 519-525;

"To Kill a Foreign Name," *World Literature Today*, 61 (Autumn 1987): 531-534;

"Blonde on Blonde," *American Film*, 13 (March 1988): 48-52.

Guillermo Cabrera Infante is one of the most important Latin-American authors since Jorge Luis Borges and ranks along with Julio Cortázar, Carlos Fuentes, Gabriel García Márquez, Alejo Carpentier, and Manuel Puig in popularity. A man whose personal style and political views have been controversial, Cabrera Infante's literature has proven even more provocative. With a style that fits no current mold, he seems to amuse the majority of his readers but cajoles and perplexes the critics. Compared more often with writers such as Petronius, Laurence Sterne, Lewis Carroll, Ernest Hemingway, and James Joyce than with his Latin-American contemporaries, Cabrera Infante is nonetheless in the vanguard of new Latin-American fiction, and he exhibits many of the characteristics and concerns of today's Latin-American writers: a radical break with the traditional plot line in favor of a fragmented format; a search for authenticity in language; a preference for the self-conscious narrator and the autocritical metanovel (a novel that comments on its own origin, structure, and style); and the presence of the cinematic in style, theme, and technique.

Cabrera Infante was born on 22 April 1929 in Gibara, a small city on the northern coast of Cuba's Oriente province; he was the first son of Guillermo Cabrera, a journalist and typographer, and his wife, the former Zoila Infante. Five years later his parents founded the Communist party in Gibara, and at the age of seven Guillermo and a younger brother, Sabá, witnessed their parents' arrest and the confiscation of their books. After the parents' jail sentence of several months, the family was reunited but destitute. When Guillermo was twelve they moved to Havana, where the boy's adventures with life in the big city began. At seventeen, inspired by a university professor, he became an avid reader, and at the age of nineteen he published a parody of Miguel Angel Asturias's *El Señor Presidente* (1946) in the journal *Bohemia* (13 June 1948). Cabrera Infante quit college to begin his literary career, editing for *Bohemia* and several newspapers and attending the Escuela Nacional de Periodismo. He founded a literary magazine, *Nueva Generación* (1948-1949), and, with a few friends, created the Cinemateca de Cuba (Film Library of Cuba).

In 1952 Cabrera Infante published a short story in *Bohemia* containing profanities in English, which resulted in his being jailed, having to pay a fine, and being barred from the School of Journalism. In 1954 he began writing a weekly movie column under the pseudonym of G. Caín for *Carteles*, Cuba's second most popular magazine. He became involved in clandestine activity against the dictator Fulgencio Batista's regime, and his writing became sufficiently political that it merited strict censorship.

In 1958 he wrote most of the stories and politically slanted vignettes that he gathered later to form *Así en la paz como en la guerra* (In Peace as in War, 1960). A response to the climate of violence prevalent in Cuba in the 1950s, the book has vignettes with a violent tone that counterpoints the lyrical tone of the stories. Although the book was nominated for the Prix International de Littérature and was published in France, Italy, and Poland, its engagé revolutionary fervor is not a

Cabrera Infante in Havana, 1952 (photograph by Nestor Almendros)

current in Cabrera Infante's later writing. Indeed he eventually disowned the book on the premise that it reflects reality instead of creating it.

Cabrera Infante was among the artists and intellectuals who enjoyed the heady freedom of the first years of the Cuban Revolution, beginning with Fidel Castro's rise to power in January 1959. The young author served briefly as head of the Consejo Nacional de Cultura and as an executive in the newly created Film Institute. He traveled through the United States, Canada, and South America in Castro's entourage and visited Europe, the Soviet Union, East Germany, and Czechoslovakia with a delegation of journalists. Also in 1959 Cabrera Infante founded and edited *Lunes*, an ambitious cultural and literary supplement of *Revolución*, the semiofficial newspaper of the revolutionary government, with a circulation of nearly a quarter of a million issues a week. The editors of *Lunes* branched out into television with a series ("Lunes de Revolución") in 1960 and invited politically oriented authors from all over the world to visit Cuba.

In 1961 Cabrera Infante and his brother Sabá became central figures in the first major clash between Cuban artists and revolutionary goals. Sabá and cameraman Orlando Jiménez-Leal made *P.M.*, a short film celebrating Havana nightlife, which was televised by *Lunes* on a program dedicated to international works of experimental cinema. When the artists submitted *P.M.* to the Film Censorship Board (of the Instituto del Cine) to obtain an exhibition stamp, the film was banned and seized. This act represented the first time in revolutionary Cuba that a work of art was censored for its form and content and not for expressing explicitly counterrevolutionary ideas. In response, the editors and collaborators of *Lunes* organized a written protest signed by more than two hundred writers and artists, directed to Nicolás Guillén, president of the Primer Congreso de Escritores y Artistas de Cuba. The scandal led to the government's postponing the congress and staging instead a series of "Conversaciones con los Intelectuales," presided over by Castro. In April 1961, at the time of the Bay of Pigs invasion, Castro had declared Cuba officially socialist. Then in June the *Lunes* magazine and TV series were banned, and Castro declared: "Con la Revolución todo, contra la Revolución nada" (With the Revolution everything, against the Revolution nothing), closing a speech that defined Cuban policy toward the arts until 1968. Ironically the unemployed Cabrera Infante was elected vice-president of the writer's union a month later.

During what became an internal exile, Cabrera Infante prepared a book of his film reviews, adding a prologue, an interlude, and an epilogue narrating the rise and fall of the film critic G. Caín (his pseudonym). *Un oficio del siglo XX* (1963; translated as *A Twentieth-Century Job*, 1991) sets out to prove that the only way a critic can survive under communism is as a fictional character.

In 1962 Cabrera Infante gave a series of lectures at the Cinemateca de Cuba that were later published as *Arcadia todas las noches* (Arcadia Every Night, 1978). These talks on five film directors—Orson Welles, Alfred Hitchcock, Howard Hawks, John Huston, and Vincente Minnelli—represented a dangerously independent act merely because Cabrera Infante chose to discuss Hollywood films. He did not, however, discuss John Ford, because the Western genre was considered reactionary, and by then most of Ford's films had been destroyed.

Also in 1962 Cabrera Infante was sent to Brussels as a cultural attaché (a Latin version of being sent to Siberia). It was there that he began writing out of an obsession to preserve the memory of the inhabitants of the cafés and cabarets of Havana nightlife depicted in *P.M.*, an ongoing concern that finds expression in almost all of Cabrera Infante's works.

The major themes in Cabrera Infante's writing are the city of Havana, language, the cinema, machismo, erotic love, and betrayal. As an exile without the privilege of returning to his homeland, Cabrera Infante has been concerned with recording his memories of the language, music, humor, folklore, and characters of the city that made up his former world. For him, literature is the verbalization of memory; but at the same time, it comes from the imagination. Above all, for Cabrera Infante, literature is a game, something to be enjoyed; it is not essentially communication. He thus amuses his readers with wordplay, alliteration, and puns, inviting readers to be creative, to get involved, and to have fun with his colloquial, fragmented, and digressive style reminiscent of the ancient *Satyricon*, by Petronius Arbiter, and Laurence Sterne's *Tristram Shandy* (9 volumes, 1760-1767).

The vein of social consciousness originally begun in *Así en la paz como en la guerra* was to continue in "Vista del amanecer en el trópico" (View of Dawn in the Tropics), which won the Biblioteca Breve prize in 1964, but the work never appeared in print in its prize-winning form. (The *Vista del amanecer en el trópico* of 1974 is a totally different work.) The 1964 book was published in a revised version, with all political overtones removed, as *Tres tristes tigres* (1967; translated as *Three Trapped Tigers*, 1971), a book which soon came to be known as the funniest book from Latin America. Cabrera Infante began writing *Tres tristes tigres* in 1961 as a reaction to the censure and confiscation of *P.M.* and to the sudden death of Fredy, a popular Cuban vocalist, in Puerto Rico. *Tres tristes tigres* captures the Spanish language spoken in Havana in the 1950s and the characters who inhabited the night scene of that decadent time. In the prologue of the book a bilingual master of ceremonies in the Tropicana club introduces the book's contents as a musical show about to begin. What follows offers little in terms of traditional plot; it is, rather, a loosely structured collage of literary fragments—vignettes, anecdotes, translations, parodies, letters, psychiatric sessions, and dreams—in which five main characters recount the intrigues, affairs, and events during a series of nights in 1958, on the eve of the revolution.

Silvestre, a journalist, narrates "Bachata," the longest section of the book, and is supposedly the writer/assembler of *Tres tristes tigres*. Arsenio Cué is an actor, radio announcer, and best friend of Silvestre. Códac is a photojournalist and narrates "Ella cantaba boleros" (She Was Singing Boleros), a story with a close approximation of a traditional plot line, which is divided into eight sections and interspersed throughout the text. Códac wants to preserve the memory of La Estrella, a *mulata* who has just died and whose singing and dancing used Afro-Cuban rhythms. Eribó, a bongo player and commercial artist who represents the lower socioeconomic class, narrates his frustrated affair with Vivian Smith-Corona, a country-club *criolla* (Creole). Bustrófedon, a deceased oral poet and former leader of the group of friends, is supposedly the author of "La muerte de Trotsky referida por varios escritores cubanos, años despues—o antes" (The Death of Trotsky as Described by Various Cuban Writers, Years After the Event—or Before), a parody of seven Cuban authors: José Martí, José Lezama Lima, Virgilio Piñera, Lydia Cabrera, Lino Novás Calvo, Alejo Carpentier, and Nicolás Guillén.

Although the unusual style of *Tres tristes tigres* lends itself to multiple interpretations, the central theme, in Cabrera Infante's own words, is betrayal: "three-fold treason (in language, in literature and in love)." The author, the character-narrators, and the reader are involved throughout in a chain reaction of betrayals, which make up the fabric of the novel and which comment on communication and literature outside the novel. This molding of an entire work around a single idea is a central feature of Menippean satire, which consists of the adventures of an idea or a truth in the world. Cabrera Infante deals with problems relevant to communication caused by the imperfect nature of language and the human tendency to deceive. Betrayal is manifested on all levels of *Tres tristes tigres* in its form, characterization, and language.

Musical forms are decisive in the structure of *Tres tristes tigres*, which is closely related to that of a rhapsody, a musical composition that is irregular in form and resembles an improvisation. The etymological roots of "rhapsody" also pertain, since the Greek rhapsodist was a professional reciter or chanter of epic poetry, a genre consid-

Cabrera Infante with his second wife, Miriam Gómez, in London, 1970 (photograph by Michael Thompson)

ered to be the forerunner of the novel. Cabrera Infante advises his readers that the book is at its best when read aloud. The fragmented and irregular sections introduced by the master of ceremonies and "spoken" by the character-narrators decidedly suggest an improvised, musical show: "Sin palabras pero con música y sana alegría y esparcimiento . . ." (Without words but with music and happiness and joy . . .).

The unity of *Tres tristes tigres* is based on its musicality. Cabrera Infante's jumps in temporal sequences, lack of a clear-cut plot, and a strong emphasis on memories, in juxtaposition with wordplay and rapid spatial movement of the characters, tend to approximate the simultaneity of music. The content of *Tres tristes tigres* is ambivalent, as can be judged by the great divergence in reader reactions and critical interpretations. The phonetic quality of the spoken word captures not only the various tones of Cuban dialects and speech patterns but also the feelings and mentalities of the characters portrayed. The book succeeds in being the musical composition it purports to be, given the limitations of the medium.

Although the novel can approximate a musical composition in content, tone, and structure, the literary form in its essentially verbal nature misrepresents the nonverbal quality of music. This tendency to deception is accentuated by the "author's" concealment of the plot and by unreliable narrators who distract and confuse the reader. Códac, Eribó, Cué, and especially Silvestre all speak directly to the reader on many occasions, thus destroying the illusion of a world unto itself usually created in a fictional work. The reader is unable and unwilling to suspend his disbelief when dealing with a narrator who follows in the footsteps of Tristram Shandy. The narrators are also found to be unreliable in the sense that they often mix up time sequences, present only partial vignettes rather than episodes, and generally cannot be trusted. As characters, they reveal a variety of treasonous attitudes, such as incipient self-betrayal, betrayal of literature for the movies, lying, delation, deceit, and artifice as a life-style.

The ephemeral and contradictory Bustrófedon is an intriguing example of the spirit of Cuban *choteo* (mocking) on an intellectual level, in that he takes nothing and no one seriously, and he reflects the central problem of the book: language as betrayal. *Boustrophedon* is an ancient method of writing in which the lines run alternately from right to left and from left to right, as in various ancient inscriptions in Egyptian, Greek, and certain other languages. More than a master of parody, Bustrófedon's very existence exposes language and literature as betrayal. The most important things readers know about this enigmatic anagrammatist are his attitudes about literature and how they correspond with his activities and his name. His constant alteration of the spoken word and his parodies of Cuban literature are distortions of realities. As a champion of "invisible" writing, Bustrófedon inspires and at times perturbs his friends by an obsession with words in their pure and chaotic state. Words are the essence of speaking and writing, both equally important according to Bustrófedon. In spite of the fact that not just words but also the conventions of written and spoken language serve as the raw materials for communication, Bustrófedon is not concerned with these conventions, for he seems to have little interest in mundane or even rational discourse. He is, rather, as described by Códac, the epitome of the surrealist metaphor: "the fortuitous encounter of a sewing machine and an umbrella on a dissection table." This passage from Comte de Lautréamont's *Les Chants de Maldoror* is written in the ancient boustrophedon method in *Tres tristes tigres*. In the spirit of surrealism, whose fundamental tenets undermine conscious, rational activity, Bustrófedon represents the spontaneous flow of spoken language, as found in folklore or conversation, which dies when dissected.

In terms of conventional characterization, however, Bustrófedon's name and the opinions he professes about literature reflect a psychotic personality split. His name is the Spanish word for *boustrophedon*, yet he refuses to leave any written work of his for posterity, going so far as to destroy the original tape of his seven parodies. His problem of identity is pointed out by Cué, who muses that of all the palindromes Bustrófedon found, he never came up with "el temible ... Yo soy" (The dreadful ... I am). In light of Bustrófedon's inherent self-betrayal and his antiliterature stance in a twentieth-century novel, he is understandably a sad or trapped tiger.

The copy of the seven parodies of Cuban writers (preserved on a tape by Códac) represents the pinnacle of Bustrófedon's "works." Bustrófedon's parodies are treasonous of the writing styles and themes of the authors, and the harshest parody imitates the best known, Alejo Carpentier. This is only natural for the *choteador*, whose goal is to reduce the exemplary figure to his own level by openly mocking his style. Since Carpentier is more esteemed, he must be dealt with more radically, for he is the highest in the literary hierarchy Bustrófedon wishes to abolish in carnivalesque spirit.

Silvestre's final narration closes with the neologism *tradittori*, formed by combining the Italian phrase *traduttore, traditore* (translator, traitor), meaning that all translation betrays the original. The written word betrays the spoken word by freezing its fluidity and removing its accompanying gestures and tone. Translation from one language to another, as evidenced in "Los visitantes" (The Visitors), or from one art form to another results in inaccuracy and distortion. Literature is travestied by translation and parody. In short, *Tres tristes tigres* is dedicated to self-exposure. The novel sets off a chain-reaction effect, beginning with the betrayal implicit in the use of words to represent the objects and feelings of an individual's reality. In the process, an important part of readers' assumptions about literature, which enable them to suspend disbelief, has been severely jostled. While other Cuban writers had already experimented with the fragmentation of form in narrative and employed popular language in a creative way, Cabrera Infante was the first Cuban successfully to employ extensive wordplay to create a truly funny book, written with the specific intent to capture the spoken word of a certain region and epoch: Havana in the 1950s. In the spirit of Borges, Cabrera Infante reminds readers that they are reading a piece of fiction, thus exposing literature for the artifice that it is. The book is extremely popular, has had a very favorable critical response, and has been translated into French, English, Portuguese, German, and Italian.

In 1965 Cabrera Infante returned to Cuba for his mother's funeral and was shocked by the dismal aspect of Havana and the paranoia of his friends. He was asked to remain in Cuba for an interview that never took place, but he finally managed to leave Cuba for good, taking with him his two daughters from his marriage to Marta Calvo, which had lasted from 1953 to 1961. The three of them lived in Madrid for about a year, with Cabrera Infante's second wife, Miriam Gómez, a successful Cuban theater and film actress, whom he had married in 1961. During this time, he rewrote the book that became *Tres tristes tigres*, stripping it of all political overtones. He soon became a persona non grata in Francisco Franco's Spain, perhaps because of his issues of *Lunes* on anti-Franco writing; the Republican literature of the Spanish Civil War; and Pablo Picasso's *Guernica* (1937). By 1967 the family was living in poverty in London.

Although Cabrera Infante was no longer officially associated with his fatherland, he once again played an unwittingly decisive role in the struggle for freedom of expression in revolutionary Cuba. Since Cabrera Infante had left Cuba in 1965, a progressive hardening toward writers and artists unwilling to defend and sustain the new culture had led to accusations of homosexuality, forced labor-camp stays, or incarceration for many. Near the end of 1967 the poet Heberto Padilla wrote a letter published in *El Caimán Barbudo*, a revolutionary publication for youth, defending Cabrera Infante's *Tres tristes tigres*, which was banned in Cuba. Cabrera Infante's position had been ambiguous up until this controversy. With his responses in an interview for *Primera Plana* (Argentina, 16 August 1968), there was no longer any doubt as to his anti-Castro stance. The writer harshly denounced the lack of artistic and intellectual freedom in revolutionary Cuba. This left Padilla in the dangerous position of having defended a "traitor" and was the beginning of a nightmare for the poet. Some of his prize-winning poems were classified as counterrevolutionary, and in 1971 Padilla was jailed for one month. His release was conditional on a statement of self-criticism as a counterrevolutionary. Both his incarceration and his confession resulted in letters from U.S., Latin-American, and European intellectuals protesting and denouncing the Stalinist procedures forced on the poet. Cabrera Infante now found himself in the painful position of being openly against a revolution that was favorably considered by many other intellectuals around the world, and at the same time knowing his friends were being silenced and tortured in Cuba or set adrift in exile like himself.

In his first years in London, Cabrera Infante made some money writing film scripts: the unfortunate *Wonderwall* (1968) and the successful *Vanishing Point* (1970), the latter of which involved extended travel in the American Southwest looking for locations. In 1972 he wrote a screenplay based on Malcolm Lowry's *Under the Volcano* (1958), the story of a mad alcoholic. The time pressures of writing scripts, plus the lunatic character of the work, caused Cabrera Infante to have a nervous breakdown, which, combined with the painful news of Alberto Mora's suicide in Cuba, was to affect Cabrera Infante's productivity for several years. After his astounding success with *Tres tristes tigres* in 1967 and his winning a Guggenheim Fellowship in 1970, his readers were naturally concerned and disheartened.

During this bleak time, however, Cabrera Infante managed to rework some old manuscripts, combine some essays, and write imaginative poems and fragments in order to publish several books: *Vista del amanecer en el trópico*, *O* (1975), *Exorcismos de esti(l)o* (Exorcisms of Style, 1976), and *Arcadia todas las noches*. Cabrera Infante began writing the new *Vista del amanecer en el trópico* during his exile in Brussels. Its nearly one hundred vignettes depict a long history of tyranny and violence in Cuba, a history that belies the placid tropical setting of the island. With a critical perspective, he provides a panorama of Cuba from its geographical origins to the present, a personal version of history made up for the most part of anonymous anecdotes. Some vignettes are commentaries on historical photographs, and most give the photographic effect of a moment frozen in time and space. The rapid succession of scenes of violence, repression, and hypocrisy suggest the persistence of such a mentality and its consequences.

O, often referred to as "zero" by Cabrera Infante, is a collection of twelve essays, many of which had been published in *Mundo Nuevo*. Four of the essays describe London from the perspective of a newcomer fascinated by its personalities, pop culture, and decadence. Two essays defend pornography, but in a humorous vein. While most of the essays are amusing, the autobiographical "Obsceno" recounts the personal trauma Cabrera Infante suffered because of the censorship of his story "Balada de plomo y yerro" (Ballad of Lead and Error), published in *Bohemia* (1952), and explains his subsequent preference for using pseudonyms. Perhaps the most interesting of these essays is "Centenario en el espejo" (Centennial in the Looking-Glass), in which Cabrera Infante pays homage to Lewis Carroll by discussing him as a *contradictorio*. He also touches on scenes from Carroll's life and on his love for words. According to Cabrera Infante, Carroll creates his own language by applying mathematical logic to conversation, thereby destroying it.

The verbal games of *Exorcismos de esti(l)o* were assembled as an homage to Raymond Queneau's *Exercises de style* (1947), in which ninety-nine versions of one story are presented. The dadaist style of "Rompecabezas" (Puzzle) in *Tres tristes tigres* is carried to extremes in *Exorcismos de esti(l)o*, in which the fragments, collages, pastiches, poems, and essays all parody stylistic considerations or play on words in one way or another. The tone of the book is humorous and ironic, with no political overtones. When serious metaphysical questions are raised no answers are offered, for not only were the fragments written during the period of Cabrera Infante's depression but the work is dedicated to literary form, not content. Several essays present meditations on particular words and pronunciation and how they change over the centuries. In a section entitled "Minotauromaquia," Cabrera Infante presents a burlesque version of Dedalus and the labyrinth. All in all, the book is a playful volume of art for art's sake.

Things took a turn for the better in 1978 when Cabrera Infante came out of seclusion to travel to the United States with his wife Miriam. He delivered a lecture at Yale University, his first public speech in sixteen years. The following year *La Habana para un Infante difunto* (1979; translated as *Infante's Inferno*, 1984) was published in Spain. According to Cabrera Infante, speaking tongue in cheek, it is the first erotic novel published in Spanish since Francisco Delicado, another exile, published his *Lozana andaluza* (Luxuriant Andalusian) in Rome in 1515. In his lengthy book, Cabrera Infante returns to the Havana of his youth, weaving tales of sexual adventure in the tenements, movie houses, and *posadas* (brothels). Similar to *Tres tristes tigres*, this book is rife with wordplay, but while *Tres tristes tigres* is colloquial, *La Habana* is literary, with more play on the written than on the spoken word. Cabrera Infante writes a double-edged dialogue in an encounter between the writer and his past. Yet another work in the Menippean tradition, its emphasis is on wordplay, parody, and sexuality. *La Habana* is a creative fantasy on the theme of erotic love. The narrator is a frustrated Don Juan who progresses from voyeur to participant during a humorous denigration of machismo.

Dust jacket for Cabrera Infante's 1979 novel, which he jokingly calls the first erotic novel published in Spanish since 1515

The story begins with a twelve-year-old boy, the unnamed narrator, in awe of everything in the big city. He is fascinated by the contrasts between Havana and the small town from which he just moved with his family. Women and the movies are of prime importance in the boy's life and become more and more intertwined as the story progresses. The early chapters touch on his sexual awakening, erotic fantasies, and masturbation. By the fifth chapter one sees clearly that the minor characters are being delineated not only through typecasting and physical description but also by their use of language. The ensuing chapters contain delightful stories of growing up in Havana. "Todo vence al amor" (Love Conquered by All) tells the story of three failures in love during the narrator's school days. Julieta sexually initiates the narrator, and Dulce provides him with his first extended sexual relationship without guilt. In "Casuales encuentros forzados" (Casual Forced Encounters) there is a portrait of the epitome of the *criaditas* (little maids) for whom the narrator feels an occasional attraction. Her body is not exceptional, but the strange way she varies her speech, from popular expressions and *dejo habanero* (local slang) to clearly enunciated, passionate statements, shocks and amazes the narrator. A line taken directly from *La Novela del Aire* (a radio soap opera), such as "Tienes que jurarme amor eterno o no conseguirás seducirme, Rodolfo" (You must swear eternal love or you won't be able to seduce me, Rudolph), is followed by something like "¿Mi chino me quiere ver encuerá?" (My baby wants to see me naked?). The *criadita* borrows not only her sentiments but also her language from radio soap operas.

The love relationship between Margarita and the narrator (in the "Amazon" chapter) is the most passionate and involved of all those in the book; both parties take each other and the relationship seriously, yet they interact, for the most part, as hunter and huntress. Margarita is the only female the narrator seems to respect as a person, and it is she who shares, to a certain extent, his voyeuristic tendencies. The voyeuristic theme, which is exploited in the chapter called "La visión de un mirón miope" (Vigil of the Naked I), is central to the novel. The protagonist revels in his tactile vision as he observes *cuerpos celestes* (heavenly bodies) during late night vigils with a pair of binoculars. The same occurs for readers of the book, as the narrator draws them into reading as a voyeuristic act. Similarly, he goes to the movies, while the reader "views" the book as if it were a film of vignettes on a theme.

In *Tres tristes tigres* the main dialogue is between two characters, Silvestre and his cowriter and double, Cué, but in *La Habana* there is an inner dialogue between two voices of the self-conscious "I," respectively the narrator and the writer. Throughout *La Habana* the reader is given the impression that the comments written in parentheses are made by the writer, correcting the narrator in his choice of words relative to the time of which he is speaking. The writer clarifies expressions used by the narrator and justifies his use of obscenities. In essence the writer provides explanatory notes on the narration, occasionally correcting temporal references and other times supplying details the narrator forgot. The comments within parentheses tend toward linguistic concerns, word usage—the writer's comments on the narration. Besides providing etymological digressions, the writer's statements often add greater depth and humor to the narration, as when he describes his technique of telescoping time, or when he winds his way back and forth through the labyrinth of time and memories. These comments include mixtures of verbal tenses, contrasting the "then" and the "now," differentiating between temporal and spatial references, and pointing out contrasts in the knowledge and awareness of the narrator with regard to the epoch to which he is referring.

These sporadic and seemingly whimsical appearances by the writer cause the focus to shift from the past back to the present, as the writer maintains a dialogue with his own past. From the reader's perspective the writer pops in and out, receding ever again behind his typewriter ribbon. Meanwhile the narrator, unaware of the intrusions, continues his story. While the writer must keep out of sight to satisfy minimally the conventions of fiction, his jack-in-the-box appearances provide distance, detachment, and irony for the reader.

The most predominant stylistic device in *La Habana* is the use of alliteration, especially in groupings of threes. For Cabrera Infante, by his own admission, alliteration is a literary way of representing sexual acts, the erotic aspect due perhaps to the linking of words by similar sounds, a coming together, or the suggestion of a ménage à trois. There are countless lighthearted parodies of famous phrases from literary and cinematic works interwoven in the narration.

The epilogue of *La Habana* takes readers from the possibly autobiographical to the fantastic, as the narrator enters a metaphysical plane that is at once phantasmagorical, mythical, and vulgar. This grotesquely humorous ending parodies the adventures of a mythological hero observed from an unusual point of view with radical changes in dimension. *La Habana*, with its innovative use of language and its burlesque treatment of machismo, has enjoyed a great deal of popularity, although its critical reception has not been nearly as favorable as that of *Tres tristes tigres*. *La Habana* has been translated into English, French, Portuguese, Italian, and Japanese.

In 1980 Cabrera Infante was a writer in residence at the University of West Virginia in Morgantown and also gave lectures all over the United States and in Mexico, Colombia, and Venezuela. He met Reinaldo Arenas and saw Heberto Padilla again, two survivors from Cuban concentration camps and jails. Cabrera Infante realized that the same fate would have befallen him had he remained in Cuba. He was a writer in residence in 1982 at the University of Virginia, in 1985 at Wellesley College, and at West Point in 1986.

During the 1980s Cabrera Infante wrote several well-researched character sketches and essays on books, films, and topics as diverse as censorship; unjust imprisonment; the lives and works of Cuban writers Lezama Lima and Piñera; and President Ronald Reagan as a political figure. Just as his more lengthy works, Cabrera Infante's essays also defy categorization. In almost all cases what seems to be a nonfictional piece turns into fiction at some point, and what begins as fiction may include some nonfiction. This facet of his writing promises to become more predominant, as evidenced by his *Holy Smoke* (1985), a witty, book-length study of the history of the cigar and its impact on popular culture. Written in English, and verbally brilliant, it muses on cigar smoking from Columbus to Castro, with a special emphasis on cinema and literature. One of the things readers learn is that tobacco was first discovered in Gibara, Cabrera Infante's birthplace.

Beginning with its oxymoronic title, *Holy Smoke* is prolific in the apparently contradictory, both in its verbal patterns and incongruities. The oxymoronic construct is naturally a dialogic relationship. In *Holy Smoke* one sees a world turned upside down, a mixture of the serious and the comic. Although the cigar is usually spoken of in relatively glowing terms, it is also described in naturalistic or grotesque terms. Other manifestations of the oxymoronic pattern, such as a mixture of genres and multivoiced, multitoned narration, are readily identifiable in *Holy Smoke*.

Inserted genres, including poetry, quotes from historical and botanical texts, letters, films, interviews, newspapers, signs, billboards, books on tobacco etiquette, and literary selections, offer a compendium of information on smoking from every conceivable source. Similar to Robert Burton in his *Anatomy of Melancholy* (1621), Cabrera Infante aspires to an encyclopedic approach, with a seemingly haphazard mixture of styles in which history, folklore, and scholarly research on tobacco and film blend with personal stories and commentary. Although the inserted materials are diverse in their original function, their inclusion in *Holy Smoke* becomes tantamount to homogeneity in that all are subjected to the double-voiced effect of irony and parody.

Ironic discourse involves the use of someone else's words to create a hostile effect. The distancing and humor imparted by the narrator's commentaries on people, films, books, and events throughout *Holy Smoke* have the dialogic function of providing that irony and parody. Due in large part to the ridiculous and incongruous nature of much of the "impossible" dialogue, the solemn quality of humanity and its works is thrown into comic relief. Whereas in his earlier books Cabrera Infante's narrators made editorial comments on their *own* writing, the narrative voice in *Holy Smoke* comments on the works of other writers, "correcting" Daniel Defoe, for example—"Please, let's have an instant rewrite"—and remarking on the latter's discourse on tobacco.

One of the narrator's many roles in *Holy Smoke* is just this sort of dialogic relationship with the materials assembled in the text. The first-person-singular narrator is also identified more closely than ever before with Cabrera Infante, as he recounts autobiographical information about himself and his family, including his personal reminiscences on cigar smoking. The conversational tone of the narration gives the sensation of a relationship between narrator and reader as well. The setting that comes to mind most frequently is that of a stand-up comedian in a club, entertaining his audience.

Multilingualism is another aspect of *Holy Smoke*, Cabrera Infante's first book written in English rather than Spanish. In this way Cabrera Infante has adroitly converted a practical necessity—*Holy Smoke* grew out of a suggested article for a U.S. magazine—into a Menippean vehicle, perfect for a writer who has been known as a master of the pun since his *Tres tristes tigres*. Cabrera Infante's capacity for paronomasia is no less brilliant in English than in Spanish, with mixed metaphors, jumbled proverbs, oxymorons, and hyperbole—techniques that draw attention to the words being played upon, at the expense of any possibility for a logical sequence of thoughts. His syntax carries over a distinctly Latinate quality from Spanish, and he continues his practice of sprinkling untranslatable words and phrases in Spanish, French, Latin, and even Catalan throughout the text, along with offering many etymologies.

This linguistic Ping-Pong serves as a substitute for character and plot development, with much more concern for topical or profoundly human issues than for history or legend. In

"Good-by, Charlie"
a playlet

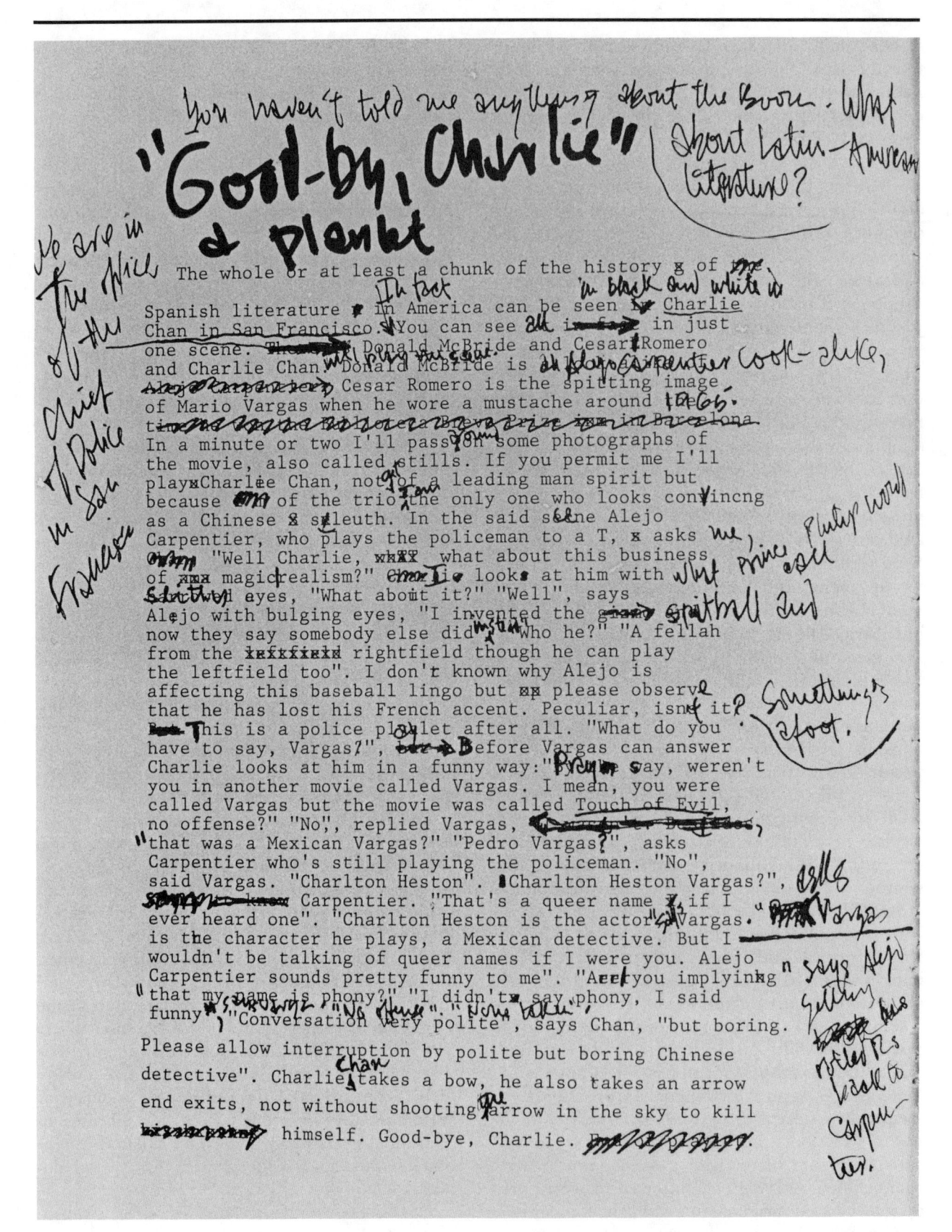

The whole or at least a chunk of the history of Spanish literature in America can be seen in Charlie Chan in San Francisco. You can see it in just one scene. Donald McBride and Cesar Romero and Charlie Chan. Donald McBride is Alejo Carpentier. Cesar Romero is the spitting image of Mario Vargas when he wore a mustache around the 60's. In a minute or two I'll pass on some photographs of the movie, also called stills. If you permit me I'll play Charlie Chan, not of a leading man spirit but because of the trio the only one who looks convincing as a Chinese sleuth. In the said scene Alejo Carpentier, who plays the policeman to a T, asks "Well Charlie, what about this business of magic realism?" Charlie looks at him with startled eyes, "What about it?" "Well", says Alejo with bulging eyes, "I invented the game and now they say somebody else did." "Who he?" "A fellah from the rightfield though he can play the leftfield too". I don't known why Alejo is affecting this baseball lingo but please observe that he has lost his French accent. Peculiar, isn't it? This is a police playlet after all. "What do you have to say, Vargas?". Before Vargas can answer Charlie looks at him in a funny way: "Say, weren't you in another movie called Vargas. I mean, you were called Vargas but the movie was called Touch of Evil, no offense?" "No", replied Vargas, "that was a Mexican Vargas?" "Pedro Vargas?", asks Carpentier who's still playing the policeman. "No", said Vargas. "Charlton Heston". "Charlton Heston Vargas?", Carpentier. "That's a queer name if I ever heard one". "Charlton Heston is the actor, Vargas is the character he plays, a Mexican detective. But I wouldn't be talking of queer names if I were you. Alejo Carpentier sounds pretty funny to me". "Are you implying that my name is phony?" "I didn't say phony, I said funny". "Conversation very polite", says Chan, "but boring. Please allow interruption by polite but boring Chinese detective". Charlie Chan takes a bow, he also takes an arrow end exits, not without shooting arrow in the sky to kill himself. Good-bye, Charlie.

Page from the revised typescript for "Good-by, Charlie," which Cabrera Infante calls "a playlet" (by permission of Guillermo Cabrera Infante)

Cabrera Infante's earlier works one sees a vision of the world in terms of an ultimate question or issue in life: in *Un oficio del siglo XX* a film critic examines his career and decides to leave it behind for a more creative endeavor, thus exorcising an aspect of his self-identity; in *Tres tristes tigres* the idea of betrayal in language, literature, and love is played out as an adventure on all levels of the text; in *La Habana para un Infante difunto* the Don Juan figure and his sexual exploits are burlesqued. The narrator of *Holy Smoke* also fulfills the function of provoking and testing an idea or truth. All aspects of an addiction are discussed by a narrator who presents himself essentially as a seeker of knowledge. As researcher-narrator he may be seen as the wise man who gathers together all supporting evidence and demonstrates its applicability to his theme that smoking a cigar is a way to be somebody in this life.

As an anatomy of a vice, *Holy Smoke* has something for everyone. It presents the story of the rise of tobacco: its historical roots, its popularity, and the many forms of use and abuse it has taken; its demise in terms of health-related effects; and its actual and symbolic presence in art forms, especially in cinema and literature. In 1986 Cabrera Infante began to translate *Holy Smoke* into Spanish as "Puro humo," but he found that "puns do not travel well, for they are the wine of prose."

In 1987 Cabrera Infante was writer in residence at the University of Oklahoma and was the featured writer at the Eleventh Puterbaugh Conference on Writers of the French-Speaking and Hispanic World. "Cuerpos divinos" (Divine Bodies), begun in 1968, and "Itaca vuelta visitar" (Ithaca Revisited), Cabrera Infante's version of a spy novel, are two long-standing projects that remain to be completed, as he gives priority to more pressing concerns, such as the essays he publishes regularly in magazines, journals, and newspapers. He is compiling his political essays in *Mea Cuba*, forthcoming in 1992. Cabrera Infante has also prepared a filmscript for Paramount Pictures entitled "The Lost City," to be filmed in 1992.

With books that defy categorization, Cabrera Infante has inspired a wealth of critical response and conjecture. David P. Gallagher asserts that Cabrera Infante aims to demolish literature as a solemn and pretentious art form by using everyday spoken language and by parodying writers, among other techniques. Since Cabrera Infante denies that he writes novels, there is an ongoing debate as to the genre of his works. While

Cabrera Infante while he was writer in residence at the University of Oklahoma, 1987 (photograph by David D. Clark)

Isabel Alvarez-Borland argues that he writes short stories, vignettes, and essays, combining them in a fragmented mosaic, Emir Rodríguez Monegal contends that his work is largely autobiographical. Other critics note that he writes carnivalized literature in the ancient style of Menippean satire.

Cabrera Infante's works have been criticized by some for their lack of ideological commitment, but they have been lauded by most for their genius. Beginning with *Tres tristes tigres*, his works have been forbidden in Cuba, where he is widely considered to be "un buen escritor, pero mal revolucionario" (a good writer, but a bad revolutionary).

Interviews:

José Corrales Egea, "Diálogo con Guillermo Cabrera Infante," *Casa de las Américas*, 3 (March-June 1963): 49-62;

Emir Rodríguez Monegal, "Las fuentes de la narración," *Mundo Nuevo*, 25 (1968): 41-58;

John Brookesmith, "Guillermo Cabrera Infante: Cantando las 40," *Imagen*, supplement 42 (February 1969): 9-16;

Kjell A. Johnson, "Una entrevista con Cabrera Infante," *Alacrán Azul*, 1, no. 1 (1970): 12-17;

Johnson, *He sido el primer proxenata creado por el socialismo* (Caracas: Cojo, 1971);

Rita Guibert, *Seven Voices: Seven Latin American Writers Talk to Rita Guibert*, translated by Frances Partridge (New York: Knopf, 1973), pp. 341-436;

Danubio Torres Fierro, "Entrevista con Guillermo Cabrera Infante," *Vuelta*, 1, no. 11 (1977): 18-27;

Sharon Magnarelli, "Una entrevista de larga distancia con Guillermo Cabrera Infante," *Prismal/Cabral: Revista de Literatura Hispánica/Cuaderno AfroBrasileiro Asiático Lusitano*, 5 (Fall 1979): 23-42;

Regina M. Janes, "From 5 to 7: An Interview with Guillermo Cabrera Infante," *Salmagundi*, 52-53 (Spring-Summer 1981): 31-56;

Antonio Prieto Taboada, "Gajes y placeres del oficio," *Escandalar*, 4, no. 3 (1981): 77-84;

Eligio García, "Guillermo Cabrera Infante: El más triste (y alegre) de los tigres," in his *Son Así: Reportaje a nueve escritores latinoamericanos* (Mexico City: La Oveja Negra, 1982), pp. 181-231;

Isabel Alvarez-Borland, "Viaje verbal a La Habana, ¡Ah Vana!: Entrevista de Isabel Alvarez-Borland con G. Cabrera Infante, arquitecto de una ciudad de palabras erigida en el tiempo," *Hispamérica*, 11 (April 1982): 51-68;

Alfred J. MacAdam, "The Art of Fiction LXXV: Guillermo Cabrera Infante," *Paris Review*, 25 (Spring 1983): 154-195.

Bibliographies:

David William Foster, *Cuban Literature: A Research Guide* (New York: Garland, 1985), pp. 125-133;

William L. Siemens, "Selected Bibliography (1960-1987)," *World Literature Today*, special Cabrera Infante issue, 61 (Autumn 1987): 535-538.

References:

Edna Acosta-Belén, "The Literary Exorcisms of Guillermo Cabrera Infante," *Crítica Hispánica*, 3, no. 2 (1981): 99-110;

Isabel Alvarez-Borland, *Discontinuidad y ruptura en G. Cabrera Infante* (Gaithersburg, Md.: Hispamérica, 1982);

Alvarez-Borland, "*La Habana para un Infante difunto*: Cabrera Infante's Self-Conscious Narrative," *Hispania*, 68 (March 1985): 44-49;

Alvarez-Borland, "The Pícaro's Journey in *La Habana para un Infante difunto*," *Hispanófila*, 30 (May 1987): 71-79;

Lourdes Casal, *El Caso Padilla: Literatura y Revolución en Cuba, Documentos* (Miami: Universal, 1971);

Edgardo Cozarinsky, "Páginas del libro de la noche: *Arcadia todas las noches*," *Escandalar*, 3, no. 1 (1980): 91-92;

David P. Gallagher, "Guillermo Cabrera Infante," in his *Modern Latin American Literature* (New York: Oxford University Press, 1973), pp. 164-185;

Rosemary Geisdorfer Feal, *Novel Lives: The Fictional Autobiographies of Guillermo Cabrera Infante and Mario Vargas Llosa* (Chapel Hill: North Carolina Studies in the Romance Languages and Literatures, 1986);

Jaime Giordano, "Función estructural del bilingüismo en algunos textos contemporáneos: Cabrera Infante, Luis R. Sánchez," in *Literatures in Transition*, edited by Rose S. Minc (Gaithersburg, Md.: Hispamérica, 1982), pp. 161-175;

Juan Goytisolo, "Lectura cervantina de *Tres tristes tigres*," *Revista Iberoamericana*, 42 (January-March 1976): 1-18;

Ivar Ivask, ed., *World Literature Today*, special Cabrera Infante issue, 61 (Autumn 1987);

Reynaldo L. Jiménez, *Guillermo Cabrera Infante y "Tres tristes tigres"* (Miami: Universal, 1977);

Djelal Kadir, "Nostalgia or Nihilism: Pop Art and the New Spanish American Novel," *Journal of Spanish Studies: Twentieth Century*, 2, no. 3 (1974): 127-135;

Suzanne Jill Levine, "La escritura como traducción: *Tres tristes tigres* y una *Cobra*," *Revista Iberoamericana*, 41 (July-December 1975): 557-567;

Jacques Lezra, "Squared Circles, Encircling Bowls: Reading Figures in *Tres tristes tigres*," *Latin American Literary Review*, 16 (June 1988): 6-23;

William T. Little, "Notas acerca de *Tres tristes tigres* de G. Cabrera Infante," *Revista Iberoamericana*, 36 (October-December 1970): 635-642;

Josefina Ludmer, "*Tres tristes tigres*: Ordenes literarios y jerarquías sociales," *Revista Iberoamericana*, 45 (July-December 1979): 493-512;

William Luis, "Autopsia de *Lunes de Revolución*," *Plural*, 11 (March 1982): 52-62;

Luis, "Cine y cultura en Cuba," *Linden Lane*, 5, no. 3 (1986): 16-18;

Alfred J. MacAdam, "*Tres tristes tigres*: El vasto fragmento," *Revista Iberoamericana*, 41 (July-December 1975): 549-556;

M.-Pierrette Malcuzynski, "*Tres tristes tigres*, or the Treacherous Play on Carnival," *Ideologies and Literature*, 3, no. 15 (1980): 33-56;

Julio Matas, "Orden y visión de *Tres tristes tigres*," *Revista Iberoamericana*, 40 (1974): 87-104;

Stephanie Merrim, "*La Habana para un Infante difunto* y su teoría topográfica de las formas," *Revista Iberoamericana*, 48 (January-June 1982): 403-413;

Merrim, "A Secret Idiom: The Grammar and Role of Language in *Tres tristes tigres*," *Latin American Literary Review*, 8 (Spring-Summer 1980): 96-116;

Merrim, "Sobre Guillermo Cabrera Infante, *Exorcismos de esti(l)o*," *Revista Iberoamericana*, 44 (January-June 1978): 276-279;

Ardis L. Nelson, *Cabrera Infante in the Menippean Tradition* (Newark, Del.: Juan de la Cuesta Hispanic Monographs, 1983);

Nelson, "El doble, el recuerdo y la muerte: Elementos de fugacidad en la narrativa de Guillermo Cabrera Infante," *Revista Iberoamericana*, 49 (April-September 1983): 509-521;

Nelson, "*Tres tristes tigres* y el cine," *Kentucky Romance Quarterly*, 29, no. 4 (1982): 391-404;

Julían Ríos, ed., *Guillermo Cabrera Infante* (Madrid: Fundamentos, 1974);

Emir Rodríguez Monegal, "Cabrera Infante: La novela como autobiografía total," *Revista Iberoamericana*, 47 (July-December 1981): 265-271;

Rodríguez Monegal, "Estructura y significaciones de *Tres tristes tigres*," *Sur*, 320 (1969): 38-51;

José Schraibman, "Cabrera Infante, tras la búsqueda del lenguaje," *Insula*, 286 (1970): 1, 15-16;

William L. Siemens, "Guillermo Cabrera Infante: *Tres tristes tigres*," in his *Worlds Reborn: The Hero in the Modern Spanish American Novel* (Morgantown: West Virginia University Press, 1984), pp. 138-171;

Siemens, "Heilsgeschichte and the Structure of *Tres tristes tigres*," *Kentucky Romance Quarterly*, 22 (1975): 77-90;

Siemens, "Women as Cosmic Phenomena in *Tres tristes tigres*," *Journal of Spanish Studies: Twentieth Century*, 3 (Winter 1975): 199-209;

Raymond D. Souza, "Cabrera Infante: Creation in Progress," in his *Major Cuban Novelists: Innovation and Tradition* (Columbia: University of Missouri Press, 1976), pp. 80-100;

Souza, "Cabrera Infante: Literatura e historia," *Linden Lane*, 1 (October-December 1982): 3-4;

Jonathan Tittler, "Intratextual Distance in *Tres tristes tigres*," *Modern Language Notes*, 93 (March 1978): 285-296;

John Updike, "Infante Terrible," *New Yorker*, 47 (29 January 1972): 91-94;

Emil Volek, "*Tres tristes tigres* en la jaula verbal: Las antinomias dialécticas y la tentativa de lo absoluto en la novela de Guillermo Cabrera Infante," in his *Cuatro claves para la modernidad* (Madrid: Gredos, 1984), pp. 154-178.

Alejo Carpentier
(26 December 1904 - 24 April 1980)

Roberto González-Echevarría
Yale University

BOOKS: *Dos poemas afro-cubanos (deux poemes afro-cubains)* (Paris: Senart, 1930);

Poèmes des Antilles (Paris: Gaillard, 1931);

¡Ecue-Yamba-O! (Madrid: España, 1933);

Viaje a la semilla (Havana: Ucar & García, 1944); translated as *Journey Back to the Source* (1970);

La música en Cuba (Mexico: Fondo de Cultura Económica, 1946);

El reino de este mundo (Mexico: Ibero Americana, 1949); translated by Harriet de Onís as *The Kingdom of This World* (New York: Knopf, 1957);

Tristan e Isolda en Tierra Firme (Caracas: Nacional, 1949);

Los pasos perdidos (Mexico City: Ibero Americana, 1953); translated by de Onís as *The Lost Steps* (New York: Knopf, 1956; London: Gollancz, 1956);

El acoso (Buenos Aires: Losada, 1956); translated as *Manhunt, Noonday*, 2 (1959): 109-180;

Guerra del tiempo (Mexico City: General, 1958); translated by Frances Partridge as *The War of Time* (New York: Knopf, 1970; London: Gollancz, 1970);

El siglo de las luces (Mexico City: General, 1962); translated by John Sturrock as *Explosion in a Cathedral* (Boston: Little, Brown, 1963; London: Gollancz, 1963);

El derecho de asilo (Mexico City: General, 1962);

Tientos y diferencias (Mexico City: Universidad Nacional Autónoma, 1964; enlarged edition, Montevideo: Arca, 1970; enlarged again, 1973);

Literatura y conciencia política en América Latina (Madrid: Corazón, 1969);

Papel social del novelista (Buenos Aires: Hombre Nuevo, 1969);

La ciudad de las columnas (Barcelona: Lumen, 1970);

Los convidados de plata (Montevideo: Sandino, 1972);

Concierto barroco (Mexico City: Siglo XXI, 1974);

Alejo Carpentier (photograph copyright by Jerry Bauer)

El recurso del método (Mexico City: Siglo XXI, 1974); translated by Partridge as *Reasons of State* (New York: Knopf, 1976; London: Gollancz, 1976);

Novelas y relatos (Havana: UNEAC, 1974?);

El periodista: Un cronista de su tiempo (Havana: Granma, 1975);

Letra y Solfa, edited by Alexis Márquez Rodríguez (Caracas: Síntesis Dosmil, 1975);

Crónicas, 2 volumes, edited by José Antonio Portuondo (Havana: Arte y Literatura, 1975 [i.e., 1976]);

Razón de ser: Conferencias (Caracas: Universidad Central, 1976);

Cuentos (Havana: Arte y Literatura, 1977);

Afirmación literaria americanista (Caracas: Universidad Central, 1978);

La consagración de la primavera (Mexico City: Siglo XXI, 1979);

Bajo el signo de La Cibeles, edited by Julio Rodríguez Puértolas (Madrid: Nuestra Cultura, 1979);

El arpa y la sombra (Mexico City: Siglo XXI, 1979);

Ese músico que llevo dentro, 3 volumes, edited by Zoila Gómez García (Havana: Letras Cubanas, 1980);

El adjetivo y sus arrugas (Buenos Aires: Galerna, 1980);

La novela latinoamericana en vísperas de un nuevo siglo y otros ensayos (Mexico City: Siglo XXI, 1981);

Ensayos (Havana: Letras Cubanas, 1984);

Historia y ficción en la narrativa hispanoamerica (Caracas: Monte Avila, 1984);

Conferencias (Havana: Letras Cubanas, 1987);

Tientos, diferencias y otros ensayos (Barcelona: Plaza & Janés, 1987).

Collection: *Obras completas*, 9 volumes (Mexico City: Siglo XXI, 1983-1986).

RECORDING: *Alejo Carpentier lee sus narraciones*, Havana, Casa de las Américas, LD-CA-6.

Alejo Carpentier, a major Latin-American novelist with a dense, allusive style that has influenced other writers, was born in Havana on 26 December 1904, St. Stephen's Day. His father, Georges, an architect, was French, and his mother was of Russian descent. The Carpentiers had arrived in Cuba two years before Alejo was born, their sights on a better lot in the newest of the Spanish-American republics. Cuba had been declared independent by the United States on 20 May 1902, after a nearly four-year occupation that followed Spain's defeat in the war of 1898. The Carpentiers were not poor immigrants, however. The house in which they settled in El Cotorro, on the outskirts of Havana, must have been of considerable size, because Carpentier would later recall roaming in his father's library, and in such novels as *El acoso* (1956; translated as *Manhunt*, 1959) and *Los pasos perdidos* (1953; translated as *The Lost Steps*, 1956) there are mentions of spacious homes and of courtyards where the younger characters frolic. In Georges Carpentier's library Alejo satisfied his curiosities as a young reader—he tells of having read works by French Romantic authors and by Pío Baroja, the modern Spanish novelist. The language spoken at home was French, but in the street the young Carpentier learned Spanish—first from the boys he played with and then in the private schools where his parents sent him. He went first to the Colegio Mimó, which had been founded by a Mason and had great intellectual pretenses. Later he attended Candler College, a Cuban-North American school that the sons of affluent families attended.

The youths Carpentier played with were different from him, not only because they spoke Spanish but because many were black. Carpentier's adult life was in many ways a struggle to bring together the two worlds of his childhood: the sheltered, refined, and European one of his home; and the livelier, more exotic and attractive world of the Cuban blacks in the street. Cuba, a mixture of several cultures, mostly African and Spanish, also included the European world of his father. Carpentier never succeeded in synthesizing the mixture of cultures from which he sprang, and perhaps it is to this failure that one can attribute the tension behind his creative impulse.

Carpentier frequently journeyed to France, and he spent many years in this, his father's homeland. When he was a teenager, the Carpentier family traveled as far as Russia to collect an inheritance. On their return, they made a long stop in Paris, where he attended the Lycée Jeanson de Sailly. In Paris, among French students, he must have felt different but at the same time in his element—a Charles Bovary from the tropics. When he returned to Havana, he finished his bachelor's degree and soon enrolled in the school of architecture at the Universidad de La Habana. Like any good, provincial, French son, Carpentier wanted to join in his father's business. He had also learned music from his father, although by the time he started at the university he had abandoned the piano. As time went on, Carpentier would acquire an impressive knowledge of music as well as architecture, even though he would never finish his degree.

Beyond knowledge and a profession, the university offered the chance to climb the social and economic ladders in Cuba, and the Carpentiers, who had sent Alejo to the best private schools, undoubtedly desired, as immigrants often do, for their young son to establish himself in their new country. But life was to deal Alejo a cruel blow that would radically change his fate. One day Georges Carpentier abandoned his family, and nothing was ever heard of him again. This forced Alejo to leave the university in order to support himself and his mother. Thus he began to write for newspapers; he even wrote a history of shoes for the shoemakers' union. For the first time, two things came together that were to have great importance in Carpentier's life: culture and business. Perhaps to compensate for the absence of his father, he became one of the most learned Spanish-American writers since Andrés Bello. And business, most specifically advertising, would bring him the economic well-being and the social position that his father's disappearance had denied him at a very crucial point in his life.

Economic stability would have to wait, however. Cuba soon began to show signs of social and political distress. Peace had not only abandoned the Carpentier household but had also left the street, where war would break out between the different factions of the unstable island society. It was the beginning of the 1920s. After various North American interventions, meant to reestablish order, the political situation in Cuba became more and more chaotic. Even though he had already abandoned his studies, Carpentier soon found himself involved in political activities at the university. The 1920s was a decade of economic growth and political turbulence in Cuba, which culminated in a full-fledged revolution against the dictatorship of Gerardo Machado y Morales, who had come to power in 1925. Machado was supported by those social classes that would stand to benefit from economic growth, and, of course, the United States; but his opposition was a coalition of groups that included the recently organized Communist party, various student groups, and other sectors, especially workers, who were affected by his politics. Machado had been gradually changing into a typical Latin-American dictator. He had amended the constitution to prolong his presidency, and he employed such violent measures against the opposition that he would soon be dubbed "el asno con garras" (the ass with claws). When the revolution was at the point of victory in 1933, the United States managed to manipulate the situation in such a way that, although Machado had to flee to the Bahamas, the revolutionaries were unable to assume power. From the ashes of Machado's dictatorship would arise the next Cuban dictator, Fulgencio Batista, who dominated island politics, directly or indirectly, until the revolution of 1959.

The students and intellectuals who fought against Machado were not alone. The student movement had begun in Córdoba, Argentina, in 1923 with the university reform that reverberated through the entire continent. The Cuban revolutionaries had the support of the Mexicans as well, who were at that time consolidating the gains of their revolution. The Cubans felt they were part of a movement that had international ramifications. Few of their leaders survived the failure of the revolution. Rafael Trejo died of a bullet wound during a demonstration, Eduardo Guiteras was assassinated in Mexico by agents of Machado, and Rubén Martínez Villena died of tuberculosis, his health destroyed in the revolutionary struggle. Villena was the most dramatic figure of the period, having been a major player in the two principal activities of the younger generation: the artistic avant-garde and politics. The so-called Revolución del '33 and its most dramatic participants left an indelible mark on Carpentier, who would incorporate it in his novels, especially in *El acoso* and *El recurso del método* (1974; translated as *Reasons of State*, 1976). The revolutionaries of 1933 were for Carpentier exemplary men of action whom he always admired but could never quite emulate.

Carpentier was, however, involved in the student movement, but he spent the most bloody years of the struggle against Machado and Batista abroad. In 1923, at the age of nineteen, he had been named editor of a new weekly magazine, *Carteles*, that would become one of the most important in Cuba, and in which his contributions would appear until 1949. Carpentier had the talent of a good business manager, with a solid middle-class sense of money and an enormous capacity for work. *Carteles* prospered in the midst of the economic growth that, in spite of the political upheaval, the country enjoyed, and Carpentier, although not rich, at least had weathered with his mother the hard times.

Around the middle of the 1920s Carpentier's political activism was increasing at the same rate as his artistic production. He joined the Grupo Minorista, a group that included political and intellectual dissidents, and participated in a protest against Machado's immediate predecessor, Alfredo Zayas, whose venality had become intolerable. By 1927 Carpentier had already begun to distinguish himself as a promoter of the nascent Afro-Cuban or Afro-Antillian movement, he was regularly asked to give lectures on the artistic avant-garde in Europe, and he had been one of the founders of *Revista de Avance*, one of the key journals of the avant-garde. He also contributed to the literary section of the very conservative (Spanish-oriented) *Diario de la Marina*, which, paradoxically, was another important vehicle of the artistic and political avant-garde in Cuba. He also began to write around this time for *Social*—an illustrated weekly geared to an upper-middle-class and aristocratic Cuban audience—which, besides concerning itself with the social activities of its readers, was one of the magazines most infused with avant-garde art in all of Spanish America. Carpentier's contributions to *Social* were frequent and prolific. Through this magazine, Carpentier rubbed elbows with Cuban high society. *Carteles* would bring him economic stability, whereas *Social* afforded him prestige.

Involvement in the new art movement and in political activism led Carpentier and his companions to look at black culture as an autochthonous source of artistic and political energy. The spirit of rebellion that moved the younger generation found inspiration in the art of black people, based in a religious faith that had helped them survive the horrors of slavery. Black culture signified a rejection of the European, which coincided, for the younger generation, with the rejection of European art by the avant-garde itself. Carpentier collaborated with two Cuban composers, Amadeo Roldán and Alejandro García Caturla, in the creation of various ballets, comic operas, and other compositions that would spread the spirit of rebellion and faith of the black people within their own culture. These activities made him even more infamous with the authorities, who arrested him during a roundup of dissidents in 1927. Carpentier went to jail with Communists, *Anarquistas*, and others who seemed suspect to the police.

Carpentier only spent forty days in jail, but upon his release he knew he was blacklisted and in danger. In spring 1928 he found a way to escape Cuba. An international convention of journalists met in Havana. The French surrealist poet Robert Desnos attended and became Carpentier's friend. Desnos allowed the Cuban to use his papers to sail back to France. In France, Carpentier completed his apprenticeship in the avant-garde. Through his connection with Desnos, he became associated with the surrealists, and he supported his friend against André Breton in 1930, when two factions clashed for motives that were partly political.

Dust jacket for Carpentier's first novel, which he began writing in 1927 while he was imprisoned in a Cuban jail with other political activists

From Paris, Carpentier continued his contributions to *Carteles* and *Social*. For *Social* Carpentier wrote almost exclusively about the art of the avant-garde. His articles on Igor Stravinsky, Pablo Picasso, Jean Cocteau, and many others kept the Cuban public informed about the artistic revolution that was developing in Europe. Carpentier also published in *Social* a column on women's fashion that he signed with the pseudonym Jacqueline. From Europe, Carpentier helped support the Cuban revolutionaries in their fight against Machado by publishing several articles on the atrocities of that government in Spanish magazines of the Left, such as *Octubre*, managed by Rafael Alberti.

His work in *Carteles*, *Social*, and other magazines could not provide Carpentier with enough to live on, because, in addition, he had gotten married shortly after his arrival in Paris. This first wife, who died soon afterward from tuberculosis, barely appeared at all in Carpentier's accounts of himself in interviews and news reports, and she was completely absent in the criticism that was written about him. According to Carpentier his first wife was Swiss and died of tuberculosis in a sanatorium in the French Pyrenees, the region he would describe many years later in *El siglo de las luces* (1962; translated as *Explosion in a Cathedral*, 1963). Pressured by economic need, Carpentier began to work in radio broadcasting, in a studio called Foniric, the property of Paul Deharme, a French businessman who employed him and promoted his radio programs. Radio and advertising would be Carpentier's occupation until the beginning of the 1960s, even after the success of the Cuban Revolution.

Shortly after the death of his first wife, Carpentier got married again, this time to Frenchwoman Eva Frejaville. He had found his calling in the country his father had abandoned. He had succeeded in reconstructing the world of his home in El Cotorro—the protected and refined orb of the French language. It would not have been difficult for him at this time to take on or reaffirm his French identity. In Havana, according to Juan Marinello, many people considered Carpentier a foreigner at this time, especially because of the guttural *r* that he was never able to eliminate from his Spanish. Carpentier's ambiguity could have been relieved if he had simply become the French writer that threatened to emerge from his father's library. Carpentier was to remain in Paris until 1939, except for a short trip to Cuba in 1936 to visit his mother—eleven years away from the Caribbean world, leading a well-established life in the French capital, where no one would take him for a foreigner. But Carpentier did not become French and, on the contrary, struggled to remain Cuban.

Paris at the end of the 1920s and the beginning of the 1930s was, as it has intermittently been since the nineteenth century, the intellectual and artistic capital of Spanish America. Cuban poets got to know Chilean poets in Parisian cafés, and Argentine composers discovered Mexican painters in the art galleries of the French capital. While in Paris, Carpentier became a friend of Latin-American novelists and poets such as the Guatemalan Miguel Angel Asturias, the Venezuelan Arturo Uslar Pietri, and the Chilean Pablo Neruda. He also became better acquainted with Cuban poets and painters, including Nicolás Guillén and Wifredo Lam. From Paris, Carpentier traveled frequently to Madrid, where he met Federico García Lorca, Rafael Alberti, Miguel Hernández, and many other Spanish and Spanish-American writers who, especially during the years of the Republic, created an intellectual and artistic flowering in the Spanish capital that Carpentier would often evoke. Spain was another homeland for Carpentier, as much for its culture as for its political ambience before the civil war. In 1937 he was part of the Cuban delegation that was present at the Congress of Intellectuals against Fascism, which Juan Marinello and Nicolás Guillén also attended. At that time, Carpentier met Octavio Paz, and artists and intellectuals from all over the world, and saw up close the devastation of the Spanish Civil War. These contacts with artists and intellectuals of other Latin-American countries provided Carpentier with a continental perspective. In Paris he realized that his attempt to integrate black culture with Cuban art had its counterpart in the "indigenist" movement prevalent in countries such as Mexico and Peru. This stimulus prompted him to attend courses in ethnology at the Sorbonne and to spend long hours sheltered at the National Library in Paris, where he read book after book on Spanish America. Years later Carpentier would attempt to substitute the Spanish America that he discovered in books in Paris for another experienced firsthand. This effort was, perhaps, together with his attempt to define himself culturally, the essence of Carpentier's spiritual and artistic life.

In 1930 Carpentier founded a literary magazine in Paris with the financial support of Elvira de Alvear, a South American millionaire for whom he apparently worked as a secretary. In it he published the work of his French and Spanish-American friends. Called *Imán* (magnet), based on his inspiration to unite the intellectual world of Paris, especially the Spanish-speaking one, the magazine only had one issue. In this issue Carpentier advanced a fragment of the novel he had begun to write during his imprisonment in Havana in 1927— *¡Ecue-Yamba-O!* (Praised Be the Lord, 1933); the title is in Lucumí, one of the African languages spoken in Cuba, though the novel was written in Spanish. Meanwhile Carpentier continued adapting plays for the radio. The two worlds of his childhood would repeat themselves in Paris: his French home, financed by regular employment; and the street, where he spoke Spanish with his Spanish-American friends. Both worlds converged in his personality: the French intellect and the Spanish American's yearning to discover his roots.

Carpentier continued in Paris the creative work he had started in Cuba. Soon after arriving in the French capital, he finished "¡Yamba-O!," a musical poem he produced in collaboration with the composer François Gaillard. He also collaborated with Gaillard in the composition of *Poèmes des Antilles* (Antillian Poems, 1931), a suite of Afro-Cuban poems written in French, much better than what their author's silence about them years later might indicate. In the magazine *Cahiers du Sud*, Carpentier published in 1930 a short story, "Histoire de lunes" (History of Moons), his first narrative work of any scope, which anticipates some of the characteristics of his mature work. The story, like *Poèmes des Antilles*, is also in French, as were his contributions to *Bifur*, an avant-garde magazine, one of whose advisers was James Joyce. But Carpentier's major work during these first years in Paris was *¡Ecue-Yamba-O!* The novel was not a great success. Years later Carpentier rejected it, and there was not another authorized edition of *¡Ecue-Yamba-O!* until a few years before his death. Marinello, one of the most prominent intellectuals of the Cuban avant-garde, devoted a piercing and negative review to it, which is one of the first important commentaries about Carpentier.

Marinello pointed out that *¡Ecue-Yamba-O!* is an odd mixture of artistic styles, which attempts without success to present a profound vision of the world of black Afro-Cubans. On the one hand, Carpentier tries to give a conventional description of the life of blacks in the sugar mills and the city. On the other hand, he attempts to capture the religious faith that inspired the blacks—through the devices of avant-garde literature, especially bold metaphors; the reduction of the landscape to primary forms, as in cubism; and the creation of an onomatopoeic language resembling the music of African rituals. One of the most innovative aspects of the novel is the inclusion of photographs of liturgical rituals and instruments, which gives the book the air of an ethnographic study or a surrealistic book-object. Carpentier attempts to demonstrate that the connection between religious doctrine, art, and a way of life among the black people would encourage in that sector of Cuban society a resistance capable of rescuing it from the cruel economic exploitation to which it was subjected. With the so-called *novelas de la tierra* (novels of the earth), such as *Doña Bárbara* (1928), by Romulo Gallegos, and *The Vortex* (1924), by José Eustacio Rivera, *¡Ecue-Yamba-O!* shares an interest in the natural Latin-American world. But unlike these books, it incorporates the characteristic array of avant-garde devices and an anthropological perspective. Carpentier tries to do too many things, and *¡Ecue-Yamba-O!* was virtually ignored by the reading public.

Neither *¡Ecue-Yamba-O!* nor the ballets, poems, songs, and stories published by Carpentier in the 1920s and 1930s transformed him into a well-known author. In addition his literary production after 1933 was almost nonexistent until around the middle of the 1940s. The first works of fiction published by Carpentier after *¡Ecue-Yamba-O!* were the stories "Oficio de tinieblas" (Officium Tenebrae, 1949) and *Viaje a la semilla* (1944; translated as *Journey Back to the Source*, 1970), published in a private edition of a hundred copies. His next work of fiction was *El reino de este mundo* (1949; translated as *The Kingdom of This World*, 1957). What did keep Carpentier continuously in the public eye in Cuba were the articles he sent from Paris to *Carteles*.

During these years, Carpentier continued reading voraciously about Latin America, especially the chronicles of the discovery and conquest, as well as works of authors who were his contemporaries. These readings were to crystallize in Carpentier's work, in his mature stage, in those works that would transform him into one of the principal Latin-American writers. That stage was to begin upon his return to Cuba, with the fulfillment of his longing to assert his Spanish-American identity, no longer through books but through direct experience.

The situation in Europe was growing tense around 1939. The civil war had ended in Spain with the defeat of the Republic, and the imminence of another world war was clear. Many of Carpentier's Spanish friends had gone into exile, many to Spanish America. Meanwhile the situation in Cuba was becoming more promising. Batista had come to an agreement with the Left, and the Cuban economy, which had always benefited from European conflict, was on the rise. Nicolás Guillén was also back in Cuba. There were funds for radio broadcasts of a cultural nature, and Carpentier was chosen to produce some of them. He returned to Havana in 1939 with his French wife. A new life was beginning for him.

In Havana, Carpentier met a group of friends eager for his knowledge about the European artistic community. He would meet with these friends in a house on the outskirts of the capital to exchange views about art. His marriage with Eva, however, did not survive the tropics, and Cuban artists and intellectuals continued to be sharply divided by politics. Carpentier participated sporadically in these activities. In October 1939 Carpentier was divorced from Eva, and he was married on 26 May 1941 to a Cuban, Lilia Esteban Hierro, a member of a well-to-do family. With Lilia, Carpentier was to acquire domestic stability that lasted for the rest of his life. To her he systematically dedicated every one of his books published after their marriage, which are the most important of his career. Carpentier's work can be divided into two periods, one before Lilia and one after her. Through his work in radio, his publications in magazines and newspapers, and his marriage with Lilia, Carpentier achieved not only stability but the kind of economic and social status that his family had sought since they arrived in Cuba.

The division in the Cuban artistic and intellectual world manifested itself in literary magazines. One side was led by José Lezama and called themselves the *Orígenes* group, after the magazine they published. The other side had a more piously political bent, and one of their leaders was Guillén, already a member of the Communist party. Guillén published *La Gaceta del Caribe*, a tabloid in which Carpentier presented a fragment of *El reino de este mundo*. But Carpentier also contributed to *Orígenes*, and although he cannot be considered a member of the group, since by the summer of 1945 he had again left the country, his mature work still shares basic features with those of Lezama and his followers. In addition Carpentier published significant stories in the magazine run by Lezama and José Rodríguez Feo, including "Oficio de tinieblas," "Semejante a la noche" (Like the Night), and fragments of *El acoso*. One should not be misled by Carpentier's apparent lack of Catholic faith, an important factor with Lezama and his disciples. In 1949, in an important essay published in Caracas, Carpentier eulogized the Catholic Paul Claudel, and soon, in the prologue to *El reino de este mundo*, Carpentier demanded that the Spanish-American artist have faith, no longer a religious one, but in the culture and art of the Continent. This particular position of Carpentier's does not differ much from that of *Orígenes*.

La música en Cuba (Music in Cuba, 1946), published in Mexico, was conceived with an enthusiasm that could be called the aesthetic of *Orígenes*. That is, Carpentier's attempt to trace the origins of Cuban music and its peculiarities was motivated by the same desire to understand the essence of Cuban culture that stimulated Lezama and his group. The background to the stories Carpentier published in *Orígenes* is the sugar region close to nineteenth-century Havana, where the most important aspects of a future national culture persevered; the research needed to recreate that environment arose from Carpentier's investigations while writing *La música en Cuba*. Furthermore the majority of the stories collected in *Guerra del tiempo* (1958; translated as *The War of Time*, 1970) came out of that research, and the same can be said of *El reino de este mundo*. The *Orígenes* artists, especially Lezama, practiced a kind of telluric transcendentalism, a search for origins that would instill in their work precisely the kind of religious aura that Carpentier suggests in his prologue to *El reino de este mundo*. In *La música en Cuba*, using the research methods he had learned in Paris, Carpentier reaches back to the sixteenth century to the first ballads Spanish mariners sang on the island, to the music of the native rituals, and to the ritual music of the Africans.

But Carpentier discovered a more recent origin of Cuban music, which led him to Haiti and the Haitian Revolution, which is the theme of *El reino de este mundo*. The catalyst in the creation of Cuban music was the combination of Cuban elements and those features brought to Cuba by Haitian exiles, who arrived mostly at Santiago de Cuba. The main importation was the *contredance* (country dance), which became in Cuba the *contradanza* and led to the habanera, which became famous in Georges Bizet's opera *Carmen* (1875). From the habanera came the *danzón*, from which contemporary forms of Cuban music are derived. Besides the importance that this theory has for the study of Cuban music, for Carpentier it meant discovering a first stage in Cuban history, a departure whose principal component was the black presence on the island. If Carpentier could suggest a new beginning for the evolution of the history of Cuba and of the Caribbean in general, what would make that history coherent and link the events that composed it? This is the problem Carpentier confronts in his fiction of the 1940s. During earlier years Carpentier had dealt with similar issues, but these had now acquired a historical dimension that would draw him back to the novel form. Carpentier would not return to the present in his fiction until *Los pasos perdidos* in 1953, at which time, faced with the dilemma of history, he recon-

Carpentier in Havana, 1962 (photograph by Paolo Gasparini)

sidered the question of origin and of a beginning.

The six years Carpentier spent in Cuba between 1939 and 1945, when he and his wife moved to Caracas, were a period of great activity. His radio programs were a great success, and he mingled with the best writers and painters of the island. In 1943 the French actor Louis Jouvet went on a tour that brought him to Cuba, and there he convinced Carpentier to accompany him to Haiti. Carpentier made the trip and was awestruck by the ruins of the Haitian Revolution at La Ferriere and Sans Souci. They inspired him, along with his research on the origins of music, to write *El reino de este mundo*. He also traveled to Mexico, where he signed a contract with Fondo de Cultura Económica for the publication of *La música en Cuba*. He then went to New York, where the Columbia Broadcasting Company proposed that he write radio programs directed to Latin America. Carpentier and Lilia stayed at the elegant Warwick Hotel in the center of Manhattan, and there they began to ponder their future.

Carpentier imagined what his life would be like in the big city, living in the suburbs, traveling daily by train and subway to work, anonymous in the immense human masses of New York. The couple decided to return to Cuba, and immediately Carpentier accepted an offer from Carlos Frías, a friend from the Paris days, who was founding Publicidad Ars, which would become one of the most important advertising agencies in Venezuela when the impact of North American capital and petroleum began to transform the Venezuelan economy. Carpentier's knowledge of radio and his proven managerial skills made him an ideal candidate for the position Frías offered.

In Caracas, Carpentier succeeded in becoming one of the best-known and most-respected writers of Latin America, but it was not easy. There was no market for Latin-American novels. Carpentier was forced to help finance the publication of *El reino de este mundo*, and *Los pasos perdidos*, the two novels that brought him fame in the 1950s. His first work of fiction from an international publishing house was *El acoso*, published by Losada in Buenos Aires in 1956. By this time Carpentier had already won two literary prizes in France. In 1954 the French translation of *El reino de este mundo* was selected as one of the most significant books of the year in France, and in 1956 the French version of *Los pasos perdidos* was given the prize for the best foreign book of the year. Carpentier was already fifty-two when Losada decided to publish *El acoso*. Two years later, in 1958, the Compañía General de Ediciones, in Mexico City, collected the stories Carpentier published in the 1940s and early 1950s, together with *El acoso*, and produced *Guerra del tiempo*, which would have great success. A year later the same company published a second edition of *Los pasos perdidos*, which was the first to have a wide circulation in the Spanish-speaking world. On the threshold of the 1959 Cuban revolution, Carpentier was becoming one of the principal novelists in Latin America.

Carpentier has often said that Venezuela widened his vision of Latin America because of the variety of landscapes and the variegated races of its people. Venezuela had all the features that characterized the New World: enormous mountains, plains, bountiful rivers, woods, the ocean, and a population composed of whites, blacks, and Indians. But Venezuela also allowed Carpentier to rethink his conception of history and his theories on the origins and characteristics of that history. This he accomplished in the process that led him to write *Los pasos perdidos*. Carpentier, in his work as a publicist for a company with strong ties to the United States, lived out in Caracas something of the experience he had rejected in New York. Caracas was undergoing a major transformation that put Carpentier in touch with a postindustrial society and in direct contact with the mass communication that characterizes it. Publicidad Ars produced television and radio commercials as well as programs for both media. During his summer vacations Carpentier took trips into the jungle, where he had an opportunity to experience the sensation of escape and a return to origins. Carpentier, in short, experienced a Latin America of the future and one of the most remote past, which furnished him with the reflective stance found in *Los pasos perdidos*.

Carpentier led a multiple existence in Caracas: he was a publicist, journalist, writer, professor, lecturer, and promoter of music festivals. His success as a publicist was definitive. In journalism "Letra y Solfa" (Letters and Music), the almost-daily column he wrote for *El Nacional*, kept the Caracan public up-to-date on music, literature, the visual arts, and the latest European news (the best of these columns were collected and published in 1975). When one remembers that he also finished or wrote *El reino de este mundo*, "El camino de Santiago" (1954; translated as "Highroad of St. James," 1970; collected in *Guerra del tiempo*), *El acoso*, *Los pasos perdidos*, and *El siglo de las luces*, one has to admire the discipline and scope of his work.

Carpentier carried the manuscript for the last of these novels in his luggage when he returned to Cuba in July 1959, after the revolution. The book was published in 1962 and became one of the so-called Spanish-American boom novels.

In order to return to Cuba, Carpentier had to close down his comfortable home in Caracas and leave behind his secure position. In Caracas, Carpentier had the prestige, the money, and the social position he had striven for much of his life. Carpentier's connection with the revolutionary Cuban government would transform him into a controversial figure in Spanish-American cultural politics, especially when many artists and intellectuals became disillusioned with the revolution as a result of its repressive politics and increasing dependence on the Soviet Union. Carpentier was always faithful to Fidel Castro's regime: he signed every manifesto, supported the policies of the government, turned his back on friends who did not, participated in all the regime's formalities, and refrained from criticism. The revolutionary government rewarded Carpentier with a privileged position. He spent from 1968 until the end of his life in France as a cultural attaché for European affairs, while life in Cuba became increasingly difficult. He was allowed privileges, such as the ability to receive royalties, when Cuba would not recognize copyright laws, and other Cuban writers could neither receive foreign payment nor publish outside the island.

Carpentier was able to travel with all the conveniences and guarantees of his diplomatic status, while José Lezama Lima was denied permission to attend foreign symposia about his work. In Paris, Carpentier aided Cuban policies by appearing before the Russell Tribunal, which denounced U.S. activities in Vietnam, but he also took advantage of his diplomatic status by traveling all through Europe. These contradictions distanced Carpentier from some of the "boom" writers, with whom he had always had a somewhat tense relationship anyway. For some of those writers rebellion was conceived more as a counterculture than Carpentier's docile and solicitous relations with the Cuban Communist bureaucracy. From 1952 to 1958 Carpentier lived a peaceful existence in Venezuela during the dictatorship of Pérez Jiménez; from 1959 until his death in 1980 he lived under the regime of Castro. Carpentier successfully directed the Editorial Nacional (national publishing firm) from 1962 to 1966, published novels and short stories, traveled all over the world, and participated in literary panels. This amounted to nearly thirty years of life under governments directed by Latin-American strongmen, during which time Carpentier prospered and wrote his most important work.

Carpentier probably saw in the Cuban revolution the culmination of a kind of theodicy similar to the one present in many of his books, a synthesis of politics and art, the unity of a desire for a utopia and its realization in history. Inspired perhaps by the feeling that life ultimately imitates art, Carpentier did not care to test too severely the connection of such lofty ideals with the practice of politics, and he looked the other way.

It would be foolish to criticize Carpentier for the privileges that his monumental work afforded him, but it is shallow to cast him as a political activist. And it is wrong to think that his life was a model of political deportment more deserving of unqualified praise than of analysis. It is much more worthwhile to study Carpentier's decisions, in all their complexity, during the revolution, including his becoming, or allowing himself to be made, a member of the Cuban Communist party. When Carpentier returned to Cuba in 1959, he was impelled to do so probably by a desire to join a victorious political movement whose beginnings glimmered in the revolution of 1933, which had marked his youth. The ambiguity that Marinello had reproached him for and the neutrality that Neruda, in his memoirs, charged him with, must have weighed Carpentier down. The battle between a life of reflection and one of action was a dilemma for Carpentier, and it is a poignant theme in some of his novels, especially *Los pasos perdidos* and *El siglo de las luces*. Once he had devoted himself to the revolution, it would have been difficult to retreat from it, even though the political situation on the island was worsening.

Remaining with the revolution in 1959, during a period when most Cubans glorified it, was easy; but breaking with it in 1968, or 1971, or during any of the crises with the intellectuals, would

Dust jacket for the 1962 best-seller that influenced writers such as Gabriel García Márquez

have been difficult. The latter would have been a truly political gesture with enormous risks, and Carpentier was not particularly the kind of man given to political acts that might run great risks. He had railed against "committed" literature in the 1940s and 1950s, and he only attempted it, with little success, in *La consagración de la primavera* (The Consecration of Spring, 1979), when it was no longer dangerous to do so. He thus passively accepted the government's demands on others while producing books that were replete with aspects of the baroque. In private he admired Jorge Luis Borges, but in public he refrained from protesting the unavailability of the Argentine's work to Cuban readers. He maintained a friendship with Carlos Fuentes in private, but he said nothing publicly about the Mexican writer's break with the Cuban revolution.

The social criticism in Carpentier's work does not emanate from a given ideological or doctrinal position. His fiction revindicates black heritage in Spanish America, especially in the Caribbean, and inexorably chronicles the injustices in the history of the New World since the conquest.

El siglo de las luces, the novel Carpentier had in his suitcase when he arrived in Havana in 1959, incited much debate about political issues. For some the novel is a kind of roman à clef about the Cuban Revolution, an idea that is absurd because the book was written in Caracas before the revolution. Others have attempted to identify any changes Carpentier made in the novel once he joined the revolution. Still others realize that Carpentier's novel not only has little Marxism in it but also seems completely at odds with Marxist doctrine. The book was a bestseller. Carpentier profited from his success as a writer, and his association with Cuba put him in a brighter limelight. *El siglo de las luces* had an immediate impact on writers such as Gabriel García Márquez and Fuentes, to a large extent because it presents a working out of the problems Carpentier introduced in *Los pasos perdidos*, and it provides a model of how to write fiction in Latin America that is based on the history of the New World. His narratives written in the 1940s, including *El reino de este mundo*, are aimed at a convergence or correspondence between the natural world of Spanish America and its history. Fiction was to be for Carpentier the fusion of both worlds, hence the circularities, repetitions, and reiterations. However, in *Los pasos perdidos* Carpentier put his romantic ideology to the test, and the result was that there is no such continuity between nature and history: only the political events of history are its points of departure. Culture is fabricated by humanity. Its origin is not in the jungle, but in those acts of foundation carried out by man. In *El siglo de las luces* echoes of the French Revolution catalyze a series of political events not linked to the natural world, as are the revolts in *El reino de este mundo*, but encompassing writing, architecture, and every cultural manifestation. *El siglo de las luces* is made up of a symbolic system like that of the Hebrew Cabala, which prioritizes hidden codes not based on reason, as the eighteenth-century philosophers and revolutionaries claimed, but on a kind of universal *superreason* that binds all cultures together. The title of Carpentier's novel (literally, The Century of the Lights) alludes, then, ironically, to the lights of reason, inasmuch as the lights also refer to the *Zohar*, or "Book of Splendors," the principal text of the Cabala, written in Spain by Moisés de León in the fifteenth century. The novel, which begins in Havana at the end of the eighteenth century, ends in Madrid after the historic events of the second of May—the last scenes of the novel are based on Francisco José de Goya's paintings. *El siglo de las luces* is a work of extraordinary figurative richness, using actual documentary sources (the protagonist, Victor Hugues, is based on a real historical figure with that name). Apart from its value as a novel, it is one of the most profound studies of the transition from the Enlightenment to the Romantic age in Latin America.

After *El siglo de las luces* there was a hiatus of twelve years in Carpentier's novelistic production, similar to the one between *¡Ecue-Yamba-O!* and *Viaje a la semilla*. However, in 1964 Carpentier published a book of essays that had an enormous impact on Latin-American literature: *Tientos y diferencias* (Probes and Differences), which contains Carpentier's recent pieces, but also has others from his stay in Caracas, especially the revised and enlarged prologue to *El reino de este mundo*, an essay originally published in *El Nacional* in 1948. In that prologue, which had received little attention even after being published in the novel, Carpentier had proposed a theory that, when it reappeared in *Tientos y diferencias*, during the boom of the Latin-American novel and at the height of the Cuban revolution, created rifts among critics of the Spanish-American novel. This theory was dubbed by Carpentier "marvelous [Latin-] American reality." In truth, during the period in which Carpentier published *Tientos y diferencias*, neither his work nor his avowed political position corresponded with the theories of the prologue. Carpentier's theories come from surrealism, Oswald Spengler, and a *lebensphilosophie* that led him to hypothesize that Spanish-American art arises from an act of faith during which the artist becomes one with nature. In reality, as one sees in *El reino de este mundo*, there has to be a gap between the premodern Spanish-American ambience and the artist's modern point of view, which is equivalent to saying that an ironic perspective persists in the novel. This is also what occurs in *El siglo de las luces*, where the origin that is pursued is not a natural one but a political one. The theories of the essay do not conform to *El siglo de las luces*, and the portion of the essay that makes up the original prologue to *El reino de este mundo* does not agree with what was added after 1959, which concerns a trip Carpentier took to China and the Soviet Union.

Carpentier's theories on the Latin-American baroque, also in *Tientos y diferencias*, are more coherent. They are also more consistent with his novels close to that time. Carpentier understood the baroque as a mixture of styles in a single work, a combination that corresponds to the different roots of each style. Spanish-American art, which always tends toward the baroque, exhibits that mixture of styles, which is at the same time a kind of temporal disconnection; the neoclassical coexists in architecture with vestiges of the *mudéjar* and the modern style. The mixture renders it impossible for each work to be centered in one idea that dominates the rest. It is not an amalgam whose metaphoric base is the natural world, a kind of chaos of Romantic origin, but a coexistence of forms whose origins are the different cultures that people the Latin-American scene—hence the apparently permanent disproportion of such art, not only in terms of size but in terms of the lack of equilibrium in the different parts. Neruda's *Canto general* (General Song), with its overly ambitious desire to encompass all of Spanish-American history, is an example of this lack of proportion. Carpentier's story "Los escogidos" (The Chosen), where the Noahs of various cultures come together during the flood that seems to be part of every mythological tradition, is another example, but with an attempt at order in diversity, restraint among disproportion, and a multiplicity of origins that only cancel one another. These are the characteristics of the Latin-American baroque, according to Carpentier. García Márquez's *Cien años de soledad* (1967; translated as *One Hundred Years of Solitude*, 1970) was evidently conceived under the influence of Carpentier's ideas.

In 1974, as if to commemorate his seventieth birthday, Carpentier finally published two more novels: *Concierto barroco* (Baroque Concert) and *El recurso del método* (translated as *Reasons of State*, 1976). *Concierto barroco* is a return to the Afro-Antillian movement, since one of its protagonists is black and it is a practical test of Carpentier's ideas on the baroque. The final moment of this brief work is a jam session in the Ospedale della Pieta, where all the characters join in with the musical instruments of their traditions. The work makes chronological leaps: it begins in the eighteenth century in Spanish America and ends in the twentieth in Europe, when Filomeno, the black Cuban slave, leaves his master to attend a Louis Armstrong concert in Paris.

El recurso del método is a novel about a dictator, which takes place in a Spanish-American country that is a synthesis of several countries; the central character is based on several dictators, the most important being Cuba's Gerardo Machado. The dictator, a tragicomic figure, or figurehead, who wants to appear refined and spends half his life in Europe, is a parody of the head of state as a product of telluric forces. Carpentier's dictator is surrounded not by natural elements but by products that are flagrantly artificial: the background for political meetings is made of cardboard, and fake palms make everything look like an opera decor. *El recurso del método*, whose title is a distortion of René Descartes's *Discours de la Méthode* (1637), is a profoundly comic novel, the only one of Carpentier's that openly demonstrates this characteristic. As in *Concierto barroco* the major focus is the mixture of elements from different cul-

Caricature of Carpentier by Pancho Grailles

tural traditions, which manifest themselves as false when they come into contact with each other, and that together are a kind of baroque summa of artifice. The dictator is the center of that proliferating artificiality and ends up having no control over anything; his own self is false and empty, the point of intersection for the various traditions. This approach constitutes not only a criticism of political authority but also the author's authority—he is a tiny dictator who controls, or tries to control, his fictive universe. Carpentier's dictator, a music lover and a Francophile who divides his life between Spanish America and France, is representative of Carpentier himself.

Carpentier's two final novels are very different from each other. *La consagración de la primavera*, whose title refers to Igor Stravinsky's work, is a long autobiographical novel in which Carpentier, among other things, rewrites *Los pasos perdidos*: modern man, looking for meaning in his life, finds it not in the remote past but in the future. The novel organizes history in a teleological way. Carpentier begins with the Spanish Civil War, which is seen as a result of the Russian October Revolution, and finishes with the Cuban Revolution. Carpentier writes his life according to how he would have liked to have led it: one character is an architect, another a writer, and another a musician. The most autobiographical of all is an advertising man, but he ends up as a revolutionary activist, wounded at the Bay of Pigs. The novel is melodramatic, poorly written, pedantic, boring, and it was a critical and commercial failure. *El arpa y la sombra* (The Harp and the Shadow, 1979) was written when Carpentier knew he was dying of cancer; the novel brings a kind of ironic balance to his work. Carpentier projects himself in the figure of Christopher Columbus, the first American "narrator," as a last resort to find the origin of American writing. The pretext is the investigation that was carried out in the nineteenth century, when canonization was being considered for the discoverer, and the trial that was held to that effect in the Vatican. In one strand of the novel Columbus is on his deathbed reminiscing about his life. Readers find out that it was by seducing Queen Isabella that Columbus convinced her to help him, thereby rendering the entire American enterprise part of an illicit love affair. Columbus, of course, is not canonized, and the negative decision undoubtedly alludes to the many occasions that Carpentier (though expected to) did not win the Nobel Prize.

The novel is based on documentary sources that reconstruct Columbus's life, as if Carpentier wished to show his hand, that is, the artifice, subtly. The result is almost more of a rococo miniature than a baroque work. The end of Carpentier's work is this refined joke, this magnificent display of technical mastery, and this ironic vision of his own literary enterprise. History is not moved by great events or by economic forces but by something more human, like passion. In the end Carpentier seems to have chosen Sigmund Freud over Marx. The origin that Carpentier sought is in a love affair, not in the depths of the jungle or the vagaries of history.

Carpentier's death came in Paris, after he had gotten up early to write and had attended an official function in his diplomatic capacity. He died in his home, with Lilia at his side, on 24 April 1980.

Interviews:

César Leante, "Confesiones sencillas de un escritor barroco," *Cuba*, 3, no. 24 (1964): 30-33;

Klaus Müller-Bergh, "Conversando con Carpentier: Paris 1974," *Casa de las Américas*, 131 (1982): 117-122;

Entrevistas (Havana: Letras Cubanas, 1985).

Bibliographies:

Roberto González-Echevarría and Klaus Müller-Bergh, *Alejo Carpentier: Bibliographical Guide* (Westport, Conn.: Greenwood, 1983);

Araceli García-Carranza, *Biobibliografía de Alejo Carpentier* (Havana: Letras Cubanas, 1984).

Biographies:

Lloyd King, *Alejo Carpentier, Caribbean Writer* (St. Augustine, Trinidad: University of the West Indies Press, 1977);

Roberto González-Echevarría, *Alejo Carpentier: The Pilgrim at Home* (Ithaca, N.Y.: Cornell University Press, 1977);

Eduardo González, *Alejo Carpentier: El tiempo del hombre* (Caracas: Monte Avila, 1978);

José Vila Selma, *El "ultimo" Carpentier* (Las Palmas, Spain: Mancomunicadad del Cabildo, 1978).

References:

Leonardo Acosta, *Música y épica en la novela de*

Alejo Carpentier (Havana: Letras Cubanas, 1981);

Carlos J. Alonso, "Viaje a la semilla," *Modern Language Notes*, 94 (March 1979): 386-393;

Salvador Arias, ed., *Recopilación de textos sobre Alejo Carpentier* (Havana: Casa de las Américas, 1977);

Frederick A. de Armas, "Metamorphosis as Revolt: Cervantes' *Persiles y Segismunda* and Carpentier's *El reino de este mundo*," *Hispanic Review*, 49 (Summer 1981): 297-316;

Antonio Benítez-Rojo, "'El camino de Santiago' de Alejo Carpentier y el *Canon perpetuus* de Juan Sebastián Bach: Paralelismo estructural," *Revista Iberoamericana*, 49 (April-September 1983): 293-322;

Benítez-Rojo, "'Semejante a la noche' de Alejo Carpentier y el *Canon per tonos* de Juan Sebastián Bach: Su paralelismo estructural," *Eco*, 43 (April 1983): 645-662;

Ramón Chao, *Palabras en el tiempo de Alejo Carpentier* (Barcelona: Argos Vergara, 1984);

Ariel Dorfman, "Entre Proust y la momia americana: Siete notas y un epílogo sobre *El recurso del método*," *Revista Iberoamericana*, 47 (January-June 1981): 95-128;

Dorfman, "El sentido de la historia en la obra de Alejo Carpentier," in his *Imaginación y violencia en América* (Caracas: Nuevo Siglo, 1976);

Helmy F. Giacoman, ed., *Homenaje a Alejo Carpentier* (New York: Las Américas, 1970);

Roberto González-Echevarría, "Socrates Among the Weeds: Blacks and History in Carpentier's *Explosion in a Cathedral*," in *Voices from Under: Black Narrative in Latin America and the Caribbean*, edited by William Luis (Westport, Conn.: Greenwood, 1984), pp. 35-53;

Frank Janny, *Alejo Carpentier and His Early Works* (London: Tamesis, 1981);

Jo Labanyi, "Nature and the Historical Process in Carpentier's *El siglo de las luces*," *Bulletin of Hispanic Studies*, 57 (1980): 55-66;

William Luis, "Historia, naturaleza y memoria en 'Viaje a la semilla,'" *Revista Iberoamericana*, 154 (1991): 151-160;

Sharon Magnarelli, "'El Camino de Santiago' de Alejo Carpentier y la picaresca," *Revista Iberoamericana*, 40, no. 86 (1974): 65-86;

Alexis Marques Rodríguez, *El barroco y lo real maravilloso en la obra de Alejo Carpentier* (Mexico City: Siglo XXI, 1982);

Marques Rodríguez, *La obra narrativa de Alejo Carpentier* (Caracas: Universidad Central, 1970);

Nora Mazziotti, ed., *Historia y mito en la obra de Alejo Carpentier* (Buenos Aires: García Cambeiro, 1972);

Klaus Müller-Bergh, ed., *Asedios a Carpentier* (Santiago, Chile: Universitaria, 1972);

Angel Rama, "Los productivos años setenta de Alejo Carpentier," *Latin American Research Review*, 16, no. 2 (1981): 224-245;

Modesto Sánchez, "El fondo histórico de *El acoso*," *Revista Iberoamericana*, 41, nos. 92-93 (1975): 397-442;

Donald L. Shaw, *Alejo Carpentier* (Boston: Twayne, 1985);

Emma S. Speratti-Piñero, *Pasos hallados en El reino de este mundo* (Mexico City: Colegio de México, 1981);

Frances Wyers Weber, "*El acoso*: Alejo Carpentier's War on Time," *Publications of the Modern Languages Association of America*, 78 (September 1963): 440-448.

Rosario Castellanos
(25 May 1925 - 7 August 1974)

Willy O. Muñoz
Kent State University

BOOKS: *Apuntes para una declaración de fe* (Mexico City: América/Educación Pública, 1948);

Sobre cultura femenina (Mexico City: América, 1950);

De la vigilia estéril (Mexico City: América, 1950);

Tablero de damas: Pieza en un acto (Mexico City: América, 1952);

Poemas: 1953-1955 (Mexico City: Metáfora, 1957);

Balún-Canán (Mexico City: Fondo de Cultura Económica, 1957); translated by Irene Nicholson as *The Nine Guardians* (London: Faber & Faber, 1959; New York: Vanguard, 1960);

Al pie de la letra (Jalapa, Mexico: Universidad Veracruzana, 1959);

Salomé y Judith (Mexico City: Jus, 1959);

Lívida luz (Mexico City: UNAM, 1960);

La constitución (Mexico City: Instituto Nacional Indigenista, 1960);

Ciudad Real (Jalapa, Mexico: Universidad Veracruzana, 1960);

Les Etoiles d'herbe (Paris: Gallimard, 1962);

Teatro Petul (Mexico City: Instituto Nacional Indigenista, 1962);

Oficio de tinieblas (Mexico City: Mortiz, 1962);

La novela mexicana contemporánea y su valor testimonial (Mexico City: Juventud Mexicana, 1964?);

Los convidados de agosto (Mexico City: Era, 1964; enlarged, 1968);

Juicios sumarios (Jalapa, Mexico: Universidad Veracruzana, 1966);

Materia memorable (Mexico City: UNAM, 1969);

Album de familia (Mexico City: Mortiz, 1971);

Poesía no eres tú; Obra poética: 1948-1971 (Mexico City: Fondo de Cultura Económica, 1972); translated by Magda Bogin as *The Selected Poems*, bilingual edition (St. Paul, Minn.: Graywolf, 1988);

Mujer que sabe latín... (Mexico City: SEP-Setentas/Educación Pública, 1973);

El uso de la palabra (Mexico City: Excélsior, 1974 [i.e., 1975]);

El mar y sus pescaditos (Mexico City: SEP-Setentas/Educación Pública, 1975);

El eterno femenino (Mexico City: Fondo de Cultura Económica, 1975);

El verso, la palabra y el recuerdo (Mexico City: Instituto Cultural Mexicano-Israelí/Costa-Amic, 1984);

Bella dama sin piedad y otros poemas (Mexico City: Fondo de Cultura Económica, 1984);

Meditación en el umbral (Mexico City: Fondo de Cultura Económica, 1985); translated by Julian Paley as *Meditation on the Threshold*, bilingual edition (Tempe, Ariz.: Bilingual Press/Editorial Bilingüe, 1988).

Editions in English: *A Rosario Castellanos Reader*, edited by Maureen Ahern, translated by Ahern and others (Austin: University of Texas Press, 1988);

Another Way to Be: Selected Works, translated and edited by Myralyn F. Allgood (Athens: University of Georgia Press, 1990).

OTHER: Susana Francis, *Habla y literatura popular en la antigua capital chiapaneca*, prologue by Castellanos (Mexico City: Instituto Nacional Indigenista, 1960);

Sergio Fernández, *Relatos del fuego y la ceniza*, prologue by Castellanos (Mexico City: Fondo de Cultura Económica, 1968);

La corrupción intelectual, prologue by Castellanos (Mexico City: Nuestro Tiempo, 1969);

"Cuando Sartre hace literatura," *Revista de la Universidad de México*, 28 (April 1973): 19-24.

Rosario Castellanos considered literature a means of understanding the world around her. Consequently her fiction sprang from a deep-felt need to respond to issues close to her own reality: mainly the problems of Indians and the oppression of women. Having been raised in Comitán, Mexico, a provincial town with a strong Mayan influx, she became acquainted at an early age with the Indian plight. Because of this familiarity, she considered Indians to be neither mysteri-

Rosario Castellanos circa 1959 (photograph by Hans Beacham)

ous nor poetic, but rather a people who lived in atrocious misery. Moreover, she felt she had to write of how misery had atrophied their best qualities. Castellanos included women in significant roles in her indigenous and neoindigenous writings, so that class, race, and sex could be seen as constitutive parts of the economics of oppression. Her loyalty, then, was divided between the despair of the Indians and the alienation of women. Castellanos's achievements are convincing evidence that she always strove to attain the maximum of her potential in a patriarchal society such as Mexico. Her feminist works reveal the self-consciousness of a writer who was keenly aware of her gender. Castellanos tried to describe the stifling consequences patriarchal expectations have on women, and the difficulties they have in overcoming cultural conditioning. Despite the noticeable bitterness in her feminist literature, Castellanos practiced a well-understood feminism: one that could lead women to collaborate efficiently with men.

Phyllis Rodríguez-Peralta summarizes the scope of Castellanos's fiction: "from the primitive Indian surroundings in the southern state of Chiapas, to the narrow ambiance of provincial towns, to the sophisticated impersonal life of the capital; at the same time the view of women is focused first from a wide lens encompassing an Indian-white panorama, to a closer proximity of provincial women restricted by traditional mores, and then to a close-up of contemporary women in the city who are emerging into the harsh glare of personal choices and personal responsibilities."

Born on 25 May 1925 in Mexico City, to César Castellanos and Adriana Figueroa de Castellanos during a business trip, Rosario Castellanos claimed Comitán, the provincial town to which she was taken when she was a few weeks old, as her birthplace. At that time Mexico was going through a period of uncertainty due to the land reform promulgated by President Lázaro Cárdenas. He sought to end the uneven distribution of wealth by giving land to the peasants. Consequently the Castellanos family lost their estate, thus suffering a significant economic blow. From that point on they seemed to lose their interest in living. Overprotected and limited by her parents,

Rosario found refuge in solitude, silence, and the reading of books she took from her father's library. Her childhood was saddened by her inability to compete successfully against her brother, Benjamin, for their parents' affection. When Benjamin died of undiagnosed appendicitis, she was guilt-ridden because she blamed herself for wishing his death.

Rosario Castellanos was raised by a nursemaid, Rufina, a peasant woman who inspired love, admiration, and respect for the Indians, and introduced Castellanos to a world of myths and legends, elements that would play an important role in her writing. When she was seventeen, in 1942, her family moved to Mexico City. It was the first time she had left the provincial life-style of Comitán. Because of her natural shyness, she felt disoriented in the big city at first and sought refuge in her books. She attended the Luis G. León high school for two years before graduating. There she met Dolores Castro, who became a lifelong friend. During this period, Castellanos avidly read diverse authors, including Rubén Darío, Gabriela Mistral, and José Gorostiza, and familiarized herself with the strategies that differentiate poetry from prose.

At school she found that a group of students under the direction of Professor Agripino Gutiérrez was publishing a weekly literary journal, the *Estudiante*. When one of her school assignments on Greek tragedy was published there, she felt encouraged to send two poems, "Un verso" and "La muerte" (Death). On 20 March 1942 they were published along with an introductory note by Gutiérrez, who predicted she would become a great poet. He noticed in her a "very special bitterness."

In 1944 she was admitted to the Universidad Nacional Autónoma de México to study law, but during the second semester she switched to philosophy and literature. She became a member of the "Generation of the 1950s," a group of intellectuals who sought to rediscover humanism after World War II. In that circle she confirmed her vocation as a writer. Literature became the reaffirmation of her existence, the companion of her solitude, and the spiritual comfort she never found at home.

Her first book of poems, *Apuntes para una declaración de fe* (Notes for a Declaration of Faith), was published in 1948, and her parents died later that year. Although there was only a weak link between parents and daughter, she was devastated by their death, which is evident in the poet-

Castellanos at age eighteen, when she was attending high school in Mexico City

ry she wrote afterward. Her uncle Jesús Figueroa took her into his house and provided much-needed support.

Two years later, in June 1950, she earned a master's degree in philosophy. The following year she received a grant from Cultura Hispánica de Madrid to study with the Spanish writer Dámaso Alonso. She invited her friend Dolores Castro to travel with her, and together they visited Paris, Rome, Florence, and Vienna. In Rapallo, Italy, they met the Chilean Nobel Prize winner Gabriela Mistral. Upon returning to Mexico in 1952, Castellanos was commissioned to work in the region where she spent her childhood, promoting cultural events as part of the activities of the Instituto de Ciencias y Artes. During the brief period she spent in Chiapas, she rediscovered the folklore and the Indian mythology that surrounded her as a child. This happy time in her life came to an abrupt end when Castellanos, ill with tuberculosis, had to return to Mexico City. Her convalescence lasted a year, in which she spent her time reading, defining herself, and thinking about the direction she would like her life to take. This period of growth was extended in 1954, when she was granted a one-year fellowship by the Centro Mexicano de Escritores, a prize she shared with Juan Rulfo.

With renewed strength, Castellanos obtained a position at the Instituto Nacional Indigenista in 1956. She was sent to the Centro Coordinador Tzetzal-Tzotzil de San Cristóbal de las Casas, in Chiapas. Following the love teachings of Simone Weil, whom she admired, Castellanos became actively involved in a social issue that had always interested her: the plight of the Indians. She championed the idea of incorporating the Indians into modern culture by educating them. To supplement their education, she wrote and acted in a series of vignettes for a theater group called Teatro Guñol Petul, in which she dramatized exemplary situations for the Indians (the vignettes were collected and published in 1962). The task was arduous since the group traveled to remote Indian villages that lacked accessible roads. Her personal aim was to incorporate the Indian into national life. To achieve this end, she wrote several pamphlets for the Indians, such as *La constitución* (1960), which explains the rights they have under Mexican law.

The return to Chiapas gave Castellanos the opportunity to come to terms with her own past. The result was her first novel. *Balún-Canán* was published in 1957, received the Premio Chiapas in 1958, and was translated as *The Nine Guardians* in 1959. Divided into three parts, the novel features the first and final sections being narrated by a seven-year-old female child, and the second by an omniscient narrator. The child's narration centers on growing up with a brother who receives preferential treatment from the parents because he is male. The narrator seeks affection from her nursemaid, an Indian who becomes her substitute mother and introduces her to an alternative world: the Mesoamerican cosmogony. Once initiated, the narrator believes in the power of Indian magic, thus explaining why she feels guilty for the role she thinks she played in her brother's death, as he is the victim of an Indian curse. In spite of the disquieting ending of the novel—with a guilt-ridden narrator—the beauty of the poetic imagery used by the child-narrator to highlight the Indian oral tradition creates a balance that offsets the theme of oppression.

The section narrated by an omniscient narrator follows the tribulations of a landholder family from Chiapas, the Argüellos, who attempt to keep their land amidst the implementation of agrarian reform in the 1930s and 1940s. With this historical context as background, the novel revolves around the antagonistic position of Indians and whites, who are at the opposite poles of an economic conflict. The novel also presents women being oppressed sexually by men who belong to the same or higher social class or race. Female Indians are the most exploited of all.

Castellanos uses language very carefully in this novel, because language is a system that is deeply embedded in the fabric of exploitation; it is one factor that determines social position. For the Indians the inability to communicate in Spanish means exclusion, but a Spanish-speaking Indian does not fare much better, since he is scorned by whites who consider Spanish to be their exclusive privilege.

In spite of the poetic language, the novel has a serious shortcoming: the limited awareness of the child-narrator. She is not capable of arriving at a satisfactory closure, one that would adequately tie up all the dynamics raised throughout the novel. Nonetheless, *Balún-Canán* was a success and contributed to Castellanos's growing reputation as a writer.

Although acclaimed for her literary achievement, Castellanos felt lonely most of her life. While other children played, she preferred to read. Since she felt guilty for her brother's death, she tried to accomplish what he was unable to do. He would have become a professional of some sort, she thought, so she became a professional writer. However, her very triumphs kept possible suitors away. One can assume that even during her mature years many men felt threatened by her and opted to keep away. After a second stay in Chiapas, her loneliness became more acute, but she fought it with an unusual amount of work. In January 1958, when Castellanos was thirty-three, late for Mexican standards, she married Ricardo Guerra, a philosopher who, according to Castellanos at the time of her wedding, not only respected her literary career but also encouraged her to pursue it further. However, she soon realized that he was not impressed with her achievements: on the contrary, he often boasted about not having read any of her works. After two miscarriages, in 1961 she gave birth to a son, Gabriel, a source of immense happiness for her. The birth of a son opened a new world for Castellanos: that of motherhood. However, the happiness Gabriel brought to her marriage was

A 1962 meeting of writers: (standing) Juan Rulfo, José Emilio Pacheco, and Juan García Ponce; (seated) Carlos Valdés, Castellanos, and Alberto Dallal

an island, since her conjugal life turned sour. As early as 1963 she stated that her marriage was strictly monogamous on her part and totally polygamous on his. They cohabitated, but led their own lives. The marriage ended in 1971.

In 1960 Castellanos published *Ciudad Real* (Royal City), a collection of short stories, which won her the Premio Xavier Villaurrutia the same year. The book was the result of her experiences while working at the Instituto Nacional Indigenista. She dedicated the book to the institute for its efforts to change the social conditions of the Indians. The ten stories offer a variety of situations that arise when two races come into contact. From the beginning the Indians are characterized as displaced people who have lost both their land and their will to the advances of the white man. Consequently they hold a justifiable distrust of individuals who are not of their own race. The collection ranges from the Indians' pagan practices to their indoctrination into Catholicism; events include lofty activities, such as educating the Indians, as well as the grotesque, as in the passage where Indians are burned alive in a hut. Throughout the book Indians are portrayed as poor, humble, superstitious, ignorant, discriminated against, exploited, and often perceived as less than humans. As is often the case in indigenous literature, their misfortunes have an economic reason. The situation in which they are trapped is illustrated by the commentary of a woman in "El círculo del hambriento" (The Circle of the Hungry). She opposes the idea of educating the Indians because, when they become aware of their rights, they demand the right price for their goods and just pay for their labor—this raises prices for the white consumer, she argues.

The exploitation also crosses sexual lines as depicted in "Modesta Gómez." In this story Jorgito, son of a well-to-do family, the Romelias, forces himself on his longtime adolescent female Indian companion, the title character. His mother reluctantly consents to his sexual activities. However, when Modesta gets pregnant, Doña Romelia throws her out of the house, saying that she would be a bad example for the Romelia daughters. The female Indian is not only objectified, she is also the victim of a hypocritical double standard. When women of the middle class have been trapped fulfilling traditional roles destined for them, or even when they fail to attain the status of mothers and wives, the narratives tend to place them in ironic situations. For example, a self-sacrificing woman is mother to a squandering son; old spinsters are viewed as ridiculous misers or pious churchgoers. This ironic distancing from women who do not transcend the patriarchal roles imposed on them was to become Castellanos's major leitmotif throughout her fiction. The narrative voice is more impartial when female Indian characters have to struggle economically just to be mothers for their children.

In the last two stories of the book, the point of view is that of humanitarian groups who come to aid the Indians in their struggle. The new kind of relation established between whites and Indians allows the stories to focus on the cultural differences that must be overcome in order to incorporate the Indians into modern society. One of these obstacles is language. Language is not only a means of communication, but above all it is a system by which a culture codifies its concept of social order. To teach the Indians a modern language consequently also means to submit them to a process of cultural colonization. This transculturization can be dangerous if only the interests of the colonizer are considered, as is the case in "Arthur Smith salva su alma" (Arthur Smith Saves His Soul). At other times, as in "El círculo del hambriento," the benefactors are just as inhumane as the oppressors: a doctor lets an Indian child die because the parents cannot afford medicine.

Ciudad Real is written in a rich, expressive prose, at times mixed with regional colloquialisms. However, the lack of variation in the narration—nine of the ten stories are narrated by an omniscient narrator—leads one to believe that Castellanos had a didactic purpose in mind: to make the reader a witness to the system of exploitation under which Indians live. She falls into the same trap that many indigenous writers have encountered: the paternalistic attitude of the writer who sees the Indians as a helpless race. Nevertheless, *Ciudad Real* established Castellanos as an important Mexican indigenous writer, one who had a deep understanding of Indian culture and a firm conviction to expose the oppression of the natives.

From 1960 to 1966 Castellanos served as chair of the Department of Journalism and Information at the Universidad Nacional Autónoma de México (UNAM), while simultaneously teaching Spanish-American literature at the same university. Her importance as a journalist was confirmed in 1963, when Julio Scherer García invited her to write a weekly editorial for the newspaper *Excélsior*, an activity she fulfilled until the end of her life. The thematic scope of her editorials—collected in *El uso de la palabra* (The Use of the Word, 1975)—ranges over a variety of aspects of Mexican society, feminism, literary criticism, biographical sketches of notable men and women, and personal notes based on her life, including her experiences as the Mexican ambassador to Israel (1971-1974).

Oficio de tinieblas (The Dark Service), published in 1962, received the Premio Sor Juana Inés de la Cruz. With this novel Castellanos established herself as a dominant author. Joseph Sommers, an important early critic of Castellanos, considered this novel to be her best work and a stepping-stone in the reorientation of the indigenous novel in Spanish America.

Catalina Díaz Puiljá, the female Indian protagonist of *Oficio de tinieblas*, emerges as a fully developed character. This is a significant accomplishment, especially in light of the fact that Latin-American novelists had not until then succeeded in portraying convincing Indian characters in the context of their own culture. Catalina is a barren woman who compensates for her shortcoming by becoming an *ilol*, a magic healer and interpreter of mystical Tzotzil Indian beliefs in the supernatural.

The novel is based on a historical event, the uprising of the Chamula Indians in San Cristóbal de las Casas in 1867, which ended with the crucifixion of one of the Indians, who was proclaimed the indigenous Christ. However, as Castellanos explained, as she was writing the novel, little by little history yielded a fictional account. She started by placing the action in a more familiar historical context: in the 1930s, during the epoch of Cárdenas and the implementation of land reform in Chiapas. Again Castellanos dialectically opposes Indians and ladinos in a situation that influences all aspects and levels of life in traditional San Cristóbal de las Casas, a provincial center in Chiapas. The novel seems conceived according to one of the principles of Weil, that when oppressor and oppressed are bound in a relation, "the current of evil goes from the strong to the weak and returns again to the strong." Thus the most striking common characteristic of white society is the degree to which its religious and political institutions and its entire system of values have been corroded by a mixture of hate and fear of the Indians, who are regarded as inferiors and basically unredeemable, but upon whom the white society depends for its livelihood.

In the novel the historical struggle for the possession of the land is interpreted according to Tzotzil beliefs. The Indians interpret the present in the light of the mysterious, and often terror-ridden, past. The reenactment of mythical structures accounts for the Tzotzils' ahistorical conception of time, in which the past is depicted as conditioning the acceptance and understanding of the present. At the end of the story the defeated Indian rebellion is synthesized, not in terms of battles won or lost, but in a newly mythologized present. Castellanos, then, transcends the narrow social objectives of the indigenous writer—a label from which she always disassociated herself—to inscribe a neo-indigenous modality, one that incorporates in the narration the Indians' mythical perception of reality.

The writing of *Los convidados de agosto* (The Guests of August), published in 1964, coincided with the failure of her marriage, and this may have influenced the tone of the three short stories and the short novel therein, where humor is absolutely eschewed. Also noticeable is the calculated contempt felt by the narrator toward female characters who seek marriage and motherhood as the limit of their expectations. Spinsterhood, the resigned acceptance of traditional roles, or the failed attempt to transcend Comitán's middle-class sexual politics are some of the themes developed in the stories. Castellanos's mastery of narrative techniques, already apparent in *Oficio de tinieblas*, and her ability to capture lyrical moments in the concise space of a poem combine in *Los convidados de agosto*.

Helene M. Anderson has rightly summarized the female characters of *Los convidados de agosto* as "restless adolescents on the threshold of womanhood, impatient to claim its experiences and rewards; or spinsters who, in a desperate attempt to break the structures that enclose them, surrender themselves on summer nights to strange men, 'without resistance, without enthusiasm, without sensuality, without remorse,' but in some last effort to give meaning to their lives.... They are women left at life's periphery, abandoned by fathers and lovers, whose role is to wait, for there is nothing more dishonorable than initiating a thrust into life. Time and again, the female characters in Castellanos' stories wait."

The title story, the best piece of the collection, dramatizes the day Emelina, an aging spinster, breaks the tedium of waiting and puts her-

Rosario Castellanos

self in a position where she may be found by a man. The first part of the story is written in the best Proustian tradition, reviving past memories and capturing strong emotions, such as the protagonist's repressed sexuality. The separation of the sexes in Comitán is strict, and the story also illustrates the duplicity that governs this society, where men are allowed to do as they please while women are supposed to stay home and wait passively for someone to come along.

In "Román, el viudo" (Román, the Widower) Romelia has just become a wife and is savoring the prestige of her newly acquired status. But the day after the wedding she is returned to her parents' home because Román alleges she was not a virgin. In reality she is the victim of Román's revenge, for he uses her to avenge the supposed affair of his deceased wife and Rafael, Romelia's older brother. Her father does not listen to her plea of innocence but believes the husband's version of the story, because he views Román as a man of honor. To carry out his perverse purpose, Román simply employs the mechanisms patriarchal society has set in place to perpetuate its way of life, thus making unjust demands on women.

After Castellanos gave up her post at UNAM in support of Dr. Ignacio Chávez, when he was asked to leave the presidency of the university in 1966, she traveled to the United States for a year as a visiting fellow at the Universities of Wisconsin, Indiana, and Colorado. Upon returning to Mexico, she was named "Woman of the Year" and also received the Premio Carlos Trouyet for her whole oeuvre. From 1967 until 1971 she again taught at UNAM.

In her 1971 book of fiction, *Album de familia*, Castellanos abandons her characteristic serious tone and presents short stories full of biting humor and irony. She invites her readers to laugh, while at the same time forcing them to ponder the events that caused the laughter. The shift in setting from the provincial town to the city allows the emergence of more contemporary themes, such as the marriage of a professional woman, extramarital affairs, homosexuality, and abortion; readers also encounter characters close to Castellanos's personal reality: women writers.

In "Lección de cocina" (Cooking Lesson) a newlywed philosophically approaches the change of responsibilities she has acquired as a consequence of her new status. Narrated in the first person in a direct, informal style, the story is built upon a binary opposition that confronts the protagonist's inner self: she is a sophisticated urban professional, but with a set of servant's activities she must perform as a married woman. The main metaphor seems to be that any illusions this newlywed may have had about marriage go up in smoke, just as the steak that burns up on the grill.

"Album de familia," the title novella—first written as a play, *Tablero de damas* (Checkerboard, 1952)—thrusts the reader into the sphere of women writers. For the most part the story maintains its initial dramatic form, for what predominates is a heated discussion between the writer Matilde's old disciples, an exchange that at times becomes confusing since most identifying rhetorical tags—"X or Y said"—have been deleted from this minimally mediated narrative. Behind the assured facade of the disciples there are women who have not yet been true to themselves. Their own discourses—mindless squabbles—reveal a behavior stereotypically attributed to women, mainly jealousy and hypocrisy, to which have been added other pitfalls such as alcoholism and promiscuity. Only Matilde, the laureate poet who has pursued poetry as a means toward self-knowledge, has lived an authentic life. However, at the end of her life, solitude is her only reward.

Although Castellanos's female characters are not able to break away from the confinements in which patriarchal society has placed them, her own life continued reaching unexpected heights. In 1971, the year of her divorce, she was named Mexican ambassador to Israel. She traveled with her son, Gabriel, who had become a major focal point in her life. Once again she kept an overwhelming pace: she performed her ambassadorial duties, disseminated fervently the Mexican culture in the Jewish state, was invited to teach Latin-American literature at the Universities of Jerusalem and Tel Aviv, completed another book of essays, and continued sending her weekly editorial to *Excélsior*. For the first time Castellanos seemed to be at peace with herself; she was perceived to be happy. Unfortunately her life came to an abrupt end on 7 August 1974, when after a bath, with her feet still wet, she tried to turn on a lamp and was electrocuted on the spot. She was forty-nine years old. Her body was returned to Mexico for burial.

Women identify with Rosario Castellanos not in spite of her ups and downs but because of them. They see in her a woman who painfully but triumphantly fought against a hostile environment that tended to devalue women just because of their gender. She longed for a family she never had, both as a child and as a married woman. But even if solitude was her eternal baggage, those who knew her remember her contagious laughter, the grace, and the humor she gave lavishly to those who came into contact with her. When she criticized her own works, she did it severely, constantly devaluing their worth. Castellanos gave herself lovingly to others without asking much in return: to the Indians, to her students, and to her readers. For Castellanos's life and her literature are reflections of each other; they present a world divided in need of reconciliation.

Interviews:

Luis Adolfo Domínguez, "Entrevista con Rosario Castellanos," *Revista de Bellas Artes* (January-February 1969): 16-23;

Augustín Antonio Albarracín, "Imagen del 'México Nuevo' en la Colina de la Primavera," *Universal* (17 September 1971): 16;

Günter W. Lorenz, "Rosario Castellanos," in his *Diálogo con Latinoamérica* (Santiago, Chile: Pomaire, 1972), pp. 187-211;

Dolores Cárdenas, "Rosario Castellanos: La mujer mexicana, cómplice de su verdugo," *Revista de Revistas*, 22 (November 1972): 24-27;

Margarita García Flores, "Rosario Castellanos: La lucidez como forma de vida," *Onda*, supplement to *Novedades* (18 August 1974): 6-7;

Mary Lou Dabdoub, "Ultima charla con Rosario Castellanos," *Revista de Revistas*, 119 (September 1974): 44-46.

Biography:

Oscar Bonifaz, *Rosario* (Mexico City: Presencia Latinoamericana, 1984).

References:

Marjorie Agosin, "Rosario Castellanos ante el espejo," *Cuadernos Americanos*, 43 (March-April 1984): 219-226;

Maureen Ahern and Mary Sealy Vásquez, eds., *Homenaje a Rosario Castellanos* (Valencia, Spain: Albatros Hispanofila, 1980);

Helene M. Anderson, "Rosario Castellanos and the Structures of Power," in *Contemporary Women Authors of Latin America*, edited by Doris Meyer and Margarite Fernández Olmos (Brooklyn: Brooklyn College Press, 1983), pp. 22-32;

Mario Benedetti, "Rosario Castellanos y la incomunicación racial," in his *Letras del continente mestizo* (Montevideo: Arca, 1967), pp. 130-135;

Julieta Campos, "La novela mexicana después de 1940," in her *La imagen en el espejo* (Mexico City: UNAM, 1965), pp. 141-157;

Emmanuel Carballo, "Rosario Castellanos: La historia de sus libros contada por ella misma," in his *Diecinueve protagonistas de la literatura mexicana del siglo XX* (Mexico City: Empresas, 1965), pp. 411-422;

Laura Lee Crumley de Pérez, "*Balún-Canán* y la construcción narrativa de una cosmovisión indígena," *Revista Iberoamericana*, 50 (April-June 1984): 491-503;

Frances R. Dorward, "The Function of Interiorization in *Oficio de tinieblas*," *Neophilologus*, 69 (July 1985): 374-385;

Rosa María Fiscal, "Identidad y lenguaje en los personajes femeninos de Rosario Castellanos," *Chasqui*, 14 (1985): 25-35;

Fiscal, *La imagen de la mujer en la narrativa de Rosario Castellanos* (Mexico City: UNAM, 1980);

María Estela Franco, *Rosario Castellanos: Semblanza psicoanalítica; Otra forma de ser humano y libre* (Mexico City: Plaza & Janes, 1984);

Donald H. Frischmann, "El sistema patriarcal y las relaciones heterosexuales en *Balún-Canán*, de Rosario Castellanos," *Revista Iberoamericana*, 51 (July-December 1985): 665-678;

Alfonso González, "Lenguaje y protesta en *Oficio de tinieblas*," *Revista de Estudios Hispánicos*, 9 (October 1975): 441-450;

Naomi Lindstrom, "Women's Expression and Narrative Technique in Rosario Castellanos's *In Darkness*," *Modern Language Studies*, 13 (Summer 1983): 71-80;

Almudena Mejías Alonso, "La narrativa de Rosario Castellanos y el indigenismo," *Cuadernos Americanos*, 44 (May-June 1985): 204-217;

Beth Miller, "Female Characterization and Contexts in Rosario Castellanos' *Album de familia*," *American Hispanist*, 32-33 (January-February 1979): 26-30;

Miller, "El feminismo mexicano de Rosario Castellanos," in her *Mujeres en la literatura* (Mexico City: Fleischer, 1978), pp. 9-19; and "Personajes y personas: Castellanos, Fuentes, Poniatowska y Sainz," pp. 65-75;

Miller, "Historia y ficción en *Oficio de tinieblas*," *Texto Crítico*, 10 (January-April 1984): 131-142;

Miller, "Rosario Castellanos' *Guests in August*: Critical Realism and the Provincial Middle Class," *Latin American Literary Review*, 7 (1979): 5-19;

Willy O. Muñoz, "*Los convidados de agosto*: Acercamiento a un texto posible," *Letras Femeninas*, 16 (1990): 51-58;

Muñoz, "Enmarcando la locura en *Los convidados de agosto*," *Hispanófila*, 101 (January 1991): 77-86;

Elena Poniatowska, "Rosario Castellanos: Rostro que ríe, rostro que llora," *Revista Canadiense de Estudios Hispánicos*, 14 (1990): 495-509;

Poniatowska, "Rosario Castellanos: !Vida, nada te debo!," in her *¡Ay vida, no me mereces! Carlos Fuentes, Rosario Castellanos, Juan Rulfo: La literatura de la onda* (Mexico City: Mortiz, 1985), pp. 43-132;

Marta Portal, "*Oficio de tinieblas*," in her *Proceso narrativo de la revolución mexicana* (Madrid: Cultura Hispánica, 1977), pp. 212-221;

Phyllis Rodríguez-Peralta, "Images of Women in Rosario Castellanos' Prose," *Latin American Literary Review*, 6 (Fall-Winter 1977): 68-80;

A Rosario Castellanos: Sus amigos (Mexico City: Año Internacional de la Mujer, 1975);

Stacey Schlau, "Conformity and Resistance to Enclosure: Female Voices in Rosario Castellanos' *Oficio de tinieblas (The Dark Service)*," *Latin American Literary Review*, 12 (Spring-Summer 1984): 45-57;

Perla Schwartz, *Rosario Castellanos: Mujer que supo latín . . .* (Mexico City: Katún, 1984);

Nina Scott, "Rosario Castellanos: Demythification Through Laughter," *Humor: International Journal of Humor Research*, 2 (1989): 19-30;

Joseph Sommers, "Changing View of the Indian in Mexican Literature," *Hispania*, 47 (March 1964): 47-55;

Sommers, "El ciclo de Chiapas: Nueva corriente literaria," *Cuadernos Americanos*, 23 (March-April 1964): 246-261;

Sommers, "Forma e ideología en *Oficio de tinieblas* de Rosario Castellanos," *Revista de Crítica Latinoamericana*, 4, nos. 7-8 (1978): 73-91;

Sommers, "The Indian-Oriented Novel in Latin America: New Spirit, New Forms, New Scope," *Journal of Inter-American Studies*, 6 (April 1964): 249-265;

Sommers, "Rosario Castellanos: Nuevo enfoque del indio mexicano," *La Palabra y el Hombre*, 29 (1964): 83-88.

Julio Cortázar

(26 August 1914 - 12 February 1984)

Steven Boldy
Emmanuel College, Cambridge

BOOKS: *Presencia*, as Julio Denis (Buenos Aires: Bibliófilo, 1938);

Los reyes (Buenos Aires: Gulab & Aldabahor, 1949);

Bestiario (Buenos Aires: Sudamericana, 1951);

Final del juego (Mexico City: Presentes, 1956; enlarged edition, Buenos Aires: Sudamericana, 1964); translated by Paul Blackburn in *End of the Game, and Other Stories* (New York: Pantheon, 1967; London: Collins, 1968); republished as *Blow-up, and Other Stories* (New York: Collier, 1968);

Las armas secretas (Buenos Aires: Sudamericana, 1959);

Los premios (Buenos Aires: Sudamericana, 1960); translated by Elaine Kerrigan as *The Winners* (New York: Pantheon, 1965);

Historias de cronopios y de famas (Buenos Aires: Minotauro, 1962); translated by Blackburn as *Cronopios and Famas* (New York: Pantheon, 1969);

Rayuela (Buenos Aires: Sudamericana, 1963); translated by Gregory Rabassa as *Hopscotch* (New York: Pantheon, 1966; London: Collins, 1967);

Todos los fuegos el fuego (Buenos Aires: Sudamericana, 1966); translated by Suzanne Jill Levine as *All Fires the Fire* (New York: Pantheon, 1973);

La vuelta al día en ochenta mundos (Mexico City: Siglo XXI, 1967); translated by Thomas Christensen as *Around the Day in Eighty Worlds* (San Francisco: North Point, 1986);

El perseguidor, y otros cuentos (Buenos Aires: América Latina, 1967);

62: Modelo para armar (Buenos Aires: Sudamericana, 1968); translated by Rabassa as *62: A Model Kit* (New York: Pantheon, 1972);

Ultimo round (Mexico City: Siglo XXI, 1969);

Viaje alrededor de una mesa (Buenos Aires: Rayuela, 1970);

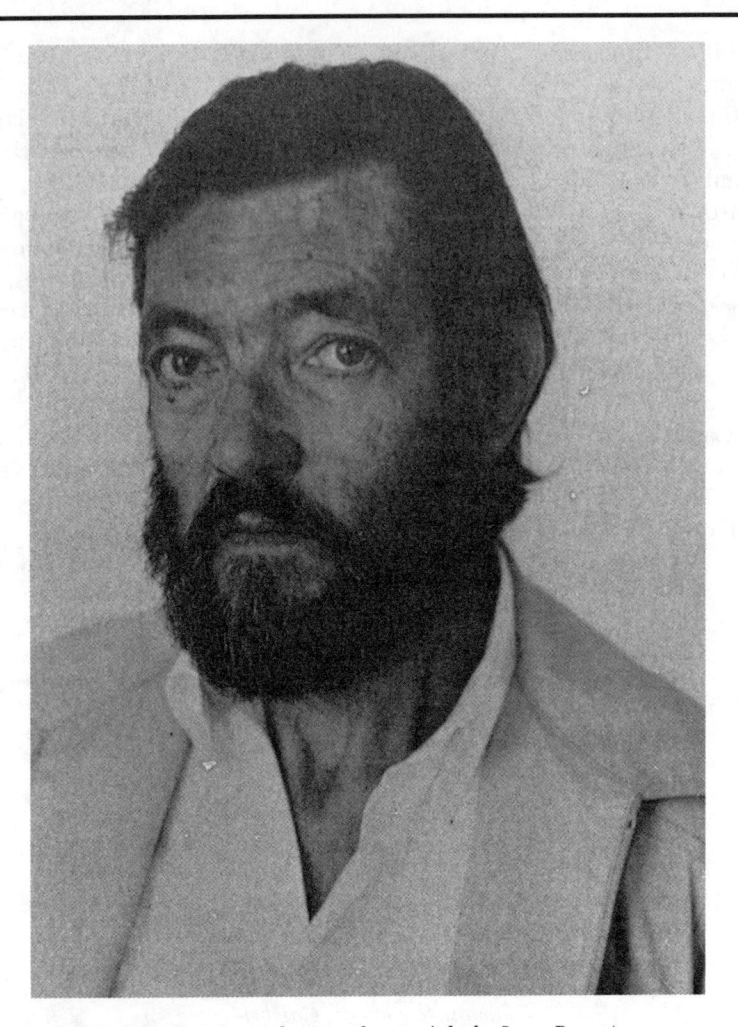

Julio Cortázar (photograph copyright by Jerry Bauer)

Pameos y meopas (Barcelona: OCNOS, 1971);
La isla a mediodía y otros relatos (Estella, Spain: Salvat, 1971);
Prosa del observatorio (Barcelona: Lumen, 1972);
Libro de Manuel (Buenos Aires: Sudamericana, 1973); translated by Rabassa as *A Manual for Manuel* (New York: Pantheon, 1978);
Reunión (Santiago, Chile: Quimantu, 1973);
La casilla de los Morelli, edited by Julio Ortega (Barcelona: Tusquets, 1973);
Octaedro (Buenos Aires: Sudamericana, 1974); translated by Rabassa in *A Change of Light and Other Stories* (New York: Knopf, 1980);
Vampiros multinacionales (Mexico City: Excélsior, 1975);
Alguien que anda por ahí (Madrid: Alfaguara, 1977); translated by Rabassa in *A Change of Light and Other Stories*;
Un tal Lucas (Madrid: Alfaguara, 1979); translated by Rabassa as *A Certain Lucas* (New York: Knopf, 1984);
Queremos tanto a Glenda (Mexico City: Nueva Imagen, 1980); translated by Rabassa in *We Love Glenda So Much and A Change of Light* (New York: Vintage, 1984);
Deshoras (Mexico City: Nueva Imagen, 1983);
Nicaragua tan violentamente dulce, by Cortázar and Carol Dunlop (Barcelona: Muchnik, 1983);
Los autonautas de la cosmopista, by Cortázar and Dunlop (Barcelona: Muchnik, 1983);
Cuaderno de bitácora de "Rayuela," by Cortázar and A. M. Barrenechea (Buenos Aires: Sudamericana, 1983);
Salvo el crepúsculo (Mexico City: Nueva Imagen, 1984);
El examen (Buenos Aires: Sudamericana, 1986).

Collections: *Cuentos*, edited by Antón Arrufat (Havana: Casa de las Américas, 1964);
Ceremonias (Barcelona: Seix Barral, 1968)—comprises *Final del juego* and *Las armas secretas*;
Relatos (Buenos Aires: Sudamericana, 1970);

Antología, edited by Nicolás Bratosevich (Buenos Aires: Librería del Colegio, 1975);
Los relatos, 3 volumes (Madrid: Alianza, 1976).

TRANSLATION: Edgar Allan Poe, *Obras en prosa* (Madrid: Ediciones de la Universidad de Puerto Rico, 1956).

In all that Julio Cortázar ever wrote, be it novel, short story, play, poem, essay, or collage, he pitted all his intelligence, passion, and playful humor against unthinking acceptance of the given, the automatic, and the imposed, and sought to discover and forge a wider, freer, more authentic definition of humanity. The explosive revelation and the tenderness of his texts together with the example of independence and solidarity of the man stand as important examples in Latin-American letters.

Born on 26 August 1914 to Argentinian parents, Julio José Cortázar and María Herminia Descotte de Cortázar, who were in Brussels on a business trip during the German invasion, Cortázar did not travel to Argentina until four years later. When he returned to Europe for good at the age of thirty-seven, his destiny as an essentially Argentinian and Latin-American writer was set. Without the European perspective, however, and the wide, eclectic European culture that is the hallmark of the Argentinian intellectual, novels such as *Rayuela* (1963; translated as *Hopscotch*, 1966) would not have been possible. Something similar is true of the complex dual perspective of novels by the Cuban Alejo Carpentier such as *Los pasos perdidos* (1953; translated as *The Lost Steps*, 1956).

Cortázar was brought up with his sister, Ofelia, in the Buenos Aires suburb of Bánfield after their father abandoned the family. Though Cortázar described to Graciela de Sola his early life in a big, animal-filled garden as paradise, he added that this memory is tinged by excessive sensitivity and frequent sadness. He soon began to feel asphyxiated by the narrowness of family life, he explained, when for example his relatives threw a party to celebrate their acquisition of a refrigerator. Cortázar was a precocious reader with a special preference for so-called fantastic literature, and at the Mariano Acosta school, where he studied, he retreated into a small group of literary-minded friends and the patronage of teachers who fostered the passion for the classics that colors his early poetry, and who tried (unsuccessfully) to publish his schoolboy essay on Pindar.

Cortázar as a young man in Buenos Aires

In 1932 he qualified to teach primary school and in 1935 as a secondary-school teacher. After he spent just one year in studies at the Universidad de Buenos Aires, his family's economic situation forced him to accept teaching posts in the remote provincial towns of Bolívar and Chivilcoy, where he read large quantities of foreign literature and polished some sonnets of his. From 1944 to 1945 he taught French literature at the Universidad de Cuyo in Mendoza but chose to resign in 1946 after being involved in political agitation against Juan Perón, for which he was briefly imprisoned. After returning to Buenos Aires, Cortázar took an administrative post in the Cámara Argentina del Libro (Argentine Book Chamber), a publishing group, and from 1948, after rapidly completing a degree as public translator, he exercised that profession until 1951. In 1949 he traveled to France and Italy. The best account of his reaction to his country on his return is to be found in the poems of "Razones de la cólera" (Reasons for Anger), some of which were published in 1971 in *Pameos y meopas* ("Peoms and Meops") but which are best read with the accompanying commentary by Cortázar in *Salvo el crepúsculo* (Save the Twilight; published in the year of his death, 1984), in which "Razones" appears in its entirety.

Cortázar's first publication was *Presencia* (Presence, 1938), a slim volume of sonnets under the pseudonym Julio Denis, which were characteristic of the "Generation of the 1940s," a group that included his friend Daniel Devoto. Cortázar had also written many stories, but he did not begin to publish them until they came up to his stringent standards. In 1944 in the magazine *Correo Literario* he published a "fantastic" short story, "La bruja" (The Witch), which he never included in any anthology, and in 1946 and then 1948, in *Los Anales de Buenos Aires*, Jorge Luis Borges published Cortázar's first major stories, "Casa tomada" (House Taken Over) and "Lejana" (Distant), which were later included in *Bestiario* (1951). In 1949 the dramatic, poetic *Los reyes* (The Kings) was published. The language is highly literary, even precious, but the reversal of accepted, ready-made structures, in this case those of myths, makes the work in many ways a paradigm of much of Cortázar's later production. The Greek king of the title, Minos, represents the repressive order of authority and the Freudian superego, while the monstrous Minotaur is the malignèd force of joy and sensuality. King Theseus of Athens is a feeble-headed automaton to whom Ariadne gives the thread so the Minotaur will be able to escape after killing Theseus (in a reversal of the legend). In most of his subsequent work, monsters will remain for Cortázar both a frightening threat to the everyday order and a source of liberation, an alternative, truer order.

By the mid 1940s, however, political events under Perón and his faction were threatening Cortázar and the Europeanist, rather elitist class of writers to which he belonged, including many of those associated with Victoria Ocampo's *Sur* magazine. A marked distaste for the atmosphere developing at the time is evident in Cortázar's *El examen* (The Examination), a novel written in 1950 but not published until 1986. After a nightmarish day in which two couples maintain endless conversations about the nature and fate of Argentina and wander the streets of Buenos Aires, where a threat that is clearly Peronism becomes a deadly plague, then a mysterious all-enveloping mist, and then causes crumbling streets, Juan and his fiancée leave for Europe. This is what Cortázar did, too, when in 1951 he left for Paris with a scholarship from the French government. In Paris he soon realized that if he were to be authentic, he could not cast off the mental and existential reality he had brought with him. Much of his later work is the chronicle of that return to his own personal, national, and continental reality. Oliveira, the hero of *Rayuela*, is his first character symbolically to return to Buenos Aires in his place.

Cortázar resided in France for the rest of his life, in Paris and later also in his summer house in Saignon, Provence. During most of those years he would spend some months working as a translator for UNESCO and then traveling widely. In 1953 he married another translator, Aurora Bernández, and their friendship was to survive their divorce some twenty years later. Late in his life he married a young Canadian writer, Carol Dunlop, who died of leukemia in 1982, and with whom he wrote several stories, including *Los autonautas de la cosmopista* (The Autonauts of the Cosmopike, 1983), an affectionate, surrealist account of a one-month trip down a French motorway. To the end Cortázar would go against the grain of the expected to try to see what the alienation of modern life makes invisible. For practical reasons he applied for French citizenship and was granted it by a special decree of President François Mitterand in 1981.

In the same year that he left Argentina (1951), Cortázar published his first collection of stories, *Bestiario*. There is much disagreement as to which is the essential Cortázar: the novelist or the short-story writer; there is little doubt, however, that together with his fellow countryman Borges he has written the best and most important corpus of short stories in the Spanish language. He was also a lucid thinker on the nature of the short-story genre and wrote some illuminating pieces, such as "Del cuento breve y sus alrededores" (Of the Short Story and Its Environs), in the collage work *Ultimo round* (Final Round, 1969), and "Del sentimiento de no estar del todo" (On the Feeling of Not Being Quite There), in another miscellany, *La vuelta al día en ochenta mundos* (1967; translated as *Around the Day in Eighty Worlds*, 1986). In the latter he argues that significant writing springs from a position of "extrañamiento" (strangeness) with regard to reality and rationality in the writer. In the *Ultimo round* piece he argues that stories are often the exorcizing of a neurosis or obsession, written in a sort of trance or "état second" (second state), as if simply transcribing an oneiric reality already formed in the deeper regions of the psyche. The story is thus autonomous from the author to an extent and deals in basically archetypal material through which it communicates directly with the reader.

These comments are generally borne out by the experience of reading his stories, except perhaps that the later stories become more self-conscious and intertextual, and are often skillfully calculated to carry a political dimension. What they manage in an unequaled manner is to question the hegemony, discrete separateness, and naturalness of the status quo, the ego, and socially accepted concepts of time, identity, and reality. These structures are questioned by being related to something different from them, what Cortázar has called "lo otro" (the other). This other might question, control, or become unexpectedly related to the given. Continuity between phenomena and dimensions occurs where one expects separateness, and discontinuity where one expects uniformity. One of the most basic structural features of the stories is analogy—between individuals, situations, and times—and a passage to another dimension suggested by such analogies. Models or forces that control the present and the lives of characters become of fundamental importance. Such models may take the form of the lives of people long dead, literary texts, myths, or even pieces of music. Related to this process is the giving of a fantastic, often vaguely animal shape to what has been repressed, feared, or ignored by an individual or group.

The discontinuity, surprise, or shock that decenters the character in some stories has varying effects. In "La autopista del Sur" (The Southern Thruway), from *Todos los fuegos el fuego* (1966; translated as *All Fires the Fire*, 1973), the traffic jam that lasts for several months causes primitive patterns of behavior as well as romances that sadly will not transfer back into normality. In "La banda" (The Band), in *Final del juego* (1956; translated in *End of the Game*, 1967), Lucio Medina, a cultured character, enters a cinema expecting to see an Anatole Litvak film but instead sees a large group of female employees of a shoe company marching up and down the stage and playing instruments awfully out of tune, while their families applaud. As a result of the experience and its philosophical aftermath, Medina abandons his profession and disappears from the country. In "Lugar llamado Kindberg" (A Place Called Kindberg), in *Octaedro* (1974; translated in *A Change of Light*, 1980), the charming encounter of the traveling salesman Marcelo with the sensual vitality of the young hitchhiker Lina drains his future life of meaning, and, after leaving her, he crashes into a plane tree at 160 KPH.

Continuities or disturbing links are established between very different sorts of realities. In *Bestiario*, for example, two stories show different but related links. When the identification is between individuals, the result is the doppelgänger: in "Lejana," for example, the middle-class Alina Reyes discovers, initially as a mental presence provoked by an anagram but later as a reality, that she has another self in a hungry, beaten beggarwoman in Budapest. The double is what she most fears, her opposite socially but also an image of her own suffering. In "Axolotl" the link is between species, as a man exchanges his identity with a fish. Continuities between individuals across time as well as space add an extra dimension, with obvious notions of metempsychosis, or an unconsciously imposed destiny. The heritage can be one of unexplainable violence, as when a fiancé is taken over by the presence of a dead Nazi rapist in the title story of *Las armas secretas* (The Secret Weapons, 1959); or a complex destiny of failure, as in stories such as "Segundo viaje" (Second Trip), in *Deshoras* (Out of Phase, 1983), where a mediocre boxer is inexplicably possessed of an enormous talent that takes him on exactly the same route through success to death as his most admired boxer and compatriot some years earlier. The lives of the musicians in

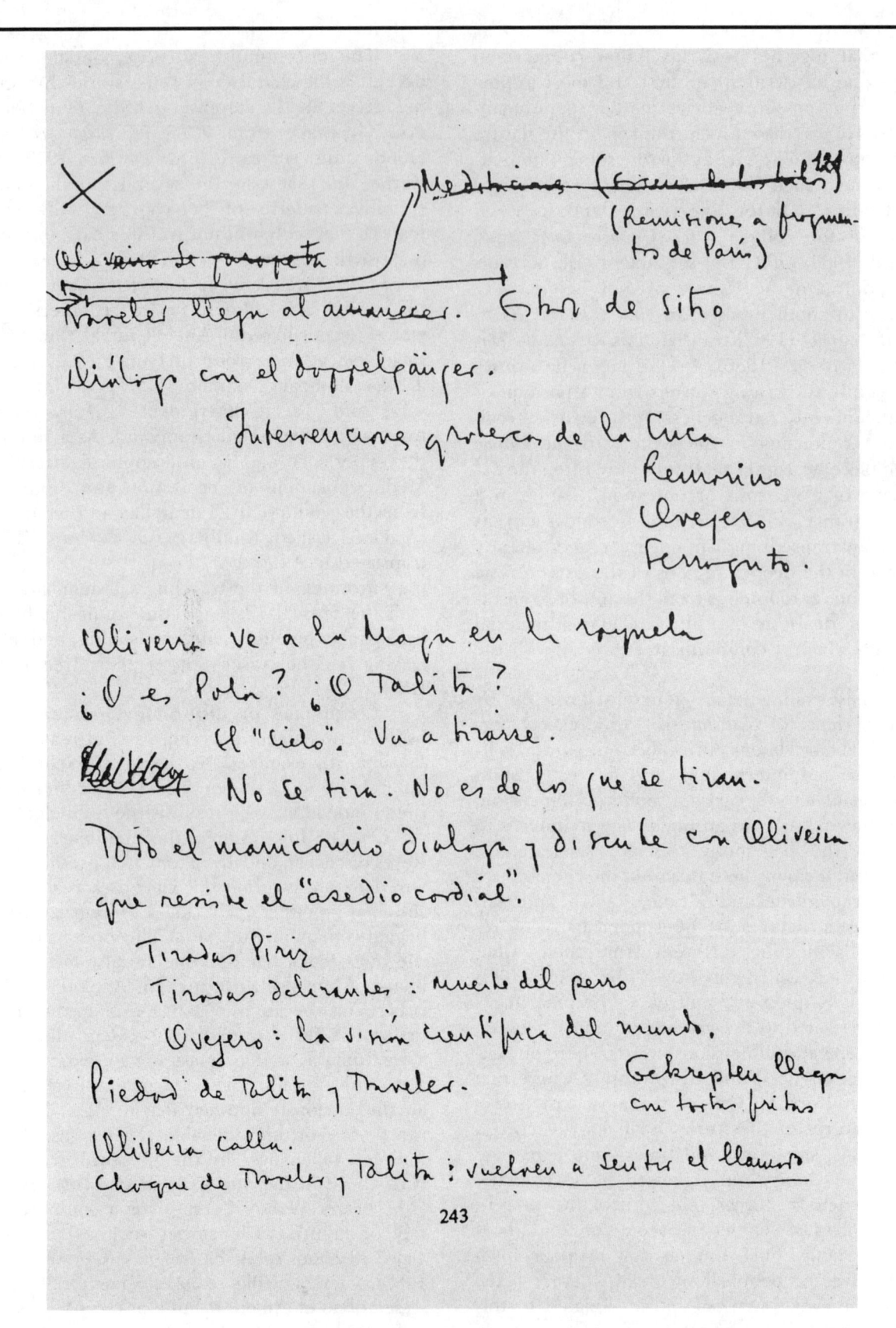

Pages from Cortázar's preliminary notes for Rayuela *(Collection of Ana Maria Barrenechea; by permission of the Estate of Julio Cortázar)*

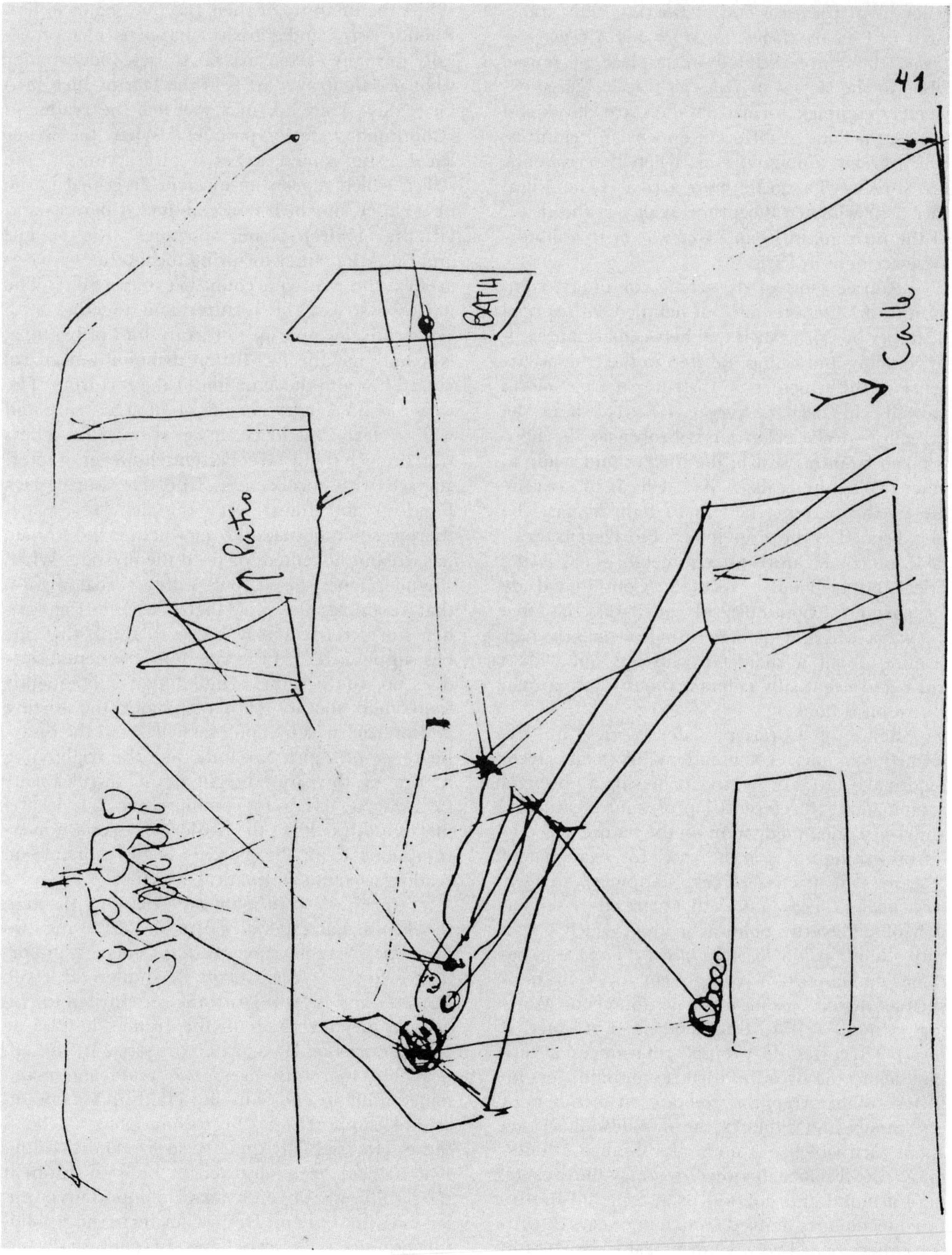
41
BATH
Calle
Patio

"Clone," in *Queremos tanto a Glenda* (1980; translated in *We Love Glenda So Much and A Change of Light*, 1984) are dictated by a piece of music, while in the stories of *Todos los fuegos el fuego* extremely complex formal parallels are developed between actions in different epochs and cultures, which create ambiguities, as when the reader is not sure in "La noche boca arriba" (The Night Face Up) whether the prime reality is the death of the protagonist in an Aztec war or in a motorcycle accident in Paris.

Another sort of disturbing continuity, common to the fantastic tale but handled with special dexterity by Cortázar, is that between art and reality, reading and acting. Related to the true occurrence of the structure is "Instrucciones para John Howell," in *Todos los fuegos el fuego*, where the spectator-spectacle barrier is broken as the hero is taken from his seat in the theater and made to enter a play; he realizes that, if he is to save the life of the heroine, he has to fight against the plot dictated by the script in order to avert its inevitable outcome. More purely metafictional is the brief and brilliantly executed "Continuidad de los parques" (Continuity of the Parks), in *Final del juego*, where a man is sitting in an armchair reading about a character who sets out with a knife and eventually enters a room where a man is reading a book....

Some of Cortázar's later stories are extremely complex combinations of many techniques and levels of writing, achieving a powerful combination of referential prose, intertextuality, and a sustained meditation on the nature and ethics of writing. This is the case, for example, of "Recortes de prensa" (Press Clippings), in *Queremos tanto a Glenda*, a story that marks the culmination of his overtly political writing, which began with "Reunión," in *Todos los fuegos el fuego*, and became an important component of collections such as *Alguien que anda por ahí* (Someone Walking Around, 1977; translated in *A Change of Light*). "Recortes de prensa" reproduces a clipping about the dreadful tortures and murders inflicted by the Argentine military on members of one family and explores the morality of writing about such violence from a safe distance. It questions the distance between writing and reality, here a moral and political issue using all the refined techniques derived from many years of writing experience. The woman narrator, in Paris, is asked by a sculptor friend to write a text to accompany some of his sculptures on the theme of violence. She then shows the sculptor the clipping. While the intensity of their reaction seems to link Buenos Aires and Paris, as happens metaphorically in many early Cortázar stories, they wonder what use their own art is in the face of such brutal reality. They are in a way like the reader in "Continuidad de los parques." When the writer leaves, she comes across a girl crying in the street, which repeats an incident described in the newspaper, in which police abducted parents and left the children alone. She goes with the girl and finds the father torturing the mother with cigarettes: the written account becomes reality. The narrator strikes the torturer and together with the victim ties him up to torture him in his turn. Not only has the fact-fiction dichotomy been reversed but also the situation of the torturers. The writer is no longer "on the good side," safe and with a clear conscience that it is only the others who do such things. Her account, however, is interspersed with recollections from literature (Jack London) and films. Over the next few pages there is some hesitation over whether the woman has dreamt, invented, or lived the episode. When she telephones the sculptor with a verbal account that resembles the plot, then tells him that it is her story, readers may begin to think that she has simply invented the tale, but her mental state does not confirm this. The sculptor subsequently sends her another clipping, about the torture and murder of a man in Marseilles and the disappearance of a girl. Not only does the frightening nature of the story heighten the awful reality Cortázar is trying to communicate, but it also makes it difficult for the reader not to question assumptions about the passivity of his own role on reading accounts of political atrocities.

Cortázar's own political evolution through the 1950s, but especially over the following two decades, was remarkable. Perhaps the most important factor was the Cuban Revolution of 1959. Cortázar and his wife, Aurora, were invited to Havana as jury members for the Premio de Casa de las Américas in 1963. After this occasion he endeavored to return every two years and maintained until the end of his life a faithful but not uncritical support for the revolutionary process there. He gradually came to realize and to admit that he had been mistaken in his evaluation of the significance of Peronism as an important popular mass movement. Despite an increasing political awareness, however, and an enthusiastic espousal of the cause of the student movement that culminated in Paris in May 1968—which Cortázar documented in a significant article in *Ultimo round*—his politics and creative literature did not really come together in a fruitful manner until the 1970s, with his novel *Libro de Manuel* (1973; translated as *A Manual for Manuel*, 1978). The main body of Cortázar's novels was published in the 1960s: *Los premios* (1960; translated as *The Winners*, 1965), *Rayuela* (1963), and *62: Modelo para armar* (1968; translated as *62: A Model Kit*, 1972). *Los premios* is a rich, readable, exciting novel, a somewhat allegorical story (though Cortázar denied it) of a sea cruise that never gets beyond the Río de la Plata; half the ship is put out of bounds by the authorities on the unconvincing excuse of the outbreak of a rare form of typhus. The prohibited stern becomes a taboo or repressed area on many levels, and the attempt by the passengers to storm it symbolizes their desire to explore these areas and incorporate "the other" into their personal and national lives. Life with the prohibited area missing is seen as absurd, a kaleidoscope, and a product of chance unratified by any deeper certainties, like the lottery that gave the passengers their winners' tickets. The inauthenticity of the characters' lives, their class snobbery, and their refusal to face their fundamental dilemmas or accept their own sexuality are translated into the illness of a child, who only recovers when the stern is reached. This illness of the child, who represents the values and intuitive contact lost or destroyed by the adult mind, is repeated in later novels. Indeed *Los premios* contains many of the key elements of later works but does not manage to combine them in their most effective manner.

The double text is an example of one of these elements. The main narrative is interrupted at regular intervals by nine chapters, in italics, of a fundamentally different sort of writing, which offers a metaphysical and linguistic commentary on the action. Its author or focus, Persio, searches for the *figuras* that would symbolically order the chaos of the various strands of the text, but the symbolism of the stern is almost too abundantly clear already, and the density of the avant-garde writing, despite its interest, jars readers too abruptly alongside the text it is supposed to complement; it possibly tempts many readers to pass over these soliloquies. The technique, however, prepares one for the "optional chapters" of *Rayuela*, which interact far more dynamically with the main text, and for the dual narrators of *62* and *Libro de Manuel*. As authorial alter ego and collective double, Persio anticipates Morelli in *Rayuela* and similar characters in later Cortázar novels. Persio's mistrustful but ironically flamboyant style of language is expanded and developed in *Rayuela*. He sees language as an accomplice of all that hides the deeper truths; of official, nationalistic rhetoric; and of the dualistic structures of rationality, which prevent a fusion between the apprehending subject and reality. The consciousness that all he possesses in order to go beyond language *is* language leads to the dialectical denouncing of one discourse by another, in this and in later texts, and to a fundamental heteroglossia.

Though a fine novel, little in *Los premios* led readers to expect the revolution in the use of language and in the novel form in Spanish effected by *Rayuela*, the story of Horacio Oliveira, a middle-aged Argentine intellectual, similar in some ways to Cortázar, who lives a bohemian existence in Paris, where he meets the mysterious La Maga; she brings to a head his dissatisfaction with life and his own hyperintellectualism and offers him the example of a more authentic, though more magical way of relating to reality. But in destroying that which separates him from her world, he destroys their relationship, and possibly (indirectly) causes the death of her son, Rocamadour, and herself. Returning in Cortázar's place to Argentina, Oliveira must try to reconcile himself with reality, perhaps through the truths he has gained in Paris. Society is represented by his old friend Traveler and Traveler's wife, Talita; and as the presence of the long-dead La Maga begins to make itself felt, much depends on how the group reads the situation. In an open-ended finale, where Oliveira is possibly going mad or committing suicide, the question of his possible reconciliation with reality and his fellows is left very much up to the reader to answer.

The novel has three parts: the thirty-six chapters of the first are set in Paris; the twenty of the second in Buenos Aires; while the third, optional part has seventy-five generally short pieces. These are intercalated, contrapuntally, into the text according to instructions given in a direction board at the beginning of the novel, and the reader physically mimics the game of hopscotch and the spiritual search of the protagonist as the reader leafs through the volume in search of the next chapter. There is thus a double opposition: between two places, as so often in the short stories; and between two sorts of writing.

Many of the "dispensable chapters" are attributed to Morelli, a fictional author within the novel, related to Cortázar but not to be confused with him. These are generally either pieces of theorizing on the novel form, or else quotations from other writers. Each sort of chapter has a dual function. On the one hand, the ones in the third section explain and offer a widening of perspectives following an earlier chapter; or else, by dint of their difference or pointed unrelatedness, they contradict the established meaning, pluralize readings, and disturb the reader by subverting his traditionally stable relationship with a univocal text. Though *Rayuela* has often been dubbed an antinovel for aspects such as these, Morelli claims that the novel form is precisely a shared, collective ground. The Russian critic Mikhail Bakhtin similarly believed what he called heteroglossia, or using the language of others, to be perhaps the essential trait of the novel. Oliveira and Morelli are concerned at the automatisms of language, at its arbitrary authority parading as naturalness; and a multivoiced text, rather than displaying the prestige of its impeccable intellectual pedigree, seriously undermines the authoritative voice of the more traditional novel.

Other "dispensable chapters" belong more firmly to the narrative, but react contrapuntally with the main chapter they follow, contrasting with it in tone, content, or even genre. The humorous will follow the tragic; the grotesque, the pathetic. However, such combinations are also present in the main text, as when, for example, in a chapter with which Cortázar was particularly pleased, Oliveira and La Maga separate while pulling faces at each other and writhing with laughter at each other's clichés. The reader who welcomes such tensions and difficulties, and abandons the inertia of a passive, cathartic relation with the story for a critical examination of his own reactions and an active involvement in the text, is referred to by Morelli as an accomplice reader. Reading becomes a critical process rather than the absorption of a message. Such multigenre characteristics are not exclusive to *Rayuela* but are also central to Cortázar's collage works and to books such as *Prosa del observatorio* (Prose from the Observatory, 1972), in which what is basically a prose poem on two apparently heterogeneous themes (eels and stars) alternates with photographs of an observatory in India, while interspersing the alien technical jargon of two French scientists.

The first phrase of *Rayuela*, "Would I find La Maga?," establishes the fact that Oliveira's quest is inseparable from La Maga. Her presence

Dust jacket for Cortázar's 1963 novel, which includes "optional" chapters that allow the novel to be read in different ways

and loss suffuse the first chapters with a haunting pathos. La Maga is a highly mythified character and belongs to the same long literary tradition as does André Breton's Nadja. She is chaotic and ignorant and neglects her child, and yet has powers of intuition and a seemingly spontaneous and unmediated relation with reality that destroys Oliveira's confidence in the power, or rather validity, of his intelligence. In a way she radicalizes or universalizes a dissatisfaction in Oliveira that had been simply local. La Maga's role is similar to that of dreams, which affect Oliveira strongly, giving him the certainty that there is a better, happier state outside the structures of the given and the waking mind. The novel attempts to produce a similar effect of strangeness in the reader through the use of disturbing techniques and discontinuities. La Maga's effect on Oliveira is to create a heightened sense of the absurd in him, a sense of the falseness of conventional society. His very lucidity, however, prevents him from essaying any solution to his predicament because he fears that the solutions he can envisage simply belong to the problem. The result is sterility, and paralysis of will and emotion. He senses that La Maga's love could be a solution; but La Maga tragically appears to Oliveira to be the most dangerous trap. His mistreatment of her and their love is the first and most painful stage in his attempted liberation from convention, biological reflexes, and civilization in general.

When Oliveira returns to La Maga's room to find that her son, Rocamadour, has died without her knowing, he refuses to follow the normal pattern of behavior and offers no gesture of compassion toward the mother. His attitude finally puts him beyond the pale; he is expelled from his group of friends and reaches the sort of zero point for which he had been looking.

Toward the end of the first part La Maga disappears, and it is not known whether she simply leaves or commits suicide, perhaps by drowning in the Seine. This ambiguity and her role for the rest of the novel are skillfully used to pose the question, which is never resolved, whether La Maga returns in some sort of fantastic way to Buenos Aires and her death takes on a deeply mythical and archetypal character, or whether these are simply figments of the imagination of an increasingly deranged Oliveira. The mythical reading is certainly prepared for by a few highly poetic erotic passages in which La Maga seems to want Oliveira to kill her during their love affair so she can be reborn like a phoenix or propitiate a release of cosmic forces.

On his return to Buenos Aires, Oliveira seems to have acquired some of the attributes of La Maga: he acts as an irritant, a messenger, and an inquisitor to the Travelers, Manuel and Talita, and denounces their life-style as La Maga had his. Manuel is Oliveira's doppelgänger, what Oliveira was before he set out for Paris, and, despite a ludic and attractive life-style, Manuel represents Oliveira's more conventional self. Talita acts as a bridge between the two men, who come gradually to represent two different forms of logic, or perhaps two different ways of reading. She is an alter ego of La Maga, but also her opposite in that she is a reader of encyclopedias, a form of classification alien to La Maga, and also a pharmacist, and thus associated with medicine, always a sign of repression in Cortázar's works. As the tension among the friends, who feel they are part of a game larger than themselves, gradually grows, they move from their jobs in a circus (life in its amusing absurdity) to jobs as warders in a lunatic asylum (life in all its fundamental and dangerous absurdity). The crisis point finally comes when Oliveira goes down to the asylum morgue with Talita and, believing her to be La Maga, kisses her. In all of Cortázar's 1960s novels one can discern a symbolic descent to Hades—like that of Orpheus, for example, to recover Eurydice—to recuperate a lost force or vital presence. La Maga comes to represent what Oliveira finds lacking in modern life and reproaches the Travelers for repressing or ignoring.

The onus is very much on Manuel, as the more conventional side of the duality formed by the two men, to react to Oliveira's kissing his wife. According to which sort of reading Manuel chooses, several "truths" are possible, including these: La Maga has returned as a ghost, or as a mythical force of vitality; Oliveira has simply tried to seduce his wife, to which the easiest response is jealousy; or Oliveira has gone mad. To declare someone mad is one of the most traditional and effective ways of dismissing what one does not accept, and Manuel is briefly tempted by this solution, as Oliveira, undecided himself as to exactly what is happening, barricades himself in his room. Madness, however, has taken on several connotations in the novel, where Oliveira muses on the possibility of "joining the world, the Great Madness." In a mad world, to go mad is to be reconciled to reality and society, to be at one with its absurd or conventional laws. It is this acceptance, of which Oliveira has always before been incapable, that his long path has prepared him to embrace. When Talita and Manuel take his side against the authorities, he feels an intense solidarity with them, a love and a harmony that no longer represent a threat or a capitulation.

The ending of the novel is open: perhaps Oliveira throws himself out the window; perhaps he goes mad; perhaps he goes home to his girlfriend. The whole experience of *Rayuela*, however, suggests that there can be no final, static reconciliation between conventionality, or closure, and that which denies it and is different from it. The reading of the book nevertheless offers a more dynamic and enriching relationship with "the other," a model for the questioning of the unthinking acceptance of the given as natural and inevitable.

Five years after *Rayuela* was published, Cortázar produced *62: Modelo para armar*, which is not as widely read as it deserves; it is his most complex and perhaps most endearing and amusing work. The overt intertextuality and theoretical apparatus of the "dispensable chapters" and endless intellectual conversations of *Rayuela* are absent in this deceptively light work. However, some of the motivating thought behind *62* is outlined in an essay in *Ultimo round*, "La muñeca rota" (The Broken Doll), and parallel texts by writers such as Felisberto Hernández, Vladimir Nabokov, and Louis Aragon are acknowledged. The impersonal or transpersonal psychology of *62* is mapped out in chapter 62 of *Rayuela*. Another form of intertextuality is offered by a series of texts cryptically alluded to in the novel but only minimally cited. Referred to as *figuras*, they seem to dictate the actions of groups of characters or at least determine the significance of these actions. Toward the end of *Rayuela* Oliveira feels that his relationship with the others was becoming like a chemical relationship outside them and beyond their control, associated with La Maga or the force or vitality she carried. *Rayuela* was marked by a search for La Maga, and *62* is also a search, but an impersonal search to go beyond the state of Homo sapiens. Juan searches throughout for Hélène, but in a novel where one is not so much the sum of one's own acts but of those of others, his search is far from straightforward. Whether Hélène is a vampire, a homosexual, or simply an anesthetist is determined by the attitudes of others in the narrative.

The suspicion of a deeper meaning or organization underneath a surface reality and psychology always haunted Cortázar, who saw chance as one of the main means of discovering such a deeper level, in that chance is not dictated by an intentionality springing from conventional aims or ideas. The image of the lottery in *Los premios* and Oliveira's wanderings through Paris to meet La Maga by coincidence, and thus on a deeper plane, are systematized in *62* and promoted to the level of theme and methodology: the instantaneous pattern formed by insects flying around a lamp is an image of the creation of meaning in the work, which Cortázar describes as a series of elements, ideas, and experiences circulating around a void, which is the text in the making. The Mexican poet and critic Octavio Paz similarly talks about the poem being signs in search of a meaning. Wordplay is consequently important in *62* insofar as it bypasses intentional signification, as in the story "Lejana," where an anagram of the protagonist's name reveals her deeper identity. The novel opens with an avalanche of wordplay, as Juan sits in a restaurant and various words come together from different sources to suggest to him a strong link between the woman he loves, Hélène, and vampirism, offering him knowledge he is not fully prepared to face.

Chance on a thematic level is present in various forms. A curious character called Monsieur Ochs makes dolls, which become something of a cult because their purchaser cannot know what they contain: anything from a hundred-franc note, to a comb, to an object of considerable obscenity. Ochs is symbolically connected with the Roman emperor Elagabalus, reputed to be the inventor of lotteries. A doll passes from character to character—apparently according to the flow of relationships between them—and carries the evolving meaning of the novel, until the doll is finally broken open to reveal the guilt of Hélène and the punishment implicit in the initial wordplay, which has been fostered by the bad faith of Juan and which controls the meaning of Hélène's relationships with others such as the young girl Celia. Other characters participate in the general aleatory thrust of the novel in a provocative and ludic fashion, such as Marrast, who builds his statue upside down and plots to send mischievous messages to the Neurotics Anonymous with unforeseeable results.

The fluid nature of the psychology of the novel is articulated through two structures developed from previous works. The action among the group of friends takes place in three European cities: Paris, London, and Vienna, known as the *zona*, a development from the geographical dualism of *Rayuela*. Dualism is restored, however, by the opposition between the *zona* and a construct known as the *ciudad* (city), which is all three cities and a separate, oneiric area to which the inhabitants have access. In the *ciudad*, the characters seem to search for each other and at the same time for toilets and showers to bathe, to cleanse themselves perhaps of the guilt that seems to come from their involvement in the *figuras*. Related to the *ciudad* is the figure of *mi paredro*, a collective double who embodies many of the substitutive or even repressive attitudes connected with the narration. *Mi paredro* develops as a synthesis of existential doubles, such as Manuel Traveler, and authorial doubles, such as Morelli. *Mi paredro* can be any one of the characters, but also takes on a separate identity and appears when characters, out of embarrassment, cowardice, or prejudice, prefer substitution or sublima-

Cortázar lecturing in November 1975 at the University of Oklahoma (photograph by Gil Jain)

tion to an acceptance of the truth.

It is through him or activity associated with him that the *figuras* function, the main *figuras*, or models, being the stories of St. Sebastian, Parsifal, and the Bloody Countess, and the myth of Actaeon and Diana. The association of monstrosity (from the Minotaur of 1949 to the vampire of 1968), guilt, and possible liberation was to be taken up again simultaneously on the sexual and political fronts in *Libro de Manuel*.

The 1970s were an important and dramatic time politically in Latin America. The decade started with great hope and elation with the Chilean Popular Unity government of Salvador Allende, whose investiture Cortázar attended, but the fascist coup there in 1973 (the protest against which Cortázar joined) was followed by others in Uruguay, Bolivia, and Argentina (in 1976), after which Cortázar considered himself truly a political exile from his country. Only in 1979, with the Sandinista victory in Nicaragua, did the tide of right-wing oppression start to turn. Such turmoil naturally provoked a great amount of debate among Latin-American writers. Though novelists including Carlos Fuentes, Mario Vargas Llosa, Gabriel García Márquez, and Cortázar aligned themselves in the 1960s with the Cuban Revolution, they, and most specifically Cortázar, were attacked from the Left for separating their politics and their writing; for the alleged irrationalism, pornography, and elitism of their work; and for their inferiority complex vis-à-vis Europe. What such critics were demanding was basically some form of social realism. Cortázar constantly countered by arguing that it was the job of the left-wing writer to promote liberation on all fronts, not just the strictly ideological, indeed that to ignore other aspects of liberation (sexual, literary, and behavioral) was simply to store up problems for the project of a future socialist man. A watershed came in 1971, when the Cuban poet Herberto Padilla was imprisoned for alleged counterrevolutionary activities, and a letter of protest was signed by a host of intellectuals from around the world. When Fidel Castro counterattacked, accusing the signatories of playing into the hands of imperialism, a second letter was sent, which Cortázar did not sign. Instead he published a poem, "Policrítica a la hora de los chacales" (Multicritical in the Time of the Jackals), in which he reasserted his strong support for the revolution but demanded a space in which to defend it his own way.

Against this background, and as a dialogue with it, *Libro de Manuel* was published in 1973. In the story of a political kidnapping in Paris, Cortázar tries to reconcile various previously incompatible demands: literary experimentation, a political message accessible to a wide public, sexual liberation, and political action. The novel was written quickly to serve the urgent purpose of offering information and opening a debate, and it cannot be judged by the same rigorous and purely literary criteria as earlier novels. Many of the techniques used to achieve his new aims were adapted from previous works. Real newspaper clippings, for example, of political events, violence in France, and torture in Vietnam are intercalated, almost in an aleatory fashion, and are read by the characters. The idea is, of course, a development of the "dispensable chapters" of *Rayuela*. The provocative, ludic attitude of Oliveira in that novel and the aleatory, absurdist activity of Marrast and the others in *62* play an important role in *Libro de Manuel*, as the revolutionaries attempt to increase the receptivity of the Parisians to alternative behavior and break their faith in the immutability of their system by Dada-like gestures, such as putting old cigarette butts into new packets and eating in restaurants while standing up.

The problematics of writing are as firmly foregrounded and debated in this novel as in *Rayuela* and are resolved in a similar way. At least three characters are concerned with writing and language. The intellectual Andrés realizes, on listening to avant-garde music, that he can only concentrate when he hears the melody of the piano and realizes that fully to abandon traditional narration, though it might carry with it values the author is impugning, is to lose the reader and fail to communicate. As elsewhere, a double text is adopted, with two authors and two sorts of writing: in this case, the straightforward narration of the kidnapping and its ideological rationale, alongside a highly metaphorical logic of personal motivation that counterpoints it, questioning and complementing it. One narrator, "el que te dije" (he who speaks to you), separates all the information into its personal and political dimensions and refuses to make any links among these dimensions. At a certain point his classification breaks down, though, and he lapses into a parody of the *Iliad* before dying or disappearing. It is left to Lonstein to reshuffle the information, and Andrés is presented as finishing the actual writing.

It is Lonstein and Andrés who wage the main war on the eroticism front. The former's dissertations on various sexual taboos, especially masturbation, hark back to the language of *Los reyes*, as he recommends turning monsters into princes by accepting them for what they are. His profession as corpse-washer in a morgue is a metaphorical projection of his cleansing of language through opening its most scabrous aspects. In a related sequence, for Andrés, the intellectual who is hovering between contemplation and action, the breaking of sexual taboo, specifically the one against sodomy, becomes an essential step in breaking down certain barriers in himself in order to allow him to take on a full and lucid commitment to the revolutionary action.

Cortázar's own generosity and active commitment to the cause of justice in Latin America throughout the 1970s and up to his death cannot be questioned. He was a member of the Russell Tribunal and campaigned tirelessly, to the detriment of his health and literary production, against the atrocities of the military regime in Argentina and in support of the Nicaraguan Revolution. The theme of political terror was portrayed with increasing intensity in his short fiction and in works where Cortázar indulged his taste for defying generic classification, such as *Vampiros multinacionales* (Multinational Vampires, 1975), which combines the form of the comic strip and its characters with real people and political analysis and information. Some of his royalties were donated to causes such as the care of political prisoners in Argentina, the Russell Tribunal, and the *Pueblo Sandinista* of Nicaragua. His preoccupations and activities are amply and often movingly illustrated in a volume of essays he wrote with Dunlop, *Nicaragua tan violentamente dulce* (Nicaragua So Violently Sweet, 1983). Cortázar died in Paris on 12 February 1984 of leukemia and heart disease.

Interviews:

Gustavo Luis Carrera and Victor Suárez, *Nuevas viejas preguntas a Julio Cortázar* (Caracas: Universidad Central de Venezuela, 1978);

Ernesto González Bermejo, *Conversaciones con Cortázar* (Barcelona: Edhasa, 1978);

Evelyn Picon Garfield, *Cortázar por Cortázar* (Jalapa, Mexico: Universidad Veracruzana, 1981).

Bibliographies:

M. V. Reyzabal, "Bibliografía de y sobre Cortázar," *Cuadernos Hispanoamericanos*, 122, nos. 364-366 (1973): 649-667;

Marta Paley de Francescato, "Bibliography of Works by and about Julio Cortázar," in *The Final Island: The Fiction of Julio Cortázar*, edited by J. Alazraki and I. Ivask (Norman: University of Oklahoma Press, 1978);

Sarah de Mundo Lo, *Julio Cortázar, His Works and His Critics: A Bibliography* (Urbana, Ill.: Albatross, 1985);

E. D. Carter, Jr., "A Chronological List of Cortázar's Works" and "Annotated Bibliography," in his *Julio Cortázar: Life, Work, and Criticism* (Fredericton, N.B.: York Press, 1986).

Biographies:

Graciela de Sola, *Julio Cortázar y el hombre nuevo* (Buenos Aires: Sudamericana, 1968);

E. D. Carter, Jr., *Julio Cortázar: Life, Work, and Criticism* (Fredericton, N.B.: York Press, 1986).

References:

Jaime Alazraki and Ivar Ivask, eds., *The Final Island: The Fiction of Julio Cortázar* (Norman: University of Oklahoma Press, 1978);

A. M. Barrenechea, "Estudio preliminar," in *Cuaderno de bitácora de "Rayuela,"* by Cortázar and Barrenechea (Buenos Aires: Sudamericana, 1983);

Steven Boldy, *The Novels of Julio Cortázar* (Cambridge: Cambridge University Press, 1980);

Fernando Burgos, ed., *Los ochenta mundos de Julio Cortázar: Ensayos* (Madrid: Edi-6, 1987);

J. C. Curutchet, *Julio Cortázar o la crítica de la razón pragmática* (Madrid: Nacional, 1972);

Carlos Fuentes, "Cortázar: La caja de Pandora," in his *La nueva novela hispanoamericana* (Mexico City: Mortiz, 1969), pp. 67-77;

N. García Canclini, *Cortázar: Una antropología poética* (Buenos Aires: Nova, 1968);

Helmy F. Giacoman, ed., *Homenaje a Julio Cortázar: variaciones interpretativas en torno a su obra* (New York: Las Americas, 1972);

Luis Harss, "Julio Cortázar, o la bofetada metafísica," in his *Los nuestros* (Buenos Aires: Sudamericana, 1969);

Ana Hernández del Castillo, *Keats, Poe and the Shaping of Cortázar's Mythopoesis* (Amsterdam: Benjamins, 1981);

David Lagmanovich, ed., *Estudios sobre los cuentos de Julio Cortázar* (Barcelona: Hispam, 1975);

Pedro Lastra, ed., *Julio Cortázar, El Escritor y la Crítica* (Madrid: Taurus, 1981);

Alfred J. MacAdam, *El individuo y el otro: Crítica a los cuentos de Julio Cortázar* (Buenos Aires: Librería, 1971);

J. Poulet, ed., *Co-Textes*, special Cortázar issue, 11 (April 1986);

Review of Contemporary Fiction, special Cortázar issue, 3 (Fall 1983);

Revista Iberoamericana, special Cortázar double issue, 84-85 (July-December 1973);

Joaquin Roy, *Julio Cortázar ante su sociedad* (Barcelona: Península, 1974);

Saúl Sosnowski, *Julio Cortázar: una búsqueda mítica* (Buenos Aires: Noé, 1973);

David Viñas, *De Sarmiento a Cortázar: Literatura argentina y realidad política* (Buenos Aires: Siglo Veinte, 1971);

Saúl Yurkievich, *Julio Cortázar: al calor de tu sombra* (Buenos Aires: Legasa, 1987).

José Donoso
(5 October 1924 -   )

Ricardo Gutiérrez Mouat
Emory University

BOOKS: *Veraneo y otros cuentos* (Santiago, Chile: Universitaria, 1955);

Dos cuentos (Santiago, Chile: Guardia Vieja, 1956);

Coronación (Santiago, Chile: Nascimento, 1957); translated by Jocasta Goodwin as *Coronation* (New York: Knopf, 1965; London: Bodley Head, 1965);

El charlestón (Santiago, Chile: Nascimento, 1960); translated by Andrée Conrad as *Charleston and Other Stories* (Boston: Godine, 1977);

El lugar sin límites (Mexico City: Mortiz, 1966); translated by Hallie D. Taylor and Suzanne Jill Levine as *Hell Has No Limits*, in *Triple Cross* (New York: Dutton, 1972);

Este domingo (Santiago, Chile: Zig-Zag, 1966); translated by Lorraine O'Grady Freeman as *This Sunday* (New York: Knopf, 1967; London: Bodley Head, 1968);

El obsceno pájaro de la noche (Barcelona: Seix Barral, 1970); translated by Hardie St. Martin and Leonard Mades as *The Obscene Bird of Night* (New York: Knopf, 1973);

Cuentos (Barcelona: Seix Barral, 1971);

Historia personal del "boom" (Barcelona: Anagrama, 1972); translated by Gregory Kolovakos as *The Boom in Spanish American Literature: A Personal History* (New York: Columbia University Press, 1977);

Tres novelitas burguesas (Barcelona: Seix Barral, 1973); translated by Conrad as *Sacred Families: Three Novellas* (New York: Knopf, 1977; London: Gollancz, 1978);

Casa de campo (Barcelona: Seix Barral, 1978); translated by Levine and David Pritchard as *A House in the Country* (New York: Knopf, 1984);

La misteriosa desaparición de la Marquesita de Loria (Barcelona: Seix Barral, 1980 [i.e., 1981]);

El jardín de al lado (Barcelona: Seix Barral, 1981);

Poemas de un novelista (Santiago, Chile: Ganymedes, 1981);

Cuatro para Delfina (Barcelona: Seix Barral, 1982);

José Donoso

Sueños de mala muerte (Santiago, Chile: Universitaria, 1985);

Seis cuentos para ganar (Santiago, Chile: Cochrane-Planeta/Teleduc, 1985);

La desesperanza (Barcelona: Seix Barral, 1986); translated as *Curfew* (New York: Weidenfeld & Nicolson, 1988);

Este domingo: Versión teatral de la novela homónima, by Donoso and Carlos Cerda (Santiago, Chile: Bello, 1990);

Taratuta; Naturaleza muerta con cachimba (Madrid: Mondadori, 1990).

Collection: *Los mejores cuentos* (Santiago, Chile: Zig-Zag, 1966).

PLAY PRODUCTION: *Sueños de mala muerte*, Santiago, Chile, ICTUS, November 1982.

SELECTED PERIODICAL PUBLICATIONS—
UNCOLLECTED: "The Blue Woman," *MSS*, 3 (November 1950): 3-7;
"The Poisoned Pastries," *MSS*, 3 (May 1951): 3-8;
"Footsteps in the Night," *Américas*, 11 (February 1959): 21-23;
"Chronology," *Review* (Fall 1973): 12-19;
"Ya nadie usa calañes," *Epoca*, 3 (2 September 1990).

José Donoso is the most prominent Chilean novelist of the twentieth century and one of that select group of Latin-American writers who achieved international notoriety in the 1960s. This was the decade of the Latin-American novel's modernization by cosmopolitan writers conversant with the most significant experiments of modernist fiction in Europe and the United States. In light of the transculturation of narrative forms that characterized the reinvention of the Latin-American novel, it is easy to forget that the early works of writers such as Donoso were more responsive to local traditions than prestigious foreign models of the moment: Donoso's early stories and novels cannot be properly understood outside the context of Chilean fiction around 1950.

During the first half of the twentieth century Chilean fiction was dominated by the regionalist novel, which interpreted national identity by documenting human, linguistic, and cultural types. The typical was found in the rural countryside and in the more remote outposts of civilization, where men and nature could remain in traditional stasis, rooted in the beginning, in the origins of the national being. But regionalist fiction (which in Chile was also known as *criollismo*, or nativism) was not a regional genre through which the inhabitants of the interior represented themselves. On the contrary, regionalism was an urban narrative form, a centralized representation of regional diversity and autonomy that inscribed the need to integrate the national territory and to standardize national life on the urban model.

The Latin-American novelists of the 1960s shared neither the aims nor the naturalist models of regionalism. Donoso in particular has denounced regionalism and the critical habits it engendered on two counts: excessive localism and the reduction of narrative to a simplistic, mimetic criterion. Donoso acknowledges the historical place of regionalism, especially championed in Chile by Mariano Latorre and Marta Brunet, both of whom achieved canonical status in the Chilean educational establishment; the regionalist novel, after all, embodied the perspective of ascending social sectors, often articulating the social and political concerns of a lower middle class formed to a significant extent by migrants from the provinces and the countryside. But Donoso cannot abide the "realist" aesthetic values of regionalist writers. If Donoso's fiction can be said to have one imperative, it is to undermine established orthodoxies and to elaborate social reality from a dialogical perspective.

Chilean critics usually situate Donoso's early works in the context of the "Generation of 1950," which refers to a group of middle- and upper-middle-class writers who changed the direction of Chilean fiction from nativism to a cosmopolitanism underscored by a renewed concern with narrative form. By the 1940s regionalism had given way to an emerging urban novel dealing with the working class and with themes of social justice best represented by the works of Nicomedes Guzmán, the leading figure of the "Generation of 1938." Predictably the proletarian novel made little or no impact on the Generation of 1950. Donoso, Jorge Edwards, Luis Alberto Heiremans, and others replaced working-class characters with their middle-class counterparts, and the family mansion usurped the space reserved for the factory or the hovel in the proletarian novel. Furthermore the heightened formal consciousness of the later writers stemmed from their careful reading, often in the original languages, of English, French, German, and North American fiction, a luxury denied to their socially disadvantaged predecessors. In this sense Donoso is a representative example of the Generation of 1950, though he has never identified himself or his work with this generational group nor with any other, including the constellation of Latin-American authors who in the 1960s protagonized the "boom" of the Latin-American novel. In fact, his 1972 chronicle of the period, *Historia personal del "boom"* (translated as *The Boom in Spanish American Literature: A Personal History*, 1977), is remarkable, among other things, for the detachment of the chronicler and for the literally *ex-centric* point of view from which the carnival of the boom is presented.

José Donoso Yáñez was born in Santiago on 5 October 1924, into a family belonging to the professional middle class (his father, José Donoso, and both of his grandfathers were physicians, and his two brothers are lawyers) but with strong ties to Chilean aristocratic culture; his mother was the former Alicia Yáñez. His genealogy includes politicians, historians, writers, and literary critics, and he himself holds a university degree, thus continuing a family tradition lasting four generations. His parents were not wealthy, but his father in particular had a literary culture he shared with his son, who spent the first ten years of his schooling in the Grange (a prestigious private school in Santiago also attended by Mexican novelist Carlos Fuentes at approximately the same time), and who at seven years of age had a private English teacher at home.

Donoso's school years were significant in ways not having to do with actually going to classes. In "Chronology" (*Review*, Fall 1973) Donoso links his remembrance of that period of his life (1932-1942) to several motifs that later were to play major roles in his fiction. For example, he remembers his fascination with dressing up and the games he and his brothers used to stage until parental authority intervened and brought them to a halt, the parents fearing excessive feminization. This early display of costume and play-acting is evoked in the later fiction and is a model for the narration process of Donoso's most important novels. He also remembers how his experience in school, and especially of organized sports, brought out his incapacity to belong to any group whatsoever, political, social, or literary. As he grew older this outsider began to make the acquaintance of the hobos and prostitutes who made their living in the outskirts of the city. These characters populate some of Donoso's novels, and the clochard in particular was to become a fantasy character elicited through psychoanalysis (to which the mature Donoso submitted himself regularly) and ambivalently displayed in his fiction, since the clochard represents both the promise of total freedom from social codes and the experience of nothingness: anarchy and nihilism.

Donoso also emphasizes the many times he feigned stomach illness to play hooky and the way in which this deception, which fooled even his father, in time became a real ulcer, intimately linked to the creative process, either precluding

Dust jacket for Donoso's first novel (1957), which was selected by the Faulkner Foundation in 1963 as the best Chilean novel published since World War II

or nourishing it. He remembers collapsing from a hemorrhage upon completing the manuscript of his first novel, *Coronación* (1957; translated as *Coronation*, 1965), and he recounts the emergency surgery performed during the long process of writing one of his later works, *El obsceno pájaro de la noche* (1970; translated as *The Obscene Bird of Night*, 1973), which actually includes a heightened version of the incident. In this version the body of the author becomes a metaphoric equivalent for the body of the text, a metaphor that bespeaks the somatic nature of much of Donoso's fiction and perhaps of all writing.

Another type of "body"—the house—plays a major role in Donoso's autobiographical recollections and in the imaginary topography of his works. He recounts how in 1929 his family moved downtown, into a large house owned by three great-aunts, "who were rich, bedridden, widowed, and 'alone in the world' although each was surrounded by her own court of relatives and servants." Then in 1938 the family moved back to their earlier home whose garden was to become a major symbol, strongly linked to filial sentiments and fears, in *El jardín de al lado* (The Garden Next Door, 1981). This is the house that as of 1939 lodged Donoso's crazy grandmother, one of the protagonists of his first novel.

After failing to graduate from school, the future novelist also failed to hold down a job and decided to escape to the desolate South of Chile, where for almost a year he worked as a shepherd in a Magallanes hacienda; he then hitchhiked to Buenos Aires, where for eight months he labored as a dockhand. Upon returning to Santiago, Donoso completed his studies and entered the Universidad de Chile to specialize in English language and literature. In 1949 he won a scholarship from the Doherty Foundation to continue his studies at Princeton, a move that proved to be of lasting impact in Donoso's literary production because it coincided with the reevaluation of Henry James and with the lectures of critics and poets such as R. P. Blackmur and Allen Tate. Furthermore at Princeton Donoso wrote his first stories, two pieces in English entitled "The Blue Woman" and "The Poisoned Pastries," which appeared in a literary magazine partially founded at the university by Donoso himself, *MSS* (November 1950 and May 1951, respectively). These stories are aesthetically unremarkable, though they present some themes that later works of his will restate with variations. "The Blue Woman," an urban story like its counterpart, deals (albeit superficially) with the fragmentation of subjectivity. A woman with an aberrantly large nose undergoes a cosmetic operation, and in the drunken celebration that follows, she is seduced by one of the reveller much to her dismay, for it is not really she who is the object of male attention but a now-unknown woman she has glimpsed in a blue mirror. The idea for the story has prestigious literary overtones (of Francisco de Quevedo and Edmond Rostand, for example), but its development is more in line with Jewish ethnic stereotypes, if only circumstantially (the protagonist's name is Myra, and the story is set in New York City). "The Poisoned Pastries" is set in the drawing room of a well-appointed and old-fashioned middle-class household and is narrated from the perspective of a child who is trying to outgrow his own exaggerated image of his father's power. There is nothing Kafkaesque in this story; the transition between the imaginary and the real father is effected by means of a tame anecdote involving the father's charity toward the needy and his underlying goodness. Yet the handling of the point of view anticipates a whole range of Donoso's later stories and novels.

By 1952 Donoso was back in Santiago after a journey through parts of the United States, Mexico, and Central America; and after he tried teaching and journalism for a while (he was briefly the literary critic for *Ercilla*, perhaps the most serious Chilean magazine of the period), he decided to move out of his parents' home to dedicate himself full-time to literature. In 1954 he wrote his first story in Spanish, "China," somewhat akin to James Joyce's "Araby" (in *Dubliners*, 1914), and published in Enrique Lafourcade's *Antología del nuevo cuento chileno* (Anthology of the New Chilean Short Story, 1954), the anthology that launched the Generation of 1950. Donoso's first book was published in 1955; a collection of short stories titled *Veraneo y otros cuentos* (Summertime and Other Stories), it was published at his expense and with the collaboration of friends, family, and subscribers. The "vanity" nature of the publication says far more about the Chilean publishing industry (unwilling to take risks with unpublished Chilean authors, financially dependent on the old regionalist "classics" and foreign products both great and mediocre) than about the quality of the stories themselves, which range from excellent to unconvincing and include various styles and themes.

The title story is the most memorable. Set in a Chilean seaside resort, it tells of two children whose friendship is compromised by the illicit relations between their parents, the father of one carrying on what appears to be a clandestine affair with the other's mother. The ambiguity of this relationship is propitiated by the oblique narrative technique, reminiscent of a novel such as Henry James's *What Maisie Knew* (1897). The children function as "reflectors" of their parents' story, which they come to know through their own limited experience and through information they pick up from their respective nannies. The story successfully depicts the world of the urban bourgeoisie and that of early adolescence, but it also elaborates, as most of Donoso's work does, the interplay between masters and servants. In fact the book is dedicated to Donoso's household servant, Teresa Vergara, who could not read. Another of these stories, "Fiesta en grande" (The Picnic), presents the world of a faceless bureaucrat who lives in boardinghouses and barely makes ends meet. What interests Donoso is the pathos of a mediocre employee, worn down by the daily grind, who one day excels in his chosen avocation but is nevertheless humbled by his unchanging circumstances. The functionary is a relatively new character in Chilean fiction, and Donoso was to return to such characters in subsequent works.

"Tocayos" (Namesakes) is also an urban story about the working class, but it would be wrong to associate it with the proletarian novel of the 1940s. "Tocayos" concerns the naive love between Juan and Juana, a mechanic and a pastry-shop maid, who in their own way are upwardly mobile, as is the pastry shop owner, whose savings will allow him someday to buy a house for his mother. The upbeat perspective of the story should not be confused with Nicomedes Guzmán's faith in the regeneration of the proletariat, which is essentially a belated, working-class positivism; nor can the motivation of Donoso's characters be ranged alongside that of Guzmán's sociologically typed men and women. There are other differences, but they all point to a break between the Generation of 1938 and that of 1950, a conflict between tradition and modernization. However, it is fair to say that in *Veraneo* Donoso is groping for some kind of synthesis of literary traditions even as he seeks to renovate Chilean fiction by appealing to postnaturalist foreign models.

Another case in point is "Dinamarquero" (The Dane's Place), Donoso's only truly regionalist venture. This story, explicitly based on his youthful Patagonian experience, emphasizes the local color of the Chilean pampas and is affected by a sentimentalism rare in Donoso's fiction. In order to gain verisimilitude, the city-bound narrator yields the narrative discourse to one of the locals, familiar with the place and with the main characters of the story: a Danish sailor beached in the Magellanic wasteland and the prostitute he marries and with whom he sets up shop. The story is less interesting than what it evinces, namely the location of Donoso's book at a kind of literary crossroads, where many directions are feasible and none dominant. *Veraneo* is after all a first book written at a moment of transition that shows Donoso's cautious approach to the question of literary renewal.

"Dinamarquero" is not the only story in the collection based to some extent on personal experience, which in itself betrays a certain literary naiveté associated with descriptive realism. "El güero" (The White Man) is a rather wooden and unconvincing incursion into what later would be called "magical realism," featuring foreign anthropologists, Indian legends, and exotic settings, which reflect Donoso's brief sojourn in Mexico on his way back to Chile from Princeton (the story is set in the Mexican interior, and the title is in Mexican Spanish). There is some exoticism also in "Dos cartas" (Two Letters), which involves a truncated epistolary exchange between two former schoolmates, an English planter in Kenya and a Chilean lawyer. The letters are meant to be trivial, but the nostalgia is not. The last story in *Veraneo* is "Una señora" (A Lady), which vaguely evokes the strangeness of an Edgar Allan Poe story and the figure of the *flâneur*, or idler (for example, in Poe's "The Man of the Crowd"). Donoso's first book made an impression on the Chilean literary scene and won the 1956 Municipal Prize for Short Stories.

The following year Donoso moved away from the bustle of the city and the workaday world and lived with a fisherman friend's family in Isla Negra, the island in the South of Chile popularized by Pablo Neruda, who had begun to use it as a retreat in the early 1950s. Perhaps Donoso was attracted by the literary magnetism of the island, since his purpose in going there was to finish his first novel. When *Coronación* was published in 1957, once again he had to display creative energy and muster the support of family and friends to ensure distribution. It is relevant that *Coronación* was published exactly a century after Gustave Flaubert's *Madame Bovary* (1857), in view of the structural procedures employed by Donoso, which are in the best Flaubertian tradition: symmetry, internal echoes, gradation, antithesis, a polished style, irony, and so on. There is also a rhetorical analogy between the two novels. Just as *Madame Bovary* was written simultaneously to appeal to and shock its bourgeois readership, *Coronación* follows the well-trodden path of Chilean realism—familiar to the mid-twentieth-century Chilean reader from the works of the country's greatest nineteenth-century novelist, Alberto Blest Gana—but departs from it in the climactic final scene, where the realist code is deformed by the grotesque. The grotesque crowning of the mad, vituperative grandmother is an attempt to transcend the traditional aesthetics within which Donoso felt imprisoned by his public, and it prefigures later scenes in more ambitious novels.

Coronación is a story of aristocratic decadence, or rather, of the deterioration of an idle bourgeoisie with aristocratic pretensions, although the notion of *fin de race* is not grasped in

María del Pilar de Donoso and José Donoso circa 1971

its economic dimension but in its operativity: Donoso simply deals with a social class that has outlived its legitimacy. He contrasts it with a more energetic and enterprising professional middle class, and especially with a proletariat equally at a dead end. The novel is structured in terms of an opposition between the oligarchic and the proletarian characters, mobilized by the gradual irruption of the proletarian world into the exclusive order of the upper bourgeoisie, an invasion signified by the inviolable mansion of the Abalos family being, at the end of the novel, penetrated and violated by common criminals. Again Donoso's treatment of the popular classes owes little to the Chilean proletarian novel, though it is plausible, effective, and relevant within the context of Chilean social and literary history. But the perspective from which the proletarian characters are presented is déclassé, as manifested by the work ethic that informs Mario's moral code and the sudden revulsion felt by the servant Estela during the robbery of the Abalos mansion. Her refusal to go ahead with the plot has as much to do with not wanting to be manipulated by her associates as with her innate sense of values, that is, her inherent subservience to bourgeois morality.

Donoso's portrayal of Andrés Abalos betrays the influence of existentialism, which characterizes the work of other members of the Generation of 1950. The most significant aspect of the portrayal of the oligarchy is the irony that undermines its hegemonic discourse. The plot centers on the desperate erotic attraction, combined with revulsion, that the gentleman Don Andrés feels or thinks he feels for his servant, Estela, and his hope that this last fling will redeem an otherwise insipid life. This liaison is grotesque, given the social norms of the bourgeoisie, and dangerously transgressive because it threatens the core of class identity. It is also one example among many in Donoso's fiction of the intertwining of masters and servants that undercuts the power of the master class (showing its dependence on the powerless) and reveals bourgeois repressions. The ironic questioning of social hegemony is also undertaken through the manipulation of the narrative point of view. The omniscient narrator represents the interiority of the protagonists through a free, indirect style, producing an interplay of perspectives ruled by irony and inviting the collaboration of the reader, who must meaningfully relate disparate segments of text. The ironic space thus created, however, was apparently not occupied by all of Donoso's early critics, who focused on more conventional aspects of the novel. Not that *Coronación* can be called, following Umberto Eco, an "open work," but the critical blindness of its reception (on the whole positive and even encouraging) makes it easier to understand why Donoso felt the imperative to seek out more responsive literary environments abroad.

In 1958 Donoso scraped together some money and set off for Buenos Aires, where he met María del Pilar Serrano—a translator and painter—whom he married in 1961. The two years he spent in Buenos Aires produced a new series of short stories, published in Santiago as *El charlestón* (1960; translated as *Charleston and Other Stories*, 1977). The title story presents the city-life routine of three lower-middle-class youths (work, soccer, women, and madcap drunkenness) and then focuses on a shared experience that momentarily interrupts it, watching an overweight reveler collapse in a bar. The story is conceptually unremarkable, but it does demonstrate Donoso's mastery of the informal, colloquial narrative monologue that he was to use so effectively in his later production. "La puerta cerrada" (The Closed Door) is a kind of fable centered on the figure of the outsider, a child whose only desire is to sleep. The child grows up to be an eccentric young man, takes a job, and makes a bet with his skeptical boss that before he dies his sleeping will open a door of perception closed to the average man. Many years later, having abandoned society and with the appearance of a hobo, he returns to his former boss's house to collect on his bet. The latter closes the door on him and the sleeper dies in the wintry cold, his expression transfigured by the attainment of a vision. The fable's topic is an exceptional sensibility—that of the modern artist—mocked and denied by the crassness of the modern world. The best-known Latin-American statement of the topic is in Rubén Darío's "El rey burgués" (The Bourgeois King), written in 1888, when the triumphant bourgeoisie had relegated poetry to the realm of the useless and the poet to the marketplace. Donoso's fable, generically akin to Darío's story, sets the dreamer's quest against the background of office and boardinghouse, spaces where average men and women live, work, and succeed or fail. But the dreamer is outside of it all in a marginal space of his own making.

"Ana María" prolongs the thematics of marginality by narrating the relationship that develops between the little girl of the title, who lives fenced in a garden and ignored by her selfish parents whose erotic play she interrupts, and a kind old vagabond with whom she walks away in the end. The story is moving rather than sentimental and has great suggestive power in that Donoso alludes only obliquely to the little girl's resentment against her parents. By the same token, the story's setting is symbolically the Garden of Eden from which the protagonist chooses to become an exile. "El hombrecito" (The Handyman) is the story of a social type familiar to the Chilean middle classes, though the narrative is not told in a *costumbrista*, or picturesque, way but with the intention of capturing the narrator's childhood, part of which is tied up with the evocation of a particular handyman.

"Paseo" (The Walk) is the last story in the collection and Donoso's most anthologized one. Like "El hombrecito" it is narrated by an adult who adopts the perspective of the child he was when the events took place, though the tone of "Paseo" is more complex than the whimsical musings of its counterpart. It narrates the mysterious and willful disappearance of a spinster, the only woman in a household of men related to her by blood, who is the enforcer of strict social convention in an asphyxiating atmosphere of bourgeois decorum. The limited point of view works effectively to convey the enigma of her disappearance since the only interiority it reveals is that of the child whose caretaker the spinster was. The story stresses the brothers' inability or unwillingness to acknowledge the perturbing family secret (the spinster's disappearance), all the more because the social code that identifies the family as a superior caste is predicated on the absence of all uncertainty and doubt, precisely the monkey wrench that Aunt Matilde throws into the family's ordered functioning. Significantly it is her contact with the abject (in the form of a stray and half-starved dog met on the way back from church) that causes her to leave, for throughout Donoso's fiction the exclusions that create the identity of the dominant classes return to haunt them. In "Paseo" the outside is shaped by two kinds of imagination. On the one hand, it is the place of the lower and criminal classes, according to the images and stereotypes current among the adults in the household; on the other, it is the ships passing in the night outside the young narrator's window, full of the promise of discovery and adventure. Both forms of the outside come together to motivate the spinster's last walk away from home.

It is easy to imagine, given other stories by Donoso, the erstwhile bourgeoise dressed in rags and impersonating a *clocharde* on the outskirts of the city.

Donoso's next published short story was "Santelices," which appeared in *El Mercurio* (the leading Chilean newspaper) in July 1962 and was subsequently collected with all the author's previous stories in *Cuentos* (Stories, 1971). It narrates the secret obsession of the eponymous character, an obscure, middle-aged bureaucrat who lives in a boardinghouse and outwardly seems tame and well-adjusted, but who has the peculiar habit of collecting and displaying pictures and color plates of wild jungle animals. Santelices's fascination with the power and ferocity of the big cats reaches a crescendo when the boardinghouse owners chastise him for having nailed the pictures to the wall, an indecent and perverse act in the estimation of toothless Don Eusebio and his obese and grotesque daughter. The boarder takes refuge in his office, where five stories below he can see an inner courtyard with a delicate young blonde surrounded by domestic cats. Santelices's obsession reaches its highest pitch when these harmless creatures become bloodthirsty wildcats in his imagination, and his only thought is to save the girl, trapped in the courtyard with hundreds of beasts around her. There are also imaginary trees and branches outside the office window, which the bureaucrat-turned-hero tries to catch hold of when he jumps out. The story is masterfully told and constructed and works on several levels, among them the caricaturesque description of the boardinghouse owners' pretentiousness and vulgarity, and the dramatic elaboration of the repressed. Above all "Santelices" is an excellent example of Donoso's penchant for the grotesque and for the kind of exaggerated deformation that was to shape his later novels of the 1960s.

Also in 1962 Donoso attended a writers' congress in the southern Chilean city of Concepción and struck up a friendship with his former schoolmate Carlos Fuentes. It was at this congress that Donoso became aware that something exciting was happening with the Latin-American novel. The following year *Coronación* was selected by the Faulkner Foundation as the best Chilean novel published in the postwar period, and in 1964 Donoso and his wife accepted an invitation by the Inter-American Foundation to participate in yet another writers' congress, this time in Mexico. They planned to be gone for only a few weeks, but they did not return to Chile until 1980.

In Mexico, Donoso made a living writing literary criticism for *Siempre* and, more important, wrote his next two novels, *El lugar sin límites* (1966; translated as *Hell Has No Limits*, 1972)—written between December 1964 and February of the following year—and *Este domingo* (also 1966; translated as *This Sunday*, 1967). *El lugar sin límites* is a brilliant deconstruction of Chilean and Latin-American regionalism, a taut and suspenseful novel that retains characters, settings, and forms of speech typical of that narrative genre (and of the vine-growing region of Chile, where the story takes place) but subverts them through the operation of mythical and symbolic languages and, above all, through the novel's generative mechanism, which rejects the mimetic principle. This mechanism can be described as a metonymic contagion that undermines the boundaries of traditional representation and authority. The story recounts the arrival of a transvestite performer in a run-down town adjacent to the property of the local landowner, who takes a paternalistic attitude toward the newcomer and tries to protect him from the threats of the local tough, a truck driver who has sworn revenge upon the transvestite. The town where the action takes place is symbolic of hell, as the epigraph taken from Christopher Marlowe's *Dr. Faustus* (1604) makes clear.

The violence implicit in the story is sexual in nature and propagates itself by means of a metonymic chain whose origin is the transvestite's ambiguity. All the traditional values enshrined by canonical narrative genres (virginity, machismo, ownership, and patriarchalism) are deformed as they become links in this chain. The driver Pancho Vega's virile stance is revealed as a mask that hides sexual ambiguity, which finally must be covered up by an act of brutal violence; the transvestite usurps the role of procreating father; his virgin daughter runs a brothel, owned by her mother who has won it in a bet with its former proprietor, the landowner. The novel is thus constructed by a series of metonymic inversions displayed on a multiplicity of levels and framed against a background of traditional verisimilitude. It is significant that the traditional expectations created by the regionalist novel (that is, scenes depicting "normal" life in the town and the hacienda) are not entirely frustrated but displaced from the foreground to the background, while the foreground is occupied by a stage (the brothel), where the characters impersonate sexual roles. The meaning of *representation* shifts from mimesis to theater, and the narrative voice itself copies the histrionic model by its own kinds of impersonation. There is no longer an authoritative narrator as there was in *Coronación* but a shifting narrative discourse, its author conscious of its rhetorical effects and deliberately ambiguous.

El lugar sin límites was the first novel published by Donoso outside of Chile, and *Este domingo* was his last novel to be originally published in his native country. However, *Este domingo*, written after *El lugar sin límites*, is not an attempt to break down the old limitations. It seems more like a novel deliberately written in a former "Donoso style," as understood by the Chilean reader of the time. Largely because of *Coronación* Donoso had been typecast as a social or realist writer, and he left Chile in search of new masks of his own, rejecting those imposed on him by the literary establishment. Furthermore, before leaving Chile, the Zig-Zag publishing house had advanced him one thousand dollars against the publication of a future novel, and with *Este domingo* the author paid his debt. To be sure, the "generous claws" of the publisher, as Donoso referred to the advance, are indirectly represented in the novel, which turns on the theme of interested charity. Doña Chepa is a wealthy social benefactress who takes a suspicious interest in Maya, a prison inmate convicted of murder. She mothers him after obtaining his release and drives him to kill Violeta, her husband Don Alvaro's former maid and sexual initiator, financially set up for life by Don Alvaro's mother. Don Alvaro, meanwhile, is dying of cancer and is the object of ridicule on the part of his grandsons, one of whom narrates sections of the novel in a tone similar to that of "Paseo." Doña Chepa, on the other hand, is a figure dear to the children because she invents games for them and neutralizes parental authority. The novel is ironically structured in terms of an opposition between legitimate and illegitimate games (the latter being the ones the society lady plays with the ex-convict, and the husband's adolescent games with the maid) and narrated with greater formal freedom than *Coronación*. *Este domingo* describes a more modern bourgeoisie than Donoso's first novel but lacks its totalizing ambition. While *Este domingo* might disappoint some readers of *El lugar sin límites*, it should be noted that the later novel is caught between the poetics of the grotesque and of deformation (which will explode in Donoso's next novel)

Cover for Donoso's 1973 collection of novellas that satirize the Barcelona bourgeoisie

and the poetics of a refined, updated kind of realism, Jamesian as opposed to Flaubertian. The grotesque in *Este domingo* is configured as much by Don Alvaro's parodic appearance as by Doña Chepa's involvement with someone far beneath her social station. This is a type of alliance that recalls *Coronación* and that in *El lugar sin límites* becomes anarchic.

After leaving Mexico, Donoso divided his time for a while between the United States (where he taught writing at the University of Iowa and at Colorado State) and Spain, where he eventually settled in Calaceite, in the Teruel region, until 1980. He spent the years between 1965 and 1969 trying to finish a project he had started in 1963, which was to become his greatest novel to date and one of the well-recognized novels of the "boom": *El obsceno pájaro de la noche*. The several drafts of this voluminous novel (which began as a short story to be called "El último Azcoitía" [The Last Azcoitía]) attest to

Donoso's major aesthetic concern of the 1960s: the transformation of his "homegrown" realism into an original and modern literary idiom, a transformation made all the more urgent by the ongoing restyling of Latin-American fiction. The creation of *El obsceno pájaro* was, by any of Donoso's accounts, an extremely traumatic process necessitating constant traveling and even serious medical attention. In fact, and if Donoso's own recollections are to be trusted, the novel's final form was suggested by his temporary experience of madness and hallucination, the result of drugs ingested during an emergency ulcer operation in Fort Collins, Colorado. It is easy and perhaps facile to refer to the novel as the delirious and paranoid monologue of an ailing writer (represented in the narrative by both Humberto Peñaloza and Mudito); more interestingly the story has the appearance of a hybrid or graft, of a cut-up body sewn back together without any attempt to erase the sutures. And this is how the novel took shape. Originally (and the original fragments are included in the text), the *Bird* was to be a fable à la Isak Dinesen, centering on the misshapen scion of an aristocratic couple, Jerónimo and Inés de Azcoitía, who cannot bear the sight of their offspring and seclude him away from the eyes of the world in La Rinconada, Jerónimo's estate, which he quickly populates with monsters more repulsive than his own first-born son. But the straightforward quality of this fable was gradually deformed as darker presences (witches, clochards, decrepit crones, and monsters) took over, and the novel began to take on the appearance of one of Goya's dark paintings, although other shaping elements derive from the Bakhtinian carnival: parody, inversions, repetitions, the proximity of the old hags and the newborn baby (recalling the Kersch statuette mentioned by Mikhail Bakhtin), games, disguises, and so on. Ultimately the novel's form is predicated on the impossibility and undesirability of a synthesis between or among the multiple strands, models, and voices involved in its creation, all made natural by the presiding figure of the crazed writer.

The content of *El obsceno pájaro* reflects its form and creative process—for instance in the description of the two main settings: the crumbling convent in which the old crones take refuge, an anarchic and labyrinthine space whose walls and doors are often mirages or trompe l'oeil; and La Rinconada, another concentric labyrinth whose center is occupied by Boy, Jerónimo's heir. But in the absence of an authoritative narrator, Boy's existence is contradictory and phantasmagoric: he could as well be Mudito (the grotesque "author" of the novel); the miraculous child fanatically worshipped by the old hags in the secrecy of the convent; or nobody. From the absent center of the labyrinth, the text proliferates in search of direction, but the narrative strands get tangled up and compose a grotesque figure in which plot, characters, and chronology are hopelessly lost. One of the representations of the novel-within-the-novel is the "imbunche," a mythological figure born with all its orifices sewn up—a macabre metaphor for a novel trapped in the imagination of a tortured writer.

Ideologically, *El obsceno pájaro* is about power and the distortions it produces in the powerless. The exercise of social, political, and economic power is linked to a classical aesthetics and to the principle of classification, which separates the dominant class from the dominated ones. The narrative discourse subverts the ideological base of power: instead of gesturing toward the transparency of language, it produces itself by a constant sliding of the signifier; instead of privileging proportion and clarity, it appeals to disproportion and ambiguity. Furthermore Donoso imagines a confabulation against the *patrón*, which unifies all the subordinated groups: women, beggars, orphans, and writers—or at least the kind of writer represented by Humberto Peñaloza, the lower-middle-class upstart who prostitutes his questionable talent by becoming Don Jerónimo's factotum. Peñaloza's chronicle of La Rinconada and of its founder's deeds is born deformed if at all. Among other things, *El obsceno pájaro* is a metanovel that puts the canons of realism on trial and sides instead with the discourse of the subaltern.

The book is Donoso's great modern novel, if modernism can be mapped according to Eugene Lunn's categories in *Marxism and Modernism* (1982): aesthetic self-consciousness or self-reflexiveness, predominance of the logic of metaphor over narrative and temporal structure, ambiguity, and the demise of the integrated subject. After 1970 Donoso shifted gears in the direction of a postmodern novel, though this does not mean that all of Lunn's categories were superseded. *Tres novelitas burguesas* (1973; translated as *Sacred Families: Three Novellas*, 1977) attests to the perseverance of the rhetoric of ambiguity and the continued exploration of fragmented subjectivity. These three short novels, in a pseudo-

Donoso circa 1973

Balzacian way, cast an ironic glance at the Catalan bourgeoisie (by then Donoso had spent some time in Barcelona and environs). Their mode is generally the fantastic, but distinct from Jorge Luis Borges's baroque version or Julio Cortázar's surrealist-inspired revision of the nineteenth-century horror story. Donoso's elaboration of this genre is subordinated to the ironic interweaving of traditional and liberated social codes or prescriptions, and it allows for an inventive freedom that situates the book outside the Manichean struggle between the old and the new. Formal "liberation," that is, is envisioned not as a rejection of tradition but as its cannibalization or transformation.

"Chatanooga [*sic*] choo choo" is the story of the sexual destruction and reconstruction (literally represented by the loss and retrieval of the phallus) of a middle-aged, old-fashioned male whose fantasy is the possession of a female model described as the incarnation of contemporaneity. The traditional male fantasy of woman as object is ironically turned against the perpetrator, whose identity is revealed as dependent on a unitary conception of self (centered on the phallic organ). "Atomo verde número cinco" (Green Atom Number Five), whose opening paragraph parodies the beginning of Jane Austen's *Pride and Prejudice* (1813), narrates the reversion of a typically middle-class couple to a state of savagery, motivated by the unexplainable and gradual disappearance of the carefully chosen objects that make up their "definitive" apartment and the concomitant mutual accusations that expose all they had repressed during their long marriage. And "Gaspard de la nuit" (Gaspard of the Night), generated to some extent by an intertextual "conversation" with Aloysius Bertrand's eponymic prose poem and Maurice Ravel's musical version of it, narrates the fantastic exchange of identities between the son of a traditional family (whose "liberated" mother seems to him just another mask of conventional female prototypes) and a clochard he meets in his wanderings through an Edenic park in the heart of Barcelona. As in Honoré de Balzac's *La Comedie Humaine* (1842), Donoso's characters reappear from novella to novella.

Tres novelitas burguesas may be considered a minor work, but Donoso's next novel is a major effort comparable in scope to *El obsceno pájaro*, though very different in texture. *Casa de campo* (1978; translated as *A House in the Country*, 1984) is a carnivalized allegory of the Chilean military coup of 1973, and an exploration—through a study of the aristocratic family—of the ideological repertoire to which the military dictatorship could appeal for legitimation at a cultural level. Accordingly the novel is set in the country residence of an extended oligarchic family—the Venturas—where internal intrigues pitting faction against faction proliferate. At the top of the social pyramid are the adults; in the middle, the thirty-three cousins; near the bottom, the army of servants who take their orders from the adults and whose duty is to keep the unpredictable children in their place; and, at the bottom, the natives who dig the gold from the Venturas' mines. Outside the vertical structure of the pyramid of power are the foreigners who control the world markets where the Venturas trade their gold. Within the neocolonial order represented by the novel, however, the foreigners wield the real power, if not social authority. These groups respond to ideologies that clearly demarcate their boundaries, but the crisis that sets the story in motion (and which allegorically refers to Salvador Allende's election to power in 1970 and the resulting right-wing coup three years later) splits the children (the middle classes) and the lackeys (the army) into warring factions, the aim being to fill the power vacuum left by the adults' excursion into the countryside. The house (the nation) is left at the mercy of the children, some of whom uphold the traditional order while others seek alliances with the natives in order to bring about radical change. The novel plots the upturn and downturn of power as different cliques accede to or fall from it, and the story ends with an apocalyptic leveling of social orders that allegorically is a call for social cooperation in the face of national chaos.

Although *Casa de campo* brings to mind novels such as Richard Hughes's *High Wind in Jamaica* (1929) and William Golding's *Lord of the Flies* (1954), its aestheticism, or *preciosismo*, is unmatched by these models and, indeed, by most modern or postmodern writing. Donoso's style is a beautifully crafted verbal mask reminiscent above all of Latin-American poetic *modernismo* at its most removed from historical reality, and of the language of painting. To a large extent the novel is conceived as a series of *tableaux vivants* of great refinement, and allusions to painting abound. The house itself features a trompe l'oeil Renaissance mural with life-size figures, which can well stand as a metaphor for the novel as a whole: beautiful but deceptive. Indeed, the narra-

Dust jacket for Donoso's 1978 novel, an allegory of the 1973 military coup in Chile

tor would have one believe that the representation proposed by the novel is an autonomous and aesthetic order with no ramifications into history and staged by a dictatorial author who does as he pleases with his characters. But some of the characters appear to be far from submissive to authorial will, and the novel is a ciphered rendering of contemporary Chilean history, which even includes fragments of speeches by Allende and Augusto Pinochet.

However, one should not discard the authorial claims to autonomy too hastily. While it is true that the text's aesthetic quality is undermined from within by scenes of brutality and cannibalism that show the poetic reverie to be mere make-believe, always on the verge of catastrophic collapse, *Casa de campo* is the response of a modern writer (that is, of a writer whose inheritance is the autonomy of literature) to the ravages of history. The imposition of a military dictatorship on a country to which Donoso felt fated to return is directly translatable as the imposition of an external authority on the writer's own creative freedom (Donoso uses the word *castración* to refer to the indignities brought upon the nation by the military takeover). The novel's self-conscious artificiality can be construed, then, as the reassertion of creative autonomy at a time of duress, when the urgency of the political agenda threatened to swallow up concerns of a purely aesthetic kind. However, and at the same time, Donoso's claim for aesthetic self-determination must be legitimated in historical terms. Thus, *Casa de campo* cannibalizes history, and, through this appropriating and reordering gesture, the novel can afford on the surface to deny the very historical reality to which it responds.

In 1980 Donoso was to make his definitive return to Chile, writing in the meantime two vastly different novels. *La misteriosa desaparición de la Marquesita de Loria* (The Mysterious Disappearance of the Marchioness of Loria, 1981) is a brief, mock-erotic novel that re-creates the Madrid of the *belle époque*, especially through the illustrated magazines of the period, some of whose drawings are included in the original Seix Barral edition (dated 1980 but published the following year). It is as if Donoso had constructed a story of aristocratic intrigue and erotic pursuit out of a sequence of these stylized illustrations depicting the life of leisure and sport led by the urban well-to-do. He weaves fairy-tale motifs into the fabric of the erotic novel, and the protagonist's disappearance at the end of the story recalls Aunt Matilde's disappearance at the end of "Paseo," in spite of the obvious differences between the short story's realist code and the novel's unabashed display of artifice.

El jardín de al lado (The Garden Next Door, 1981) is a somber and bitter semi-autobiographical narrative focusing on a failed Latin-American novelist (in the midst of the boom), whose family life crumbles all around him partially as a result of his political exile. It is thus the story of a triple defeat in which the author lays bare his intimacy, movingly at times, often with alienating results. The novel is sharp, biting, and uncompromising in its depiction of the Latin-American exile community in Spain and in the rendering of the protagonist's marriage, though Donoso assumes a nostalgic tone when narrating the prolonged agony of the protagonist's mother in faraway Chile (Donoso's mother passed away in 1975, and he briefly returned to Chile for the funeral).

It would be wrong, however, to exaggerate the novel's autobiographical value. Donoso has always held the view that fiction is a kind of exorcism of personal demons, and in *El jardín de al lado* he confronts them publicly. But the novel's structural model is the mirror, which has some Stendhalian aspects but also distorts and tricks. Thus the failed novelist at the center of the plot is a Donoso left out of the boom's movable feast, not one of the actual protagonists of the Latin-American novel's reinvigoration. Furthermore the closing chapter performs an astonishing reversal of perspective, and it turns out that the novel's narrator is in fact the assumed narrator's wife. Beyond the putative merits or flaws of its narrative strategy, *El jardín de al lado* represents Donoso's second attempt to come to terms with the trauma of Chilean contemporary history. In *Casa de campo* Donoso dons the mask of an eighteenth-century author who can intervene at will in his narrative; in *El jardín de al lado* he attempts to doff all masks and integrate his personal demons into the historical nightmare.

El jardín de al lado was the last novel Donoso wrote in Spain. Since that time he has been busy directing literary workshops, writing a monthly column for the Agencia EFE, and producing new fiction. However, it was his involvement with theater that characterized the early years of his return. In November 1982 his play *Sueños de mala muerte* (Dreams of a Bad Death, published in book form in 1985) was staged by Chile's leading dramatic group, ICTUS, and opened to rave reviews and significant audience response; it was later performed in Caracas. Other major Latin-American novelists have tried their hand at dramatic writing, and the theater in Chile has been perhaps the most significant form of artistic endeavor since the coup of 1973, much of this having to do with the superior sense of communal protest and of solidarity that the theater affords when compared to poetry or fiction. Not that *Sueños de mala muerte* is overtly political, but it does set out to capture the sense of despair that hangs over a country asphyxiated by a military dictatorship and (temporarily) ruined by an economic depression.

Sueños de mala muerte—an ironic, tragic, and somewhat buffoonish story of petit bourgeois characters aspiring to own property and coming to blows over the only property they can afford to own: a mausoleum—started out as a rough draft for a short story that grew to the size of a full-fledged play in an ongoing creative exchange between the author and the ICTUS actors. A separate version of this project grew out of one of these many drafts and was published as a novella in Donoso's *Cuatro para Delfina* (Four for Delfina, 1982), his first book of fiction to be written after his return to Chile. The title alludes to the four novellas that make up the book and to Delfina Guzmán, the leading Chilean actress and the instigator of Donoso's involvement with ICTUS.

In general, and as expected, these short novels are profoundly marked by their author's reencounter with his native country and the Chilean vernacular. Thus "Los habitantes de una ruina inconclusa" (The Inhabitants of a Unfinished Ruin) is an allegory depicting the economic shambles of Chile in the early 1980s, the social tensions generated by the shortage of capital and its concentration in the hands of a few, and the rise of a new entrepreneurial class to replace the traditional bourgeoisie. The story is based on the confrontation between the comfortable middle class and the lumpen element that invades the older residential neighborhoods. Ideologically Donoso elaborates the bourgeoisie's bad consciousness and identifies the new speculators as the enemy of the disenfranchised. "El tiempo perdido" (Lost Time) is an ingenious and poignant homage to Marcel Proust's great novel, *A la recherche du temps perdu* (7 volumes, 1913-1927), whose characters are emulated and impersonated by a group of bohemian provincials with literary aspirations. Donoso had read Proust forty years earlier (the temporal frame of "El tiempo perdido") and played the role of society dandy for a while, probably with the same poor results as one or two of his characters. The last of the four novellas is "Jolie Madame," which focuses on a trio of middle-age females on holiday.

In 1986 Donoso published *La desesperanza* (translated as *Curfew*, 1988), a sober and disenchanted novel dealing with contemporary Chilean politics. The form is classical in its tripartite division and in its observance of the canonical unities of time, place, and action. Its recurring icon is Arnold Böcklin's painting *Island of the Dead*. The story takes place in the twenty-four hours between Matilde Neruda's death and her funeral (Neruda's widow died in Santiago in January 1985). The first part is set in the widow's house during her wake and focuses mostly on the triangular relationship among the protagonists: Mañungo Vera, a successful folksinger who returns to Chile for the first time after the coup; Judit Torre, the beautiful scion of a powerful family who sympathizes with the Left; and Lopito, a bohemian poet, physically and morally abject, who prods Mañungo's nationalist consciousness. Outside this triangle stand other characters that give the novel depth and range: a local literary glory; a militant member of the Communist youth and his right-wing counterpart; an old friend and confidant of Neruda; and others. The second part presents Judit and Mañungo taking a nightmarish journey through Santiago in the hour after curfew. The focus is restricted to Judit's story of prison and torture, and to her sudden encounter in the darkened streets with an officer ambiguously implicated in her detention. The tension resumes in the third and final section, which narrates Matilde's multitudinous funeral and Lopito's ill treatment at the hands of the police, which results in his death. Lopito's death, in turn, motivates Mañungo's self-knowledge and his decision to assume his Chilean identity fully, overcoming the identity of the self-exiled pop idol he was in Europe. This individual tragedy is counterpointed with a larger one whose victim is Matilde Neruda herself, or, rather, her wishes that her funeral should be an occasion for reconciliation and not a vituperative demonstration against the regime.

La desesperanza (which literally translates into English as *Despair*) fuses, then, the personal and the political in a way that combines the despair of the many with the newly found faith of the few. The theme of Mañungo and Judit's story is not so much the retrieval of one's origins as the creation of a new, authentic identity with the materials offered by history, no matter how degraded these may be. The narrator makes it clear that this is a step that the nation as a whole has yet to take, lost as it is in a fantasy of progress and well-being that cuts it off from present-day reality.

Donoso's latest fiction to date is a pair of novellas published together as *Taratuta; Naturaleza muerta con cachimba* (Taratuta; Still Life with Pipe, 1990). "Taratuta" is a kind of metafictional variation of Sigmund Freud's "family romance" theory. The story recounts its own production as well as the invention of an identity for one of the characters, who bears the same improbable name as a minor and shadowy protagonist of the Bolshevik Revolution, mentioned in Gerard Walter's biography of Lenin and in other accounts of the period. The piece bears witness once again to Donoso's lifelong interest in the travails of identity, but it represents a new solution to the con-

Donoso and Ricardo Gutiérrez Mouat in Washington, D.C., 1986

flict between culture and politics that the author had previously dealt with in *Casa de campo* and *El jardín de al lado*. The story reads like an unfinished draft of one of its many possibilities, all of which involve an interweaving of history and fiction. Its ultimate effect is to balance the historical status of the Russian Taratuta and his fictional nomadic descendant, whose uncertain identity and undefined physiognomy range him alongside the clochard in such stories as "Gaspard de la Nuit" and "Los habitantes de una ruina inconclusa." This character's possessive woman companion is an avatar of the witch figure who appears in novels such as *El obsceno pájaro* and *La desesperanza*.

The title of the second novella, "Naturaleza muerta con cachimba," refers to an avant-garde painting that the narrator finds by chance in a dilapidated provincial museum housing the works of the fictional painter Larco, whose real-life model seems to be the Bavarian artist Mauricio Rugendas, the subject of a 1980 play Donoso has never finished writing. The plot of the novella centers on the encounter between the narrator—a mediocre bureaucrat—and the museum's decrepit caretaker, who turns out to be the master painter himself. Upon the latter's death, the erstwhile functionary usurps his identity and retires to live in the former museum. The topic of artistic incomprehension functions as one of the story's themes, but at a deeper level "Naturaleza muerta con cachimba," like its companion piece, is about the power of artistic creation to absorb and transform mundane existence.

In 1990 José Donoso was awarded the Chilean Premio Nacional de Literatura. His break with *costumbrismo* (nativism) and with the social novel of an earlier generation powerfully ushered in the modern Chilean novel, a form Donoso used to explore the relationships and identity of the dominant classes.

Bibliographies:

Luis Domínguez, ed., *Los mejores cuentos de José Donoso: Recopilación, introducción y nota bibliográfica* (Santiago, Chile: Zig-Zag, 1966);

John J. Hassett and others, "Biobibliography— José Donoso," *Chasqui*, 2 (November 1972): 15-30.

References:

Hugo Achugar, *Ideología y estructuras narrativas en José Donoso* (Caracas: Centro de Estudios "Rómulo Gallegos," 1979);

Pamela Bacarisse, "*El obsceno pájaro de la noche*: A Willed Process of Evasion," in *Contemporary Latin American Fiction*, edited by Salvador Bacarisse (Edinburgh: Scottish Academic Press, 1980), pp. 18-33;

John Barth, "Postmodernism Revisited," *Review of Contemporary Fiction*, 8 (Fall 1988): 16-24;

Ricardo Gutiérrez Mouat, "Aesthetics, Ethics, and Politics in Donoso's *El jardín de al lado*," *PMLA*, 106 (January 1991): 60-70;

Gutiérrez Mouat, "El desclasamiento como ideología y forma en la narrativa de José Donoso," in his *El espacio de la crítica* (Madrid: Orígenes, 1989);

Gutiérrez Mouat, *José Donoso: Impostura e impostación* (Gaithersburg, Md.: Hispamérica, 1983);

Alfred J. MacAdam, "Countries of the Mind: Literary Space in Joseph Conrad and José Donoso," in his *Textual Confrontations* (Chicago: University of Chicago Press, 1987), pp. 61-87;

Sharon Magnarelli, "José Donoso's *El obsceno pájaro de la noche*: Witches Everywhere and Nowhere," in her *The Lost Rib* (Lewisburg, Pa.: Bucknell University Press, 1985), pp. 147-168;

Oscar Montero, "*El jardín de al lado:* La escritura y el fracaso del éxito," *Revista Iberoamericana*, 123-124 (April-September 1983): 449-467;

Emir Rodríguez Monegal, "El mundo de José Donoso," *Mundo Nuevo*, 12 (June 1967): 77-85;

Rodríguez Monegal, "The Novel as Happening: An Interview with José Donoso," *Review 73* (Center for Inter-American Relations, 1973): 34-39;

Severo Sarduy, "Writing/Transvestism," *Review* (Fall 1973): 31-33;

Philip Swanson, "Donoso and the Post-Boom: Simplicity and Subversion," *Contemporary Literature*, 4 (Winter 1987): 520-529;

Swanson, "Structure and Meaning in *La misteriosa desaparición de la Marquesita de Loria*," *BHS*, 3 (July 1986): 247-256.

Carlos Fuentes
(11 November 1928 -   )

Lanin A. Gyurko
University of Arizona

BOOKS: *Los días enmascarados* (Mexico City: Los Presentes, 1954); translated in part by Margaret Sayers Peden in *Burnt Water* (New York: Farrar, Straus & Giroux, 1980);

La región más transparente (Mexico City: Fondo de Cultura Económica, 1958); translated by Sam Hileman as *Where the Air is Clear* (New York: Obolensky, 1960; London: Deutsch, 1986);

Las buenas conciencias (Mexico City: Fondo de Cultura Económica, 1959); translated by Hileman as *The Good Conscience* (New York: Obolensky, 1961);

La muerte de Artemio Cruz (Mexico City: Fondo de Cultura Económica, 1962); translated by Hileman as *The Death of Artemio Cruz* (New York: Obolensky, 1964; London: Secker & Warburg, 1977);

Aura (Mexico City: Era, 1962); translated by Lysander Kemp (New York: Farrar, Straus & Giroux, 1968);

Cantar de ciegos (Mexico City: Mortiz, 1964); translated in part by Peden in *Burnt Water*;

Zona sagrada (Mexico City: Siglo XXI, 1967); translated by Suzanne Jill Levine as *Holy Place*, in *Triple Cross* (New York: Dutton, 1972);

Cambio de piel (Mexico City: Mortiz, 1967); translated by Hileman as *A Change of Skin* (New York: Farrar, Straus & Giroux, 1968);

París: La revolución de Mayo (Mexico City: Era, 1968);

Righe per Adami (Venice: Alpieri, 1968);

La nueva novela hispanoamericana (Mexico City: Mortiz, 1969);

Cumpleaños (Mexico City: Mortiz, 1969);

El mundo de José Luis Cuevas, bilingual edition, translated by Consuelo de Aerenlund (Mexico City: Galería de Arte Misrachi, 1969);

Todos los gatos son pardos (Mexico City: Siglo XXI, 1970); revised in *Los reinos originarios: Teatro hispanomexicano* (Barcelona: Barral, 1971);

El tuerto es rey (Mexico City: Mortiz, 1970); republished in *Los reinos originarios: Teatro hispanomexicano*;

Casa con dos puertas (Mexico City: Mortiz, 1970);

Tiempo mexicano (Mexico City: Mortiz, 1971);

Terra nostra (Barcelona: Seix Barral, 1975); translated by Peden as *Terra Nostra* (New York: Farrar, Straus & Giroux, 1976; London: Secker & Warburg, 1977);

Cervantes o la crítica de la lectura (Mexico City: Mortiz, 1976); translated in part by Fuentes as *Don Quixote or the Critique of Reading* (Austin, Tex.: Institute of Latin American Studies, 1976);

La cabeza de la hidra (Barcelona: Argos, 1978); translated by Peden as *The Hydra Head* (New York: Farrar, Straus & Giroux, 1978; London: Secker & Warburg, 1979);

Una familia lejana (Mexico City: Era, 1980); translated by Peden as *Distant Relations* (New York: Farrar, Straus & Giroux, 1982; London: Secker & Warburg, 1982);

Agua quemada (Mexico City: Fondo de Cultura Económica, 1981); translated in part by Peden in *Burnt Water*;

Cuerpos y ofrendas (Madrid: Alianza, 1981);

Orquídeas a la luz de la luna (Barcelona: Seix Barral, 1982);

Gringo viejo (Mexico City: Fondo de Cultura Económica, 1985); translated by Fuentes and Peden as *The Old Gringo* (New York: Farrar, Straus & Giroux, 1985);

Cristóbal nonato (Mexico City: Fondo de Cultura Económica, 1987); translated by Alfred MacAdam as *Christopher Unborn* (New York: Farrar, Straus & Giroux, 1989);

Myself with Others: Selected Essays (New York: Farrar, Straus & Giroux, 1988);

Constancia y otras novelas para vírgenes (Mexico City: Fondo de Cultura Económica, 1990); translated by Thomas Christensen as *Constancia and Other Stories for Virgins* (New York: Farrar, Straus & Giroux, 1990);

La campaña (Buenos Aires & Mexico City: Fondo de Cultura Económica, 1990); translated by MacAdam as *The Campaign* (London:

Deutsch, 1991; New York: Farrar, Straus & Giroux, 1991);
Valiente mundo nuevo (Madrid: Mondadori, 1990).

OTHER: Autobiographical overview, in *Los narradores ante el público*, first series (Mexico City: Mortiz, 1966), pp. 137-155.

Born in Panama City on 11 November 1928, under the astrological sign of Scorpio, as he is fond of mentioning, Carlos Fuentes, one of Mexico's premier novelists, is the son of Rafael Fuentes Boettiger, a career diplomat and at the time attaché to the Mexican legation in Panama, and the former Berta Macías Rivas. The young Fuentes spent much of his childhood in the capital cities of Latin America, including Montevideo and Rio de Janeiro, where his father was secretary to the Mexican ambassador to Brazil—the distinguished poet and essayist Alfonso Reyes, who later became Fuentes's literary mentor. From 1934 to 1940 Fuentes attended the Henry D. Cooke public school in Washington, D.C., where his father was counselor to the Mexican Embassy, and where his sister Berta was born. In contrast with this international experience, a decisive occurrence, which led to his recognizing himself as Mexican, was the appearance of headlines in the Washington newspapers declaring the nationalization and expropriation of the oil wells in Mexico by President Lázaro Cárdenas. Fuentes says that, although up to that time he had been very popular with his North American classmates, he suddenly found himself snubbed and then shunned.

For the first time he became aware of the ambivalent relationship, at times cordial and at other periods antagonistic, between the United States and Mexico, a theme he would later develop in several of his works, culminating in *Gringo viejo* (1985; translated as *The Old Gringo*, also 1985), his novel of border crossings and cultural shock, which depicts the experiences of two North Americans in the turbulent Mexico of the 1910 revolution and which rapidly became a best-seller in the United States. Fuentes possesses a cosmopolitan nature and has been friends with leading North American writers, such as Arthur Miller, to whom Fuentes's 1970 drama *Todos los gatos son pardos* (All the Cats Are Gray) is dedicated; Norman Mailer; and William Styron, to whose father *Gringo viejo* is dedicated.

When Fuentes's father was named chargé d'affaires in Santiago, Chile, Fuentes attended the Grange school, where one of his classmates was José Donoso, who credits Fuentes with being the founder of the Latin-American "boom" novel. A constellation of novelists, including Argentina's Julio Cortázar, Colombia's Gabriel García Márquez, Peru's Mario Vargas Llosa, and Donoso himself, developed the all-encompassing *novela totalizante*, an exuberant fusion of social, psychological, and metaphysical concerns, and experiments in language, time, space, and point of view. Donoso's long essay *Historia personal del "boom"* (1972; translated as *The Boom in Spanish American Literature: A Personal History*, 1977) provides a glowing tribute to Fuentes, to both his artistic inspiration and his efforts to open the publishing houses of the United States to contemporary Latin-American authors. In the 1940s Fuentes lived in Buenos Aires, where his father was in charge of the Mexican Business Affairs Department, a Buenos Aires that Fuentes would later evoke nostalgically in his novel *Cambio de piel* (1967; translated as *A Change of Skin*, 1968). In 1946 Fuentes attended the Colegio de México, later studying at the Institut des Hautes Etudes in Geneva before returning to Mexico to become a student in the school of law at the Universidad Nacional Autónoma de México. During the early 1950s he was press secretary for the United Nations Information Center in Mexico City and secretary in the Bureau of Cultural Diffusion at the university.

In 1954 Fuentes published his first book, a collection of short stories that emphasized the supernatural combined with trenchant social satire, *Los días enmascarados* (The Masked Days; translated in part in *Burnt Water*, 1980), and he struck a fascinating theme that would reappear throughout his works: the violent irruption into twentieth-century, bourgeois Mexican society of the ancient Mayan gods (as in the story "Chac Mool") and Aztec deities (as in "Por boca de los dioses" [Through the Mouth of the Gods])—the point of which being to excoriate commercial and technological Mexican society for its rampant materialism, status-striving, and (figurative) incessant demands for victims of blood sacrifices. Several of the stories in this collection are important in that they constitute direct antecedents of Fuentes's first and one of his most important novels, *La región más transparente* (1958; translated as *Where the Air is Clear*, 1960), which focuses on all social classes, from the exploited and marginalized lower classes, to the precarious middle class, formed after the revolution of 1910, to the dazzling nouveaux riches, a class of entrepreneurs and socialites that sprang up after the ancien régime—the followers of Porfirio Díaz—was defeated. The strikingly original aspect of this work is that the Mexico of the 1950s is evoked from the perspective of Ixca Cienfuegos, who functions both as individual participant and as a collective unconsciousness and who assumes human form but is in fact an ancient Aztec god—the god of war, Huitzilopochtli—returned to Mexico not to provide spiritual regeneration for a vapid and soulless society but to take vengeance on the descendants of the sixteenth-century conquistadores for having overthrown the ancient Aztec deities. With *La región más transparente* Fuentes boldly initiated the *novela totalizante*, changing the course of Mexican literature by producing a dazzling fusion of anthropology, sociology, music, painting, and film. Similar to the gigantic, explosive murals of Diego Rivera that inspired him, Fuentes combines all epochs of Mexican history and mythifies them, from the founding of the ancient capital city Mexico-Tenochtitlán in 1326 to the conquest, the colonial period, the War of Reform, and the French Intervention, culminating in the Mexican Revolution of 1910, which forms a basic theme of this work as it does for several of Fuentes's subsequent novels.

In 1956 Fuentes and the literary critic Emmanuel Carballo founded the *Revista Mexicana de Literatura* (Mexican Review of Literature). Following in the diplomatic footsteps of his father, Fuentes served from 1957 until 1959 as director of international cultural relations for Mexico's Ministry of Foreign Affairs, and from

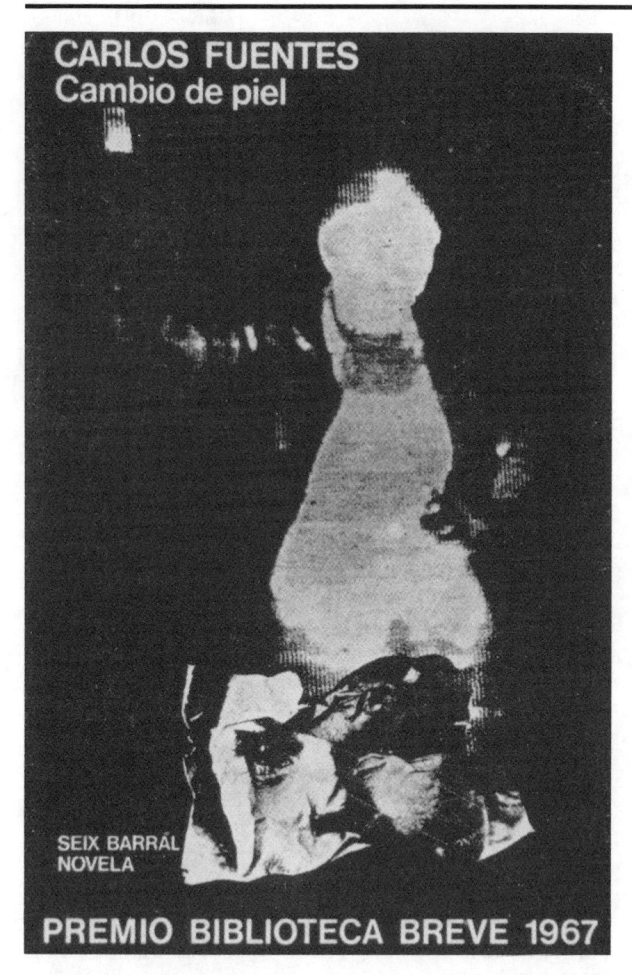

Dust jacket for the Barcelona edition of Fuentes's nostalgic novel set in Buenos Aires, where he lived in the early 1940s

1975 to 1977 he served as the ambassador from Mexico to France, having been appointed by President Luis Echeverría. In 1959 Fuentes married Rita Macedo, a screen actress, and in 1962 their daughter Cecilia was born. He was elected to the Colegio Nacional in 1972, and his welcoming address was delivered by the Mexican essayist, poet, and Nobel Prize winner Octavio Paz.

Divorced from Macedo in 1969, Fuentes married Sylvia Lemus, a journalist, in 1972. Their son, Carlos Rafael, was born in 1973 and their daughter, Natascha, in 1974. Throughout his many articles in leading newspapers and journals in Mexico and in the United States, Fuentes has acted as "ambassador without portfolio," seeking to define the relationship between the United States and Latin America and to promote international understanding. He has lectured at Cambridge University and at Princeton and Harvard, where he was Robert F. Kennedy Professor in Latin American Studies and taught courses in comparative literature.

Among Fuentes's major themes are the quest for Mexican national identity—influenced by the writings of the Mexican philosophers José Vasconcelos and Samuel Ramos, and by the seminal work on the Mexican national character by Octavio Paz, *El laberinto de la soledad* (The Labyrinth of Solitude, 1950)—and a continued and profound exploration of the components of that identity: political, historic, social, psychological, and mythic. One of Fuentes's most compelling themes is the world of ancient indigenous myths, the gods and goddesses of the Aztec pantheon, including the god of life and love, Quetzalcoatl, his downfall and self-banishment from the New World, and his supposed return in the form of the Spanish conquistador Hernán Cortés, examined in *Terra nostra* (1975; translated, 1976) and in his drama *Todos los gatos son pardos*. The play fuses the epoch of the Conquest of Mexico with the student massacre of Nonoalco Tlatelolco in 1968, in the same setting of the blood sacrifices rendered by the Aztecs to their gods and the last fierce battle between the Spanish invaders and the indigenous defenders: the historic Plaza de las Tres Culturas. Tlazoltéotl, the ancient Aztec goddess of filth and carnal love, is evoked in Fuentes's novel *Zona sagrada* (1967; translated as *Holy Place*, in *Triple Cross*, 1972), which expertly fuses Aztec, classical Greek, and Egyptian myths. And the *mater terribilis*, Coatlicue, whose huge stone idol, with its serpent heads, its necklace of severed human hands, and its skirt of serpents, in the Museo Nacional de la Antropología, is a sinister presence in *La región más transparente* and in a more disguised form in his novella *Aura* (1962; translated, 1968).

Fuentes has also explored the Latin-American identity, inspired by the Cuban novelist Alejo Carpentier who has examined the clash of European and New World cultures in his novels. In *La campaña* (1990; translated as *The Campaign*, 1991) Fuentes evokes the struggle for Latin-American independence from Spain at the beginning of the nineteenth century, creating one of his most idealistic protagonists, Baltasar Bustos, who is determined to convert the ideals of liberty and equality of Jean-Jacques Rousseau into direct and immediate action, and who serves under José de San Martín, evoked by Fuentes as a stern and implacable force of social justice to liberate Argentina. Baltasar subsequently travels to Mexico, where he joins the forces of the insurgents under the command of the valiant priest Quintana, who represents the continuation of the valorous and savvy priest Morelos. But Quintana is shadowed by Morelos's tragic fate; both will become martyrs to the cause of independence, and their lives and heroic goals will be assumed symbolically by Baltasar. In *Una familia lejana* (1980; translated as *Distant Relations*, 1982), which, in contrast to so many of the works of Fuentes, demonstrates the complex and powerful influence of the New World on the Old, Fuentes includes as characters writers such as José María de Heredia, grandson of the well-known Cuban lyric poet José María Heredia. In *Una familia lejana* also appear Jules Lafforgue, Jules Supervielle, and the most famous of the émigrés, the Uruguayan author Isadore-Lucien Ducasse, who assumed the name Comte de Lautreamont and authored the gruesome work of demonic possession, *Les Chants de Maldoror*, to which Fuentes pays homage in this, his own novel of demonism and blood sacrifice.

Another theme that appears throughout Fuentes's work is that of the United States and the tremendous social, cultural, and political impact it has exerted on his homeland. Fuentes is decidedly ambivalent toward the country viewed in Latin America as the Colossus of the North. Although he has spent much of his life traveling and lecturing in the United States, teaching at major North American universities, and collaborating on Public Broadcast System projects, such as the one commemorating the voyage of Christopher Columbus in 1492, in his fictional works Fuentes ironically emphasizes the fact that the greatest revolutionary force in Mexico is not the rebellious but ultimately defeated *los de abajo* (lower class) but the North American presence. And in *Gringo viejo*, in an attempt to come to grips with the North American-Mexican cultural clash, Fuentes evokes a revolutionary Mexico at the beginning of the twentieth century through North American eyes and from a feminist perspective. Thus the narrator and the most important character is neither the acerbic and misanthropic Ambrose Bierce, to whom the title refers, nor the revolutionary general in the army of Pancho Villa, Tomás Arroyo—who in a fit of rage kills Bierce, ironically granting Bierce the death he has sought in Mexico—but the recluse, Harriet Winslow.

The structure of Fuentes's first novel, *La región más transparente*, an epic of modern Mexico inspired in part by John Dos Passos's *Manhattan Transfer* (1925), is loose, disjointed, fragmentary, and kaleidoscopic, as the narrative moves relentlessly from one social class to another, constantly shifting its perspective to evoke a panorama of city life. This highly fluid structure mirrors the postrevolutionary society of Mexico as unstable, in constant tension and flux. The remnants of the Porfirian elite, defeated in the revolution of 1910, such as Fuentes's haughty character Doña Lorenza and her ambitious niece, Pimpinela de Ovando, struggle to hold on to their wealth by trading "class for cash" with the nouveaux riches, such as the pretentious Norma Larragoiti de Robles and her husband, Fernando Robles, one of the central figures in the work, both catapulted to a position of economic power and social prominence after the revolution and both desperately seeking the confirmation of their status by the former aristocrats, including the once-prestigious Ovando family. Robles, a fighter in the revolution who has served under Alvaro Obregón and helped defeat the forces of Pancho Villa in the crucial battle of Celaya, quickly seizes the power that his being on the winning side gives him to construct a financial and industrial empire for himself. He rapidly distances himself from his origins, from the lower classes for whose benefit the revolution was ostensibly fought, and gives up revolutionary ideals of land, labor, and educational reform. Robles constructs a lavish neocolonial mansion to isolate himself from the masses. The lack of national unity—the extreme alienation of one group or class from another—is strikingly conveyed through the technique of presenting only fragments of conversations or encounters, as Fuentes first evokes Gladys García, a prostitute in awe of the nouveaux riches, then shifts to focus on the lavish and seemingly endless parties of the jet set, then evokes the stoic survivors of Villa's once-glorious northern division, who meet to recall past victories that have led to nothing, as they still remain mired in poverty and insignificance. Instead of acknowledging his responsibility for his own people, for whom the revolution was fought, Robles dons expensive cashmere suits and, ashamed of his Indian features, even powders his face white, thereby emulating the dictator whom he had overthrown, the mestizo Porfirio Díaz, who glorified everything that was not Mexican.

In *La región más transparente* Fuentes creates a series of characters who are developed not merely as individuals but as complex, ambivalent symbols of postrevolutionary Mexico. The most important character and the most enigmatic is

Ixca Cienfuegos. As an individual, the aloof and highly evasive Ixca can never be precisely defined. He plays many roles, from business adviser, to go-between, to gigolo, and elicits confessions from the persons whose confidence he gains, then suddenly betrays them, bringing about their downfall. Acting as a best friend of the vain and highly insecure Rodrigo Pola, Ixca seeks to claim him as a victim of sacrifice. He seduces then attempts to murder Robles's wife, Norma, and is instrumental in precipitating the financial ruin of Robles. Ixca's role is vague and protean because he is meant to symbolize a collective consciousness—the spirit of ancient indigenous Mexico, which throughout the history of the nation, from the time of the conquest of Mexico-Tenochtitlán by the Spanish, has remained defeated, unincorporated into the dominant society. Symbolic of this estrangement is a twentieth-century descendant of the ancient Aztecs, Gladys García, the prostitute who opens and closes the narrative, a symbol of hopelessness, poverty, and fatalistic resignation. Ironically, she never establishes contact with Ixca, the fellow Indian who reaches out to her, but she is in awe of the New Gods, the members of the jet set with their endless partying and social ostentation. Ixca is portrayed as a perpetual outsider, a marginal man who moves incessantly through modern Mexican society without ever gaining acceptance by any class or group. Teódula Moctezuma, Ixca's mother, represents the mother of the gods. When Teódula is initially seen in the book, she seems to be praying to the Catholic Virgin, yet the emphases in her prayers, on the offering up of her heart and on the skirt of serpents worn by the deity, indicate she is really praying to the ancient Aztec goddess Coatlicue.

In Aztec cosmology Coatlicue, the great earth goddess, was the mother of Huitzilopochtli, the god of the fiery sun, symbolized by Ixca Cienfuegos, whose last name means "one hundred fires." Thus did the Aztecs explain the natural universe, in which the sun was seen daily to be born out of the earth, to rise to a fiery zenith, and then to sink and die, as it was again swallowed up by the earth. The dread Coatlicue is represented, in the immense stone statue that stands in the Museo Nacional de la Antropología in Mexico City, as wearing a necklace of human skulls and hands. She thus symbolizes the earth not only as a life-giving womb but as a tomb. Coatlicue gives birth to death. Immediately after his birth, her son Huitzilopochtli, venerated as the god of war, puts to death her other children, who had been plotting to kill her. Like her patron goddess, Teódula, too, has given birth to death. She has lost all of her children but one—Ixca. She is fanatically engaged in a death cult, as she prays over the skeletons of her dead husband and children and paints their skulls blue. Her last name, Moctezuma, indicates the human side of this sinister and ambivalent character creation, her link with the Aztec emperor defeated by Cortés, Moctezuma, whose vacillating and paranoid character Fuentes was to explore in his first drama, *Todos los gatos son pardos*. Teódula's donning of elaborate jewels signifies that she holds part of the famed lost treasure of Moctezuma, kept hidden from the avaricious conquistadores. And as a twentieth-century descendant of Moctezuma, she incarnates the Aztec demand for retribution against the descendants of the conquerors. Ixca is compelled to become the instrument of that vengeance, as Teódula insistently demands that he bring her a blood sacrifice; only by death can they be redeemed.

The implacable Ixca discounts both the present and the future of Mexico, because for him the whole of the national identity is resident in its Aztec past, both Mexico's glorious origin and its inalterable fate. Yet, unlike the so-called indigenist writers, whose position is represented forcefully and eloquently by Ixca, Fuentes himself sees the national identity as far more complex. Thus he develops several other characters who represent opposing points of view, such as Robles, who, although he is an Indian, dismisses the Aztec past as barbaric and irrelevant. Ashamed of his origins, Robles sees the past as representing only poverty and backwardness. He extols himself as a self-made man who has overcome his origins as the son of campesinos and by dint of his great energy and perseverance has achieved a well-deserved position as financier and industrialist. He suppresses the fact that only the sacrifices of true idealists, such as his cousin Froilán Reyero or the labor leader Feliciano Sánchez, made possible the victory of the revolution and enabled him to gain his vaunted position. Just as Ixca touts himself as a national savior, in contact with what he glorifies as the only authentic Mexico, so, too, does Robles exalt himself as a national redeemer, but for entirely different reasons. Robles pompously claims to be the single-handed architect of a progressive and prosperous new Mexico, the creator of a now-burgeoning new middle class that did not exist before the revolution.

Yet Robles, although he exalts himself as a vibrant present, is really an emanation of the past. In his marrying of a glittering but sterile mask of international chic, Norma Larragoiti, whose social chattering Robles turns on and off as he mixes entertainment of his guests with entrepreneurial dealings, the pompous Robles continues the *afrancesamiento*, the cult of European values, practiced by Porfirio Díaz. But Fuentes chooses as his most explicit symbol of postrevolutionary Mexico not the brash and authoritative Robles but a person who in almost every respect is his opposite—Rodrigo Pola, an introspective, self-doubting, constantly frustrated youth incapable of any sustained action. Fuentes evokes contemporary Mexico as a country in flux, created anew out of the revolution of 1910, still groping for a national definition and for an effective way to assert itself.

The failure of idealism, the impossibility of spiritual regeneration for both the individual and the nation, is underscored throughout this fatalistic narrative by the somber motif of the mother, symbolic of Mexico, who is linked not with creation but with death. For example, the anguished, overprotective Rosenda Pola is obsessed by the desire to reabsorb her child Rodrigo into her womb so that she can be eternally giving birth. When Ixca buries her, he ironically describes her shriveled body as resembling that of a grotesque, stillborn child. As a mother who has given birth to death, Rosenda parallels the demonic Teódula and also becomes a grim symbol of Mexico City, which Fuentes evokes as a huge womb endlessly giving birth to millions who are condemned to a death-in-life existence, a theme he later develops in *Cristóbal nonato* (1987; translated as *Christopher Unborn*, 1989).

In contrast to *La región más transparente*, *La muerte de Artemio Cruz* (1962; translated as *The Death of Artemio Cruz*, 1964) is a tightly organized work in which every fragment of narrative, every incident, and every motif is related either directly or indirectly to the life of the protagonist. One of Fuentes's prime goals in this novel was to create a single character powerful and complex enough to be convincing as a national symbol, representing both the new nation that has emerged out of the revolution and the way in which revolutionary reform, instead of being a permanent process—the ideal of Fuentes—has stagnated and in many cases even ossified. The disintegrating Cruz represents a revolution that in Fuentes's opinion is dying; the legacy of the moribund Cruz, officially touted through the newspaper he controls, is one of revolutionary glory and idealism, but the narrative reveals another legacy, that of power-mongering, corruption, venality, opportunism, and constant betrayals of the ideals of the revolution, which will be inherited by the hordes of flatterers and fawners surrounding Cruz, such as his lackey Padilla or Jaime Ceballos, who like Cruz had begun as an idealist with empathy for the plight of the dispossessed but who rapidly suppresses his idealism in order to pursue fortune and social status and to become one of the "easy consciences" Fuentes rails against in his second novel, *Las buenas conciencias* (1959; translated as *The Good Conscience*, 1961).

La muerte de Artemio Cruz, regarded by many critics as Fuentes's finest novel, exemplifies his definition of what the ideal novel should be: a paradoxical fusion of the novel of adventures and the novel of linguistic experimentation. *La muerte* examines the career of Cruz, whose very name (meaning "Cross") symbolizes his state, a fusion of Spanish and mulatto. Cruz, through a series of mental flashbacks as he lies dying, relives key moments when his life was at a crossroads, demanding decisions that would limit all his future options. And, in an allusion to the cross of Christ, the protagonist is seen as an ironic martyr whose deathbed agonies symbolize a burden not only of excruciating pain but of guilt and despair.

From the time of his birth, Cruz's existence is surrounded by violence and death, an allusion by Fuentes to the bloodshed that encompasses Mexican history. Even on his deathbed Cruz is portrayed as a conglomeration of warring selves. Undefeated in the revolution, emerging unscathed from the sanguinary atmosphere of the 1920s, Cruz defeats all his enemies except time. The complexity of Cruz's identity, a fusion of cowardice and bravery, idealism and treachery, rampant greed and materialism, and a capacity for self-sacrifice, is underscored by the structure of the novel. Instead of being portrayed as a coherent whole, Cruz's identity is fragmented into three narrative voices—first, second, and third person—in separate segments. His physical disintegration and spiritual dissolution, his incapacity to master self by integrating ego, conscience, self-serving ambition, and sense of social responsibility, are underscored in that the three voices keep alternating but always remain separate. Each nar-

Fuentes circa 1982 (photograph by Carlos Fuentes, Jr.)

rative voice, or inner double of the protagonist, reflects a different aspect of Cruz's paradoxical character. His anguished, dying self is expressed through the fragmented, chaotic style of the first-person monologue. His conscience and his subconscious are dramatized in the authoritative, convoluted style of the second-person narration. And Cruz's outer life, key incidents from the past in which he was called upon to make a choice—for example between sacrifice on the battlefield or self-preservation, or between a loveless but socially respectable marriage with the aristocrat Catalina and divorce and remarriage to the woman Cruz genuinely loves, Laura Riviere—is dramatized through the terse, third-person accounts. These diverse aspects of self are fused only negatively, at the end of the novel, as all three voices condense and collapse, abolished by death.

Cruz himself negates the opportunities for deliverance. In order to feel secure and powerful, he chooses to create a world in which everyone around him will be an image of himself, a world of fawners and opportunists strikingly dramatized in the third-person narrative of 31 December 1955. Cruz summons to his mansion one hundred guests, ostensibly to celebrate the New Year but in fact to pay court to him, as he sits aloof and unapproachable, exulting in his control over the crowd of arrivistes and deal makers, all created in his image. On the surface the celebration is of new life, but Cruz is secretly mocked by his guests as the "mummy of Coyoacán," and in vengeance he imagines in his twisted mind the unleashing upon them of the hordes of enormous rats that inhabit this old monastery converted into Cruz's palace. Rejecting the genuine love of Laura Riviere, Cruz remains with his paid mistress Lilia, who despises him but clings to him in a relationship as spurious and as spiteful as that between Robles and Norma in *La región*.

Even the details of structure have been carefully, exactingly worked out to mirror the basic themes of the novel. The last third-person segment, that of 9 April 1889 (the sections are antichronological), provides a flashback to the moment of Cruz's birth. This third-person segment is followed immediately by a section of first-person narrative evoking the exact moment of the protagonist's death. Structurally, therefore, there is but an instant between birth and death, an ironic juxtaposition severely undercutting Cruz's vaunted pretensions to be an all-powerful ruler who can rival even God. So great is Cruz's egomania that, even on his deathbed, as on the one hand he envies the lowly sponge for its ability to regenerate the whole of the self from but a fragment, a capacity which he lacks, on the other hand he attempts brashly to bargain with God, offering to believe in him in return for terrestrial immortality. The trinity of selves in Cruz refers to the divine Trinity: the Father and Son are ironically represented in Cruz and his son Lorenzo. Cruz is the godlike father who impels his son toward blood sacrifice, as he takes Lorenzo away from the overly protective Catalina and impels him toward a life of adventure in Cocuya, where Cruz has had the ancestral Menchaca estate restored. Cruz nurtures Lorenzo's idealism, until finally the youth, believing he is emulating his father's heroism in the Mexican revolution, leaves for Spain, where he will subsequently give his life in the Spanish Civil War—a heroic death Cruz regards as redeeming his own cowardice on the battlefield.

The juxtaposition of birthday and deathday, also essential to Fuentes's novel *Cumpleaños* (Birthdays, 1969), is not a mere aesthetic tour de force: it transmits through the structure of the work one of its central themes, the abnormal closeness of life and death throughout the whole of Cruz's existence and the corresponding importance Cruz places on having survived. From the moment of his birth, death hovers close to Cruz, in the form of his father, Atanasio Menchaca, a hacendado, who approaches the hut where Cruz's mother, Isabel Cruz, is giving birth, in order to kill his illegitimate son. Ironically death allows Cruz's life. Only because the ruthless Menchaca himself is killed is the life of the infant Cruz possible. Over and over again Cruz's existence is extended only because someone else dies in his place. With horrible irony Cruz on his deathbed, instead of displaying gratitude toward those who sacrificed their lives so that he could live, commands them to sacrifice themselves again so he can continue to live. Thus Cruz, who at the beginning of his life has represented the "new man," the opportunity for social reform, instead develops symbolically in terms of fatalistic archetypes—first as a hacendado, then as a conquistador, and finally as the Aztec emperor and the god of war, Huitzilopochtli, nourishing himself on the blood sacrifice of his victims. The culminating irony is that the death spasm of Cruz is depicted in terms of the obsidian knife of the grisly, ancient Aztec ritual of sacrifice.

Unlike *La muerte*, but similar to *La región*, *Gringo viejo* exemplifies Fuentes's capacity to write a novel of adventures that functions on many different levels: as a quest for identity on the part of the three main characters; as a historical novel, which continues the vibrant tradition of the novel of the Mexican revolution, begun in 1915 with the publication of *Los de abajo* (The Underdogs) by Mariano Azuela; and as a complex metaphysical work that interweaves dream sequences with intertextuality—incorporation of key scenes not only from the life of the historical Bierce but also from his short stories. Bierce is evoked as both a historical personage—as the flamboyant, cynical curmudgeon who authored *The Devil's Dictionary* (1911) and who was one of the few American authors to have fought in the Civil War and to have written works of fiction based on his gruesome battle experiences—and as a character in several of his own stories, including the hauntingly parricidal "A Horseman in the Sky." The inspiration for the character of the Gibson girl Harriet Winslow in *Gringo viejo* came to him while he was conversing with Jane Fonda, who later produced the film version of the novel, starring Gregory Peck as Ambrose Bierce, Jimmy Smits as the Villista general Tomás Arroyo, and Fonda herself as the strong-willed and uncompromising Winslow.

In *Gringo viejo*, from within old age and solitude, paralleling the recluse Consuelo in *Aura* (1962; translated, 1968), Harriet Winslow endlessly relives her experiences as a young and headstrong woman in Mexico, when she became the mistress of Tomás Arroyo, who offered her emotional and sexual fulfillment, in contrast to her prissy North American beau Delaney. And yet she suddenly rejects the relationship and departs from Mexico forever, to lock herself away and to live, as do so many of Fuentes's characters, including Rosenda Pola in *La región*, primarily in memory and imagination. Early in the novel Winslow, on the model of her impulsive and adventurous father, a soldier who abandons the family and lives the rest of his life in Cuba with his black mistress, leaves her mother to travel to Mexico to become a governess on the estate of the Miranda family. Only when she arrives does she find that her employers, like so many of the Porfirian aristocrats, have fled to France. Winslow stays, channeling her energies into educating "revolutionary children." There she encounters Bierce. Alienated from his wife and hated by his daughter, who holds him responsible for the suicide of one of his sons and the untimely death of another, Bierce has entered the extremely dangerous world of revolutionary Mexico, not in search of a new life, as is Winslow, but determined to die, preferably to be shot by Pancho Villa himself. Possessed by a deep Thanatos instinct but too cowardly to commit suicide, Bierce, who has fought valiantly for the North in the U.S. Civil War, longs to die on the battlefield. The historical Bierce crossed the frontier from El Paso into Mexico in 1913. He joined the forces of Villa and was never heard from again after the battle of Ojinaga. Some sources maintain that Bierce died as the result of malnutrition and disease; others say he was slain on the spot by an enraged Villa when the cantankerous Bierce declared he was abandoning Villa to fight on the side of Alvaro Obregón and Venustiano Carranza. In any case the ambiguity that surrounds the sudden disappearance of Bierce provides fertile terrain for fantasy making, 'and Fuentes has supplied still another ending to the Bierce conundrum.

As occurs so often in Fuentes's fatalistic world, the central characters of *Gringo viejo* are unable to achieve redemption. Although the weary and depressed Bierce, the impetuous Winslow, and the resentful Arroyo all attempt to break away from fruitless past lives and sterile past relationships, and in the case of the aged Bierce from past failures and inadequacies, all are ultimately defined not in terms of the new existences they have been given the opportunity by the revolution to create for themselves, but as inextricably bound to the old ones. As in so many of Fuentes's works, the characters are united, ironically, only in death. The sudden death of Bierce, shot in the back by a crazed Arroyo after Bierce has deliberately provoked him by setting fire to Arroyo's prized document—the land grant from the king of Spain legitimizing the claims of the people to the lands of the North—marks an ironic triumph for "Old Bitters" (Bierce), who has finally consummated his Thanatos desire. *Gringo viejo* both begins and ends with the contemplation of death. At the outset the focus is on the disinterment of Bierce's body, seeming in the fierce expression on his face to be more alive in death than in life. Bierce dies twice: Villa has him shot again, this time from the front, so he can claim the North American was executed by federal troops. The action of disinterment provides a thematic reflection of the narrative process itself, as the tormented Winslow endlessly resurrects the spirits of Bierce and of Arroyo in her stricken conscience. Arroyo is the reluctant revolutionary, just the opposite of the fanatic and unstoppable Demetrio Macías in Azuela's *Los de abajo*. Ironically, although Arroyo burns almost all of the Miranda mansion to the ground, an act not only of revolutionary destruction but of personal vengeance against his father, the cold and spiteful Don Miranda, who gave him life but refused to recognize him, Arroyo leaves the huge mirrored ballroom, modeled on the ballrooms of Versailles, intact.

Like Cruz and Robles, Arroyo initially represents the new, but he rapidly becomes linked with the old; he longs not only to slay his father but to become him, to rule over the hacienda. Thus can be explained his mesmeric state, as he lingers at the hacienda and must be impelled by his own troops to rejoin the revolution. Villa, another of the false fathers of the narrative, addresses Arroyo using the affective diminutive, right before executing him for not displaying total loyalty to him and to the revolutionary cause. And the novel ends with a focus on death, as it flashes back to evoke the tyrannical Miranda as an aged Don Juan. The disinterment and contemplation of the cadaver of Bierce at the outset is paralleled by the grisly ending, a view of the body of Miranda, hanging in a well somewhere in the Yucatán—the corpse Arroyo has longed to gaze upon and gloat over. The physical deaths of Bierce, Arroyo, and Miranda are paralleled by the life-in-death existence to which Winslow condemns herself. In *La región más transparente*, the narrator Ixca states cynically that the only hero acceptable in Mexico is the dead hero; death is the only proof that the hero is not a mere poseur, such as Robles and Cruz. Arroyo is at the end consecrated as a revolutionary hero because his untimely death impedes him from betraying his ideals. It is the outsider, the perceptive Bierce, who sees that Arroyo would emulate not only the initial phases of the military career of Porfirio Díaz, when he defended his homeland against the French Intervention and became a valiant and heroic supporter of Benito Juárez, in the struggle against the imperial authority of Maximilian and Carlota, but also the end of his career, when he became a virtual dictator of Mexico, ruling the nation single-handedly for thirty years and allowing rampant foreign exploitation, to the extent that Mexico became known as "the mother of foreigners, and the stepmother of Mexicans."

In *Gringo viejo*, a novel that Fuentes said in an interview was originally to be entitled "Frontiers," he is concerned with both North American and Mexican national identities. The evangelical Winslow at first expresses the attitude that Mexico must be Americanized, remolded according to Yankee Puritan virtues of thrift, energy, and committee administration, which she fervently attempts to actualize as she goes about organizing the revolutionaries so they can one day run the hacienda themselves, without hacendados. Yet the narrative traces her change of attitude. At the end she seems to become the spokesperson for Fuentes, as she declares that instead of Mexico being re-created in the image of the United States, it must be understood and accepted as it is.

Cristóbal nonato demonstrates that Fuentes has the capacity continually to expand and renew his artistic vision, charting new directions. Similar to *Terra nostra* in its prodigious length and verbal intricacies, but limiting its focus primarily to Mexico and providing much more emphasis on the development of its characters—who, rather than

Fuentes circa 1987, the year his novel Cristóbal nonato *was published (photograph copyright by Jerry Bauer)*

being primarily allegorical symbols, as are many of the characters in *Terra nostra*, are humanized and imbued with social and psychological depth—*Cristóbal nonato* is distinct from most of the other novels of Fuentes in tone. Many of these other works are characterized by a solemn tone that coincides with their often rhetorical style, but *Cristóbal nonato* is a humorous work in which slapstick, caricature, farce, satire, and incessant wordplay balance its depressing theme, which centers on Mexico City in 1992, wracked by myriad social and ecological problems, and plagued by black acid rain, by roving street gangs, and by a government that constantly substitutes contests, diversions, ceremonies, and celebrations for social action and amelioration.

In contrast, *Terra nostra*, for example, begins and ends in Paris in the year 1999, on the verge of the millennium. Thus Fuentes creates an air of tension, of apocalyptic expectancy, from the very start. There occurs a massive communal birthing, as if in desperate response to the imminent catastrophe. And at the end, after the apocalypse, only two characters, Polo Febo and Celestina, who become metamorphosed into the creative Aztec deities Quetzalcoatl and Quetzalpilli, fuse to repopulate the universe, as Fuentes posits a new genesis. Yet it is significant that the idealistic center of the work, the stage for the creation of a New World utopia, is not any Latin-American society but Paris, the physical and in many cases the spiritual homeland of the "boom" authors. In *Cristóbal nonato* the utopian dream that preoccupies Fuentes throughout his work is also located away from Mexico, this time in the world of the Orient, referred to as Pacifica. In a strange and wondrous scene at the end, three caravels appear to take the protagonist, Angel, and his lover Angeles, the central (and parental) characters of *Cristóbal nonato*, away from the New World, which Fuentes depicts as degenerating into incessant factionalism, endless fratricidal conflict, and horrendous and seemingly unsolvable ecological problems. Yet, significantly, Angel refuses the temptation; thus once again Fuentes emphasizes the Mexican capacity to endure and to survive despite the adversities, including earthquakes, fires, floods, man-made catastrophes, revolutions, and uprisings, that have afflicted Mexico.

In direct contrast with *La muerte*, a novel of death and of death-in-life, *Cristóbal nonato* is a novel of life. It is narrated by a fetal voice and is divided into nine major units to symbolize the nine months of Cristóbal's sometimes rapturous and sometimes traumatic fetal existence. His joy at being conceived is undercut when his mother, Angeles, is subsequently raped by the archenemy of Angel, Matamoros, and when she is abandoned by Angel and kidnapped by the Indian youth Jipi "Hippy" Toltec. *La muerte* ends with the sudden collapse of the various selves within Cruz; in contrast, *Cristóbal nonato* ends triumphantly with a proliferation of selves, the birth of twins: Cristóbal and his sister, Niña Ba, who throughout the narrative has been evoked as an invisible presence. Cruz's narrative, in particular the sonorous second-person sections, rolls over the reader, who many times is swirled along in its torrential flux, whereas the reader in *Cristóbal nonato* is personalized and repeatedly called upon, being referred to as the Elector, a word that, like so many of the characters and episodes in the narrative, has a dual significance. It underscores first of all the role of the reader as coauthor of the text. Many times the Elector is implored by the anguished Cristóbal to keep on reading; indeed the completing of the work is the only way that the incipient protagonist can be born, brought to full life in the imagination of the Elector. The reader is at times presented with embryonic scenes, which symbolize Cristóbal's own state, or with multiple choices on how a particular episode is to be completed, and encouraged to create the destinies of the character. A page of the novel is even left blank and the Elector is given guidelines on how to fill it.

In *Cristóbal nonato* the fate of Cristóbal, who desperately wants to be born, often seems to force him into the status of the heroine of the movie serial *The Perils of Pauline*, and the Elector is implored to come to the rescue. The fate of Fernando Benítez, the "good uncle" of Angel—in contrast with the avaricious Uncle Homero Fagoaga, who attempts to kill his nephew in order to claim his inheritance—is held in dramatic abeyance. Throughout the work the octogenarian Benítez (based on the eponymous eminent Mexican anthropologist and mentor of Fuentes who dedicated his career to the study of Mexico's many indigenous cultures) is a heroic figure, as he attempts morally to shape the inchoate Angel and to impel Homero, who like so many of Fuentes's characters defends the revolution rhetorically and then proceeds to acquire an immense private fortune, to dedicate his efforts to ameliorating the situation of the underdogs.

Many of Fuentes's works contain pyrotechnical endings, as in *La región*, in which the day of national independence is devastatingly presented as but the "Skull of Independence," an allusion referring not only to the head of Father Hidalgo—which was displayed in a cage in the same city he had taken, Guanajuato—but foreshadowing the multiple deaths with which *La región* ends. In *Cristóbal nonato* an immense conflagration that begins in the squatter district rapidly spreads to all of Mexico City.

Two manifestations of the Virgin Mother compete in *Cristóbal nonato*. In contrast to the self-sacrificing, serene, long-suffering mother Angeles is the false virgin, the carnivalesque goddess Mamadoc, "Mother and Doctor of All Mexicans," who is "created" by the cabinet minister Robles Chacón. The shrewd politician seeks to neutralize the great frustration and the pent-up urge for violence in the downtrodden populace by giving them a new, glittering symbol in which their resentment and vindictiveness can be sublimated. It is ironic that Mamadoc, a secretary from the office pool who is laboriously transformed by Robles into a mythic figure, should be venerated as a national mother, because her womb is sewn shut. She is prohibited from bearing children by natural means, since she is a modern emanation of the Holy Virgin. The sole public function of Mamadoc is to appear once a year, on the national holiday of 16 September, to utter before the assembled faithful the famous Grito de Dolores (Cry of Independence). Fuentes satirizes the penchant for national mythmaking; Mamadoc is incarcerated in her role, kept imprisoned in a lavish mansion in which all the mirrors have been removed so she will finally lose all awareness or memory of her previous identity. Thus the anguished cry of Mamadoc is not a theatrical one but rather a genuine expression of her constant victimization.

Ironically, even though he is the son of Federico Robles, who has fought heroically in the revolution, and of an Indian woman who spends most of her life in poverty, Robles Chacón views with horror the popular revolutionary leaders such as Pancho Villa and Emiliano Zapata, and he posits instead an eternal oligarchy for Mexico.

He links the heroes of the people with anarchy and mindless destruction, and, significantly, the rebel leader in the novel, Matamoros, is evoked negatively, as leading a revolution of plunder and slaughter, bereft of idealism. Robles Chacón emerges as the consummate politician, who first and last seeks to co-opt all opposition rather than inciting conflict, in a world presented as constantly threatening to fall apart. Throughout the novel Fuentes puns searingly on the names of the two principal cities used as settings: Mexico City becomes Mugsicko and Makesicko City; and Acapulco is transmogrified into Kafkapulco, Sacapulco, Rajapulco, Akapulque, and Acapulcalipsis.

Despite the temporary infidelity of Angel, who slavers after the Mexican "Valley Girl" Penny López and allows himself to be seduced by her mother as the price of obtaining Penny's affections, he finally returns to Angeles. Indeed *Cristóbal nonato* is one of the few works of Fuentes in which love triumphs. In *La muerte*, for example, the protagonist loves genuinely only once; his affair with Regina is thwarted by her untimely death. Yet her memory will be evoked throughout his life; she represents the elusive idealistic epoch of the revolution, which in the pessimistic world of Fuentes can never be permanently recovered.

The ancient Aztec presence, erupting violently into the present, a powerful, insistent, yet deceptive and ever elusive phenomenon in Fuentes's works, is evoked with a mixture of horror and humor, a marginalized force, but just as deadly, in *Cristóbal nonato*. Significantly the cover of the Spanish edition of the novel bears a picture of an ancient Aztec deity, Xipe Totec. This is the same god, by the way, whose spirit presides over *Cambio de piel*, whose title alludes to this young god, the god of spring, when the earth literally "changes its skin," becoming green to mark the renewal of life, and when snakes shed their old skins. Xipe Totec is a concretization of the desire for redemptive change on both the individual and national levels. Xipe is burlesqued in *Cristóbal nonato*, where he appears in the form of the flippant young musician Jipi Toltec, who gives new meaning to the term *flaky* as he literally sheds pieces of his skin throughout the narrative. Xipe was god of the seed, which "dies" in order to be reborn, as it falls to the earth then breaks out of its husk. The priests of this god sacrificed victims by skinning them, then donned the skins; and statues of Xipe reflect this "double skin." The demonic Jipi leads the revolt of the dispossessed campesinos in Acapulco, who attempt to regain their lands, once communal and now in the hands of private developers. Burying two young women, international models, in the sand, he suffocates them to death then does a bizarre "Dance of the Deer" over their bodies. It is Jipi who kidnaps Angeles and who kills Rigoberto Palomar, the grandfather of Angel, who has led a successful rescue mission but dies as he is struck by a flaming lance.

In the fatalistic world of *La región*, in which mythic determinism finds a parallel in economic oppression, the lower classes are portrayed as constantly victimized by those above them and preyed upon by their own class. Yet they remain politically passive, resigned to their adverse fate, symbolized at the end by the hopelessness of the situation of Gladys García. In *Cristóbal nonato* their plight has markedly worsened. The Bay of Acapulco is depicted as covered by a huge oil slick, while elaborate theme parks with swimming pools inhabited by huge plastic whales lure the tourists. The dehumanizing treatment the peasants receive, as they are pushed farther and farther into the mountains, sparks a clandestine revolt, as an immense tide of offal rapidly flows into the luxurious hotels, drowning the patrons in their rooms, while others die after imbibing cocktails that have been poisoned, on the model of the way in which the black slaves in Haiti take vengeance on the French planters in Alejo Carpentier's *El reino de este mundo* (1949; translated as *The Kingdom of This World*, 1957), a work that significantly influenced Fuentes. Both novels demonstrate the ultimate futility of rebellion. In Carpentier's work the oppressiveness of the colonial power is substituted by the tyranny of Henri Christophe. In *Cristóbal nonato* the apparently successful revolt of the dispossessed gains them nothing; it is co-opted by the federal government, which allows the rebels to eradicate the local political leadership in the state of Guerrero, which has been inimical to the central government.

Counterpointing the vast, expansive, epic novels, such as *La región*, *Gringo viejo*, and *Cristóbal nonato*, and testifying to the versatility of Fuentes, are three brief, compact, powerful works whose collective theme is that of physical and metaphysical possession, of the supernatural and the demonic: *Aura*, *Cumpleaños*, and *Una familia lejana*. These reflect the Borgesian themes of time and eternity, death and immortality, self and monstrous double, orthodoxy and heresy, reality and dream, and, as in so many of the short stories of Jorge Luis Borges, the creation of a demonized space—of an architectural, geometric hell world, which Fuentes at times presents in the shape of the ancient Aztec pyramid, as in *Cambio de piel* or *Una familia lejana*, and at other times as a sinuous and darkened labyrinth, as in *Aura* and *Cumpleaños*.

Aura is a complex, ambiguous narrative that can be interpreted either as a supernatural story—as the possession of the mind and soul of the narrator, Felipe Montero, by the revenant spirit of Llorente, summoned up by the sorceress Consuelo, with the assistance of the devil—or as a psychological work in which Aura becomes a product of the extremely unstable mind of Felipe, under the influence of the hallucinogenic drugs administered to him by Consuelo. The theme of psychological possession is reinforced by the style of the novel, narrated from the point of view of Felipe, but in the second-person singular, which a hypnotist uses to entrance the subject. However, a person cannot be hypnotized unless he or she is willing. Felipe is a weak and malleable character, literally without an "I," bereft of a strong ego. From start to finish of the narrative he is always distanced from himself; he is the "you," the "other." Underscoring the complexity of *Aura* is that the insistent quest of Felipe to rescue Aura, whom he perceives as exploited and even enslaved by her harridan aunt, is but a reflection of an internal quest, the desperate search by the inchoate and pusillanimous Felipe for identity, self-actualization, and self-transcendence. Yet the fundamental irony of *Aura* is that the nebulous self of Felipe can find and assert itself only in the other, in the ghost of General Llorente, soldier in the Imperial Army of Maximilian, whose subsequent defeat and execution at Querétaro by Juárez adumbrates the rapid demise of Llorente's ambitions. Felipe never mentions family or friends; he has no attachments in the outside world, a social vacuum that is quickly filled by his experiences in the realm of Consuelo, both horrifying and yet strangely pleasurable. Stalled in his doctoral dissertation, bored with his profession as a secondary-school teacher, Felipe is the perfect vessel for invasion by an alternate self. Thus Felipe's entering into the bizarre world of Consuelo, his acceptance of her offer of employment—he is to revise the moldering memoirs of Llorente—initially infuses his limbo existence with new purpose. Throughout his experiences Felipe responds ambivalently, repeatedly deciding to flee, yet each time compelled to remain, hypnotized by the green eyes of Aura. Only at very end, when it is too late, when the terrified Felipe clutches at his features, being torn from him by a supernatural force, does he realize that he has been caught in a trap, that the hunter—his last name, Montero, signifies "one who hunts"—has become the hunted.

Fuentes has defined his literary style as a hybrid form, as symbolic realism. Throughout his briefer narratives, he creates a world in which apparently realistic structures, objects, characters, and settings symbolize the fantastic. For example, the weird labyrinthine castle in the Yugoslav city of Split—in which the thirteenth-century theologian Siger de Brabante, the insane protagonist of *Cumpleaños*, dwells—symbolizes the rancorous, tyrannical, and self-divided personality of Siger himself. The passageways of the strange, demonic structure suddenly constrict and entrap the equivalent to Felipe in *Aura*: the twentieth-century architect George, who from his comfortable suburban home in London is abruptly and mysteriously thrown into the turbulent world of Siger, evoked as the parallel of Consuelo, as a voracious demiurge who seeks victims of sacrifice to sustain his identity. (That the mausoleumlike house of Consuelo, located in the very center of Mexico City, is built of tezontle symbolizes it as a mysterious house of time, similar to the castle of Siger, or to the mansion on the Clos de Renards of the mysterious André Heredia in *Una familia lejana*. Tezontle is a volcanic stone, material that was originally part of the Aztec pyramids destroyed by the conquistadores, who used the stones again to erect their cathedrals and dwellings.)

The peculiar combination of theology and violence, masterfully parodied by Borges in his short story "Los teólogos" (The Theologians, in the 1952 edition of *El Aleph*), also characterizes *Cumpleaños*, which portrays the multiple, supernatural lives of Siger de Brabante, a historical figure who becomes the object of Fuentes's fantasizing, just as Bierce does in *Gringo viejo*. The real Siger was denounced by Etienne Tempier and Thomas Aquinas, and fled from the Université de Paris to Italy, where he was assassinated by a crazed servant in 1281. Fuentes's Siger loves power and desires to live forever. For many of the egomaniacal protagonists of Fuentes's works, immortality is an obsessive goal, one that signifies the domination of the corrosive and ultimately ruinous course of chronological time, the nemesis of so many of Fuentes's characters.

Fuentes circa 1991 (photograph by Carlos Fuentes, Jr.)

The warped André in *Una familia lejana* is consumed by hatred and a desire for vengeance against mother figures. Like Siger, he seeks to perpetuate the self, as a means of demonstrating his complete independence of women and of the biological processes. Yet André succeeds in producing only an incomplete, feral successor. And the self-perpetuation fanatically pursued by Siger is also a sterile process. The various identities he assumes throughout the centuries are not cumulative, do not enhance his prestige or power, but rather are cyclical. His ultimate identity is as a hunter of wild beasts, the same caveman existence that was his first identity centuries earlier. In Borges's short story "El inmortal" (The Immortal, in the first [1949] edition of *El Aleph*) the precious gift of immortality for the Roman tribune Flaminius Rufus is the result of drinking the water of a sacred river. In Fuentes's works, however, immortality is obtained only as the result of the blood sacrifice of the other. For Siger as demonic master, immortality seems to hold the promise of infinitely expanding identities and experiences. For the architect George—like Felipe in *Aura* suddenly reduced to the status of hapless victim, like the human being designated in the Aztec world to represent a god and die as a victim of sacrifice—the only choice he has is the time and manner of his dying. Siger is similar to the demonic and ravenous Ixca Cienfuegos; both operate on the model of the ancient Aztec gods, who supposedly derived new strength and power from the hearts torn from human victims of sacrifice. The concept of the parasitic gods who nourish themselves on human blood is symbolized by the constant emphasis on the stiletto Siger uses to wound George in the forearm as a prelude to their blood mingling, as he gives a demonic twist to the phenomenon of "blood brothers."

The epigraph to *Cumpleaños*, "Time suffers from a hunger of incarnation," is from the work of another of the Latin-American authors who have exerted a considerable influence on Fuentes's vision: his fellow Mexican Octavio Paz. The sensitive Manuel Zamacona in *La región* and Artemio Cruz dramatize many of the concepts of Mexican national identity that Paz develops. The emphasis on wearing of multiple masks; the importance in Mexico of the verb of violation, *chingar*; the fundamental solitude of individual and nation; and the attempts to transcend this solitude—all found in Paz's work—find narrative and dramatic parallels in the art of Fuentes.

In *Cumpleaños* the all-powerful time that insistently seeks incarnation is personified in the form of Siger, who parallels the killer-narrator of *La región* and of *La muerte*. The geometrical hell world that is the domain of Siger finds a source in the weird, frightening, and monstrous Library of Babel in Borges's story "La biblioteca de Babel." In these works the hell world is not a Dantesque vision of flames and sulphur, but one of incessant and punishing geometrical repetition, fierce and inhuman. Borges's story evokes the terror of the infinite, the horrendous maniacal repetition of galleries, corridors, volumes, and letters. Details of this hellish structure, such as the hexagonal, prisonlike cubicles of the library, find their equivalent in the house of Siger.

Many of Fuentes's works of the fantastic and the supernatural are stories of impossible exorcism. *Cumpleaños* traces the various means, all ultimately futile, through which George attempts to battle against the demon that has encroached upon his integrity and freedom and that threatens to possess his soul. His name is an allusion to Saint George, the patron saint of England, who slew the dragon. In Fuentes's story, however, the opposite occurs, as the dragon slays George. The tyrannical Siger orders his servant Nuncia to keep the cages always filled, with animals such as the bear, the owl, and the tiger, which symbolize his own feral nature. It is significant that the one animal cage remaining to be filled is that of the dragon.

Paralleling the means through which the frantic George attempts to exorcise himself of the demonic Siger is the way that the artist, perhaps even Fuentes himself, harnesses his personal demons and obsessions, exorcising them by transforming them into works of art, thereby objectifying and controlling them. After an apocalyptic scene in which much of the palace/city of Siger is destroyed by a brutal horseman, another emanation of Siger, the creative vitality of George impels him to seek to restore the ruined city. Thus begins the battle between the destructive impulses of Siger, linked with the demonic, and the constructive, unifying genius of the architect George, who at this point seems to become a symbol of Fuentes himself, as an author committed to a realistic sociopolitical stance, as opposed to the far more abstract stance of Borges, who, to some, represents the epitome of art for art's sake. In contrast to the regressive and suppressive instincts of Siger, who is dedicated to blocking windows and doors, George desperately strives for unity, with Nuncia, who becomes George's lover, linked with the Annunciation, with Eve, and ironically with the Virgin Mary—a presence seen often in Fuentes's works, culminating in a series of novellas, *Constancia y otras novelas para vírgenes* (1990; translated as *Constancia and Other Stories for Virgins*, 1990), in which she is evoked as a revenant presence in twentieth-century Mexico. George desperately strives for unity, with Nuncia—as they become Adam and Eve in a paradise that turns into a metallic hell world—or with Siger himself, toward whom George responds as a father figure, and whom George is on the verge of slaying, but toward whom he suddenly feels compassion. If one interprets these confrontations and quests for redemptive unity allegorically, they may symbolize the struggle between the author—often seen in Latin-American culture—who speaks out against dictatorship, economic oppression, and the abuses of power, as opposed to the solipsistic and reclusive writer who, in the extreme, remains incarcerated within the self, refusing to become a national spokesperson (as Fuentes over and over again has not refused to be), and instead constructs what some view as sterile intellectual paradigms and dream palaces. George is attuned to the sounds of the industrious activity in the outside world, to the work of building a society, and he emerges as a civilizing principle; in contrast, Siger, despite his great erudition, is linked with the bestial. George's visualized and treasured column of stone exemplifies a key theme of Fuentes's art: the anti-Manichaean principle of fusion, the redemptive unity of opposites, seen in *Cambio de piel* and at the end of *Terra nostra*. Yet in the somber world of Fuentes, when opposites fuse, it is most often not to gain a transcendental and liberating synthesis but rather a destructive one. In *Cambio de piel* the fierce locust gods, symbol of this destructive fusion of opposites, as they are protective of both the harvest and its destroyers, preside over the ending. The weird metaphysical fusion of the youths Víctor and André in *Una familia lejana* marks the death of the ironically named Víctor, another example of the *conquistador conquistado*, as his identity is transfused to sustain a new form of André Heredia. Ironically, in *Cumpleaños*, the Janus column, symbolic of redemptive time, which is contemplated by the wistful George, never gets beyond the dream stage. The end of the novella marks the domination by the closed, ascetic, and oppressive Siger, who does not want an aesthetic structure of openness but rather to seal himself off from the outside world, to construct an impenetrable fortress to protect himself against assassination.

Fuentes's achievements in the novel genre have been recognized through his being awarded several distinguished prizes including the Premio Alfonso Reyes (for his entire oeuvre to that time) in 1980. *Cambio de piel*, one of his most intricate and problematic novels, was awarded the Premio Biblioteca Breve by the Barcelona publishing house Seix Barral. In 1975 Fuentes received the Premio Xavier Villaurrutia in Mexico City and in 1977 was awarded the Rómulo Gallegos prize in Venezuela, both honors for his novel *Terra nostra*, which he wrote while a fellow at the Woodrow Wilson International Center for Scholars in Washington, D.C. In 1984 he was awarded the Mexican Premio Nacional de la Literatura by President Miguel de la Madrid, and in 1987 he received the Spanish Premio Cervantes in Madrid, awarded by King Juan Carlos.

Interviews:
Emmanuel Carballo, "Carlos Fuentes," *Diecinueve protagonistas de la literatura mexicana del siglo XX* (Mexico City: Empresas, 1965), pp. 427-448;

Luis Harss and Barbara Dohman, "Carlos Fuentes, or the New Heresy," in their *Into the Mainstream: Conversations with Latin American Writers* (New York: Harper & Row, 1967), pp. 276-309;

Emir Rodríguez Monegal, "Carlos Fuentes," in his *El arte de narrar: Diálogos* (Caracas: Monte Avila, 1968), pp. 113-146;

Herman P. Doezma, "An Interview with Carlos Fuentes," *Modern Fiction Studies*, 18 (Winter 1972-1973): 491-503;

James R. Fortson, *Perspectivas mexicanas desde París: Un diálogo con Carlos Fuentes* (Mexico City: Corporación Editorial, 1973);

Jonathan Tittler, "Interview: Carlos Fuentes," *Diacritics*, 10 (September 1980): 46-56.

Bibliographies:
Richard Reeve, "An Annotated Bibliography on Carlos Fuentes," *Hispania*, 53 (1970): 595-652;

Reeve, "Selected Bibliography (1949-1982)," *World Literature Today*, 57 (Autumn 1983): 541-586;

L. Teresa Valdivieso, "Bibliografía de/sobre Carlos Fuentes (1981-1985)," in *La obra de Carlos Fuentes: Una visión múltiple*, edited by Ana María Hernández de López (Madrid: Pliegos, 1988), pp. 377-383.

References:
Liliana Befumo Boschi and Elisa Calabresi, *Nostalgia del futuro en la obra de Carlos Fuentes* (Buenos Aires: García Cambeiro, 1974);

Robert Brody and Charles Rossman, eds., *Carlos Fuentes: A Critical View* (Austin: University of Texas Press, 1982);

John S. Brushwood, "Sobre el referente y la transformación narrativa en las novelas de Carlos Fuentes y Gustavo Sainz," *Revista Iberoamericana*, 47, nos. 116-117 (1981): pp. 49-54;

Gloria Durán, *La magia y las brujas en la obra de Carlos Fuentes* (Mexico City: Universidad Nacional Autónoma de México, 1976); translated by Durán as *The Archetypes of Carlos Fuentes: From Witch to Androgyne* (Hamden, Conn.: Shoe String, 1980);

Manuel Durán, "Carlos Fuentes," in his *Tríptico mexicano: Juan Rulfo, Carlos Fuentes, Salvador Elizondo* (Mexico City: Secretaría de Educación Pública, 1973);

Wendy B. Faris, *Carlos Fuentes* (New York: Ungar, 1983);

David W. Foster, "*La región más transparente* and the Limits of Prophetic Art," *Hispania*, 56 (March 1973): 35-42;

Georgina García Gutiérrez, *Los disfraces: La obra mestiza de Carlos Fuentes* (Mexico City: Colegio de México, 1981);

Helmy F. Giacoman, ed., *Homenaje a Carlos Fuentes: Variaciones interpretativas en torno a su obra* (New York: Las Américas, 1971);

Juan Goytisolo, "*Terra nostra*, Our Old New World," *Review*, 19 (Winter 1976): 5-24;

Daniel de Guzmán, *Carlos Fuentes* (New York: Twayne, 1972);

Lanin A. Gyurko, "Freedom and Fate in Fuentes' *Cambio de piel*," *Revista/Review Interamericana*, 7 (Winter 1977-1978): 701-739;

Gyurko, "Fuentes, Guzmán, and the Mexican Political Novel," *Ibero-Amerikanisches Archiv*, 16, no. 4 (1990): 545-610;

Gyurko, "Identity and the Mask in Fuentes' *La región más transparente*," *Hispanófila*, 65 (January 1979): 75-103;

Gyurko, "The Image of Cortés in Fuentes' *Todos los gatos son pardos*," *Káñina*, 5, no. 1 (1981): 55-69;

Gyurko, "Myth and Demythification in Fuentes and Wilder," *Hispanic Journal*, 7 (Fall 1985): 91-113;

Gyurko, "The Myths of Ulysses in Fuentes's *Zona sagrada*," *Modern Language Review*, 69 (April 1974): 316-324;

Gyurko, "Novel into Essay: Fuentes' *Terra nostra* as Generator of *Cervantes o la crítica de la lectura*," *Mester*, 11 (Spring 1983): 16-35;

Gyurko, "Role Playing and the Double in Fuentes' *Orquídeas a la luz de la luna*," *Horizontes*, 30 (October-April 1987): 57-92;

Gyurko, "The Self and the Demonic in Fuentes' *Una familia lejana*," *Revista/Review Interamericana*, 12 (Winter 1982-1983): 572-620;

Gyurko, "Self, Double, and Mask in Fuentes' *La muerte de Artemio Cruz*," *Texas Studies in Literature and Language*, 16 (Summer 1974): 363-384;

Gyurko, "Social Satire and the Ancient Mexican Gods in the Narrative of Fuentes," *Ibero-Amerikanisches Archiv*, 1, no. 2 (1975): 113-150;

Gyurko, "Women in Mexico: Fuentes' Portrayal of Oppression," *Revista Hispánica Moderna*, 38, no. 4 (1974-1975): 206-229;

Ana María Hernández de López, *La obra de Carlos Fuentes: Una visión múltiple* (Madrid: Pliegos, 1988);

Juan Loveluck, "Intención y forma en *La muerte de Artemio Cruz*," *Nueva Narrativa Latinoamericana*, 1, no. 1 (1971): 105-116;

Loveluck and Isaac Levy, eds., *Simposio Carlos Fuentes: Actas* (Columbia: University of South Carolina Hispanic Studies, 1980);

Mary Seale-Vásquez, "Character Development in Fuentes' *A Change of Skin*," *Latin American Literary Review*, 6, no. 12 (1978): 68-85;

Joseph Sommers, "The Field of Choice: Carlos Fuentes," in his *After the Storm: Landmarks of the Modern Mexican Novel* (Albuquerque: University of New Mexico Press, 1968), pp. 133-164;

M. L. Valdés, "Myth and History in *Cien años de soledad* and *La muerte de Artemio Cruz*," *Reflexión*, 2, nos. 3-4 (1974-1975): 243-255;

Michael Wood, "The New World and the Old Novel," *INTI*, 5-6 (1977): 109-112.

Gabriel García Márquez
(6 March 1928 -)

Alicia Borinsky
Boston University

BOOKS: *La hojarasca* (Bogotá: Sipa, 1955); translated by Gregory Rabassa as *Leaf Storm and Other Stories* (New York: Harper & Row, 1972; London: Cape, 1972);

El coronel no tiene quien le escriba (Medellín: Aguirre, 1961); translated by J. S. Bernstein in *No One Writes to the Colonel and Other Stories* (New York: Harper & Row, 1968; London: Cape, 1971);

La mala hora (Madrid: Pérez, 1962); translated by Rabassa as *In Evil Hour* (New York: Harper & Row, 1979; London: Cape, 1980);

Los funerales de la Mamá Grande (Jalapa, Mexico: Editorial de la Universidad Veracruzana, 1962); translated by Bernstein as *Big Mama's Funeral* in *No One Writes to the Colonel and Other Stories*;

Cien años de soledad (Buenos Aires: Sudamericana, 1967); translated by Rabassa as *One Hundred Years of Solitude* (New York: Harper & Row, 1970; London: Cape, 1970);

Isabel viendo llover en Macondo (Buenos Aires: Estuario, 1967);

La novela en América Latina: Diálogo, by García Márquez and Mario Vargas Llosa (Lima, Peru: Milla Batres, 1969);

Relato de un naúfrago (Barcelona: Tusquets, 1970); translated by Randolph Hogan as *The Story of a Shipwrecked Sailor* (New York: Knopf, 1986);

La increíble y triste historia de la cándida Eréndira y de su abuela desalmada (Barcelona: Barral, 1972); translated by Rabassa as *Innocent Eréndira and Other Stories* (New York: Harper & Row, 1978; London: Cape, 1979);

Ojos de perro azul (Rosario, Argentina: Equiseditorial, 1972);

El negro que hizo esperar a los ángeles (Rosario, Argentina: Alfil, 1972);

Cuando era feliz e indocumentado (Caracas: Ojo del Camello, 1973);

Chile, el golpe y los gringos (Bogotá: Latina, 1974);

Cuatro cuentos (Mexico City: Comunidad Latinoaméricana de Escritores, 1974);

Gabriel García Márquez in 1982

El otoño del patriarca (Barcelona: Plaza & Janes, 1975); translated by Rabassa as *The Autumn of the Patriarch* (New York: Harper & Row, 1976; London: Cape, 1977);

Todos los cuentos (Barcelona: Plaza & Janes, 1975);

Crónicas y reportajes (Bogotá: Instituto Colombiano de Cultura, 1976);

Operación Carlota (Lima, Peru: Mosca Azul, 1977);

Periodismo militante (Bogotá: Son de Máquina, 1978);

De viaje por los países socialistas (Cali, Colombia: Macondo, 1978);

Crónica de una muerte anunciada (Bogotá: Oveja Negra, 1981); translated by Rabassa as *Chronicle of a Death Foretold* (New York: Harper & Row, 1982; London: Cape, 1982);

Obra periodística, 4 volumes, edited by Jacques Gilard (Barcelona: Bruguera, 1981-1984);

El rastro de tu sangre en la nieve; El verano feliz de la Señora Forbes (Bogotá: Dampier, 1982);

El secuestro: Relato cinematográfico (Salamanca, Spain: Lóguez, 1983);

El amor en los tiempos del cólera (Bogotá: Oveja Negra, 1985); translated by Edith Grossman as *Love in the Time of Cholera* (New York: Knopf, 1988);

La aventura de Miguel Littín, clandestino en Chile (Madrid: El País, 1986); translated by Asa Zatz as *Clandestine in Chile: The Adventures of Miguel Littín* (New York: Holt, 1987);

El general en su laberinto (Madrid: Mondadori, 1989).

Edition in English: *Collected Stories*, translated by Gregory Rabassa and J. S. Bernstein (New York: Harper & Row, 1984; London: Cape, 1991).

The work of Gabriel García Márquez owes much of its popularity to the seemingly easy access it offers to readers and to the way it departs from the highly intellectualized, self-reflective mode that characterizes other Latin-American fiction of the mid twentieth century by restoring the coherence of plot. An immediate understanding of the facts narrated is possible. The most trivial aspects of such a change in sensibility may be understood in terms of the attraction for readers to form conventional projections into characters and actions; the less obvious reasons behind the appeal of García Márquez's fiction reveal a different kind of lucidity at work, a new sense of how literature may better reflect on its own making.

García Márquez has authored many short stories and several novels, as well as journalistic articles that, since 1948, have appeared in such Colombian publications as the *Universal* and *Espectador*, and the Spanish newspaper *El País*, among others. Although his subjects cover a wide range of interests, which includes film criticism, there is a prevailing emphasis on Latin America, its history, landscape, and political realities. A shrewd observer of Latin-American societies, García Márquez has tried to fuse factual and literary events while undoing linear narratives. His short stories are formally austere, favoring rural settings with surprising elements that sometimes also appear in his novels. Because of the interconnections among his various works of fiction—featuring the reappearance of characters such as Eréndira and members of the Buendía family, as well as the frequent setting of events in the town of Macondo—he has been compared to William Faulkner. Similarities between works of these two authors, though, do not go beyond superficial aspects.

García Márquez has been an attentive reader of the chronicles of travelers to the New World during the discovery and colonization of the Americas. Traces of such interests are to be found in many of his works, especially in his best-known novel, *Cien años de soledad* (1967; translated as *One Hundred Years of Solitude*, 1970), and in *El otoño del patriarca* (1975; translated as *The Autumn of the Patriarch*, 1976). His sometime friend and admirer, Peruvian writer Mario Vargas Llosa, records in *Gabriel García Márquez: Historia de un deicidio* (1971) that García Márquez has a fondness for Daniel Defoe's *Journal of the Plague Year* (1722), which plays a most important role in understanding *El amor en los tiempos del cólera* (1985; translated as *Love in the Time of Cholera*, 1988). Well read in European and American literatures, both in English and Spanish, García Márquez also recaptures for the contemporary reader echoes of narrative modes of the Spanish chevalieresque and Renaissance traditions. In 1982 he received the Nobel Prize for Literature, one of many honors bestowed on him in recognition of his art.

Gabriel García Márquez was born in Aracataca, Colombia, on 6 March 1928 to Gabriel Eligio García and Luisa Santiaga Márquez de García, but he spent the first eight years of his life with his maternal grandparents, Col. Nicolás Márquez and Tranquilina Iguarán de Márquez. After the colonel's death Gabriel went to live with his parents in Sucre, a river port. In 1940 the young García Márquez went, on a scholarship, to the Liceo Nacional de Zipaquirá, a high school near Bogotá. Seven years later he enrolled in law school at the Universidad Nacional in the capital. Political unrest closed the university in 1948, and García Márquez transferred to the Universidad de Cartagena but never graduated. Instead he became a writer for the Cartagena newspaper *Universal*, then later—from 1950 through 1952—for the *Heraldo* in Barranquilla. By 1955 he was a well-known journalist at the

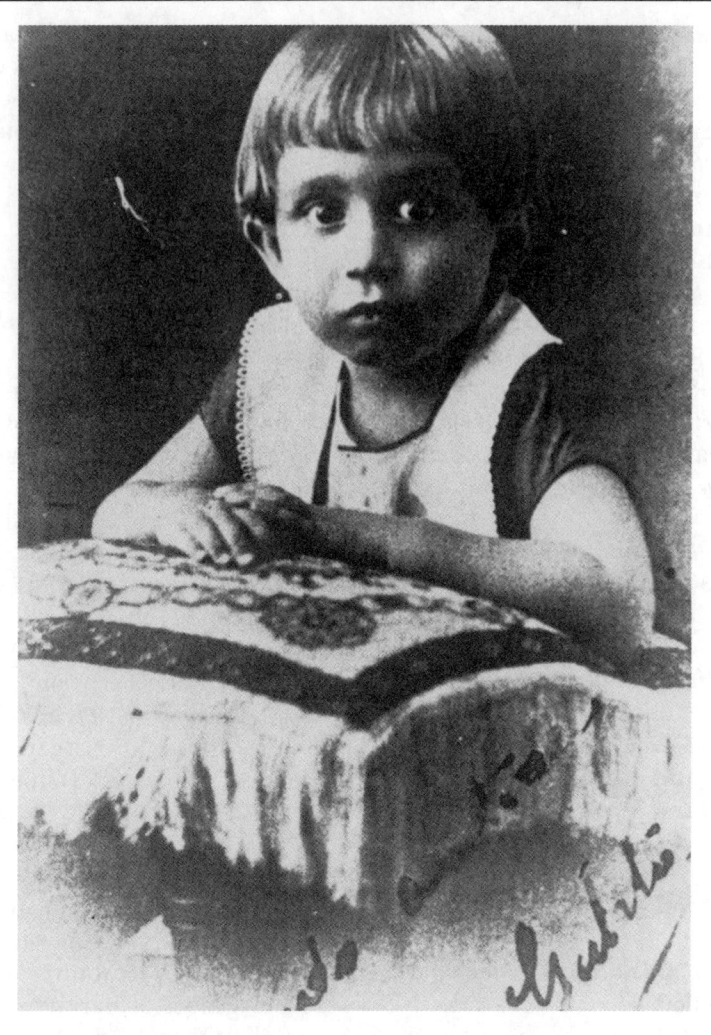

García Márquez at the age of two in Aracataca, Colombia

Espectador in Bogotá. From 1956 to 1958 he wrote fiction and was a free-lance journalist in Paris, London, and Caracas, before returning to Barranquilla to marry his childhood sweetheart, Mercedes Barcha, in March 1958. They moved to Caracas, where García Márquez worked for the magazine *Momento*. In May 1959 he was instrumental in launching a branch of Prensa Latina in Bogotá, where he and his wife had moved; in August their first child, Rodrigo, was born. García Márquez and his family relocated to New York City in 1961. He worked at the Prensa Latina branch there briefly but then resigned to tour the southern United States and look for film-writing work in Mexico City. He eventually wrote for magazines there and then took an advertising job with J. Walter Thompson's Mexico City branch in 1963. A second son, Gonzalo, had been born in 1962.

Meanwhile his fiction-writing career had begun seriously and successfully with *El coronel no tiene quien le escriba* (1961; translated in *No One Writes to the Colonel and Other Stories*, 1968), which portrays the stillness of a small Latin-American town and focuses on the long wait for a pension that the protagonist endures throughout the novel. Concerns about plot and the nature of writing are woven together in a way that reappears only much later in García Márquez's work—in particular in his novel *El general en su laberinto* (The General in His Labyrinth, 1989) dealing with Simón Bolívar's last days.

His most important volume in the short-story genre is *Los funerales de la Mamá Grande* (1962; translated as *Big Mama's Funeral* in *No One Writes to the Colonel*, 1968). In this book the reader is offered a glimpse of some characters who are developed further in *Cien años de soledad*. *Los funerales de la Mamá Grande*, together with *La hojarasca* (1955; translated as *Leaf Storm*, 1972), serves as an introduction to the gallery of eccentrics and adventurers found later in his novels.

Cien años de soledad presents a plot—the narrative element so derided by the likes of Macedonio Fernandez and Ramon Gomez de la Serna—that is not an obstacle to thought. However, the "manuscript" (supposedly written by the character Melquíades and found and deciphered at the end of the novel by Aureliano) has the general effect of reweaving the beginning. From this perspective, the ending of the novel is nostalgic: the story of the family is over, the reader is made to leave the scene of psychological projection with the awareness that no continuation is possible, given the apocalyptic ending (the world has come to a point of total obliteration).

The abandonment of naive reading is worked into the novel in two strands: the ending is the end of the Buendía family (the focus of the plot) and the beginning of critical awareness (through the notion of a manuscript that holds all the clues). *Cien años de soledad* thus closes, asking the reader to recover from the dizziness of fiction. The remedy is conceived in the form of an exercise in literary interpretation, stemming from the recognition that the plot has been filtered through a dubious "translation."

García Márquez, in *Cien años de soledad*, takes issue with the contempt for plot and celebrates criticism as a way out of its illusions—*within* the framework of the novel. A totalizing intention underlies the project from this perspective. In an earlier formulation of the issue—as it appears in Julio Cortázar's *Rayuela* (1963; translated as *Hopscotch*, 1966)—the reader may choose between two avenues of pursuit: the delight in the linear sequence of events with Cortázar's "La Maga" character as a central node of meaning, or the disjointed critical view stemming from Morelli's notes. In *Cien años de soledad* García Márquez masks the seams of his fiction until that crucial moment, the ending of the book, where they become decisive in the materiality of what is being read. In a literary figuration of Jorge Luis Borges's *El Aleph* (1949; translated, 1970), the events of the novel are embodied in an instant: "The final projection which Aureliano [Buendía] had begun to glimpse when he let himself be confused by the love of Amaranta Úrsula, was based on the fact that Melquíades [the author of the manuscript] had not put events in the order of man's conventional time but had concentrated a century of daily episodes in such a way that they coex-

Dust jacket for the novel that, according to the Nobel Prize committee, solidified García Márquez's reputation as "a rare storyteller richly endowed with a material . . . which seems inexhaustible"

isted in an instant." In learning at the end of *Cien años de soledad* that everything one has read is in Melquíades's manuscript, the reader is forced to perform somewhat the same movements of the character (Aureliano), who shuts himself up in order to decipher it, managing in the process to ignore the death of the last baby of the family—whose body is being carried away by ants as the avid reading starts. Aureliano's is, of course, no *simple* reading.

The character is hoping to find his origins; the price he pays is high because, in doing so, he has to forget about his future. The choice this time, in favor of literature, pushes "real life" aside. As he reads he not only brutally refuses to acknowledge the solemnity of the demise of the family by not paying due respect to his offspring, but he also defines himself as a character in the

Gabriel García Márquez

sense of Melquíades's manuscript. Borges's *El Aleph* summarizes in one simultaneous, privileged perception all the occurrences that can be expressed only successively by language. Borges and Miguel de Cervantes are summoned up by García Márquez as persuasive crafters of the entanglements that take readers—and characters—away from the certainty of physical death into the pleasures and relative eternity of literature, albeit in a room that has been firmly shut.

It has been repeatedly noted that this ending places the novel in the long tradition of self-reflective literature. But a quite different sense of the text might be elicited once the final pages are considered in context. The decipherer, alone in the room, arrives at his discovery through an active dismissal of reality: "Herido por las lanzas mortales de las nostalgias propias y ajenas, admiró la impavidez de la telaraña en los rosales muertos, la perseverancia de la cizaña, la paciencia del aire en el radiante amanecer de febrero. Y entonces vió al niño. Era un pellejo hinchado y reseco que todas las hormigas del mundo iban arrastrando hacia sus madrigueras por el sendero de piedras del jardín. Aureliano no pudo moverse. No porque lo hubiera paralizado el estupor, sino porque en aquel instante prodigioso se le revelaron las claves definitivas de Melquíades" (Wounded by the fatal lances of his own nostalgia and that of others, he admired the persistence of the spider webs on the dead rose bushes, the perseverance of the rye grass, the patience of the air in the radiant February dawn. And then he saw the child. It was a dry and bloated bag of skin that all the ants in the world were dragging toward their holes along the stone path in the garden. Aureliano could not move. Not because he was paralyzed by horror but because at that prodigious instant Melquíades's final keys were revealed to him).

Aureliano's task as an interpreter is thus rooted in an act of violent oblivion. Remembering his past is as one with the forgetting of the immediate destiny of his offspring. Interpretation is located in a temporal sequence where looking back into the past becomes, paradoxically, simultaneous with oblivion from the facts constituting it.

The conceit of the book within the book in *Cien años de soledad* produces the figure of a reader-decipherer who—from within the fiction—is charged with giving shape to events leading to his own inception as a character. His intelligence is not without bounds: the outer limit of its reach is indicated in his dismissal of the events that make up the concrete conditions for the very act of interpretation.

While the decipherer is the most recognizable reader-figure in the novel, another character of a very different sort embodies the qualities attributable to fiction itself. Remedios, the beauty, has an evanescent presence. The nature of her intelligence is an object of discussion for the other characters, who are divided in their opinions about her. There are those who think she is retarded or merely stupid, and others, such as Aureliano, who believe she has a special lucidity that makes traditional ways of thought dispensable. The nature of the passion she ignites in the males who pursue her makes the reader understand her as the ever-elusive object of a desire destined to remain unsatisfied. Her figure is evocative of a long tradition in which female beauty is portrayed as dangerous and ultimately fatal to those who succumb to its spell. Her speech, unschooled in metaphor, works with a literality occasionally hilarious in its effects.

Remedios is larger than life but has—as a fictional figure—an intensity that stands for the notion of reality itself. Her presence has an extreme carnality. One of the arguments against her intelligence is that she does not like to wear clothes. Her almost naked body is a constant reminder of her ahistorical nature. This refusal to participate in culture places her either above or beneath it. As the novel evolves, Remedios literally levitates away, leaving behind a nostalgia for solving the doubts she inspired.

There is an unknown in the question about Remedios. The unfolding of her enigma within the novel brings one back to the way in which Melquíades's prophecy is deciphered. Her eloquence may be mistaken for lack of intelligent speech because of the inadequacy of her language in the context of everyday conversation. Melquíades's manuscript remains virtually invisible until a revelatory moment sets the deciphering in motion; in very much the same way, Remedios's lucidity is accessible through an act of belief in the sophistication of her mind. The instantaneous perception of her beauty invests her carnality with a nondiscursive meaning. Thus, her literal use of language turns into a series of wise aphorisms for readers. Her character encapsulates everything that may be said about the representational level in the novel. Remedios seems to exist in a deeper context, beyond words, as a privileged representative of the literary tradition preceding the novel, a powerful entity precipitating changes in the destinies of others by her mere presence.

The other female characters are partial embodiments of the mystery of Remedios. They share with her the capacity for hiding part of their motivations; the novel portrays them as being part of a world of gravitating secrets. Such are the traits of Amaranta, Amaranta Ursula, Pilar Ternera, Rebeca, and Fernanda, who remain virtually unknown to readers in spite of the many anecdotes they help develop. The nature of their secrecy is, perhaps, their femininity and is seen as constituting a potential danger to other characters who belong to the more recognizable world of adventure, where action is a measure of time.

Aside from the inevitable considerations linking this representation of women to ideologies of the eternal feminine, their supernatural power lies in their lack of participation in the discursive world of the other characters. The reasons for the kind of gravitation they each attain are varied: Fernanda has a mysterious ailment and, like Rebeca, a past unknown to the reader. Ursula sees, through her eventual, literal blindness and her intuition, beyond any explanations about the sources of her power; Pilar Ternera's physical energy is matched only by nature itself; Amaranta has an uncanny apathy that endows her with a patience turned into an obsessive strategy; Amaranta Ursula seems a combination of the two other female characters present in her name. Her powers are enormous, and her physical energy is portrayed as almost impersonal because of its similarity to a "natural" force. This rapid inventory of traits provides the register in which the notion of Remedios, the beauty, becomes an image for understanding the role that her privileged energy plays in the assessment of how the novel works.

The female characters, as described, possess something beyond intelligence, ways of understanding and interacting through what appears to be a leap in which the rational is acknowledged but always marginalized. Remedios is the most hyperbolic figuration of the process that turns these women into emblems for a secret source of energy. When she levitates out of the novel, Remedios intensifies the kind of nostalgia created by the other female characters. Her loss is the absence of something that takes on the virtuality of reality because of her overt carnality.

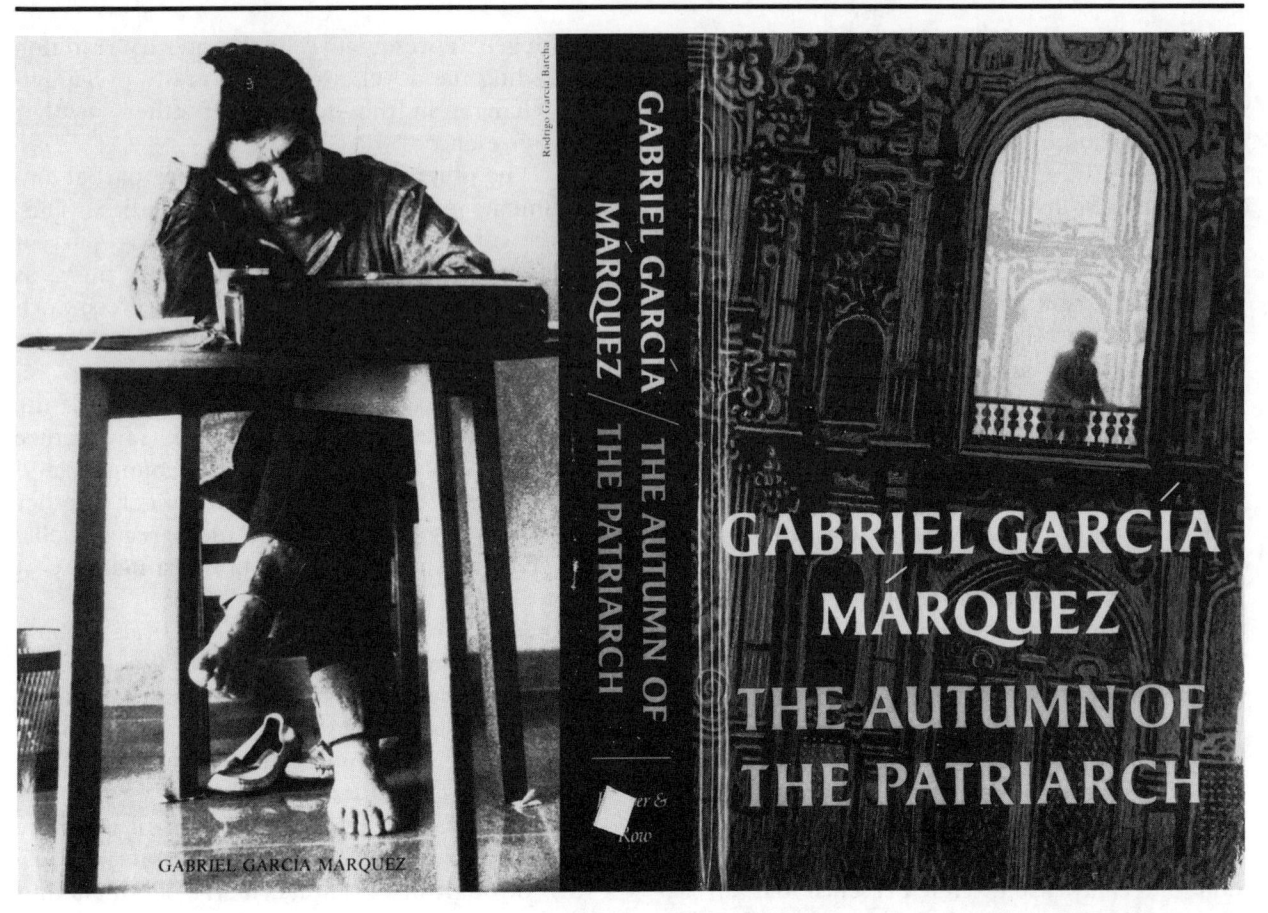

Dust jacket for the English translation of García Márquez's 1975 novel, which examines the illusions that a Latin-American dictator uses to maintain his power

Melquíades's manuscript is attuned to the nature of Remedios. Its language is not discursive or sequential, although it abounds in effects sustaining the desire to understand it. Remedios's otherworldliness attracts characters to a fatal destiny. The manuscript to be deciphered has, as does the love generated by Remedios, a frightening capacity for causing violence. Aureliano forgets about his own child as he starts to understand Melquíades's message. Paradoxically, in forgetting his offspring, he has the hope of finding himself: "Fascinado por el hallazgo, Aureliano leyó en voz alta, sin saltos, las encíclicas cantadas por el propio Melquíades que le hizo escuchar a Arcadio, y que eran en realidad las predicciones de su ejecución, y encontró anunciado el nacimiento de la mujer más bella del mundo que estaba subiendo al cielo en cuerpo y alma, y conoció el origen de dos gemelos póstumos que renunciaban a descifrar los pergaminos, no sólo por su incapacidad e inconstancia, sino porque sus tentativas eran prematuras. En este punto, impaciente por conocer su propio origen, Aureliano dió un salto" (Fascinated by the discovery, Aureliano read aloud without skipping the chanted encyclicals that Melquíades himself had made Arcadio listen to and that were in reality the prediction of his execution, and he found the announcement of the birth of the most beautiful woman in the world who was rising up to heaven in body and soul, and he found the origin of the posthumous twins who gave up deciphering the parchments, not simply through incapacity and lack of drive, but also because their attempts were premature. At that point, impatient to know his own origin, Aureliano skipped ahead).

Aureliano's "intelligent" reading feeds on partiality. His being a reader and a character is not a device that facilitates a projection for the reader of the novel. Aureliano strives to find himself through a double betrayal that sustains the fiction in which he participates. In forgetting his offspring, he is being unfaithful to that level of plot that might give him a "future" as a member of a continuing family. He also betrays the reader of

Jorge Amado and García Márquez

the novel—that implicit entity in every book—by not being interested in following every avatar of the manuscript. As he skips passages in order to find his own origins, he ceases to be a neutral embodiment of reading to become, more explicitly, what he has always already been: a fictional character whose limitations are the result of hedonistic self-interest.

In thinking of Aureliano's role as a decipherer and Remedios, the beauty, as an embodiment of a nondiscursive enigma, one constitutes a basic scene of reading and writing: the reader (Aureliano), on the one hand, and the subject (Remedios), on the other. The stability of this arrangement disappears as Aureliano's unfaithful reading of the manuscript emerges in the novel. The will to partiality as a means of self-understanding returns him to the same level as the other characters in the novel. Such a perspective questions the place of the reader in the novel, since the awareness of a shared ground with a character makes it necessary to find another point of departure for critical reading.

Other works by García Márquez take up the issue and elaborate further on its many reverberations.

El otoño del patriarca, a novel with a texture often bordering on a prose poem, presents an anonymous Latin-American dictator with recognizable traits drawn from different countries. In dense, repetitive images, the reader is introduced to the complex support structure for the leader's power. The dictator's absolute authority stems, to a large extent, from his capacity to draw on the mystery his persona has created. The issue of whether he is dead or alive is discussed by the people; the unpredictability of his reactions grants him a specificity that intensifies the sense that his "being" is beyond the grasp of the common man.

In reading the novel, one is made aware, though, of the fact that his government is sustained by a complicated system of staged illusions. The substantial presence attained by the dictator in the eyes of his contemporaries is shown from the inside of the artifice of power. There are some hilarious moments, such as the one in which the dictator's own mother says that had she known the position her son would hold, she would have made sure he learned how to read and write. Aside from the situational humor and the abundant social comment that may be drawn from the statement, one should reflect on how this dictator is given the attributes of a triumphant will shorn of all intelligence.

The texture of the novel allows the reader to see two strands of the repressive tapestry woven by the dictatorship: one is the ruthless violence exercised against the opposition, replete with shifts in motives for striking out at hastily defined enemies; the other is the seams that hold the image of the dictator together for the people to behold. His speeches—made out of clichés—save him from the travails of originality in language. His lovesickness for a female character, Manuela Sánchez, who spurns him with her final disappearance, grants him a sense of humanity—insofar as she represents the beauty of the poor ("la belleza del muladar")—and the kind of vulnerability frequently associated with demagogy.

The dictator is an elusive object whose language and being are subjects of interpretation. The novel brings back in a new framework the problems of how to translate (interpret) the presence of a character who, devoid of intelligence of his own, precipitates, nevertheless, everything of importance that goes on in the narrative. Because the dictator does not have an analytical mind, he becomes an ideal subject for analysis. His virtual silence triggers the need for the speech of others.

El otoño del patriarca is an extended meditation on the authority granted to a character because of ignorance of his origins; the less the reader knows about the reasons determining the character, the more attracted he is to study him and fall within his aura. The illusion of depth that such a development gives to fiction is seen in the novel in its political aspect, as well as in its ludic literary implications.

The system that was put into play in *Cien años de soledad* reappears in *El otoño del patriarca*, establishing the limits of objects to be read with increased analytical clarity: the reader is drawn to a secret. The dictator, Remedios, and Melquíades's manuscript offer several faces, one of which is an all-embracing intelligence; another is staggering stupidity and ignorance. The reader has, as in the previous novel, an entity into which he might project himself; in *El otoño del patriarca* it is no longer one of the Buendías but "the people," who see the dictator from afar, as he passes in a car without their being able to tell whether it is really he, or what his face looks like, but they are sure, nevertheless, of the pressing nature of the question. In this partial system of projection, the reader is less fortunate that he was in *Cien años de soledad*, because this time there is no way out of the reading enclosure. It was possible to frame Aureliano's reading of Melquíades in a specific room and look at it from another level, an *outside*, but in *El otoño del patriarca* that space *beyond* does not exist. For the novel is conceived as the world itself, and the reader is drawn from this dictator to all others, *outside* the book but within a society that turns mystery and stupidity into absolute authority.

In the short novel *Crónica de una muerte anunciada* (1981; translated as *Chronicle of a Death Foretold*, 1982), readers know the subject from the outset—the death of Santiago Nasar. The novel, therefore, does not deal with a mystery but with something self-evident. A fact, more tangible than comprehensible, initiates the narrative: a man has been murdered. The characters of the novel are presented in a lineup with opinions and certainties that were not enough to stop the occurrence. The death has taken place in the context of a tightly knit community; its motive is simple and traditional. It involves a marriage, a virginity lost by the bride at the wrong time, an explanation that may not have been true and the death of the alleged male culprit at the hands of avenging men. The bride's family's honor has been tainted by her sexual encounter; the Hispanic literary tradition offers the violent solution as a commonplace.

The event and its resolution are already part of common experience. Given the profoundly *known* nature of what is being told, how does this novel produce the tension of suspense? The pleasure involved in reading this book is a celebration of reality. The murder is invested with the weight of a necessary element. The role of the characters is none other than attesting to the existence of the event that holds them together by making it "happen" over and over again.

The reader contemplates the fabrication of the event and ends up convinced of its inevitability. Inevitability can be confused with necessity, as the grounding subject of the book becomes the *necessity* of the event. Common sense, with its incapacity to generate new solutions and its eminently conservative rhythm, dominates a narration that, paradoxically, grants great importance to the role of dreams and local superstitions.

García Márquez in Stockholm after receiving the 1982 Nobel Prize for Literature (photograph copyright 1982 by The Nobel Foundation)

When thinking about the murder, all characters are trapped in the destructive defense of the family's honor. While the novel starts by stating the fact of the murder, its suspense is built around the credibility of the motives leading to its occurrence. The success of the book resides in silencing that level of reading that might want to question the event, that is, the silencing of a more intelligent and suspicious look at the information.

In drawing the scenes of reading as they appear in each of these novels, one finds a need for a distinction between reading and readers *within fiction* (as part of a plot), and reading and readers in the sense commonly understood as *critical*. Following closely such developments in *Cien años de soledad*, a model of reading emerges where understanding the book is tied to the enigma behind Remedios, the beauty's silence as a ground for fiction—while a hostile reaction to Aureliano's partial interest in deciphering the past embodies the beginning of critical awareness on the part of a detached reader.

El otoño del patriarca intensifies these problems by making of the mystery (eloquence and elusiveness) of Remedios, a haunting and urgent political problem in the figure of the dictator. In *Crónica de una muerte anunciada* the celebration of conformity creates a fissure through which a critical reader, performing his task against the grain of the book, understands his own exclusion as central to what is being narrated. *El amor en los tiempos del cólera* presents another series of scenes of reading and writing, this time as the very thread of its plot.

El amor en los tiempos del cólera derives its charm, in part, from the anachronistic movements of the long courtship between two elderly characters. Theirs is a romance that appears to be woven by the memories of a bygone youth. Love letters from the man, Florentino Ariza, to the woman, Fermina Daza, are the thread that keeps them attentive to each other until—after more than four hundred pages—readers are presented with a change in the perception of the importance of the epistolary link. Florentino first goes to Fermina's house after he has sent her a letter he had written in a state of depression, caused by the embarrassment of anticipating his first visit to her house. The encounter goes smoothly, overcoming the difficulties that had caused the composition of the letter.

A new system of mail delivery in the town makes it possible for the letter to arrive precisely at the time that Florentino is visiting with Fermina. He asks Fermina not to read the letter. She says:

> "Claro.... Al fin y al cabo, las cartas son del que las escribe. ¿No es cierto?"
> El dio un paso firme.
> "Así es"—dijo—"Por eso es lo primero que se devuelve cuando hay una ruptura."
> Ella pasó por alto la intención y le devolvió la carta, diciendo: "Es una lástima que no pueda leerla, porque las otras me han servido mucho." El respiró a fondo, sorprendido de que ella hubiera dicho de un modo tan espontáneo mucho más de lo que él esperaba, y le dijo: "No se imagina qué feliz me hace saberlo." Pero ella cambió el tema, y él no consiguió que lo reanudara en el resto de la tarde.

> ("Of course.... After all, letters belong to the one who writes them, don't they?"
> He stepped with decision.
> "That's the way it is"—he said—"That's why they are the first things to be returned when there is a breakup."
> She overlooked his intention and returned the letter to him saying: "It is a pity that I can't read it, because the others were very helpful to me." He took a deep breath, amazed at the spontaneity with which she had said much more than he had expected, and told her: "You have no idea at the happiness that this knowledge gives me." But she changed the subject and he could not get her to come back to it for the rest of the afternoon.)

After having been the only link between two characters who had been physically apart, the letters, through Fermina's reaction, enter into another realm. They become something different from the weighty reality that brought the lovers together, something that Florentino dares define as literature.

The novel thus takes two routes simultaneously: one that leads in the direction of litera-

Dust jacket for the English translation of García Márquez's 1985 novel, which deals with the long epistolary courtship of an elderly couple

ture, and the other portrayed as divergent, bringing readers closer to feelings seen as more real than the ones in the hypothetical book. The hypothesis of *El amor en los tiempos del cólera* serves to show that, at age seventy-two, Fermina Daza can still be a cunning reader and a blushing inspirer of courtship. She returns the letters to Florentino, thereby freeing herself from his "book." In returning the letters and safely confining them to a book, Fermina is able to make the transition from potential gullible reader (a believer in illusions who is unable to take action, a dreamer unconnected to the present) to a credible lover. Literature has been given a place; it has served the purpose of bringing Fermina and Florentino together and now must be pushed aside so that the romance may, indeed, continue. Fermina has been seduced by the letters but is capable of maintaining the kind of distance that leaves room for the reality of Florentino, the man, not the character constructed by the letters.

Fermina has the steadiness of parochialism. She has common sense; therein lies the source of her strength that allows her to act out the love attachment she has had for so many years with Florentino. The letters are necessary conventions very much like the imported furniture in some of her rooms, but the heart of it all is the reality of their lives, which has the same ring of authenticity as the local furniture in her home.

As in other works by García Márquez, notably *Cien años de soledad*, the particularly female virtues of intuition and common sense are emphasized in contrast to the relative lack of them in the male characters. Florentino is interested in literature in a way that could make him a victim of it, since he was ready to suffer the consequences of taking the letters "seriously" and risking the end of his relationship with Fermina, had she not so readily disregarded them by accepting their being literature. Dr. Urbino, her longtime husband, now deceased, is also portrayed as an intellectual. Although he is a solid member of the community and enjoys reading history books, he has one fanciful occupation that leads him to his death. Replicating the contrasts between the local and the imported furniture in his house, Dr. Urbino owns a pet parrot to whom he speaks in French and Spanish. (When he was younger he had succeeded in teaching French so well to one of his parrots that it could speak it as a true scholar.) One day, as he is engaged in speaking with another parrot—this time in Spanish—it tries to fly away. Dr. Urbino calls it back and then attempts to reach it by climbing a ladder. At this point in the novel Dr. Urbino has already passed his eightieth birthday, and he dies as a result of falling from the ladder. Unlike Fermina, Dr. Urbino cannot free himself from the friction generated by the two differing halves of his existence. He is killed because he is unable to judge properly the distance (the parrot was perched higher than he had calculated) between them—between life and literature. Fermina's expertise is the result of a fundamental lack of interest in the conventions of art, literature, and the intellect.

Fermina and Florentino are said to carry the scent of old age in their bodies, at a time of sickness and death. Nevertheless they embody the ideal of the stability of youthful passion in remaining true to the intensity of their first liaison, decades before their permanent reunion. That such a resolution is possible under the aegis of the refusal of literature, rather than the opposite, is, indeed, a sign of the kind of reevaluation of the role of the metafictional mode presently under way in Latin-American writing.

In *Cien años de soledad* the explicit ending of the novel inflects the reading toward disregarding the lives of the family in favor of a manuscript being unfolded and in urgent need of elucidation. In that way, critical elucidation rather than the multiple projections in plot is asserted as the purpose of both writing and reading. *El amor en los tiempos del cólera* works toward an opposite effect. The hypothetical book being written through Florentino's letters is made into a mere moment—to be disregarded—in the couple's "true" story. The accent is on the weight of that which is being told as rooted in experience.

In *El general en su laberinto*, in stark contrast to *El otoño del patriarca*, the historical references are meticulously documented, and the central character is clearly identified as Simón Bolívar. As readers follows the last days of Bolívar, they are made aware of the complex web of intrigue and betrayal surrounding him. He is portrayed as a physically diminished man, prone to fevers and melancholic sentiments. Memories of dances, songs, and lovemaking are interspersed with the reality of his departure from home and the extreme conditions of the journey. The vulnerability of Bolívar in this novel stands in opposition to the patriotic images through which he has been traditionally represented. In writing this historical fiction, García Márquez has joined the contemporary Latin-American writers who think of the novel as an ideal medium for critical reinterpretation of the past. In this case, the persona of the reader, who has the task of rethinking the terms of Bolívar's cult, is parallel to the persona of Bolívar himself, coming to terms with his career and associates.

El general en su laberinto repeats and expands in an intimate tone some of the preoccupations developed in the rest of the García Márquez literary corpus: the link between power and solitude, as in *Cien años de soledad* and *El otoño del patriarca*, as well as the evocation of the aging, ailing body, as seen in *El amor en los tiempos del cólera*. The many people who see Bolívar in the course of his journey remind the reader of the characters in *Crónica de una muerte anunciada*. The rhythm of the narrative is slow, intending to provoke a pace of reading that would mimic Bolívar's own personal journal.

Most recently, García Márquez has pursued an interest in film, already present in his journalism. He has made a series of six films for Span-

García Márquez circa 1987

ish television that have received critical and popular approval.

Interviews:

Leopoldo Azancot, "Gabriel García Márquez habla de política y de literatura," *Indice*, 237 (1968): 30-31;

José Domingo, "Entrevista a García Márquez," *Insula*, 259 (1968): 45-47;

Armando Durán, "Conversaciones con Gabriel García Márquez," *Revista Nacional de Cultura*, 29, no. 185 (1968): 23-43;

Rosa Castro, "Con Gabriel García Márquez," in *Recopilación de textos sobre García Márquez* (Havana: Casa de las Americas, 1969), pp. 29-33;

Claude Couffon, "Gabriel García Márquez habla de *Cien años de soledad*," in *Recopilación de textos sobre García Márquez*, pp. 45-47;

Ernesto González Bermejo, "García Márquez: Ahora doscientos años de soledad," *Triunfo*, 441 (1970): 12-18;

Rita Guibert, *Seven Voices: Seven Latin American Writers Talk to Rita Guibert* (New York: Knopf, 1973), pp. 303-338;

Ramón Oviero, "He sido un escritor explotado," *Ahora*, 656 (1976): 34-39;

Guillermo Sheridan and Armando Pereira, "García Márquez en México," *Revista de la Universidad de México*, 30, no. 6 (1976);

Alfonso Rentería Mantilla, ed., *García Márquez habla de García Márquez, 33 reportajes* (Bogotá: Rentería, 1979);

Plinio Apuleyo Mendoza, *El olor de la guayaba* (Barcelona: Bruguera, 1982);

Marlise Simons, "A Talk With Gabriel García Márquez," *New York Times Book Review*, 5 December 1982, pp. 7, 60-61.

Bibliographies:

Margaret Eustalia Fau, *Gabriel García Márquez: An Annotated Bibliography, 1947-1979* (Westport, Conn.: Greenwood, 1980);

Fau and Nelly Sfeir de González, *Bibliographic Guide to Gabriel García Márquez, 1979-1985* (Westport, Conn.: Greenwood, 1986).

Biography:

Stephen Minta, *García Márquez: Writer of Colombia* (New York, 1987).

References:

John Benson, "Disyunción en los cuentos de García Márquez," *Chasqui*, 8, no. 1 (1978): 18-22;

Birute Ciplijauskaité, "Foreshadowing as a Technique and Theme in *One Hundred Years of Solitude*," *Books Abroad*, 47 (Summer 1973): 479-484;

Frank Dauster, "The Short Stories of García Márquez," *Books Abroad*, 47 (Summer 1973): 466-470;

Mary E. Davis, "The Voyage Beyond the Map: 'El ahogado más hermoso del mundo,'" *Kentucky Romance Quarterly*, 26, no. 1 (1979): 25-33;

David William Foster, "The Double Inscription of the *Narrataire* in 'Los funerales de la Mamá Grande,'" in his *Studies in the Contemporary Spanish-American Short Story* (Columbia: University of Missouri Press, 1979), pp. 51-62;

Foster, "García Márquez and the *Ecriture* of Complicity: 'La prodigiosa tarde de Baltazar,'" in his *Studies in the Contemporary Spanish-American Short Story*, pp. 39-50;

Carlos Fuentes, "Macondo, Seat of Time," *Review*, 70 (1971): 119-121;

David P. Gallagher, "Gabriel García Márquez," in his *Modern Latin American Literature* (London: Oxford University Press, 1973), pp. 144-163;

Helmy F. Giacoman, ed., *Homenaje a Gabriel García Márquez* (New York: Las Américas, 1972);

Judith A. Goetzinger, "The Emergence of a Folk Myth in *Los funerales de la Mamá Grande*," *Revista de Estudios Hispánicos*, 6 (May 1972): 237-248;

Joel Hancock, "Gabriel García Márquez's *Eréndira* and the Brothers Grimm," *Studies in Twentieth Century Literature*, 3, no. 1 (1978): 45-52;

Luis Harss and Barbara Dohmann, "Gabriel García Márquez, or the Lost Chord," in their *Into the Mainstream* (New York: Harper & Row, 1967), pp. 310-341;

Paul M. Hedeen, "Gabriel García Márquez's Dialectic of Solitude," *Southwest Review*, 68 (Autumn 1983): 350-364;

Regina Janes, *Gabriel García Márquez: Revolutions in Wonderland* (Columbia: University of Missouri Press, 1981);

Djelal Kadir, "The Architectonic Principle of *Cien años de soledad* and the Vichian Theory of History," *Kentucky Romance Quarterly*, 24, no. 3 (1977): 251-261;

William Kennedy, "The Yellow Trolley Car in Barcelona and Other Visions: A Profile of Gabriel García Márquez," *Atlantic Monthly*, 231 (January 1973): 50-59;

Latin American Literary Review, special García Márquez issue, 13 (January-June 1985);

Kurt L. Levy, "Planes of Reality in *El otoño del patriarca*," in *Studies in Honor of Gerald E. Wade*, edited by Sylvia Bowman and others (Madrid: Porrúa Turganzas, 1979), pp. 133-141;

Wolfgang A. Luchting, "Gabriel García Márquez: The Boom and the Whimper," *Books Abroad*, 44 (Winter 1970): 26-30;

Luchting, "Lampooning Literature: *La mala hora*," *Books Abroad*, 47 (Summer 1973): 471-478;

John P. McGowan, "A la recherche du temps perdu in *One Hundred Years of Solitude*," *Modern Fiction Studies*, 28 (Winter 1982-1983): 557-567;

Bernard McGuirk and Richard Cardwell, *Gabriel García Márquez: New Readings* (Cambridge, U.K.: Cambridge University Press, 1987);

George R. McMurray, *Gabriel García Márquez* (New York: Ungar, 1977);

Floyd Merrel, "José Arcadio Buendía's Scientific Paradigms: Man in Search of Himself," *Latin American Literary Review*, 2 (Spring-Summer 1974): 59-70;

Klaus Müller-Bergh, "*Relato de un náufrago*: García Márquez's Tale of Shipwreck and Survival at Sea," *Books Abroad*, 47 (Summer 1973): 460-466;

Harley D. Oberhelman, *The Presence of Faulkner in the Writings of García Márquez* (Lubbock: Texas Tech Press, 1980);

Julio Ortega, "*One Hundred Years of Solitude* and *The Autumn of the Patriarch*: Text and Culture," in his *Poetics of Change: The New Spanish-American Narrative* (Austin: University of Texas Press, 1984), pp. 85-95; 96-119;

Roger M. Peel, "The Short Stories of Gabriel García Márquez," *Studies in Short Fiction*, 8 (Winter 1971): 159-168;

Arnold M. Penuel, "Death and the Maiden: Demythologization of Virginity in García Márquez's *Cien años de soledad*," *Hispania*, 66 (December 1983): 552-560;

Penuel, "The Sleep of Vital Reason in García Márquez's *Crónica de una muerte anunciada*," *Hispania*, 68 (December 1985): 753-766;

Emir Rodriguez Monegal, "*One Hundred Years of Solitude*: The Last Three Pages," *Books Abroad*, 47 (Summer 1973): 485-489;

Robert Lewis Sims, "The Banana Massacre in *Cien años de soledad*: A Micro-structural Example of Myth, History and Bricolage," *Chasqui*, 8, no. 3 (1979): 3-23;

Sims, "Theme, Narrative, Bricolage and Myth in García Márquez," *Journal of Spanish Studies: Twentieth Century*, 8 (Spring and Fall 1980): 143-159;

Mario Vargas Llosa, *Gabriel García Márquez: Historia de un deicidio* (Barcelona: Barral, 1971);

Vargas Llosa, "García Márquez: From Aracataca to Macondo," *Review*, 70 (1971): 129-142;

Raymond L. Williams, "The Dynamic Structure of García Márquez's *El otoño del patriarca*," *Symposium*, 32 (Spring 1978): 56-75;

Williams, *Gabriel García Márquez* (Boston: Twayne, 1984);

Richard D. Woods, "Time and Futility in the Novel *El coronel no tiene quien le escriba*," *Kentucky Romance Quarterly*, 17, no. 4 (1970): 287-295;

Lois Parkinson Zamora, "The End of Innocence: Myth and Narrative Structure in Faulkner's *Absalom, Absalom!* and García Márquez's *Cien años de soledad*," *Hispanic Journal*, 4, no. 1 (1982): 23-40;

Zamora, "The Myth of Apocalypse and Human Temporality in García Márquez's *Cien años de soledad* and *El otcño del patriarca*," *Symposium*, 32 (Winter 1978): 341-355.

José Lezama Lima

(19 December 1910 - 9 August 1976)

J. C. Ulloa
Virginia Tech
and
L. A. de Ulloa
Radford University

BOOKS: *Muerte de Narciso* (Havana: Ucar, García, 1937);

Enemigo rumor (Havana: Ucar, García, 1941);

Aventuras sigilosas (Havana: Orígenes, 1945);

La fijeza (Havana: Orígenes, 1949);

Analecta del reloj (Havana: Orígenes, 1953);

La expresión americana (Havana: Instituto Nacional de Cultura, Ministerio de Educación, 1957; enlarged edition, Montevideo: Arca, 1969);

Tratados en La Habana (Havana: Universidad Central de Las Villas, 1958);

Dador (Havana: Ucar, García, 1960);

Paradiso (Havana: Unión Nacional de Escritores y Artistas de Cuba, 1966; revised edition, Mexico City: Era, 1968); translated by Gregory Rabassa as *Paradise* (New York: Farrar, Straus & Giroux, 1974; London: Secker & Warburg, 1974);

Orbita de Lezama Lima, edited by Armando Alvarez Bravo (Havana: UNEAC, 1966);

Los grandes todos (Montevideo: Arca, 1968); also published as *Lezama Lima* (Buenos Aires: Alvarez, 1968);

Posible imagen (Barcelona: Sinera, 1969);

Poesía completa (Havana: Instituto del Libro, 1970; enlarged edition, Havana: Letras Cubanas, 1985);

La cantidad hechizada (Havana: UNEAC, 1970);

Esferaimagen: Sierpe de don Luis de Góngora; Las imágenes posibles (Barcelona: Tusquets, 1970);

Introducción a los vasos órficos (Barcelona: Barral, 1971);

Las eras imaginarias (Madrid: Fundamentos, 1971);

Obras completas, 2 volumes, edited by Cintio Vitier (Mexico City: Aguilar, 1975, 1977);

Cangrejos, golondrinas (Buenos Aires: Calicanto, 1977);

Fragmentos a su imán (Havana: Arte & Literatura, 1977);

Oppiano Licario (Havana: Arte & Literatura, 1977);

Imagen y posibilidad, edited by Ciro Bianchi Ross (Havana: Letras Cubanas, 1981);

El reino de la imagen (Caracas: Ayacucho, 1981);

Juego de las decapitaciones (Barcelona: Montesinos, 1982);

Cuentos (Havana: Letras Cubanas, 1987);

Relatos (Madrid: Alianza, 1987);

Confluencias (Havana: Letras Cubanas, 1988).

OTHER: *Verbum*, edited by Lezama Lima and René Villarnovo (Havana, June-November 1937);

Espuela de Plata, edited by Lezama Lima and others (Havana, 1939-1941);

Nadie Parecía, edited by Lezama Lima (Havana, 1942-1944);

Orígenes, edited by Lezama Lima (Havana, 1944-1956);

Angel Gaztelu, *Gradual de laudes*, introduction by Lezama Lima (Havana: Orígenes, 1955);

Antología de la poesía cubana, 3 volumes, edited by Lezama Lima (Havana: Consejo Nacional de Cultura, 1965);

Juan Clemente Zenea: Poesía, selected, with an introduction, by Lezama Lima (Havana: Academia de Ciencias de Cuba, 1966).

In 1966, after the publication of his first novel, *Paradiso* (translated, 1974), José Lezama Lima emerged as a writer of astounding imagination capable of creating the most intricate and allusive metaphors. He was proclaimed by Julio Cortázar, Mario Vargas Llosa, Octavio Paz, Severo Sarduy, and other Hispano-American writers as one of the most brilliant and complex authors of the latter half of the twentieth century. Cortázar, the first serious reader outside of Cuba of Lezama's work and editor of the Mexican edition of *Paradiso*, was the most enthusiastic spokesman for the aesthetic values of the novel. According to Cortázar, Lezama's novel and poetic works, all of clearly hermetic character, are made more accessible to readers who take into account the poetic principles discussed by Lezama in his essays written throughout a lifetime dedicated to culture. In its totality, Lezama's oeuvre is a conjunction of fragments, a dialogue conducted between early poetic conceptions expressed in his essays, taken up again in his poems, and realized in its fullest expression in his novelistic work. *Paradiso* and its sequel, *Oppiano Licario* (1977), gather themes, preoccupations, and dialogues initiated years earlier and bring them to full development. The publication of *Paradiso*, as was the case with some of Lezama's previous works, was accompanied by considerable uproar and resistance. The Cuban edition created a scandal, and there was an unsuccessful attempt to suppress its circulation since it was considered pernicious to revolutionary ideology. However, Lezama is now acclaimed in Cuba as one of the greatest writers of the revolution. His controversial stature has led many of his critics to take opposing sides as to his political ideology and his participation in the revolutionary process. For some, he is a revolutionary writer; for others, an intellectual preoccupied only with poetry and culture and detached from ties with the political system launched in 1959 with the advent of Fidel Castro's government.

Born on 19 December 1910 in the military camp Columbia, near Havana, José María Andrés Fernando Lezama Lima was the second child of José María Lezama y Rodda and the former Rosa Lima y Rosado. Lezama y Rodda, an artillery lieutenant in the Cuban army, died in 1919, a victim of an influenza epidemic at Ft. Barrancas in Pensacola, Florida, where he was serving as an Allied forces volunteer. His death put an end to a promising military career, which had begun in the Fortaleza de la Cabaña as commandant of the El Morro Military Academy. Rosa Lima y Rosado, daughter of revolutionary exiles residing in the United States during the Cuban War of Independence from Spain, resisted accepting the death of her husband and inculcated in her three children, Rosa, José, and Eloísa, a great respect for the gallant military figure. After his death, the family moved into Rosa Lima y Rosado's mother's house in Havana. In time, the thirty-one-year-old widow formed with her children a subfamily within the larger family unit, and the image of the dead lieutenant became the center of their existence. In 1929 she moved with her children into a house of their own. After her daughters married, she continued to live alone with her son until her death in 1964. During their life together he and she developed a close relationship, which proved to be decisive in his writing and in his development as a poet. He did not marry until after her death, and only because she had requested him to do so. On 5 December 1964, only a few months after his mother's death, Lezama married María Luisa Bautista Treviño, an old friend of the family. They continued to live in the maternal house until his sudden death on 9 August 1976.

As a child, José Lezama Lima, even more than his sisters, felt his father's invisible presence, and he identified so completely with his mother that he acquired her peculiar way of modulating her speech. The absence of his father created within the young Lezama an anxiety that moved him to meditate intensely upon death. In fact, the feeling of unreality that characterizes his poetry has its provenance in this youthful search for answers to the unknown. The desire to give meaning to absence and the unexplored is the most representative paradigmatic aspect of his work. It was discontinuity, the void caused by death, that attracted this persistent explorer of the arcane. But in his works one does not perceive any desperation, because he found in the image of resurrection a justification for the unknown of death. In a 1971 interview with Jean-Michel Fossey (collected in *Interrogando a Lezama*) Lezama affirmed that the recurring motif of absence in his work and his obsession with overcoming the void of the unknown are directly related to the death of his father. His father's death was also put in poetic form many years later in *Paradiso*, in which the image of the father returns and the tragedy of his death is re-created. Passages in which an image fills the void caused by absence abound in *Paradiso* and in the rest of his oeuvre.

Lezama's childhood education began in 1920 and continued until 1928 without major interruption. He pursued his primary and secondary studies principally at the Colegio San Francisco de Paula, where the educator Pablo Mimó was headmaster and where Lezama's father had also been educated. The intense asthma attacks Lezama suffered from an early age recurred upon the death of his father to such a degree that he spent a great part of his childhood closed up in his room and not participating in the games of his friends. During this period of his life he began the readings that would lead him to live within his incomparable world of poetry.

In secondary school, the avid, asthmatic reader, though a dedicated student, won neither prizes nor medals for academic success. He was able to distinguish himself, however, in humanities courses, above all in the history of Spanish literature, taught by Professor Fernando Sirgo. What Lezama learned in class was not sufficient for him. Having begun studies for his *bachillerato* two years before other boys of his age, Lezama complemented his assigned readings with works by Miguel de Cervantes, Lope de Vega, Pedro Calderón de la Barca, Luis de Góngora, and other Spanish classics. All of these, especially Cervantes and Góngora, notably influenced his literary formation. He also amused himself by reading the French symbolists as well as the books of G. K. Chesterton and Jacques Maritain. In *Paradiso* the years in Mimó's Colegio are re-created in minute detail, although the veil of fantasy that covers most of the episodes diminishes the autobiographical elements. Lezama's avid readings of this period as well as his long, wakeful nights are also evoked in *Paradiso*, with allusions to the classics and to those texts that most challenged him.

By 1927 Lezama began to take seriously his vocation as a poet. In this period he wrote his first poems in a lined notebook with a red cover, decorated with vegetative motifs and entitled "Inicio y escape" (Beginning and Escape). The twenty-one poems included suggest some of the poetic constants of his future poetry: silence, murmurs, interrogatives, night, the underworlds of the sea and rivers, and the universe of the unknown. On the first page of "Inicio y escape" appears the date 1927 followed by a question mark. There is evidence, however, that the poet used this notebook until June 1932. The manuscript

Lezama Lima in 1960, when he was the director of the Departamento de Literatura y Publicaciones in Cuba (photograph by Berestein)

was recovered in 1983 by Emilio de Armas and is part of the enlarged edition of *Poesía completa* published in 1985.

According to Armando Alvarez Bravo, in 1929 the intense emotional fusion began between Lezama and his mother, becoming more enveloping as they remained alone together after his sisters married. The year 1929 also saw Lezama's matriculation at the Universidad de La Habana as a law student, and a series of political events abruptly awakened his civic consciousness. Cuba was going through one of the most difficult times in its history: the dictatorship of Gerardo Machado. University students formed a political nucleus in order to lead protest activities against the regime, and on 30 September 1930 they participated in a demonstration during which several of them were injured. Lezama found himself involved in this act of protest in spite of the torment that asthma caused him. He re-created in *Paradiso* this episode of his life, fused with another one he had witnessed in 1925: the student demonstration led by the student president Julio Antonio Mella. The 1930 demonstration and Mella's heroic figure provided sources of imagery for Lezama. He would compare Mella with the leaders of the War of Independence, such as Antonio Maceo, and develop Mella as a character until he is changed in *Paradiso* into a mythical Apolline figure.

For Lezama, the recent history of Cuba, from a revolutionary point of view, was founded precisely on that day in September 1930. His participation in politics would not be that of an activist but rather that of an intellectual who develops within his writing a philosophy of redemption, conceived as a response to the national disintegration he observes. Through writing he could redeem that which is essentially Cuban, which he saw being lost among the political detritus of his time.

Due to the student protests, Machado closed the university and all cultural centers. For Lezama the closing did not represent a tragedy.

The university environment appeared to him to be like a bazaar, and the professors like ventriloquists repeating without emotion the same knowledge year after year. Without employment opportunities, Lezama made use of this period of nearly four years while the university was closed to read all the books he could buy with his modest means or could borrow from his friends. It was also in this period that he began to smoke cigars with regularity, making the cigar an integral part of his image. He immersed himself, with the smoke of his inseparable *Habano* for company, in the Spanish, French, Italian, and German classics; in oriental philosophy; in the Roman, Greek, and Egyptian classics; in the Chinese classics of the sixth century B.C.; and in everything that could challenge and free his imagination from the era of political and cultural disintegration that Cuba was experiencing. He avidly explored every source of knowledge, and his internal world was nourished by various texts, among them the most inaccessible and arcane. Yet he did not intend to isolate himself in an ivory tower but rather to find answers that would permit him to address his intellectual anxieties caused by death, discontinuity, and the dilemma between the occult and the profane.

As his copious readings increased, Lezama's circle of friends became more selective. If he was not reading, he conversed with those who, like him, saw the necessity for a change in Cuban culture. Lezama was an insatiable conversationalist. There are many anecdotes concerning the wit and sardonic tone he often used to poke fun at nearly everyone and everything. Generally his mockery was accompanied by obvious sympathy or a playful tone that did not cause any rancor or bruised feelings.

In 1932 he met a young Spanish poet, some four years his junior, who was studying for the priesthood at the Seminario de San Carlos. Lezama's friendship with Angel Gaztelu lasted until Lezama's death and was punctuated by animated *tertulias* (literary talks) in the back room of La Victoria bookstore on Calle Obispo and by long walks through the streets of Havana. Lezama and Gaztelu's walks blossomed into intense conversations, generally about literature, but also about philosophy and religion. Lezama helped Gaztelu to pursue his literary vocation, and the latter encouraged Lezama to continue his religious studies. Lezama's Catholicism owes much to these conversations with the young priest and to readings of the Bible and oriental mysticism. In Lezama's works one finds an eclectic Catholicism founded on various philosophies and studies. In his discussions with Gaztelu, Lezama often concluded that he was a Catholic in his own way, a statement Gaztelu invariably countered by saying it was the best way not to be one.

As soon as he was ordained, Gaztelu was sent to the small towns of the interior of Cuba. His stay in Bauta, near Havana, was the most fruitful for his friendship with Lezama and for the impact that both young men began to have on the island toward the end of the 1930s. Every weekend, especially Sundays, Lezama went with other friends and intellectuals to visit the priest and continue the *tertulias* begun the previous week at La Victoria. These were friendly gatherings of painters, musicians, writers, sculptors, and poets. They talked about everything, and at the head of it all was Lezama. From these meetings sprang artworks created specifically for the little church at Bauta, which eventually became known as the "Iglesia de Orígenes" (Church of Orígenes), because it houses some work by the intellectuals who five years later would join together around Lezama to form the highly esteemed group known as "Orígenes."

With the fall of Machado and the reopening of Havana's university in 1934, Lezama resumed his law studies to please his mother, who wanted him to have a worthwhile career. But his numerous readings and new friendships had changed the affable young asthmatic. His vision of reality and of poetry began to show definitive features. He was now ready to live fully his true life: one of culture and poetry.

The year 1937 was crucial in determining Lezama's literary direction. On 2 January he read to the Círculo de Amigos de la Cultura Francesa (the Circle of Friends of French Culture) an essay entitled "El secreto de Garcilaso" (Garcilaso's Secret; collected in *Obras completas*, volume one, 1975), which caused an uproar among the listeners because of the daring of its metaphors. He had recently met Juan Ramón Jiménez, a Spanish poet preoccupied with the attainment of "pure" poetry. In those days, Lezama was already known among the poets of his generation for the authority and skill with which he expressed his opinion on literary matters and because of his belief in the role that poetry should play in Cuban culture. This local recognition of his intellect and the timorous admiration that his obscure eloquence sometimes inspired in his listeners encouraged him to establish a cordial, yet intense and poetically focused, dialogue on insularity and the cultural destiny of Cuba. In 1937 he published his most consequential poem, *Muerte de Narciso* (The Death of Narcissus), and began to edit his first review, *Verbum* (1937). *Verbum* is the prototype of a series of literary notebooks that would culminate in the foundation of *Orígenes* (1944-1956). *Verbum* attracted a following of law students and intellectuals who in time formed part of the *Orígenes* group. The objective of the review was to promote culture, avoid controversy, and look for essential elements of national expression. Nevertheless, there were gainsayers who called the review "Plomum" (Lead), alluding to the "weight" of Lezama's style and the obscure thematics, remote from law students' immediate interests. *Verbum* lasted only six months.

In 1939 *Verbum* was replaced by *Espuela de Plata* (Silver Spur, 1939-1941), which was also of short duration because of financial problems and internal squabbles. In this new literary review, edited by Lezama, Mariano Rodríguez, and Guy Pérez Cisneros, art became a sister to literature. It had been decided to include vignettes and illustrations in each issue. Lezama's interest in painting had already been evident. He often showed up at Rodríguez's studio with a package of salt crackers to talk about painting and literature, and in Lezama's work one finds abundant references to the plastic arts. Besides its managing editors, the following grouped themselves around *Espuela de Plata*: Angel Gaztelu, Eliseo Diego, Cintio Vitier, Gastón Baquero, Alfredo Lozano, Justo Rodríguez Santos, José Ardevol, Virgilio Piñera, Amelia Peláez, René Portocarrero, Arche, and Ernesto González Puig. Lezama wanted to create with this review a tradition in Cuban letters, to fill the cultural vacuum with art and literature.

The *Espuela de Plata* group was soon attacked by other intellectuals (in such journals as the *Revista de Avance* and *Gaceta del Caribe*) for not participating in the crisis that Cuba was experiencing. Internal conflicts among the members followed these external pressures. Differences between Lezama and Piñera arose for religious and personal reasons, and these, among other factors, led to the disbanding of the review in 1941.

Espuela de Plata went through six issues and introduced the vitality of contemporary European currents of thought. In this period Lezama's *Enemigo rumor* (Hostile Murmur, 1941) was published a short time before his thirty-first birthday. *Enemigo rumor* is the book of poems that definitively classified Lezama as a poet. The collection contains daring, carefully written poems of great metric, thematic, and conceptual variety. The difficulty in comprehension is due to the original use of metaphor and arbitrary and abstruse syntactical constructions. The poems present varying levels of difficulty as well as different levels of experimentation, since fragments alluding to classical literature, mythology, and religion are embedded in a bold, original style. In this collection themes reappear that Lezama alluded to in *Muerte de Narciso* and included in previous writings: death and the great extent of the unknown that he wanted to see reduced down onto a page through the means of poetry.

During this period, Lezama had already begun to work with the Consejo Superior de Defensa Social at the Castillo del Príncipe, which was then the Havana prison. He was the counsellor in charge of judicial matters. This work terrified him because he had to deal with common delinquents whom he believed he recognized in the cafés and streets of Old Havana. This occupation, nonetheless, allowed him the money he needed to pay for his publications. Thus in September 1942, after the break with Piñera, Lezama and Gaztelu collected enough funds to found another review, *Nadie Parecía* (Nobody Could Interfere), which lasted until 1944.

After the cessation of *Espuela de Plata*, that group of intellectuals dispersed. Piñera founded and edited *Poeta* (1942-1943), a review of antagonistic character. Gastón Baquero, Cintio Vitier, Eliseo Diego, and others from the original group founded *Clavileño* (1942-1943), a publication interested in recovering Cuba's poetic past. Lezama's response to this polemical period was the founding of *Nadie Parecía*. The founders and contributors of these three reviews joined together a little later in the founding of the most important of all Lezama's publications, *Orígenes*.

In *Nadie Parecía* Lezama continued the work begun in his previous journals, but he determinedly added a religious orientation, which had been a cause for the split with Piñera. Thus the review carried as a subtitle *Cuaderno de lo bello con Dios* (Notebook on Beauty with God). In its first issue a verse appeared by San Juan de la Cruz, taken from the last strophe of his "Canciones entre el alma y el amado" (Songs Between the Soul and the Lover, 1577), which synthesizes the mystic union with God in which the devil and immediate obstacles are vanquished. This seems to

José Lezama Lima (photograph by Jesse A. Fernández)

imply, within the context of *Nadie Parecía*, a conscientious effort on the part of the editors to divorce themselves from the polemical milieu. The review included texts by Lezama, Gaztelu, Juan Ramón Jiménez, Adolfo Fernández Obieta, José Morena Villa, and others. The review also published translations of Latin, French, and English classics, and notes by and about Cuban painters.

All of Lezama's poems published in *Nadie Parecía* were collected later in 1949 in the first two parts of a poetry collection entitled *La fijeza* (Persistence), which also contains, in the third part, several poems that appeared in *Orígenes*.

The poems of this period in Lezama's life refer in an abstruse way to the difficulties the poet experienced concerning his relationship with his former contributors to previous reviews; the poems return to the theme of poetry and the role of the poet; and, finally, they show a more marked religious sentiment.

The early journals founded and edited by Lezama prepared the way for the appearance in 1944 of *Orígenes*. The previous year Lezama had met José Rodríguez Feo through the painter Rodríguez, with whom he had collaborated in the founding of *Espuela de Plata* in 1939. From their conversations the idea arose of founding another review, more ambitious than the previous ones. Rodríguez Feo was the patron who made possible the publication of *Orígenes*.

Orígenes, which began to circulate in the spring of 1944 with the subtitle *Revista de Arte y Literatura*, welcomed not only various poets, musicians, and painters who had collaborated on former reviews edited by Lezama, but also new members who came to fill the ranks. For several years it published writings by Cuban authors; made accessible to the public previously unpublished translations of well-known foreign authors; reviewed art exhibitions; and furnished information on concerts and musical events. It was the most intense and influential literary organ of the era. In it Lezama published his first short stories—"Cangrejos, golondrinas" (Crabs, Swallows) and "Juego de las decapitaciones" (The Decapitation Game); ten poems; fundamental essays on poetry—"Imágenes posibles" (Possible Images), "X y XX," "La dignidad de la poesía" (The Dignity of Poetry), "Exámenes" (Inquiries), and "Introducción a un sistema poético" (Introduction to a Poetical System); and the first five chapters of *Paradiso*. Many of his essays are collected in *Introducción a los vasos órficos* (Introduction to the Orphic Vessels, 1971), in which the vital elements of his poetics are developed in chronological order, from 1945 to 1968. Other *Orígenes* essays were included in 1970 in *La cantidad hechizada* (The Magic Quantity).

What most interested Lezama in this review was precisely to return to the origins, to the roots of creation itself, to testify to the act of poetry's birth. At the same time, he was interested in achieving a state of introspection that would permit him to approach the origins of poetry, of things Cuban, and of the unknown. This search for the unknown, a characteristic that strongly marks Lezama's work and is repeated throughout it, also came to be a leading objective of this literary organ. In the development of *Orígenes*, Lezama did not accept any dualism. He surrendered himself with passion and devotion to the cultivation of poetry and the intellect. This part of his life is characterized by voracity, an insatiable thirst for knowledge. This is also his most fruitful period in that he was able to formulate more precisely his poetic principles and also to begin the novel that would bring him more fame.

In 1945 the review established its own publishing house. Three years later Ediciones Orígenes published Vitier's anthology entitled *Diez poetas cubanos, 1937-1947* (Ten Cuban Poets, 1937-1947), an homage to the quiet, persistent work of the poets in the group. The anthology includes several of Lezama's well-known poems previously published in other collections. Ediciones Orígenes also published some of Lezama's books: *Aventuras sigilosas* (Secret Adventures, 1945), *La fijeza* (1949), and *Analecta del reloj* (Analects of the Clock, 1953). Through the issues of the review and the books published by Ediciones Orígenes, the members of the group succeeded in making visible and accessible to Cuban and foreign readers their poetic efforts. Unfortunately, in 1953 problems began with the publication of Jorge Guillén's "Epigramas," which made fun of Jiménez's "pure" poetry. The antagonism between the two Spanish poets created in turn a split between Rodríguez Feo and Lezama, since the latter supported Jiménez while the former favored Guillén. The withdrawal of economic support by Rodríguez Feo finally brought about the extinction of the review. Because of the disagreement between the two editors of *Orígenes*, the review published two different versions of numbers 35 and 36 (vol. 11, 1954): one edited by Lezama and the other by Rodríguez Feo.

Undoubtedly, Lezama was the most prominent figure of the *Orígenes* group. During the years the review was in circulation he exercised great influence on all those who were associated with it. But this was not a unilateral influence. Lezama benefited greatly from the interchange with the others' ideas and modes of expression. His greatest contribution to the review was in the essay genre, since the studies published there contain some of the basic ideas of his poetics, of great impact not only on the members of the group but also on his novels.

In the first essays of *Introducción a los vasos órficos* one can observe a process of amplification in the search for images that already prefigure Lezama's later concepts of *vivencia oblicua* (oblique experience), *súbito* (the unexpected), and *eras imaginarias* (imaginary eras). These conceptions are key elements in his writing, which is dominated by poetic derivations and associations and not by causal relationships. In "Introducción a un sistema poético," which appeared in *Orígenes* in 1954, he delineates the essential qualities of his system. He insists upon the fact that poetry alone finds its true realization in a hyperbolic situation and within primordial superabundance and an environment of infinite possibilities. In "La dignidad de la poesía," from 1956, Lezama adds charity as a necessary element for acting within superabundance. The poet perceives himself as the "begetter of the possible," the high priest charged with attaining resurrection through poetry, with creating a new causality capable of shortening the distance between man and the unknown. The poet becomes the intermediary between man and God or the gods. Lezama knows that what he is looking for is absurd, and it is precisely this absurdity that brought him to investigate fundamental texts. He was interested in philosophical beliefs and in primitive Christianity, from which he extracted basic elements for intertextual composition—a process of constant borrowing that is summarized in one of his well-

mensity—in short, for the obliteration of all limits, to be replaced with an infinite extension, the orb of the ineffable. Related to his poetical goals are the conceptions of *vivencia oblicua* and the *súbito*. With *vivencia oblicua* Lezama creates a system of associations linked to the unreal and able to penetrate the unknown, and to illuminate it, while with the *súbito*, a surprising and unforeseen enlightenment of causal links occurs. Both literary mechanisms would become the cornerstone of his novels, where there are no causal concatenations, but rather contrapuntal encounters, where reality, unreality, poetic causality, and the unconditional contend with one another. That is, the connection between antecedent and consequence is not important; what is important is the multifarious aspect of the image, the intertextual counterpoint, and the tangential or sudden inferences that they evoke.

It is precisely the obstinate nature of Lezama's inquiring mind as well as his immeasurable thirst for knowledge that drove him in 1960 toward the configuration of *eras imaginarias*. In "A partir de la poesía" (Beginning with Poetry; in *Introducción a los vasos órficos*) one finds the amplification of ideas he had delineated for the first time in "Mitos y cansancio clásico" (Myths and Classical Stupor), the first chapter of *La expresión americana* (American Countenance, 1957). Lezama proposes a radical change; he suggests new critical directions and underlines the potential and importance of reflective reasoning, which can bring to an end the American subjection to European culture. One observes also that his attraction to the unknown persists in his search for eras in which exceptional circumstances and periods of superabundance allow the flourishing of a surprising metaphorical causality. He was very interested in Orphic myths; in Egyptian conceptions of death and the afterlife; in Taoism, with its seminal potential for exploring the creative vacuum of ancient China; and in the productive intermingling of the yin and the yang in the philosophy and literature of the Orient.

In *La expresión americana* Lezama observes, in his definition of the metaphorical subject, that causal concatenations must be overcome and that imaginary eras with all their synchronic and intertextual force can present surprising perspectives and open up new creative fields to the imagination; yet his objective in this book of essays is more immediate. Lezama returns to what is essentially American in the search for a center of radiance. The idea of the Incan era obsessed him.

Dust jacket for the 1970 collection that includes some of the essays Lezama Lima wrote for the journal Orígenes

known statements: "The impossible acting on the possible creates an actuating possible within infinity." That is, the impossible and the absurd create their own reason. The impossibility for man to justify death makes resurrection possible. The definition of faith by which Lezama justifies his postulates comes from Paul's Epistles, and these postulates take on their full meaning if one considers "faith" as the "substance" of that which is not seen, of that which is hoped for. Faith, as concretism, as the substance of the unknown, is fundamental to Lezama's conception of the poetic image or the materialization of the unknown.

Both essays, "Introducción a un sistema poético" and "La dignidad de la poesía," have as a common denominator Lezama's desire to do away with obstacles to his poetic formulation. There is an eagerness for liberation, for im-

For this reason *La expresión americana* does not have the generalizing intent found in the essays of *Introducción a los vasos órficos*, but rather the objective of investigating American culture profoundly and in a critical-creative way.

In mid January 1957 Lezama read five lectures at the Centro de Altos Estudios of the Instituto Nacional de Cultura in Havana. Also in early 1957 Lezama was verbally attacked by the dissidents of *Orígenes*, who had affiliated with *Ciclón*, the new review that Rodríguez Feo had begun to publish. The members of *Ciclón* advocated a more direct type of literature than that found in *Orígenes* and with more possibility of communication with readers. The dissidents' sympathies were not with Spanish and French writers, but rather with English and Hispano-American poets, such as T. S. Eliot and Pablo Neruda. In the pages of *Ciclón* treatises were published attacking the literature found in *Orígenes* and denying the value of this publication for Cuban culture. Also during the late 1950s, Lezama experienced personally the political uneasiness that Cuba was going through: his house was broken into by the dictator's police in a futile attempt to link him with anti-Batista forces. In spite of these misfortunes, Lezama succeeded, as before, with his characteristic obstinacy, in concentrating on his lectures and other work, without worrying too much about any dialogue with the public. The lectures at the Centro de Altos Estudios are collected in *La expresión americana*.

The Cuban Revolution of 1959 appeared to bring about the changes in Cuban culture for which Lezama had hoped. With greater importance bestowed upon the arts, Lezama no longer had to preoccupy himself with obtaining necessary funds to pay for his publications. Although he saw himself attacked in November and December of 1959 by Guillermo Cabrera Infante, Antón Arrufat, Heberto Padilla, César Leante, and other collaborators of *Lunes de Revolución*, who wanted to do away with his powerful literary influence, Lezama in time forgot the wrongs done him and agreed to take part in the cultural process. This same year he accepted the post as director of the Departamento de Literatura y Publicaciones of the Consejo Nacional de Cultura and participated in a series of lectures organized by the student association of the Universidad de La Habana. In 1961 he was elected as one of the six presidents of the Unión de Escritores y Artistas de Cuba (UNEAC)—the Cuban Writers and Artists Union. In 1962 he began work as ad-

Lezama Lima (photograph by Mariano Ferré)

viser at the Centro Cubano de Investigaciones Literarias (Cuban Center for Literary Research). This initial revolutionary period offered writers such as Lezama the opportunity to write and publish their works without financial worries.

Lezama published *Paradiso* at the age of fifty-six, when many thought his fame as a writer would be limited to that group of friends with whom he regularly met in the bars and cafés of Havana, in the bookstores, and at the Ucar, García Publishing Company. If international fame had not reached him because of his poems and erudite essays, the publication of *Paradiso* served as a bridge between the imaginary world he had forged and the public outside his limited circle of friends. Even though he had published the first five chapters in issues of *Orígenes* in 1949, 1952, and 1955, as well as several episodes in an anthology of the Cuban novel published in 1960 by the Cuban Ministry of Education, the total conception of the work was realized upon the death of his mother in 1964. The novel therefore became another attempt to fill the void caused by death. In *Paradiso* Lezama finally found the best and most fruitful way to unite his knowledge with the experiences of a life totally dedicated to poetry.

The structure of the novel is a product of Lezama's poetical conceptions. The work can be divided into four extensive planes with marked exterior differences: 1) the familiar, which includes the most distinctive events pertaining to the main character, José Cemí, and which is distinguished by its autobiographical flavor and by the experiences entwined around the image of the genealogical tree; 2) one that introduces a world alien to the familiar one, containing phallic allusions and descriptions, and references to man's sexual origins, as well as to their multiple manifestations; 3) one for events that occur without apparent causality, thereby destroying the temporal dimension; and 4) the one that contains the final encounter between Cemí and Oppiano Licario, his poetic and intellectual mentor. Lezama's force of poetic causality prevents the reader from perceiving any sequential link between the different planes, and it is for this reason that some critics initially saw the novel as a discordant medley.

The novel begins with a decisive event in Cemí's infancy. Baldovina, the family servant, attends to Cemí during one of his asthma attacks. Asthma, a constant in the novel and in the life of Lezama, tempts the reader from the very beginning to identify the protagonist with the author of the novel. The whole first part is therefore dominated by a family atmosphere and by the image of the father's untimely death, which motivates an attempt to fill the void of his absence. In *Paradiso*, as well as in Lezama's concept of *eras imaginarias*, two great themes stand out: death and the return to origins. The latter theme is synthesized in the image of the genealogical tree that serves as a center or *axis mundi* around which the most significant events of the protagonist's childhood revolve. In the first part of the novel, the symbolism of the tree forms a cosmic-paradisiacal image and acquires hierophant characteristics precisely attributable to Lezama's religious experiences. Because of its verticality, the image of the *axis mundi* is projected toward infinity in an attempt at penetrating the unknown.

The world outside the family center is introduced by events related to Cemí's school and university life. In this part there are long, complex dialogues on erotic love and the origin of sexuality. Sexual relations of all types among the different characters are described in vivid detail. In general they are presented without evasiveness and are embedded in dazzling metaphorical imagery pregnant with multiple connotations. Phallic images range from those related to experiences at school to those referring to primitive beliefs of the sixth century B.C. Like the genealogical tree, the image of the phallus has a structural function and serves by its verticality to facilitate the union of the now with the unknown. Several Cuban intellectuals have seen in this part of *Paradiso* obvious connections with Lezama's personal life. Cabrera Infante, for example, in an essay entitled "Vidas para leerlas" (Lives to be Read), makes an astute comparison between Lezama's and Piñera's homosexual preferences. For Cabrera Infante, many of the episodes in *Paradiso* were conceived by Lezama as a silent protest against the oppression homosexuals suffered in communist Cuba.

The last three chapters of *Paradiso* form an intratextual synthesis of the novel's key parts. Time and space are destroyed, and poetical concepts that Lezama had amply discussed in his essays are put into action. As in several abstruse episodes found in the first part of the novel, the writing in these chapters is metaphorical, dazzling, and obscure. Poetical analogies, the *súbito*, and *vivencia oblicua*, with imprecise connections lacking apparent causal links, predominate when the enigmatic character Cemí had met in his childhood beside his father's deathbed, Oppiano Licario, mysteriously reappears.

The last chapter contains Cemí's encounter with Licario, the fictive author of *Súmula, nunca infusa de excepciones morfológicas* (Never Infused Compendium of Morphological Exceptions). Through meetings with Licario, Cemí learns to control the rhythm of his respiration. Cemí achieves a state of internal breathing, a universal rhythm of self-knowledge that will facilitate his poetical investigations and his incursions into the void toward the beginning of time, toward the unknown.

The first edition of *Paradiso* was prepared by UNEAC in 1966. Bound in a very simple cover, this edition is marred by numerous typographical errors. Its appearance in the bookstores of Havana caused a furor. Several minor government officials classified the novel as pornographic and as an open manifesto in favor of homosexuality. Therefore, they took measures to take the four thousand copies already printed out of circulation and even to intercept those that had already left Cuba. This censorship lasted only a few months, since the novel eventually began to circulate freely within and outside Cuba thanks to the official approval of the revolutionary government. The second edition of *Paradiso*, dated 1968, was published in Mexico City. This edition, revised by the author, contains illustrations by René Portocarrero, the Cuban painter and former associate of *Orígenes*. The cover, also by Portocarrero, is dark pink with an illustration of a primitive head wearing a hat in the shape of an emblematic baroque cornucopia with white, black, green, red, pink, and orange colors.

International critics received *Paradiso* with excitement, although the homosexual aspect continued to stir up a certain amount of controversy. In November 1967 *Mundo Nuevo* included two letters, one by the writer Mario Vargas Llosa and the other by the Uruguayan critic Emir Rodríguez Monegal, in which the importance of the novel's homosexual episodes are debated. Rodríguez Monegal suggests an allegorical interpretation that reflects the poet's *eras imaginarias*. The Argentinian novelist and critic Julio Cortázar published "Para llegar a Lezama Lima" (How to Approach Lezama Lima) in his 1967 collection of essays *La vuelta al día en ochenta mundos* (Around the Day in Eighty Worlds). Cortázar was the first critic who seriously and systematically devoted himself to analyzing some of the levels for possible interpretation found in *Paradiso*. He finds intertextual connections between obscure episodes in the novel and *A Journey to the Center of the Earth* (1864) by Jules Verne.

Apparently disturbed by certain statements made by critics concerning *Paradiso*, Lezama wrote to his sister Eloísa in June 1966, announcing a continuation of his opus, intending to clarify the earlier novel. In 1977 the unfinished sequel to *Paradiso*, entitled *Oppiano Licario*, was published posthumously.

In *Oppiano Licario* one reencounters many of the main characters of *Paradiso*, as well as Inaca Eco Licario, Oppiano's mysterious sister. The reader enters a world of derivative associations far removed from a causal chain of events. *Oppiano Licario* represents a point of juncture of many of the postulates discussed by Lezama in his poetry, in his essays, and especially in *Paradiso*.

In *Oppiano Licario* Cemí continues his poetic apprenticeship, which culminates in his union with Inaca Eco Licario, from whom he obtains the vision of reconstructing fragments into a whole, which is Inaca's metaphorical representation as the sister and complement to Oppiano. In this sequel Lezama wanted to tie up loose ends and resolve some of the unknowns in *Paradiso*, but his endeavor was cut short by his unexpected death, brought about by pneumonia, in 1976.

According to Enrico Mario Santí, *Oppiano Licario* is the ultimate fragment and must be read as an integral part of a greater text that was interrupted by Lezama's death. During a trip to Cuba in 1979, Santí succeeded in obtaining the original outline of the novel from Lezama's widow. Comparing this outline with the posthumous novel, Santí concludes in his 1982 essay "*Oppiano Licario*: La poética del fragmento" (Oppiano Licario: The Poetics of the Fragment) that the text of the novel itself anticipates and discusses its own fragmentation.

In the last few years of his life, Lezama gained a lot of weight. During his lifetime he had been a great gourmand of food and drink, which he consumed with the same intensity with which he devoured a good book. He had a lust for smells and flavors, as can be appreciated in some of his descriptions of Creole cooking found in *Paradiso* and in some of the poems in *Fragmentos a su imán* (Fragments of His Magnet, 1977). Lezama's disabling obesity kept him from moving about with facility or leaving his house. Walking a few blocks fatigued him and made his breathing difficult. He no longer attended the *tertulias* in cafés and bookstores, nor could he stroll through the beloved streets of Havana. After a time he became a recluse, an immobile pilgrim who was limited to making fantastic imaginary voyages or spending long periods conversing with the few friends who remembered to visit him. From 1971 on, after having been accused by Heberto Padilla of being guilty of antirevolutionary activities, Lezama became isolated, and many of his former friends became afraid of reprisals and stopped visiting him. In correspondence published by Eloísa Lezama Lima under the title *Cartas* (Letters, 1979), Lezama alludes to his difficulties within the revolutionary regime and his lack of freedom to travel abroad. Some of his Cuban friends state, nevertheless, that Lezama was not deprived of his liberties and that, if he did not travel, it was because he did not choose to do so.

In the decade of the 1980s the Cuban government, motivated by the controversy concerning Lezama's political position in Cuba and reacting to the letters published by his sister, sponsored a series of publications with the intention of redeem-

Lezama Lima circa 1974

ing and completing Lezama's image. In 1981 Ciro Bianchi Ross published *Imagen y posibilidad* (Image and Possibility), a collection of some of Lezama's essays, with the purpose of profiling a Lezama more politically committed to the revolution than his other writings or letters generally reveal. At the same time, Bianchi Ross attempted to portray a Lezama who was provided by the revolutionary government with all the facilities possible to publish his work. Bianchi Ross wanted to contradict any insinuation of ostracism during the last years of Lezama's life.

In 1986 Carlos Espinosa completed a series of interviews, which he transcribed as testimonials in his book *Cercanía de Lezama Lima* (Intimate Lezama Lima). The book offers details on Lezama's personal life that would otherwise be difficult to obtain. Beneath the surface this book is also a veiled response to the *Cartas*, which are manipulated by Espinosa to support some of the collected testimonials. As one might expect, testimonials by several dissidents associated with Lezama, but living now outside of Cuba, are missing.

In reality the political question raised during Lezama's last years confuses his political views with his aesthetics. Lezama had long hoped for revolutionary change, as some of his writings, especially in the essay genre, demonstrate. Lezama's political response to social conditions was clearly on the side of change. His creative writing, however, is highly metaphorical and allusive. He even meditates on the potentiality of the image as the secret cause of history. But beyond the political overtones of his primary interest in the *imagen histórica*, the bulk of his work, conceived before the revolution and completed in the 1970s, cannot be considered as revolutionary or political literature. Lezama was a universal poet, impossible to label with political nomenclature. His obsession was poetry, and his life was literature.

Letters:

Cartas, edited by Eloísa Lezama Lima (Madrid: Orígenes, 1979).

Interviews:

Armando Alvarez Bravo, "Conversación con Lezama Lima," *Mundo Nuevo*, 24 (June 1968): 33-39;

Tomás Eloy Martínez, "El peregrino inmóvil," *Indice*, 232 (June 1968): 22-26;

Interrogando a Lezama, edited by the Centro de Investigaciones Literarias de la Casa de las Américas (Barcelona: Anagrama, 1971);

Jean-Michel Fossey, "Entrevista con Lezama," in *Galaxia latinoamericana: Siete años de entrevistas* (Las Palmas, Grand Canary: Inventarios Provisionales, 1973), pp. 29-50;

Fossey, "Antes de morir Lezama," *Indice*, 401-402 (September-October 1976): 45-49;

Ciro Bianchi Ross, "Asedio a Lezama Lima," *Quimera*, 30 (April 1983): 30-46;

Cercanía de Lezama Lima, edited by Carlos Espinosa (Havana: Letras Cubanas, 1986).

Bibliography:

Justo C. Ulloa, *Sobre José Lezama Lima y sus lectores: Guía y compendio bibliográfico* (Boulder, Colo.: Society of Spanish and Spanish-American Studies, 1987).

References:

Armando Alvarez Bravo, ed., Introduction to *Orbita de Lezama Lima* (Havana: UNEAC, 1966);

Leonor Alvarez de Ulloa, "Ordenamiento secreto de la poética de Lezama," in *José Lezama Lima: Textos críticos*, edited by Justo C. Ulloa (Miami & Madrid: Universal, 1979), pp. 38-65;

Emilo Bejel, *José Lezama Lima, Poet of the Image* (Gainesville: University of Florida Press, 1990);

Ciro Bianchi Ross, ed., *José Lezama Lima: Imagen y posibilidad* (Havana: Letras Cubanas, 1981);

Guillermo Cabrera Infante, "Vidas para leerlas," *Vuelta*, 41 (April 1980): 4-16;

Julio Cortázar, "Para llegar a Lezama Lima," in his *La vuelta al día en ochenta mundos* (Mexico City: Siglo XXI, 1967), pp. 135-155;

James Irby, "Lezama's Early Poetry: Intertextuality in *Enemigo Rumor*," in *Transformations of Literary Languages in Latin American Literature: From Machado de Assis to the Vanguards*, edited by K. David Jackson (Austin, Tex.: Abaporu, 1987), pp. 165-186;

Julio Ortega, "*La expresión americana*: Una teoría de la cultura," in *José Lezama Lima: Textos críticos*, pp. 66-74;

Enrico Mario Santí, "Lezama, Vitier y la crítica de la razón reminiscente," *Revista Iberoamericana*, 92-93 (July-December 1975): 535-546;

Santí, "*Oppiano Licario*: La poética del fragmento," *Revista de la Universidad de México*, 19 (November 1982): 8-13;

Mario Vargas Llosa and Emir Rodríguez Monegal, "Cartas: Sobre el *Paradiso* de Lezama Lima," *Mundo Nuevo*, 16 (1967): 89-95.

Clarice Lispector

(10 December 1925 - 9 December 1977)

Earl E. Fitz
Pennsylvania State University

BOOKS: *Perto do coração selvagem* (Rio de Janeiro: Noite, 1944); translated by Giovanni Pontiero as *Near to the Wild Heart* (New York: New Directions, 1990; Manchester, U.K.: Carcanet, 1990);

O lustre (Rio de Janeiro: AGIR, 1946);

A cidade sitiada (Rio de Janeiro: Noite, 1949; revised edition, Rio de Janeiro: Alvaro, 1964);

Alguns contos (Rio de Janeiro: Ministério de Educação e Saúde, 1952);

Laços de família (São Paulo: Alves, 1960); translated by Pontiero as *Family Ties* (Austin: University of Texas Press, 1972; Manchester, U.K.: Carcanet, 1985);

A maçã no escuro (Rio de Janeiro: Alves, 1961); translated by Gregory Rabassa as *The Apple in the Dark* (New York: Knopf, 1967; London: Virago, 1985);

A paixão segundo G. H. (Rio de Janeiro: Autor, 1964); translated by Ronald W. Sousa as *The Passion According to G. H.* (Minneapolis: University of Minnesota Press, 1988);

A legião estrangeira (Rio de Janeiro: Autor, 1964); translated by Pontiero as *The Foreign Legion* (New York: Center for Inter-American Relations, 1979; Manchester, U.K.: Carcanet, 1986);

O mistério do coelho pensante (Rio de Janeiro: Alvaro, 1967);

A mulher que matou os peixes (Rio de Janeiro: Sabiá, 1968); translated by Earl E. Fitz as *The Woman Who Killed the Fish*, Latin American Literary Review, 11 (Fall-Winter 1982): 89-101;

Uma aprendizagem; ou, O livro dos prazeres (Rio de Janeiro: Sabiá, 1969); translated by Richard A. Mazzara and Lorri A. Parris as *An Apprenticeship; or, The Book of Delights* (Austin: University of Texas Press, 1986);

Felicidade clandestina (Rio de Janeiro: Sabiá, 1971);

A imitação da rosa (Rio de Janeiro: Artenova, 1973);

Agua viva (Rio de Janeiro: Artenova, 1973); translated by Fitz and Elizabeth Lowe as *The Stream of Life* (Minneapolis: University of Minnesota Press, 1989);

Onde estivestes de noite (Rio de Janeiro: Artenova, 1974); translated by Alexis Levitin in *Soulstorm* (New York: New Directions, 1989);

A via crucis do corpo (Rio de Janeiro: Artenova, 1974); translated by Levitin in *Soulstorm*;

A vida íntima de Laura (Rio de Janeiro: Olympio, 1974);

Visão do esplendor: Impressões leves (Rio de Janeiro: Alves, 1975);

De corpo inteiro (Rio de Janeiro: Artenova, 1975);

A hora da estrela (Rio de Janeiro: Olympio, 1977); translated by Pontiero as *The Hour of the Star* (Manchester, U.K.: Carcanet, 1986);

Um sopro de vida: Pulsações (Rio de Janeiro: Nova Fronteira, 1978);

Quase de verdade (Rio de Janeiro: Rocco, 1978);

Para não esquecer (São Paulo: Atica, 1978);

A bela e a fera (Rio de Janeiro: Nova Fronteira, 1979);

A descoberta do mundo (Rio de Janeiro: Nova Fronteira, 1984).

Collection: *Seleta*, edited by Renato Cordeiro Gomes (Rio de Janeiro: Olympio, 1975).

TRANSLATION: Oscar Wilde, *O retrato de Dorian Gray* (Rio de Janeiro: Ouro, 1974).

At the time of her death in 1977, Clarice Lispector was widely viewed not only as Brazil's leading writer but as one of the most extraordinary writers of narratives ever to emerge from Latin America. A brilliantly original stylist whose lyrically rendered and philosophically oriented texts revolutionized Brazilian fiction in the post-World War II era, Lispector is also becoming celebrated as a prototypical practitioner of *l'écriture féminine* (feminist writing) and of poststructuralist writing in general. Her reputation as an experimental novelist and short-story writer has spread well beyond the confines of Latin America. As this process of international recognition contin-

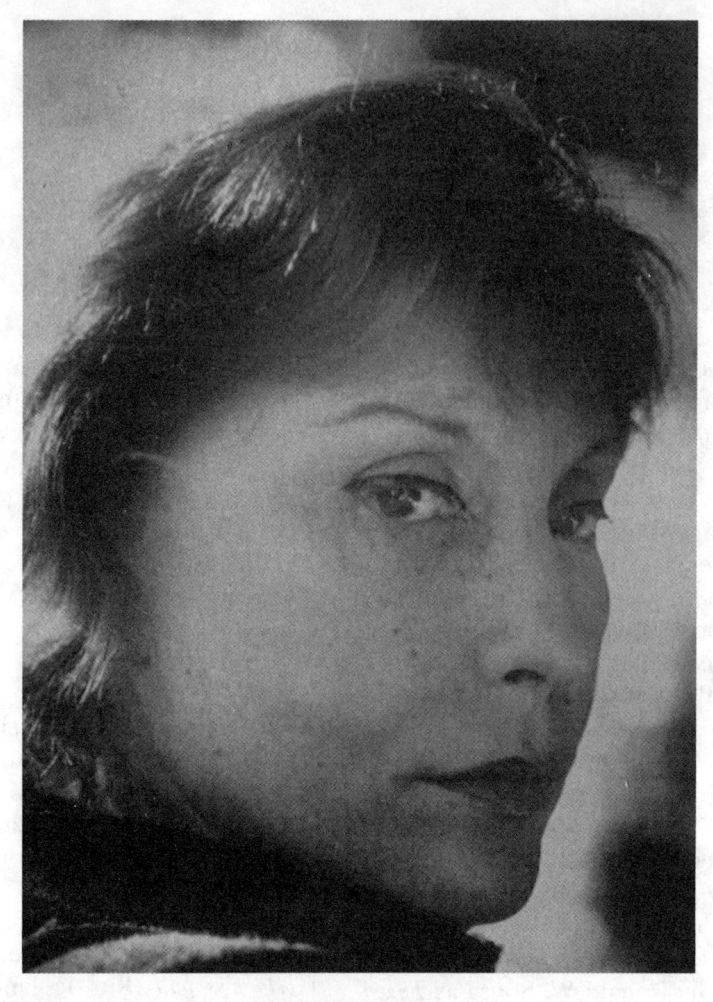

Clarice Lispector

ues, it seems likely that Lispector will eventually gain her rightful place as one of Western literature's major late-twentieth-century authors.

Born in Tchetchelnik, a tiny Ukrainian village, on 10 December 1925, Lispector was the daughter of Pedro and Marian Lispector and immigrated with her family to Brazil when she was two months old. The family disembarked in the port city of Alagoas in 1926, and it was there, in Brazil's poverty-stricken Northeast, that Clarice would spend the first eleven years of her life. Looking back much later on the hardships of those early days, she would say that although her family lacked many things, she did not think of herself as being poor.

The northeastern experience had a minimal impact on Lispector the mature artist, however, since only her late novel *A hora da estrela* (1977; translated as *The Hour of the Star*, 1986) deals directly with it. As a child of six she had learned to read and exhibited a precocious interest in composing tales for her family and friends. In addition, she had also begun about this time to write simple stories, which she would send off to local newspapers in the hope of seeing some published. None ever was.

In 1932 the family moved from the isolated and economically depressed Northeast to the great urban center of Rio de Janeiro, the intellectual and artistic milieu which had an immediate and profound effect on Lispector's growth, both as a literary artist and as an educated human being. Taking advantage of the cultural and educational possibilities available to her, she began to read such diverse writers as Machado de Assis, Graciliano Ramos, Fyodor Dostoyevski, Herman Hesse, and Katherine Mansfield. Particularly influenced by the last three, Lispector decided that she, too, would become an author. By 1940 she had begun to study for her law degree at the National Faculty of Law and to work as an editor at the prestigious Agência Nacional. It was there, while also working for the evening paper, *A Noite*, that she got to know such fellow writers and intellectuals as Antônio Callado, Lúcio Cardoso, Adonias Filho, Otávio de Faria, and Cornélio Pena, all of whom were engaged in the renovation of Brazilian narrative, a process that Lispector would dramatically bring to a head with the publication of her first novel, *Perto do coração selvagem* (1944; translated as *Near to the Wild Heart*, 1990), the same year she graduated from law school. In 1943 she had married Mauro Gurgel Valente, a fellow law student. They were to have two sons, Pedro and Paulo.

With its title coming from James Joyce's *Portrait of the Artist as a Young Man* (1916), *Perto do coração selvagem* can be seen as Brazil's earliest "new novel," the first to depart decisively from the traditions and restrictions of the past. A richly symbolic work in which a woman's inner identity is contrasted with her outer world and in which the conflict between the inner and outer is reflected in a poetic fusion of language and existence, *Perto do coração selvagem* dramatically altered the way Brazilian critics and writers would think of the novel genre. Always concerned with the problems of identity, communication, language, and being, Lispector would continue to be a highly complex and iconoclastic writer through her novels, short stories, children's books, translations, and nonfiction pieces.

Though almost entirely unknown outside Brazil during the early years of her career (and never a "popular" writer even within her homeland), Lispector first began to achieve international attention in 1960 with the publication of *Laços de família* (translated as *Family Ties*, 1972), a collection of tightly written stories in which the existential drama of everyday existence is intensely scrutinized. Combining a laconic, highly compressed style with structural moments of intense psychological revelation in which the characters, nearly always female, make themselves known to the reader, her extensive work in this genre made her one of the most respected short-fiction writers of the late twentieth century, in Brazil, in Europe, and throughout the Americas.

Lispector's international reputation continued to grow in 1961, when her fourth novel, *A maçã no escuro* (translated as *The Apple in the Dark*, 1967), was published. This lyrical, ironic study of a man who undergoes both a discovery and loss of self amounts to a turning point in her career, one that initiates her later, better-known works. Of the later novels, three stand out—*A paixão segundo G. H.* (1964; translated as *The Passion According to G. H.*, 1988), *Agua viva* (1973; translated as *The Stream of Life*, 1989), and *A hora da estrela*—as do the story collections *Onde estivestes de noite* (Where Were You at Night, 1974; translated in *Soulstorm*, 1989) and *A via crucis do corpo* (The Cross Way of the Flesh, 1974; also translated in *Soulstorm*). Embodying many of the philosophical and literary problems associated with poststructuralism Lispector's fluid, poetic, and mythic texts have won a large and devoted following, both nationally and internationally.

Since the 1960s, critics have tended to see Lispector's contribution to Brazilian literature as occurring in three primary areas: helping to revolutionize Brazilian narrative by turning it inward; urbanizing it; and giving it a female (if not necessarily "feminist") orientation. Very much ahead of their time in the 1940s, her enigmatic, often mystical texts continue to exert a profound influence on Brazilian literature.

The first step in this process of revitalization was an extraordinary one. Published in 1944, in the midst of a literature still dominated by the social realism of the 1930s, *Perto do coração selvagem* was a stunning breakthrough for its fledgling author. Critics applauded its poetic language and its probing treatment of a woman's psychological growth and development. Divided into two interlocking parts (childhood and adulthood), the novel chronicles decisive moments in the life of its protagonist, Joana, and the various psychological repercussions these events cause. In general Lispector's fiction is not so much about events or actions in the external world as it is about the psychic reactions these actions and events elicit in the minds of her characters. In this sense her works take on their phenomenological dimension. They are, in essence, studies of the constantly fluctuating relationships between things in the universe (including other consciousnesses) and a single human consciousness. For all that the novel's conflicts lie in Joana's mind, however, *Perto do coração selvagem* is not, properly speaking, a "psychological novel." Less analytical than evocative, the work is structured around recurring patterns of symbols and motifs, such as darkness, water, and silence, that then integrate themselves into larger narrative units reflecting Joana's restless introspectiveness. Reminiscent of the works of James Joyce and Virginia Woolf, Lispector's first novel broke new ground for Brazilian narrative, showing how it could benefit from such staples of modern fiction as the interior monologue; temporal dislocation; rejection of external orientation; structural fragmentation; and an emphasis on the ebb and flow of psychological, rather than chronological, time.

The use of a poetic structure and a fragmentary, incomplete main character continues in Lispector's second novel, *O lustre* (The Chandelier, 1946). As in her first work, she focuses on the inner vicissitudes of her female protagonist, Virgínia, who is struggling to reconcile her present with her past. Finding solace in neither the big city, where she unhappily resides, nor her family's Eden-like country estate (from which she had been cast out for a childhood indiscretion), Virgínia oscillates between these two poles in a futile attempt to secure a sense of self-worth. Lispector uses an anguished female consciousness to shape the text and hold it together. Yet, while there is less structural and temporal dislocation in *O lustre* than in *Perto do coração selvagem*, there is a more definitive sense of closure; Virgínia dies, the victim of a fatal traffic accident, whereas Joana is left pondering her none-too-certain future.

Lispector's third novel, *A cidade sitiada* (The Besieged City, 1949), differs from its predecessors in that, for the first time, a particular physical environment, the town of São Geraldo, plays a dominant role in the narrative. Another feature that distinguishes this often-overlooked work is its comic dimension. Satiric in its treatment of certain bourgeois customs and social types, *A cidade sitiada* is also a commentary on the false appearances (or multiple realities) of things (including people); on the changes wrought by time; and on the diverse ways that objects reflect and are reflected in other objects. Technically *A cidade sitiada* stands out for its orchestrated symbolism, its caricatures, and the degree to which the development of the female protagonist, Lucrécia Neves, is distanced from the narrative voice.

The years 1952 to 1959 were significant for Lispector because she began to experiment with the short-story genre. The collection *Laços de família* did for the story form what she had already done for the novel, that is, altered basic structure, content, and style. Citing the dramatic intensity, the economy of expression, and the internalized conflicts of her short fiction, many critics believe she is a better story writer than she is a novelist, though this assertion involves very different standards of evaluation. A close reading of all her works, however, suggests that, although they have many thematic and technical features in common (such as the use of the epiphany as a structuring device), her longer, novel-length narratives differ markedly from her short fictions, the former being more lyrical in style and structure than the latter. At any rate, such tales as "Love," "Family Ties," and "The Buffalo" have established themselves as classics of the genre in modern Latin-American literature.

Lispector returned to the novel form in 1961 with *A maçã no escuro*, which ranks among her most impressive achievements. This long, complex novel is based, albeit ironically, on the motif of the quest. Martim, the novel's protagonist (and one of the few highly developed male characters in her fictive world), is a man struggling to gain some sense of personal identity. The mechanism by which he attempts to do this is language, that most complex and maddening of human attributes. When the novel opens, Martim is running away from something. The reader soon learns that Martim has committed a crime, the attempted murder of his wife, and that he is trying to escape from the police. Alone in the desertlike countryside and in the dark, physically as well as psychologically, Martim begins to reject both the sociopolitical consequences of his crime (which, for him, was a liberating act of self-affirmation) and the psycholinguistic attributes of his former self. For both processes, language shows itself to be a simultaneously stabilizing and destabilizing force, one that both helps and hinders him in his process of self-discovery. Martim, an "antihero" who is confused both about what he wants to do and how it might be done, becomes ever more deeply entangled in a web of words, a condition summed up by the omniscient narrative voice that declares, "At some unidentifiable point, that man had become prisoner in a ring of words."

Gradually this novel becomes a poststructuralist discourse on the ever-elusive linkages between language, human cognition, and being. Relying heavily on what is essentially a phenomenological approach to the relationships between things (including human beings, presented here as both perceivers and objects perceived), Lispector supplants the cause-and-effect-related plot of the realistic novel with the open, fluid structures of the lyrical novel. Building her narrative on patterns of symbolically rendered self-reflection, repeated in ever-expanding and interlocking contextual codes (social, sexual, political, and psychological, to cite the main ones), she subtly presents a world in which language inevitably determines who and what people are. *A maçã no*

Frontispiece and title page for the 1972 English translation of the 1960 short-story collection that established Lispector's literary reputation

escuro can be read as a poststructuralist treatise on the drama of language and being. Her inherently deconstructive impulse is effectively demonstrated in the work's final few pages, when Martim, who has labored mightily, if none too clearly, to attain a satisfying sense of personal identity, suddenly presents himself as anxious to reject his hard-won goal and return to the unthinking condition of nonauthentic being. Unexpectedly contrite, Martim now appears as a repentant apostate, one meekly willing to be led back into the folds of the stifling society from which he was seen to be fleeing at the outset of the novel.

As reflected in his and the narrator's language, Martim's insecurities and fears undercut, or deconstruct, his ability to sustain a stable "presence" in his self-consciously defined existence. Thus does Lispector achieve the simultaneous and paradoxical interplay of "presence" and "absence" that Jacques Derrida considers to be the inescapably destabilizing force of language. This linguistic decentering continues into the narrative's final lines, when Martim is utterly passive and is hopeful that someone else can give him the identity he so anxiously seeks (but cannot or will not sustain himself).

Lispector's increasingly overt preoccupation with problems of language and being continues in her next two publications, *A legião estrangeira* (1964; translated as *The Foreign Legion*, 1979)—an anthology of stories and nonfiction pieces—and *A paixão segundo G. H.* The first of these works reflects her ongoing interest in short fiction as well as a new interest in literary theory and criticism. Although none of the nonfiction pieces is very long (indeed, most are little more than brief aphoristic notations), many of them are self-referential in that they comment on or explain how and why she writes as she does. Several of these auto-critical observations offer perspectives on her concept of the nature and the function of language. At one point she says, "writing for me is a necessity.... I write because of my inability to understand except through the process of writing."

The mysticism implicit in these lines comes to full fruition in *A paixão segundo G. H.*, a novel that ranks among the most powerful works produced during the 1960s. Through her main, and virtually only, character, an upper-middle-class woman known to the reader only by her initials, G. H. (which are embossed on her luggage), Lispector presents a mystical quest for self-realization and fulfillment. Early in the story, reflecting on her condition, G. H. suddenly and with an unexpected savagery crushes a cockroach. This outwardly insignificant act, coming as G. H.'s psychic self-inquisition has weakened her sense of who and what she is, precipitates an extraordinary flood of mental and emotional divagation in which her own discourse self-consciously becomes both the object of narration and the narration itself. In a structural sense the novel is unusual in that this climax occurs early in the work. Primitive in significance for G. H. and an ambiguous blend of revulsion and attraction, the cockroach had exerted a powerfully subversive force over her. Aware of its vertiginous enthrallment, G. H., struggling to retain control of her self, lashed out at the roach, suddenly unable to endure the tension any longer.

The destruction of the insect dramatically constitutes a natural crisis. After this turning point the narrative ebbs and flows through what might be described as a protracted and lyrically rendered dénouement, in which G. H. anguishes over her nascent sense of suddenly authentic being and her now-unknown place within the universe.

The final two-thirds of the book amount to a lengthy and time-stopped epiphany, one that fluctuates between the poles of anxiety and ecstasy. As the intensity of G. H.'s epiphanic experience wanes, the novel draws to a close. Reflecting on her mystical journey, G. H. suspects that she may well be a fundamentally changed woman. The unsettling question that concludes the text, however, is whether she will be able to sustain her newly won knowledge in the life that lies ahead of her.

As the 1960s wore on, Lispector began to write quasi-political "children's" literature, such as *O mistério do coelho pensante* (The Mystery of the Thinking Rabbit, 1967), in which a clever, determined rabbit keeps getting out of its cage, and *A mulher que matou os peixes* (1968; translated as *The Woman Who Killed the Fish*, 1982), a somber, slightly chilling tale of responsibility, death, and guilt.

Recovering from serious burns suffered in an apartment fire in Rio de Janeiro, Lispector published in 1969 another of her most singular novels, *Uma aprendizagem; ou, O livro dos prazeres* (translated as *An Apprenticeship; or, The Book of Delights*, 1986). The story of a love affair between two people, Lori and Ulysses, this sixth novel stands apart from Lispector's other novels principally because it is structured not around a single, self-absorbed character but around two main characters, a man and a woman. This same distinction is borne out in the novel's structure, which is based on dialogue rather than monologue. A further difference is that—in a work implying that in life, as in any labor, one can learn through an apprenticeship to do things better—Lispector makes her most optimistic statement about the potentially salubrious effect love may have on human existence.

Lori and Ulysses unite in a satisfying way only after each has attained a separate sense of identity, this being a singular feature of their relationship and one that is underscored repeatedly in the novel. Paradox is a fundamental characteristic of Lispector's fiction, and it is sharply apparent: Lori and Ulysses can, through the unifying power of love, become one only after each has learned to exist alone. In the end, then, as this much-overlooked novel implies, one can only discover the phenomenological "other" by first discovering—and sustaining—the truths of one's self.

In 1971, with *Felicidade clandestina* (Clandestine Happiness), Lispector returned to the cryptic, dramatically intense, enigmatic story form. Two years later, however, she published one of her greatest achievements, the powerful, poetic novel *Agua viva*. Written in the form of a woman's unbroken monologue to an erstwhile lover, the novel is a self-conscious study of several interrelated issues: the process of signification; the nature of language as a medium of communication; the relative advantages of writing and painting as modes of expression; the religious and erotic impulses in human existence; freedom and servitude; and love and hate.

Reflecting on the mysterious and elusive ontological "presence" of words, the voice in *Agua viva* also comes to deal with what paradoxically is simultaneously "absent" from all linguistic discourse—that is, all one takes, gratuitously, to be stable and verifiable in regard to reality, meaning, and knowledge. Formally and thematically, all is process, flow, and movement in *Agua viva*; there is no solidly referential center to the text, nothing that corresponds to what Derrida conceives of as "presence." A powerful manifestation of the principles of poststructuralist theory, *Agua viva* is gaining recognition as one of the best narratives of the 1970s.

Another 1970s work by Lispector, *Onde estivestes de noite*, is a collection of short stories. Although these tales offer much that is vintage Lispector, such as the eternal human quest for identity, the psychological process of "becoming," and a heavily metaphoric style, they also show her giving a freer rein to her wry sense of humor, to the nature of androgynous existence, and to the possibilities inherent in self-conscious narrator/protagonists. An unusual feature of this collection of droll, mysterious tales is the extent to which she begins to develop elderly people as protagonists. In "A procura de identidade" (The Search for Identity), for example, a nearly sixty-year-old woman, Mrs. Jorge B. Xavier, finds herself both physically lost (in the labyrinthine corridors of the huge football stadium of Maracanã) and, increasingly, psychologically lost (in the even more labyrinthine corridors of her mind). As she struggles to find a way out of the stadium, she begins to perceive that, like Maracanã, her life is a maze, a futile, trivial, and inauthentic process from which she can neither escape nor find respite.

Published the same year as *Onde estivestes de noite?* was *A via crucis do corpo*, another compilation of stories. These pieces, however, stand out for three reasons: the extent to which they openly invite the reader to imbue the texts with meaning; the frankness of their sexuality; and the rare focus, lyrical or philosophical, on a character's inner sense of development and being. These often wry tales are also striking for the darkly ironic sense of life that they generate and for their relative lack of the lush lyricism that characterizes Lispector's novels. "Via crucis," for example, ironically parallels Christ's virgin birth and crucifixion with the human condition. The story's sardonic conclusion suggests that in this life of hope, doubt, and betrayal, people all walk "the Way of the Cross." *A via crucis do corpo*, the last story collection she was to publish before her death in 1977, gives ample evidence of why she is widely perceived as one of Latin America's most gifted short-story writers. Comparable to such better-known Spanish-American masters of the genre as Horacio Quiroga, Julio Cortázar, and Jorge Luis Borges, Lispector helped revolutionize the modern Latin-American short story.

After publishing two collections of chronicles and profiles—*Visão do esplendor* (Vision of Splendor) and *De corpo inteiro* (Sound of Body)—in 1975, Lispector returned to the novel form with *A hora da estrela*. Another of her most respected works, this novel was turned into an excellent 1985 film by Suzana Amaral. Lispector attempts to merge in this book the intensely lyrical subjectivity and ontological meditations of earlier novels with themes and problems of a more overtly sociopolitical nature. The protagonist of this self-conscious, tragicomic text is a poorly educated young woman, Macabéa, who, representing a real sociological phenomenon in Brazil, emigrates from the poverty-plagued Northeast in search of a job and a better life in the big city. Woefully ill equipped to handle the demands that urban life makes on her, Macabéa struggles merely to survive. Told by an artistically and politically astute narrator called Rodrigo S. M., Macabéa's story symbolizes, on the sociological plane, the plight of countless northeasterners.

Fusing his own fictive identity as a literary character with that of Macabéa, Rodrigo draws the story to a close by saying, in response to Macabéa's death: "Macabéa has murdered me. She is finally free of herself and of me . . . for I have just died with the girl."

Composed and assembled with the help of Lispector's friend Olga Borelli, *Um sopro de vida* (A Breath of Life) was published posthumously in 1978. More a confession than a novel, *Um sopro de vida* develops into a long, lyrical paean to life, to love, and to what was, for Clarice Lispector, the mysteriously symbiotic relationship between language and existence. At times agonizing, at times soothing, *Um sopro de vida* can be taken as her final statement on life and its magical relationship to art. Facing death from cancer, as she knew she was, Lispector imbued the term *sopro* (breath) with a double meaning: as a metaphor for the creative act, in all its manifold forms; and, in a larger sense, for life itself, for the act of living, which she had always seen in terms of mystery, mysticism, ceaseless self-scrutiny, and language. Often overlooked, *Um sopro de vida* is perhaps the most poignant—and the most revealing—of all her works.

Interviews:

Elaine Zagury, "O que diz Clarice de Clarice," *Cadernos Brasileiros*, 50 (November-December 1968): 60-79;

Maryvonne Laponge and Clelia Pisa, "Brasileiras: Voix, écrits du Brésil," *Des Femmes* (1977): 198;

María Ester Gilio, "Tristes Trópicos," *Crisis*, 4 (July 1978): 44;

Elizabeth Lowe, "The Passion According to C. L.," *Review*, 24 (June 1979): 34-37.

Bibliographies:

Earl E. Fitz, "Bibliografia de e sôbre Clarice Lispector," *Revista Iberoamericana*, 50 (January-March 1984): 293-304;

Fitz, "Bibliografia de e sôbre Clarice Lispector," *Travessia*, 14 (1987): 180-205;

Cathy Giffuni, "Clarice Lispector: A Complete English Bibliography," *Lyra*, 1, no. 3 (1988): 26-31.

References:

Olga Borelli, *Clarice Lispector* (Rio de Janeiro: Nova Fronteira, 1981);

Assis Brasil, *Clarice Lispector* (Rio de Janeiro: Organização Simões, 1969);

Samira Yousef Campedelli and Benjamin Abdala, *Clarice Lispector* (São Paulo: Abril Educação, 1981);

Hélène Cixous, *Vivre L'orange* (Paris: Des Femmes, 1979);

Roberto Corrêa dos Santos, *Clarice Lispector* (São Paulo: Atual, 1986);

Earl E. Fitz, *Clarice Lispector* (Boston: Twayne, 1985);

Benedito Nunes, *Leitura de Clarice Lispector* (São Paulo: Quirón, 1974);

Nunes, *O Mundo de Clarice Lispector* (Manaus, Brazil: Govêrno do Estado do Amazonas, 1966);

Teresinha Alves Pereira, *Estudo sôbre Clarice Lispector* (Coimbra, Portugal: Nova Era, 1975);

Olga de Sá, *A Escritura de Clarice Lispector* (Petrópolis, Brazil: Vozes / Lorena, Brazil: Faculdades Integradas Teresa d'Avila, 1979).

René Marqués

(4 October 1919 - 22 March 1979)

Aníbal González
Michigan State University

BOOKS: *Peregrinación* (Arecibo, P.R.: Privately printed, 1944);

Otro día nuestro (San Juan, P.R.: Imprenta Venezuela, 1955);

Juan Bobo y la Dama de Occidente (Río Piedras, P.R.: Antillana, 1956);

Cuentos puertorriqueños de hoy, by Marqués and others (Río Piedras, P.R.: Cultural, 1959);

La víspera del hombre (San Juan, P.R.: Club del Libro de Puerto Rico, 1959);

Teatro, 3 volumes: volume 1 (Mexico City: Arrecife, 1959); volumes 2 and 3 (Río Piedras, P.R.: Cultural, 1971);

En una ciudad llamada San Juan (Mexico City: Universidad Central de México, 1960);

El puertorriqueño dócil (Río Piedras, P.R.: Privately printed, 1962);

La casa sin reloj (Jalapa: Universidad Veracruzana, 1962);

La carreta (Río Piedras, P.R.: Editorial Cultural, 1963); translated by Charles Pilditch as *The Oxcart* (New York: Scribners, 1969);

Ensayos (Río Piedras, P.R.: Antillana, 1966; revised and enlarged, 1971); translated by Barbara Bockus Aponte as *The Docile Puerto Rican: Essays* (Philadelphia: Temple University Press, 1976);

El apartamiento (Barcelona: Rumbos, 1966);

Las manos y el ingenio del hombre (San Juan: Departamento de Instrucción Pública, 1966);

Mariana o el alba (Río Piedras, P.R.: Antillana, 1968);

Sacrificio en el Monte Moriah (Río Piedras, P.R.: Antillana, 1969);

La muerte no entrará en palacio (Río Piedras, P.R.: Cultural, 1970);

David y Jonatán; Tito y Berenice: Dos dramas de amor, poder y desamor (Río Piedras, P.R.: Antillana, 1970);

Un niño azul para esa sombra (Río Piedras, P.R.: Cultural, 1970);

Carnaval afuera, carnaval adentro (Río Piedras, P.R.: Antillana, 1971);

Vía crucis del hombre puertorriqueño (Río Piedras, P.R.: Antillana, 1971);

Ese mosaico fresco sobre aquel mosaico antiguo (Río Piedras, P.R.: Cultural, 1975);

Inmersos en el silencio (Río Piedras, P.R.: Antillana, 1976);

La mirada (Río Piedras, P.R.: Antillana, 1976).

Playwright, short-story writer, novelist, and essayist, René Marqués was the most gifted and internationally visible member of the group of Puerto Rican writers of the 1950s that the poet Juan Antonio Corretjer called the "Desperate Generation." Marqués raised the technical standards of each of the genres he cultivated, and he set the tone for much of the prose writing of his generation. The tone of that writing was generally one of existential anguish and profound anxiety, permeated by a nostalgia for the vanishing (and idealized) rural way of life. Invoking the works of existentialist thinkers from Miguel de Unamuno to Martin Heidegger and Jean-Paul Sartre, Marqués produced a violent, tragic vision of Puerto Rican culture, which left a significant imprint in the Puerto Rican literature of the 1950s and 1960s. Throughout these two decades Marqués was the dominant literary figure of his country. A perennial prizewinner at the Ateneo Puertorriqueño literary competition, he wrote plays that were performed to great public acclaim, and when, because of their polemical political content, they could not be staged, they were still widely read and admired. Marqués also actively promoted literary production among the writers of his own and of younger generations by encouraging the formation of publishing houses, book clubs, and theater groups, and by editing anthologies of Puerto Rican narratives.

Flamboyant, charismatic, and controversial, Marqués was a firm believer in his island's independence from the United States. Near his last years of life his reputation as a deeply patriotic writer was so firmly established that, as Luis Rafael Sánchez has noted, it became almost cus-

René Marqués

tomary at every performance of his plays to hold a brief, solemn ceremony after the play's end to give the author a standing ovation and a Puerto Rican flag. By the early 1970s, however, Marqués's influence among Puerto Rican writers had waned considerably; his last dramatic and narrative works were little understood, and his ideas about Puerto Rican culture were subjected to scathing criticism by younger intellectuals. Marqués's literary and personal trajectory can be summed up in his transition from the hyperactive "angry young man" of the 1950s to the unpredictable, controversial, and frequently embarrassing *vieillard terrible* of the late 1960s and early 1970s to the silent and brooding figure, looking far older than his sixty years, who withdrew to the hills of Cubuy muttering apocalyptic statements.

Shortly after Marqués's death in March 1979, however, a more balanced critical reappraisal of the man and his literary achievement began to emerge and is still in progress. More and more Marqués is being regarded as a superb literary craftsman, a stylistic innovator, and as the initiator of the professionalization of Puerto Rican writing.

To fully understand the reasons behind the prophetic stance Marqués often exhibited in his writings and the intensity and bitterness of his social criticism, one must take into account the traumatic circumstances in which Marqués, as well as the other members of the Desperate Generation—José Luis Gonzáles, Pedro Juan Soto, José Luis Vivas Maldonado, and Emilio Díaz Valcárcel—wrote their works. The late 1940s and early 1950s in Puerto Rico saw the persecution and dismemberment of a widespread and influential nationalist movement that had found its political expression during the 1930s in the Nationalista party headed by Pedro Albizu Campos. The social reformism of the Franklin D. Roosevelt administration during the Depression, along with the Americans' renewed realization of Puerto Rico's strategic importance during World War II, caused American influence to be exerted on Puerto Rican society during those years as never before, and in different ways. New military and naval installations on the island were established, and the existing ones were enlarged, although Puerto Rico was granted a degree of autonomous government. The Puerto Rican government began a crash industrialization program, aimed at changing the island from a predominantly agrarian, sugar-producing country into an industrial one, a sort of Caribbean Hong Kong. Soon after, the large-scale immigration of Puerto Ricans to New York was encouraged as a safety valve for the problems of rural unemployment and urban overcrowding caused by industrialization. The intellectuals of the 1940s, all of whom were nationalists of one sort or another, saw the fortunes of nationalism wax and wane, and saw the Hispanic essence of Puerto Rican nationality appropriated and diluted by the government. If one adds to this the impact of McCarthyism in Puerto Rican politics of the 1950s, it is not surprising that these writers grew "desperate."

Marqués's life story reads like the plot of one of his stories or plays. Many of his most striking characters are people of rural origin, endowed with an innate nobility, who usually possess some special talent or gift not appreciated by the rest of humanity, and who are therefore hounded to death, insanity, or internal exile. Examples that come to mind are Juan Santos, the carver of wooden saints, in "Pasión y huida de Juan Santos, santero" (Passion and Flight of Juan Santos, Wooden Saint Carver; in *Otro día nuestro* [Another Day of Ours, 1955]), the old women who live in Christ Street in *Los soles truncos* (The Truncated Suns, in *Teatro*, volume one, 1959), and the aging Nationalist leader (Albizu Campos) under house arrest in "Otro día nuestro." Although Marqués—who, unlike other members of the Desperate Generation, was never affiliated with either the Nationalist or the Communist party—was never literally persecuted, he felt himself to be among those that the changing Puerto Rican social and political system was trying to eliminate. He thus became their spokesman, although from a culturally conservative standpoint. From the beginning of his career, Marqués saw himself as a Creole Jeremiah, weeping for the old, rural Puerto Rican values that were being swept away, and cursing those who wished to deny Puerto Rico its identity.

Marqués was born on 4 October 1919 in Arecibo, Puerto Rico. The grandson of farmers, his early childhood was spent in the countryside, in the family farms of San Isidro and Carrizales. Marqués's parents divorced when he was nine, and he spent the rest of his childhood with his maternal grandparents, whose conservative, agrarian values he absorbed. True to those values, he studied agronomy at the Colegio de Agricultura y Artes Mecánicas in Mayagües, receiving his degree in 1942. That same year, he married Serena Velasco, whom he was to divorce fifteen years later.

Marqués, however, did not find agronomy as exciting as the profession of letters. His love of literature, as well as his nationalism, had been nurtured during his youth by a relative, Padrina Padilla de Sanz, the daughter of a well-known Puerto Rican poet and patriot of the nineteenth century, José Gundal Padilla; she was herself a poet, musician, feminist, and cultural animator in Arecibo. In 1944 Marqués resigned his job with the Department of Agriculture. That same year he published in Arecibo his first and only book of poems, *Peregrinación*. The book attracted little attention, and only recently have critics scrutinized it, seeking early intimations of Marqués's literary obsessions.

Salient characteristics of these poems—besides their clumsiness—are their tone of anger and prophetic denunciation, and the anticolonialist feelings Marqués expressed in them. Also significant is the vision of anticolonialism in terms of a rejection of city life—seen as corrupted by foreign, North American values—and a nostalgia for the agrarian, Hispanic, and Catholic values Marqués considered the true expression of Puerto Rican nationhood.

In 1946, married and with a family to care for, Marqués left for Spain to study Spanish literature at the Universidad de la Madrid. Contact with the relatively rich theatrical life of the Spanish capital, along with his readings of classical and modern drama at the university, led him to write his first play, *El hombre y sus sueños* (Man and His Dreams, in *Teatro*, volume two, 1971), an allegorical piece that shows a stronger influence from the Spanish Golden Age dramatist Calderón de la Barca than from the absurdist theater then in vogue. *El sol y los MacDonald* (The Sun and the MacDonalds, also in *Teatro*, volume two) also dates from this period, but the most visible influence on the style of this play is from Eugene O'Neill, particularly from *Mourning Becomes Electra* (1931). Marqués, although a nationalist in every respect, was not averse to adopting and adapting aspects of North American culture to his needs. Indeed, as Arcadio Díaz Quiñones has pointed out, Marqués presents the paradox of a culturally conservative writer who is stylistically modern and concerned with keeping the formal aspect of his works up to date.

While in Madrid, Marqués wrote for *El Mundo* a series of journalistic chronicles on Spanish life, titled "Crónicas de España," which began to make him known as a writer. Upon his return to his native island in 1947, the ever-active Marqués worked as a manager in a commercial firm owned by his father-in-law in Arecibo, while simultaneously presiding over the Sociedad Pro Arte and contributing chronicles and reviews to the main newspapers and journals of the capital: *El Mundo*, *Puerto Rico Illustrado*, and *Asomante*. The following year Marqués left Arecibo to work on the newspaper *Diario de Puerto Rico*, where he published book and theater reviews.

In 1949 Marqués was once again on the move, this time to New York, where a Rockefeller Foundation scholarship allowed him to study drama at Columbia University and at the Piscator's Dramatic Workshop. There he wrote as part of a course his only English-language play, *Palm Sunday*, based on real-life events and dealing with the massacre of Nationalist party members by police in the city of Ponce in 1937. (The play was never published.) Also in 1949 Marqués won the first of his many prizes at the Ateneo Puertorriqueño's annual literary contest, with his existentialist-inspired short story "El miedo" (Fear; in *Otro día nuestro*).

Marqués's return to Puerto Rico in 1950 marks the beginning of his most active, creative period. He immediately accepted a position with the División de Educación de la Communidad of the Puerto Rican Departamento de Instrucción Pública. His division's task was to increase literacy and raise the cultural level of the Puerto Rican rural population; the division was at that time one of the most innovative agencies in the Puerto Rican government and a refuge for many nationalist writers and artists. Marqués worked as a writer and chief editor, producing educational pamphlets on such diverse subjects as hurricanes and the ancient Taino Indians of Puerto Rico, as well as several short-story anthologies and film scripts.

But aside from his projects for the division, Marqués was, as usual, extremely active, writing and producing some of his best plays and many of the short stories he would collect in 1955 and 1960, respectively, in his first two books of stories, *Otro día nuestro* and *En una ciudad llamada San Juan* (In a City Called San Juan). Although *El sol y los MacDonald* and *Palm Sunday* were successfully staged in 1950 and 1956 respectively, the play that was to give Marqués an international reputation, *La carreta* (published as a book in 1963; translated as *The Oxcart*, 1969), was originally published in several issues of *Asomante* from 1951 to 1952. It was first staged in New York in 1953, the following year in San Juan, and in 1957 in Madrid.

From the beginning, *La carreta* was a critical and popular success. It is, in a sense, Marqués's most typical work, because it exhibits most of the ideas and motifs that recur in his other plays as well as in his essays and narratives. Chief among these is the notion that the countryside (particularly the island's coffee-growing highlands) is the foundation of Puerto Ricans' cultural identity and a source of spiritual and moral regeneration. A corollary of this idea is Marqués's vision of the city as a corrupt and corrupting milieu, as a spiritual prison, and as the focus of U.S. colonialism.

Although it has many tragic elements, *La carreta* is essentially a melodrama. The play tells the story of the breakup of a family of Puerto Rican peasants—the elderly Don Chago, his widowed daughter Doña Gabriela, her adopted son Luis, and her other children, Juanita and Chaguito—as the imposition of a sugarcane monoculture forces them to abandon their land and move to the city to seek economic betterment. Once in San Juan the characters live in a slum, where their old-fashioned values are severely put to the test. The oxcart of the play's title is a symbol of these characters' circuitous route from alienation to self-recovery. Unlike Marqués's other plays, which make use of "poetic realism," *La carreta* aspires to an almost documentary realism in its stage settings and in the characters' speech, in which Marqués mimics the peculiarities of Puerto Rican rural speech. Although he was not a profound theatrical innovator, he experimented constantly with different techniques, always seeking to achieve a high level of professionalism in his plays and to communicate his message more effectively to his audience.

As time went by, the prophetic stance evident in *Peregrinación* became more pronounced in Marqués's work. His increasing prestige allowed him to present his social message more explicitly and to a larger audience. His next dramatic work immediately after *La carreta* was the pantomime *Juan Bobo y la Dama de Occidente* (Juan Bobo and the Lady from the West, 1956), an overt satire on the rejection of Puerto Rican values and ideas exemplified by the plans of the rector of the Universidad de Puerto Rico, Jaime Benítez, to instill in students North American and European values.

A year before, in 1955, Marqués had published his first book of short stories, *Otro día nuestro*. In these narratives Marqués deals with a constellation of related topics: the persecution of nationalists, the change in Puerto Rican religious values brought on by the Protestantism imported from the United States, the increasing cultural assimilation of Puerto Ricans who migrate to the United States, and the fear, alienation, and self-destructiveness with which, according to Marqués, Puerto Ricans face their colonial experience.

With this book Marqués showed his technical mastery of the short-story genre and began the introduction of existentialist ideas into Puerto Rican narrative—"La muerte," for example, bears an epigraph from Martin Heidegger. Furthermore, Marqués also contributed to the development of a modern Puerto Rican urban narrative since, despite his ideological preference for the country over the city, Marqués wrote mostly about city people. Previously, during the 1920s and 1930s, Puerto Rican authors had preferred to write about the *jíbaro* (peasant) and his troubles in the countryside; Marqués remained faithful to this interest in Puerto Rican peasants, but the changing historical circumstances impelled him to chronicle—disapprovingly—the transformation of the peasant into city dweller. Marqués thus strengthened the return to an urban thematic in Puerto Rican literature that had been initiated by José Luis González with his book of stories *El hombre en la calle* (The Man in the Street, 1948).

Another characteristic of Marqués's work is the connection between his dramatic writings and his narrative. Not only are Marqués's stories highly melodramatic and full of symbolism, but some of them are actually rewritings of parts of certain plays: such is the case with "Isla en Manhattan," based on the second act of *La carreta*. Others serve as preliminary sketches for plays, as occurs with "Purificación en la calle del Cristo" (Purification on Christ Street), in *En una ciudad llamada San Juan*; the story served as the basis for *Los soles truncos*. Conversely, Marqués's plays are also highly narrative. Unlike the relatively spare stage directions favored by many modern playwrights, Marqués's are notoriously detailed and "literary," making it possible to read his dramas almost as if they were short novels.

In 1958 Marqués won four of the five first prizes given by the Ateneo Puertorriqueño: in drama, for his play *Un niño azul para esa sombra* (A Blue Child for that Shadow, 1970); in the short story, for "La sala" (The Living-Room; in *En una ciudad llamada San Juan*); in the novel, for *La víspera del hombre* (The Eve of Manhood, 1959), written during 1957 with the aid of a Guggenheim Fellowship; and in the essay, for "Pesimismo literario y optimismo político: Su coexistencia en el Puerto Rico actual" (Literary Pessimism and Political Optimism: Their Coexistence in the Puerto Rico of Today, in *Ensayos*, 1966; translated as *The Docile Puerto Rican: Essays*, 1976). That same year (1958) saw the successful staging of *Los soles truncos* during the First Puerto Rican Theater Festival, sponsored by the Institute of Puerto Rican Culture.

Los soles truncos is one of Marqués's most popular and frequently staged plays. It is the story of three elderly sisters—Hortensia, Emilia, and Inés—who live in an old house in San Juan. Hortensia has died before the action of the play begins, but she reappears in the two surviving sisters' memories. The women are the daughters of a German naturalist who came to the island in the mid nineteenth century and a woman from the Puerto Rican Creole aristocracy. They had been brought up essentially as aliens in their own country, having been educated in Europe, and lived a life of Europeanized luxury and refinement amid the tropics. Paradoxically, however, after the American invasion of 1898 and the increasing Americanization of the island, the sisters began to see themselves as symbols and defenders of the Hispanic and Creole heritage. Hortensia used to tell Emilia, "To resist is the password, Emilia. Resistance. In spite of hunger, time, and misery." Assailed on all sides by modernization—symbolized by the blaring of car horns and other street sounds as well as their creditors' knocks on the door—the two surviving sisters make a suicide pact, vowing to kill themselves and destroy their house before selling it to the developers who would turn it into a luxury hotel. Unlike the sisters in *Los soles truncos*, Marqués's cultural conservatism never led him to become an elitist intellectual. As Díaz Quiñones has noted, there is in Marqués's work some of the populism he professed to dislike in the political sphere. At a more ideological level, *Los soles truncos* may be seen as Marqués's trenchant analysis of the historical failings and contradictions of the Puerto Rican Creole elite: particularly their attempt to mimic Europe while ignoring the Puerto Rican reality, as well as their fear of modernity, expressed as an opposition to North American colonial domination.

René Marqués

The year that followed the premiere of *Los soles truncos* saw the publication of another of Marqués's major works, his first novel, *La víspera del hombre*. In this "coming-of-age" novel, set in late-1930s Puerto Rico, Marqués evokes his childhood and adolescence. Nevertheless, although there are numerous autobiographical references in the novel, it is not an autobiography. Unlike Marqués, Pirulo, the protagonist, is of direct peasant origins, and his situation is not at all like that of Marqués at the same age; for example, Pirulo does not know—until late in the novel—who his true father is. He lives as a ward in Carrizal, the estate of Don Rafa, a big landowner from the Arecibo region, who is later revealed as Pirulo's father.

Pirulo's highly melodramatic story—similar to Marqués's plays—may be seen as a political allegory and prophecy. Pirulo serves to focus Marqués's depiction of the economic and social dislocation produced by North American colonialism in Puerto Rico since the 1898 invasion. Marqués presents the breakup of the coffee plantations (like the ones where Pirulo lived with his stepfather before moving to Carrizal); the rise of the American-owned sugar mills; the Puerto Rican peasants' loss of their land to these sugar mills; the campaign by the colonial government to culturally assimilate Puerto Rican school children (such as Pirulo) by forcing them to study in English and to recite the Pledge of Allegiance to the U.S. flag; and many other negative effects of North American domination. Marqués also presents the efforts by Puerto Ricans to resist such domination: from the historical fables told to Pirulo by Marcela—a mysterious woman said to be a witch—to the more conventional political struggles of figures such as Nationalista leader Don Pedro Albizu Campos (who appears in a scene in the novel along with Marqués's relative Padilla de Sanz). After much suffering—including a love affair that ends tragically—Pirulo reaches "the eve of manhood" with a growing anticolonial vision, a deep sympathy for the struggles of the peasantry, and a hatred of cities (Arecibo is portrayed as a foul, prostitution-ridden place). Pirulo's progress toward manhood can be seen as an allegory of the political maturation Marqués wished to see in his fellow countrymen.

What makes this novel more than a mere expression of Marqués's ideology is its impressive display of narrative artistry. Marqués uses techniques of flashback, anticipation, and symbolization derived in part from his readings of William Faulkner. As in his short stories, Marqués's prose style in *La víspera del hombre* is flexible, although generally solemn in tone and highly Hispanicized. Marqués rarely made use of slang terms, and his narration is written in a pure Castillian that is quite different from the standard Puerto Rican vernacular.

After *La víspera del hombre* Marqués's next major publication was his second collection of short stories, *En una ciudad llamada San Juan*. These stories show a more mature, more nuanced writer than the somewhat strident author of *Otro día nuestro*. Although their content is as sensationalist and melodramatic as that of the earlier book and of Marqués's writing for the theater, Marqués brings into play his literary skills to give his characters greater psychological depth and to endow each story with deeper symbolic resonances.

Despite the urban thematic announced in its title, the book begins with "Tres hombres junto al río" (Three Men Near the River). This story serves as a prelude, and it is placed in a separate section titled "Antes de la ciudad" (Before the City). "Tres hombres junto al río" is, at first glance, one of Marqués's forays into historical fiction—a tendency that would intensify in his later works. Nevertheless, as in other "historical" texts by Marqués, the narrative soon becomes a political allegory: three Indians who have just murdered a Spanish conquistador fearfully await his resurrection, since the Spanish friars have given them to understand that all Christians, when killed, revive after three days. At the end of that period, of course, the Spaniard's rotten corpse swells and explodes, and the Indians conclude that the conquistadors are human and can therefore be fought. "My nation will be free," prophesies one of the Indian protagonists; "It will be free." This prophecy in the case of the Indians was never fulfilled, and it must be understood as referring to modern Puerto Rico.

Another political allegory is "Purificación en la calle del Cristo." However, although allegories also abound in the other stories, Marqués is more concerned with exploring the psychological effects of colonialism and of urban society in general.

As in his previous works, Marqués's vision of urban life in these stories is grim. Furthermore his views on the effect of colonialism on the Puerto Rican psyche parallel those of Francophone Caribbean and North African writers such as Franz Fanon and Albert Memmi. Marqués believes that colonialism engenders a profound but often unconscious resentment in the colonized, a resentment that frequently surfaces as violence and aggression by the colonized individual against himself—in suicide or mutilation—or against his peers. Rarely is this violence directed against the colonizers, who are usually far away, hidden, or well protected from their subjects, although when violence against them happens, it has a therapeutic, liberating effect on the colonized.

The stories having to do with urban life in *En una ciudad llamada San Juan* explore a wide range of psychosocial conditions produced by colonialism and urbanization: the loss of cultural and personal identity brought about by Americanization; prostitution and vice; existential boredom and insanity; the repression of the nationalists; the loss of political freedom; the emasculation of the Puerto Rican male—in Marqués's view—by a rising matriarchy; and the individual and spasmodic acts of violent resistance by the colonized against the colonizer.

In many ways Marqués's next important publication after *En una ciudad llamada San Juan*, the long essay *El puertorriqueño dócil* (The Docile Puerto Rican, 1962), later collected in *Ensayos*, can be seen as the discursive reformulation of the ideas about the pernicious effects of colonialism in his short stories and plays. A great deal of controversy initially surrounded this essay, since in it Puerto Rico's foremost writer claimed that his countrymen were congenitally incapable of organized rebellion against foreign domination. Marqués further claimed that most Puerto Ricans had a profoundly self-destructive propensity that led them to engage in suicidal acts of rebellion, such as the ones historically performed by members of the Nationalista party during the 1950s, or those portrayed by writers such as José Luis González, Pedro Juan Soto, and Marqués himself in their narratives. Today Marqués's thesis—which was always viewed with skepticism by those cognizant of Puerto Rico's century-old history of organized resistance to colonialism—is essentially discredited, and his generalizations about the

Puerto Ricans' "collective psychology" are considered mostly a projection of Marqués's own personal beliefs and fears. Marqués, in any event, argued his case in a rather topsy-turvy fashion, since most of the instances of suicidal rebellion he cites are taken from narrative fiction, and he was unwilling to recognize that this might simply be a literary topic and not a direct reflection of Puerto Rican reality.

Although Marqués continued to be a presence in the Puerto Rican literary and theatrical scene throughout most of the late 1960s, this was also the period in which he began to lose touch with the social and historical developments taking place on the island, and even to ignore them. It is true that the struggle against the drafting of Puerto Ricans to fight in the Vietnam War, for instance, stimulated Marqués to produce his "oratorio" *Vía crucis del hombre puertorriqueño* (Way of the Cross of the Puerto Rican Man, 1971). But even in this text it is clear that Marqués's Creole ideology, his cultural conservatism, no longer had anything important to say to a younger generation that derived its ideology and rhetoric from Marxism and from such diverse events as the Cuban Revolution and the civil rights struggle in the United States. Another of Marqués's vulnerable points began to make itself evident during this time: his antifeminism. His negative or stereotypical representation of women began to be seen as the expression not only of his personal misogyny, of his machismo, but also of his nostalgia for the conservative agrarian, patriarchal values that had been deeply eroded by Puerto Rico's industrialization and urbanization.

Marqués's last plays either look back nostalgically toward the old patriarchal days of Puerto Rico, as in the historical drama about the 1868 Lares Uprising, *Mariana o el alba* (Mariana or the Dawn, 1968), or move even further backward in time and the literary tradition to the biblical past, as in *Sacrificio en el Monte Moriah* (Sacrifice on Mount Moriah, 1969) and *David y Jonatán; Tito y Berenice: Dos dramas de amor, poder y desamor* (David and Jonathan; Titus and Berenice: Two Plays of Love, Power and Hate, 1970). These last plays are the most blatantly allegorical of Marqués's productions, and they show not only his increasing isolation from the Puerto Rican actuality but also his desire to find a more powerful and transcendent set of symbols, derived from biblical imagery, with which to transmit his values to his audience. However, these plays were neither well received nor understood at the time of their publication.

During the late 1960s and early 1970s younger writers such as Luis Rafael Sánchez and Rosario Ferré began transforming Puerto Rican fiction through the introduction of vernacular usage into narrative discourse and the abandonment of the realist mode that had predominated in the island's fiction. The Spanish-American narrative "boom" began to reach the island and was further promoted by such visiting Spanish-American critics and writers as Angel Rama, Marta Traba, and Mario Vargas Llosa in their courses at the Universidad de Puerto Rico in 1970. Soon Marqués's work began to seem outdated and anachronistic.

Marqués was not unaware of this, however, and his last major published work, his second novel, *La mirada* (The Glance, 1976), is a valiant, if flawed, attempt to come to grips not only with the style of the Spanish-American boom but with his own personal conflicts, particularly his homosexuality, which Marqués never publicly acknowledged. The protagonist of *La mirada*, a nameless young man, is a university student who tires of the strike, the violence, the noise, and the urban decay of San Juan. He leaves the university, despite his good grades, and goes to visit his brother Humberto, who lives in Washington, D.C. To his disgust he finds that, in front of Americans, Humberto denies being a Puerto Rican and refers to his brother as a "distant relative." The protagonist then returns to the island, and tries to start a farm. His land is invaded by a group of hippies, however, with whom he gets involved. One day, under the influence of drugs, he injures some of the hippies and kills a woman. He is captured and jailed, and his prison experiences are even more harrowing. He is not allowed access to books and culture, and he is sodomized by his fellow inmates. The protagonist's only moments of happiness have been his latently homosexual adolescent friendship with his schoolmate Julito and his later incestuous relationship with his niece María. Significantly both Julito and María are killed together in a nightclub fire. The protagonist's search for love is symbolized in the novel by a lonely, Christ-like individual with whom the protagonist at various moments in his life has exchanged a penetrating glance. Nevertheless, this mysterious figure has been castrated.

La mirada presents an absurdist vision of Puerto Rican society, and despite its occasional flashes of humor—a rare trait in Marqués's work—

it is still deeply pessimistic. Marqués follows some of the boom's innovations in his use of a mythical substratum for his narrative (the myth of Cronus, who decapitates Gaea and castrates Uranus), in the complex zigzag structure of his narrative, and in his unusually explicit erotic allusions (Marqués was never a prudish writer, however). One of the boom's authors with whom Marqués felt great affinity was the Mexican Carlos Fuentes, and echoes of the latter's novels, particularly *Zona sagrada* (Sacred Zone) and *Cambio de piel* (A Change of Skin)—both from 1967—are evident in *La mirada*.

Puerto Rican society is unusual in the Hispanic world in containing a strong anti-intellectual component—a trait attributable not only to American influence, but to Puerto Rico's history as an impoverished colonial backwater. In countries such as Mexico or Peru, the opinions of poets and novelists such as Octavio Paz, Fuentes, or Vargas Llosa are sought by the press and are highly respected. In Puerto Rico, high culture survives in academia and in elitist institutions such as the Ateneo Puertorriqueño but has little contact with or impact on the mass media. René Marqués was an important exception and a precursor. In his plays, stories, novels, and essays, in organizations like the Club del Libro (Book Club), and in his readiness to engage in political polemics in the press, he was able partially to bridge the gap between high culture and mass culture and to enhance the status of the Puerto Rican writer as social critic. Despite his now-outmoded agrarian and patriarchal ideology, Marqués still remains a key figure in Puerto Rican literary history. Although his works are no longer influential even at the level of their style, the example of his professionalism, his devotion to the writer's craft, and his struggle to raise the status of the writer in Puerto Rican society are still elements of his legacy that are worth recovering.

References:

María Teresa Babín, "Apuntes sobre *La carreta*, in Marqués's *La carreta*, fifth edition (Río Piedras, P.R.: Cultural, 1963), pp. v-xxi;

Babín, *La carreta en el tiempo*," *Sin Nombre*, 10 (October-December 1979): 45-57;

Efraín Barradas, "El machismo existencialista de René Marqués," *Sin Nombre*, 8 (October-December 1977): 69-81;

Pedro M. Barreda Tomás, "Lo universal, lo nacional y lo personal en el teatro de René Marqués," in his *El teatro en Iberoamérica* (Mexico City: Instituto Internacional de Literatura Iberoamericana, 1966), pp. 135-147;

María M. Caballero, *La narrativa de René Marqués* (Madrid: Playor, 1985);

Frank Dauster, "René Marqués y el tiempo culpable," in his *Ensayos sobre teatro hispanoamericano* (Mexico City: AgoSetentas, 1975), pp. 102-126;

Dauster, "The Theater of René Marqués," *Symposium* (Spring 1964): 35-45;

Arcadio Díaz Quiñones, "Los desastres de la guerra: para leer a René Marqués," in his *El almuerzo en la hierba (Lloréns Torres, Palés Matos, René Marqués)* (Río Piedras, P.R.: Huracán, 1982), pp. 133-168;

Carlos R. Hortas, "René Marqués' *La mirada*: A Closer Look," *Latin American Literary Review*, 8 (Spring-Summer 1980): 196-212;

José M. Lacomba, "Corte transversal en la obra cuentística de René Marqués: 1955-1975," introduction to Marqués's *Inmersos en el silencio* (Río Piedras, P.R.: Antillana, 1976), pp. 9-26;

Eleanor J. Martin, *René Marqués* (Boston: Twayne, 1979);

Concha Meléndez, "Sobre *Las víspera del hombre*, de René Marqués," *Asomante*, 16 (April-June 1960): 102-107;

José Luis Méndez, "Sartre y la literatura puertorriqueña," *Sin Nombre*, 11 (January-March 1981): 68-84;

Vernon L. Peterson, *Idea y representación literaria en René Marqués* (Madrid: Pliegos, 1986);

Charles R. Pilditch, *René Marqués: A Study of His Fiction* (New York: Plus Ultra, 1977);

Esther Rodríguez Ramos, *Los cuentos de René Marqués* (Río Piedras, P.R.: Editorial de la Universidad de Puerto Rico, 1975);

Luis Rafael Sánchez, "Las divinas palabras de René Marqués," *Sin Nombre*, 10 (October-December 1979): 11-14;

D. L. Shaw, "René Marqués' *La muerte no entrará en palacio*: An Analysis," *Latin American Theater Review*, 1 (Fall 1968): 31-38.

Manuel Mejía Vallejo

(23 April 1923 -)

Raymond Leslie Williams
University of Colorado

BOOKS: *La tierra éramos nosotros* (Medellín: Alvarez, 1945);

Tiempo de sequía (Medellín: Alvarez, 1957);

Al pie de la ciudad (Buenos Aires: Losada, 1958);

Cielo cerrado (Medellín: Tertulia, 1963);

El día señalado (Barcelona: Destino, 1964);

Cuentos de la zona tórrida (Medellín: Carpel-Antorcha, 1967);

Aire de tango (Medellín: Bedout, 1973);

Las noches de la vigilia (Bogotá: Instituto Colombiano de Cultura, 1975);

Prácticas para el olvido (Medellín: Publicaciones Técnicas, 1977);

Las muertes ajenas (Bogotá: Plaza & Janés, 1979);

Tarde de verano (Bogotá: Plaza & Janés, 1980);

El viento lo dijo (Medellín: Universidad de Antioquia, 1981);

Y el mundo sigue andando (Bogotá: Planeta, 1984);

El hombre que parecía un fantasma (Medellín: Biblioteca Pública, 1984);

María, más allá del paraíso (Cali, Colombia: Quijada, 1984);

Hojas de papel (Bogotá: Universidad Nacional, 1985);

La sombra de tu paso (Bogotá: Planeta, 1987);

La casa de las dos palmas (Bogotá: Planeta, 1988);

Colombia campesina (Bogotá: Villegas, 1989);

Otras historias de Balandú (Bogotá: Intermedio, 1990);

Memoria de olvido (Medellín: Universidad de Antioquia, 1990).

Collection: *Manuel Mejía Vallejo* (Bogotá: Procultura, 1989).

Manuel Mejía Vallejo is a Colombian writer whose work emanates from the traditions of his native region of Antioquia. Antioquia's rich oral tradition is an integral element in his fiction. Paradoxically, despite this traditionalism, his work is not only modern, but in effect his 1964 novel, *El día señalado* (The Special Day), heralded modern, new fiction in Antioquia. Like many writers from this region, Mejía Vallejo frequently employs nostalgic elements in his fiction and says: "I am in favor of a literature of past memory when the memory is something active, when it's not an excessive nostalgia, but a discovery of something that has gone and consequently continues alive." Antioquia's history and traditions, modernity with respect to narrative technique, and a special kind of nostalgia are constant elements in Mejía Vallejo's work.

Born in Jerico, Antioquia, on 23 April 1923, Mejía Vallejo was reared in a rural setting. His parents owned a large farm near the small town of Jardín in western Antioquia, where the young Mejía Vallejo spent his childhood. They sent him to Medellín, the capital of Antioquia, to study in high school. Mejía Vallejo has stated that perhaps during those high school years his literary vocation was born. He was enthused about writing letters to his parents after his mother once wrote to him that "what we like most is the correctness and ease with which you write letters." In the 1940s he became more actively involved in writing while pursuing studies at the Universidad de Bolivariana in Medellín. While studying there he wrote for a small local newspaper and composed his first novel, *La tierra éramos nosotros* (We Were the Land, 1945). Looking back on that first amateurish novel, Mejía Vallejo stated years later: "I don't defend that work except in that sense that it was made honestly, with characters I had lived with on my parents' farm. I tell the story of my youth, and with so much innocence that I didn't even change the characters' names. They are still alive with the names that appear in the book."

La tierra éramos nosotros is a first-person account of Mejía Vallejo's childhood in rural Antioquia. The narrator-protagonist of this novel relates in the present tense his experiences with the campesino life after returning to his region from an extended absence. The absolute peace and tranquillity of such a rural life contrasts with the decaying nation he leaves behind in the city. From the moment he returns to the farm, he begins making systematic connections between him-

Manuel Mejía Vallejo

self and the land: upon arriving he proclaims, "La tierra éramos nosotros." This work is primarily a celebration of the simple things of rural life, from what he calls "nontranscendent afternoons" to local customs.

Colombia in the 1940s, and particularly Antioquia, suffered increasing violence and civil unrest. This conflict reached a moment of explosive tension on 9 April 1948, when Liberal presidential candidate Jorge Eliécer Gaitán was assassinated in Bogotá, and the city erupted in violence. Deep-seated tensions between the Liberal and Conservative parties resulted in a ten-year civil war in which approximately two hundred thousand people died. This period is commonly referred to as "La Violencia" (The Violence) in Colombia. From 1953 to 1957 the military dictator Gustavo Rojas Pinilla was in power; his effect on writers and intellectuals was repression and censorship.

Mejía Vallejo spent the period of "La Violencia" working as a journalist and writing fiction in Venezuela and Central America. Much of the time he worked with the Colombian newspaper *El Espectador*, although he claims to have lived for eight months playing poker. During this period he wrote and published the stories collected in *Tiempo de sequía* (Time of Drought, 1957). In Maracaibo, Venezuela, in 1951 he wrote and published the short story "El milagro" (The Miracle), which was selected among the best stories in a national short-story contest sponsored by the Venezuelan newspaper the *Nacional*. That same year he published "La guitarra" (The Guitar), this time winning the *Nacional* contest outright. In 1952 he wrote the short stories "Un fantasma para Diógenes" (A Ghost for Diógenes) and "Caballo para toda la eternidad" (Horse for All Eternity) in Maracaibo and then moved to San José, Costa Rica, where he completed "Una canoa baja el Orinoco" (A Canoe Goes Down the

Mejía Vallejo in 1958, his first year as director of Imprenta Departamental

Orinoco). He wrote "Luna de tiempo seco" (Moon of Dry Time) in San Salvador in 1953, and moved once again, this time to Guatemala, where he composed "Los julianes" and "Tiempo de sequía." The latter won a national short-story contest in Mexico in 1955. Later Mejía Vallejo wrote "La muerte de Pedro Canales" (The Death of Pedro Canales) and "Al pie de la ciudad" (both in Guatemala, 1955), "Miedo" (Fear; in Panama, 1956), and "Palo caído" (Fallen Tree; in Medellín, 1956).

In the stories of *Tiempo de sequía* Mejía Vallejo is interested in capturing the essence of rural life. In "Al pie de la ciudad" the reader finds the opening pages of what later will be the 1958 novel of the same title: the anecdotal story of humble folk in the neighborhood of Los Barrancos in Medellín, who live, as the title indicates, at the foot of the city. In "Caballo para toda la eternidad" the author tries a new experiment, with some success, telling the entire story in dialogue form. The title story, "Tiempo de sequía," deals with characters who barely survive, who are in absolute human misery, and who are without the most basic necessities.

The political situation in Colombia changed radically on 10 May 1957 with the downfall of Rojas Pinilla. In late 1957 Mejía Vallejo experienced a series of favorable events: the completion of his novel *Al pie de la ciudad* (At the Foot of the City, 1958), which he sent to a contest sponsored by the prestigious publisher Losada in Buenos Aires; his being named director of Medellín's important publishing house Imprenta Departamental; and the publication of *Tiempo de sequía*.

These events set the stage for one of the most active and vibrant periods of Mejía Vallejo's career, from 1958 to 1964. Returning to Colombia to accept his position as director of Imprenta Departamental, he became immediately involved in the cultural life of Antioquia. Once in charge of the publishing house, he aggressively launched the "Colección de Autores Antioqueños." The collection became a national controversy when public attacks were published in newspapers, questioning the objectivity of his selection of writers. In 1960 he began another important collection of Antioquian literature, the "Festival del Libro Antioqueño."

During this period of fervent activity in Medellín, Mejía Vallejo wrote two books that represent early contributions to the modern novel in Spanish America: *Al pie de la ciudad* and *El día señalado*. His modern narrative techniques involve the innovative use of narrators and structures. *Al pie de la ciudad* is divided into three parts, offering the reader three visions of the events. In the "Primera Parte" the focus is on the Los Barrancos area and the process of maturation of a boy in a poor family that lives there. The perspective totally changes in the "Segunda Parte": the problems of Los Barrancos are seen through the eyes of Dr. Salomón Arenas, of the upper middle class. These two perspectives are synthesized in the "Tercera Parte," which contains stories from both of the previous story lines. Because of its denunciation of social injustice and its incorporation of the modern and the traditional, *Al pie de la ciudad* is similar to the Guatemalan Miguel Angel Asturias's *El Señor Presidente* (1946; translated as *The President*, 1963).

Mejía Vallejo's most successful novel, *El día señalado*, is a synthesis of various elements from his previous fiction. The narrator develops two narrative lines: one in third person, which deals with a small town, and another in first person, telling a story of personal revenge. The novel begins with a six-page prologue, narrated in the third person, which relates the life story of José Miguel Pérez, a common man with a common name who lives (as indicated in the novel's first line) from December 1936 to January 1960. He lives a typical childhood and is instructed by his mother from an early age that he must "ser alguien" (be someone) in his life. Nevertheless, he lives a life dedicated to the simple work and simple pleasure of the rural life. Both *guerrilleros* and soldiers pass through his land, and on one occasion the soldiers steal his horse. He decides to pursue the thieves and recover his horse. In the countryside he sees the visible evidence of "La Violencia": mutilated bodies of *guerrilleros*. The narrative perspective then changes to that of the townsfolk and Pérez's mother: several cadavers are brought to the town, including that of José Miguel Pérez. This prologue sets the tone of useless, irrational violence that will be developed in the novel.

Pérez is only a background character rarely mentioned in the remainder of the novel, which is developed in three parts, each preceded by a prologue. The third-person prologues relate the conflicts of "La Violencia": the power structure, associated with the government and soldiers, is in conflict with rural guerrillas. The first-person stories tell of the final stages of the narrator's lifelong search for his father, in order to murder him as an act of revenge. The narrator's search is presented as both an obsession and an inevitable process, destined to result in an encounter between father and son. The narrator's only emotions throughout the story, in fact, are related to the hatred he feels for his father and his obsession with revenge. The structure reaches a turning point at the end of the second part: the son encounters the father, setting the stage for the inevitable violence of the third part. In the first-person section of the third part this encounter between father and son culminates in the son finally consummating the revenge in the novel's final pages.

Mejía Vallejo manipulates a series of dualities in this novel, beginning with the structure's narrative lines. Critics have pointed out dualities such as the father-son pair, the contrast between the "good" *guerrillero* (Antonio Roble) and the "bad" *guerrillero* (Pedro Canales), the contrast between the prostitute and the local church ladies, and, of course, the conflict between the *guerrilleros* and the soldiers. Indeed, some readers have found the use of dualities so consistent as to be excessive.

Set in the mythical Antioquian town of "Tambo," *El día señalado* represents an important synthesis in Mejía Vallejo's writing career and a turning point for the novel in Antioquia. The synthesis involves incorporating elements from the traditional novel in Antioquia—above all, traditional, oral language—with elements from the "new novel," or modern Spanish-American novel. Mejía Vallejo's use of structure and point of view represented an innovation in Antioquia in 1964. In addition, *El día señalado* is one of the most outstanding works to deal with the period of "La Violencia" in Colombia. When asked years later which was his best work, Mejía Vallejo responded, "Perhaps *El día señalado* because I captured a critical moment for Colombia."

With *El día señalado* Mejía Vallejo gained national and international recognition. An important factor in this new recognition was his being awarded for this novel the prestigious Premio Nadal in Spain. With the publication of *El día señalado* in 1964 Mejía Vallejo's period of intellectual maturity began. After completing his tenure as director of Imprenta Departamental in the early 1960s, Mejía Vallejo's next professional commitment besides writing was with a group called "Papel Sobrante" (Extra Paper). Oscar Hernández Monsalve conceived the idea of selling extra paper and using the money to publish books. The group consisted of Mejía Vallejo, Hernández Monsalve, Darío Ruiz Gómez, Dora Ramírez, Antonio Osorio Díaz, and John Alvarez García. The collection of books published by the group set the direction for Antioquian letters during the 1960s, the last of its eight volumes being Mejía Vallejo's *Cuentos de la zona tórrida* (Tales of the Torrid Zone, 1967). During the late 1960s and early 1970s Mejía Vallejo was virtually invisible on the literary scene. Colombians and readers of Colombian literature were captivated in 1967 with Gabriel García Márquez's *Cien años de soledad* (translated as *One Hundred Years of Solitude*, 1970). García Márquez's shadow was an insurmountable factor for all other Colombian writers, including Mejía Vallejo. He spent his time teaching literature classes at the Universidad Nacional de Medellín and writing on his farm outside the city.

One of the most outstanding stories of *Cuentos de la zona tórrida*, "La venganza" (The Vengeance), was written in 1960 and was the original seed for the novel *El día señalado*. The short story deals with the love-hate relationship between the narrator/protagonist and his father. As in the novel, the protagonist searches for the father in order to murder him. The subtle handling of point of view is this story's main achievement. The reader observes the protagonist's mental processes and motives from the very first line. The narrator then reveals a series of details about the other characters and the setting.

Of Mejía Vallejo's production during the 1965-1988 period, his major novel is *Aire de tango* (1973), his homage to the music of the tango and the city of Medellín. He captures the essence of the language and spirit of a working-class neighborhood in Medellín, the "Barrio Guayaquil," and that neighborhood's cult of the tango. It is a novel of several achievements. The narrator transforms everyday reality into an ideal, idealized world. A first reading of *Aire de tango* reveals a novel that deals primarily with the celebrated Argentine tango singer Carlos Gardel. A first-person narrator relates in the novel a series of anecdotes about the world of the tango in Medellín: about Gardel; about a great admirer of his, Jairo; and, finally, about the life of the narrator himself. The story is told in an oral style in which the narrator answers a series of questions, even though neither the listener nor his questions ever appear in the text. It is as if the speaker were in a bar in the Barrio Guayaquil, telling stories among friends. Beyond these particular characters, the novel deals with something intangible: the spirit of a past epoch, with an "air" of the tango.

The points of confluence among the three principal characters—Gardel, Jairo, and the narrator—make the reality of *Aire de tango* complex and in constant flux. On the one hand, Jairo dedicates his life to a type of imitation of and search for Gardel. Jairo's participation in bar fights, for example, is justified in the text when he realizes that Gardel himself acted in this way. Jairo dedicates himself to forming himself as well as possible around the character of Gardel. In this sense his life consists of a search: he studies the most minute details of Gardel's life; at the same time he attempts to incorporate that lifestyle into his own. Gardel incarnates the tango, and Jairo incarnates Gardel. The narrator becomes obsessed with both Gardel and the tango. His narration is an extensive homage to them.

The main achievement of *Aire de tango* is the creative impulse that constantly transforms reality. It is a mythifying process. This myth is not classical myth or Jungian myth. Rather, Mejía Vallejo uses material from popular myths. In the end, *Aire de tango* is a novel that mythifies everyday people and their music, the tango.

With the publication of *Aire de tango* Mejía Vallejo's isolation of the late 1960s ended. The novel was awarded a national novel prize (the Premio Vivencias) and was well received by Colombian critics and the press. Consequently since 1973 Mejía Vallejo has been a visible, respected intellectual figure in Colombia. His high level of productivity since 1973 has contributed to his public visibility, culminating in 1983 with his invitation to the presidential palace to give a lecture to celebrate his sixtieth birthday.

The fiction published since *Aire de tango* represents a variety of Mejía Vallejo's interests. With *Las noches de la vigilia* (Vigilant Nights, 1975) he experimented with brief narratives almost entirely unrelated to his previous work. The volume con-

Dust jacket for Mejía Vallejo's 1980 novel, a traditional narrative dealing with miraculous events

sists of sixty-two short narratives, which vary in length from a few lines to several pages, but which in general are one or two pages. The shortest, "Testigo de cargo" (Responsible Witness), consists of only three lines. The total volume narrates stories of a small town called Balandú, "pueblo en vía de sueño" (Sleepy Village), which frequently appears in Mejía Vallejo's fiction. The novel *Las muertes ajenas* (Foreign Deaths, 1979) deals with a young man who unjustly suffers six years in jail and looks for revenge. As in much of his work, Mejía Vallejo laments the loss of traditional human values in the new, modern Antioquia. As one of the characters poignantly states in the last chapter, "Es una verguenza la humanidad" (Humanity is a shame). The novel's denouement, with images of human corpses, certainly underlines this negative vision. One critic has noted that this novel's "magical" quality is intimately related to Mejía Vallejo's evocation of the local setting. The structure and narrative technique of *Las muertes ajenas* are traditional, although some sections feature changes in point of view. The opening chapter, for example, is narrated in the second person, *tú*. *Tarde de verano* (Summer Afternoon, 1980) is also traditional in narrative technique. It begins with the line "Algunas tardes suceden cosas extrañas" (Some afternoons strange things happen), and the narrator describes the intimate world of Paula and Eusebio Morales in a fashion that justifies this initial statement. As one critic has noted, this novel portrays a world of stagnation and isolation. *Tarde de verano* also contains elements of magic and fantasy, with the ghosts and miracles one associates with the fiction of García Márquez. *Y el mundo sigue andando* (And the World Follows Walking, 1984) is one of Mejía Vallejo's most experimental fictions, divided into three parts to carry out three types of narrative experiments. The thematic content, nevertheless, is similar to *Las muertes ajenas* and *Tarde de verano*.

In two recent novels, *La sombra de tu paso* (The Ghost of Your Step, 1987) and *La casa de las dos palmas* (The House of Two Palms, 1988), Mejía Vallejo creates two distinctly different fictional worlds. *La sombra de tu paso* has as its source those years in the 1960s when Mejía Vallejo was intimately involved with the intellectual world of Medellín. A first-person narrator/protagonist takes a nostalgic look at those intellectually vibrant years in the capital of Antioquia, writing a story of his romantic relationship with a woman named Claudia. Each chapter begins with a brief dialogue between the protagonist and Claudia, which takes place in a "present" several years after the period of the main anecdote. The chapter then moves to the narrator's anecdotes of the 1960s. Many characters are intellectuals and writers well known among Colombian literary circles, such as the poets Gonzalo Arango and Jaime Jaramillo. Both were leaders in the scandalous and irreverent *nadaísta* movement in Colombia during the 1960s, centered in Antioquia. A subtle subtext is the story of the protagonist becoming a writer: the formative years narrated in this novel are, in fact, the years during which Mejía Vallejo matured as a writer.

Typical of Colombian and Spanish-American fiction of the 1970s and 1980s, *La sombra de tu paso* also includes a level of metafiction: the narrator occasionally comments on the act of creating while he is in the process of fabricating his story. *La casa de las dos palmas* synthesizes many of Mejía Vallejo's motifs and major themes; a tone of nostalgia predominates. Nevertheless, it is not as experimental as *Y el mundo sigue andando* or *La sombra de tu paso*: a conventional, omniscient narrator tells the story in chronological order. This narrator assumes such a traditional role that he occasionally makes generalizations about the nature of life. *La casa de las dos palmas* relates the story of Efrén Herreros in Mejía Vallejo's mythical town of Balandú. Most of the action takes place in the early twentieth century, the period of the "War of a Thousand Days," when traditional values still dominated. This novel celebrates such values. A novel of nostalgic impulses, *La casa de las dos palmas* gives thematic importance to memory and the dreams of an ideal humanity that often appear in Mejía Vallejo's work.

His major work, and certainly the writing for which he will be remembered, is unquestionably his fiction. Nevertheless, he has also published some poetry and essays. *Prácticas para el olvido* (Practices for Oblivion, 1977) consists of two hundred brief love poems, each of four lines, which express much of the same nostalgia and many of the human values found in Mejía Vallejo's fiction. The pieces in *Las noches de la vigilia* are best described as prose poems, exercises in writing briefly about his favorite dreams and obsessions. The book of essays *Hojas de papel* (Leaves of Paper, 1985) contains twenty-three articles, mostly dealing with writers from Antioquia.

Manuel Mejía Vallejo has stated that "the road to literature is an entirely personal one; it is the labor of the solitary man." Indeed, the profound voice of Mejía Vallejo is often personal in tone. It is the voice of a writer who has spent a lifetime meditating on his past in Antioquia and the relationship of the individual to that region's history and traditions. Yet the strength of Mejía Vallejo's best fiction lies in its ability to communicate universal experiences by means of subtle narrative techniques and well-conceived structures, making him one of Colombia's best modern writers of the twentieth century.

Biographies:

Otto Morales Benítez, *Conozca a Manuel Mejía Vallejo* (Mendellín: Extensión Cultural Universidad de Antioquia, 1982);

Jaime Montoya Candamil, *Manuel Mejía Vallejo* (Bogotá: Avance, 1984).

References:

Kurt Levy, "El Oficio de Manuel," in *Ensayos de literatura colombiana*, edited by Raymond L. Williams (Bogotá: Plaza & Janés, 1985), pp. 35-42;

Seymour Menton, "*El día señalado*: Un análisis ambivalente precedido de una esquematización imposible de la novela de la Violencia," in his *La novela colombiana: Planetas y satélites* (Bogotá: Plaza & Janés, 1978), pp. 219-245;

Luis Marino Troncoso, *Proceso creativo y visión del mundo en Manuel Mejía Vallejo* (Bogotá: Procultura, 1986);

Raymond L. Williams, "Manuel Mejía Vallejo, *Aire de tango*," in his *Una década de la novela colombiana: La experiencia de los setenta* (Bogotá: Plaza & Janés, 1981), pp. 77-85.

Juan Carlos Onetti
(1 July 1909 -   )

Zunilda Gertel
University of California, Davis

BOOKS: *El pozo* (Montevideo: Signo, 1939; revised edition, Montevideo: Arca, 1965);
Tierra de nadie (Buenos Aires: Losada, 1941);
Para esta noche (Buenos Aires: Poseidón, 1943);
La vida breve (Buenos Aires: Sudamericana, 1950); translated by Hortense Carpentier as *A Brief Life* (New York: Grossman, 1976);
Un sueño realizado y otros cuentos (Montevideo: Número, 1951); title story translated by Inés de Torres Kinnell as "A Dream Come True," in *Door and Mirrors: Fiction and Poetry from Spanish America*, edited by Carpentier and Janet Brof (New York: Grossman, 1972), pp. 190-203;
Los adioses (Buenos Aires: Sur, 1954); translated in *Goodbyes and Stories* (Austin: University of Texas Press, 1990);
Una tumba sin nombre (Montevideo: Marcha, 1959); republished as *Para una tumba sin nombre* (Montevideo: Arca, 1967);
La cara de la desgracia (Montevideo: Alfa, 1960);
El astillero (Buenos Aires: General Fabril, 1961); translated by Rachel Caffyn as *The Shipyard* (New York: Scribners, 1968);
El infierno tan temido (Montevideo: Asir, 1962); translated by Jean Franco as "Dreaded Hell," in *Latin American Writing Today*, edited by J. M. Cohen (Baltimore: Penguin, 1967), pp. 34-48;
Tan triste como ella (Montevideo: Alfa, 1963);
Juntacadáveres (Montevideo: Alfa, 1964); fragments translated by Lynn Tricario and Suzanne Jill Levine as "Junta, the Bodysnatcher," *Fiction*, 5, no. 1 (1976): 14-16;
Jacob y el otro; Un sueño realizado y otros cuentos (Montevideo: Banda Oriental, 1965); first story translated by Izaak A. Langnas as "Jacob and the Other," in his *Prize Stories from Latin America: Winners of the Life en Español Literary Contest* (New York: Doubleday, 1963);
Cuentos completos (Buenos Aires: Centro Editor de América Latina, 1967);
Tres novelas (Montevideo: Alfa, 1967);
Novelas cortas completas (Caracas: Monte Avila, 1968);
La novia robada y otros cuentos (Buenos Aires: Centro Editor de América Latina, 1968);
Los rostros del amor, edited by Emir Rodríguez Monegal (Buenos Aires: Centro Editor de América Latina, 1968);
Obras completas, edited by Rodríguez Monegal (Mexico City: Aguilar, 1970);
La muerte y la niña (Buenos Aires: Corregidor, 1973);

Tiempo de abrazar y los cuentos de 1933 a 1950 (Montevideo: Arca, 1974);
Onetti (Buenos Aires: Del Noroeste, 1974);
Requiem por Faulkner y otros artículos, edited by Jorge Ruffinelli (Montevideo: Arca/Calicanto, 1976);
Tan triste como ella y otros cuentos (Barcelona: Lumen, 1976);
Dejemos hablar al viento (Barcelona: Bruguera Alfaguara, 1979);
Cuentos secretos (Montevideo: Marcha, 1986);
Presencia y otros cuentos (Madrid: Almarabu, 1986);
Cuando entonces (Madrid: Mondadori, 1987);
Obra selecta (Caracas: Ayacucho, 1989).

RECORDING: *Juan Carlos Onetti lee sus narraciones*, Havana, Casa de las Américas, LC-CA-7.

TRANSLATIONS: William Faulkner, "Todos los aviadores muertos," *Marcha* 52 (21 June 1940): 20-21; 53 (28 June 1940): 22-23;
Phobe Atwood Taylor, *El misterio de Cabo Cod*, translated by Onetti and E. M. Pekeharing (Buenos Aires: Poseidón, 1946);
Erskine Caldwell, *La verdadera tierra*, (Buenos Aires: Schapire, 1954);
Burgess Drake, *Hijos del viento* (Buenos Aires: Acme, 1957).

SELECTED PERIODICAL PUBLICATIONS—
UNCOLLECTED: "Felisberto, el 'naif,'" *Cuadernos Hispanoamericanos*, 302 (August 1975): 257-259;
"Confesiones de un lector," *Mundo Hispánico*, 338 (May 1976): 6-7;
"Presencia," *Cuadernos Hispanoamericanos*, 339 (September 1978): 369-374.

Juan Carlos Onetti, a major novelist and short-story writer in Latin America, achieved international notoriety with the publication of *La vida breve* (1950; translated as *A Brief Life*, 1976), one of the most original novels of the 1950s to emerge from writers in the Río de la Plata area. In his fiction Onetti has developed an innovative point of view along with a semantic change in narrative, which, combined with his particular philosophy, has produced a new kind of existential novel in South America. His writing posits neither an ideology nor an intellectual analysis of the characters but explores a way of being that reflects a critical, distinctive attitude toward social and ethical values. In this vein, his fiction anticipated the so-called 1960s Boom in the Spanish-American novel.

Juan Carlos Onetti was born in Montevideo, Uruguay, on 1 July 1909; he is the son of Carlos Onetti, a customs employee, and Honoria Borges de Onetti, from southern Brazil. Onetti's personal memories do not figure directly in his works nor in his conversations and interviews, but he occasionally mentions his childhood as a happy time.

His early schooling was irregular and frequently interrupted due to his family's moving from place to place. In high school he abandoned formal study and began to lead an unconventional, bohemian life, working at many different jobs—as a doorman, waiter, official guard, and wheat sifter. In those years, however, he became an avid reader, and the works of Knut Hamsun, which he admired passionately, prompted him to invent narratives with both imaginary and real episodes. He was also aware of the sociopolitical changes in America and Europe at that time and was attracted to the socialism of the Soviet Union.

When he was twenty-one, he married his cousin María Amalia Onetti, and they settled in Buenos Aires, where their son, Jorge, was born in 1931. (Eventually, Jorge himself became a well-known novelist in Uruguay.) Also in 1931 Onetti completed the manuscript of *El pozo* (The Pit), his first novelette; unfortunately it was lost before it could be offered to a publisher. Later the manuscript was found, reworked, and finally published in 1939. His first-known publication, however, was "Avenida de Mayo—Diagonal—Avenida de Mayo," which won a prize from the journal in which it was published, the *Prensa* (Buenos Aires), in 1933. He also wrote the first draft of *Tiempo de abrazar* (Time to Embrace), a short novel that circulated in manuscript among his friends but was not published until 1974.

In 1934 he returned to Montevideo and, having divorced María, got married again, this time to María Julia, his first wife's sister. Onetti's literary attempts were encouraged by the publication of two short stories, "El obstáculo" (1935) and "El posible Baldi" (1936) in the *Nación* (Buenos Aires).

In his narratives Onetti is preoccupied with social and political problems; his personal concern with both national and international affairs led him to support the Spanish Republican cause. Intending to volunteer for their civil war, he planned a trip to Spain but did not go. Remain-

A 1945 photograph of Onetti in Buenos Aires, where he worked for Reuters news service from 1941 to 1954

ing in Montevideo he openly criticized the corruption, excessive materialism, and lack of authentic values Uruguay was experiencing as a result of the rapid increase in immigration to cities along the Río de la Plata. Onetti was also involved in the intellectual preoccupations of a group of his contemporaries who met regularly at the Café Metro, where, in 1939, the literary magazine *Marcha*, founded by Juan Carlos Quijano, came into being. During three decades, from 1939 to 1974, this weekly magazine was a very influential and important voice within the Uruguayan cultural world. From 1939 to 1941 Onetti was managing editor of *Marcha* as well as an active contributor of acerbic and incisive articles, signed with the pseudonyms Periquito el Aguador (Watering Parrot) and Grucho [sic] Marx.

El pozo was first published in a limited edition of five hundred copies. Not until twenty-six years had passed did this work reappear in a new edition. In 1965 it became a critical success, recognized as an existential novel prefiguring the technical and narrative changes that would culminate in the "new novel" of the 1960s in Spanish America. *El pozo* reflects the scepticism of the genera-

tion that defined itself just before and during the first years of World War II. According to Onetti, this was a generation facing sociopolitical problems and conscious of its existential limitations. The protagonist, Eladio Linacero, secluded within the solitude of his room, on the night of his fortieth birthday writes his memories as an interior monologue, keeping pace with his recollections throughout the night. The lack of communication and the alienation of the character emerge as the result of an obsessive existential consciousness confronting a strange, hostile world. Linacero finds that his dreams are the only possible means of escape; however, these offer merely a brief refuge. The existentialism of Onetti's characters resembles Jean-Paul Sartre's ideas. Even so, a more probable direct influence on the radical attitude shown by Onetti's characters may be found in the novels of the Argentine writer Roberto Arlt.

In 1940 Onetti submitted the novel *Tiempo de abrazar* to a national jury empowered to select the best Uruguayan work for competition in an international contest promoted by Rinehart and Farrar of New York. Onetti's novel was not selected,

Dust jacket for Onetti's 1950 novel, which focuses on Juan María Brausen and the two imaginary doubles that he has created

and the typescript was subsequently lost. Some fragments of the manuscript were eventually recovered and published in *Marcha* in 1943. In 1941 Onetti became an editor for Reuters news in Montevideo; soon afterward he began working for the same agency in Buenos Aires, where he remained until 1954.

During this period he also worked for the *Nación* and published in it in 1942 the story "Un sueño realizado" (translated as "A Dream Come True," 1972)—collected in *Un sueño realizado y otros cuentos* (1951). The novel *Tierra de nadie* (No Man's Land, 1941) won second place in a competition sponsored by Editorial Losada, on whose jury Jorge Luis Borges served. In *Tierra de nadie* Onetti defined his stance as a writer—a resentful, independent attitude toward both the reality he recreates and his own existential absurdity: "The fact is that in the most important South American country the morally indifferent type, the man with neither faith nor interest in his destiny, thrives. The novelist should not be reproached for confronting and depicting this human type with an equal spirit of indifference."

In 1943 Onetti published the novel *Para esta noche* (For Tonight). Then, in 1945, Elizabeth María Pekelharing became Onetti's third wife, and they had a daughter, Isabel María, born in 1951. With the publication of *La vida breve* in 1950, Onetti was recognized as a writer worthy of note in the international literary world, and since then his name has stood with those of the founders of the contemporary Spanish-American novel.

La vida breve marks an important shift in his narrative perspective. Breaking away from the rational, logical order of the traditional novel, Onetti finds in fragmentary structure an apt vehicle for expressing the existential angst of his protagonist, Juan María Brausen, who is facing a failed marriage and the economic uncertainty of a mediocre world. Aspiring to transcend everyday reality, this character invents his own personal world. Thus Brausen creates not only his doubles—the physician Díaz Grey and his antagonist Arce—but also his own city: Santa María, a nontemporal, nonspatial place, a mythical port somewhere on the Río de la Plata coast. Santa María, accessible by both land and water, was to become the setting for several Onetti sagas. Within *La vida breve* the double characters Brausen/Díaz Grey and Brausen/Arce, along with the imagined space of Santa María, are intertwined with the situations of daily life, thereby creating a constant, unlimited oscillation between the possible and the impossible.

In 1951 Onetti collected his short stories in *Un sueño realizado y otros cuentos*. Two years later he published the story "El álbum" in the literary journal *Sur* (Buenos Aires). The Sur Publishing Company also published Onetti's short novel *Los adioses* (1954; translated in *Goodbyes and Stories*, 1990), yet another work expressing the isolation and loneliness typical of his characters; this time two are involved in an impossible love story. Around 1954 he left Buenos Aires and moved to Montevideo, where he concentrated his main activities on journalism, working for the newspaper *Acción* run by Battle Berres; there Onetti wrote and published literary articles that attracted positive critical attention. In 1955 Onetti married his fourth wife, Dorotea (Dolly) Muhr. They remained in Montevideo, where he was named director of the municipal libraries. *Una tumba sin nombre* (A Nameless Tomb, 1959), one of his most inventive novels, is set is Santa María and focuses on the housemaid and prostitute Rita, a woman physically absent yet omnipresent within the text, which is created through the interplay of numerous versions of her story told by the different characters. This interweaving of the continuous reiterations and excursions of new versions of the tale gives an uneasy, distinctive ambivalence to the narrative, leading finally to the uncertainty of the story and the impossibility of knowing any definitive truth.

In Onetti's *El astillero* (1961; translated as *The Shipyard*, 1968) and *Juntacadáveres* (1964; partially translated as "Junta, the Bodysnatcher," 1976), characters from earlier narratives reappear and, along with new protagonists, revitalize the Onettian saga of Santa María. Both these novels received unanimous critical praise. *El astillero* was awarded the certificate of merit by the Faulkner Foundation in 1963; *Juntacadáveres* was not only selected for publication by the jury of the literary contest sponsored by Abril Editors of Buenos Aires but was also included in 1967 among the finalists for the prestigious Premio Rómulo Gallegos, awarded every five years to the best Spanish-American novel. In 1962 the government of Uruguay awarded the Premio Nacional de Literatura to Onetti for the literary and artistic achievement of all his published work.

In subsequent years literary critics interested in Latin-American novels frequently dealt with Onetti's works as he gained wider notice from the international public. He participated in conferences of Spanish-American writers, and in 1966 he visited the United States for the first time, when he was invited to attend the conference of the PEN Club held in New York. In 1967 Onetti traveled to Venezuela and in 1969 to Chile. His complete works, with a perceptive introduction by Emir Rodríguez Monegal, were published the following year. Onetti was acclaimed in 1972 in a survey conducted by *Marcha* as the best Uruguayan novelist of the last fifty years. Subsequently he published *La muerte y la niña* (Death and the Girl, 1973) and, a year later, *Tiempo de abrazar y los cuentos de 1933 a 1950*.

In 1974 an unexpected event drastically changed Onetti's daily life. As a member of the jury in a literary contest sponsored by *Marcha*, he participated in selecting the year's best short story written in Uruguay. The prize was awarded to "El guardaespalda" (The Bodyguard), by Nelson Marra. This story, which was published in *Marcha* in February of that same year, recounts the agony of a member of a torture squad, who,

wounded by *guerilleros*, recalls and assesses his life as well as his dependence on the regime and his relations with the military authorities. As a consequence of the selection of this story, Marra and the members of the jury were arrested. After more than three months in prison, Onetti was released, mainly because of the protests of the press and international institutions. At the time Onetti was not permitted to travel to Italy, where his novel *El astillero*, which seems to evoke a Felliniesque world, was chosen as the best Latin-American novel translated and published in Italian (1972). Then, confronted by the intolerable situation of living under the power of a dictatorship, in constant political unrest in his own country, Onetti renounced his position as director of the municipal libraries, traveled to Europe and, invited by the Instituto de Cultura Hispánica, settled in Spain in 1975. Since then, Onetti has lived in Madrid with his wife, Dolly, who left her position as first violinist with the Uruguayan symphony in order to accompany her husband to Spain.

Many countries have honored Onetti with invitations and testimonials. In 1976 he was a member of the international jury for a Mexican novel contest; two years later, he was honored by the Sorbonne in Paris; in 1979, he participated in the First International Congress of Spanish Language Writers held in Las Palmas, Canary Islands. He went to Mexico in 1980 to attend a testimonial in his honor given by the Universidad Veracruzana. In that same year, Onetti was nominated for the Nobel Prize in Literature by the Latin-American PEN Club because his works gave voice to "a silent population representing the cultural world of three-hundred million Hispanic speakers." Also in 1980 Onetti was awarded the prestigious Premio Miguel de Cervantes by the Spanish Ministerio de Cultura and Información. Upon being interviewed by the *New York Times*, Onetti observed that in Spanish America he was "discovered" relatively late in life, and that commercial success and translations of his novels into English, French, Italian, Swedish, Polish, and Japanese increased considerably after he moved to Spain.

Although Onetti has participated more actively in public life recently than he did before, he remains much like many of his protagonists: a solitary being who grants few interviews, seldom ventures out, and prefers the anonymity and seclusion of the Madrid apartment he shares with his wife. As the critic Omar Prego observed (in *Juan*

Onetti in Barcelona, 1979

Carlos Onetti, 1986), in his home Onetti seems to be one of his own characters: " . . . lying upon his bed, he smokes one cigarette after another. Books are scattered everywhere: on the shelves, under the bed, in cardboard boxes. He has doubts with respect to the long trip from Madrid to Montevideo to accept an invitation extended by President Sanguineti to visit Uruguay. With his peculiar humor, Onetti claims to feel as old as one of those Fords manufactured to last ten years, when all of the parts begin simultaneously to fall apart."

Onetti's attitude of the indifferent and distant man has never curtailed his consistent activity and production as a writer. Two important novels, *Dejemos hablar al viento* (Let's Allow the Wind to Speak, 1979) and *Cuando entonces* (When Then, 1987), were published after Onetti established his residence in Madrid. Both depart from the Santa María setting of his previous writing to a new location in Lavanda, a name suggesting the country of Uruguay, which is also known as "La Banda Oriental." As would be expected of an Onettian milieu, however, this place is neither concrete nor geographically precise and has, at one and the same time, realistic and fantastic dimensions. The characters in these novels, like those in his previous works, are pushed to the edge by society and live in a nightmare world of ruin and corruption.

Dejemos hablar al viento consists of two parts. It is first the story of Medina, a failure in life, and his lovers. As in other Onetti texts the characters seem to be created by the narrator as figures reflecting themselves in multiple other figures. At the end of the first part of the narrative, Medina confronts a figment of his imagination, Carreño. This character is none other than the phantasmagorical recreation of Larsen, a character imagined by Brausen in *La vida breve* and re-created as a frustrated artist in *Juntacadáveres*, who is ultimately killed in *El astillero*. Consequently it is significant that in the second part of *Dejemos hablar al viento*, as the wind increases, it becomes an elemental force of purification and destruction, ultimately doing away with the decadent city of Santa María, originally invented by Brausen's dream in *La vida breve*. The final fire is symbolic: a scarlet light that spreads throughout the city, accompanied by the asphyxiating smell and heat of inevitable final destruction.

Onetti's *Cuando entonces* is a tragic tale of love, involving prostitution, failure, and pessimism. Like the detective genre, this narrative reconstructs disperse fragments of the life and death of Magda. Magda is remembered by two characters in a beer hall in Lavanda. Her story takes place on the other bank of the river, in Buenos Aires. The end of the novel is indeterminate, but it is the affirmation of fantasy and reality as invented, independent worlds.

In 1991 Onetti was working on a novel, as well as on occasional short essays for publication in newspapers and journals. In the contemporary literary world, his narrative cosmos has been compared to that of such great masters as Sartre, William Faulkner, and Samuel Beckett. Within the context of the twentieth-century Latin-American narrative, Onetti's work remains one of the most authentic expressions of the innovative experience of the 1960s, a self-reflexive attitude that led to a reevaluation of the absurdity of the human condition in an uncertain, contradictory universe.

Interviews:

Luis Harss and Barbara Dohmann, *Los nuestros* (Buenos Aires: Sudamericana, 1966);

Emir Rodríguez Monegal, "Conversación con Juan Carlos Onetti," *Eco*, 119 (March 1970): 442-475;

Jorge Ruffinelli, "Juan Carlos Onetti: Creación y muerte de Santa María," in his *Palabras en orden* (Buenos Aires: Crisis, 1974), pp. 69-88;

José Manuel García Ramos, "Entrevista con Juan Carlos Onetti," *Camp del 'Arpa*, 45-46 (June-July 1977);

Omar Prego and María Angélica Petit, "Onetti habla," in *Juan Carlos Onetti o la salvación por la escritura* (Madrid: Sociedad General Española de Librería, 1981).

Bibliographies:

Hugo J. Verani, "Contribución a la bibliografía de Juan Carlos Onetti," in *Onetti*, edited by Jorge Ruffinelli (Montevideo: Marcha, 1973), pp. 267-291;

Aurora Ocampo, "Bibliografía de Onetti," in her *Novelistas iberoamericanos contemporáneos* (Mexico City: UNAM, 1981).

References:

Fernando Aínsa, *Las trampas de Onetti* (Montevideo: Alfa, 1970);

Mario Benedetti, "Juan Carlos Onetti y la aventura del hombre," in his *Literatura uruguaya del siglo XX* (Montevideo: Alfa, 1963);

Jaime Concha, "Juan Carlos: *El pozo*," *Anales de la Universidad de Chile*, 139 (1966);

Concha, "*Tierra de nadie* de J. C. O.," *Atenea*, 417 (1967);

Crisis, special Onetti issue, 6 (1974);

Cuadernos Hispanoamericanos, special Onetti triple issue, 292-294 (October-December 1974);

Fernando Curiel, *Onetti: Obra y calculado infortunio* (Mexico City: Universidad Nacional Autónoma de México, 1980);

Jean Franco, "La máquina rota," *Texto Crítico*, 18-19 (July-December 1980): 33-46;

Zunilda Gertel, "*Para una tumba sin nombre*: ficción y teoría de la ficción," *Texto Crítico*, 18-19 (July-December 1980): 178-194;

H. Giacoman, ed., *Homenaje a Juan Carlos Onetti* (New York: Las Américas, 1974);

Djelal Kadir, *Juan Carlos Onetti* (Boston: Twayne, 1977);

Kadir, ed., *Review*, special Onetti issue, 16 (Winter 1975);

Josefina Ludmer, *Onetti: Los procesos de construcción del relato* (Buenos Aires: Sudamericana, 1977);

Omar Prego, *Juan Carlos Onetti: Perfil de un solitario* (Montevideo: Trilce, 1986);

Angel Rama, "Origen de un novelista y de una generación literaria," in Onetti's *El pozo* (Montevideo: Arca, 1965);

Emir Rodríguez Monegal, "La fortuna de Onetti," in his *Literatura uruguaya del medio siglo* (Montevideo: Alfa, 1962);

Rodríguez Monegal, ed., Prologue to *Obras completas de Juan Carlos Onetti* (Mexico City: Aguilar, 1970);

Jorge Ruffinelli, "Onetti antes de Onetti," in Onetti's *Tiempo de abrazar y los cuentos de 1933 a 1950* (Montevideo: Arca, 1974), pp. xi-liv;

Ruffinelli, ed., *Onetti* (Montevideo: Marcha, 1973);

Ruffinelli, ed., "Onetti en Xalapa," *Texto Crítico*, special Onetti double issue, 18-19 (July-December 1980);

Peter Turton, "Las permutaciones de la desgracia o 'Esbjerg, en la costa' de Juan Carlos Onetti," *Revista Canadiense de Estudios Hispánicos*, 1 (1983);

H. Verani, ed., *Juan Carlos Onetti, el escritor ante la crítica* (Madrid: Taurus, 1987).

Elena Poniatowska
(19 May 1933 -)

María-Inés Lagos
Washington University in St. Louis
(Translated by Ben Heller)

BOOKS: *Lilus Kikus* (Mexico City: Los Presentes, 1954);
Melés y Teleo (Mexico City: Revista Panoramas, 1956);
Palabras cruzadas (Mexico City: Era, 1961);
Todo empezó el domingo (Mexico City: Fondo de Cultura Económica, 1963);
Los cuentos de Lilus Kikus (Veracruz: Universidad Veracruzana, 1967);
México visto a ojo de pájaro (Mexico City: Colibrí, SEP, 1968);
Hasta no verte Jesús mío (Mexico City: Era, 1969);
La noche de Tlatelolco (Mexico City: Era, 1971); translated by Helen Lane as *Massacre in Mexico* (New York: Viking, 1975);
Querido Diego, te abraza Quiela (Mexico City: Era, 1978); translated by Katherine Silver as *Dear Diego* (New York: Pantheon, 1986);
De noche vienes (Mexico City: Grijalbo, 1979);
Gaby Brimmer, by Poniatowska and Brimmer (Mexico City: Grijalbo, 1979);
La vendedora de nubes (Mexico City: Colibrí, SEP, 1979);
El león no es como lo pintan (Mexico City: Colibrí, 1979);
Fuerte es el silencio (Mexico City: Era, 1980);
La casa en la tierra, by Poniatowska and Mariana Yampolsky (Mexico City: INI-Fonapas, 1980);
El último guajolote (Mexico City: Cultura, 1982);
Domingo siete (Mexico City: Océano, 1982);
¡Ay vida, no me mereces! (Mexico City: Mortiz, 1985);
La raíz y el camino, by Poniatowska and Yampolsky (Mexico City: Fondo de Cultura Económica, 1985);
Estancias del olvido, by Poniatowska and Yampolsky (Mexico City: INI-Centro Hidalguense de Investigaciones Históricas, 1986);
Tlacotalpan, by Poniatowska and Yampolsky (Mexico City: 1987);
Hablando en plata, by Poniatowska and David Maawad (Mexico City: Centro Hidalguense de Investigaciones Históricas, 1987);
México sin retoque, by Poniatowska and Héctor García (Mexico City: UNAM, 1987);
La "Flor de Lis" (Mexico City: Era, 1988);
Nada, nadie: Las voces del temblor (Mexico City: Era, 1988);
Juchitán de las mujeres, by Poniatowska and Graciela Iturbide (Mexico City: Toledo, 1989);
Compañeras de México (Riverside: University Art Gallery, University of California, 1990).

Elena Poniatowska has devoted much of her fiction and journalism to giving a voice to the anonymous masses that do not have access to the printed word or to other modes of communication. In her chronicles she has rescued from obscurity and oblivion aspects of Mexican society and politics related to the lower classes and has spoken out about certain facts the government has attempted to hide or ignore. Poniatowska includes women in the category of the oppressed, of those without a voice, because the female experience has been traditionally ignored or silenced, especially in societies such as Mexico's, which are overwhelmingly patriarchal. Females are often the protagonists in her fiction. Generally placed in disadvantageous situations by their age, social standing, or simply by being women, Poniatowska's characters are noted for their rebelliousness, for breaking the rules. Examples of such characters are the eponymous protagonist of *Lilus Kikus* (1954), Jesusa of *Hasta no verte Jesús mío* (Until I See You, Dear Jesus, 1969), and Esmeralda in "De noche vienes" (The Night Visitor), the title story of her 1979 collection. A compassionate humor and subtle irony characterize Poniatowska's style, as does a great adeptness in the use of colloquial language. Early on in her writing career Poniatowska became known primarily as a journalist and interviewer, and she has contin-

Elena Poniatowska

ued her work as a journalist while developing her fiction. Because of this, and because some of her fictional characters have been inspired by real people, her narratives are usually associated with the genre of the testimonial or the documentary novel.

Elena Poniatowska was born in Paris on 19 May 1933. Her mother, the former Paula Amor Iturbide, was Mexican, though also born in France; her father, Yvan E. Poniatowski, was of Polish origin. As a result of the Mexican Revolution of 1910 her family on her mother's side lost part of its landholdings and fortune. On her father's side Poniatowska descends from a family of Polish nobles, who were expelled from the country after the partition of Poland. Upon the outbreak of World War II she and her mother and sister moved to the south of France, where they lived with Yvan Poniatowski's parents. There Elena and her younger sister attended public school. When Elena was eight years old, they moved to Mexico to live with her mother's family, while her father remained in France fighting the Nazis. As a child she spoke French; only after moving to Mexico did she learn Spanish. In Mexico City she began her studies at a British high school, then attended the Liceo Francés de México for a year, and finished her last two years of secondary school at the Convent of the Sacred Heart's Eden Hall, in Torresdale, Pennsylvania. After studying at Manhattanville College on a scholarship, Poniatowska began her literary career in 1953 in Mexico City, interviewing important Mexican literary and political personalities. She has worked as a journalist for more than thirty-five years, writing first for *Excelsior* in 1954 and, since 1955, for *Novedades*. She recounts that in her years as a reporter she did an interview a day, and that, when she went to work for *Novedades*, she was supposed to produce three articles every week. She has referred in interviews to the difficulties of combining the responsibilities of a mother, a wife, and a professional. She is a regular contributor to such reviews as *Vuelta* and

Plural, and is a member of the editorial board of *fem.*, a feminist journal directed by university women. She has lectured all over Mexico, and is one of the founders of the Cineteca Nacional (Mexican Film Library), and the publishing house Siglo XXI. Her husband, the astrophysicist Guillermo Haro, died in April 1988. Poniatowska has three children, Emmanuel, Felipe, and Paula, and lives in Mexico City. Although she does not teach professionally, she has led workshops for young journalists, especially women.

Poniatowska's first novel, *Lilus Kikus*, is short and composed of scenes or vignettes narrated in the third person, which present the intimate feelings and experiences of the protagonist at different moments of her childhood and adolescence. A subtle irony and a playful ingenuousness reveals Lilus's nonconformity to the values adults wish to inculcate in her. Thus the work acquires a subversive and contentious tone regarding the reasons with which the adult world attempts to induce the protagonist to accept social conventions.

The book underscores how the mechanisms of power function upon girls, forcing them to remain in a position of subordination and docility, and, above all, coercing them to be like other girls. But Lilus is not a conventional girl; she believes in superstitions, plays with little animals instead of dolls, and when she is taken to Acapulco for a vacation, she amuses herself with the crabs she finds on the sand, with starfish, and with the water. At times Lilus becomes absorbed observing a cat playing with its tail, or looking at a drop of dew sliding down a leaf, thinking about stones and the rain, or wondering about the mysterious light of the fireflies. All of this disconcerts her father, because it is not the type of behavior one expects from a girl, and he reproves her for her unconventional habits. Her mother also feels uncomfortable with Lilus's inclinations and predilections, and her parents send her to be educated at a religious school to learn to behave like a young lady. The nuns try to teach her submissiveness and patience, and the story ends there. The irony with which the narrative voice refers to these lessons indicates that, although the ending is open, it will be difficult to "reform" Lilus. In the year following the publication of this first novel, Poniatowska had her first child, Emmanuel.

Poniatowska published her novel *Hasta no verte Jesús mío* in 1969. The person who served as inspiration for the novel was a poor and uneducated woman Poniatowska saw in a public washing area; the woman's manner of speaking was so attractive that Poniatowska sought her out for a series of interviews. In an article published in *Vuelta* (November 1978), Poniatowska explained the difficulties she experienced in interviewing her subject; the informant was very distrustful and did not understand why the writer was interested in her. Poniatowska's book is not a transcription of the interviews nor an ethnological or anthropological study; rather, taking as a point of departure this woman's story, Poniatowska selects, transforms, and elaborates in order to create her narrative. She has complained about the critical reception of those works possessing a testimonial basis, in that they are perceived as less valuable than pure fiction. She asks herself why certain novels, which refer to concrete historical circumstances and whose authors have investigated and informed themselves about their topic before writing, should be considered pure fiction and others not. Nevertheless, even if Poniatowska created the character Jesusa by combining traits of her nannies, the interviewee, and of other women she has known, she also treats the character as if she were a real person. In Poniatowska's 1985 book of essays *¡Ay vida, no me mereces!* (O Life, You Don't Deserve Me!) Jesusa is referred to as if she were an author, in spite of the fact that Jesusa Palancares is not the name of the interviewee but rather the name Poniatowska gave to her character.

Hasta no verte Jesús mío tells the story of Jesusa from her childhood in Tehuantepec until her old age in Mexico City. She is a complex, contradictory character who resists definition. Her childhood and adolescence are marked by the deaths of her mother and of her brother Emilio, with whom she was very close and toward whom she has shown love and tenderness. After the death of her mother, Jesusa's childhood ends for all practical purposes. Though she is at the time only five, she never plays again; she says, "Si todo era puro trabajar desde chica" (Everything was work work work since I was a little girl). Her family frequently moves, and when they live in Tehuantepec the father works nights to be able to care for his children during the day. The father seems exceptional in many respects. Jesusa says her father combed her hair with his smooth hands, and he chastised his son Efrén because the recently wed Efrén has abused his wife. Nevertheless, Jesusa's father has many lovers, and this is one of the reasons Jesusa finally quarrels with him.

During this period the protagonist enjoys a good deal of liberty; she likes to walk through the hills and do what the young boys do. She does not learn to make tortillas and instead enjoys playing war. Unlike other girls of her age, Jesusa has no interest in sexuality, nor does she show any curiosity about it. Neither is she given to fantasy; she lives in the present, and since she is not of a passive or a resigned nature, she makes her own decisions. She is overtly hostile toward religion and the priests and severely criticizes the education she receives from the nuns, who, in her opinion, have taught her nothing whatsoever. As for her relationships with others, they are marked by silence: she usually speaks with no one.

During the 1910 revolution she weds Pedro, an officer who practically forces her to marry him. At the time, she is fifteen years old, her husband seventeen. From the very first day, he treats her poorly, locking her in the house and going out carousing. Thus he imposes his authority on the rebellious woman who had resisted him; he seems to have married her because of his desire to subjugate her. Marriage means for Jesusa the loss of her freedom and the submission to the desires of her husband. She no longer has her own money, she must stay in the house, and her husband controls all her movements. After accepting this treatment for some time, Jesusa rebels and threatens him with a gun. However, although they end up fighting in the revolution side by side, Pedro continues having lovers, and when Jesusa, as an old woman, remembers him, she confesses that she never felt love for him. Jesusa sees relationships with men as confrontations in which one is constantly comparing forces. She is a rebellious woman who does not want to surrender herself; she values her liberty and wants to be in control at all times.

Again and again the protagonist compares how things were before with how they are now. These comparisons underscore the distance between the narrator Jesusa, whose discourse is an oral testimony, and the character being created. Readers are dealing, therefore, with a reconstruction in which forgetting intervenes, as does the distorting lens of the narrator, which at times magnifies or interprets memories in a fantastic manner. The autobiographical mode allows the reader to accept more easily certain imaginary episodes that are presented as if they were historical events, and makes it seem normal for the narrator to add fictional scenes, such as her encounter with Emiliano Zapata, or her brief command of the troops after the death of her husband and in the absence of the general officially in charge.

An important facet of Jesusa is her religious perspective. After having been a rebel and a nonconformist all her life, rejecting Catholicism, she joins a religious group named the Obra Espiritual (Spiritual Work). However, she discovers that this religious sect suffers the same defects as the traditional institution, and she quarrels with its directors because she thinks they look down on her for her lack of money. One observes in Jesusa's religious convictions a mixture of beliefs that derive from various origins, but the basic tenets of Christianity predominate. For example, the ideas that the earth is a valley of tears in which people pay for their sins in order to be worthy of Heaven and that one should accept the will of the all-seeing God are derived from the teachings of the Catholic church. On the other hand, she believes in reincarnation and in spiritualist ceremonies. She feels guilty for her errors and believes she is paying for her sins in the present reincarnation because she has had to suffer so much.

Although on one hand the protagonist is an exceptional character in that she will not permit her liberty to be limited, on the other hand she accepts masculine polygamy as something natural, and she places the responsibility for men's errors on women. In spite of her rebelliousness and her sense of autonomy, shown by her refusal to accept the hegemony of a husband, of the church, or of the religious sect, Jesusa has adopted the social principles that have kept women and the poor subjugated to the dominant order.

But in spite of the contradictory docility exhibited by Jesusa with regard to the social system, *Hasta no verte Jesús mío* is a novel that contributes much to women's struggles to be recognized as human beings with the right to be treated with dignity and to enjoy the same privileges and opportunities as men. By naming, presenting, and describing a woman's experience, she bears witness to a life. Jesusa not only dramatizes the oppression that a woman from the lower classes experiences for being poor and uneducated, but also for simply being a woman. Jesusa wants to have liberty and the capacity to decide her own fate; she does not want to live the life of a subordinate. The frustration revealed by the character alludes to that of women from all social strata, who find themselves in a similar situation.

In 1978 Poniatowska published *Querido Diego, te abraza Quiela* (translated as *Dear Diego*, 1986), inspired by the story of the artist Diego Rivera and Angelina Beloff, an exiled Russian painter who was Rivera's lover in Paris for ten years. In the epistolary mode Poniatowska fictitiously reconstructs the letters that Quiela (Angelina) could have sent to Rivera after he left her to return to Mexico. Poniatowska read the 1963 biography of Rivera written by Bertram Wolfe, *The Fabulous Life of Diego Rivera*, which contains one letter and fragments of two others, but she did not know when writing her novel that Angelina Beloff's memoirs existed in unpublished form. Readers find in *Querido Diego* a situation similar to that of Jesusa. Although Poniatowska may have been inspired by Beloff, she states that she used her only as a pretext, because the substance of the letters is Poniatowska's creation. Nevertheless, in her epilogue she refers to the historical characters by their true names and mentions that, thirteen years after this Parisian episode, Beloff went to live in Mexico but never contacted Rivera, not wanting to bother him. This colophon seems to indicate that the writer seeks a handle in historical reality that will lend authority to her words.

The protagonist of the novel is a woman who suffers and laments her desertion by her lover, and in her letters she converses with him in the hope that he will return. Quiela depends on love relationships, and although she experiences sporadic fits of independence and autonomy, the feeling that predominates is that it is impossible for her to go on living apart from Rivera.

Poniatowska has been criticized for having created such a submissive, dependent protagonist. In her defense one must take into account that, on the one hand, the letters encompass a period of only nine months, the months that follow the desertion of the lover; on the other hand, the text shows how the socialization of women can lead them to self-destruction if they are not capable of cutting their affective ties to those who have rejected them. In addition, by emphasizing the untiring fidelity of Quiela, who is presented as a victim of her dependency, the novel suggests that, if she were to lead an autonomous life, she would free herself from the constant humiliations to which she submits herself.

The short-story collection *De noche vienes* reveals her search for a personal style. She says that in "Cine prado" (Prado Cinema) she consciously strove to write in a literary manner, that is, according to accepted literary conventions, but in "De noche vienes," which was written especially for this volume, she writes in a style she feels to be her own.

It has been observed that humor and irony are frequently used by women writers as subtle means to subvert traditional, patriarchal values. Although Hispanic literature is not especially noted for its humor (indeed the reverse is the case), women writers often make use of this strategy in order to offer a critical perspective on the dominant order. In Mexican literature there is the example of a woman writer much admired by Poniatowska, Rosario Castellanos, who employs this tactic; other contemporary examples are Rosario Ferré of Puerto Rico and Mireya Robles of Cuba. Thus, in the same way Poniatowska uses the testimonial genre to neutralize a highly subversive discourse, as in *Hasta no verte Jesús mío*, in the title story of *De noche vienes* she uses humor to create situations that radically alter conventional modes of conduct. Beneath an appearance of naiveté that would seem to exalt certain traditional feminine characteristics, such as the eagerness to serve others while ignoring one's own needs, Poniatowska allows the reader to laugh and celebrate an event that undermines the basis of society, mocking not only the ridiculousness of the double standard in relationships between the sexes, but also the Mexican Revolution, religion, and the law.

In the story a nurse, Esmeralda, an ingenuous woman with what are considered to be typical feminine qualities, such as compassion and a concern for others, is accused of polygamy by one of her five husbands. Esmeralda had lived happily and in peace for several years, devoting one day of the week to each of her spouses (unknown to each other) and the weekends to her father. The relationship established between the accused and the judge repeats the pattern of her previous conduct. With her naiveté, or perhaps astuteness (an ambiguity which is never clarified), she seduces the judge, who, although he cannot but condemn her, becomes another of her admirers, and along with the five husbands visits her in jail on Sundays.

The art and humor of Poniatowska transforms a situation that could be grotesque into a suggestive, ambiguous story in which masculine and feminine stereotypes are reversed to subvert the established order without breaking with conventional values. Bear in mind that, because the law should be respected, the protagonist is condemned and incarcerated for her crimes, though much to the chagrin of all her consorts. Life and feelings do not always agree with the legal system, inasmuch as all of Esmeralda's admirers, including the judge who must condemn her to several years in jail, lament her having to be punished.

During the 1960s and 1970s Poniatowska continued to develop as a journalist. *Palabras cruzadas* (Crossword Puzzle, 1961) is a collection of her interviews, including conversations with François Mauriac, Luis Buñuel, Lázaro Cárdenas, and Fidel Castro. *Todo empezó el domingo* (It All Began on Sunday, 1963) documents what poor people do on Sundays and was illustrated by Alberto Beltrán.

Her journalistic pieces are important documents of oral history; they recount the intrahistory of Mexico. Among them *La noche de Tlatelolco* (1971; translated as *Massacre in Mexico*, 1975) stands out, as does *Fuerte es el silencio* (Silence So Strong, 1980) and *Nada, Nadie* (Nothing, Nobody, 1988), which contains testimonies about the earthquake in Mexico City in 1985.

La noche de Tlatelolco documents through a multitude of voices the massacre that occurred on 2 October 1968, when the Mexican police and army fired on a peaceful protest crowd in the Plaza de las Tres Culturas, after months of conflict between university students and the authorities. Poniatowska's chronicle brings together testimony from many witnesses of different political orientations, including parents and students; statements that appeared in the newspapers; headlines and news items; documents of student organizations; transcripts of tape recordings; army dispatches; and Poniatowska's own comments.

Although Poniatowska appears reserved in person—she is a soft-spoken woman—when she writes she does not hesitate to denounce repression, both personal and governmental, which is exercised upon those who dissent or protest against the establishment. In 1980 she published *Fuerte es el silencio*, a searing document that exposes the struggle of the thousands that migrate to the cities to establish themselves, and which goes on to record the daily history that is suppressed within the country but often noted in the foreign press. Of the five chronicles in the book, the last one, "La colonia Rubén Jaramillo" (The Rubén Jaramillo Settlement), best exemplifies Poniatowska's creative journalistic style. There she recreates Florencio Medrano's struggle to convince slum dwellers to follow him and settle in unused land outside Cuernavaca. Also in 1980 she wrote the text for a book of photographs of poor rural houses, *La casa en la tierra* (The House On The Land). In 1979 *Gaby Brimmer* had been published—based on an interview with a girl suffering from cerebral palsy. Other books of her journalism years include *El último guajolote* (The Last Turkey, 1982) and *Domingo siete* (Sunday the Seventh, 1982).

Her book of critical essays *¡Ay vida, no me mereces!* contains studies of the works of Carlos Fuentes, Juan Rulfo, and Rosario Castellanos, and the literature of the so-called Onda (Wave), which developed between the mid 1960s and the beginning of the 1970s. The essay on Castellanos reveals not only Castellanos's role in the process of change in how women are treated in Mexico but also shows how Poniatowska shares much of Castellanos's feminist ideology.

Poniatowska's novel *La "Flor de Lis"* (The "Fleur de Lis"), published in 1988, reveals a change to a more intimate tone. She recounts the story of Mariana, a girl born in France to a Mexican mother and a French father, who moves to Mexico during World War II. Mariana is in touch with diverse facets of Mexican social reality. On one hand, she is brought up in the midst of an aristocratic family with its European traditions and rituals, and attends an exclusive Catholic boarding school in the United States. On the other hand, since she lives in Mexico City, where she takes typing and stenography classes to become a bilingual secretary, she has the opportunity to observe how it is to live in the city, riding the crowded buses and strolling in the old, no-longer-fashionable downtown area. At the end of the narrative, Mariana's confusion begins to unravel when she embraces her country and what it represents, and decides to have a tamale at a diner called "Flor de Lis," thus timidly trespassing the rules of her upper-class upbringing. Although one suspects that there is a great deal of autobiographical material in this text, the narrative still exposes those social mechanisms that have kept women in their traditional roles.

Poniatowska ranks among the most distinguished women writers of Mexico today: she has received an honorary degree from the Universidad de Sinaloa, and in 1979 was the first woman to be awarded the Premio Nacional de Periodismo (journalism). She was awarded the prestigious Premio Xavier Villaurrutia in 1970, but rejected it because she did not agree with Mexican government policies, and she has received numerous other honors in her country and abroad. Although her works treat polemical and urgent themes, they have enjoyed great public success, as attested by the many editions of her work. She is constantly invited to give lectures and take part in literary conferences all over the world.

Elena Poniatowska has dared to record the suffering of those who are "nobody," as well as the corruption of the authorities. With regard to her own life she has undoubtedly exercised a process of self-censorship, and only recently has she decided to explore in her fiction the theme of childhood experiences, the relationship between parents and child, and the full influence of religion. She no longer utilizes Jesusa, nor Quiela; her own voice seems to have emerged, unmediated. As her tenacity and untiring activity demonstrate, Poniatowska continues to be an effective speaker for those who have endured, as she says in *Fuerte es el silencio*, "un silencio de siglos" (a silence of centuries).

Interviews:

Beth Miller, "Interview with Elena Poniatowska," *Latin American Literary Review*, 4, no. 7 (1975): 73-78;

Miller and Alfonso González, "Elena Poniatowska," *26 autoras del México actual* (Mexico City: Costa-Amic, 1978), pp. 301-321;

Teresa Méndez-Faith, "Entrevista con Elena Poniatowska," *Inti*, 15 (Spring 1982): 54-60;

Magdalena García-Pinto, *Historias Intimas* (Hanover, N.H.: Del Norte, 1988), pp. 173-198.

References:

Miriam Balboa Echeverría, "Notas a una escritura testimonial: *Fuerte es el silencio* de Elena Poniatowska," *Discurso Literario*, 5 (Spring 1988): 365-373;

Bell Gale Chevigny, "The Transformation of Privilege in the Work of Elena Poniatowska," *Latin American Literary Review*, 13, no. 26 (1985): 49-62;

Lisa Davis, "An Invitation to Understanding among Poor Women of the Americas: *The Color Purple* and *Hasta no verte Jesús mío*," in *Re-inventing the Americas: Comparative Studies of the Literature of the United States and Spanish America*, edited by Chevigny and Gari Laguardia (New York: Cambridge University Press, 1986), pp. 224-241;

Margarite Fernández Olmos, "El género testimonial: aproximaciones feministas," *Revista/Review Interamericana*, 2, no. 1 (1981): 69-75;

Joel Hancock, "Elena Poniatowska's *Hasta no verte Jesús mío*: The Remaking of the Image of Woman," *Hispania*, 66, no. 3 (1983): 353-359;

Julia A. Kushigian, "Transgresión de la autobiografía y el *Bildungsroman* en *Hasta no verte Jesús mío*," *Revista Iberoamericana*, 140 (1987): 667-677;

María-Inés Lagos-Pope, "El testimonio creativo de *Hasta no verte Jesús mío*," *Revista Iberoamericana*, 150 (January-March 1990): 243-253;

Monique J. Lemaître, "Jesusa Palancares y la dialéctica de la emancipación femenina," *Revista Iberoamericana*, 132-133 (1985): 751-763;

Elizabeth Starcêvic, "Breaking the Silence: Elena Poniatowska, a Writer in Transition," *Literatures in Transition: The Many Voices of the Caribbean Area: A Symposium*, edited by Rose S. Minc (Gaithersburg, Md.: Hispamérica, 1982), pp. 63-68;

Starcêvic, "Elena Poniatowska: Witness for the People," *Contemporary Women Authors of Latin America: Introductory Essays*, edited by Doris Meyer and Margarite Fernández Olmos (Brooklyn: Brooklyn College Press, 1983), pp. 72-77;

Cynthia Steele, "La creatividad y el deseo en *Querido Diego, te abraza Quiela*, de Elena Poniatowska," *Hispamérica*, 14, no. 41 (1985): 17-28;

Charles Tatum, "Elena Poniatowska's *Hasta no verte Jesús mío* (Until I See You, Dear Jesus)," *Latin American Women Writers: Yesterday and Today*, edited by Tatum and Yvette Miller (Pittsburgh: Latin American Literary Review Press, 1977), pp. 49-58.

Manuel Puig

(28 December 1932 - 22 July 1990)

Lucille Kerr
University of Southern California

BOOKS: *La traición de Rita Hayworth* (Buenos Aires: Alvarez, 1968; revised edition, Barcelona: Seix Barral, 1976); translated by Suzanne Jill Levine as *Betrayed by Rita Hayworth* (New York: Dutton, 1971; London: Arena, 1984);

Boquitas pintadas: Folletín (Buenos Aires: Sudamericana, 1969); translated by Levine as *Heartbreak Tango: A Serial* (New York: Dutton, 1973);

The Buenos Aires Affair: Novela policial (Buenos Aires: Sudamericana, 1973); translated by Levine as *The Buenos Aires Affair: A Detective Novel* (New York: Dutton, 1976);

El beso de la mujer araña (Barcelona: Seix Barral, 1976); translated by Thomas Colchie as *Kiss of the Spider Woman* (New York: Knopf, 1979; London: Arena, 1984);

Pubis angelical (Barcelona: Seix Barral, 1979); translated by Elena Brunet (New York: Vintage, 1986; London: Faber, 1987);

Maldición eterna a quien lea estas páginas (Barcelona: Seix Barral, 1980); also published (in English) as *Eternal Curse on the Reader of These Pages* (New York: Random House, 1982; London: Arena, 1985);

Sangre de amor correspondido (Barcelona: Seix Barral, 1982); translated by Jan L. Grayson as *Blood of Requited Love* (New York: Vintage, 1984);

Bajo un manto de estrellas; El beso de la mujer araña [plays] (Barcelona: Seix Barral, 1983); *Bajo un manto de estrellas* translated by Ronald Christ as *Under a Mantle of Stars* (New York: Lumen, 1985); *El beso de la mujer araña* translated by Michael Feingold as *Kiss of the Spider Woman*, in *Latin America: Plays*, edited by George W. Woodyard and Marion Peter Holt (New York, 1986);

La cara del villano; Recuerdo de Tijuana (Barcelona: Seix Barral, 1985);

Mystery of a Rose Bouquet, translated by Allan Baker (London & Boston: Faber & Faber, 1988);

Cae la noche tropical (Barcelona: Seix Barral, 1988); translated by Levine as *Tropical Night Falling* (New York: Simon & Schuster, 1991).

SELECTED PERIODICAL PUBLICATION—
UNCOLLECTED: "Growing Up at the Movies: A Chronology," *Review*, 4-5 (1971-1972): 49-51.

Though Manuel Puig has most recently come to the attention of the general public through the successful 1985 filming of his novel *El beso de la mujer araña* (1976; translated as *Kiss of the Spider Woman*, 1979), he has been a well-known figure in Latin-American letters since the late 1960s, when he began to publish his experimental novels. Puig's work exemplifies modern Latin-American writing's most adventurous contribution to contemporary literary trends, which include a return to popular culture. His writing pertains to the traditions of both "high" and "low" art, and leads readers to examine the distinctions between these traditions and the hierarchy of values implicit in their labels. Puig's writing challenges conventional notions of literature and art as it draws on literary, subliterary, and nonliterary forms and languages to fashion new narrative models and radical ways of thinking about fiction.

Since the publication of his first novel, *La traición de Rita Hayworth* (1968; translated as *Betrayed by Rita Hayworth*, 1971), Puig has been accorded an important place within Latin-American literary tradition, which the so-called Boom of the 1960s helped to reshape. At one time critics tried to classify generationally the fiction writers who came to represent the extraordinary production and reception of the "new" narrative, and Puig was initially situated with the younger writers who emerged in the late 1960s, including Reinaldo Arenas, Guillermo Cabrera Infante, and Severo Sarduy. However, today one is more likely to read the work of Puig and others, such as Arenas, Cabrera Infante, Sarduy, Julio Cortázar, José Donoso, Gabriel García Márquez, Carlos Fuentes, and Mario Vargas Llosa, not as representative of radically different phases but rather as a continuum of contemporary Latin-American narrative.

Though Puig, like many other prominent writers, had lived outside Latin America for some time, and his writing deals with issues in contemporary culture and society that cross national boundaries, his work is also firmly rooted in the realities of his own country (Argentina) and Latin America as a whole. He was born on 28 December 1932 in General Villegas, where he spent his formative years with his family. His father, Baldomero Puig, was a businessman, and his mother, María Elena Delledonne de Puig, was a chemist. His early schooling and his introduction to the world of films, which had a great impact on his writing, took place in General Villegas, a provincial town in the pampas that became a model for the setting in his first two novels, *La traición de Rita Hayworth* and *Boquitas pintadas* (1969; translated as *Heartbreak Tango*, 1973).

Puig's attachment to films began even before he went to grade school. As he remarks in an autobiographical piece in *Review* (1971-1972), sometime in 1936 he had "started going to the movies almost every evening at six o'clock." His interest in Hollywood films, especially the melodramas and musicals of the 1930s and 1940s that figure as important thematic and formal motifs in *La traición de Rita Hayworth*, *The Buenos Aires Affair* (1973; translated, 1976), *El beso de la mujer araña*, and *Pubis angelical* (1979; translated, 1986), continued, especially during the time he spent in Buenos Aires as a high-school boarder: "School was awful; the children were cruel. I missed my mother tremendously. The only consolation was the Sunday matinee at a first-run theatre." Throughout his secondary education (and, presumably, even when his parents moved the family to Buenos Aires in 1949) his moviegoing schedule did not change.

Though after high school (at his parents' insistence) he tried studying architecture for a brief time and then switched to philosophy at the Universidad de Buenos Aires, Puig eventually decided he wanted to become a film director. In the mid 1950s he won a scholarship to study in Rome, where he studied at the Centro Sperimentale di Cinematografia. He also had a chance to work with some directors at Cinecittà during this period, as well as some years later (1961-1962), when he returned to Rome and translated film subtitles. During the late 1950s and early 1960s Puig also taught Spanish and Italian and worked as a translator in London and Rome (1956-1957), had jobs as a dishwasher in London and Stockholm (1958-1959), and worked as an assistant film director in Europe and Argentina (1957-1960). During the mid 1960s he came to the United States and worked as a clerk for Air France at what was then Idlewild Airport (1963-1967). It was during this period that he began his writing career.

The shift to narrative fiction came by way of trying to write film scripts, first in English (during his first stay in Rome in the 1950s) and then in Spanish (after his 1960 return to Argentina). He began what would later become *La traición de Rita Hayworth* in March 1962. In the *Review* piece, Puig says he was trying to write a script "about something I had really experienced.... In order to put some distance between me and the autobiographical stuff, I planned to write a description (for my exclusive use) of each leading character.... Suddenly the voice of an aunt came out quite clearly.... The description of my aunt was supposed to take one page, but it took almost twenty-five! It was all her talking, all in the first person, and I could play with it all I wanted. By the second day it was clearly a novel."

Though Puig finished *La traición de Rita Hayworth* by February 1965, and in December of that same year it was a finalist in the Seix Barral novel contest, it was not published until three years later. Though publication contracts had been signed as early as 1965, censorship problems initially presented serious obstacles. Puig describes the 1968 publication of the novel as the result of the "risk" taken by a small Buenos Aires publishing house (Alvarez). Just a year or so later, however, the book not only became a best-seller but was also named one of the best novels of 1968-1969 by *Le Monde*.

La traición de Rita Hayworth deals with small-town life in the Argentine provinces (the town is called Coronel Vallejos) and focuses on the life of Toto, son of Mita and Berto Casals. With the exception of the final chapter, dated 1933 and temporally displaced from a position at the beginning of the novel to the end, the novel's chapters progress chronologically from 1933, when Toto is born, to 1948, when he is a high-school student. However, since the story as such is told mostly through spoken and written monologues and dialogues in which different characters reveal themselves, Toto's central position emerges only gradually. The reader soon discovers, however, that attention is focused on Toto not only through his own three chapters (his two interior monologues at ages six and nine, and his high-school composition at age fourteen), but also through the chapters of other characters whose revelations about him and his family help to fill in some of the gaps of their story.

In a 1977 interview with Katherine Bouman, Puig asserted that the story is essentially his own: "Ninety-five percent of the novel is real. Sometimes for the sake of economy two characters from the films [that Toto relives or reworks into fantasies in his monologues] became one; but it was about me, and the people close to me. The characters were the family that didn't have time for me as a child." Toto is a character who is obsessed with, and regularly escapes into fantasies based on, films he has seen with his mother, who shares his fascination with the era's films, especially musicals and melodramas. Puig has drawn attention to the important influence of Hollywood films on Argentine culture in the 1930s and 1940s, the era on which he focuses in *La traición de Rita Hayworth* and *Boquitas pintadas*. He suggested in the same interview, moreover, that those films provided "escape from an impossible system of machismo, aggression and dominance."

Though other characters also serve to reveal the strictures of the social system to which Puig refers, Toto, as the future artist/homosexual, is the principal subject through whom this critique is developed. Moreover, in his siesta-hour movie fantasies (chapters 3 and 6), in which he often expresses fear of his father and devo-

detalles; a continuación quedó callada. La joven se disponía a hacer cualquier comentario para evitar el silencio cuando la visitante, con voz más alta de lo acostumbrado en ella, pidió que la cena fuera lo más tarde posible, porque tenía intención de hablar antes con el director de cierta galería municipal, y no sabría cuando la recibiría en su despacho; agregó

só, dejaría sola a la visitante unos minutos porque debía ir hasta la azotea, donde había olvidado pañales tendidos en la soga. La mujer quedó sola, miró hacia el balcón, cuya puerta de acceso había permanecido abierta. El niño seguía llorando. La mujer no fue hasta el cuarto contiguo a verlo, en cambio se dirigió al baño, revisó el botiquín y halló disimulada tras el paquete de algodón una vasija de jalea anticonceptiva. La destapó para olerla. Volvió a taparla y la dejó en su lugar, cubierta debidamente por el paquete de algodón. De allí fue a la cama matrimonial. Descorrió totalmente la sábana de arriba, aparecieron dos vellos negros crespos, atribuibles a la zona púbica. Volvió la sábana a su lugar. Miró en derredor, sobre una silla yacía aún el piyama de hombre. La visitante lo revisó, olió el saco y después el pantalón.

Se oyó ruido en el pasillo, reapareció la joven con los pañales, humedecidos por la llovizna; encendió el horno de la cocina y allí los colocó. Pidió disculpas por la tardanza y por el fastidio que ocasionaba el llanto del niño. La joven madre lo tomó en brazos y lo mostró a la visitante, *le* preguntó además si ya habían precisado con su marido la hora en que se reunirían para cenar. La visitante miraba al niño como si nunca hubiese visto otro en su vida, respondió que el joven le había pedido antes de colgar que entre ellas dos fijaran los ~~detalles; agregó~~ que el niño le parecía hermosísimo. La joven madre dijo que debía cambiar inmediatamente al bebé, y *volvió a ofrecer a* ~~repitió si~~ la visitante ~~lo quería~~ otro vaso de leche para acompañar la tajada de torta ya cortada. La visitante inesperadamente aceptó. La joven madre *se sorprendió más aún* ~~cuando aquélla le pidió una pastilla para dormir. Como avergonzada, la mujer acotó que si bien esa noche había bebido demasiado, ya habían pasado muchas horas y no se produciría conflicto alguno entre alcohol y barbitúricos.~~ Tragó *la pastilla* con un sorbo de leche. La joven madre sacó del horno los pañales ya secos, los extendió sobre la cama matrimonial y allí puso al niño. Pidió a la visitante que se sentara junto a ella para no darle la espalda durante la operación y le rogó que le contara algo de sus planes artísticos, pero en seguida se corrigió, pues eso debería contarlo durante la cena y quería evitarle repeticiones tediosas. Le pidió en cambio que le hablara de las cosas que le causaban miedo. La visitante, sentada en la cabecera de la cama y con la cabeza apoyada contra el respaldo de seda capitoné, dijo que le causaban miedo las tormentas. La joven no permitió

Page from the typescript for The Buenos Aires Affair *(by permission of Editorial Joaquín Mortiz)*

tion to his mother, or in his high-school composition about his favorite movie (chapter 13), which becomes a personal oedipal drama woven from scenes of idyllic romance and conflictive encounter, readers find virtually all the thematic threads that run through the other characters' chapters as well. Questions about social roles and sexual identity, and about the problematic nature of cultural myths and social norms (men must be Don Juan/macho figures; women must be submissive), act as an implicit critique of the established order with which Puig has sought to take issue.

More specifically, Puig remarked in a 1977 interview with Ronald Christ that in the "first book, I was dealing with the oppression of women, with a latent homosexual child growing up, and I didn't want to make any judgment about those cases." Though he claims that his initial aim was merely to describe such realities, he has later agreed with interviewers that his early work, with its potentially critical emphasis, prepared the way for more explicit social criticism in other novels. For example, he emphasized to Christ that he initially "didn't understand why the women were like that or why the child was being modeled into a homosexual.... When I wrote *Rita Hayworth*, I still believed in Clark Gable as a force of Nature. I thought it was a cruel Nature that had made this strong man and these weak Harlows but that it was, in fact, Nature's law. Now I am convinced that Clark Gable is an historical-cultural product, not Nature's creature."

That Puig's critical project is serious has not always been understood by his readers. For example, given the "trivial" nature of the story told in *La traición de Rita Hayworth* (it is a simple story of a family living in the provinces, where nothing very important happens and where ordinary small-town characters do no more than talk about themselves or write inconsequential pages), one might not immediately see the social, cultural, and literary issues raised. However, from *La traición de Rita Hayworth* on, Puig's work has exemplified a radical questioning of both social institutions and artistic (more specifically, literary) values. This is the kind of questioning that has become associated with contemporary Latin-American writing as a whole.

Puig's novels are works of literary experimentation as well as social and cultural criticism. *Boquitas pintadas* and *The Buenos Aires Affair* extend the challenge to established literary conventions and cultural hierarchies a good deal further than his first novel, as they reveal more pointedly the complexity of his experimentation with narrative structure and language. However, *La traición de Rita Hayworth* begins to reveal that his focus is as much on literary matters as on social questions; his concern is as much with conventions of fiction writing as with issues of modern culture. The story in Puig's first novel is told by the characters themselves, who speak or write in their own voices throughout the novel's sixteen chapters. *La traición de Rita Hayworth* is a collection of languages derived from the quotidian and popular models that have shaped modern Argentine culture. Many of them, as they are used by Argentines of the period Puig has in mind in the novel, can be considered "alienated languages" (Puig's term) that have been appropriated in his characters' speech and writing.

These forms of discourse play a crucial role because the identities of the characters in *La traición de Rita Hayworth* are created not so much by the incidents to which they refer as by the language they produce, and which produces them, as they speak or write. As Puig suggested in a 1972 interview with Emir Rodríguez Monegal, these were the only models available to first-generation Argentines (the sons and daughters of Italian or Spanish immigrants), who, lacking an appropriate and original linguistic model at home, turned to movies, radio, sports and fashion magazines, and popular literature, fashioning themselves on those models. Puig's representation of the popular language of the 1930s and 1940s, which is the language of *La traición de Rita Hayworth* and *Boquitas pintadas*, dramatically reveals this influence.

Puig's interest in the forms and languages of popular culture, as well as the world of films, is evident from the modes of writing and speech he incorporated into his texts (tango lyrics, fashion magazine columns and interviews, church confessions, personal diary rhetoric, sports vocabulary, and official medical, legal, and police prose), as well as the generic models with which he works (serial fiction and the detective novel). Thus chapters in *La traición de Rita Hayworth* present Toto's high-school composition about his favorite Hollywood movie, his friend Esther's sentimentalized and dramatic diary prose, his small-town neighbor Herminia's pseudo-intellectual notebook ruminations, his mother's friend Choli's fashion-magazine vocabulary, and his classmate Cobito's voice as a gangster-movie hoodlum. These, as well as other instances of popular

Puig circa 1974 (photograph by J. E. Lamarca)

discourse represented in the novel, reveal both the characters' personal fantasies and emotional situations and the borrowed cultural models that shape their perception of the world.

Boquitas pintadas not only plays with the narrative devices and temporality of serial fiction, its chapters—called "entregas" (episodes)—are also headed by lyrics from popular tangos. Its story, temporally deformed by a variety of chronological displacements of episodes that resemble the devices of mystery fiction, is told through narration in third person, stream of consciousness, dialogue, "hidden dialogue" (in which one character's voice is heard but another's is inferred), official documents, and letters. *The Buenos Aires Affair*, subtitled *Novela policial* (detective novel), works with the conventions of detective fiction, has passages from Hollywood movie scripts as its chapters' epigraphs, and uses written documents, interior monologues, dialogues, and footnotes, among other techniques, to tell its story.

Though the dialogue form dominates Puig's next five novels, none of those texts follows a completely homogeneous narrative plan. In *El beso de la mujer araña* there are also interior monologues, hidden dialogue, official documents, and a set of authorial footnotes used to advance its narrative; *Pubis angelical* also has first-person diary texts, omniscient third-person narration, and stream of consciousness segments; several letters and documents form the epilogue of *Maldición eterna a quien lea estas páginas* (1980; also published as *Eternal Curse on the Reader of These Pages*, 1982), the rest of which is in dialogue form; *Sangre de amor correspondido* (1982; translated as *Blood of Requited Love*, 1984) combines monologue, hidden dialogue, and third-person narration with its dialogues; and *Cae la noche tropical* (1988; translated as *Tropical Night Falling*, 1991) incorporates letters, newspaper articles, and police documents among its narrative forms. The display of technical virtuosity in Puig's novels draws attention to the procedures of narrative fiction. It demonstrates one of the ways Puig's writing challenges conventional ideas about the forms and languages appropriate for works of fiction. Indeed, readers can hardly remain unaware that they are reading works of narrative as they grapple with the structural complexity and discursive heterogeneity of his novels.

Boquitas pintadas and *The Buenos Aires Affair*, structurally the most complex of Puig's texts, tell complicated stories filled with soap-opera intrigues and melodramatic scenarios typical of the popular genres named in their subtitles (*Folletín* [serial novel] and *Novela policial*). Each story seems to match the structure that shapes it, and each story calls attention to Puig's popular sources. *Boquitas pintadas* matches up the serial novel with the Don Juan figure; *The Buenos Aires Affair* plots out a psychosexual drama in the form of a detective novel. Though Puig's treatment of popular literature genres in these novels and his presentation of the characters' speech and writing in his first novel have been read as parodies, he has often asserted a different attitude and intention in those works. For example, he remarked in the Christ interview that "parody is a word I don't trust too much because it carries some degree of scorn. Very seldom do I let myself go in the direction of scorn. What's more, there's a difficulty in distinguishing the degrees of parody in my works. Sometimes I deal with parodic characters; that is, characters who are mimicking some kind of remote model, and they are a parody in themselves. It's not me who's doing the parody. Then I've been told that *Heartbreak Tango* [*Boquitas pintadas*] is a parody of serials and that *The Buenos Aires Affair* is a parody of detective stories. That's not right. At least that was not my intention. I like those two underrated genres and I tried to use them seriously, downright artistically."

Puig's writing takes a radical position with respect to such "underrated genres." His playful version of a serial novel in *Boquitas pintadas* rescues the popular form from its "lowly" position as a subliterary genre, transforming it into the foundation for an exemplary work of experimental fiction. His manipulation of the conventions of detective fiction give a new (and decidedly "high") turn to that popular model in *The Buenos Aires Affair*. Both of these texts lay bare the narrative mechanisms that support the popular forms. Yet the reflexive turn given their conventions produces texts that represent some of the most radical practices of contemporary fiction and readily lend themselves to the vocabulary and theories proposed by modern criticism.

Both *Boquitas pintadas* and *The Buenos Aires Affair* emphasize the process of reading, which Puig himself likened to a process of seduction. (In fact, he stated on several occasions that he has written each novel with a specific reader in mind. Though he did not identify any of those figures, he claimed that his purpose was to convince each of those readers of some point, perhaps even to seduce them to see things his way.) This may well be the appropriate metaphor to describe the author/reader relation in these two novels, and even in *La traición de Rita Hayworth*. Their narrative structures follow and also play with the procedures of mystery fiction, making use of temporal deformation to produce radical disjunctions between story and plot. Such disjunctions involve the reader in activities of detection and, in the process, also emphasize the novels' reflexive qualities. In *La traición de Rita Hayworth* Puig places Berto's (Toto's father's) 1933 chapter at the end of the novel, instead of at the beginning with others from its own temporal frame. This displacement creates both the illusion of mystery and the suggestion of a final solution to the novel. It creates a problematic turn for a text that otherwise proceeds in an ordered, though in its own way also difficult, fashion.

Boquitas pintadas is structured around multiple narrative inversions; they occur within individual chapters and also span its sixteen episodes. Key pieces of information are alternately denied and supplied to the reader, whose activity thus becomes an effort to fill in gaps of information and keep track of multiple narrative mysteries throughout the entire reading process. As its subtitle suggests, *The Buenos Aires Affair* follows the conventional narrative inversion of the detective genre (we start with the "scene of the crime" and move back in time to an "explanation" before moving forward to the final "solution"), while also turning that formulaic model upside-down so as to transform it into something quite original. In addition, the fragmentary nature of these texts (most of the episodes of *Boquitas pintadas* and the chapters of *The Buenos Aires Affair* comprise several different narrative methods in separate, juxtaposed textual fragments) creates a disjointed narrative that the reader can reconstruct as a more or less complete, chronological story only at the end of the novel.

The stories told in *Boquitas pintadas* and *The Buenos Aires Affair* are matched with narrative models and techniques that seem to seduce and betray the reader, whose position thus comes to resemble that of some of the fictional characters in the narratives themselves. For example, *Boquitas pintadas* tells a tale of simultaneous and serial small-town seductions and betrayals. Its central character is a provincial Don Juan (Juan Carlos), a master of manipulation and deception, whose attitude and actions are virtually duplicated in the behavior of the other main characters in the novel. According to Puig the models for these characters were people from Villegas, where he began to write his second novel when he returned in 1967 to Argentina from Europe and the United States and caught up on the news about many of the people among whom he had once lived.

Boquitas pintadas is a tale of lives intertwined in passionate illusion and treacherous action, strategies aimed at pleasure and schemes designed for power, in a small Argentine town in the 1930s and 1940s. The time and town are the same as for *La traición de Rita Hayworth*. In the first novel readers see the beginning of Puig's exploration of popular myths and social forms from inside a particular family; in his second novel he expands the frame to include the social network of the whole town, represented by characters from different social strata. However, the working-class as well as the middle-class characters are equally affected by the popular cultural models (soap operas, tangos) and myths (the Don Juan/macho figure) through which they fashion (and also betray) their own lives and loves.

In *The Buenos Aires Affair*, the protagonists (Leo, a sadist, and Gladys, a masochist) form the paradigmatically criminal couple of the popular detective novel. Puig sets this novel principally in Buenos Aires (the settings of his novels follow the general geographical path taken by his own life), where the protagonists are born, meet, and become entangled sexually and, apparently, criminally with one another. In telling their stories by focusing on the psychosexual details of their biographies, which include scenes of sexual violence, and in seeing those details and scenes lead toward a criminal plot that fits the conventions of popular detective fiction, Puig plays with the connections between popular ideas about psychoanalysis and popular literature.

Puig also begins to address questions about art and politics more explicitly than in his earlier works. He confronts issues of artistic value not only in his recuperation of the detective novel but also in the development of his main characters. Gladys is an artist, whose original attachment to "low" forms of culture is emphasized by the novel, which also charts her development into an important figure of modern "high" art. Leo is an art critic, whose involvement with "high" currents ultimately brings him into contact with Gladys, his criminal and sexual partner.

Puig develops considerations of cultural and political matters more explicitly in *El beso de la mujer araña*, *Pubis angelical*, and *Maldición eterna a quien lea estas páginas*, the three novels that follow. In *The Buenos Aires Affair*, considered pornographic and banned in the 1970s by both Juan Perón and then the military government (Puig again left Argentina when it was first banned), Puig presents both ends of the political spectrum in a critical light by including in the protagonists' biographical sketches brief references to their political opinions or activities (Gladys is anti-Castro and Leo is anti-Perón). The discussion of political matters becomes, however, one of the primary concerns in *El beso de la mujer araña*, whose protagonists virtually incarnate its two principal thematic poles: politics and homosexuality. The story deals with the relationship between two prisoners—Valentín, a political activist, and Molina, a homosexual—who share an Argentine prison cell for six months in 1975. Puig wrote the novel after leaving Argentina in 1973 and returning to New York, though he had begun his research for it while still in Buenos Aires, where he was able to meet with some political prisoners.

The dialogues between Valentín, the proponent of Marxist political theory and activity, and Molina, the spokesman for sentimentality, popular culture, and homosexuality, develop around the latter's narration of Hollywood films to his cellmate. The film stories act as a mediator between the two, eventually allowing for some kind of reconciliation between what appear to be such radically opposed characters and ideologies. Some of the films narrated by Molina are real 1940s movies (such as *Cat People* and *I Walked with a Zombie*), while others are inventions by Puig, who did considerable research for the book. Each of the protagonists seems determined to seduce the other into seeing things his own way;

Dust jacket for the 1976 novel that was adapted for the screen as Kiss of the Spider Woman

each seems to want to instruct his cellmate about his own beliefs and desires. The characters' talks about the movies narrated by Molina or the political theories and activities described by Valentín are plotted so as to captivate readers through devices of serial fiction (stories are interrupted and information is withheld to create suspense). The dialogue between author and reader becomes most explicit in the footnotes, where an explanation of the origins and nature of homosexuality is developed.

Though the notes were not meant to advance the fictional story, they are an important component of the novel. They signal the seriousness with which Puig considered contemporary cultural issues and the intellectual climate surrounding the production and reception of works of literature in which such issues are explored. The success of the novel clearly speaks not only of the power of Puig's fiction and style but also of the public's interest in the issues about which he chose to write. The novel spawned the acclaimed film *Kiss of the Spider Woman*, and Puig also adapted it for the stage, publishing it in 1983 with his first work written directly for the theater, *Bajo un manto de estrellas* (translated as *Under a Mantle of Stars*, 1985).

Pubis angelical, Puig's fifth novel, goes a bit further to expose, but not necessarily to resolve, questions about politics, history, psychology, and sexuality, while also continuing to utilize and recuperate popular-culture models. When he was still working on the novel, Puig explained in the conversation with Christ that in this phase of his work he was interested in the clash between political ideals and personal needs: "even if there were a perfect Marxist society, where everything was shared in the best human spirit, there would still be one capital—physical beauty, sexual beauty. That wouldn't be shared.... There are many ways to hunger in life and we're conscious of the need for food, for a roof, but repression has stopped the need for sex from being clarified." Besides fashioning a science-fiction fantasy as a model of how such needs might be met in a future society, Puig has the female protagonist's fantasies, diary monologues, and talks with two other characters revolve around male-female relationships, politics, history, and contemporary culture as she tries to sort out her own desires and duties.

The main character is Ana, who is hospitalized in Mexico in 1975. As in *La traición de Rita Hayworth* and *El beso de la mujer araña*, much of the novel's action is discursive. The narrative presents Ana's diary pages and her alternating conversations with two friends (a feminist and a political activist lawyer) as part of the same narrative frame. This narrative, however, alternates with another, which, the author himself has suggested, plots out an unconscious story line of which Ana is vaguely aware and which is told by an omniscient narrator. The diary texts and dialogues openly thematize political and cultural questions, while the narrative over which Ana has no control may well act out, as it were, some of the protagonist's fantasies, fears, and desires. The novel thus shifts between an essentially realistic setting (Ana in the hospital in 1975) and one that, as it unfolds in its own chronological order, resembles first a 1940s Hollywood romantic melodrama and later a science-fiction adventure.

The dialogues between Molina and Valentín and the authorial footnotes in *El beso de la mujer araña*, combined with the explicit discussions of the recent political history of Argentina, Lacanian theories of psychoanalysis, women's liberation, and contemporary culture in the dialogues of Ana and her two friends in *Pubis angelical*, suggest that Puig seems to have shifted toward open declarations of his themes via his characters' explicit statements. Indeed, as the dialogues in *Maldición eterna a quien lea estas páginas* seem to follow this pattern (for example, the two protagonists discuss the Argentine political situation in general and specific terms), Puig's sixth novel appears to support further, if not solidify definitively, such a reading of his work's development. While this trend toward overt discussion of political and cultural issues has become a characteristic feature of some fictions that appear deliberately to draw attention to their own thematic directions, what Puig develops in his novels is a debate, not a conclusive statement, about each issue.

In *Maldición eterna a quien lea estas páginas* the two protagonists (Larry, a twenty-six-year-old former history teacher, and Ramírez, a seventy-four-year-old Argentine exile) talk throughout the novel. Though the dialogue form responds to Puig's technical preferences for developing certain thematic topics, the device in this novel also derives from the material on which the text is based. The novel is presumably a translation of interview materials in English that Puig gathered in talks with a young man he met in New York in 1977, where Puig had returned to live after residing for a time in Mexico. Puig developed a heart problem, and since the Mexico City altitude would be detrimental to his health and thus prohibited his return there, he decided to stay in New York. His doctor advised swimming as an exercise, and, at the public pool on Carmine Street, he met the man he was to befriend and interview.

Puig shaped the original dialogue into the story of the relationship between Larry and Ramírez, who talk about and analyze themselves and one another. The fictional situation is a simple one: set in 1978, the novel presents a series of conversations between Ramírez, recently arrived in New York and bound to a wheelchair, and Larry, who becomes his companion by taking him for walks in Greenwich Village. However, the dialogue becomes a confusing exchange of conflicting memories and stories about whose truth value the novel gives no definitive or final statement. Indeed, *Maldición eterna a quien lea estas páginas* (whose title supposedly refers to a phrase Larry deciphers by accident while scanning some of Ramírez's books from his time spent as a political prisoner, and whose meaning remains obscure) implicitly questions the possibility of establishing an authoritative conclusion to the debatable issues of politics and culture.

Like *Maldición eterna a quien lea estas páginas*, *Sangre de amor correspondido* also emphasizes the difficulty of fixing truth through memory or language, the virtual impossibility of telling a completely truthful story. Set in Brazil (Puig lived in Rio de Janeiro at the time), the story is not so much a narrative as a set of scenes that are retold, revised, and reperformed, so that the reader (and also the characters, it seems) can never be quite sure what has happened. Though the original truth of the scenes remains inaccessi-

Puig in 1984 (photograph copyright by Jerry Bauer)

ble, enough information is provided in monologues, dialogues, and third-person segments to establish the central relationship between Josemar—a small-town figure one might connect to Don Juan types in Puig's earlier novels (for example, Toto's cousin Héctor in *La traición de Rita Hayworth* and Juan Carlos in *Boquitas pintadas*)—and Maria da Gloria, the girl he "deflowers" in a scene that is contradictorily retold as their tale of adolescent passion is remembered, relived, and repeated throughout the novel.

Cae la noche tropical, Puig's last novel, published two years before his untimely death in 1990, is also situated in Brazil, where the novel's principal characters—Nidia and Luci, sisters, the former eighty-three and the latter eighty-one years old—are presented. The discourse of gossip and the intricacies of interpersonal and familial relations inform the novel, which is set mainly in Rio de Janeiro and whose action unfolds during the last few months of 1987 and ends in February 1988. The spoken and epistolary dialogues between the sisters and other characters close to them sustain much of the novel. Its discourse is that of everyday conversation; its topics, like those in some of Puig's other novels, might be characterized as somewhat trivial: Nidia and Luci's colloquial discourse focuses on incidents and themes characteristic of the *novela rosa* (romance novel) and soap operas. The story of old-age concerns and the characterization of the elderly women through their poignant and nostalgic ruminations seem to take Puig's writing to the end of a "story" his novels began to tell in *La traición de Rita Hayworth*.

Puig's novelistic "story" was begun, however, not as the basis for a literary project but as an attempt to produce a successful script for the cinema. Indeed, the emphasis on direct discourse in his last and some of his other novels may remind one that Puig began his literary career after trying to write screenplays, one of which turned into his first novel. Though he established himself as a novelist, he had what he called a "forced return" to script writing when he was asked to do the screenplay for *Boquitas pintadas*. The Argentine director Leopoldo Torre Nilsson had requested the rights to the novel in 1973, and though Puig felt uncomfortable with the project, as he explains in the autobiographical prologue to two recent screenplays (*La cara del villano; Recuerdo de Tijuana* [Face of the Scoundrel; Memory of Tijuana, 1985]), he did adapt his novel for the screen. He also remarks in the 1985 prologue that, even though Torre Nilsson had allowed him complete creative freedom, he felt uncomfortable with the task of adaptation, since it required him to synthesize and summarize, to follow the dictates of the film, rather than the literary, form.

Until his death from heart failure on 22 July 1990, Puig continued to write works of fiction and drama, and to collaborate on film projects, which undoubtedly would have found audiences in Europe, the United States, and Latin America. Puig became a truly international literary figure, as well as a celebrated author in Latin America. His challenge to conventional notions about literary genres and languages, as well as his call for an examination of the cultural norms that shape modern society, has been recognized as part of an important critical current in modern writing. Puig's work has refashioned some of the rules for reading and writing works of fiction. His texts have changed the way people think about literature and culture. Writing such as Puig's assures the vitality of modern fiction and its future.

Interviews:
Emir Rodríguez Monegal, "El folletín rescatado," *Revista de la Universidad de México*, 27 (October 1972): 25-35;

Saúl Sosnowski, "Entrevista [a Manuel Puig]," *Hispamérica*, 3 (May 1973): 69-80;

Suzanne Jill Levine, "Author and Translator: A Discussion of *Heartbreak Tango*," *Translation*, 2, nos. 1-2 (1974): 32-41;

Danubio Torres Fierro, "Conversación con Manuel Puig: La redención de la cursilería," *Eco*, 28 (March 1975): 507-515;

Katherine Bouman, "Manuel Puig at the University of Missouri-Columbia," *American Hispanist*, 2, no. 7 (1977): 11-12;

Marcelo Coddou, "Seis preguntas a Manuel Puig sobre su última novela: *El beso de la mujer araña*," *American Hispanist*, 2, no. 18 (1977): 12-13;

Ronald Christ, "An Interview with Manuel Puig," *Partisan Review*, 44 (1977): 52-61;

Christ, "Interview with Manuel Puig," *Christopher Street* (April 1979): 25-31;

Nora Catelli, "Entrevista con Manuel Puig: Una narrativa de lo melífluo," *Quimera* (April 1982): 22-25;

Jorgelina Corbatta, "Encuentros con Manuel Puig," *Revista iberoamericana*, 49 (April-September 1983): 591-620.

References:
Pamela Bacarisse, *The Necessary Dream: A Study of the Novels of Manuel Puig* (Cardiff: University of Wales Press, 1988);

Alicia Borinsky, "Castration: Artifices; Notes on the Writing of Manuel Puig," *Georgia Review*, 29 (Spring 1975): 95-114;

René Alberto Campos, *Espejos: la textura cinemática en La traición de Rita Hayworth* (Madrid: Pliegos, 1985);

Lori Chamberlain, "The Subject in Exile: Puig's *Eternal Curse on the Reader of These Pages*," *Novel*, 20 (1987): 260-275;

Marcelo Coddou, "Complejidad estructural de *El beso de la mujer araña*, de Manuel Puig," *Inti*, 7 (Spring 1978): 15-27;

Michelle Débax, Milagros Ezquerro, and Michèle Ramond, "La marginalité des personnages et ses effets sur le discours dans *El beso de la mujer araña* de Manuel Puig," *Imprévue*, 1 (1980): 91-112;

Roberto Echevarren and Jaime Giordano, *Manuel Puig: montaje y alteridad del sujeto* (Santiago, Chile: Maitén, 1985);

Juan Armando Epple, "'The Buenos Aires Affair' y la estructura de la novela policíaca," *Estudios filológicos*, 10 (1974): 43-65;

Milagros Ezquerro, "Le fonctionnement sémiologique des personnages dans *Bajo un manto de estrellas* de Manuel Puig," *Caravelle/Cahiers du monde hispanique et luso-brésilien*, 40 (1983): 47-58;

James Ray Green, Jr., "*El beso de la mujer araña*: Sexual Repression and Textual Repression," in *LA CHISPA '81: Selected Proceedings*, edited by Gilbert Paolini (New Orleans: Tulane University, Louisiana Conference on Hispanic Languages and Literatures, 1981), pp. 133-139;

Bella Jozef, "Manuel Puig: Reflexión al nivel de la enunciación," *Nueva narrativa hispanomericana*, 4 (January and September 1974): 111-115;

Lucille Kerr, *Suspended Fictions: Reading Novels by Manuel Puig* (Urbana: University of Illinois Press, 1987);

Bart L. Lewis, "Narrative Structure in Manuel Puig's *Maldición eterna a quien lea estas páginas*," *Hispanic Journal*, 7, no. 2 (1986): 81-85;

Raquel Linenberg-Fressard, "La motivation des noms de personnage dans *Pubis angelical* de Manuel Puig," *Imprévue*, 1 (1986): 99-109;

Alfred J. MacAdam, "Manuel Puig's Chronicles of Provincial Life," *Revista hispánica moderna*, 36 (1970-1971): 50-65;

Sharon Magnarelli, "Manuel Puig's *La traición de Rita Hayworth*: Betrayed by the Cross-Stitch," in her *The Lost Rib: Female Characters in the Spanish-American Novel* (Lewisburg, Pa.: Bucknell University Press, 1985), pp. 117-146;

Francine R. Masiello, "Jail House Flicks: Projections by Manuel Puig," *Symposium*, 32 (Spring 1978): 15-24;

Stephanie Merrim, "For a New (Psychological) Novel in the Works of Manuel Puig," *Novel*, 17 (Winter 1984): 141-157;

Marta Morello Frosch, "Usos y abusos de la cultura popular: *Pubis angelical* de Manuel Puig," in *Literature and Popular Culture in the Hispanic World: A Symposium*, edited by Rose S. Minc (Gaithersburg, Md.: Montclair State College/Ediciones Hispamérica, 1981), pp. 31-41;

Angelo Morino, "Tanghi e pellicole hollywoodiane nei romanzi di Manuel Puig," *Belfagor*, 32 (1977): 395-408;

Elías Miguel Muñoz, *El discurso utópico de la sexualidad en Manuel Puig* (Madrid: Pliegos, 1987);

José Miguel Oviedo, "La doble exposición de Manuel Puig," *Eco*, 31 (October 1977): 607-626;

Jorge Panesi, "Manuel Puig: las relaciones peligrosas," *Revista iberoamericana*, 49, no. 125 (October-December 1983): 903-917;

Gustavo Pellón, "Manuel Puig's Contradictory Strategy: Kitsch Paradigms *versus* Paradigmatic Structures in *El beso de la mujer araña* and *Pubis angelical*," *Symposium*, 36 (1983): 186-201;

Ricardo Piglia, "Clase media: cuerpo y destino (Una lectura de *La traición de Rita Hayworth* de Manuel Puig)," in *Nueva novela latinoamericana*, two volumes, edited by Jorge Lafforgue (Buenos Aires: Paidós, 1972), II: 350-362;

Julio Rodríguez-Luis, "*Boquitas pintadas* ¿Folletín unanimista?," *Sin nombre*, 5, no. 1 (1974): 50-56;

Emir Rodríquez Monegal, "A Literary Myth Exploded," *Review*, 4-5 (Winter 1971-Spring 1972): 56-64;

Severo Sarduy, "Notas a las notas a las notas . . . : A propósito de Manuel Puig," *Revista iberoamericana*, 37, nos. 76-77 (1971): 555-567;

Flora H. Schiminovich, "El juego narcisista y ficcional en *Sangre de amor correspondido*," *Discurso literario*, 1, no. 2 (1984): 295-301;

Jonathan Tittler, "*Betrayed by Rita Hayworth*: The Androgynous Text," in his *Narrative Irony in the Contemporary Spanish American Novel* (Ithaca, N.Y.: Cornell University Press, 1984), pp. 78-100;

World Literature Today, special Puig issue, 65 (Autumn 1991);

Frances Wyers, "Manuel Puig at the Movies," *Hispanic Review*, 49 (Spring 1981): 163-181;

George Yúdice, "*El beso de la mujer araña* y *Pubis angelical*: Entre el placer y el saber," in *Literature and Popular Culture in the Hispanic World: A Symposium*, pp. 43-57;

Carlos Raúl Yujnovsky, "*Boquitas pintadas* ¿folletín?," *Nuevos Aires*, 8 (1972): 49-58.

Augusto Roa Bastos
(13 June 1917 -)

Randolph D. Pope
Washington University in St. Louis

BOOKS: *El ruiseñor de la aurora, y otros poemas* (Asunción: Nacional, 1942);

El trueno entre las hojas (Buenos Aires: Losada, 1953);

Hijo de hombre (Buenos Aires: Losada, 1960); translated by Rachel Caffyn as *Son of Man* (London: Gollancz, 1965);

El naranjal ardiente: Nocturno paraguayo, 1947-1949 (Asunción: Diálogo/Cuadernos de la Piririta, 1960);

El baldío (Buenos Aires: Losada, 1966);

Los pies sobre el agua (Buenos Aires: América Latina, 1967);

Madera quemada (Santiago, Chile: Universitaria, 1967);

Moriencia (Caracas: Monte Avila, 1969);

El génesis de los Apapokura-Guaraní (Asunción: Alcor, 1971);

Cuerpo presente y otros textos (Buenos Aires: América Latina, 1972);

Yo, el Supremo (Buenos Aires: Siglo XXI, 1974); translated by Helen Lane as *I, the Supreme* (New York: Vintage, 1987);

El pollito de fuego (Buenos Aires: Flor, 1974);

Los juegos, 2 volumes (Buenos Aires: Flor, 1979, 1981);

Lucha hasta el alba (Asunción: Arte Nuevo, 1979);

Antología personal (Mexico City: Nueva Imagen, 1980);

Rafael Barrett (Stockholm: Estudios Latinoamericanos, 1981);

Contar un cuento (Buenos Aires: Kapelusz, 1984);

Escritos politicos (Buenos Aires: Estudios de Literatura Latinoamericana, 1984);

Carta abierta a mi pueblo (Buenos Aires: Frente Paraguayo, 1986);

El tiranosaurio del Paraguay da sus ultimas boqueadas (Buenos Aires: Frente Paraguayo, 1986);

Semana del autor: Augusto Roa Bastos, by Roa Bastos and others (Madrid: ICI Cultura Hispánica, 1986).

OTHER: "La narrativa paraguaya en el contexto de la narrativa Hispanoamericana actual," in *Augusto Roa Bastos y la producción cultural americana*, edited by Saúl Sosnowski (Buenos Aires: Flor, 1986), pp. 119-138.

SELECTED PERIODICAL PUBLICATIONS—
UNCOLLECTED: "Silenciario," *Cuadernos Hispanoamericanos*, 399 (September 1983): 5-19;

"El dilema de la integración iberoamericana," *Cuadernos Hispanoamericanos*, 427 (January 1986): 21-39.

Augusto Roa Bastos has created in his many short stories and two novels a monumental, complex, interrelated, and vast world. With a rich, experimental language he rewrites the history of his native land, Paraguay. While Roa's description of the violence, injustice, and repression of the colonial society of Latin America has many antecedents, his interweaving of European and Guaraní myths, the native culture of Paraguay, a depth and openness of analysis, and the diversity of his literary craft have assured him a position among the best writers of Latin America.

Roa was born in Asunción, but grew up in Iturbe, a provincial village where his father worked as a clerk on a sugar plantation. At his family's house the young Roa learned Guaraní and heard traditional stories from an old woman who lived with the family. When he was eight years old, he was sent to Asunción to continue his studies at a prestigious school, the Colegio de San José. The library of his uncle, Bishop Hermenegildo Roa, in Asunción developed the child's interest in literature, mostly fed then by Siglo de Oro (Golden Age) Spanish authors. Augusto Roa Bastos volunteered when he was fourteen to fight in the war against Bolivia. The conflict was called the Guerra del Chaco (1932-1935), after the northwestern region of Paraguay, the Chaco, where most of the fighting took place. He was assigned to the rear guard, working as warden of Bolivian prisoners and keeping track of deaths.

Augusto Roa Bastos circa 1986 (photograph by Jean Dieuzaide/NYT Pictures)

At some point during the 1930s, at his home in Iturbe, writing on the stationery of his father's employer and using the light of glowworms in a jar, Roa wrote his first short story, published decades later as *Lucha hasta el alba* (Fight until Dawn, 1979). The story begins with a father, Pedro, punishing his son, Jacob, in an attempt to squelch his strong character, since the father fears his son might become a dictator. The negative model of José Gaspar de Francia, who took absolute power in Paraguay in 1814 and was dictator until his death in 1840, motivates the father, whose methods paradoxically imitate those of Francia. The boy, using the light of glowworms, in the refuge of his room at night, reads and writes about Jacob's story in the Bible. The boy remembers a local tradition about women who dance naked in the moonlight to implore the moon for rain. He resents the better treatment afforded to his brother, Esaú. Jacob walks into the night and has a long fight with an enemy that he strangles and beheads. He has a vision of himself carrying the severed head of Francia, but the head also has the features of his own father. The boy ages prodigiously fast and dies. This melodramatic narrative contains the seeds of Roa Bastos's later fiction: the detailed description of the activity of writing, the relation of the writer with power, the biblical and mythical background, and the exploration of violence.

After interrupting his formal education when he was fifteen and going to fight in the war in the Chaco region, Roa took a low-level position at the Bank of London and South America, and he soon became well known in the cultural circles of Asunción. In 1937 he wrote a novel, "Fulgencio Miranda," which won the Premio Ateneo Paraguayo but was never published. He became a journalist for the Asunción newspaper *El País* in 1942, coming into contact with everyday social problems, among them the plight of the peasants, virtual slaves, who harvested Paraguayan tea, yerba maté. A grant from the British Council allowed Roa to travel to London in 1944, while V-2s were still bombarding the city, a traumatic experience that reinforced Roa's unromantic conception of war. He interviewed Gen. Charles de Gaulle in Paris and narrated several cultural programs for the BBC. In 1946 he was named Paraguayan cultural attaché to Buenos Aires, but he also continued with his journalism and was promoted to editor in chief of *El País*. The newspaper was seized in 1947 by the troops of Gen. Higinio Moríñigo when an uprising threatened his dictatorship. Roa had to flee via the rooftops, while soldiers set fire to the building. He went into exile in Buenos Aires and continued to live there until he moved in 1976 to France. He returned to Paraguay for several brief visits, but in 1982 he was arrested and officially expelled for life. However, after the fall of the dictator Alfredo Stroesser, Roa moved back to Paraguay in 1989.

His first published book was a collection of poems, *El ruiseñor de la aurora* (The Nightingale of Dawn, 1942), heavily influenced by his readings of Spanish poets of the sixteenth and seventeenth centuries, which would soon be put into perspective by Roa's discovery of works by Federico García Lorca, Rainer Maria Rilke, and Paul Valéry. Roa's second poetry book, *El naranjal ardiente: Nocturno paraguayo* (The Burning Orange Grove: Paraguayan Nocturne, 1960), offers sonnets on the theme of exile and two longer poems in which he remembers friends and country.

Paraguay, Roa felt, was being suffocated by a succession of dictatorships and wars that did not foster the free development of art. While Roa's own poetry is derivative, he played an important role in the belated introduction of avant-garde literature into Paraguay, sharing the limelight with the Spanish-born Josefina Plá and Hérib Campos Cervera. From this period of apprenticeship, Roa kept a flair for unexpected images and a language that delights readers with puns and symbolism.

While surviving in exile as a journalist, book reviewer, lecturer, and screenwriter, who had to keep attuned to his Argentinean surroundings, Roa wrote stories that take place in Paraguay or are immediately related to Paraguayan exiles. Yet his writing is a broad quest to understand the place of human beings in history. Who is the individual and what characterizes his relations with others? How is history transmitted and by whom? What are the obligations of the intellectual? How does language help and obstruct in the understanding of a given situation? What forms the active process of memory in remembering and forgetting? These are the recurrent themes of Roa's narratives.

His first collection of short stories, *El trueno entre las hojas* (Thunder in the Leaves, 1953), is dedicated to the Guatemalan novelist Miguel Angel Asturias, and it reflects the influence of Asturias, who tried in most of his novels to reconstruct the indigenous world, not only as a place where trees and animals have exotic names but as a different world altogether, where a self-sufficient cosmogony generates a parallel world to the European, even if based on the same material objects. From epiphanies that illuminate a common misunderstanding, the mistaken belief that sharing the same boat or drink means sharing the same world, comes the uneasy experience of most of the stories in *El trueno entre las hojas*. In "Carpincheros" (Capybara Hunters), the first story, a German couple and their daughter live on a sugar plantation next to a river. The gap between Europeans and natives is magnified by these German settlers. The eight-year-old daughter, Margaret, is fascinated by families that live on boats on the river, hunting the capybara, the largest living rodent, which grows to be about four feet long and one hundred pounds in weight. These hunters have not become enslaved by the pervasive European exploitation represented by Margaret's father and his business. They are free, and they make a wondrous appearance on the Night of St. John, when the villagers send rafts of burning logs down the river. For Margaret nothing else will live up to this ideal icon of absolute freedom, silent rowers sliding through islands of fire. After a melancholy year spent observing the enslaved existence of the workers at the sugar plantation, Margaret leaves with the hunters, rejecting her own past.

The call of "the other" is, in Roa's stories, a dangerous fascination. In "Cigarrillos 'Máuser'" (Mauser Cigarettes) a black female servant almost kills a twelve-year-old boy when she provides him with a pack of cigarettes without any instructions regarding how many to smoke at once. The excessive ending—the servant hangs herself—shows the trauma of a violent coming together of radically different cultures and languages. In a country where 95 percent of the people use Guaraní

Roa Bastos in Asunción, Paraguay, before he went into exile in 1947

as the language of everyday life, yet Spanish is the language of schooling, culture, and government, Roa has often referred to a pathological situation that he characterizes as linguistic schizophrenia. Many Guaraní words sprinkled in the stories of *El trueno entre las hojas* retain an exotic opacity that resists incorporation into the flow of Spanish, even though 168 such expressions are translated in the glossary appendix. Roa's struggle to bridge the gap between languages and cultures is not altogether successful, since the point of view remains on the white, Spanish side of the conflict.

Two of the best stories of *El trueno entre las hojas* explore the difficulties of making amends for centuries of discrimination and exploitation. "Esos rostros oscuros" (Those Dark Faces) tells of Amelia, the daughter of an important political figure in the capital, who has been sent to the countryside to cure her of the influence of romantic ideas and excessive reading. Yet the bucolic land, which she loves to explore alone, especially at sunset, contains also the workers, who grow exasperated by Amelia's provocative way of dressing and behavior. She is gang raped by "those dark faces," her white body like a dead fish out of water and far away from the safe territory of home. "Esos rostros oscuros" points at the violence lurking in others, while "Audiencia privada" (Private Meeting), by far the best story of *El trueno entre las hojas*, brings out the weakness in the individual self. A man who has studied engineering visits a high government official at home to show him a project that could benefit many homeless families. The government official is surrounded by his children and is drinking his maté tea from a silver gourd with a golden straw that shines like a flame. The project appears to be good, and the influential official is ready to accept it when a catastrophe happens: the visitor drops from his pocket the golden straw that he had tried to steal; he is a victim of kleptomania.

The struggle between the admiration for the native inhabitants of the Americas and the uncontrollable thirst for gold is at the foundation of Latin-American culture, and "Audiencia privada" shows the divided Spanish mind, torn between altruistic projects and the theft of the land, gold, and work of the natives. Some other stories are less accomplished: "El trueno entre las hojas" itself is marred by anti-Semitic stereotyping and a simplistic confrontation between good and bad.

Roa's subsequent books of short stories contain diverse combinations of old and new stories and chapters from his novels. A good example of an early story is "Kurupí," written in 1959 but published in 1967 in *Madera quemada* (Burnt Wood). It is an understated account of the abusive behavior of Melitón Isasi, who is sent to a small town to whip up recruitment for the Chaco war and keep peace and order. He sends the men away and seduces the women, with the connivance of a priest and an old woman. An adolescent he has seduced, Felicita, is about to have a son when her twin brothers arrive. They kill Melitón and nail him to a cross, where he is discovered by his wife. The crisp dialogue, subdued intensity of feelings, well-delineated atmosphere, and mounting tension make this a model short story comparable to the best of Gabriel García Márquez or Juan Rulfo.

"Borrador de un informe" (Rough Copy of a Report), dated 1958 and published in *El baldío* (The Wasteland) in 1966, has merited the attention of several critics, for it combines a double version of a complicated series of events leading to the deaths of three people. Another excellent story is "Cuerpo presente" (The Wake), published in *Cuerpo presente y otros textos* (The Wake and Other Texts) in 1972. While the civil war surrounds a small town, villagers and performers in an itinerant circus attend the wake of Chepé Bolívar, the telegrapher, a local hero. Yet they cannot reach the cemetery because of the chaos of the war. Images of solidarity and chaos, the sharp edge of nature and the background of war, and the homage to the small hero and his muted life run through most of Roa's stories. Even if his style spans from an early form of social realism to a highly experimental flow of consciousness and from an early rough opposition between civilization and barbarism to a sophisticated ironic ambiguity, the stories work together and take much of their suggestive force from their place in Roa's work, more a giant mural painting of a country than a series of single intimate portraits.

In 1959 Roa's *Hijo de hombre* (1960; translated as *Son of Man*, 1965) received the first prize in an international contest organized by the important Argentinean publishing house Losada. One of the members of the jury was Asturias. The novel also received the coveted first prize of the city of Buenos Aires and an award of distinction from the Faulkner Foundation. *Hijo de hombre* has nine chapters, five of them narrated by Miguel Vera, a veteran of the war against Bolivia in Chaco, and four chapters narrated by what seems to be the voice of tradition. In the first chapter Halley's comet in 1910 heralds the birth of a new wooden Christ, carved by Gaspar Mora, a maker of musical instruments who suffers from leprosy and hides in the mountains. The new Christ is rejected by the local church, but the inhabitants of the town, Itapé, defend it, and the priest allows the statue to be placed on a hill outside town. The sexton, who fails in his attempts to burn the image, hangs himself, like Judas. The second chapter reuses the theme of the conflict between altruism and rapacity seen in "Audencia privada." A foreign doctor is stranded accidentally in Itapé and takes care of the poor. He finds coins of gold and silver in an old image of St. Ignatius, and from then on he demands to be paid with images of the saints, which he beheads searching for more hidden treasures. From a saintly figure, he degenerates into a drunken madman who ultimately leaves in search of more gold.

The third chapter happens chronologically before the second, since it is here that the doctor is thrown off the train when he tries to help a sick baby but is mistaken for a baby snatcher. The main event of the chapter is the trip of Miguel Vera, when a boy, from his small town of Itapé to the capital, where he will study in a military school. He is accompanied by a woman, Damiana, and her sick baby. They must spend the night at Sapukai, and during the night Miguel drinks the milk from Damiana's breasts, stealing nourishment from the weak baby. The fourth chapter backtracks again, to tell the story of the birth of Cristóbal Jara, a contemporary of Vera. After Jara's birth his father and mother run away from a tea plantation where they are basically slaves. There is a clear, if unspoken, parallel with the birth of Christ, also born while his parents were in a strange place, away from their hometown. Cristóbal's mother is called Natividad,

Augusto Roa Bastos

and the lecherous colonel in charge of security in the plantation shows traits of Herod. The Jara family manages to escape and return to their town of Sapukai, where they move into an abandoned railroad carriage. It is this railroad carriage that is at the center of chapter 5, since the Jaras have moved it inch-by-inch at night into the jungle, a proof of their independence and determination. Vera, who has been sent by the army to Sapukai, wishes to see the fabled house of the Jaras and hires Cristóbal, now a grown man, to be his guide. At the site of the railroad car, some guerrilla fighters request the help of Vera to train them, since they have heard that he was disciplined for insubordination at the military school and is, therefore, a likely candidate to lead their cause. He accepts, yet in the next chapter the reader finds out that Vera has betrayed the men while he was drunk, and they have been captured, except Cristóbal, who is hiding at the cemetery. A party in town allows Cristóbal the chance to escape with the help of a community of lepers who surround him and take him away to safety.

Chapter 7 is the diary of Vera, imprisoned for his actions in Sapukai, then sent to the Chaco war. The description of the desperate situation of the combatants, their thirst, and their lack of resources is masterful. A powerful scene closes Vera's diary: the company under his command is mostly dead, thinned down by the enemy but also by thirst, since they are trapped in a scorched dust-bowl area away from the main army. The feverish, hallucinating Vera sees at long last—and much too late—a truck carrying water appear in the distance, and he empties the rounds of his machine gun, killing the driver, in the mistaken belief that the saving water is only a cruel phantom of imagination. Chapter 8 goes back in time to show that the driver of the saving cistern is Cristóbal Jara, who has volunteered for the mission. After many obstacles, his is the only truck that crosses the enemy lines. His hands are wounded, so he must tie himself to the driving wheel, as a modern reincarnation of the crucified Christ who tries to bring the water of life to his fellow human beings only to be shot down by the new Judas, Miguel Vera.

The last chapter, "Ex combatientes" (Veterans), shows Vera in charge of Itapé after the war, when another veteran, Crisanto Villalba, returns dazzled from the front, unable to face the return to normal life. His response is to throw all the hand grenades he still carries in his satchel into what was once his home and is now an abandoned building to which he cannot relate. Vera is saddened, lonely, immersed in memories, and wanting a change. His sympathies are with the oppressed—the human beings crucified by other human beings—yet he is still serving the oppressors. An accident, or a suicide, ends Vera's life. A final report says that he was horrified by suffering but knew not what to do about it. Roa's novel, by etching the parallel between the life and passion of Christ and Cristóbal Jara, represents a call to compassion and action, a rejection of uncommitted observers—the Miguel Veras who end up being unwitting accomplices of a situation they detest. The symphonic structure of *Hijo de hombre*, with its apparently independent chapters that could be seen as short stories, proves that past and present, the individual and society, and peace and war are deeply interrelated, inevitably contaminating the space of the so-called detached observer—Vera or the reader.

Roa's second novel, written partly with the help of a Guggenheim Foundation grant that he received in 1971, is *Yo, el Supremo* (1974; translated as *I, the Supreme*, 1987). It has been considered his masterpiece and takes its place alongside other classic descriptions of Latin-American dictators: the Spaniard Ramón María del Valle Inclán's *Tirano Banderas* (1926; translated as *The Tyrant*, 1929), Miguel Angel Asturias's *El señor Presidente* (1946), Alejo Carpentier's *El recurso del método* (1974; translated as *Reasons of State*, 1976), and Gabriel García Márquez's *El otoño del patriarca* (1975; translated as *The Autumn of the Patriarch*, 1976). The main difference is that, while those other novels are loosely based on historical facts, their dictators being composites of several well-known historical villains, Roa's novel closely follows the life of Paraguay's José Gaspar Francia, who led the country from 1914 until his death in 1940 and was called El Supremo in his own time. He sealed off Paraguay to defend the nation, faced by the combined attacks of Argentina and Brazil. The results of his policies are paradoxical: on one hand, he forbade emigration and immigration; suffocated culture, education, and science; and was ruthless against his enemies; on the other hand, his isolationist policies assured that the Indian population was not overrun by Europeans, that the Guaraní language held a prestige no other native language has in Latin America, that new crops were introduced, that the economy was buttressed, and that a national pride grew, which was important to the survival of this landlocked country surrounded by aggressive giants.

Yo, el Supremo presents itself as the compilation by a twentieth-century narrator of a large amount of material about Francia and his period. The narrator adopts from time to time the historian's style of footnotes and the sifting of contradictory evidence. Yet simultaneously a pretense reminiscent of Miguel de Cervantes's *Don Quixote* complicates the reliability of the narrative: most of the text pretends to be dictated by Francia himself to his secretary Patiño, who in turn changes sentences to suit his own convenience. Francia, Patiño, and the compiler, plus various voices quoted from historical documents, struggle in vain to impose one version of the events, to resolve all ambiguities, and to arrive at a conclusion, a verdict about Francia's government.

The novel begins in 1840, with Francia irritated because someone has forged his signature in a pamphlet that calls for the dictator's beheading after his death. His obstinate and futile search for the forger becomes an uphill battle against all who have written and will write about him, those who manipulate his public image. He asserts his differences with Simón Bolívar and José de San Martín, with Brazil and Argentina, he explains how he dealt with foreign scientists and with his enemies, and how he studied in his own library and conducted scientific experiments, while keeping his countrymen in the bliss of ignorance recommended by his hero Jean-Jacques Rousseau. Culture is considered dangerous by Francia, silence and action being the only places where truth can reside. In writing, claims the dictator, words lose their true significance and can be misinterpreted. He distrusts the official scribes, and he writes his private diary, of which the reader gets a glimpse before it is, at the end of the novel, destroyed by a fire. But as readers get closer to the man, the fantastic elements increase: in his diary his favorite dog talks and the dictator's pen—inherited by the main narrator, the compiler—is like a movie projector showing images of the past. Remembrance becomes for the dictator a dialogue with his own conscience, which addresses the old man with the emerging and devastating truth that he has betrayed his true self. In the Faustian price he has paid for power, he is like his Mexican counterpart, the title character of Carlos Fuentes's novel *La muerte de Artemio Cruz* (1962; translated as *The Death of Artemio Cruz*, 1964).

Francia delights in puns and etymology, shows himself as a sophisticated, resourceful speaker, sends fatherly and clever memos, and shows an excellent grasp of Paraguayan history. While Roa has declared that he was not interested in writing a novel that would follow history in every detail, he has stayed close enough to make the text tantalizing. The reader who is encouraged to turn to history to complement Francia's fictional portrait will find that he has been the subject of encomiastic and denigrating biographies, and that even the most trivial documents are suspect in a country where history has been written and rewritten incessantly under the guidance and scrutiny of harsh dictatorships. Some of these historical documents are slightly modified in the novel—for example, the number of toys Francia bought in 1837 for the children of Asunción is augmented: 77 soldiers become

770, 12 rifles become 12,000, and a sentry is magnified to 1,000 sentries. Events are conveniently modified for the sake of dramatic force, such as the interview between Francia and the English merchant John Parish Robertson, who in the novel is given one day to leave Paraguay, though the real Robertson wrote that he was granted two months to settle his affairs and leave the country. Since the novel insists on the unreliable nature of all writing, and of the author, the discrepancies introduced by Roa confirm that readers must practice active questioning, never getting lulled by the false promise of the veracity of historians or narrators. Despite the concluding summation of the compiler, where he deplores Francia's big words, fraudulent rhetoric, perverse ambition, and pride, Francia has grown through the novel to be a brilliant, disturbingly powerful, and enduring character, in the same category as Domingo Sarmiento's Facundo Quiroga or Rómulo Gallegos's Doña Bárbara.

Roa left Argentina in 1976, because a military dictatorship had made his haven unsafe, and he was hired as an associate professor by the Université de Toulouse, where he taught until 1985. His reputation as one of the major Latin-American writers has consistently grown. In 1989 he received Spain's Premio Cervantes. The translation into English of *Yo, el Supremo* was greeted by Fuentes on the first page of the *New York Times Book Review* (6 April 1986) as "a richly textured, brilliant book—an impressive portrait"; Paul West in the *Washington Post* (11 May 1986) claimed that "Augusto Roa Bastos is himself a supreme find, maybe the most complex and brilliant, the densest-textured Latin-American novelist of all." While there are other Latin-American writers who are equally complex—notably José Lezama Lima and Severo Sarduy—Augusto Roa Bastos stands alone as a master of his own created world, a vast, sophisticated, and profound network of texts that can be valued for inventiveness and narrative excellence but also for his refined and fascinating portrait of Paraguay.

Interviews:

Jean L. Andreu, "Entretiens avec Roa Bastos," *Caravelle: Cahiers du monde hispanique et lusobrésilien*, 14 (1970): 207-218;

David Maldavsky, "Autocrítica: reportaje a Augusto Roa Bastos," *Los libros*, 12 (1970): 11-12;

"La cultura como rebelión: Entrevista con Augusto Roa Bastos," *Quimera: Revista de Literatura*, 23 (September 1982): 23-29;

Javier M. González, "An Interview with Augusto Roa Bastos," *Salmagundi*, 72 (Fall 1986): 21-30;

Juan González, "Augusto Roa Bastos: Entrevista," *Siglo XX/20th Century*, 4 (1986-1987): 64-67.

Biography:

Rubén Bareiro Saguier, *Augusto Roa Bastos* (Montevideo: Trilce, 1989).

References:

Augusto Roa Bastos: Actas del Coloquio Franco-Alemán, Düsseldorf, 1-3 junio de 1982 (Tübingen: Niemeyer, 1984);

Salvador Bacarisse, "La filosofía de la historia del compilador de *Yo, el Supremo*, de Augusto Roa Bastos," *Revista Iberoamericana*, 51, nos. 130-131 (1985): 249-259;

Fernando Burgos, ed., *Las voces del Karaí: Estudios sobre Augusto Roa Bastos* (Madrid: Edelsa, 1988);

David William Foster, *Augusto Roa Bastos* (Boston: Twayne, 1978);

Helmy F. Giacoman, *Homenaje a Augusto Roa Bastos* (New York: Anaya/Las Américas, 1973);

Adolfo León Aldana, *La cuentística de Augusto Roa Bastos* (Montevideo: Géminis, 1975);

Juan Manuel Marcos, *Roa Bastos, precursor del postboom* (Mexico City: Katún, 1983);

Saúl Sosnowski, ed., *Augusto Roa Bastos y la producción cultural americana* (Buenos Aires: Flor, 1986);

Francisco Tovar, *Las historias del dictador Yo, el Supremo, de Augusto Roa Bastos* (Barcelona: Mall, 1987).

João Guimarães Rosa
(27 June 1908 - 19 November 1967)

Jon S. Vincent
University of Kansas

BOOKS: *Sagarana* (Rio de Janeiro: Universal, 1946); translated by Harriet de Onís (New York: Knopf, 1966);

Corpo de Baile, 2 volumes (Rio de Janeiro: Olympio, 1956; republished in 3 volumes, 1964-1965);

Grande Sertão: Veredas (Rio de Janeiro: Olympio, 1956); translated by Onís and James L. Taylor as *The Devil to Pay in the Backlands* (New York: Knopf, 1963);

Primeiras Estórias (Rio de Janeiro: Olympio, 1962); translated by Barbara Shelby as *The Third Bank of the River and Other Stories* (New York: Knopf, 1968);

Tutaméia: Terceiras Estórias (Rio de Janeiro: Olympio, 1967);

Estas Estórias, edited by Paulo Rónai (Rio de Janeiro: Olympio, 1969);

Ave, Palavra, edited by Rónai (Rio de Janeiro: Olympio, 1970);

Rosiana (Rio de Janeiro: Salamandra, 1983);

Jardins e Riachinhos (Rio de Janeiro: Salamandra/Ipiranga, 1983);

A Volta do Marido Pródigo (Porto Alegre, Brazil: Tchê, 1987).

Collections: *Seleta*, edited by Rónai (Rio de Janeiro: Olympio, 1973);

Contos, edited by Heitor Megale and Marilena Matsuoka (São Paulo: Nacional, 1978).

OTHER: José Condé, ed., *O Mistério dos M M M*, includes chapter by Guimarães Rosa (Rio de Janeiro: Cruzeiro, 1962).

João Guimarães Rosa made his debut in Brazilian letters with *Sagarana* (1946; translated, 1966), a volume of short stories that appeared to be fashioned in the perennially popular regionalist vein, but the stories were informed by a mystic vision not usually considered a part of that tradition. The language of the narratives appeared to be an amalgam of traditional Brazilian regionalist diction and some other unidentifiable idiom, perhaps an invented one. The title itself is a neologism, an agglutination of the Germanic root that produced the word *saga*, and a Tupi suffix meaning "rough, crude." Had Guimarães Rosa not written another word, his authorship of *Sagarana* would have assured him a place in Brazilian literary history as a great but minor writer. As a decade of silence from him drew to a close, it indeed appeared that he had exhausted his imagination on one volume. But in 1956 he published not only a second book but a third one as well, and, since that time, he has been generally considered not merely an important writer but the twentieth century's single standard of excellence in Brazilian prose fiction, the first writer to have achieved such acclaim on a national scale since Joaquim María Machado de Assis in the last century. Almost as astonishing as the singularity of his position in literary history is the fact that he produced seven volumes of prose in what would have to be termed "spare time," since he was a full-time diplomat during his entire literary career.

Guimarães Rosa was born on 27 June 1908 in the small provincial town of Cordisburgo, Minas Gerais, in central Brazil; he was the eldest of six children of Francisca Guimarães Rosa and Florduardo Pinto Rosa, a well-to-do businessman. The young writer attended high school in Belo Horizonte, the state capital. He was an enthusiastic student and an avid reader. His favorite subjects were natural history and languages, which he studied from early childhood. He began studying French at the age of six; later, as a young man, he no doubt surprised and pleased a Russian he happened to meet by insisting on hearing for the first time the correct pronunciation of a language he had already taught himself to read; he improved his Russian further still when a cossack chorus showed up to give a show in Barbacena.

Guimarães Rosa entered medical school in Belo Horizonte in 1925. His first literary publication, "The Mystery of Highmore Hall," a short story, appeared in the magazine *O Cruzeiro* in

João Guimarães Rosa

1929. In 1930 he graduated from medical school, and on 27 June of that year he married Lygia Cabral Pena. In 1931 he established a private practice in the town of Itaguara, Minas Gerais, and subsequently volunteered his services as a doctor with the Brazilian Força Publica (national guard), where he was eventually named a staff physician. In 1934 he passed the Brazilian foreign service examination and entered the Ministry of Foreign Affairs. He served the Brazilian government in a variety of diplomatic posts during a distinguished career, eventually attaining the rank of ambassador.

Like all great writers, Guimarães Rosa wrote inexhaustible texts that seem to demand a second and a third reading and that offer something new with every rereading. Because of the density and richness of his stories, Guimarães Rosa has seldom been a popular author in terms of sales, but his name is known to almost all literate Brazilians, and those who have taken the trouble to read him are almost worshipful. His texts have been translated into other languages only sporadically and with widely varying success, probably less as a result of the different skills of the translators than because of the novelty of his use of language.

His first three books share certain similarities of concept and execution because they all derive in one way or another from remembered or experienced events in Brazil's *sertão*, the bleak interior backlands. But because none of these books is in the least sense conventionally regionalistic, except in a superficial way, the term *transcendent regionalism* is used to describe the combination of picturesque setting and spiritual inquiry contained in them.

Sagarana has a curious history. In 1937 Guimarães Rosa submitted a volume of his poetry to a national contest sponsored by the Brazilian Academy of Letters. His book, "Magma," won the contest. Oddly, it has never been published, but the success with verse probably encouraged Guimarães Rosa to consider writing fiction. In 1938 he submitted a one-thousand-page collection of short stories to the Humberto de Campos fiction contest. His collection missed the first prize by the margin of one vote, and even though some judges and at least one publisher were interested in publishing the second-place entry, the author, who entered the contest under the pseudonym Viator, could not be located. "Contos" was reportedly written in a period of only seven months, and its author, apparently disappointed with only a second place in the contest, seemed disposed to let the manuscript gather dust. Guimarães Rosa got the news of his second-place finish in Hamburg, Germany, where he had been named to a vice-consulate that year. In Germany he met Aracy Moebius de Carvalho, who would become his second wife. He had two daughters, Agnes and Vilma, by his first wife and had no children by his second wife.

Brazil broke diplomatic relations with Germany in 1942, and Guimarães Rosa was interned for four months in Baden-Baden with several other Brazilians. During the internment he showed the manuscript of his book to the painter Cícero Dias, who reacted to the work with enthusiasm and encouraged him to find a publisher. Released in May, Guimarães Rosa returned to Brazil and was named secretary of the Brazilian embassy in Bogotá, Colombia, where he remained for two years.

Guimarães Rosa was named head of the Brazilian state department's documentation service in 1945. Now back in Rio, he finally decided to do something with the manuscript of his short stories, and in five months of intensive work he revised "Contos," eliminating one story completely and editing the others down to about half their original length. In 1946 "Contos," transformed into *Sagarana*, was published.

The story behind *Corpo de Baile* (Ballet Corps, 1956) is less clear, and it is not known whether Guimarães Rosa worked simultaneously on these tales and on *Grande Sertão: Veredas* (1956; translated as *The Devil to Pay in the Backlands*, 1963) or whether he finished the first and then began the other. But the two books, both quite long, appeared only five months apart, and it is probable that he had worked on both during the decade of his publishing hiatus. The stories in *Sagarana* average just over forty printed pages in length, one feature that distinguishes them from the run-of-the-mill Brazilian short story, usually about a quarter that length. Those of *Corpo de Baile* average over seventy pages in length, the longest being over a hundred and twenty pages. The first edition of the book was in two volumes. *Grande Sertão*, his only novel, is a chapterless monologue of almost six hundred pages. If anything can be deduced from the external design of these narratives, it would be that a trend toward gigantism is in process, and indeed one notable feature of Guimarães Rosa's prose is an ongoing experimentalism with narrative form, a seemingly endless search for an appropriate structure for his fictions.

The principal similarity among these three works is that they all appear to be about rustics from the Brazilian hinterland, but that feature amounts to little more than setting, a contribution to atmosphere but little else. Unlike traditional works of regionalism, these tales are less descriptions or evocations of place than stories about character—arguably the essence of the modern short story. Another feature that might be considered essential to modern fiction is that there is progressively a greater difference in the tales between what the Russian formalists called *fabula* and *sujet*: the chronological order of the story versus the disposition of motifs and other narrative strategies employed to produce aesthetic effect. A reader is likely to sense this opposition in the reading of *Sagarana*, when it becomes apparent that the traditional notion of "single effect" is almost impossible to pin down in the stories, because they seem to have more than one purpose. One of the clearest of these purposes, and one that makes these modern tales look rather old-fashioned, is the importance of the narrators. Some are hidden, some are retellers of another's tale, and some appear merely to be liars, but whatever their relationship to the text, there is a sense of narrative play in all these tales that must be considered part of the *sujet*. Another curious anachronism of the stories in this volume is that the structural models for most of them are antiques—one is a fable, one a trickster tale, one a story with talking animals, one a magician's tale, and so on. These two features—the prominence of the narrator and the old-fashioned structures—might suggest an unsophisticated or at least conventional narrative form, but the stories are in fact quite complex. One embellishing element impossible to overlook is the originality of language—the tales are riddled with alliteration, neologisms, syntactic reversal, internal rhyme, ellipses, and odd turns of phrase. Other intricacies are the persistent presence of irony and ambiguity, the constant viewing of events from a moral perspective, the sharp comic sense, and the contrapuntals (framing devices, tales within tales, epigraphs, and drawings).

What emerges from the reading of these stories is a curious combination of something akin to an echo effect, offset by an almost constant surprise element, largely a function of the aggressive originality of diction. The echo is produced by the likely familiarity with the models, some of the conventions of oral tale-telling, and the frequently cozy and comforting narrator. On a second or third reading, it is not unlikely for readers to find the stories familiar not only because the book was read before but also because of the sense that the narratives must have been read, or heard, someplace other than in the pages of *Sagarana*. But that sense of familiarity is dispelled by a potently defamiliarizing use of language, so that the comfort a reader feels with a known text is constantly being disrupted by the mode in which the story is told. Both the familiar and the unfamiliar contribute to the pleasure of the reading.

The complexity of this first effect is compounded by an inescapable awareness that not only is the mode of telling odd but nothing else is quite what it should be, either. The opening tale, which appears to be about not much more than an old donkey dragooned into being a mount on a cattle drive, is so shot through with ironies, misleading asides, aphorisms, and object lessons, that the reader must conclude that the donkey is either a fraud or part of a larger metaphor, because the tale is really about reality, fate, death, and survival more than it is about beasts of burden or cattle drives. Another tale, which appears to be an adventure tale about a rural con artist, likewise becomes a disquisition on love, power, and the moral use of lies. A tale about two old men dying of malaria is about not only death but also trust, honor, loyalty, and, oddly, the devotion of pets. Another, about the seeking of revenge, is again about honor, but it is also about errors (including sin), even those brought about serendipitously. Another, which appears to be only a memoir, is, among other things, a love story. Every story has a rural setting, but in none of them are the flora and fauna, nor even the folkways, the meat of the narrative, because each tale hinges on a concept of a higher order, whether it be spiritual, moral, or the irony of good and ill fortune.

If the narratives of *Sagarana* are unsettling to readers who like their stories straightforward and to the point, those of *Corpo de Baile* are likely to provoke extreme distress. To begin with, the narratives in this second work are even less like traditional short stories than those of *Sagarana*. Worse, the author was not only aware of this fact but flouted the convention openly, first by categorizing the narratives as *novelas* (novelettes) on the title pages, switching the term to *poems* on the following page, and listing four of them as *romances* (novels) and three as *contos* (short stories) in the table of contents. As a final blow to critics who like to determine the genre of narrative on the basis of girth alone, one of the so-called short stories is thirteen pages longer than the shortest "novel." And, like the stories of *Sagarana*, all are too long to qualify as normal short stories.

The stories are not only long—they are, by turns, improbably dense, highly ornamented, and extremely suggestive. So much so that only years after the appearance of the volume have some of the arcane referential codes been discovered by scholars. It is almost as if Guimarães Rosa had designed the book for exactly that audience, since he clearly could not have expected the ordinary reader to be inclined, much less equipped, to undertake the unraveling of such mysteries in the process of reading.

Guimarães Rosa is now often referred to by critics as a baroque writer, probably more in reference to this volume than to any other of the author's works. The very density of the stories is surely one of the reasons the term has been used, but there is also the ornamented, decorative quality of structure and the almost stagy quality of diction. Beyond that, a view of a reality composed of sets of theses and antitheses always in flux appears to inform all the stories, with the result that the reader's attention is drawn as much to the process of narration as to the narration itself. The tales might, in fact, be called "process narratives," since many of the conventional satisfactions of narrative (closure, revelation, resolution of tension) are absent or displaced, and others (enigma, code systems, code deformation) are principal sources of effect.

The dislocation of the reader's usual relationship with the text begins with the fact that the language is not conventional Portuguese. But neither is it any other known form of the language. The first two paragraphs of "Cara-de-Bronze"

Dust jacket for the English translation (1963) of Grande Sertão: Veredas, *Guimarães Rosa's only novel*

(Bronze-Face), for example, contain at least a dozen neologisms or obscure usages, several ellipses, reversals of word order, and assorted examples of internal rhyme, alliteration, onomatopoeia, and repetition, as well as a representative sample of Guimarães Rosa's own inimitable system of punctuation. This passage also contains an example of typographical alteration, the purposeful double spacing of the word *buritizais* (fields of buriti palms) as it occurs fifth in a series of six forms of *buriti*. Some lines are in unmarked metric feet. Bound morphemes occur as if they were words.

What appears to be happening here is that any rules that writers and readers had observed about language no longer apply; from the phoneme, through the morpheme and word, up through syntax into an entirely new rhetoric, the poetics of a new and startling reality emerges. It is difficult to resist the temptation to read Guimarães Rosa aloud, and one reason for this is that many of what appear to be nonsensical sound strings on paper begin to make sense when produced orally. But it is also tempting to appreciate his language for the totality of effect, since it is, in and of itself, both challenging and richly satisfying. However, readers who take their satisfaction only from the language will be cheated. Indeed the bulk of the criticism on Guimarães Rosa has some kind of linguistic orientation, which is in a sense a professional validation of the impression that language alone is the point of the stories.

Yet another reason for taking language as the central source of effect is that it is difficult if not impossible to summarize the stories. Each one appears to have a central narrative core, but any reader who has read one of the stories would be reluctant to recount that core and be satisfied that the essence had been retold. Part of the difficulty is that all have numerous lateral narratives, some of them so compelling that readers may spend much of the time reading a story and following what is essentially a false trail. Another complicating factor is that many of the central characters defy easy categorization—some appear intentionally to have been drawn as symbolic personages, but in no case is it easy or even feasible to establish unambiguous referential meanings for such characters. Finally, every tale in the book could be read with some preconceived notion and still work as a piece of fiction. That is, a reader disposed to read for plot would get a successful plot story; one inclined to read for character revelation would get that; and one who reads for ideas, emotional effects, or atmosphere would find all those things in abundance.

The stories, while fluid in form, all operate within a finite field of meaning—what changes each story from one reading to another is the degree to which a given reader is prepared to respond to a broad variety of signals. In "O Recado do Morro" (The Message of the Mountain), for example, the plot appears to be about a rural lothario and his jealous rivals. The story ends in a brawl in which the protagonist takes on six of these men and then flees to safety. But the critic Ana Maria Machado has discovered that the week-long sojourn which takes place in the middle of the plot is structured on a kind of secret code, with each night's stopping place and companion having a symbolic name and each place having a god, an attribute, a planet, or an event connected with it. On Tuesday, for example, the day of Mars, the god of war, the characters stay at the ranch of Marciano; the hero goes out with his friend Martinho; and there is a fight. All the other days have equally related sequences of symbols and attributes.

It is not likely that Guimarães Rosa expected all his readers to decipher this curious cryptogram—obviously, he was having fun with the arcane, imbedded code—but a reader who knows about it can scarcely read the story again in the same way he might have on a first reading, when it probably seemed like nothing more than a simple adventure story. The story also contains a hilarious Danish scientist and a half-dozen bizarre madmen, all with symbolic or suggestive names, whose interpretation depends less on a knowledge of classical mythology than on a sensitivity to Christian and Portuguese nomenclature and an appreciation of the inherent "sanity" of madness. Thus, each narrative ingredient has its own justification for existence, and each requires different kinds of knowledge and sensitivity for a full understanding.

Another story, "Campo Geral" (High Plains Field), perhaps less arcane, appears to be about the coming of age of an eight-year-old boy. Readers familiar with Guimarães Rosa's life would likely recognize the tale as semi-autobiographical, because the central plot turn is based on the discovery that the boy's ineptitude is not a character flaw but the result of acute myopia, a condition Guimarães Rosa had himself. The relative simplicity and straightforwardness of the basic plot, however, omits most of the principal sidelight effects of the story—the tragic and moving death of a younger brother, a disquisition on God and death, the story of a demented neighbor, a tapir hunt, a frightening and comic episode with a group of monkeys, and a dissertation on good and evil.

All seven of the stories have rural settings, and all seem to be about characters one might expect to find in the backlands of Brazil. But the book is full of surprises, not the least of which is that the real themes of the stories are not picturesque but timeless: life and death, sin and virtue, good and evil, free will and destiny, madness and sanity. And each is an inquiry more than it is an object lesson or a moral statement. In the process, a baffling array of symbols, myths, and folk motifs appear, not always in ways that are likely to satisfy wholly the reader whose cultural tradition emphasizes a sense of precision. The cast of characters includes cowboys with metaphysical anxieties, aged sex symbols, holy idiots, blind prophets, and even trees and animals. Some stories have extensive footnotes, including quotes from the Upanishads. Characters change names in the middle of a story. Nothing is easy.

Much of the complexity of the work no doubt derives from the breadth of education and interest of its author. A physician who was from a small town in the interior and who had spent years practicing in even smaller towns, Guimarães Rosa was also an amateur naturalist of considerable knowledge and an avid student of folkways. But he was also a cosmopolitan man, a professional diplomat who had spent years in the world's major cities, a man of broad humanistic education, and a polyglot (he spoke six languages and read fourteen others). Like most regionalist writers, then, he knew his territory very well indeed, but he knew a lot of other territories as well, which helps to explain references to Norse legends in the middle of a story about a local swain, or quotations from ancient Hindu theology in the middle of what is ostensibly a cowboy story. What complicates things immensely for the reader, even if he is a Brazilian, is that the author never gives away anything free, which leaves each reader to decide whether or not it is really necessary to track down the provenance and significance of a given signal to understand the story fully, or whether an impressionistic reading, which relies mainly on resonance and guesswork, is sufficient.

Guimarães Rosa's third antiregionalist book is his most famous work, his only novel, *Grande*

Dust jacket for the English translation (1968) of Primeiras Estórias, *a collection of twenty-one stories focusing on socially marginal characters*

Sertão. Probably no single work of Brazilian fiction of this century has been the recipient of such lavish praise as this six-hundred-page monologue, though there appear to be almost as many ideas about what it "really means" as there are critics. Whether or not they agreed on its meaning, the members of Brazil's National Book Institute gathered in 1956 to decide which of the many books of fiction published that year deserved the Prêmio Machado de Assis, comparable to the U.S. National Book Award. In an almost unprecedented display of harmony, the prize was unanimously awarded to *Grande Sertão*.

The plot is generally thought to be based on an interview Guimarães Rosa conducted in 1952 while accompanying a cattle drive from Andrequicé to Araçaí, Mato Grosso. He had just returned to Brazil as cabinet chief of the Ministry of Foreign Affairs from a post in Paris, where he had been counselor of the Brazilian embassy. The original interview was published in newspapers in Rio and São Paulo and was eventually included, at the author's instructions, in *Estas Estórias* (These Stories, 1969). The cowboy interviewed, José Mariano da Silva, shares with the narrator of the novel a flair for storytelling but very little else; if the interview was the basis for the novel, it is a clear demonstration of the distance Guimarães Rosa was able to put between his field notes and his completed fictions.

The novel has been compared to everything from Homer's *Odyssey* to James Joyce's *Ulysses* (1922), at times apparently by way of praise by association, more often because the work seems to demand some kind of context before it makes much sense. It is such a suggestive work that it invites, and has received, a plethora of readings of every imaginable sort—linguistic, psychiatric, thematic, mythic, symbolic, hermeneutic, and philosophical. What is really striking about the narrative is that an undogmatic reader can accept, to varying degrees, any of these readings as at least partly cogent.

A fictional interlocutor spends three days listening to the autobiographical account of several years in the life of the narrator, Riobaldo, a former rural gunslinger, now retired and living in relative ease. The principal themes are the power struggles and assorted treacheries of rival bandit gangs, the narrator's possible pact with the devil, and the narrator's beclouded affection for a fellow bandit. One barrier to a clean, linear reading of the text is the rhetorical design, which not only tricks the reader into participating in the unfolding of the narrative (Riobaldo frequently asks questions and apparently gets answers), but also allows for the action to follow an affective rather than a chronological order. As in real speech, some events are recounted more than once and in different ways, and remarks about a given sequence of happenings will often trigger references to unrelated events. The narrator is a storyteller who is obviously conscious that he is speaking to an educated person, and he indulges in a variety of narrative strategies to keep interest high and to reinforce the plausibility of implausible events. But he is not attempting merely to make himself look good to his interlocutor—the narrative is a sort of inquiry, in which the speaker attempts to determine his relationship to the world by telling about it: Did he really behave honorably? Did he in fact enter into a pact with Satan? Did he really fall in love with a man?

Near the end of the book a climactic battle takes place between the rival bandit gangs, the opponents clearly aligned, by various associations, with the devil. The evil bandit leader, Hermógenes, and the narrator's equivocal love interest, Diadorim, kill each other in combat. The forces of evil are defeated, but at great cost. When Riobaldo and his gang prepare Diadorim's body for burial, they discover that he is in fact a beautiful woman, fighting in male disguise to avenge the death by treachery of her father.

Since the author is Guimarães Rosa, things are, of course, not as simple as they appear. To begin with, the language of the novel is his most "deformed" (or inventive) to date—the narrator's speech is larded with agglutinations, Latinisms, Indianisms, expletives, pleonasms, syntactic inversions, back formations, and various kinds of "display language," much of which is based on, but does not officially exist in, Brazilian Portuguese. The reader, even a native speaker, is thus constantly both surprised and confused by the text at its primary level—language—while at the same time trying to make sense of a rambling, chapterless treatise on life and the world, narrated by an implausibly erudite rustic.

Some of the conventions of the narrative are clearly derived from European literary tradition, including the motif of the girl disguised as a man, and the entire tale has an undeniable epic quality. Readers familiar with that tradition are sure to recognize the central quest motif, which is taken, according to some, from a cycle of Holy Grail tales. But many of the sources are from oral rather than written literature, and some features of the narrative can be traced to non-European and even non-Western sources. The critic William Myron Davis has even identified elements of the story that might be of Japanese origin. Wherever the motifs might have originated, the book is a masterpiece of design and inventiveness, and few other works of this century, Brazilian or otherwise, are as certain to endure as sources both of reading pleasure and critical controversy.

In 1957, less than a year after the release of *Grande Sertão*, Guimarães Rosa was presented as a candidate for membership in Brazil's most exclusive and often most capricious authors' club, the Brazilian Academy of Letters. Since balloting is secret and blackballing is still possible, it is difficult to know exactly how the voting went, but he was not admitted into the ranks of the "immortals" that time. The next year, at the age of fifty, he suffered a near-fatal heart attack.

But his diplomatic career went well. In 1958 he was promoted to minister first class with the rank of ambassador. Three years later, in 1961, the Brazilian Academy reinforced its reputation for capriciousness by presenting Guimarães Rosa with its award for excellence of collected works.

In 1962 Guimarães Rosa published his forth book, *Primeiras Estórias*, which was published in English in 1968 as *The Third Bank of the River and Other Stories*. Friends claim that the severity of the heart attack he suffered in 1958 changed his outlook on life and on writing, but whether or not that is true, this volume could not have been what anybody expected. The title literally means "first stories," which in many ways is a fitting title, because the narratives here seem not to proceed logically from anything in the first three books. (*Estórias* is a term for "story" that he rescued from disuse to avoid the ambiguity of *história*, which means both "story" and "history.") Had his critics and readers hazarded a guess as to what he would do after his novel, logic would have led to the probability of something even vaster and more ambitious than *Grande Sertão*. Perhaps Guimarães Rosa considered that possibility and rejected it; perhaps the illness really changed his mind.

Many of the features of his early books are still present in the *estórias*, but the predicted ever-expanding vision has turned back on itself, the focus is microscopic rather than cosmic, and the narrative process relies less on carefully paced climax than on epiphany. The controlled turbulence of the earlier diction has also been replaced by an incisive, condensed vocabulary and syntax, something beyond mere economy of expression.

The book is under two hundred pages in length, but there are twenty-one stories. In addition to the narrative compression implicit in each story is the fact that the *sertão*, the backlands of Brazil, are no longer of much importance. In some stories, in fact, the locale could be almost any small village or town.

Instead of a regionalism that transcends its boundaries, what seems to be going on is a process of persons transcending a state of gracelessness. The anthropological concept of "liminality" or "being at the threshold" is easily applicable to the tales in this book, because in every story a creature identified as being out of the mainstream of society either precipitates or perceives a transformation in the world. Some of the threshold beings are children, some are animals, some are outright lunatics. But they all share a peculiar relationship to society at large, since they are in it but not of it, and they all have either heightened sensibilities or heightened powers to bring about or to perceive the transformations.

The brevity of the tales has a parallel in their diction. None of the first three books contains anything that might be identified as economy of expression, and indeed by the time Guimarães Rosa reached his third book, it was as if he were experimenting with the limits of hyperexpression. Here, however, rather than the grand symphonic cascades of language found in the earlier books, is a subtle, laconic shorthand, in which the reader may lose a disproportionate amount of effect by missing a single phrase, however brief. That is not to say that the language has in any sense become conventional—indeed some critics found the language deformations in *Primeiras Estórias* so extreme as to suggest self-parody.

There is also great variety in the stories. Some are tone pieces, some are basically humorous, and some appear not to have a narrator at all. The unifying element is the transformation that generally takes place in the closing moments of each story, and in many cases it is a change the reader can accept only if his suspension of disbelief is absolute. It is appropriate that the English version of the book bears the title of one tale, "The Third Bank of the River," because it might be taken as a caveat for possible readers. Those who cannot imagine that third bank are probably going to find these stories at best difficult, at worst infuriating. Those willing to consider the possibility of the third bank will find the stories richly rewarding.

As if the third bank were not sufficient, Guimarães Rosa also instructed the artist for the Brazilian edition to include a sort of pictographic resumé of each story in the index: representational figures such as men on horseback, cattle, birds, and a train. There are also quite a few infinity symbols.

In May of 1963 Guimarães Rosa again was presented as a candidate for membership in the Brazilian Academy of Letters. The election took place on 8 August, and this time he won unanimous approval. No date for the formal ceremony of entrance was set. In 1965 Guimarães Rosa represented his country at a conference on cultural relations in Genoa and participated in the First Latin-American Writers Conference in Mexico City as vice-president. His books also began appearing in translation in the mid 1960s. French, Italian, American, and German versions, of somewhat uneven quality, appeared during the decade. His texts also began to interest the Brazilian film industry. *Grande Sertão* and "A Hora e Vez de Augusto Matraga" (Augusto Matraga's Hour and Turn), the last story in *Sagarana*, were both adapted and filmed, though only the latter enjoyed much critical success. In 1967 he was invited to be a member of the jury of Brazil's prestigious Walmap National Novel Contest. In July of that year his fifth book, *Tutaméia: Terceiras Estórias*, was released.

The main title of this book, characteristically, is not a real word but a personally streamlined version of the expression *tuta-e-meia*, meaning "trifle." The book's subtitle means "third stories," the progression from "first" to "third" possibly being a contrivance to upset faithful readers, who might have thought that they had somehow missed an entire volume of his writing.

More likely, the numerical sequence is merely another way to avoid the cliché, which holds that two, not three, follows one.

Most of the narratives in this book were published between 1965 and 1967 in a medical journal called *Pulso*. *Tutaméia* contains forty narratives and four "prefaces," which are spaced throughout the book. In a sense the stories in this volume appear to be a refinement of the compression in *Primeiras Estórias*, which makes the stories appear to be something like a distillation of a condensation, not on the face of it a promising form for narrative. Some critics, including Assis Brasil, have faulted the book for what they take to be an affectation of brevity, because they find that the result is a sense of abruptness or even incompleteness. Others consider the work not only rewarding as a reading experience but also important as a kind of gloss on Guimarães Rosa's attitudes about writing. This is especially evident in the "prefaces," which are less introductory statements than essays on the transcendent truth of fiction.

Plot in these stories is reduced to little more than anecdote and fragment, and a diction that in the previous volume was already shorthand is now concentrated, seemingly demanding a very attentive reading, or, as Guimarães Rosa suggested, a second or third reading. All the anecdotes in the book are person-centered pieces in which a principal character is separated from, or separates himself from, another character, and though some of these personages seem not much more than abstractions, the process of alienation or withdrawal is the thematic core of the book, even in anecdotes that appear to be about love. The prose is also almost aggressively gnomic, to the point that one of the frequent aphorisms will often stay with the reader longer than any notion of a sequence of events.

On 16 November 1967, some four months after the publication of *Tutaméia*, Guimarães Rosa was formally seated in the Brazilian Academy of Letters, just three days after his daughter Vilma made her literary debut with a book called *Acontecências* ("Occurencings"—not surprisingly, the title is an invented word). His acceptance speech was literate, cosmopolitan, and inventive, like everything he wrote. And there were, as always, memorable lines, such as the one near the end of the speech: "As pessoas não morrem, ficam encantadas" (People do not die—they become enchanted). Three days later, on 19 November, João Guimarães Rosa had a fatal heart attack while writing in his study. The last page he wrote in his life was a note to his daughter Vilma, which she read at a late-1967 autograph session in the Rio Yacht Club. The last page he probably read was a poem she wrote for him, which appeared in the São Paulo newspaper *Diário de Notícias* on the day of his death.

In 1969, two years to the month after the death of Guimarães Rosa, the first of his posthumous works (*Estas Estórias*) was released. He had worked with his publisher on the organization of the book before his death: the title was already selected, most of the tales had been edited, and two different indexes had been drafted. Three of the tales had appeared in different forms in the Brazilian magazine *Senhor*; four had never been published.

Estas Estórias is particularly interesting as to narrative form, because it seems in many ways to be a denial of the progression to ever-more-microscopic texts in the last two books published during his life. Something over two hundred pages in length, the book contains nine narratives, which seem to share more with the tales of *Sagarana* than with those of more recent vintage. Besides length, certain features of pace, tone, and narrative gusto link these stories with the first volume of his tales. There are two principal elements that differentiate the stories in this book from those of *Sagarana*: one is the lack of importance of the *sertão* as a locale and as a source of mystery; the other is a modification in the narrative design. In *Sagarana* the narrators are important because of the proximity of the tales to oral models, but here the narrators seem to take pleasure in flaunting the fictionality of their narratives rather than indulging in the strategies storytellers use to make their tales more believable. The telling of the tale appears as a sort of terminus in itself, as if the act of narrating were more important than any events that might or might not have taken place.

One story deals with the bizarre nature of the ordinary, one with the ordinary nature of the bizarre, one takes place in a pseudomythic space, and another is a pseudohistory. But in none of them is there any indication that the "history" has as much importance as the "story"—fiction is presented as both more important and more real than historical fact, and fabulization is not only a worthy activity, it is the only way to give order to a disordered world. Even the interview with the cowboy José Mariano da Silva, which appears to be no more than a report, has a confessed fic-

Title page for a 1983 selection of Guimarães Rosa's work

tional component that may make the reader wonder whether the interview actually took place or was invented.

Estas Estórias is probably Guimarães Rosa's least organic work, no doubt in part because its components were conceived and at least drafted over a period of almost three decades. Four of the narratives had not yet received the author's finishing touches, so there is a certain unevenness in the work. But even the least ambitious and least polished of the stories has a technical quality and intensity of effect rarely seen in fiction.

Guimarães Rosa's second posthumous book was published in 1970. *Ave, Palavra* (Hail, Word) contains the miscellany of some thirty years of writing, much of it previously published in newspapers or magazines. He had intended for most of these pieces to be published or republished in such a volume, and the title is his choice. Some of the choices about what to include were also made by Guimarães Rosa; other items were selected by the volume's editor, Paulo Rónai.

The material is arranged to provide a variety of length, pace, form, and style, but the sequence is of interest only to readers who go through the volume from beginning to end. Many readers, sensing early that there is no real organizing principle in the volume other than variety, will go ahead and take a random sampling of the assorted tidbits in the smorgasbord. It is not likely that many will read this book before reading the other works of Guimarães Rosa, which is probably just as well, because so many features of it are intensified and better appreciated through an echo effect. Mannerisms of style, characters, situations, themes—all resonate with fragments from earlier works, and neophytes may find either irritating or impenetrable such things as the catalogues, tales that refuse to end, and assorted incongruities.

The book largely comprises "occasional" pieces. Some are in verse, some are bestiaries, and others are memoirs of incidents from Guimarães Rosa's diplomatic career. Some are childhood evocations, some are funny, and some are impenetrable on first reading. The unexpected takes place with frequency; time expands and contracts.

The essence of the book is a combination of oddity of perception and originality of diction. Everything is perceived as slightly off center, and the narrative about it is phrased in that unmistakable, impossible language that can only be Guimarães Rosa's. The world is, as usual, a complex and contradictory place, and the experience of reading is by turns mystifying, illuminating, and even irritating. It is never dull.

For a writer of such extraordinary virtuosity, Guimarães Rosa lived a life of distinguished normality. No event in his life would appear to furnish any reason to surmise that a modest doctor from the interior would enjoy such success as a representative of his country to the world, much less that he would produce not one but several milestones in fiction, almost as a hobby. His was a literary career replete with contradictions and logical inconsistencies: though his work first appears to be merely a continuation of the venerable regionalist mode, certain canons of form are violated, and other, older ones are enshrined in their place, only to be replaced in the next volume; time and space gratuitously expand and contract; precision of expression produces ambiguity of purpose; truths keep emerging from lies. It is all done in a previously nonexistent, antigrammatical style, which forces the reader to do more than his share of the work. Finally, each volume is affiliated with the other six in a relationship of serial mutation, as if something in the hereditary chain has been omitted. Every book seems to start from a different narrative concept. Yet the reader familiar with one of them could perceive the others' kinship by the reading of a single line.

Guimarães Rosa's books generally sold well on publication, but in a small book market the saturation point for a readership willing to read such works was reached in a relatively short time. His works have never rivaled truly popular fiction in terms of sales. It would also be misleading to indicate that all Brazilians have reacted to his works with unqualified ecstasy. Some critics and not a few readers find the style gratuitously ornamented, the prose all but unintelligible, and the stories hard to follow. He did not attempt to make things easy for his readers, and the fact that his works are highly ambitious has no doubt had the effect of limiting his readership.

Several of the books are available in translation in the major European languages (English, French, German, Italian, and Spanish), but in no language are there more than three. Those translated have sold respectably but not spectacularly; internationally, the most vocal enthusiasm for Guimarães Rosa seems to have come from other writers and from the translators themselves. A reading of the three works now in English (*Sagarana*, *The Devil to Pay in the Backlands*, and *The Third Bank of the River and Other Stories*) would provide a reasonable basis for an appreciation of his talents, but it would not really be enough to admit a full appreciation of what has so excited the Brazilians and translators, because it would not give a full sense of reading the same three in the original. That has always been a limitation of translations, but it is fair to say that in this case the translators have had to make more than the usual compromises, and that the results of those compromises are not poor translations but books that accomplish things different from the originals.

João Guimarães Rosa was not the first gifted Brazilian writer of this century nor the last, but his works will undoubtedly remain milestones in Brazilian letters. This is not to suggest that he created a new school of writing, because his combination of exquisite style and mystic vision are inimitable. But the legacy of Luso-Brazilian literature, indeed, of world literature, is simply not what it was before his books existed.

Letters:
Correspondência com o Tradutor Italiano, by Guimarães Rosa and Edoardo Bizzarri (São Paulo: Instituto Cultural Italo-Brasileiro, 1972);
Sagarana Emotiva: Cartas de J. Guimarães Rosa, edited by Paulo Dantas (São Paulo: Duas Cidades, 1975).

Interviews:
Luis Harss and Barbara Dohmann, *Into the Mainstream: Conversations with Latin-American Writers* (New York: Harper & Row, 1967), pp. 137-172;

Günter W. Lorenz, "Diálogo con Guimarães Rosa," *Mundo Nuevo*, 45 (March 1970): 27-47.

Bibliography:
Exposição Bibliográfica de Guimarães Rosa (Lisbon: Coimbra, 1968).

Biography:
Renard Perez, *Escritores Brasileiros Contemporâneos* (Rio de Janeiro: Civilização Brasileira, 1960), pp. 177-184.

References:
Consuelo Albergaria, *Bruxo da Linguagem no Grande Sertão* (Rio de Janeiro: Tempo Brasileiro, 1977);

Sônia Maria Viegas Andrade, *A Vereda Trágica do "Grande Sertão: Veredas"* (Belo Horizonte, Brazil: Loyola, 1985);

Leonardo Arroyo, *A Cultura Popular em Grande Sertão: Veredas* (Rio de Janeiro: Olympio, 1984);

Alaor Barbosa, *A Epopéia Brasileira ou: Para Ler Guimarães Rosa* (Goiânia, Brazil: Imery, 1981);

Willi Bolle, *Fórmula e Fábula: Teste de uma Gramática Narrativa, Aplicada aos Contos de Guimarães Rosa* (São Paulo: Perspectiva, 1973);

Assis Brasil, *Guimarães Rosa* (Rio de Janeiro: Simões, 1969);

Antônio Cândido, "O Homem dos Avessos," in his *Tese e Antítese* (São Paulo: Nacional, 1964), pp. 119-140;

Maurice Capovilla, "'O Recado do Morro' de João Guimarães Rosa," *Revista do Livro*, 25 (March 1964): 131-142;

Manuel Antônio Castro, *O Homem Provisório no Grande Ser-Tão* (Rio de Janeiro: Tempo Brasileiro, 1976);

Nei Leandro de Castro, *Universo e Vocabulário do Grande Sertão* (Rio de Janeiro: Olympio, 1970);

Nelly Novaes Coelho and Ivana Versiani, *Guimarães Rosa: Dois Estudos* (São Paulo: Quíron/INL, 1975);

Irlemar Chiampi Cortez, "Narração e Metalinguagem em *Grande Sertão: Veredas*," *Língua e Literatura*, 2 (1973): 63-91.

Eduardo F. Coutinho, ed., *Guimarães Rosa* (Rio de Janeiro: Civilização Brasileira/INL, 1983);

Lenira Marques Covizzi, *O Insólito em Guimarães Rosa e Borges* (São Paulo: Atica, 1978):

José Hildebrando Dacanal, *Nova Narrativa Épica no Brasil* (Porto Alegre, Brazil: Sulina, 1973);

Dacanal, *Realismo Mágico* (Porto Alegre, Brazil: Movimento, 1970);

Mary L. Daniel, "João Guimarães Rosa," *Studies in Short Fiction*, 8 (Winter 1971): 209-216;

Daniel, *João Guimarães Rosa: Travessia Literária* (Rio de Janeiro: Olympio, 1968);

Daniel, "Word Formation and Deformation in *Grande Sertão: Veredas*," *Luso-Brazilian Review*, 2 (Summer 1965): 81-97;

William Myron Davis, "Japanese Elements in Grande Sertão: Veredas," *Romance Philology*, 29 (May 1976): 409-434;

Diálogo (Revista de Cultura), special Guimarães Rosa issue, 8 (November 1956);

Aglaêda Facó, *Guimarães Rosa: Do Icone ao Símbolo* (Rio de Janeiro: Olympio, 1982);

Adonias Filho and others, *Guimarães Rosa* (Lisbon: Instituto Luso-Brasileiro, 1969);

David William Foster and Virginia Ramos Foster, eds., *Modern Latin American Literature*, 2 volumes (New York: Ungar, 1975), II: 282-295;

Fábio Freixeiro, *Da Razão à Emoção* (São Paulo: Nacional, 1968);

Walnice Nogueira Galvão, *As Formas do Falso* (São Paulo: Perspectiva, 1972);

Galvão, *Mitológica Rosiana* (São Paulo: Atica, 1978);

José Carlos Garbuglio, *O Mundo Movente de Guimarães Rosa* (São Paulo: Atica, 1972);

Agrippino Grieco, *Poetas e Prosadores do Brasil* (Rio de Janeiro: Conquista, 1968), pp. 276-278;

Russell G. Hamilton, Jr., "The Contemporary Brazilian Short Story," in *To Find Something New: Studies in Contemporary Literature*, edited by Henry Grosshans (Pullman: Washington State University Press, 1969), pp. 118-135;

Dante Moreira Leite, *O Amor Romântico e Outros Temas* (São Paulo: Conselho Estadual de Cultura, 1964);

Luís Costa Lima, *A Metamorfose do Silêncio* (Rio de Janeiro: Eldorado, 1974);

Ana Maria Machado, *Recado do Nome: Leitura de Guimarães Rosa à Luz do Nome de Seus Personagens* (Rio de Janeiro: Imago, 1976);

Oswaldino Marques, "Canto e Plumagem das Palavras," in his *A Seta e o Alvo* (Rio de Janeiro: Instituto Nacional do Livro, 1957);

Wilson Martins, "Structural Perspectivism in Guimarães Rosa," in *The Brazilian Novel*, edited by Heitor Martins (Bloomington: Indiana University Publications, 1976), pp. 59-76;

Stephanie Merrim, *Logos and the Word* (New York: Lang, 1983);

Adolfo Casais Monteiro, *O Romance (Teoria e Crítica)* (Rio de Janeiro: Olympio, 1964), pp. 235-247;

Vera Novais, *Tutaméia: Engenho e Arte* (São Paulo: Perspectiva, 1989);

Benedito Nunes, *O Dorso do Tigre* (São Paulo: Perspectiva, 1969);

Franklin de Oliveira, "Guimarães Rosa," in *A Literatura no Brasil*, edited by Afrânio Coutinho (Rio de Janeiro: Sul Americana, 1970), V: 402-449;

M. Cavalcanti Proença, *Trilhas no Grande Sertão* (Rio de Janeiro: Instituto Nacional do Livro, 1960);

Myriam Ramsay, *Uma Concordância do Romance Grande Sertão: Veredas* (Chapel Hill: University of North Carolina, Department of Romance Languages, 1989);

Gilvan P. Ribeiro, "O Alegórico em Guimarães Rosa," in his *Realismo e Anti-Realismo na Literatura Brasileira* (Rio de Janeiro: Paz & Terra, 1974);

Júlia Conceição Fonseca Santos, *Nomes de Personagens em Guimarães Rosa* (Rio de Janeiro: Instituto Nacional do Livro, 1971);

Paulo de Tarso Santos, *O Diálogo no Grande Sertão: Veredas* (São Paulo: Hucitec, 1978);

Wendel Santos, *A Construção do Romance em Guimarães Rosa* (São Paulo: Atica, 1978);

Roberto Schwarz, *A Sereia e o Desconfiado* (Rio de Janeiro: Civilização Brasileira, 1965);

Suzi Frankl Sperber, *Caos e Cosmos: Leituras de Guimarães Rosa* (São Paulo: Duas Cidades, 1976);

Sperber, *Guimarães Rosa: Signo e Sentimento* (São Paulo: Atica, 1982);

Alan Viggiano, *Itinerário de Riobaldo Tatarana* (Belo Horizonte, Brazil: Comunicação/INL, 1974);

Jon S. Vincent, *João Guimarães Rosa* (Boston: Twayne, 1978);

Teresinha Souto Ward, *O Discurso Oral em Grande Sertão: Veredas* (São Paulo: Livraria Duas Cidades, 1984);

Pedro Xisto, Augusto de Campos, and Haroldo de Campos, *Guimarães Rosa em Tres Dimensões* (São Paulo: Conselho Estadual de Cultura, 1970).

Papers:

Guimarães Rosa's private library, including manuscripts and notes, is housed at the Instituto de Estudos Brasileiros da Universidade de São Paulo.

Juan Rulfo
(16 May 1918 - 7 January 1986)

Luis Leal
University of California, Santa Barbara

BOOKS: *El llano en llamas* (Mexico City: Fondo de Cultura Económica, 1953; enlarged, 1970); translated by George D. Schade as *The Burning Plain and Other Stories* (Austin: University of Texas Press, 1967);

Pedro Páramo (Mexico City: Fondo de Cultura Económica, 1955; revised, 1980); translated by Lysander Kemp (New York: Grove, 1959);

Pedro Páramo y El llano en llamas (Barcelona: Planeta, 1969);

Autobiografía armada, edited by Reina Roffé (Buenos Aires: Corregidor, 1973);

Obras completas, edited by Jorge Ruffinelli (Caracas: Ayacucho, 1977);

Antología personal (Mexico City: Nueva Imagen, 1978);

El gallo de oro y otros textos para cine (Mexico City: Era, 1980);

Juan Rulfo: Homenaje nacional, by Rulfo and others (Mexico City: Instituto Nacional de Bellas Artes/SEP, 1980); translated by Frank Janney as *Inframundo: The Mexico of Juan Rulfo* (Hanover, N.H.: Ediciones del Norte, 1983);

Para cuando yo me ausente (Mexico City: Grijalvo, 1982).

Although Juan Rulfo's literary production was meager, it has had an impact on Latin-American narrative fiction that surpasses that of many prolific novelists or short-story writers. His popularity, not only in Latin America but also in Europe, may be explained by the fact that his collection of short stories *El llano en llamas* (1953; translated as *The Burning Plain and Other Stories*, 1967) and his novel *Pedro Páramo* (1955; translated, 1959) capture in a powerful way the essence of rural Mexico and its people. There may be another reason for this popularity, and that is the introduction by Rulfo of a new type of fiction into Latin-American letters, a fiction that was soon to explode into the so-called Boom, with the novels of Carlos Fuentes, Gabriel García Márquez, Julio Cortázar, and Mario Vargas Llosa, among others.

Rulfo's two major works of fiction, his film scripts—collected in *El gallo de oro* (The Golden Cock, 1980)—and his photographs, many of which were published in *Juan Rulfo: Homenaje nacional* (1980; translated as *Inframundo*, 1983), deal with the countryside of his native region, the southern, bare, arid, economically deprived part of the central Mexican state of Jalisco, where he was born on 16 May 1918 in the town of Apulco. Juan Nepomuceno Carlos Pérez Rulfo Vizcaíno (his full name) was the son of Juan Nepomuceno Pérez, a civil servant, and María Vizcaíno Arias de Pérez, both also born in the same region. Soon after Rulfo's birth, his family moved to nearby San Gabriel, the city that left an indelible image in his mind and was later to be integrated into his fiction.

In San Gabriel, Rulfo attended elementary school with his two brothers and experienced the Cristero revolt (1926-1927), a religious war that broke out in central Mexico against the federal government. His father was assassinated in 1925, which left a profound emotional wound in the young boy, and two years later his mother died of a heart attack. In 1928 Rulfo and his brothers were sent to Guadalajara and were placed in the Luis Silva school for orphans, where Rulfo remained until 1932.

Wishing to continue his education, he registered at the Universidad de la Guadalajara, but on the same day he entered school, a strike was declared by the students and the university was closed. Because of the strike he went to Mexico City early in 1934, where he attended the national university to study law. As soon as his financial aid provided by an uncle stopped, Rulfo abandoned the university and began to seek employment. From 1935 to 1945 he worked in the Department of the Interior as an immigration agent.

In Mexico City, Rulfo soon wrote a novel, of which little is known except the title, "El hijo

Juan Rulfo

del desaliento" (Son of Affliction), and a short fragment, "Un pedazo de noche" (A Piece of Night), dated January 1940 but not published until 1959 (in the *Revista Mexicana de Literatura*)—it was later collected in *Antología personal* (1978). Although this fragment seems to be a chapter of a longer work—perhaps the unpublished novel—it has the structure of a short story. The fragment reflects the style and narrative technique of later stories by Rulfo, such as the aura of vagueness that hovers over the identification of people and things, as well as the indecisiveness of the characters, who are surrounded by a sense of mystery. Also present in the story is the stylistic device of personifying the emotions, which Rulfo was later to bring to a high degree of perfection. No less conspicuous in this early prose work is Rulfo's keenness in character descriptions. Unlike his predecessors, he seems to remove himself completely from the scene and allow the personages to characterize themselves. Pilar, the protagonist, does not need to say she is a prostitute; her profession is revealed by her words and actions.

In the story, Rulfo makes use of certain narrative techniques that were to become his trademarks. The first-person narrator (Pilar) tells the story in the present about an incident that occurred long ago, but she relates it as if it has just happened or is happening. The narration gives the reader the sense that the action is taking place in the present, and therefore interest in the development of the plot is heightened.

Rulfo had the fortune to have as an immigration coworker Efrén Hernández, an accomplished short-story writer from whom he learned a great deal about the art of writing. Hernández introduced Rulfo to Marco Antonio Millán, the editor of the literary periodical *América*, where in 1945 Rulfo published his first story, "La vida no es muy seria en sus cosas" (Life is not Very Serious About Things; collected in *Antología personal*). The story is about an expectant mother who has

Rulfo as a young man

lost her husband and therefore puts all her hope of happiness on her future child, whom she is sure will be a boy. However, her concern for her dead husband leads her to a second tragedy, the death of the unborn baby. The story, although melodramatic, is of interest because the main preoccupation is with death.

The story, at one time rejected by Rulfo as unworthy of his ability, can only be considered inferior when compared with the two others he published the same year, 1945, while visiting Guadalajara. There he joined Juan José Arreola and Antonio Alatorre in the publication of the literary periodical *Pan*, where two of Rulfo's best stories, "Macario" and "Nos han dado la tierra" (They Gave Us the Land), appeared in July and November of that year. Both stories were collected in *El llano en llamas*. In these two stories Rulfo demonstrates a mastery of technique and style not present in his earlier efforts. These two *Pan* stories are his first significant works.

"Macario" reflects the assuredness of the master storyteller, well versed in the psychology of his characters, especially the eponymous protagonist, whose mentality is limited. Rulfo presents in depth the experiences of a young boy (or perhaps a young man, since his age is never revealed) whose world is very confined. Macario characterizes himself by means of a long interior monologue; through Macario's limited perspective the reader becomes acquainted with his world. The technique is the same as that used by William Faulkner in *The Sound and the Fury* (1929), where Benjy describes his world. In "Macario" Rulfo has created a unity of impression that has a powerful impact on the reader.

In "Nos han dado la tierra" Rulfo approaches a sociopolitical subject, the distribution of land by the revolutionary government of Mexico. The story tells of a simple incident regarding the delivery of land to the heads of families of a small rural community. The campesinos leave their homes at daybreak in order to receive the promised land parcels. It is a very hot day, and the group begins to dwindle. By early afternoon only the narrator and three others are left. Finally the government representative appears to deliver the deeds. The campesinos want the land near the river, but they are given the *llano*, more like a desert than farmland. They protest but to no avail. The desperate situation is made all the more dramatic by the description of the desolated plains, the first description by Rulfo of his native region. As is characteristic of Rulfo's work, the social content in the story is not stated explicitly as was done by most of the writers of the revolution. His stories are usually expressed by the actions of the characters and not by any editorializing on the part of the author.

In 1947 Rulfo married Clara Aparicio, with whom he had three sons (Francisco, Pablo, and Juan Carlos) and a daughter, Claudia. Back in Mexico City that same year, he began to work in the publicity department of F. G. Goodrich, a position he held until 1954. Meanwhile, in 1952 he had received a fellowship from the Centro de Escritores Mexicanos, which made it possible for him to dedicate more time to writing. He decided to collect his stories, both published and unpublished. This first book, which was an immediate success, was published the following year under the title of one of the stories, "El llano en llamas." The Centro fellowship was extended for another year, and it is assumed that during this period he wrote the novel *Pedro Páramo* (1955). In 1954 he had already published its first chapter in the January-March issue of the periodical *Las Letras Patrias* under the title "Un cuento" (A Short Story). In 1955 he accepted a position with the government to develop the Papaloapan river basin in southern Mexico. The project was discontinued in 1956, and Rulfo was back in Mexico City. Two years later he returned to office work, this time in charge of the archives of the Sociedad Mexicana de Geografía y Estadística. He apparently liked this type of work, which was suitable for his rather quiet, withdrawn nature.

Dissatisfied, though, with life in metropolitan Mexico City, in 1959 he went back to Guadalajara with his family in search of peace and tranquillity. However, in the provincial capital things went from bad to worse, his life being complicated by his heavy drinking and ill health. While working at Televicentro, he found time to write a short novel, "El gallero" (The Cockfighter), which he did not publish, and the script for a short film, "El despojo" (The Plunder). But in 1962 he went back to Mexico City, this time to stay for the rest of his life.

By this time Rulfo had become quite popular outside of Mexico, since his fiction was being translated into many languages. In spite of this fame, he had to go back to work at another archive, this time at the Instituto Nacional Indigenista, where he was also in charge of publishing the periodical *México Indígena*. It was about this time that he began writing a new novel, to be called "La cordillera" (The Packtrain), another work that was never published.

The public had to wait until 1980 to read another new book of fiction by Rulfo: *El gallo de oro y otros textos para cine* (The Golden Cock and Other Film Scripts), a slender volume of only 143 pages. It is not clear whether these texts were reconstructed from the films, from the original scripts, or if they are the original versions written by Rulfo during the early 1960s.

In *El gallo de oro* folkloric elements predominate, as in some of the stories collected in *El llano en llamas*. The characters (Dionisio the cockfighter and Bernarda the singer), the ambiance (the small towns in Jalisco during fair time), and the imagery are all related to Mexican folklore. The story is rather common. By raising and gambling on fighting cocks, and with the help of his wife, Bernarda, who brings him good luck, Dionisio is able to amass a fortune. When Bernarda dies, though, he loses everything. Suicide is the only way out for Dionisio, who blames Bernarda for not having warned him that she was mortally ill. Bernarda's tragedy is that her magic powers bring success to others but not to her: she is desired by men for her powers and not for the love she desires. Although this work does not compare to *Pedro Páramo*, Rulfo's personal style still enlivens the world created in the story.

Even though Rulfo published only three books, his skill as a fiction writer has been recognized throughout the world. In 1970 the Mexican government awarded him the Premio Nacional de Letras. Ten years later Mexico again recognized Rulfo with additional ceremonies. In September 1980 he was admitted to the Academia Mexicana de la Lengua, and, the same year, the Instituto Nacional de Bellas Artes held conferences in his honor and published deluxe editions of his works. In 1986 the Museum of the National University of Mexico in San Antonio, Texas, held an exhibit of his photographs.

Portrait of Rulfo by Oswaldo Guayasamín

Rulfo was extremely well read. His favorite authors were, of course, novelists, especially the leading Russians, Scandinavians, Italians, Americans, and Brazilians. His interest in literature, and above all fiction, dates back to his early years in San Gabriel. The local priest had left Rulfo's grandmother a small library that Rulfo utilized. The first novels he read were those of the Italian Emilio Salgari and the Frenchman Alexandre Dumas, books of adventure liked by most boys. Then he became interested in English, American, and northern European novelists. The novel *Hunger* by Knut Hamsun left a deep impression on him. Later he went on to read more sophisticated novels, by James Joyce, William Faulkner, John Dos Passos, Ernest Hemingway, and others. Among the contemporary French writers, one of his favorites was Jean Giono; among the Germans, Günter Grass; and among the Italians, Vasco Pratolini.

Rulfo also acknowledged that he learned a great deal about writing from Efrén Hernández. Among the many writers influenced by Hernández three stand out: José Revueltas, Juan José Arreola, and Juan Rulfo.

Arreola began to publish his short stories in Guadalajara in the 1940s and represents another trend in the Mexican short story of the period, the fantastic. His fiction, like that of Jorge Luis Borges, does not normally reflect the national milieu. When Rulfo's stories appeared, critics immediately contrasted his fiction with that of Arreola. The two writers became the representatives of the two trends predominating at the time in Mexican literature: the national and the cosmopolitan. One year after Rulfo's first book was published, the critic Emmanuel Carballo published a lengthy article comparing the two writers. He observed that while Arreola universalizes his experiences, Rulfo introduces personal subject matter: "Arreola proposes problems that could occur any-

Rulfo in his Mexico City office during the 1970s

where, while Rulfo, starting from a localized place and digging deeply, gives what is national, and even regional, a universal tone."

Two of the stories that appear in *El llano en llamas* foreshadow Rulfo's novel *Pedro Páramo*. "En la madrugada" (At Daybreak) and "Luvina" have the same locale as the novel, a region Rulfo described as depopulated, the people having gone either to the Pacific Coast, the high plains, or the United States. As Ricardo Estrada has pointed out, "Luvina" can be considered "the strongest evidence available regarding the gestation of the ambience of *Pedro Páramo*, and perhaps it could be stated that it contains the germ from which the novel grew." The description of the ghost town named Luvina, for example, anticipates, to a certain extent, that of the novel's Comala, after the cacique has died and the community has become a dead town.

In "En la madrugada" the town appears with its original, actual name, San Gabriel, while in the novel it is called Comala. Rulfo explained the reason for the change: "The name does not exist, no.... But the derivation of comal—an earthenware utensil that is placed over the embers for the purpose of heating the tortillas—and the heat that prevails in that town was what gave me the idea of the name. Comala: the place over the embers" (*Autobiografía armada*, 1973). Although there is no Comala in Jalisco, where the action of the novel takes place, there is one in the neighboring state of Colima, situated at the foot of the Volcán del Fuego. The selection of the name Comala was appropriate, as it underscores the fiery nature of Pedro Páramo, the protagonist. This change, however, came much later, perhaps after the novel was completed. The year before it was published, the first chapter appeared in a periodical, and there the town is called Tuxcacuexco, a real town not far from San Gabriel.

Rulfo said that the idea of writing a novel about San Gabriel, the town where he had spent his boyhood, came to him "from an earlier period. It was, it can be said, almost planned about ten years before. I had not written a single line

Rulfo with Juan Carlos Onetti circa 1985

when it was already turning in my mind" (*Autobiografía armada*). The setting, the characters, the tone, and the narrative devices found in his short stories appear in the novel. The great difference is that in the novel all the people are dead. The idea of creating a ghost town where the inhabitants continue living after they have died came to Rulfo after a visit he made to San Gabriel, where, instead of finding the idealized town he had carried in his mind for years, he found a ghost town. The novel is the result of a desire to bring this town back to life.

In *Pedro Páramo* the presence of death predominates. This preoccupation with death as a theme is also characteristic of most of Rulfo's short stories. The stories serve as a prelude for the novel, which is an orchestration of the theme of death. It begins when Juan Preciado arrives at Comala in search of his father, Pedro Páramo, the cacique who has disinherited him, and ends with the death of Pedro, killed by another of his sons, Abundio. In the town the dead talk about killings and death, and in their graves they continue their conversations about death. The novel ends with the following description of Pedro Páramo's death: "He leaned against Damiana and tried to walk. After a few steps he fell down, pleading within but not speaking a single word. He struck a feeble blow against the ground and then crumbled to pieces as if he were a heap of stones."

Rulfo's preoccupation with death and violence was perhaps due to the many encounters he himself had with death—the revolution, the Cristero revolt of the late 1920s, and the violent deaths of some of his relatives: his father and his uncle were assassinated; his grandfather was strung up by his thumbs and lost them.

Critics are in agreement that with the publication of *Pedro Páramo* the Mexican novel reached a high degree of perfection. In his essay "Landscape and the Novel in Mexico" Octavio Paz says, "Juan Rulfo is the only Mexican novelist to have provided us an image—rather than a mere description—of our physical surroundings. Like [D. H.] Lawrence and [Malcolm] Lowry, what he has given us is not photographic documentation or an impressionist painting; he has incarnated his intuitions and his personal obsessions in stone, in dust, in desert sand. His vision of this world is really a vision of *another world*." In Carlos Fuentes's *La nueva novela hispanoamericana*

(The New Spanish-American Novel), Fuentes writes, "The work of Juan Rulfo is not only the highest expression which the Mexican novel has attained until now: through *Pedro Páramo* we can find the thread that leads us to the new Latin-American novel."

Juan Rulfo died on 7 January 1986 of lung cancer, which had been diagnosed in October 1985. One of his friends, the writer Fernando Benítez, successfully recommended to the president of Mexico that Rulfo be buried in the Rotunda de Hombres Ilustres, the resting place of most famous Mexican writers and artists. Rulfo, then Mexico's most widely read writer, had revitalized prose style, had introduced complex narrative structures, and had revealed to the world Mexico's other side, such as the strength of the rural people in spite of their suffering, their attachment to the land, and their tragic sense of life. In short, Rulfo can be considered as the representative, par excellence, of Mexican fiction writing.

Bibliographies:

Arthur Ramírez, "Hacia una bibliografía de y sobre Juan Rulfo," *Revista Iberoamericana*, 50, no. 86 (1974): 135-171;

David William Foster, "Juan Rulfo," in his *Mexican Literature: A Bibliography of Secondary Sources* (Metuchen, N.J.: Scarecrow Press, 1981), 306-323.

References:

María Elena Ascanio, "Juan Rulfo examina su narrativa," *Escritura*, 2 (1976): 305-317;

Paul W. Borgeson, Jr., "The Turbulent Flow: Stream of Consciousness Techniques in the Short Stories of Juan Rulfo," *Revista de Estudios Hispánicos*, 13 (1979): 227-252;

Julianne Burton, "Sexuality and the Mythic Dimension in Juan Rulfo's *Pedro Páramo*," *Symposium*, 28 (1974): 228-247;

Emmanuel Carballo, "Arreola y Rulfo," *Revista de la Universidad de México*, 8 (March 1954): 28-29, 32;

Stephen T. Clinton, "Form and Meaning in Juan Rulfo's 'Talpa,'" *Romance Notes*, 16 (1975): 520-525;

Margaret Virginia Ekstrom, "Frustrated Quest in the Narratives of Juan Rulfo," *American Hispanist*, 12 (1976): 13-16;

Ricardo Estrada, "Los indicios de Pedro Páramo," in *Homenaje a Juan Rulfo*, edited by Helmy F. Giacoman (New York: Las Américas, 1974), pp. 110-132;

George Ronald Freeman, *Paradise and Fall in Rulfo's "Pedro Páramo": Archetype and Structural Unity* (Cuernavaca, Mexico: Centro Intercultural de Documentación, 1970);

Carlos Fuentes, *La nueva novela hispanoamericana* (Mexico City: Mortiz, 1969);

Helmy F. Giacoman, ed., *Homenaje a Juan Rulfo* (New York: Las Américas, 1974);

Donald K. Gordon, *Los cuentos de Juan Rulfo* (Madrid: Playor, 1976);

Donald K. Gyurko, "Rulfo's Aesthetic Nihilism: Narrative Antecedents of Pedro Páramo," *Hispanic Review*, 40 (1972): 451-466;

Luis Harrs and Barbara Dohmann, "Juan Rulfo, or the Souls of the Departed," in their *Into the Mainstream* (New York: Harper & Row, 1967), pp. 246-275;

Aden W. Hayes, "Rulfo's Counter-epic: Pedro Páramo and the Stasis of History," *Journal of Spanish Studies: Twentieth Century*, 7 (1979): 279-296;

Luis Leal, *Juan Rulfo* (Boston: Twayne, 1983);

Howard Mancing, "The Art of Literary Allusion in Juan Rulfo," *Modern Fiction Studies*, 23 (1977): 242-244;

Los narradores ante el público (Mexico City: Mortiz, 1966);

Octavio Paz, "Landscape and the Novel in Mexico," in his *Alternating Current*, translated by Helen R. Lane (New York: Viking, 1973), pp. 15-16;

Terry J. Peavler, "Textual Problems in *Pedro Páramo*," *Revista de Estudios Hispánicos*, 19 (1985): 91-99;

Humberto E. Robles, "Variantes en Pedro Páramo," *Nueva Revista de Filología Hispánica*, 31 (1982): 106-116;

William Rowe, *Rulfo: El llano en llamas* (London: Grant & Cutler, 1987);

Earl Shorris, "Homage to Juan Rulfo," *Nation*, 15 May 1982, pp. 597-599;

Joseph Sommers, "Through the Window of the Grave: Juan Rulfo," in his *After the Storm: Landmarks of the Modern Mexican Novel* (Albuquerque: University of New Mexico Press, 1968), pp. 69-94.

Severo Sarduy
(25 February 1937 -   )

Julia A. Kushigian
Connecticut College

BOOKS: *Gestos* (Barcelona: Seix Barral, 1963);
De donde son los cantantes (Mexico City: Mortiz, 1967); translated by Suzanne Jill Levine as *From Cuba with a Song*, in *Triple Cross* (New York: Dutton, 1972);
Escrito sobre un cuerpo (Buenos Aires: Sudamericana, 1969);
Flamenco (Stuttgart: Manus, 1969);
Mood Indigo (Stuttgart: Manus, 1970);
Merveilles de la nature (Paris: Pauvet, 1971);
Overdose (Las Palmas, Grand Canary: Inventarios Provisionales, 1972);
Cobra (Buenos Aires: Sudamericana, 1972); translated by Levine (New York: Dutton, 1975);
Barroco (Buenos Aires: Sudamericana, 1974);
Big Bang (Barcelona: Tusquets, 1974);
Maitreya (Madrid: Seix Barral, 1978); translated by Levine (Hanover, N.H.: Ediciones del Norte, 1987);
Para la voz (Madrid: Fundamentos, 1978); translated by Philip Barnard as *For Voice* (Pittsburgh: Latin American Literary Review, 1985);
Daiquirí (Santa Cruz, Tenerife: Poéticas 2, 1980);
La simulación (Caracas: Monte Avila, 1982);
Colibrí (Barcelona: Argos Vergara, 1984);
Un testigo fugaz y disfrazado (Barcelona: Mall, 1985);
El Cristo de la rue Jacob (Barcelona: Mall, 1987);
Nueva inestabilidad (Mexico City: Vuelta, 1987);
Cocuyo (Barcelona: Tusquets, 1990).

OTHER: "Cronología," in *Severo Sarduy*, edited by Julián Ríos (Caracas & Madrid: Fundamentos/Espiral, 1976), pp. 8-14.

From poetry, to essay, to drama and the novel, Severo Sarduy's works span a literary horizon that is unconventional and enigmatic. Characterized by his complex view of the baroque in Latin-American literature, which he terms neobaroque; his questioning of the capacity of language to mediate between reality and fantasy, in association with the structuralists; and his renovative interpretation of orientalism in Latin-American literature, Sarduy's work moves beyond the time-honored structures of genres—the traditional novel, for example—to establish another sense of the literary. His experimentation with language is examined in his collections of essays and is practiced in his poetry, but it is with his novels that Sarduy has achieved international acclaim. Sarduy's ruminations on the signifier/signified relationship in language brings him into close contact with the structuralists of the *Tel Quel* group in Paris and the work of Russian critic Mikhail Bakhtin, whose theories on carnivalized literature have been elaborated on and taken in another direction by Sarduy in his redefinition of parody.

Born on 25 February 1937 in Camagüey, Cuba, into a working-class family, Severo Sarduy, the son of a stationmaster, spent his formative years in Camagüey with his family, including a younger sister. Sarduy attended a public elementary school and graduated in 1955 from the Instituto de Segunda Enseñanza in Camagüey. Sarduy became interested in literature as a vocation early on, which made his family uneasy as it seemed a dangerous route to take. He wrote and published poetry in a local newspaper and in a collection of poetry by the poets of Camagüey. In 1958 Sarduy was delighted when one of his poems was published in an important Havana literary magazine, *Ciclón*, directed by José Rodríguez Feo.

Sarduy moved to Havana in 1956 and enrolled in the school of medicine at the Universidad de La Habana. Sarduy had to earn a living while he studied, so he quickly found a job at an advertising agency, where he wrote jingles for radio and television. In 1957 Guillermo Cabrera Infante published Sarduy's "El seguro" (The Certainty), a short story of social protest, in the magazine *Carteles*. The following year Sarduy entered the world of literary criticism with a generally favorable review of José Lezama Lima's collection of essays, *Tratados en La Habana* (Treatises in Ha-

Severo Sarduy (photograph by D. Roche; copyright by Seuil)

vana, 1958). Although still aligned with the group of younger critics and authors who wrote for *Ciclón*, Sarduy began to show his admiration for Lezama Lima and those who wrote for *Orígenes*, a more conservative magazine of Catholic and nationalistic views.

When the Fulgencio Batista government fell and Fidel Castro's followers took their place in the capital, Sarduy became one of the most important young intellectuals of the revolution. In mid January 1959 Sarduy published two revolutionary poems in the newspaper *Revolución*, whose contributors had fought against the Batista dictatorship. At the end of March of that same year, Sarduy was named art critic for a new art and literature weekly, *Lunes de Revolución*, which represented a much larger and younger group than had previously written exclusively about art and literature in Cuba. Sarduy did not limit himself to these publications, though. He managed the literary page of *Diario Libre* and collaborated on the journals *Nueva Revista Cubana* and the *Artes Plásticas*. His political activities continued when he signed, in a special issue of *Lunes* (March 1959), a manifesto from writers and artists to protest the blowing up of a Belgian ship in Havana's harbor. In November of the same year, he protested the air attacks perpetrated by the United States against Cuba.

In fall 1959 Sarduy was awarded a scholarship to study art criticism at the Ecole du Louvre in Paris. When his courses were completed in 1961, Sarduy decided to stay in France. The group of young writers who had contributed to *Lunes* had disbanded, and the Cuban government was in censorial control of all publishing there.

Sarduy dedicated the next few years to further studies on art in Paris and to writing his first novel, *Gestos* (Gestures, 1963). Sarduy also began to study structuralist methodology with Roland Barthes at the Ecole Pratique des Hautes Etudes at the Sorbonne and started his creative collaboration with two important literary magazines in France, *Tel Quel* and *Mundo Nuevo*. Using structuralism, Sarduy reread the works of the Cuban literary tradition in an effort to rediscover Cuban culture and history. Sarduy's collaboration with the structuralists writing for *Tel Quel* allowed him to explore the novel and create literature in a new mode. It also introduced him to the work of Bakhtin and the concept of carnivalized literature, through which Sarduy was to analyze

Cover for Sarduy's 1972 novel, in which a transsexual travels to Tangiers for a sex-change operation

Hispanic-American literature.

Gestos is his first attempt to move away from realism in literature. The success of *Gestos* was evident through its many positive reviews in Europe and Latin America and through the subsequent translation of the novel into several other languages, including French, Danish, and German. Influenced by the psychological theories of Maurice Merleau-Ponty, Sarduy studies gestures, movements, and voices in the novel. *Gestos* relates the prehistory of the Cuban Revolution in a parody of the Batista dictatorship, in an effort to summarize "Cubanness." The plot is not the focal point and is generally not logically detailed. In *Gestos* an unnamed mulatto woman who does laundry by day and sings by night comes to symbolize the Cuban people. Readers learn about her activities through the description of her comings and goings through the streets of Havana, and through her conversations and interior monologues, which paint pictures and record gestures of Cuban society before the revolution. Other characters are presented in terms of their relationship to her, the protagonist. Her lover, a young white man, asks her to place a bomb in an electrical plant in Havana, and so become an accomplice in the clandestine battle against the Batista dictatorship. That same evening, after placing the bomb, the woman performs in a Greek tragedy, and during the performance a fire breaks out in the theater. Finally readers see her wrapped in a Cuban flag and riding in a parade to encourage everyone to vote. The electoral parade ends with shooting and a fire that appears to be engulfing the entire city. This apparent parody of the violence that engulfed Havana during the final days of the Batista dictatorship, and the destruction of a way of life for all involved, is made evident through the verbal pictures of those characters who live through the chaos and violence. The "pop lyricism" of the novel is derived from its precedents in other Cuban novels, soap operas, and musical lyrics from the popular boleros and cha-cha's of the time. Although *Gestos* is not considered one of Sarduy's most important novels, his focus on lyricism and the psychology examined through gestures makes this an exemplary work.

Sarduy's next novel, *De donde son los cantantes* (1967; translated as *From Cuba with a Song*, 1972) endeavors to answer the question raised in *Gestos* as to what is Cubanness, its essence, and its history. *De donde* is probably the most experimental of all Sarduy's novels. There are three narratives or sections, preceded by a "Cuban curriculum" and followed by a "Nota." The title (literally, "From Where Are the Singers") is enigmatic in that it may be a question or statement, which revolves around the essence of Cuba. In the first narrative a Spanish general falls in love with Flor de Loto, a singer in the Shanghai, a burlesque theater in Havana. Flor avails herself of many tricks to elude the general. Two members of the chorus, Auxilio and Socorro, who are transvestites and prostitutes, act as go-betweens for the general and Flor, taking advantage of the general's overwhelming interest in Flor to get money and gifts out of him. After they ransack the general's house, the general, in a sadistic mood, plots to kill Flor because of her numerous rejections. He sends her a gift of a bracelet that, when put on, will slash the veins of her wrist, and he waits for her corpse to be taken out of the theater, as the first narrative ends.

The second narrative traces the career of the mulatto singer Dolores Rondón, who was first developed as a character in *Gestos*. Rondón's story is told through an animated discussion between two narrators who argue about aspects of the linguistic and rhetorical composition of the story and also talk with Auxilio and Socorro. This unusual format, though obviously not that of a traditional, written history, reveals the black component of Cuban culture. The principal characters are Rondón, who represents popular speech and thought, and Mortal Pérez, her lover, who represents the typical, corrupt, and provincial politician. After their marriage Pérez becomes a senator, and they move to Havana, where they lead a lavish, wasteful life with other leaders of what is, one imagines, the Batista dictatorship.

Pérez furnishes the president with a supposedly Hawaiian dancer for his pleasure, but when

Cover for the English translation (1985) of Para la voz, *a collection of four radio plays written between 1965 and 1975*

it is learned that she is Rondón, a mulatto from Camagüey, Pérez falls into disfavor with the government. Rondón's subsequent disgrace is explained through her not having appeased the Afro-Cuban gods during her vain period of excess and luxury. The second narrator suggests that perhaps Pérez's downfall came at the hands of Auxilio and Socorro, who were probably jealous of Rondón, who returns to Camagüey and dies in poverty.

The third story represents the white, or European (specifically Spanish), component of Cuban culture. The narration begins in Spain, where Auxilio and Socorro are pursuing Pérez, the absent lover for whom they are consumed with desire. Leaving from Cádiz, Spain, they arrive in Santiago, Cuba, on their pilgrimage. There Auxilio and Socorro learn about music in the cathedral from a mulatto who seduces them. In the Santiago cathedral they discover a wooden figure of Christ, which they make into a hypostasis of Pérez. They take it and engender a procession throughout the island, from Santiago to Havana, passing through Camagüey, where the procession is confused with one of Pérez's political meetings. The group arrives in Havana in the middle of a snowstorm that blankets everything in white. The statue of Christ, which had been gradually decaying, crumbles into many pieces. The faithful, as they pick up the pieces and run for shelter, are greeted with bullets from helicopters.

This third section, titled "Entry of Christ into Havana," may suggest the entry of Fidel Castro and his troops into the capital in 1959. Castro may be the Pérez that the protagonists are pursuing. *De donde son los cantantes* is a novel of a search for power and for origins; it is also a parody of the strata of Cuban culture and society.

Sarduy's next two novels, *Cobra* (1972; translated, 1975) and *Maitreya* (1978; translated, 1987), in addition to two of his collections of essays, *Barroco* (Baroque, 1974) and *La simulación* (1982), explore the geographic and historical essence of the Americas as well as the Spanish-American representation of the Orient in America, in the same vein as the seminal works of Lezama Lima and Octavio Paz. For *Cobra* Sarduy was awarded the Prix Medicis from France. He attempts to incorporate the subconscious of the typical Spanish-American narrative into *Cobra*, and its language is enigmatic—it remains one of Sarduy's most difficult novels. *Cobra* consists of two interwoven narratives presented principally as dialogues. The first part of the novel takes place in the Teatro Lírico de Muñecas (Lyrical Theater of Dolls), a burlesque house. The protagonist, Cobra, the transsexual star at the theater, is involved with La Señora, the owner of the house, in a process to reduce Cobra's feet, which because of their size are seen as a physical defect. The drug the two use is so powerful that it reduces Cobra and the madam to dwarfs, who are named Pup and La Señorita. But then Cobra, back to normal size, goes to India with the artist Eustaquio el Sabrosón, in search of colors and paints for an Oriental number they are planning for the theater. These adventures are accompanied by a series of authorial judgments on the art of writing.

In the next sequence Cobra has gone to Tangiers in search of Dr. Ktazob, who is famous for his sex-change operations. La Señora and her disciples go to Spain looking for Cobra, where they meet up with Auxilio and Socorro, the two characters from *De donde son los cantantes*. Once in Tangiers, four drug pushers from Amsterdam direct them to Dr. Ktazob, who performs an operation on Cobra.

Sarduy's version of orientalism (seen in the Tangiers section) derives from his interests since childhood in Buddhism and theosophy, his visit to the Orient in the 1970s, and includes his amending and redefining of concepts as diverse as parody, simulation, and anamorphosis. In *Cobra* orientalism is fused with the baroque.

A connection is formed between the Tangiers section and the next scene in *Cobra* (which takes place in an unnamed ultramodern city) through the presence of the young drug pushers, who are transformed into a motorcycle gang that is adept at Tantrism and has allied with a group of Tibetan monks, in exile after the Chinese invasion. The members of the motorcycle gang are Totem, Tigre, Escorpión, and Tundra, and they submit Cobra (now a female) to an initiation rite that eventually kills her. A complex, funereal, Tantric ritual is then performed, which ends with a series of prayers, in a new section entitled "Blanco." The members have learned liturgical practices from the Tibetan monks, and Totem dispenses drugs, advice, and religious relics. The details of rites performed by the members echo the activities practiced by La Señora in the theater and Dr. Ktazob in his operation in Tangiers. *Cobra* ends with "Diario Indio," where the motorcycle gang reappears with the Tibetan monks. On their way to Tibet the gang asks for help from the Grand Lama. The story concludes in the snow at the Chinese border; in the utter desolation the only sound that is heard is the spinning of the prayer wheels at an abandoned monastery. *Cobra* is a blending of East and West, of past and present (the motorcyclists influence the monks as much as they are influenced by them), and of histories that repeat themselves (the invasion of Tibet, and the invasion of Cuba by Castro and his forces).

Sarduy's *Maitreya* is a novel whose central theme is exile. Maitreya, in Buddhism, is the future Buddha who will restore peace and truth to the world. The novel begins with the death of the Master, a Tibetan monk, at the time of the Chinese invasion of Tibet (1950), when the monks abandon their monasteries and flee to save their lives. After predicting his reincarnation as the Instructor, the Master dies, and the other monks burn the body in a funeral rite and escape to India. There they find a young boy who is being cared for by two Chinese women, the Leng sisters. The situation and the child himself corre-

Cover for the 1976 collection of critical articles that includes an autobiographical essay by Sarduy

spond more or less to the Master's prophecy, so after administering a few prescribed tests, the monks declare the boy the new Lama, the Instructor. The Leng sisters, wanting to save the child from a life of poverty and abstention in a monastery, flee with him to Ceylon, where they open a vegetarian hotel and set up the child as a priest from an ad hoc Buddhist sect. The child sells advice and religious artifacts and is joined by a niece of the Leng sisters, Iluminada Leng, who is also interested in being prosperous. But the child, who has become the young Instructor, meets a group of monks who have dedicated their lives to meditation, and he promptly becomes disillusioned with his own calling. The young Instructor then refuses to respond to his clients' questions. Iluminada, realizing the impending financial disaster, leaves with her friend, El Dulce, for Cuba. Meanwhile the Instructor dies, and the Leng sisters perform a funeral rite that resembles the one for the Master in the first part of the novel.

The second part of *Maitreya*—divided into four sections titled alternately "El Puño" and "El Doble"—includes the birth of "Las Tremendas," twin sisters, in Sagua la Grande, a city in the north of Cuba. Luis Leng, son of Iluminada and El Dulce, has gone to live there also, possibly because of the city's large Chinese population. The twins discover they have powers that allow them to tell the future and heal others. They live off these powers until they discover that, after passing through their first menstrual cycle, their powers are lost to them. They then try singing and performing on stage and are later seduced by Leng.

The scene shifts from Sagua to Miami, where La Tremenda (one of the twins), Luis Leng, and a dwarf painter from Sagua have gone to live. La Divina (the other twin) joins them there, and later they all move to New York, where Leng opens a restaurant and Las Tremendas dedicate themselves to a new sect based on rigid practices and closely allied to Marxism and Leninism. The Leng sisters reappear as two witches called Las Tétricas, and they attempt with electronic equipment to cause La Tremenda to lose her voice. La Tremenda, though, enlists the aid of a sculptor, John de Andrea, who makes a perfect double for her, which attracts the rays of the equipment used by Las Tétricas.

One evening while drugged, La Tremenda roller-skates down a New York City street until she reaches the fountain at Washington Square. From out of the fountain appears an Iranian chauffeur with whom she falls in love. Through a cultural and geographic displacement, all of the characters in the novel suddenly appear in the Middle East. In Iran they open a massage parlor that specializes in sadomasochistic practices for their wealthy clients, the sheiks. When the dwarf is accused by a sheik of abusive practices, they are all taken prisoner by the authorities and forced into exile across the desert. In an old hotel, probably in Algeria, La Tremenda and the dwarf drink a potion and are able to see the letters of the name of a prophet. Staring at the burning name of the prophet and in ritual fashion, the Iranian chauffeur makes love to La Tremenda. Within a month a fetus with membranes between its fingers and toes is expelled from her womb. The dwarf and the fetus die and are buried together. La Tremenda then appears in Afghanistan, where she is considered the object of a local cult, which she later renounces, and heads toward the South.

Maitreya, in its many cultural displacements and transformations, is very difficult, as is *Cobra* and the other Sarduy novels, to synthesize in a plot description. Unlike *Cobra*, where the prose is reduced to a series of rigid formulas, *Maitreya* unfolds register upon register of rhetorical devices, whose goal seems a rather conventional search for beauty in literature but whose composition is so visually and phonically overwhelming that the unifying sense of each component as well as that of the entire work is lost. The characters in *Maitreya* exist in exile, running from an invasion, or takeover, fleeing one history-making event after another. Events are repeated; places change but remain the same; reincarnation is in evidence. In *Maitreya* geopolitical oppositions are dissolved, and the licit and the illicit are joined, as well as the profane and the sacred. Opposition also ceases to exist when, through dialogization, the language of oriental themes is mixed with the rhetorical language of the baroque, or the neobaroque. The Tantric banquet and the parody of the koan, a Zen Buddhist exercise, for example, are united—through the fusion of opposites and the philosophic concept of the impermanence of everything in life—with the baroque.

The more recent works of Sarduy deal once again with an analysis of the Latin-American tradi-

Sarduy circa 1989 (photograph by Antonio Gálvez)

tion in literature and of what it means to be a Latin-American author. This introspection is evident in his collection of essays *La simulación* and his collection of poetry *Un testigo fugaz y disfrazado* (A Passing and Disguised Witness, 1985). Sarduy's novel *Colibrí* (Hummingbird, 1984) abandons the specific Cuban culture and theme, in evidence in his other novels, to examine a relationship pondered by other Latin-American novelists, the relationship between nature and culture in the New World. The plot of *Colibrí* opens near a river at the entrance to a jungle, in a world of drugs, money, waste, and perversion, much as was seen at the end of *Maitreya*. There La Regenta presides as madam in a house where handsome young men wrestle for the viewing pleasure of rich men and the military. La Regenta runs her business ambitiously and is assisted by a giant, various helpers, cooks, and a dwarf, who also serves as referee in the matches.

A young, extremely handsome blond man arrives one day and is given the name Colibrí, for his grace and agility in eluding the holds of his opponents. His first match is against an obese Japanese man who tries but is unsuccessful in getting Colibrí down in a wrestling hold. Colibrí becomes the hero of this small club, but because the madam has fallen desperately in love with him, Colibrí runs away into the jungle, pursued by her aides. In the jungle Colibrí meets up with El Japonesón, the fat wrestler, and they become friends and then lovers. The men who are after Colibrí find him, so he separates from El Japonesón and goes off toward the capital. There La Regenta's men find him again, and he is obliged to wrestle again with El Japonesón and with the giant. But Colibrí escapes successfully once more, going back into the jungle. Once deep inside the jungle he is captured by those who have been pursuing him, and they return him to La Regenta. But this time they treat him like a divinity. Colibrí orders the house burnt and built again, demanding that young people be brought to enliven the activities there. In the end Colibrí replaces La Regenta, becoming the new "dictator," and the novel is brought full circle (with a new manager in charge of the club).

Colibrí can be associated with other heroes, either mythical or poetic. In an anthropological approach Colibrí could be studied in terms of his initiation, or rite of passage into manhood. Colibrí is forced to leave the world he knows to be tested as a man, and then returns to assume power. Colibrí also symbolizes simulation, appearance, and fakery, and he represents the pursuit of inaccessible beauty, which in order to be possessed must first be altered or destroyed. The "strangeness" of the protagonists is underscored through the baroque rhetorical expressions and through the distancing from comparable heroic literary figures.

Sarduy's later work includes a collection of essays *Nueva inestabilidad* (New Instability, 1987), and two prose works, *El Cristo de la rue Jacob* (The Christ of Jacob Street, 1987) and *Cocuyo* (1990). Sarduy defines *El Cristo de la rue Jacob* as a series of short narratives, or "epiphanies," a term borrowed from James Joyce. The work is divided into two parts. The narratives of the first part explore violent, difficult moments of life, such as the pain of birth itself and the first scar. It is a compilation of the marks or physical scars people carry with them through life. The second part also refers to marks, but these are mental. It is an exploration of that which remains in the memory longer than a recollection but shorter than an obsession. Rather than establishing a unifying theme for the narratives of the second part, a unifying poetic impulse explores the universe, the everyday, the excessive, the essence of Cubanness, and the essence of friendship.

In praise of Sarduy's work Michael Wood concludes, "There is a dizzy freedom in such writing" (*New York Review of Books*, 20 March 1975). For Sarduy, the writer is a modern hero. It is ironic then that he goes to great lengths in his literature to eliminate the author, to destroy the opposition between creator and creation, and to pulverize the ego. Yet the strength of Sarduy's work lies paradoxically in his ability to duplicate the world through the chaotic, creative process—mixing times, histories, cultures, and genders in an effort to stimulate readers through the brilliance and complexity of his prose.

Interviews:

Emir Rodríguez Monegal, "Las estructuras de la narración," *Mundo Nuevo*, 2 (1966): 15-26;

Rodríguez Monegal, "Conversación con Severo Sarduy," *Revista de Occidente*, 93 (1970): 315-343;

Roberto González Echevarría, "Guapachá barroco: Conversación con Severo Sarduy," *Papeles*, 16 (1972): 25-47;

González Echevarría, "Severo Sarduy/Interview," translated by Jane E. French in *Diacritics*, 2 (Summer 1972): 41-45;

Harold Alvardo Tenorio, "Con Severo Sarduy en el Café de Flore," *El Mundo*, 24 November 1979, p. 15;

Francisco Pérez Rivera, "Budismo y barroco en Severo Sarduy," *Linden Lane*, 1 (1983): 6;

Julia A. Kushigian, "La serpiente en la sinagoga," *Vuelta*, 89 (April 1984): 14-20;

Julio Ortega, "Severo Sarduy: Escribir con colores," *Diario 16*, 23 June 1985, pp. 4-5.

Bibliographies:

Roberto González Echevarría, "Para una Bibliografía de y sobre Severo Sarduy (1955-1971)," *Revista Iberoamericana*, 38 (April-June 1972): 333-343;

González Echevarría, *La ruta de Severo Sarduy* (Hanover, N.H.: Ediciones del Norte, 1987), pp. 255-269.

References:

Ana María Barrenechea, "Severo Sarduy o la aventura textual," in her *Textos hispanoamericanos de Sarmiento a Sarduy* (Caracas: Monte Avila, 1978), pp. 221-234;

Roland Barthes, "Sarduy: La faz barroca," *Mundo Nuevo*, 14 (1967): 70-71;

Andrew Bush, "Literature, History, and Literary History: A Cuban Family Romance," *Latin American Literary Review*, 8 (Spring-Summer 1980): 161-172;

"Focus on *Cobra*," *Review*, special issue (Winter 1974);

Eduardo González, "Baroque Endings: Carpentier, Sarduy and Some Textual Contingencies," *Modern Language Notes*, 92, (March 1977): 269-295;

Roberto González Echevarría, "El primer relato de Severo Sarduy," in his *Isla a su vuelo fugitiva* (Madrid: Porrúa, 1983), pp. 123-144;

González Echevarría, *La ruta de Severo Sarduy* (Hanover, N.H.: Ediciones del Norte, 1987);

Juan Goytisolo, "El lenguaje del cuerpo (sobre Octavio Paz y Severo Sarduy)," in his *Disidencias* (Barcelona: Seix Barral, 1977), pp. 171-192;

Adriana Méndez Rodenas, *Severo Sarduy: El neobarroco de la transgresión* (Mexico City: Universidad Nacional Autónoma de México, 1983);

Julio Ortega, "Nota sobre Sarduy," in his *La contemplación y la fiesta* (Caracas: Monte Avila, 1969), pp. 205-211;

Gustavo Pellón, "Severo Sarduy's Strategy of Irony: Paradigmatic Indecision in *Cobra* and *Maitreya*," *Latin American Literary Review*, 12 (Fall-Winter 1983): 7-13;

René Prieto, "The Ambivalent Fiction of Severo Sarduy," *Symposium*, 1 (1985): 49-60;

Enrico Mario Santí, "Textual Politics: Severo Sarduy," *Latin American Literary Review*, 8 (Spring-Summer 1980): 152-160;

Ivan A. Schulman, "Severo Sarduy," in *Narrativa y crítica de Nuestra América*, edited by Joaquín Roy (Madrid: Castalia, 1978), pp. 387-404;

Justo C. Ulloa and Leonor A. de Ulloa, "Leyendo las huellas de Auxilio y Socorro," *Hispamérica*, 10 (1975): 9-24;

Ulloa and de Ulloa, "Proyecciones y ramificaciones del deseo en 'Junto al río de cenizas de rosa,'" *Revista Iberoamericana*, 41 (July-December 1975): 569-578.

Lygia Fagundes Telles

(19 April 1924 -   )

Fábio Lucas
Universidade de Brasilia

BOOKS: *Porão e sobrado* (São Paulo, 1938);
Praia viva (São Paulo: Martins, 1944 [i.e., 1943]);
O cacto vermelho (Rio de Janeiro: Mérito, 1949);
Ciranda de pedra (Rio de Janeiro: Nova Fronteira, 1954); translated by Margareth A. Neves as *The Marble Dance* (New York: Avon, 1986);
Histórias do desencontro (Rio de Janeiro: Olympio, 1958);
Histórias escolhidas (São Paulo: Boa Leitura, 1961);
Verão no aquário (Rio de Janeiro: Martins, 1963);
A confissão de Leontina (Sá da Bandeira, Brazil: Angola, 1964);
O jardim selvagem (São Paulo: Martins, 1965);
Antes do baile verde (Rio de Janeiro: Bloch, 1970; revised and enlarged edition, Rio de Janeiro: Olympio, 1971);
As meninas (Rio de Janeiro: Olympio, 1973); translated by Neves as *The Girl in the Photograph* (New York: Avon, 1982);
Seminário dos ratos (Rio de Janeiro: Nova Fronteira, 1977); translated by Neves as *Tigrela and Other Stories* (New York: Avon, 1986);
Filhos pródigos (São Paulo: Cultura Editora, 1978);
A disciplina do amor: Fragmentos (Rio de Janeiro: Nova Fronteira, 1980);
Mistérios (Rio de Janeiro: Nova Fronteira, 1981);
10 contos escolhidos (Brasilia: Horizonte, 1984);
As horas nuas (Rio de Janeiro: Nova Fronteira, 1989).

Collections: *Seleta*, edited by Nelly Novais Coelho (Rio de Janeiro: Olympio, 1971);
Lygia Fagundes Telles, edited by Leonardo Monteiro (São Paulo: Abril Educação, 1980);
Os melhores contos (São Paulo: Global, 1984).

Lygia Fagundes Telles

Lygia Fagundes Telles, one of Brazil's most popular writers, was born on 19 April 1924 in São Paulo; she is the daughter of Durval de Azeredo Fagundes, a district chief of police and public prosecutor, and Maria do Rosário Azeredo Fagundes. The family often moved, and Lygia spent her childhood in several towns in the interior of São Paulo state, such as Areias, Assis, Apiaí, and Sertãozinho. Her restless childhood left deep marks on her: constant change must have sharpened her sensations of fear and insecurity.

Telles studied law in São Paulo and began to free herself from her shyness and from the rigid conventions still prevailing in Brazilian society at that time. As society underwent succeeding transformations in the years that followed, Telles gradually gained freedom and assurance.

She is in the habit of saying that she has followed two men's professions, those of lawyer and writer. Coincidentally, she has been married twice, first to Gofredo da Silva Telles, a lawyer, whom she divorced in 1961, and then to Paulo Emílio Salles Gomes, a writer and film critic, who died in 1977.

In *A disciplina do amor* (The Discipline of Love), a collection of confessions and literary fragments published in 1980, Telles sketches short plot outlines and fables, and mentions topics from her formative years that have affected both her intellectual interests and her emotional life. She discusses feminism, to which she is receptive, and she analyzes love, its discipline and its lack of discipline.

Telles was twenty-one years old when World War II ended. She was already a writer, having published *Porão e sobrado* (Basement and Two-Story House, 1938) and *Praia viva* (Living Beach, 1943), both volumes of short stories. Another volume of stories, *O cacto vermelho* (The Red Cactus), followed in 1949, winning the Afonso Arinos prize awarded by the Brazilian Academy of Letters. However, she regards these juvenilia as literary exercises and has not had them republished, except for a few of the stories. She surprised the public in 1954 with *Ciranda de pedra* (translated as *The Marble Dance*, 1986), a fully rounded novel displaying features that came to be recognized as characteristic of her work. *Ciranda de pedra* won wide public acceptance and was serialized for television.

Telles's prose is laden with features characterizing post-1945 literature. In Brazil she is regarded as a member of the "Generation of 1945," a designation mainly applied to a group of poets who reacted against modernism and its revolutionary experiments of the 1920s and 1930s. The Generation of 1945 was imbued with a taste for the neoclassical, preferring traditional forms of composition such as the sonnet, though also influenced by the modern spirit. Telles's prose is, however, more attuned to the cultural atmosphere of the time, when existentialism was a keynote.

Apart from this spirit, literary processes arising from avant-garde experimentation, such as those of expressionism and surrealism, were also influential. Resources such as stream of consciousness were widely adopted for recording characters' inner lives. Telles incorporates all these developments. As a well-informed reader of new writers who were emerging in other countries, she assimilated the values of modernity and made abundant use of them. Given her innate tendencies and her spirit, she readily adopted a style punctuated with colloquial usage, alongside a strong inclination for exploring the manifestations of the unconscious. The demotic register lends a fluency to her prose, while her exploration of the unconscious gives her writing density.

A third feature was to be added to those two: a taste for magic and fantasy—touches of Romanticism, of the Gothic novel, and of the horror story. She and other writers who were her contemporaries were responsible for an innovation in Brazilian literature, inasmuch as they abandoned the realistic heritage, so important in the 1930s, when social realism predominated. She avoided, at the same time, the technique of the psychological novel, with eccentrics and psychopaths behaving according to preset patterns.

There is a special tonality to Telles's work, which consists of addressing the female psychology from a female viewpoint. The novel has been a predominantly male tradition. When the modern narrative began to portray the inner movements of the human mind, the nuances of female psychology were observed by male writers.

Female viewpoints began to be widely expressed only after World War II, with women novelists concentrating mainly on the themes of love and sexuality. Strongly rooted taboos prevented the more assertive women writers from gaining a wide readership. Telles was an innovator in this respect, since she brought to her prose fiction a freedom that only a few women poets had achieved. Furthermore, one notices in her work moments of feminist demands, pioneeringly—though in a toned-down form—in her early works, but gradually becoming firmer until they figure explicitly in *A disciplina do amor*.

Telles had an intrinsic vocation for the short-story form, which requires foreshortening, a technical virtuosity capable of creating characters in a few brief paragraphs, and the infusing of dramatic tension into objective scenes and short dialogues. An overt poetic tendency enriches her work. She was always an assiduous reader of poetry, and she leaves room for poetry in her prose, both in the purely verbal sphere, with a richness of rhythm and musicality, and in her choice of themes and situations, punctuated with mystery.

Telles's stories thus arise as polysemous units, despite the brevity of the narrative and the preparation for the effect. She continued to write short stories after establishing a reputation as a novelist. No less than twelve of her books are collections of short stories. Some stories, with minor

Cover for Telles's 1977 collection, whose title story depicts Brazilian technocrats as participants in a series of "rats' seminars"

alterations, are repeated in more than one collection, and she frequently resorts to a basic set of themes.

In 1958 Telles published a collection of short stories titled *Histórias do desencontro* (Stories of Missed Encounter). She has mastered the art of constructing human, amorous situations that are charged with expectation but are nearly always interrupted, with dramatic effect, by a failure to effect a planned meeting. A cruel determinism seems to condemn her characters to failure.

O jardim selvagem (The Wild Garden) was published in 1965. The image of a garden has a special meaning in Telles's fiction. The garden is a setting in which characters meet, act out their conflicts, or give vent to horrifying or supernatural visions. In her stories and novels, the garden evokes Eden, where history has not yet happened, a mythical entity. This is where characters feel the effusion of the unconscious.

An example of this is "Noturno amarelo" (Yellow Nocturne), in which the main character momentarily leaves her lover, walks along a path, and finds her "house of atonement." After a meeting with the demons of her past, she leaves and goes back to where she came from. It is uncertain whether the events are dreams or reality.

Alongside the garden motif there is another recurring image: greenness, as in "Antes do baile verde" (Before the Green Dance), the title story in her collection published in 1970. Green designates a state of mind engendered by a proximity to nature and its secrets.

The fiction of Telles displays another aspect: the realm of fantasy and wonder. Outside the possibilities of narrative realism, in which the characters collide with each other in their missed encounters and become entangled in their weaknesses, there remains a vast territory to be explored. This is the region of mystery, magic, and enchantment, in which she delights. Her short story "A caçada" (The Hunt, in *Antes do baile verde*), for example, makes a particular appeal to the imagination: it tells of a plunge through dark layers of being, in search of a remote and unknown past.

Tension is a constant theme in Telles's work. In "Antes do baile verde" she builds up a conflict between illusion and duty. In "Natal na barca" (Christmas Aboard the Ferry) characters stand before the presence of death. The theme of maladjustment winds through "Eu era mudo e só" (I Was Dumb and Alone), just as that of treachery permeates "O menino" (The Child). All Telles's short stories are shaped by the impact of strong tension. The reader is also entertained by the nature of the dialogue—vivid, elliptical, and packed with colloquialisms. Her texts resemble networks of interwoven spokes, combining the effect of reality with that of fantasy.

Reality is sometimes seen under an indirect, symbolic light. This occurs, for example, in the story "O seminário dos ratos" (Rats' Seminars), the title story of *Seminário dos ratos* (1977; translated as *Tigrela and Other Stories*, 1986). An elaborate descriptive apparatus, showing work procedures among technocrats, conceals another reality: that of Brazil in the 1970s, at the time its economy was swollen with the indiscriminate influx of foreign capital in the form of bank lending. The banks, awash with petrodollars, triggered what was called "the Brazilian miracle." This suddenly brought high economic growth rates, at the cost—it was discovered later—of building up a vast, unpayable foreign debt and a form of economic, cultural, and technical dependence reminiscent of the colonial era. "O seminário dos ratos" mirrors that reality, not transcribing it directly but suggesting it. The reader who lived through that period will recall the dictatorship, the censorship, the official secrecy, the repression for some, and the privileges for others.

In 1981 Telles gathered together those of her stories that seemed to concentrate on the fantasy effect or, rather, that were most closely involved with the supernatural, the miraculous, or what is commonly termed the fantastic. To this collection she gave the title *Mistérios* (Mysteries). In *Mistérios* she seeks to show her intimacy with the most profound laws of the cosmos, in a pantheistic vision in which animate and inanimate beings are coded messages. She deals with sorcery, the sacred, and the deification of nature, thus in literature taking possession of the inheritance bequeathed by religions, exploring the mystical states induced by solitude. Her fiction also absorbs the intellectual consequences of perception. The reader of Telles's short stories is made aware of recurring details, such as ants, mice, birds, cats, fragments of dreams, volcanoes, fingernails, fingers, hands, and gestures—stray syntagmas in search of a meaning, messages urging decipherment.

The alternating play of love and death is a frequently recurring theme: situations of perfect love or utter innocence are extremely fragile. A return to childhood, or even the simple search for the distant past, is an experience of atonement, as in the short story "Noturno amarelo" (Yellow Nocturne). And erotic meetings are overshadowed by death, which transcends the calculations of reason.

Her characters frequently disclose their dreams, as in "A caçada," "As formigas" (The Ants), and "A mão no ombro" (The Hand on the Shoulder). Oneiric states are found in "Emanuel" and "O encontro" (The Encounter). Her capacity for creating fables and phantasmagorias is clearly prodigious. The dream fragments are neither cumulative nor even interconnected, but supply a strange climate of discontinuity, an uncontrolled inrush of unreality. They are sometimes used for a poetic purpose, as polysemous existential signs.

Humor usually takes the form of a pause within her serious intent, providing momentary relief from the tension of the narrative. These jocular or comic interludes appear as scenic or narrative episodes and are enriched with plays on words, with distorted recollections of things read, or with amusing or ironic comments on everyday events, in which her characters surprisingly expose ridiculous aspects of themselves or their mechanically governed nervous tics. Telles employs her gift for irony and the grotesque to call the reader's attention to a social evil or to express a criticism of human relationships.

Sometimes tense, sometimes dramatic, sometimes comic, her dialogues form a harmonious whole with the fictional fabric and help the reader form a clear idea of the characters, variously presented with natural oscillations of temperament and values. It is common in her work for the supernatural to mingle with the secular order of things, as though there were no discontinuity between the real and the surreal. Secret nighttime and daytime fantasies pervade her texts, stressing sometimes life, sometimes death. The rational is thus interwoven with recurring instances of the unexpected, of the miraculous and magical. The logic of reality appears in a state of trance.

Telles offers a kind of palimpsest, a fiction punctuated with subplots, thematic ramifications, and ambiguities, in which the prevailing current is that of thought with all its ambivalences, as in the story "Senhor diretor" (Mr. Director), in which a walk through a city provides an old lady with a chain of value judgments in opposition to modern life. Similarly "A sauna" projects two planes of consciousness dealing simultaneously with the sauna and with the main character's love life.

To compose her palimpsest Telles has assimilated all the modern narrative techniques. As well as imparting great flexibility to her dialogue, she makes generous use of the free, indirect style, a technique in which the speaker alternates—at one time the narrator, at another the character—enabling the reader to encounter the latter's changing consciousness. From this emanates the confidential tone, which is the intrinsic element of her prose. She explores the Protean aspect of desire, endowing Eros with ambivalence and spontaneity and displaying even a certain attraction for the abyss, for the closeness of death.

Human beings, in her stories, are as intimidated by the realization of desires as they are by death. It is as if, in the light of Sigmund Freud, the phantoms that may give pleasure to the reader are at the root of unsatisfied desires. It is as if, in Telles's magical prose, phantoms are sent to correct reality when it is not conducive to pleasure. The qualities exhibited in her short stories are developed at greater length in the novels, as she makes use of the greater complexity this narrative form permits.

Telles emerged on the Brazilian literary scene when realistic and psychological models were becoming outworn. In *Ciranda de pedra* the fertility of her imagination is the first striking impression the work conveys. She weaves a plot so intricate in its episodes and accidents that the reader is occasionally left with a sense of delirium in which simultaneous waves of consciousness cross and recross. In this first novel her imagination, set free from the constrictions of the short-story format, is better able to reveal the characters' inner rhythms. She makes constant use of strategic interruptions—ideas are left suspended to be brought to a conclusion only further on. She enigmatically explores the *other*, laying bare the labyrinth of consciousness.

Telles with her cat

The main character, Virgínia, is, according to Telles's own assessment, the most intriguing of all her creations. Virgínia is lonely, the daughter of a divorced couple; she is torn between two homes and happy in neither. At first she lives with her mother, while her sisters live with their father. The mother, Laura, has an affair with Daniel, who used to be her doctor, but she shows distressing signs of physical and mental illness. When her condition worsens, Virgínia leaves her and moves to her father's house.

Her father, a lawyer named Natércio, already looking after her sisters, Bruna and Otávia, welcomes her. She now finds herself in an unstable environment, dominated by the housekeeper, Fraulein Herta, and the family's friends Conrado, Afonso, and Letícia. And she finds her sisters hateful. Virgínia is unable to break into this closed circle. At this point readers are given a description of the *ciranda de pedra*, or stone ring—strictly, *ciranda* is a children's game—represented by ornamental gnomes arranged in a circle in the garden.

Virgínia is shown as a child, in one episode, joyfully meeting Conrado, her childhood sweetheart. However, the first part of the novel concludes with her mother's death, Virgínia's shattering discovery that her true father is not Natércio but Daniel, and Daniel's suicide. She asks to be sent to boarding school, to escape from the "stone ring."

The second part opens with her return home at the end of her school days. Afonso is now married to Bruna; Otávia has devoted herself to painting and occasional lovers. Letícia has thrown herself into sports and a marked interest in women. And Conrado is now assailed with sexual problems. It is the same routine of frustration all over again.

Virgínia thus encounters the "stone ring" once again, and again works on a means of escape, this time a long journey. Her story is the case history of a rejection complex: farewells have always proved the solution to her difficulties.

In *Ciranda de pedra* readers are presented with the three sisters' failure to communicate. This triangular pattern of irredeemable solitude is reencountered in Telles's third novel, *As meninas* (1973; translated as *The Girl in the Photograph*, 1982).

In her second novel, *Verão no aquário* (Summer in the Aquarium, 1963), the same rejection complex is apparent from the beginning in the first-person narration by the central character, Raíza. Raíza suspects, throughout the novel, that she and her mother are rivals for the same man's love. In Telles's works the mother is usually presented as a provider, though a contradictory figure. Raíza's fond memories of her father, an alcoholic druggist, portray him as a frightened stranger, while her friend Marfa's father, Uncle Samuel, is a lunatic.

Raíza becomes infatuated with André, a mystic unconcerned with the flesh. She tries to seduce him, believing him to be her mother's lover. Her plan is to escape from her "aquarium" and gain life's wide-open spaces, in accordance with her mother's advice. But Raíza is too closely involved with her surroundings, and her strongest attachment is to her mother, whom she constantly defies and challenges in a vain attempt to lay bare her secrets. Telles employs, with grace and irony, the methods of psychoanalysis, without recognizing in it any power of redemption, since her characters follow their insecure paths to chaos and tragedy.

As meninas features three girls, Lorena, Lia, and Ana Clara, who meet by chance in a boardinghouse. The novel was written when Brazil was suffering the worst excesses of the military dictatorship. For this reason it features more political and social preoccupations than Telles's other books. There is even a scene in which an innocent person is tortured, a common event in the period of political repression. Telles perfects her narrative technique in this novel, exploring minds affected by drugs, insecurity, and fear. She thus takes the opportunity to define, in literary terms, states of psychological indefinition, between sanity and madness. A noteworthy example occurs in an episode of love and drugs in which Ana Clara, with her lover Max, gives free rein to her unconscious, with interventions from her conscious mind acting as censor, and the two characters' memories interweave.

Lorena, the most sensible of the three friends, at one point extols irrationality. She is studying law and asks: "Why shouldn't delirium have its corresponding reality?" Ana Clara imagines in her delirium "the mad reigning over the living and the dead." Lia, the materialist, engaged in the struggle for the redemption of society, sees life and death as complementary to each other, since "life needs death to live." Ana Clara is doomed. For her there is no way out. But Lia, the progressive, eventually finds victory in escape.

The richness of *As meninas* is apparent on several levels. There are passages of humor and satire, a certain metalanguage, in which Lygia Fagundes Telles formulates a criticism of the novel of the past, inasmuch as it claims to classify its characters as "good" or "bad." In her critical awareness and her fiction, circumstances often prevail as stark realities.

References:

Cristina Ferreira Pinto, "A Decadência da Família Brasileira ou a Descentralizaçao do Pai," in her *O bildengsroman feminino: Quatro exemplos brasileiros* (São Paulo: Perspectiva, 1990), pp. 109-145;

Vera Maria Tietzmann Silva, *A metamorfose nos contos de Lygia Fagundes Telles* (Rio de Janeiro: Presença, 1985);

Malcolm Silverman, "O mundo ficcional de Lygia Fagundes Telles," in *Moderna ficção brasileira*, volume 2 (Rio de Janeiro: Civilização Brasileira, 1981), pp. 162-184.

Arturo Uslar Pietri
(16 May 1906 -   )

Jorge Marbán
College of Charleston

BOOKS: *Barrabás y otros relatos* (Caracas: Vargas, 1928);
Las lanzas coloradas (Madrid: Zeus, 1931); translated by Harriet de Onís as *The Red Lances* (New York: Knopf, 1963);
Red (Caracas: Elite, 1936);
Sumario de economía venezolana para alivio de estudiantes (Caracas: Centro de Estudiantes de Derecho, 1945);
El camino de El Dorado (Buenos Aires: Losada, 1947);
Letras y hombres de Venezuela (Mexico City: Fondo de Cultura Económica, 1948; enlarged edition, Caracas, EDIME, 1958);
Treinta hombres y sus sombras (Buenos Aires: Losada, 1949);
De una a otra Venezuela (Caracas: Mesa Redonda, 1950);
Las nubes (Caracas: Ministerio de Educación, 1951);
Apuntes para retratos (Caracas: Asociación de Escritores Venezolanos, 1952);
Arístides Rojas, 1826-1894 (Caracas: Fundación Eugenio Mendoza, 1953);
Obras selectas (Madrid: EDIME, 1953; enlarged, 1956; enlarged again, 1967; further enlarged, 1977);
Tierra venezolana (Caracas: EDIME, 1953);
Breve historia de la novela hispanoamericana (Caracas: EDIME, 1954);
Tiempo de contar (Caracas: López Elias, 1954);
El otoño en Europa (Caracas: Mesa Redonda, 1954);
Pizarrón (Caracas: EDIME, 1955);
Valores humanos (Caracas: EDIME, 1955; enlarged, 4 volumes, 1964);
Teatro (Caracas: EDIME, 1958);
Materiales para la construcción de Venezuela (Caracas: Orinoco, 1959);
Sumario de la civilización occidental (Caracas: EDIME, 1959);

Arturo Uslar Pietri

Chúo Gil y las tejedoras (Caracas: Vargas, 1960);
La ciudad de nadie (Buenos Aires: Losada, 1960);
Del hacer y deshacer de Venezuela (Caracas: Ateneo de Caracas, 1962);

El laberinto de fortuna: Un retrato en la geografía (Buenos Aires: Losada, 1962);
El laberinto de fortuna: Estación de máscaras (Buenos Aires: Losada, 1964);
La palabra compartida (Caracas: Pensamiento Vivo, 1964);
Hacia el humanismo democrático (Caracas: FND, 1965);
Los libros de Miranda (Caracas: Cuatricentenario de Caracas, 1966);
Pasos y pasajeros (Madrid: Taurus, 1966);
Oraciones para despertar (Caracas: Comité de Obras Culturales, 1967);
Las vacas gordas y las vacas flacas (Caracas: Concejo Municipal del Distrito Federal, 1968);
La lluvia y otros cuentos (Santiago, Chile: Zig-Zag, 1968);
Treinta cuentos (Caracas: Monte Avila, 1969);
Catorce cuentos venezolanos (Madrid: Revista de Occidente, 1969);
En busca del Nuevo Mundo (Mexico City: Fondo de Cultura Económica, 1969);
Veinticinco ensayos (Caracas: Monte Avila, 1969);
Vista desde un punto (Caracas: Monte Avila, 1971);
La vuelta al mundo en diez trancos (Caracas: Tiempo Nuevo, 1971);
Bolivariana (Caracas: Horizonte, 1972);
Manoa (Caracas: Arte, 1972);
Moscas, árboles y hombres (Barcelona: Planeta, 1973);
La otra América (Madrid: Alianza, 1974);
El globo de colores (Caracas: Monte Avila, 1975);
Viva voz (Caracas: Italgráfica, 1975);
Oficio de difuntos (Barcelona: Seix Barral, 1976);
El projimo y otros cuentos (Barcelona: Bruguera, 1978);
Fantasmas de dos mundos (Barcelona: Seix Barral, 1979):
Los ganadores (Barcelona: Seix Barral, 1980);
La isla de Róbinson (Barcelona, Caracas & Mexico City: Seix Barral, 1981);
Cuéntame a Venezuela (Caracas: Lisbona, 1981);
Educar para Venezuela (Caracas & Madrid: Reunidas, 1981);
Fachas, fechas y fichas (Caracas: Ateneo de Caracas, 1982);
Bolivar hoy (Caracas: Monte Avila, 1983);
El conuco de Tio Conejo (Caracas: Di Mase, 1984);
Godos, insurgentes y visionarios (Barcelona: Seix Barral, 1986);
El hombre que voy siendo (Caracas: Monte Avila, 1986);
33 cuentos (Caracas: Petróleos de Venezuela, 1986);
Venezuela en seis ensayos (Caracas: Monte Avila, 1987);
Giotto y compañia (Caracas: Fundación Eugenio Montale, 1987);
La visita en el tiempo (Bogotá: Norma, 1990);
Cuarenta ensayos (Caracas: Monte Avila, 1990).

Arturo Uslar Pietri has been acclaimed as one of the best short-story writers in contemporary Latin-American literature. Although his novelistic talent has not received the unanimous recognition given to his skill in the other narrative genre, he deserves to be considered as one of the most able practitioners of the historical novel in Latin America. His works of fiction are, however, only one aspect of his literary output. Uslar has also written two volumes of verse, several theatrical pieces, dozens of essays, and thousands of newspaper articles. In addition, he has played a significant role in Venezuelan politics. His contribution to education—through political or academic offices, books, articles, and television programs—is unrivaled.

Uslar was born in Caracas on 16 May 1906, in a house whose facade still stands in the heart of Venezuela's capital. Some of Uslar's political critics have referred to his *mantuano* lineage, referring to the local aristocracy of colonial times. Uslar has justly refuted that characterization by pointing out his ancestors' relatively recent arrival in the country. Nevertheless, his background is far from ordinary. Uslar's paternal great-grandfather, Johann Uslar, was a German-born English officer who came to fight for Venezuelan independence after participating in the Spanish campaign and the Battle of Waterloo. After taking part in the battle of Carabobo, he settled in Valencia, Venezuela, where he married and started a family.

Juan Pietri, Arturo Uslar Pietri's maternal grandfather, the descendant of a Corsican immigrant, was a doctor and army general who occupied several important government positions (including the vice-presidency) before he died in 1911. Arturo Uslar Santamaría, Uslar's father, was also a general and a close friend of Cipriano Castro, Venezuela's president from 1899 to 1908. When Juan Vicente Gómez displaced Castro, General Uslar's friendship with the former president brought him some problems. Eventually, though, General Uslar was able to continue his military career and was appointed to several administrative positions during Gómez's dictatorship (1908-1935).

When Arturo was eight years old, he and his family moved to Cagua, a rural town southwest of Caracas, where his father had been designated civil administrator. For the young Uslar this association with the Venezuelan countryside was an unforgettable experience. During this first contact with Cagua and later during his stay in Maracay (1916-1923), Uslar was charmed by the wild nature that surrounded him and the almost magical atmosphere in which people lived. He collected and retained in his memory the superstitions, legends, fables, and tales of mysterious or extraordinary happenings circulating among peasants and farm workers. Uslar's preference for rural settings in most of his short stories and his familiarity with the environment and psychology of country people cannot be understood without taking into consideration his Cagua and Maracay experience.

In 1916, when Uslar's father was appointed attorney general of the state of Aragua, the family moved to Maracay. This city west of Caracas had at that time a small population and a rustic atmosphere, which pleased President Gómez's peasant tastes. The Venezuelan dictator made it his favorite place of residence. Uslar made friends with two of Gómez's younger sons. The dictator would sometimes stop and chat with the three children when they were playing. Uslar still recalls a morning when he almost collided with Gómez while reading a book on the way to school.

Uslar was—to use his term—"addicted" to books since his childhood. At age fourteen he published his first article, "El plátano o banano" (Plantain or Banana), in the *Comercio* in Maracay (28 August 1920). During successive years he continued to publish poems, short stories, and a variety of articles in magazines and newspapers in Caracas and Maracay. When Uslar was sixteen he fell ill with malaria. Fearing for his life, his parents sent him to the better climate of Los Teques, south of Caracas, where he recovered and completed his secondary education.

From 1924 to 1929 Uslar studied law at the Universidad Central in Caracas. These were important formative years in his life. He took part, with other members of his generation, in several *tertulias*, or social-literary gatherings. He was not only attracted by Spanish-American *modernistas* but also by a variety of foreign writers: Henri Barbusse, Gabriel Miró, Azorín, Antonio Machado, Oscar Wilde, Leo Tolstoy, Vladimir Korolenko, and especially Leonid Andreyev. His early inclination to modernism, evident in his first poems and short stories, gave way to an increasingly sympathetic appreciation for the avant-garde movements. His reading of Guillermo de la Torre's *Literaturas europeas de vanguardía* (European Avant-Garde Literature, 1925) and José Ortega y Gasset's *Revista de Occidente* (Western Journal) opened new cultural horizons for him.

The year 1928 was very important in the literary life of Uslar. In January he and a few other young associates published the first and only issue of *Válvula* (Valve), a literary journal that espoused the newest trends in art. Uslar not only invented the journal's name but was also the author of a defiant editorial in which he attacked "rancid" tradition, "soft" tones and "all forms of discretion."

In February 1928 the university was rocked by a student rebellion against Gómez's dictatorship. Although young Uslar was not a *gomecista*, he made the fateful decision not to join the movement. He did not want to compromise his father, and he did not see any possibility of success.

Besides, he had chosen artistic instead of political rebellion. A few months after the university events, he dazzled Venezuela's literary world with *Barrabás y otros relatos* (Barrabás and Other Stories, 1928), a collection of thirteen short stories. The impact of the book was extraordinary. *Criollismo* (local color) had dominated Venezuela's literary world until then and was especially prevalent in the short story: use of regional attire, local symbols, countryside dialect, and a "picturesque" approach to reality was common. *Barrabás y otros relatos* was a striking departure from that tradition. Three of its stories have oriental settings; two have urban backgrounds; and another two take place on the high seas.

The influence of the avant-garde is evident in the original metaphors sprinkled throughout many of the stories. Even though a considerable number of the stories are set in environments easily recognized as the Venezuelan countryside, local flavor is absent from them. Uslar avoids identification with *criollismo* by presenting moral conflicts and personal obsessions that transcend local concerns. He shows an impressive array of techniques, and his choice of language and themes demonstrates a mastery of the narrative art absent in the first stories he wrote in the early 1920s. He also resorts to magical realism, a term first used by Uslar himself in 1948 (in *Letras y hombres de Venezuela*) to describe "the depiction of man as an element of mystery surrounded by realistic data," or "a poetic intuition or denial of reality."

Although Uslar received some criticism from traditional quarters, the reception given to *Barrabás* and its author was overwhelmingly favorable. Pedro Sotillo, a respected Venezuelan critic, stated prophetically: "This young man is an intellectual new reality in our world of letters. I am afraid that he is going to spoil our literary tribe's dance of mummies" (*El Universal*, 8 September 1928). Rafael Angarita was more emphatic. *Barrabás*, according to him, was a dividing scaffold in Venezuelan literature, "the farewell to plastic and superficial landscapes, to vernacularism and nativism" (*El Universal*, 9 September 1928).

After graduating from law school in 1929, Uslar accepted an appointment as civil attaché to the Venezuelan embassy in France and left for Paris. The next five years (1929-1934) were decisive in his intellectual and cultural development, as he told Margarita Eskenazi: "I left a backward, marginal and rural country without a publishing house, a symphonic orchestra or any signs of intellectual life. I felt privileged to arrive in the Paris of surrealism, a city with all kinds of literary opportunities. My life made a 180-degree turn."

Uslar took full advantage of the favorable circumstances offered by the new milieu. No free political life existed in his tyrannically ruled country. In France there was a parliamentary democracy in full swing. Uslar was fascinated by the speeches and the debates he heard in the French Assembly. He also attended the League of Nations meetings in Geneva and listened to Aristide Briand, Gustav Stresemann, and Arthur Henderson. He got to know artists and writers such as Paul Valéry, André Breton, Salvador Dalí, Luis Buñuel, Rafael Alberti, Jean Cassou, and Massimo Bontempelli. Two of the Latin-American exiles he met in Paris, Alejo Carpentier and Miguel Angel Asturias, remained his close friends until the end of their lives. When they went out together they often discussed the different aspects of languages and culture that absorbed their interest. Uslar read to them excerpts from his first novel, which he finished in 1930: *Las lanzas coloradas* (1931; translated as *The Red Lances*, 1963) received critical acclaim from the first year of its publication. It has been widely considered as one of the best Latin-American novels of the first half of the twentieth century.

Las lanzas coloradas offers a panorama of the Venezuelan War of Independence, with the sheer brutality of its destructive forces. Uslar presents three distinct levels: the atmosphere of fantasy and superstition of the black slaves; a legendary vision of history seen mainly by Fernando Fonta, the main character; and the realistic presentation of the sordid life in the slave barracks and the orgy of violence among José Tomás Boves's *lanceros*. This is not an idyllic version of the war for independence, and yet it has an epic aura. Mariano Picón Salas has pointed out its cinematographic qualities and refers to the "pictorial impressionism and great splashes of color."

In February 1934, when Uslar returned to Venezuela after living five years in the dazzling environment of Paris, he had already made the conscious decision to try to uplift the cultural and intellectual awareness of his fellow countrymen. In newspapers and journals he soon began to inform his country of the newest literary figures and artistic trends abroad. In 1935 he founded, with some friends, a literary journal, *El Ingenioso Hidalgo*, which unfortunately floundered financially after the third number. In December 1935 President Gómez died in power, and three stifling decades of autocratic rule came to an end. Shortly afterward (on 14 July 1936) Uslar wrote an editorial entitled "Sembrar el petróleo" (We Must Harvest Our Oil; in the Caracas newspaper *Ahora*), in which he prophetically advised his countrymen not to waste the income derived from oil but to use it to diversify the country's economy and provide the means to weather future price fluctuations or the eventual depletion of the fields.

That same year, Uslar published his second collection of short stories, *Red* (Net), which marked a new development in his narrative art. Avant-garde images have practically disappeared. All but one of the stories have Venezuelan rural settings, and magic realism pervades them. Sensorial elements play a new, striking role in creating poetic atmospheres. In "Negramenta" (A Negro Mob) there is a masterful mimicry of African rhythms and an ingenious use of synaesthesia. In "La siembra de ajos" (Garlic Fields) a strong garlic smell casts an irresistible erotic spell on the protagonist. In "La lluvia" (Rain) ambiguity is created through the use of powerful visual images. José Fabbiani has commented on Uslar's differences with traditional *criollistas*: "Instead of resorting to physical objects (solitary trees or shores) to portray his characters' isolation, the author appeals to a psychological element: the anguished wait for rain, adroitly suggesting it in four or five lines."

In 1937 Uslar began teaching economics at Universidad Central and continued lecturing there during the next four years. Joined by other professionals, he eventually succeeded in adding this new academic school to the university. Until 1945 he was also actively involved in Venezuelan politics. In July 1939 he was appointed secretary of education in Gen. López Contreras's government, becoming the youngest cabinet member in Venezuelan history. Three months later (on 29 October 1939) he married Isabel Braun Kerdel, a member of a prominent family from Valencia, to whom he had been engaged for two years. They eventually had two sons. In May 1941 Gen. Isaías Medina, the new president of Venezuela, impressed by Uslar's intelligence, knowledge, and proven administrative and political skills, appointed him as presidential secretary. For the next four and a half years, with a brief interregnum in 1943, when he acted as treasury secretary for a few months, Uslar had a decisive role in shaping government policies. Many steps, most of them advised by Uslar, were taken toward the process of modernization and democratization of the country. Nevertheless, in October 1945 a coup d'état led by a group of military officers and civilian elements of the opposition Acción Democrática party toppled the government. Uslar was arrested, kept in prison for more than a month, and expelled from the country. It was a surprising and undeserved fate for a member of a government that, despite some possible mistakes, had ensured the greatest political freedom the country had enjoyed in modern times.

Deprived of economic means (his estate was eventually confiscated by the government), Uslar settled with his family in New York City. That was undoubtedly one of the most difficult periods of his life. Undaunted by adversity, he earned his living by doing a variety of odd jobs until he joined the faculty of Columbia University in the fall of 1946 as a professor of Latin-American literature. The four years he spent at Columbia were very important in determining the course of his life. He was able to resume his literary career, interrupted during his intense involvement in Venezuelan politics. In 1947 he published *El camino de El Dorado* (The Road to El Dorado), a historical novel about Lope de Aguirre, the mad rebel who died in Venezuela in 1565. In 1948 Uslar began to publish *Pizarrón* (Blackboard), a column in a Caracas newspaper that would be carried eventually by forty newspapers in eighteen countries and would still be printed four decades later. In 1949 he published his third collection of short stories, *Treinta hombres y sus sombras* (Thirty Men and Their Shadows), and in 1950, *De una a otra Venezuela* (From One to Another Venezuela), the first of his many sociopolitical essays.

Uslar demonstrates again in this collection his outstanding qualities as a master of the brief narrative genre. He admits he made a conscious effort to shun rhetorical tricks. Although all but one of the stories deal with native themes, he avoids excessive local details or the picturesque approach of the *costumbristas* (local-color writers). *Treinta hombres* offers an appealing variety: the element of humor negligible in previous collections is present in three of its sixteen stories; mystery is prevalent in five; picaresque aspects are developed in two. Uslar enriches his book with sources from the oral tradition: "Maichak" is a literary remake of an old legend of the Camaracoto Indians; "El conuco de Tío Conejo" (Uncle Rabbit's Vegetable Garden) has characters from old fables of the Venezuelan countryside; the picaresque stories of José Gabino were inspired by a tune from a collection of folkloric songs.

Treinta hombres is a departure from *Red*. Its relative lack of images (in contrast with the former book) is compensated for by the development of new imaginative means. Alliteration of demonstrative adjectives conveys in "Los herejes" (The Heretics) the feeling of fearful surprise in a girl facing a hostile mob: "*Aquellos* rostros, *aquellos* palos, *aquellas* miradas" (Those faces, those sticks, those looks). The foreboding echo of the wind is reproduced with a similar technique in another story: "Se oye re*s*onar con un *s*ordo eco de *s*oledad" (The Resounding Can Be Heard with an Echo of Solitude). Interior monologues, a dynamic use of the first-person narrative, and multiple perspectives are also used in the book. Uslar skillfully combines verb tenses. In "Los herejes" the present indicative signals dramatically the instant in which the mob decides to act violently. In another story, "El baile del tambor" (The Dance of the Drum), the same tense indicates the decisive moment in which a fugitive, bewitched by the drumbeat, heads toward the dance hall where he will be captured.

On 24 November 1948 the Acción Democrática government of Rómulo Gallegos was overthrown and replaced by a military junta. Shortly afterward most of the confiscated proper-

Uslar Pietri in 1975, when he was named Venezuelan ambassador to UNESCO

ties of General Medina's government officials were returned to their owners. Uslar was able to travel to Venezuela for a brief visit in May 1949 and decided to return permanently in July 1950.

Representatives of the military junta offered Uslar several diplomatic positions, but he turned them down. He did not want to collaborate with an undemocratic regime. He decided instead to start working for ARS, an advertising agency headed by a close friend, Carlos Eduardo Frías. He also began to teach Venezuelan literature at Caracas's Universidad Central. The military junta gave way after 1951 to the increasingly repressive dictatorship of Marcos Pérez Jiménez. In July 1952 Uslar resigned his professorship at the university in order to avoid granting the allegiance to the government then required from the faculty.

On 25 November 1953 Uslar began to broadcast a weekly cultural program, "Valores Humanos" (Achievements of Mankind), on the newly established Venezuelan television station, Radio Caracas Televisión. With only one notable interruption (1975-1979) he maintained that program until February 1987. In 1954 Uslar received Venezuela's Premio Nacional de Literatura in recognition of his literary career. Removed from political concerns, he published articles, travel accounts, plays, essays, and a literature manual during the next four years. Resistance to Pérez Jiménez's repressive regime increased in 1957. Uslar could not remain aloof, and he signed, together with other distinguished public figures, a document asking for the dictator's removal from power. Shortly thereafter (on 12 January 1958) Uslar was arrested and sent to Modelo Prison. He was still there when the government of Pérez Jiménez was finally toppled on 23 January.

In December 1958 Uslar was back into national politics with his election as a senator from Caracas. He was a voice of reason, pragmatism, and reflection in the senate, and although his moderate views were often attacked by radical elements, he gained respect for his objectivity and honesty. In 1962 Uslar published *Un retrato en la geografía* (A Portrait in Geography), the first part of a projected trilogy of novels—*El laberinto de fortuna* (The Labyrinth of Fortune)—about the post-

Gómez era. *Estación de máscaras* (Carnival Season) followed in 1964. Neither of these two books received the overwhelmingly favorable reception given to his previous two novels, and he abandoned the trilogy idea.

In October 1963 Uslar became an independent presidential candidate for the December election. Although he was reelected as a senator, he failed to win the presidency: "No gané electorado, gané lectorado" (I won over the literate but lost the electoral vote), he said in an interview with Alfredo Peña. In February 1964 Uslar and his supporters founded a new political party, the FND—Frente Nacional Democrático (National Democratic Front). They joined Raúl Leoni's government in August. Even though Uslar did not derive any personal benefit from the "broad base" coalition and had expressed reservations about the pact, he was accused of opportunism and received the brunt of the attack from the radical elements opposed to Leoni. In March 1966 a weaker FND left the coalition government. Uslar ran again for his senate seat in December 1968 and won, but he soon became less active in partisan political matters. The FND eventually disappeared from the political stage during the following decade.

Uslar continued to find time for writing. In November 1966 he published *Pasos y pasajeros* (Passages and Passengers), his fourth collection of short stories. Uslar again applies the technique of direct presentation used in *Treinta hombres*. With a sensitivity perhaps related to the *nouveau roman*, he focuses on particular objects and develops new and revealing dimensions in them. This book signals a new importance of the political theme and of urban environments in his short stories, elements that would also be important in Uslar's next collection, *Los ganadores* (The Winners, 1980).

In 1969 Uslar became the editor of the *Nacional*, one of the two leading newspapers in Caracas. Indefatigable, he maintained a very busy schedule, with his work as senator, newspaper editor, television programmer, occasional lecturer, traveler, and writer. In 1972 and 1973 he received three important awards for his writing: the Mergenthaler and the Maria Moors Cabot prizes in New York and the Premio de Miguel de Cervantes in Madrid.

In August 1973, in a memorable, patriotic speech in the senate, Uslar announced his retirement from politics. He also resigned as editor of the *Nacional* in April 1974. During the following

Uslar Pietri circa 1991

months he undertook several trips to Switzerland, Italy, England, France, and the Soviet Union.

Uslar's days of public service, though, were not yet over. In May 1975 he accepted the designation of Venezuelan ambassador to UNESCO and moved to Paris, where for four years he would ably represent his country. In 1976 *Oficio de difuntos* (Funeral Mass) was published. This novel centers on the life and times of the Venezuelan dictator Juan Vicente Gómez, but his name and those of other historical figures are changed. Uslar had previously tried to dispel what he thought was the mistake of confusing two distinct historical entities: the Latin-American dictator and the caudillo. The caudillo, in his estimation, was "a man directly related to a historical era, to a certain social situation, to a given order: that of the *hacienda*, the plantation, the farmhands," a man who appeared as "a simple, direct, and representative political formula" in times of anarchy. *Oficio de difuntos*, according to Uslar, tries to reconstruct "in the most faithful and truthful manner" the psychology and historical reality of the last caudillo of Venezuela.

Uslar begins his novel at the moment in which Gómez's death is announced. Through the character of Solana, the dictator's chaplain, Uslar rebuilds retrospectively the main events in Gómez's life. Uslar's book proved to be polemic. Some critics praised it; others pointed out historical inaccuracies or attacked what they considered to be an incomplete or mostly favorable depiction of Gómez and his regime. In reality, Uslar did change some historical facts, using the freedom the fictional frame afforded him. Although his unobtrusive narrator fails to condemn explicitly Gómez's abuses, he does not fail to reveal most of them. The novel's structural frame is simple and its language is at times monotonous. Nevertheless, *Oficio de difuntos* is an excellent attempt to capture the psychology and the internal processes of one of the most enigmatic figures in Latin-American history.

In June 1979 Uslar returned to Venezuela. His intense preoccupation with his country's welfare was seen in his involvement with televised cultural programs and his lectures on the need to improve the nation's educational system. His literary activity, in the meantime, continued unabated. During the next two years he published two new books of fiction.

Los ganadores confirmed Uslar's reputation as a master of the short story. His new directions, already revealed in *Pasos y pasajeros*, are again in evidence. City environments predominate. Some of the stories deal with modern issues. The title story presents the apocalyptical vision of a world without water. Three others develop the theme of urban terrorism.

La isla de Róbinson (Robinson's Island, 1981) is Uslar's sixth novel. The protagonist is Simón Rodríguez, Simón Bolívar's mentor and one of the most original Latin-American thinkers of the nineteenth century. Uslar, who had previously studied and written about Rodríguez, demonstrates a profound knowledge of his life and ideas. Uslar also reveals an artistic imagination mostly absent from the other historical novels he wrote after *Las lanzas coloradas*. He skillfully develops a suggestive system of symbols by utilizing the first name of Daniel Defoe's well-known solitary character. (Robinson was a name actually assumed by Rodríguez at one time.)

Two temporal streams run through the novel: one presents the protagonist advancing toward his death; the other is a collection of memories dating back to his earlier life. Many ideas expressed in Rodríguez's books are adroitly brought forth by presenting them as part of his mental process of introspection. A sober prose dotted with suggestive images complements the novel's structure. Uslar's artistry in *La isla de Róbinson* won for him, for the second time, Venezuela's Premio Nacional de Literatura (in 1982).

The popular appeal of some of Uslar's narrative works was demonstrated during the following years when they were presented in other artistic media. Angel Ferreyra's rock-opera version of *Las lanzas coloradas* began to circulate in 1982. In 1985 three of his short stories ("Simeón Calamaris," "El Cachorro," and "El enemigo") were shown as programs on Venezuelan television.

In 1986 Uslar published his second book of poems, *Godos, insurgentes y visionarios* (Conservatives, Insurgents, and Visionaries), an important ideological work that was sold out in a matter of weeks. Uslar's eightieth birthday in May 1986 was the occasion for a national celebration. He not only received homage from Venezuela's professional world but also from its political establishment. A special session of the Venezuelan congress was organized to pay him tribute. Ironically and significantly, a representative of Acción Democrática, the party of his former political enemies, honored him with a speech in the legislative body.

Uslar's many activities continued unabated during the next few years. He traveled to ten different countries in a period of four years, taking frequent trips to France and Spain. He also presided over two important government committees in Venezuela. In September 1986 one of them produced an impressively detailed account of the state of Venezuelan education and forwarded important suggestions for improvement. The second committee organized the program of events commemorating the bicentennial of the French Revolution. In November 1989 Uslar attended the International Book Fair in Miami, where he gave several lectures and received homage from the Hispanic intellectual community of that city.

Uslar's important contribution to Spanish letters was recognized once more on 20 April 1990, when he was granted, in Oviedo, Spain, the prestigious Príncipe de Asturias literary award. Uslar had been quietly but steadily working on the manuscript of a novel dealing with the life of Don John of Austria—the illegitimate son of Charles V, and the victor in the battle of Lepanto. *La visita en el tiempo* (A Visit in Time) was published in Bogotá at the end of 1990. In this novel Uslar adroitly uses a circumstance in the life of Don John as the basis for imaginative re-creation: during the first decade of his life the prince lived the humble life of a peasant, ignorant of his royal lineage.

Uslar proves to be familiar with the sources that illuminate the life of the illustrious bastard. Uslar explores in great detail the contradictory traits of Don John's character and brings him to life as a tormented but fascinating human being.

The plentiful historical information is supplemented in the novel with artful mythical development. Uslar endows his character with a passionate dedication to physical love that makes him appear as a lively representation of the mythical Don Juan. However, Don John's sudden elevation to prominence in childhood and his ultimate dependence on the will of a sly, irresolute, and probably jealous half-brother give him a sense of insecurity and precariousness.

Uslar's poetic language and artistic imagination in *La visita en el tiempo* are evidence that his creative and intellectual powers have not diminished. His knowledge of the historical period in which Don John of Austria lived is another factor that enhances the novel. Uslar presents the dense atmosphere of court intrigues, religious fanaticism, and hypocrisy characteristic of Philip II's reign. *La visita en el tiempo* may well be the best literary depiction of those dynamic, eventful times since the publication of *La gloria de don Ramiro* (Enrique Larreta's historical novel) in 1908.

Uslar's contribution to Latin-American fiction is outstanding. The first book he published (*Barrabás y otros relatos*) is a landmark in Venezuelan literature. Uslar is one of the masters of the short story in the Hispanic world and is represented in most of the anthologies published in the field. Through five decades he has continuously renewed his techniques and brought new, revealing insights to that narrative genre.

Unfortunately Uslar's novelistic work has not received the same acclaim. Most critics think that he has not been able to match in later decades the success he achieved when he was twenty-five. *Las lanzas coloradas*, as Mario Vargas Llosa says, is the work that opened the gates of recognition for the Latin-American novel in the world (quoted by Eskenazi). Guillermo Morón believes that the lack of acceptance of the Uslar novels that followed *Las lanzas coloradas* may be explained by the absence in them of the experimentation with the newest techniques observed in the works of more successful contemporary novelists. Their historical character is in that sense an obstacle.

It is also evident that Uslar's wish to remain faithful to historical facts has played a part in his choice of traditional formats. Nevertheless, Uslar's *La isla de Róbinson* and *La visita en el tiempo* show the most varied techniques in any of his historical novels since the publication of *Las lanzas coloradas*. In an interview with Efraín Subero in September 1986, Arturo Uslar Pietri announced that he did not intend to publish any more short stories but still wanted to write two or three additional novels. The great innovator in the short story may possibly break new ground in these future works.

Interviews:
Alfredo Peña, *Conversaciones con Uslar Pietri* (Caracas: Ateneo de Caracas, 1978);

Efraín Subero, ed., "La cuentística de Arturo Uslar Pietri: Libros y etapas," in his *Treinta y tres cuentos* (Caracas: Petróleos de Venezuela, 1986) pp. xv-xxxv;

Margarita Eskenazi, *Uslar Pietri: Muchos hombres en un solo nombre* (Caracas: Caralex, 1988).

Bibliographies:
Dunia García, "Contribución a la bibliografía de Arturo Uslar Pietri," *Boletín de la Biblioteca General*, 17-18 (August 1970 - June 1971): 287-317;

Universidad Católica Andrés Bello, *Contribución a la bibliografía de Arturo Uslar Pietri (1906)* (Caracas: Gobernación del Distrito Federal, 1973);

Angel T. González, "Biobibliografía de Arturo Uslar Pietri," Ph.D. dissertation, Florida State University, 1986;

Fundación Polar, *Contribución a la Biblio-Hemerografía de Arturo Uslar Pietri* (Caracas: Ex Libris, 1989).

References:
Aida M. Beaupied and Luz María Umpierre, "Ecriture de ambigüedad en 'La lluvia' de Arturo Uslar Pietri," *Hispanic Journal*, 3 (Spring 1982): 105-111;

José Fabbiani, *Cuentos y cuentistas* (Caracas: Cruz del Sur, 1951), pp. 112-128;

Emilio González López, "Uslar Pietri y la novela histórica venezolana," *Revista Hispánica Moderna*, 1 (January-April 1947): 44-49;

Jorge Marbán, "Técnicas narrativas y perspectivas temporales en *La isla de Róbinson* de Uslar Pietri," *Círculo: Revista de Cultura*, 15 (1986): 109-115;

Domingo Miliani, "La sociedad venezolana en una novela de Arturo Uslar Pietri," *Thesaurus*, 23, no. 2 (1968): 280-323;

Miliani, *Uslar Pietri: renovador del cuento venezolano* (Caracas: Universidad Central de Venezuela, 1963);

Guillermo Morón, *Dos novelistas latinoamericanos: Arturo Uslar Pietri, Ernesto Sábato* (Buenos Aires: Embajada de Venezuela, 1979);

José Napoleón Oropeza, *Para fijar un rostro: Notas sobre la novelística venezolana actual* (Valencia, Venezuela: Vadell, 1984), pp. 192-217;

Nelson Osorio, ed., *La formación de la vanguardia literaria en Venezuela* (Caracas: Academia Nacional de la Historia, 1985), pp. 349-361;

Carlos Pacheco, "La palabra y el poder: Contradicciones de la palabra sometida en *Oficio de Difuntos*, de Arturo Uslar Pietri," *Revista de Crítica Literaria Latinoamericana*, 7, no. 14 (1981): 65-86;

Mariano Picón Salas, *Estudios de literatura venezolana* (Caracas: EDIME, 1961);

José Luis Vivas, *La cuentística de Arturo Uslar Pietri* (Caracas: Universidad Central de Venezuela, 1963).

Luisa Valenzuela
(26 November 1938 -   )

Leticia Reyes-Tatinclaux
Community College of Vermont

BOOKS: *Hay que sonreír* (Buenos Aires: Américalee, 1966); translated by Hortense Carpentier and J. Jorge Castello as *Clara*, in *Clara: Thirteen Short Stories and a Novel* (New York: Harcourt Brace Jovanovich, 1976);

Los heréticos (Buenos Aires: Paidós, 1967); translated by Carpentier and Castello in *Clara: Thirteen Short Stories and a Novel*;

El gato eficaz (Mexico City: Mortiz, 1972);

Aquí pasan cosas raras (Buenos Aires: Flor, 1975); translated by Helen Lane as *Strange Things Happen Here* (New York: Harcourt Brace Jovanovich, 1979);

Como en la guerra (Buenos Aires: Sudamericana, 1977); translated by Lane as *He Who Searches* (Elmwood Park, N.J.: Dalkey Archive, 1987);

Libro que no muerde (Mexico City: UNAM, 1980);

Cambio de armas (Hanover, N.H.: Ediciones del Norte, 1982; Mexico City: Casillas, 1982); translated by Deborah Bonner as *Other Weapons* (Hanover, N.H.: Ediciones del Norte, 1985);

Donde viven las águilas (Buenos Aires: Celtia, 1983); translated by Carpentier and others as *Up Among the Eagles*, in *Open Door* (San Francisco: North Point, 1988);

Cola de lagartija (Buenos Aires: Bruguera, 1983); translated by Gregory Rabassa as *The Lizard's Tail* (New York: Farrar, Straus & Giroux, 1983; London: Serpent's Tail, 1987);

Novela negra con argentinos (Hanover, N.H.: Ediciones del Norte, 1990);

Realidad nacional desde la cama (Buenos Aires: Grupo Editor Latinoamericano, 1990).

Luisa Valenzuela is one of the first outstanding Latin-American female authors to enjoy increasing readership and interest in the 1980s. *Time* and *Newsweek* have featured articles in which Valenzuela's name appeared next to the likes of Jorge Luis Borges, Carlos Fuentes, and Julio Cortázar; and her works are being analyzed in comparative literature, women's studies, and Latin-American studies courses. Valenzuela's varied literary production may be explored from different critical perspectives: traditional approaches show Valenzuela's mastery as a storyteller; sociological and Marxist critics refer to her sociopolitical awareness; feminist critics have discovered a distinctly feminine voice in the way Valenzuela articulates her fictional worlds.

Born in Buenos Aires on 26 November 1938, Luisa Valenzuela started writing at a very early age. But as a young child she seemed more inclined to math and the sciences, to the point that her language teacher once requested from her mother—the well-known writer Luisa Mercedes Levinson, for whom Valenzuela felt an admiration and reverence that verged on idolatry—that she help the child with her compositions. Valenzuela's mother was a powerful influence since childhood and provided her with the intellectual background and incentive for reading and writing. As a young girl, Valenzuela was an omnivorous reader of Jack London, Somerset Maugham, Graham Greene, and William Faulkner, among others, whose works she first read in translation. Of the Latin-American writers, Borges and Cortázar, both of whom she knew personally, are among the most evident influences in Valenzuela's early fiction. Cortázar and Fuentes praised her work. In the United States it was Susan Sontag who first discovered her.

At age twenty Valenzuela married a French sailor and went to Paris. (She has one daughter from this marriage, Analisa, a painter living in Argentina.) While in Paris, Valenzuela observed the young prostitutes of the Bois de Boulogne and developed an interest in this human type, as attested by her first novel, *Hay que sonreír* (1966; translated as *Clara*, 1976), which she wrote when she was only twenty-one. *Hay que sonreír* tells of the misfortunes of Clara, a young, simpleminded prostitute who is seeking her identity and longing to use her mind instead of her body. Her wishes are met when she gets to perform in

Luisa Valenzuela in the late 1980s

a circus act called "La flor azteca" (The Aztec Flower), in which her body is artfully concealed and only her head is visible. Prostitute characters, with their ambiguous role in society, are also in one of the stories in *Los heréticos* (1967; translated, 1976) and in the novels *Como en la guerra* (1977; translated as *He Who Searches*, 1987) and *Novela negra con argentinos* (Black Novel with Argentines, 1990).

During the early 1960s Valenzuela was part of a group involved with "pataphysics," or the study of the exceptions rather than the rules that govern the physical world. Its main inspirator was the French writer Alfred Jarry. Valenzuela has also been very interested in sociology, anthropology, and psychoanalysis, as well as the esoteric and the occult—an interest shared by her mother. Valenzuela not only has read extensively about the religious and mythical mind of primitive societies but also has a firsthand knowledge of them: some of her travels to remote regions of Latin America made her familiar with many beliefs and rituals, including those of the Afro-Brazilian *Macumba*; the Guaraní people from Paraguay and northern Argentina; the Mapuche Indians of Chile; and the shamans in Mexico. Thus, though basically an urban writer—Valenzuela has spent a great deal of her life in cities such as Buenos Aires, New York, Barcelona, and Paris—she incorporates into her fiction those aspects of existence that one would not likely associate with the city: magic, incantatory rituals, witchcraft, masks, and shamanic knowledge. This is especially evident in the collection *Los heréticos*, which explores different aspects of superstitious beliefs and religious fanaticism, and in some stories in *Donde viven las águilas* (1983; translated as *Up Among the Eagles*, 1988). The second part of the novel *Como en la guerra* draws on Valenzuela's personal experiences of the *temazcal*, or purification bath, in Tepoztlán, Mexico, and her trip to the Mexican town of Huautla, famous for its hallucinogenic mushrooms. In Huautla, Valenzuela met the shaman María Sabina, who appears as a character in the novel. Another novel, *Cola de lagartija* (1983; translated as *The Lizard's Tail*, 1983), eclectically draws elements from quite different traditions: black (*Quimbanda*) and white (*Umbanda*) magic of the Afro-Brazilian *Candomblé*; the white African mask personifying the goddess Oya, which in the novel becomes the patriotic blue of Argentina's flag; the cleansing ceremony of the egg, which Valenzuela witnessed in Tepoztlán. *Cola de lagartija* is set in the frontier zone of Corrientes, in northern Argentina, in a region called Esteros del Iberá. *Iberá* is a Guaraní word that means "brilliant water." Valenzuela's father was from this region, where, as a child, she once sat on a giant anthill, or *tacuru*, and was not bitten, an experience transformed and ascribed to the witch doctor in the novel.

Valenzuela's sense of perception and adventure grew during her years as a journalist, which started when she was seventeen and which included travel assignments to northern Argentina, Paraguay, Bolivia, and Brazil. She wrote for well-known Argentinian publications, most notably for the *Nación*, where she spent nine years; for the glamorous *Gente*, where she was the star writer; and for the leftist journal *Crisis*. Not surprisingly, Valenzuela's fiction displays an extraordinary sensitivity capable of capturing nuances of light, time, and space, not in a purely pictorial, representational, or even lyrical sense, but rather in a powerful language that conveys and reveals the peculiar mental and spiritual atmosphere of a place and its inhabitants. She freely combines elements from different cultural backgrounds to create new myths, in which a pressing contemporaneity is also invoked. A case in point is the collection of short stories *Donde viven las águilas*. Six of the stories, including the title story, constitute a thematically distinct cluster, where man's primeval state, in close contact with nature, is evoked through the allegorical re-creation of myths and legends. The story "Crónicas de Puebloroj" (The Redtown Chronicles) renders the mythical foundation of a ghost town, its subsequent destruction, and its reconstruction by means of language and narration. "Donde viven las águilas," whose setting in the heights of a timeless mountain was inspired by her journey to Huautla, confronts aging with rites of passage and images of the life beyond. The myth of the primeval fire, seen as the source of knowledge, is retold in "Para alcanzar el conocimiento" (The Attainment of Knowledge). Valenzuela's stories convey the syncretism—the fusion of Christian and non-Christian elements—which pervades the Latin-American hinterlands. A certain nostalgia for a way of life closer to earth permeates these stories, though they are not exempt from the ironic perspective of the narrator, who often blends the edenic side of life into the larger context of perverted politics.

In 1969 Valenzuela came to the United States for the first time, as a recipient of a Fulbright scholarship to participate in the International Writers Workshop of the University of Iowa. Among the participants were Néstor Sánchez, Carmen Naranjo, Juan Sánchez Peláez, Nicolás Suescún, and Fernando del Paso. There Valenzuela began writing the novel *El gato eficaz* (Cat-O-Nine-Deaths, 1972), which she finished in Mexico. It was then that she discovered in the small town of Tepoztlán a magical Mexico, with which she fully identified. In 1972 she went to Barcelona for one year and started her novel *Como en la guerra*. She had some contact there with Alberto Custe, Cristina Peri Rossi, and José Donoso. From 1978 to 1990, Valenzuela's literary life was increasingly linked to New York City. She was writer in residence at Columbia University (1978) and at New York University (1985), and a faculty member in the Creative Writing Division of NYU for several years.

El gato eficaz constitutes an important phase in Valenzuela's literary development, for it embodies what French feminist critics, such as Luce Irigaray and Hélène Cixous, consider a feminine way of writing: the avoidance of univocal, logical narrative discourse; a multiple and ambiguous representation; and the simultaneous presence of different levels of experience. *El gato eficaz* demands a reading that allows its dizzily intricate network of signifiers to work simultaneously into the mind and senses: Valenzuela's articulates sensuous, erotic, mostly tactile images and horrifying meaning through an intensive verbal play that often interweaves opposites. Eros and Thanatos form the most recurrent symbiosis, symbolically and emblematically represented by the black cats of death. These animals (cats appear frequently in Valenzuela's fiction from her first novel *Clara*) along with an uninhibited first-person female narrator-observer, who identifies herself with the cats of death, work toward establishing the textual contiguity in the series of loosely connected mininarratives that constitute the novel.

The female character-narrator follows a feline, nocturnal itinerary through the underworld of Greenwich Village in New York City, though the physically distant sociopolitical contexts of Buenos Aires are often invoked, mainly through the opposite symbol, the white dogs of life. *El gato eficaz* displays a succession of haunting scenes of immolation, physical pain, sexual transgression, and expiation. Its language is visceral, erotic, ludic, and ironic. The cats of death symbolically represent life's inner forces and impulses, including the destructive and the creative drives. They celebrate uninhibited freedom, sexual desire, and antiestablishment feelings, all of which can be identified with the feminine, according to feminist tenets. On the opposite side of the spectrum stand the dogs of life, evoking order, logic, political and sexual repression, and bourgeois values, all of which supposedly correspond to the masculine side of existence. This opposition of the masculine and the feminine is not articulated in the text in terms of male and female individuals. It is rather a corollary that may be inferred from the sets of oppositions alluded to but never explicitly expressed. Another important feature that was to constitute one of Valenzuela's characteristic traits is the ambiguity—the fluidity of the fictional world, wrought through multiple representations. The narrator ironically searches for irrefutable categorical assertions, but this is precisely what Valenzuela's fiction tries to avoid: freezing the representation or giving the illusion of a knowable, unified, and univocally representable reality.

Valenzuela's stories and novels partake of the mysterious, the magic, and the hidden forces that compel women and men to act. However, her fictional work is always closely linked to reality, not so-called objective reality, but an inner, elusive, more intangible reality. Thus anecdote is secondary, for what interests her is not so much to create a fictional work for its own sake but to use it as a bridge that allows her and the reader to perceive the evasive *otherness* that resists representation: she seeks "to name the unnameable." Likewise she is very intent in breaking the resistances, the interior censorship, imposed by tradition and linguistic habits that prevent that *otherness* from emerging. Her fictional world is both detached from any partisan or ideologically tinted worldview and strongly committed to exploring and unveiling those aspects of human experience that escape easy conceptualization. With important variants, this preoccupation with the intangible—unmasking and naming all areas of experience, from the most intimate and personal to the more social and political—has been a constant trait of her fiction.

Political awareness also constitutes an important dimension of Valenzuela's writing. She belongs to the younger generation of Argentinian writers who lived through the tumultuous political upheaval of the 1970s and early 1980s. When Valenzuela returned to Buenos Aires in 1974—the year of Juan Perón's death and of Isabel Perón's ascent to power—she was astounded to find not only a more overtly repressive regime but also a sort of complicity, imposed by fear, in the silence and inactivity of most citizens. Late Peronism paved the way for the consolidation of military dictatorial rule. The collection of short stories *Aquí pasan cosas raras* (1975; translated as *Strange Things Happen Here*, 1979) is the first in a series of works to reflect the violence and paranoia rampant in the streets of Argentina. These stories exhibit Valenzuela's typically elliptical, condensed, and mordantly ironic style. She often proceeds in a metonymic fashion; that is, she carries the narrative thread from one anecdotal element to another either through association of meanings or through depiction of physical contiguity. For example, the title story follows the misadventures of Mario and Pedro from the moment they find an abandoned briefcase in a café. As they leave, they also find a man's jacket on top of a car. These two objects become an obsessive burden to the characters who found them. At one point the narrator ironically calls Mario and Pedro a briefcase and a jacket. What the story conveys is the paranoiac fear of persecution that prevailed in Argentina from 1974 to 1982.

The stories of *Aquí pasan cosas raras* could take place in any repressive society, for they avoid concrete references to place and time. Indeed, Valenzuela's writings never express denunciation, ideology, or political stances overtly. To allow the atrocities that besieged her country to manifest themselves in her fiction, Valenzuela resorts to the subtle vehicles of black humor, irony, erotic language, and satire.

With the military coup of 1976 the Argentine political scenario became even more repressive. Until then Valenzuela's fiction had escaped the strict censorship of the military, but her novel *Como en la guerra* had its first page and a

Dust jacket for Valenzuela's 1982 collection, which includes stories about political repression in Argentina during the late 1970s

half, containing a scene of torture, eliminated by a censor. The scene really constitutes the end of the novel and is crucial for understanding the political implications. Thus Spanish readers had a more politically innocuous book than English readers who read the translated full version. In the following years Valenzuela became actively involved in the underground task of securing political asylum for some of her fellow citizens. She befriended an ambassador, who provided shelter and safe conduits for her endangered friends. Many autobiographical details found their way into the novella "Fourth Version," published in *Cambio de armas* (1982; translated as *Other Weapons*, 1985). Valenzuela continued writing short stories in which the political and social developments of the 1970s form a very intensive background (some of these stories are in the second half of *Donde viven las águilas*). Around 1981 she also began the allegory of power titled *Cola de lagartija*. The historical context reflected in this novel is based on the repressive rule of José López Rega, who was Perón's astrological adviser and who, upon Perón's death in 1974, became the minister of social welfare but was in fact the number-one man in Argentina from 1974 to 1976, the Isabel Perón years. He was truly called, as in Valenzuela's fiction, the Sorcerer, and he had written books on witchcraft.

According to Valenzuela, she wrote this novel in an attempt to understand why a sophisticated society such as the Argentinian had been literally under the spell of a sorcerer. She also intended to show the persistence in modern Argentinian society of a syncretic form of thinking that includes superstition and knowledge of the occult sciences—a form of thinking usually attributed to primitive societies—and its connection to economic, political, and social power.

Valenzuela's knowledge of psychoanalytic theory is evident in several of her works, most notably in *Como en la guerra*. She became familiar with the works of Sigmund Freud and Jacques Lacan in the early 1970s, primarily through the teachings of the Argentinian philosopher and psychoanalyst Guillermo Maci—who himself participated in Lacan's seminars. Her novel *Como en la guerra* carries on some of the essential themes of her fiction in a very structured and demanding narrative that draws many of its clues from the psychoanalytic ideas of Lacan, though there is also the influence of Tibetan Buddhism. On one level the text is a locus where the various stages of the constitution of the psychological subject are enacted, and where the Lacanian levels of the imaginary, the symbolic, and the real come into conflict, as Maci has pointed out. However, Emily Hicks asserts that one cannot read this novel as a case history of psychoanalysis, for many of the most basic assumptions of this discipline appear ironized in the text. Instead of an increasing recapturing of the character's identity, there is a progressive dilution and quasi-disintegration of the self. In addition, the elusive plot involves revolutionary terrorism, repression, and torture. The opening segment (censored) shows the as-yet-unidentified protagonist about to be blown to pieces with a gun by his torturers, but he emerges slowly through the narrative, giving the endless search for identity a supraindividual, historical dimension.

The main character is a semiotician turned psychoanalyst—identified only as AZ—who is obsessed with deciphering the personality of his patient, an Argentinian prostitute living in Barcelona. But the reader probably perceives him as a lost soul who slowly realizes that his urge to reach outward responds in fact to a stronger need to turn inward, though he is resisting the need to delve into himself. AZ visits his patient in disguise, often wearing feminine attire, ludicrous in believing he has deceived her. The Lacanian mirror phase, where the child discovers himself as another, as an object of his own gaze, is evoked. The main character begins to recognize, in his own transvestism and in the displaced image of the prostitute he is purportedly analyzing, his own disturbed image of a fragmented self. The psychoanalyst painfully transcribes his patient's tape-recorded conversations, which, together with his own writings, constitute the bulk of the narrative. Thus Valenzuela also plays with the assumption of Lacanian psychoanalysis that the reconstitution of the subject occurs through language, meaning, and writing.

The first of the three sections of *Como en la guerra* ends when the female patient disappears and AZ decides to look for her. In the allegorical trek that ensues, the process of reconstituting the unity of the personality is enacted. His quest / search takes him in metaphoric displacement from Barcelona, to Mexico, to Buenos Aires, and each of these stages introduces new dimensions to the narrative. There is a significant shift from chronological and linear time to psychological and mythical, cyclical time, then to historical time. The character sees himself carrying a heavy knapsack loaded with accumulated knowledge that is more overpowering than useful as he attempts to experience myth and the sacred through ritual, witchcraft, and hallucinogenic mushrooms. After his purification ceremony at the *temzacal* (steam bath), the protagonist comments: "Here I am: traveling the Moebius strip through America because the space where she is to be found is not Euclidian space nor is her time the same time of which we're dimly aware when we see our skin aging." The final stage of his search takes him to his native Argentina, where he perceives a ghastly, inhuman Buenos Aires, filled with an endless row of waiting people who, not surprisingly, have also lost their identities. AZ suddenly thrusts himself into a swirl of political activism and succeeds in detonating a bomb that destroys a building. He catches a final glimpse of "her" in a female corpse that for everyone else is "the Saint" (perhaps Evita Perón), as the structure that concealed her explodes, making the final encounter the more ironic as it constitutes a definite loss.

Feminist concerns have increasingly emerged in Valenzuela's fiction. From the late 1970s on, Valenzuela has participated in many events and international conferences on women's writing, and she has shared ideas and concerns on the nature of feminine writing with writers, such as Margo Glantz, Alicia Dujovne Ortiz, Elvira Orphée, and Helena Araújo, among others. Of the two major trends of feminist thought one finds in Latin America—French psychoanalytic theory, which addresses issues of gender identification in writing, and Marxist theory, which sees women's struggles and marginalization as part of the broader class struggle—Valenzuela is clearly closer to the first. Her declarations on writing reflect the theories of French feminists. *El gato eficaz*, an evident sample of what French feminists would consider *écriture feminine*, was written at a time when she did not believe in a distinctly feminine way of writing. Valenzuela believed then that language is asexual. It was during the 1978 Third Inter-American Conference of Women Writers, which took place in Ottawa, that she realized there existed a female voice in literature, just as she was trying to assert the contrary. Valenzuela thinks that women are still trying to carve a space in the eminently male domain of language, a domain ruled by reason and authority and referred to as "phallogocentrism," a popular neologism coined by Derrida. Valenzuela believes that in assuming her new role, a female writer must perform the formidable task of appropriating and transforming language, and avoid mimicking phallocratic-logocentric discourse.

Valenzuela's fiction, in particular her more mature writing published in the 1980s, has contributed significantly to achieving a more truly feminine body of writing. Valenzuela's genuinely feminist perspective subverts traditional modes of perception and storytelling. This does not imply a clear-cut "opposite sex" point of view, but the replacement or inversion of topoi traditionally associated with one sex or the other. Already in earlier books, such as *El gato eficaz* and *Como en la guerra*, there is the attempt to reject or simply efface gender identification in the narrative perspective. Likewise, the recurrence of transvestism and transsexuality in Valenzuela's fiction, beyond their psychological basis and implications, may be seen as the rejection of the traditional binary opposition. The protagonist of *Cola de lagartija* is endowed with three testicles, but this does not reinforce his masculinity—quite the contrary: his third testicle is the feminine side of him, which controls his violent excesses and which will serve as a vehicle to engender his own offspring.

Valenzuela's writing disconcerts those feminist critics who expect women's writing to be an open critique of, or a response to, male domination in society. In the intricate worlds of *Cambio de armas*, for example, female characters may enjoy sex unabashedly, and they often subject themselves to subtle or even violent games of domination by male counterparts; at the same time, they appear entrapped in a large paranoiac sociopolitical environment. In the five stories of this collection all the main characters are women, and in four of them they are women in love. But beyond the apparent rendition of male-female relationships, in which often sex and politics or violence are closely knit, what these stories explore is the imaginary and imaginative dimension of feminine desire, which transcends sexuality: it translates the attempt to reach out physically, grasp the world, and, in so doing, break away from linguistic, literary, and societal molds that have marginalized woman. In a highly erotic, sensual, and ultimately metaphoric language, in which tactile and olfactory images prevail, Valenzuela shows the connectedness of desire and language.

The title story of the collection provides an excellent sample of Valenzuela's unusual style. The heroine, Laura, is devoid of memory, will, or conscience, and is prey to the sexual whims of a military torturer. Marta Morello-Frosch analyzes the way in which the narrative transcends the common political scenario of the capturer-tortured relationship to play out metaphorically a woman's severance from herself and the world. Language is deliberately brought to the foreground. At first, words simply help Laura regain contact with reality when she is able to name her surroundings, though she lives a confined existence in a present devoid of meaning. She refuses even to glance at her past, but certain words impose themselves on her. For the reader, words also become all-important, as the messengers of secret codes that only the unfolding of the narrative is able to decode. Each segment of the story has a subtitle that focuses on certain aspects of Laura's dramatic situation: that of a woman who has been totally separated from her past, from herself, and from others. Thus the mirrors, the window, the photograph, the keys, the peephole, the whip, and the well are key terms that function both in the realm of Laura's constricting external reality and in the realm of the powerful symbolism they introduce. The story stages the overlapping of the political and the feminine levels through language, but also through the skillful use of the narrative point of view, which suggests the lens of a movie camera. Through most of the story the focal perspective seems to emerge from Laura's physical position in the apartment: it "moves" with her. However, in the segment focusing on the peephole, the narrative focus shifts toward this small opening. Thus the episode dramatizes Laura's helplessness by suggesting sexual voyeurism, not only in the two guards who peep from the other side of the door—the outside world—but also in the reader.

Valenzuela circa 1984 (photograph by Gil Jain)

Cola de lagartija is another example of Valenzuela's distinct writing at its best. This novel imbricates several narrative codes into a dynamic pattern, thus providing several levels and layers of meaning. Here the mythical, the historical, the political, the allegoric, the psychoanalytic, and the symbolic are brought to coexist in a discourse that is multivoiced and includes self-parody and humor. On a purely fictional level, *Cola de lagartija* is the story of an exotic and monstrous wizard, endowed with three testicles, who gives free expression to his perversion through black magic, haunting the people of the marshlands, where he rules with unlimited power. The historicopolitical context is encoded in the fictionalized rendition of José López Rega, Isabel Perón's minister of social welfare. But the fictional present alludes to the context of the increased disappearances, executions, and state terrorism that followed the fall of Perónism: the late 1970s and the deadly military junta. The clues to historical characters and time and place references are minimal: the Sorcerer is the same nickname López Rega had in real life, Juan Perón is evoked with the obvious military epithet the "Generalississimo," Isabel Perón is the "Intruder," and Eva Perón is remembered as the "Dead Woman." Anonymous voices in the novel question the whereabouts of the Sorcerer and even his very survival after the military took power. (After the coup the real López Rega vanished mysteriously. He was probably spared by the military since he had too much compromising information—as the unidentified general suggests in the novel—that would have come to light had he been caught by the international agencies hunting him.) The novel shows him resurfacing in the mythical Kingdom of the Black Lagoon, wherefrom he spreads his nets of power like a black spider. Thus a fictional, mythical resonance is pitted against a historical context.

The mythical and psychoanalytical levels in the novel demand a reading beyond the concrete historical framework that prompted it. The novel is an allegory of power. In *Cola de lagartija* Valenzuela exposes and dismantles the mechanisms of repressive power and, ultimately, of authoritarian/male discourse. The narrative framework makes the Sorcerer a character of mythical proportions from the outset, through several devices: he is a first-person narrator who uses an incantatory, parabolic, almost biblical language. He describes himself in godly, hyperbolic terms: the Immanent, the High Priest, the great syncretizer who orders a pyramid built, with its interior like the Egyptian models and its exterior like the sacrificial structures of the Aztecs. He is also Lord of the Tacurú, Red Ant, the Sawman, the Witchdoc, and Sixfingers, among other names. In addition to narrating in the present, he is also writing his biography, which he expects to become a sacred book to obliterate all other books. Thus the Sorcerer's formidable power stems not only from his witchcraft but from his being a manipulator of language. Symbolically he represents the consolidation of repressive authority through the empty, manipulative rhetoric of official discourse. His witchcraft power feeds on the superstitious beliefs and populist cults he helped create in the collective memory: the Dead Woman (Eva Perón, whose veneration is tied to another popular cult, that of "La difunta Correa" [The Dead Correa]) and the Sacred Finger. (The historical López Rega attempted to resurrect Eva Perón; in the novel, he keeps her finger alive.)

Valenzuela again playfully draws from Lacanian psychoanalysis to portray her main character as a sadist and misogynist, a self-aggrandizing figure. The sorcerer's implicit homosexuality appears in connection with his servant, the castrated Egret. Thus the allusions to the Lacanian stage of the mirror—the Sorcerer's altar has a huge mirror, and later he has the interior halls of his pyramidal palace lined with a myriad of mirrors—are played out to symbolize the narcissistic obsessions of military tyrants. The fetid and translucent black waters, where there is an abundance of putrefaction and viscosity—the Sorcerer's habitat—are explicitly linked to the unconscious in the novel; however, they also refer to the collective unconscious and to the devious mechanisms used by the government to control the people. Likewise, the Sorcerer's vain attempt to generate his own offspring, via the transformation of his third testicle into a female receptacle that he inseminates, may be read metaphorically as the desire of repressive regimes to achieve their main goal: perpetuating themselves in power.

The novel opposes two competing narrators: the Sorcerer and the author/character-narrator Luisa Valenzuela, also called Rulitos, who in the second part of the text questions her ability to counter the Sorcerer's discourse. Within its own ingenious rhetoric, the novel poses these serious questions: Can the discourse of power be vanquished by the power of narrative discourse? Should the writer abandon fiction in favor of more active political involvement? These are valid questions for the Latin-American writer, for whom the act of writing is often a pressing, courageous act of demasking. Valenzuela, as a sorcerer herself, wields effectively a writer's most effective weapon: the written word.

For over a decade (1978-1990) Luisa Valenzuela was sharing her time between New York City, Buenos Aires, and Tepoztlán. In 1983 she was the recipient of a Guggenheim Fellowship, which took her to Argentina at the onset of the democratic regime of President Alfonsín. As a permanent member of the New York Institute for the Humanities, she participated in seminars on writing along with Susan Sontag, William Kennedy, Heberto Padilla, Ishmael Reed, Thomas Bishop, and Joseph Brodsky, and she attended seminars conducted by critics such as Roland Barthes, Jacques Derrida, and Michel Foucault. Valenzuela resettled in Buenos Aires in 1990. She is invited to lecture worldwide and continues to write ground-breaking fiction.

Interviews:
Sharon Magnarelli, "Censorship and the Female Writer—An Interview/Dialogue with Luisa Valenzuela," *Letras Femeninas*, 10 (Spring 1984): 61;

Magnarelli, "Luisa Valenzuela: Desenmascaramientos," video interview (Hanover, N.H.: Ediciones del Norte, 1985);

Montserrat Ordóñez, "Máscaras de espejos, un juego especular: Entrevista-asociaciones con la escritora argentina Luisa Valenzuela," *Revista Iberoamericana*, 132-133 (1985): 511-517;

Dorothy S. Mull and Elsa B. Angulo, "An Afternoon with Luisa Valenzuela," *Hispania*, 69 (May 1986): 350-352;

Magdalena García Pinto, "Entrevista con Luisa Valenzuela," in her *Historias íntimas: Conversaciones con diez escritoras latinoamericanas* (Hanover, N.H.: Ediciones del Norte, 1988), pp. 217-249.

References:
Alfonso Callejo, "Literatura e irregularidad en *Cambio de armas*, de Luisa Valenzuela," *Revista Iberoamericana*, 132-133 (1985): 575-580;

Ana M. Fores, "Valenzuela's *Cat-O-Nine-Deaths*," *Review of Contemporary Fiction*, 6 (Fall 1986): 39-47;

Marie-Lise Gazarian Gautier, "The Sorcerer and Luisa Valenzuela: Double Narrators of the Novel/Biography, Myth/History," *Review of Contemporary Fiction*, 6 (Fall 1986): 105-108;

Margo Glantz, "Luisa Valenzuela's *He Who Searches*," *Review of Contemporary Fiction*, 6 (Fall 1986): 62-66;

Emily Hicks, "That Which Resists: The Code of the Real in Luisa Valenzuela's *He Who Searches*," *Review of Contemporary Fiction*, 6 (Fall 1986): 55-61;

María-Inés Lagos-Pope, "Mujer y política en *Cambio de armas* de Luisa Valenzuela," *Hispamérica*, 46-67 (1987): 71-83;

Guillermo Maci, "The Symbolic, the Imaginary and the Real in Luisa Valenzuela's *He Who Searches*," *Review of Contemporary Fiction*, 6 (Fall 1986): 67-77;

Sharon Magnarelli, "Juego/fuego: En torno a *El gato eficaz* de Luisa Valenzuela," *Cuadernos Americanos*, 247, no. 2 (1983): 199-208;

Magnarelli, "*The Lizard's Tail*: Discourse Denatured," *Review of Contemporary Fiction*, 6 (Fall 1986): 97-101;

Magnarelli, "Luisa Valenzuela: From *Hay que sonreír* to *Cambio de armas*," *World Literature Today*, 58 (1984): 12-13;

Magnarelli, "Luisa Valenzuela's *Cambio de armas*: Subversion and Narrative Weaponry," *Kentucky Romance Quarterly* (1986);

Magnarelli, *Reflections/Refractions: Reading Luisa Valenzuela* (New York: Lang, 1988);

Z. Nelly Martínez, "*El gato eficaz* de Luisa Valenzuela: La productividad del texto," *Revista Canadiense de Estudios Hispánicos*, 4 (1979): 73-80;

Martínez, "Luisa Valenzuela's *The Lizard's Tail*: Deconstruction of the Peronist Mythology," in *El Cono Sur: Dinámica y dimensiones de su literatura: A Symposium*, edited by Rose S. Minc (Upper Montclair, N.J.: Montclair State College, 1985);

Martínez, "Luisa Valenzuela's 'Where the Eagles Dwell': From Fragmentation to Holism,' *Review of Contemporary Fiction*, 6 (Fall 1986): 109-115;

Diane Marting, "Female Sexuality in Selected Short Stories by Luisa Valenzuela: Toward an Ontology of Her Work," *Review of Contemporary Fiction*, 6 (Fall 1986): 48-54;

Marta Morello-Frosch, " 'Other Weapons': When Metaphors Become Real," *Review of Contemporary Fiction*, 6 (Fall 1986): 82-87;

Martha Paley Francescato, "*Cola de lagartija*: Látigo de la palabra y la triple P.," *Revista Iberoamericana*, 132-133 (1985): 875-882;

Evelyn Picón-Garfield, "Muerte-metamorfosis-modernidad: *El gato eficaz* de Luisa Valenzuela," *Insula: Revista de Letras y Ciencias Humanas*, 35 (1980): 17-23.

Manuel Zapata Olivella

(17 March 1920 -   )

Antonio Olliz Boyd
Temple University

BOOKS: *Tierra mojada* (Bogotá: Espiral, 1947);
Pasión vagabunda (Bogotá: Santafé, 1949);
He visto la noche (Bogotá: Los Andes, 1953);
China, 6 A.M. (Bogotá: S.L.B., 1954);
Hotel de vagabundos: Teatro (Bogotá: Espiral, 1955);
La calle 10 (Bogotá: Casa de la Cultura, 1960);
Cuentos de muerte y libertad (Bogotá: Iqueima Narradores Colombianos de Hoy, 1961);
El galeón sumergido (Cartagena: Extensión Cultural de Bolívar, 1963);
Detrás del rostro (Madrid: Aguilar, 1963);
Corral de negros (Havana: Casa de las Américas, 1963); republished as *Chambacú, corral de negros* (Medellín: Bedout, 1967); translated as *Chambacu, Black Slum* (Pittsburgh: Latin American Literary Review, 1989);
En Chimá nace un santo (Barcelona: Seix Barral, 1964);
¿Quién dió el fusil a Oswald? (Bogotá: Revista Colombiana Populibro, 1967);
He visto la noche; Las raíces de la furia negra (Medellín: Bedout, 1969);
Teatro (Bogotá: Ministerio de Educación Nacional, 1972);
Tradición oral y conducta en Córdoba (Bogotá: INCORA, 1972);
El hombre colombiano: Enciclopedia del desarrollo colombiano (Bogotá: Canal Ramírez-Antares, 1974);
El folclor en los puertos colombianos (Bogotá: Puertos de Colombia/Fundación Colombiana de Investigaciones Folclóricas, 1977);
Identidad del negro en la América Latina (Bogotá: Fundación Colombiana de Investigaciones Folclóricas, 1977);
Las claves profundas: El gran libro de Colombia (Spain: Círculo de Lectores, 1982);
Changó, el gran putas (Bogotá: Novela Saga Oveja Negra, 1983);
Las Costa Atlántica: Maravillosa Colombia (Spain: Círculo de Lectores, 1984);
Etnografía colombiana (Bogotá: Ministerio de Educación/ICFES, 1984);
El fusilamiento del Diablo (Bogotá: Plaza & Janés, 1986);
Nuestra voz: Aportes del habla popular latinoamericana al idioma español (Bogotá: Ecoe, 1987);
Lève-toi mulatre (Paris: Payot, 1987);
Las claves mágicas de América (Bogotá: Plaza & Janés, 1989);
Fábulas de Tamalameque (Bogotá: Rei Andes, 1990).

TELEVISION: *Las siete mujeres*, Channel 1, Bogotá, 1985.

RADIO: *Murallas de pasión*, Caracol, Bogotá, 1954;
Amor salvaje, Caracol, Bogotá, 1955;
Ojos vendados, Caracol, Bogotá, 1956.

OTHER: "La dialéctica aplicada al diagnóstico clinico," M.D. dissertation, National University of Colombia, 1949.

Manuel Zapata Olivella occupies a position of importance because of his straightforward approach in the areas of protest and ethnicity within the Latin-American perspective. Although it is popular to speak of the magic of realism as a backdrop to some literary social protest in Latin America, Zapata Olivella seems to have added another dimension to realism, where the force of cultural myths has become a possibility for defining cultural reality. The underlying morphology of his art form has an artistic dimension that provides a multivalent semiology. This technique extends reader participation.

The one basic difference in this approach, if one were to compare Zapata Olivella with most of his contemporaries, is that Zapata Olivella writes with what he has termed the associative relationship of myth, protest, and ethnic integration. His thematic thrust of protest is against group oppression, which he expresses in terms of economic deprivation, political abuses, racism, and violent miscegenation. His artistic use of regional

Manuel Zapata Olivella

and cultural myths highlights his contribution to Latin-American literature.

Manuel Zapata Olivella was born on 17 March 1920 in Lorica, Córdoba, Colombia, and named after his paternal grandfather, Manuel Zapata Granados. As one of the seven children of Antonio María Zapata Vásquez and Edelmira Olivella de la Barrera de Zapata, Zapata Olivella seems to have been born into a world where everyday reality is confirmed by the survival of myths. Lorica is situated on the banks of the Río Sinú, next to the Lorica marshlands. In the pre-Columbian era, this was the site of the often-mentioned kingdom of the Zenúes, a branch of the Arawak-Carib Indians. Subsequently, with the arrival of the Spaniards, Africans were introduced into the area to develop the cattle and agricultural industries. The result was a tri-ethnic population in which biological amalgamation often gave birth to cultural crossbreeding. Nor was it uncommon for the myths of the Indians, the spiritual support system of the Africans, and the religious tenets of the Spanish to operate in parallel fashion.

Zapata Olivella's mother was the daughter of a Zenúe Indian mother and a Spanish father from the Catalonian region of Spain. Her father had been attracted to the area of Lorica by the mining industry and by the possibility of finding the oil deposits that had become part of local Indian lore. The reality of this Indian heritage never became lost to Zapata Olivella. Visits with his maternal grandmother, aunts, and uncles helped to direct the formative fibers of his youth. His mother often talked to him and her other children about the traditions, tales, and rituals of her tribe, and about the legends of caciques and spirits who lived in the nearby mountains and marshes. Furthermore, Zapata Olivella feels that both his character and personality, as a writer, have likewise been richly rewarded with the African descendancy that he traces through his paternal grandparents, especially his paternal grandmother, Angela Vásquez. It was this environment with its confluence of cultures that awakened in Zapata Olivella his *conciencia mágica*, the consciousness of magic reality.

Zapata Olivella's family moved from the rural area of Lorica, in 1927, to the urban center of Cartagena, where he attended school up to and including the first year of premedicine. In 1939 he set out for Bogotá to pursue medical training, which he finished in 1948, with a brief hiatus in 1943 and 1944. He had begun writing and publishing at a very early age. At fifteen he had published articles in *El Fígaro* and *Diario de la Costa*, two newspapers in Cartagena. Other articles began to appear in 1939 in magazines in Bogotá (*Cromos, Semana,* and *Sábado*) and in the literary supplements of the *Tiempo* and the *Espectador*.

The 1943-1944 period is the time Zapata Olivella refers to as the beginning of his inclination to be a vagabond. Subsequently this vagabond yearning would take him throughout the Americas, to Europe, Africa, and Asia. In Barcelona he met Rosa Bosch, the daughter of a Catalonian painter. They were married in Bogotá in 1960 and have two daughters: Harlem and Edelma. The names of Zapata Olivella's daughters recall the ethnic imagery to which he has devoted himself in his literature. (Edelma, by the way, has been recognized as a promising poet).

The vagabond spirit of Zapata Olivella had an important influence on his literary career, especially in the investigation of myths. Most of his chronicles (*relatos*) that were published from 1949 to 1955 reflect this inclination to wander and observe. These experiences also serve as an introduction to many of the concepts used in his novels. For example, in 1943, after taking his fifth-year examinations in medical studies, Zapata Olivella left school and set out on foot to explore Central America from Panama to Mexico over a period of three months. His adventures are described in *Pasión vagabunda* (Passion of a Vagabond, 1949). In 1946 he was in the United States, where aggressive racial discrimination helped him understand both covert and overt facets of racism. In a comparative sense, this enabled him to consider more accurately the race question in Latin America. His stay in the United States resulted in *He visto la noche* (I Have Seen the Night, 1953).

In 1947 his first novel was published: *Tierra mojada* (Wet Land), which seems an introductory, schematic approach to the novel of social protest. All of the ingredients are there to demonstrate both man's injustice to man and the plight of the oppressed. There is the metaphoric struggle of man against nature and nature against man. A group of poor, landless peasants reclaims some unused marshland on which to eke out a living. Not only do the elements operate against their efforts, there are also abusive latifundists who usurp the land of the peasants, their rights, and their dignity. Hope for a better future, however, comes through the socially oriented efforts of Marco Olivares, an enlightened schoolteacher. He fights for the poor and advises them on social issues. Most of all, he helps them to organize and make the system work in their behalf. While the end of the novel offers an inference of the possibility of a better tomorrow, no solution is provided.

Various critics have spoken for and against Zapata Olivella's ending to this novel. Yet the sociopolitical reality in Colombia in 1947 precluded an ending that did more than suggest possibilities for a more progressive future. National disunity and attacks on the Liberals were occurring in Colombia between 1942 and 1946. Even with the government of Conservative Mariano Ospina Pérez (1946-1950), political anarchy still kept the nation in virtual civil war. More important in the study of Zapata Olivella's literary trajectory is the fact that this first work is an outline of the perspective he wanted his artistic direction to follow. Three basic constituent parts are presented: a context within which the author can place himself as an actuator; a spatial dimension that both supports and confirms the ethnic context; and a temporal consideration that provides context and space with philosophical and psychological dimensions of culture. The concept of African-Indian-Spanish miscegenation is especially highlighted. These are the areas that become increasingly complex and technically sophisticated as his craft develops.

Zapata Olivella's restricted emphasis caused some analysts to label him "an Afro-Hispanic writer." Zapata Olivella's ethnic viewpoint is both an outgrowth of the geographical parameters that control his context and the realization of himself as an integral part of the artistic stimuli within this geocontextual dimension. From *Tierra mojada* to *El fusilamiento del Diablo* (The Execution of the Devil, 1986), there is a consistency in thematic control: the protest for human rights and social justice, and the effects of racial amalgamation. However, he achieves movement in the

Zapata Olivella in 1976, while he was organizing the First Congress of Black Cultures in the Americas, held in Calí, Colombia, the following year

areas of contextual contours, spatial parameters, and time sequences by developing narrator/perspective and synchronic/diachronic confluence. This technical activity is a part of the dynamic literary range of contemporary Latin-American literature, which continues to explore a cultural reality in which myths are inextricable as day-to-day motivators. Zapata Olivella, as part of his technical evolution, uses myths with exceptional insight to illuminate human existence in the Latin-American context.

In the prologue to a 1964 edition of *Tierra mojada*, the Peruvian writer Ciro Alegría states that Zapata Olivella, as a writer, both suffers and enjoys life along with his heroes. His personal alliance with his characters is the first step toward a special type of contextual revelation. Because of this context, for Zapata Olivella, the myth can become reality; the African, the Indian, and the Hispanic European can become constants for the racial gamut created by miscegenation; and that oppression seems to exist because of the confluence of mythical reality, ethnicity, and culture.

The spatial dimension within which Zapata Olivella works has usually been in those areas with which he has a personal relationship: Lorica, where he was born; Cartagena, where he grew up and went to school; Quibdó (or Chocó), the region in Colombia that has a predominant ethnic grouping of African descendants, mulattos, zambos (of African and Indian heritage), and a small Indian presence. Zapata Olivella often speaks of his tri-ethnic legacy, which has produced a cultural vibrancy in the Latin-American environment. Many authors allude to the idea but never explore it. This reluctance is not new. Admission of the range of miscegenation, and its concomitant effect on social reality, is difficult for many Latin Americans to accept. Rubén Darío in his prologue to *Prosas profanas* was reacting to provocation when he stated that a drop of African or Indian blood would not prevent him from writing with the hands of a (European) marquess. *Tierra mojada*, set in the rural area of Lorica, reflects the ethnicity and the problems of the area with verisimilitude.

In *La calle 10* (Tenth Street, 1960) there is a geographical shift to Bogotá, Colombia's capital. The novel reflects street life among the homeless in Bogotá. Dehumanization is overwhelming in the scenes of hunger, murder, and prostitution. It is not unusual for such descriptions to assume metaphoric qualities. For example, poverty is an ever-present reality with ramifications that continue after death: a woman's body is given to a medical school because her husband is too poor to bury her. While the many problems of the poor are not solved at the end of this novel, there is an apparent potential for collective action. Such collective action in subsequent novels by Zapata Olivella will be the means for people to live out their mythic reality. There are inescapable aspects, in this 1960 novel, that reflect his observation of life while he lived in the capital. In 1948 Zapata Olivella was in residency at the Psychiatric Hospital for Women in Bogotá. By 1960 he had become chief physician in the Division of Health Education for the Ministry of Health in Bogotá. He remained there until 1965.

Detrás del rostro (Behind the Face), published in 1963, is also from the Bogotá period and demonstrates its author's move toward a more complex literary structure: myth begins to control both context and time. Marvin A. Lewis has found that one of the keys to understanding the story line is through deciphering the narrative structure; the narrative voice leads the reader astray: "the thin line between appearance and reality, between truth and lie, is totally blurred in the multiplicity of interpretations of the central episode" (*Treading the Ebony Path*, 1987). There is still a thematic concern with social change, which draws on aspects of violence in the countryside and the miserable life of the street urchins in Bogotá. The shooting of a street person controls the central story line. The novel ends with a note of mystery, and the reality of destitute boys, wandering in the streets of Bogotá, remains the only plausible actuality.

Corral de negros (1963; translated as *Chambacu, Black Slum*, 1989) focuses on Chambacú, an island ghetto outside Cartagena, with "diez mil casuchas apretadas, todas de paja y papel" (ten thousand huts, all made out of straw and paper, and all bunched together). Its inhabitants are mostly black Colombians whose phenotypical representations are indicative of the vagaries of miscegenation.

In *Corral de negros* Zapata Olivella explores racism as a common denominator for oppression. Only after he left Colombia in the 1940s to satisfy his "vagabond passion" did his awareness of the race situation in Colombia, and Latin America in general, become more clearly focused, with him as part of the context. In an unpublished 26 May 1989 letter, Zapata Olivella admits that the awakening of his racial consciousness was a slow process, in spite of the fact that in Cartagena in particular, and in Colombia in general, all non-Caucasian ethnic groups suffer an inherent form of prejudice. Zapata Olivella goes on to say that the hypocrisy and the false rhetoric so typical of the Latin-American environment tend to cover up most racist acts.

Discrimination against Indians in Central America and Mexico; acts of racial violence against blacks in the United States; and personal affronts of a racist nature that Zapata Olivella has experienced in Colombia, Central America, and the United States have solidified his approach to racism in his novels. For example, in *Corral de negros*, the interrelationship of Máximo, Cotena, Clotilde, and José Raquel, who are black Colombians, and Inge, who is white and Swedish, prevents any character development. Each protagonist represents a static formation of ideas.

The novel opens with the statement that "the people [of Chambacú] were waking up after being asleep for four hundred years." There is a valiant struggle against the hunger, oppression, and illiteracy exacerbated by racism. The people's leader, Máximo, is killed in the struggle to bring equality to the *chambucanos*, and the novel ends on the hopeful note that, although Máximo's eyes were closed in death, "many [of the *chambucanos*] now had their eyes open." Along with this exploration of the collective application of racism, one can clearly perceive Zapata Olivella's personal examination of popular myths that, on first reading, seem to distort reality.

José Raquel has gone to fight with the Colombian troops sent to do battle alongside Americans in the Korean War. He meets Inge in Europe, marries her, and brings her back with him to Chambacú. This ghetto of poor blacks was originally José Raquel's home. There is a suggestion that Inge follows José Raquel because of his sexual prowess. Sex, as a literary construct, affords Zapata Olivella the potential for exploring the concept of mythic reality. Once in Colombia, José Raquel abandons Inge, but she remains at his mother's house and lives in total economic deprivation. In *Corral de negros* Zapata Olivella explores the relationship between black men and white women, in addition to questioning the sexual imagery associated with the use of the black person as a primitive sexual force in literature. The reader later learns, but not from Inge, that José Raquel has been castrated because of an injury in the Korean War.

In addition to the sexual myth, which is not Inge's real reason for wanting to leave Europe, there is also the contrast of two differing realities. Inge realizes that the world vision of Chambacú has a lot to offer humanity. By contrast, it is a question of culture more than race when Máximo says to her: "Your presence makes us feel strange. . . . It is not because of the difference in skin color. You reveal to us our cultural limitations, we are stifled by misery. . . . Our ancestral culture has also been drowned. It expresses itself in magic formulae. Superstitions. For four hundred years we have been kept from saying 'this is mine.'"

Zapata Olivella's immediate environment has had a profound influence on both his cultural leanings and his philosophical outlook, and these concepts help direct his craft. The cultural ambience of Cartagena, with the backdrop of Chambacú, was a second home for Zapata Olivella. In Cartagena, Zapata Olivella became aware of the nexus that joined him to that city's black population and history. In Cartagena he also became immersed in the powerful African spiritualism of his grandmother's personal and social worlds, in spite of the veneer of Roman Catholicism that she displayed. The history of this period of his life is vividly documented in his *Lève-toi mulatre* (Rise Up Mulatto, 1987).

In his formative years, the conflict he saw created by the juxtaposition of New World exigencies and African spiritualism was a direct legacy from his father: an atheist, anticlericist, freethinker, schoolteacher, and owner of a sizable library with volumes on science, philosophy, evolutionist theories, and radical liberalism. Yet there is no indication that Zapata Olivella found these trends of thought perturbing. In his writing there is a certain correlation between the portrayal of some characters and the picture of his father that Zapata Olivella offers researchers in interviews and letters. Displays of atheistic tendencies, inculcated by his father, although subdued in his novels, are still discernible to some degree.

A strong anticlerical sentiment is unequivocal. Anticlericalism, as a semiotic construct, is an overt part of the thematic direction of social protest and mythic reality in *En Chimá nace un santo* (In Chimá a Saint Is Born, 1964). The plot focuses on the people, as a collective, in Chimá, who discover saintlike qualities in Dominguito, one of their villagers. The driving force of this novel is the concept of the many myths that give the poor and common people in Chimá an understandable grasp on reality. Dominguito is seen as the apex and the center of radiation in the etiology of their mythic cosmovision. The orthodox church, in this world of differing spiritual values, is seen in two distinct dimensions: Father Barrocal, who considers this unorthodox creation of a saint to be heresy; and Father Jeremías, the scheming sacristan who connives, for his personal gain, to take advantage of a reality to which he does not subscribe. In a certain sense, both priests represent a clash between the ontological arguments of their Western orthodoxy and the mythos that explains tangible, observable phenomena. For Zapata Olivella, it is not a question of the literate versus the illiterate, or of right or wrong. It is the concept of personal gain dressed in clerical dogma, in opposition to the basic spiritual needs of a society. In the end, the people unite against the church for a cause that confirms and continues the world that gives them philosophical strength. *En Chimá nace un santo*, from the standpoint of structure, brings Zapata Olivella to an important juncture in his development of the metamyth and the technical control of content.

Some twenty years elapsed between the publication of *En Chimá nace un santo* and Zapata Olivella's next novel, *Changó, el gran putas* (Changó, the Great Magician, 1983). There was, nonetheless, literary activity in the interim, with the publishing of a collection of short stories; other short stories that appeared in anthologies; and essays and articles in various newspapers and magazines in Colombia. There were also brief visiting professorships at the University of Toronto (1968-1969); Howard University, in Washington, D.C. (1969-1970); and the University of Kansas (1970-1971).

Zapata Olivella is a popular lecturer and interviewee, and the recognition of his literary

Zapata Olivella, 10 March 1989

worth became a fait accompli during his visits to North America, especially among those critics and academicians avidly interested in the Afro-Hispanic world. His views on Afro-Colombian culture, from his vantage point as anthropologist, psychologist, and writer, have been requested at conferences and seminars in Latin America, Africa, Europe, and North America. Zapata Olivella acknowledges that these trips, conferences, and seminars have contributed to his intellectual growth and to the honing of his craft as an author. In August 1977 he was promoter, organizer, and president of the First Congress of Black Cultures in the Americas, held in Calí, Colombia. This was followed by Congress II in Panama in 1980, and Congress III in São Paulo, Brazil, in 1983. Zapata Olivella was vice-president and one of the principle presenters at both. Prior to this, from 1967 to 1970, he was president of the Colombia chapter of the Community of Latin-American Writers.

Zapata Olivella's narrative technique came to fruition in *Changó, el gran putas*. This complex novel, with the structure of an epic, is the result of Zapata Olivella's investigation into the spiritual existence of the neo-African in Latin America and North America. The localized mythic reality of his previous novels has been expanded to combine both the ontology and the cosmology of the black man in the Americas. *Changó, el gran putas* is divided into five sections: "The Origins," "The American Muntu," "The Rebellion of the Voodoos," "A Meeting of the Bloods," and "The Fighting Ancestors." The novel is best approached by considering the dimensions of history and philosophical religiosity. Instead of one hundred years of solitude that exclude a vital part of American ethnicity, Zapata Olivella offers the reader, by means of a narrative consciousness, the trajectory of five hundred years of omission.

In his 1984 interview with Gilberto Gómez and Raymond L. Williams, Zapata Olivella admitted that his intention in *Changó, el gran putas* was to present a Latin-American novel with a new and different cosmos vision. This viewpoint would encompass a perspective that does not rely only on a Colombian point of view, an Indian point of view, or a European view, but also that of an African perspective—not that of the pure African, whose culture is undiluted, but that of the amalgamated American-African whose world vision has become enriched by the visions of the Indian and the white man. This approach enables Zapata Olivella to go beyond the mythic reality of Lorica, Cartagena, and Bogotá and to examine the extended *muntu*, or psychospiritual realism, that makes Africa and the Americas contiguous. It is precisely because of this psychospiritual dimension that time is not seen as lineal and confined into separate divisions of synchrony or diachrony. Mythic time (synchronic) and historical time (diachronic) intertwine to conform to the African *hantu*—the concept of time and place in constant evolution involving the spirits of the dead speaking through the living in an ambience of metaphysical perpetuity. All of the literary elements of this novel function as intrasupportive constructs: the application of the metamyth, the temporal-spatial concept, and the superimposed narrative voices speaking in poemlike prose.

Changó, el gran putas, as a title, is an interesting metaphor that conceptualizes the book. It combines a classical African mythos, *Changó*, with a Colombian/New World vernacular term, *el putas*. Zapata Olivella advises that *el putas*, in popular Colombian speech, has a somewhat magical dimension and designates maximum transcendency in all of what is good, evil, beautiful, and ugly. *Changó, el gran putas* required some twenty years to write, and Zapata Olivella employed approximately ten thousand file cards from research at libraries in Washington, D.C., Colombia, Senegal, Spain, Mexico, Venezuela, and Haiti.

El fusilamiento del Diablo is not as ambitious in scope but is based on the technical and thematic strengths and skills seen in *Changó, el gran putas*. Zapata Olivella applies the *muntu* theory as reality and sets the pace for other writers in Latin America. The protagonist of *El fusilamiento del Diablo*, Saturio Valencia, alias El Diablo, displays all the tendencies of his inherited *muntu*, or ancestral spirituality. He refuses to be submissive and defends his right to be a free man; in so doing he is condemned to death. In *Changó, el gran putas* Zapata Olivella referred to all those who applied the *muntu* myth in their struggle to overcome oppression as *ekobios*, a Bantu term indicating members of a brotherhood. Thus Zapata Olivella shows that the application of *muntu* would make American Indians, Afro-Hispanics, South African blacks, coloreds, and whites in the struggle against apartheid—including St. Peter Claver, José María Morelos y Pavón of Mexico, Martin Luther King, and Malcolm X—all *ekobios*. In *El fusilamiento del Diablo* Valencia is thwarted in his efforts to be free by Mr. MacDonald, a North American black man. Regardless of his skin color, MacDonald represents the white North American and white Latin-American oppressors. MacDonald does not understand his *muntu* and consequently operates beyond the pale of *ekobioism*. After valiant attempts by his followers to release him from prison, Valencia is shot and buried. True to the mythic concepts around which this novel is structured, his death produces the requisite miracles that enable reality to conform to myth: his blind aunt recovers her sight, and the children of the village (the hope of the future, the inheritors of the *muntu* spirit) see the much-longed-for miracle that proves Valencia is the Devil incarnate.

In the 26 May 1989 letter, Zapata Olivella revealed his future literary projects: "I have just finished my novel *Hemingway el cazador de la muerte* [Hemingway the Hunter of Death]. It is a fictionalized version of the reason behind the suicide of this great North American writer. It takes place in Kenya, Spain, and the United States. It has a theme that also enables me to cry out against the massacre of elephants and other African species."

In each of his careers (as physician, psychologist, anthropologist, and writer) Zapata Olivella has been recognized as an important contributor. His many recognitions include the New Human Rights prize for literature granted by the National Assembly of France in Paris (1988), for his chronicle-essay *Lève-toi mulatre*.

The vitality of contemporary Latin-American literature reflects a spirit that can readily be attributed to its cultural history. Zapata Olivella brings to this vitality a dynamism that is overtly couched in an acceptance of the multiethnic components of Hispanic America's racial cosmos. For this, his country has paid tribute to his literary efforts with special recognitions. Córdoba, Colombia, awarded him the José María Córdoba Grand Cross, by decree, on 4 May 1977. The mayor's office of Cartagena decorated Zapata Olivella with the Order of Pedro Romero on 9 April 1985, for his dedication to Colombian letters, for the furthering of science in Colombia, and for serving as a model example and stimulus to future generations. The work of Manuel Zapata Olivella confirms that a consideration of aesthetics and ethnicity in Latin-American literature adds an important dimension to his narrative technique.

Interviews:

Raymond L. Williams and Gilberto Gómez, "Interview with Manuel Zapata Olivella," *Hispania*, 67 (1984): 657-658;

Yvonne Captain-Hidalgo, "Conversación con el Doctor Manuel Zapata Olivella, Bogotá 1980, 1983," *Afro-Hispanic Review*, 4, no. 1 (1985): 26-32.

References:

Ciro Alegría, Prologue to Zapata Olivella's *Tierra mojada* (Bogotá: Bullón, 1964), pp. 1-14;

François Bogliolo, *La négritude et les problèmes du noir dans l'oeuvre de Manuel Zapata Olivella* (Dakar, Senegal & Abidjan, Ivory Coast: Nouvelles Editions Africaines, 1978);

Sylvia G. Carullo, "La dialéctica hambre-agresión en *Chambacú, corral de negros*," *Afro-Hispanic Review*, 2 (September 1983): 19-22;

Brenda Frazier Clemons, "Manuel Zapata Olivella's 'Un extraño bajo mi piel': A Study of Repression," *Afro-Hispanic Review*, 2 (September 1983): 5-7;

Aida Heredia, "Figuras arquetípicas y la armonía racial en *Chambacú: corral de negros* de Manuel Zapata Olivella," *Afro-Hispanic Review*, 6 (May 1987): 3-8;

Roberto Herrera Soto, "Zapata Olivella o las perspectivas de la negritud en las Américas," *La República* (Bogotá), Sunday supplement, 18 March 1984, pp. 1-12;

Richard Jackson, "Myth, History and Narrative Structure in Manuel Zapata Olivella's *Changó, el gran putas*," *Revista/Review Interamericana*, 13, nos. 1-4 (1983): 108-119;

Shirley Jackson, "African World View in Five Afro-Hispanic Novels," *Afro-Hispanic Review*, 5 (January-May-September 1986): 37-41;

Thomas E. Kooreman, "Integración artística de la protesta social en las novelas de Manuel Zapata Olivella," *Afro-Hispanic Review*, 6 (January 1987): 27-30;

Kooreman, "Two Novelists' Views of Bogotazo," *Latin American Literary Review*, 3 (1974): 131-135;

Marvin A. Lewis, "*En Chimá nace un santo*: Myth and Violence," *Kentucky Romance Quarterly*, 25, no. 2 (1978): 21-26;

Lewis, "La trayectoria novelística de Manuel Zapata Olivella: de la opresión a la liberación," in *Ensayos de literatura colombiana*, edited by Raymond L. Williams (Bogotá: Plaza & Janés, 1985), pp. 137-148;

Lewis, *Treading the Ebony Path: Ideology and Violence in Contemporary Afro-Colombian Prose Fiction* (Columbia: University of Missouri Press, 1987);

Ramón López Tamés, "La soledad de las razas," in his *La narrativa actual de Colombia y su contexto social* (Valladolid: Universidad de Valladolid, 1975), pp. 64-103;

Nestor Madrid-Malo, "Estado actual de la novela en Colombia," *Revista interamericana de bibliografía*, 17 (1967): 68-82;

Darío Ruiz Gómez, "La crítica como beligerencia verbal," *Letras nacionales*, 12 (1967): 17-24;

Ian Smart, "*Changó, el gran putas*, una nueva novela poemática," in *Ensayos de literatura colombiana*, pp. 149-156;

Gerardo Suárez Rondón, "Sintesis temática de la novela de violencia," in *La novela sobre la violencia en Colombia*, edited by Luis E. Serrano (Bogotá, 1966), pp. 11-44.

Checklist of Further Readings

Acker, Bertie. *El cuento mexicano contemporáneo. Rulfo, Arreola y Fuentes: Temas y cosmovisión*. Madrid: Playor, 1984.

Alan, M., and Evelyn Rugg, eds. *Actas del Sexto Congreso Internacional de Hispanistas*. Toronto: University of Toronto Press, 1980.

Alegría, Fernando. *Literatura y revolución*. Mexico City: Fondo de Cultura Económica, 1971.

Anderson Imbert, Enrique. *El realismo mágico y otros ensayos*. Caracas: Monte Avila, 1976.

Aparicio López, Teófilo. *El "boom" americano: Estudios de crítica literaria*. Valladolid: Estudio Agustiniano, 1980.

Avalle-Arce, Juan Bautista, ed. *Narradores hispanoamericanos de hoy*. Chapel Hill: U.N.C. Department of Romance Languages, 1973.

Bacarisse, Salvador, ed. *Contemporary Latin American Fiction*. Edinburgh: Scottish Academic Press, 1980.

Bassnett, Susan, ed. *Knives and Angels: Women Writers in Latin America*. London: Zed, 1990.

Bella, Jozef. *A mascara e o enigma: A modernidade da representação a transgressão*. Rio de Janeiro: Alves, 1986.

Bleznick, Donald W., ed. *Variaciones interpretativas en torno a la nueva narrativa hispanoamericana*. Santiago, Chile: Universitaria, 1972.

Boldy, Steven. *Before the Boom: Four Essays on Latin American Literature Before 1940*. Liverpool: Center for Latin American Studies, University of Liverpool, 1981.

Brushwood, John. *La novela mexicana (1967-1982)*. Mexico City: Grijalbo, 1985.

Carballo, Emmanuel. *Diecinueve protagonistas de la literatura mexicana del siglo xx*. Mexico City: Empresas, 1965.

Chang-Rodríguez, Raquel, and Gabriella de Beer, eds. *La historia en la literatura iberoamericana*. Hanover, N.H.: Ediciones del Norte, 1989.

Chevigny, Bell Gale, and Gari Laguardia, eds. *Reinventing the Americas: Comparative Studies of the Literature of the United States and Spanish America*. New York: Cambridge University Press, 1986.

Cornejo-Polar, Antonio. *Sobre literatura y crítica latinoamericanas*. Caracas: Ediciones de la Facultad de Humanidades y Educación, Universidad Central de Venezuela, 1982.

Coutinho, Afranio, ed. *A Literatura no Brasil*, 6 volumes. Rio de Janeiro: Sud Americana, 1968-1971.

Covizzi, Lenira Marques. *O Insólito em Guimarães Rosa e Borges*. São Paulo: Atica, 1978.

Dacanal, José Hildebrando. *Nova Narrativa Epica no Brasil*. Porto Alegre, Brazil: Sulina, 1973.

Dacanal. *Realismo Mágico*. Porto Alegre, Brazil: Movimento, 1970.

DeCosta, Miriam, ed. *Blacks in Hispanic Literature*. Port Washington, N.Y.: Kennikat, 1977.

Díaz, Nancy Gray. *The Radical Self: Metamorphosis to Animal Form in Modern Latin American Narrative*. Columbia: University of Missouri Press, 1988.

Dorfman, Ariel. *Hacia la liberación del lector latinoamericano*. Hanover, N.H.: Ediciones del Norte, 1984.

Dorfman. *Some Write to the Future: Essays on Contemporary Latin American Fiction*. Durham, N.C.: Duke University Press, 1991.

Durán, Manuel. *Tríptico mexicano: Rulfo, Fuentes, Elizondo*. Mexico City: Sepsetentas, 1973.

Ellison, Fred P. *Brazil's New Novel*. Berkeley: University of California Press, 1954.

Feal, Rosemary Geisdorfer. *Novel Lives: The Fictional Autobiographies of Guillermo Cabrera Infante and Mario Vargas Llosa*. Chapel Hill: North Carolina Studies in the Romance Languages and Literatures, 1986.

Fitz, Earl E. *Rediscovering the New World: Inter-American Literature in a Comparative Context*. Iowa City: University of Iowa Press, 1991.

Fleischmann, Ulrich, ed. *El Caribe y América Latina: Actas del III. Coloquio Interdisciplinario sobre el Caribe*. Frankfurt am Main: Vervuert, 1987.

Foster, David William, and Virginia Ramos Foster, eds. *Alternate Voices in the Contemporary Latin American Narrative*. Columbia: University of Missouri Press, 1985.

Foster and Foster, eds. *Gay and Lesbian Themes in Latin American Writing*. Austin: University of Texas Press, 1991.

Foster and Foster, eds. *Modern Latin American Literature*, 2 volumes. New York: Ungar, 1975.

Gallagher, David Patrick. *Modern Latin American Literature*. London: Oxford University Press, 1973.

Genro, Tarso Fernando. *Literatura e ideologia: Um novo romance latino-americano*. Curitiba, Brazil: Criar, 1982.

Gertel, Zunilda. *La novela hispanoamericana contemporánea*. Buenos Aires: Columbia, 1970.

González del Valle, Luis, and Vicente Cabrera. *La nueva ficción hispanoamericana a través de Miguel Angel Asturias y Gabriel García Márquez*. New York: Torres, 1972.

González Echevarría, Roberto. *Myth and Archive: A Theory of Latin American Narrative*. Cambridge: Cambridge University Press, 1990.

González Echevarría. *The Voice of the Masters: Writing and Authority in Modern Latin American Literature*. Austin: University of Texas Press, 1985.

Guelfi, Maria Lucia Fernandes. *Novissima: Contribuição para o estudo do Modernismo*. São Paulo: Universidade de São Paulo, Instituto de estudos Brasileiros, 1987.

Jackson, David, ed. *Transformations of Literary Language in Latin American Literature: From Machado de Assis to the Vanguards*. Austin, Tex.: Abaporu, 1987.

Jackson, Richard. *Black Literature and Humanism in Latin America*. Athens: University of Georgia Press, 1988.

Jackson. *Black Writers in Latin America*. Albuquerque: University of New Mexico Press, 1979.

Jara, René, and Hernán Vidal, eds. *Testimonio y literatura*. Minneapolis: Institute for the Study of Ideologies and Literature, 1986.

Kulin, Katalin. *Modern Latin American Fiction: A Return to Didacticism*. Translated by Aszter Molnar. Budapest: Akademiai Kiado, 1988.

Larson, Neil, ed. *The Discourse of Power: Culture, Hegemony, and the Authoritarian State*. Minneapolis: Institute for the Study of Ideologies and Literature, 1983.

Leite, Dante Moreira. *O Amor Romantico e Outros Temas*. São Paulo: Conselho Estadual de Cultura, 1964.

Lewis, Marvin. *Treading the Ebony Path: Ideology and Violence in Contemporary Afro-Columbian Prose Fiction*. Columbia: University of Missouri Press, 1987.

Lima, Luís Costa. *A Metamorfose do Silêncio*. Rio de Janeiro: Eldorado, 1974.

Lindstrom, Naomi. *Women's Voice in Latin American Literature*. Washington, D.C.: Three Continents, 1989.

Lockert, Lucía Fox, ed. *Mitos en Hispanoamérica—Interpretación y literatura*. East Lansing, Mich.: Imprenta la Nueva Crónica, 1989.

Luis, William, ed. *Literary Bondage: Slavery in Cuban Narrative*. Austin: University of Texas Press, 1990.

Luis, ed. *Voices from Under: Black Narrative in Latin America and the Caribbean*. Westport, Conn.: Greenwood, 1984.

Luis and Julio Rodríguez-Luis, eds. *Translating Latin America: Culture as Text*, special issue of *Translating Perspectives*, 6 (1991).

Magnarelli, Sharon. *The Lost Rib*. Lewisburg, Pa.: Bucknell University Press, 1985.

Martins, Heitor, ed. *The Brazilian Novel*. Bloomington: Indiana University Publications, 1976.

McDuffie, Keith, and Alfredo Roggiano, eds. *Texto/Contexto en la literatura iberoamericana*. Madrid: Artes Gráficas Benzal, 1981.

Menton, Seymour. *Prose Fiction of the Cuban Revolution*. Austin: University of Texas Press, 1975.

Meyer, Doris, and Margarite Fernandez Olmos, eds. *Contemporary Women Authors of Latin America*. Brooklyn, N.Y.: Brooklyn College Press, 1983.

Miller, Yvette E., and Charles Tatum, eds. *Latin American Women Writers: Yesterday and Today*. Pittsburgh: Latin American Literary Review, 1977.

Minc, Rose, ed. *The Contemporary Latin American Short Story*. New York: Senda Nueva de Ediciones, 1979.

Minc, ed. *Literature and Popular Culture in the Hispanic World: A Symposium*. Gaithersburg, Md.: Montclair State College/Ediciones Hispamérica, 1981.

Minc, ed. *Literatures in Transition: The Many Voices of the Caribbean Area: A Symposium*. Gaithersburg, Md.: Montclair State College/Ediciones Hispamérica, 1982.

Morón, Guillermo. *Dos novelistas latinoamericanos: Arturo Uslar Pietri, Ernesto Sábato*. Buenos Aires: Publicaciones de la Embajada de Venezuela, 1979.

Nunes, Benedito. *O Dorso do Tigre*. São Paulo: Editora Perspectiva, 1969.

Oropeza, José Napoleón. *Para fijar un rostro: Notas sobre la novelística venezolana actual*. Valencia, Venezuela: Vadell Hermanos, 1984.

Ortega, Julio. *La imaginación crítica: ensayos sobre la modernidad en el Perú*. Lima: Ediciones Peisa, 1974.

Ortega. *Poetics of Change: The New Spanish-American Narrative*. Austin: University of Texas Press, 1984.

Osorio, Nelson, ed. *La formación de la vanguardia literaria en Venezuela*. Caracas: Academia Nacional de la Historia, 1985.

Perez, Renard. *Escritores Brasileiros Contemporâneos*. Rio de Janeiro: Civilização Brasileira, 1960.

Perus, Francoise. *Historia y crítica literaria: El realismo social y la crisis de la dominacion oligárquica*. Havana: Casa de las Américas, 1982.

Picón Salas, Mariano. *Estudios de literatura venezolana*. Caracas: Edime, 1961.

Rabassa, Clementine Christos. *Demetrio Aguilera-Malta and Social Justice: The Tertiary Phase of Epic Tradition in Latin American Literature*. Rutherford, N.J.: Fairleigh Dickinson University Press, 1980.

Rincón, Carlos. *El cambio de la noción de la literatura*. Bogotá: Instituto Colombiano de Cultura, 1978.

Rivero Potter, Alicia. *Autor/lector: Huidobro, Borges, Fuentes y Sarduy*. Detroit: Wayne State University Press, 1991.

Rodríguez de Laguna, Asela, ed. *Images and Identities: The Puerto Rican in Two World Contexts*. New Brunswick, N.J.: Transaction, 1987.

Rodríguez Monegal, Emir. *El Boom de la novela latinoamericana*. Caracas: Tiempo Nuevo, 1972.

Rodríguez Monegal. *Narradores de esta América*. Montevideo: Editorial Alfa, 1969.

Rodríguez-Luis, Julio. *Hermenéutica y praxis del indigenismo*. Mexico City: Tierra Firme, 1980.

Rodríguez-Luis. *La literatura hispanoamericana entre compromiso y experimento*. Madrid: Espiral, 1984.

Rosas, Patricia, and Lourdes Madrid. *Las torturas de la imaginación*. Mexico City: Premiá, 1982.

Ruffinelli, Jorge. *Crítica en marcha: ensayos sobre literatura latinoamericana*. Mexico City: Premiá, 1979.

Ruffinelli. *La escritura invisible: Arlt, Borges, García Márquez, Roa Bastos, Rulfo, Cortázar, Fuentes, Vargas Llosa*. Mexico: Universidad Veracruzana, 1986.

Santiago, Silviano. *Nas malhas da letra: Ensaios*. São Paulo: Companhia das Letras, 1989.

Siemens, William L. *Worlds Reborn: The Hero in the Modern Spanish American Novel*. Morgantown: West Virginia University Press, 1984.

Silva-Velázquez, Caridad, and Nora Erro-Orthman. *Puerta abierta: La nueva escritora latinoamericana*. Mexico City: Mortiz, 1986.

Silverman, Malcolm. *Moderna ficção brasileira*. Translated by J. G. Linke. Rio de Janeiro: Civilização Brasileira, 1978.

Sole, Carlos A. ed. *Latin American Writers*, 3 volumes. New York: Scribners, 1989.

Souza, Raymond D. *Major Cuban Novelists: Innovation and Tradition*. Columbia: University of Missouri Press, 1976.

Viñas, David. *De Sarmiento a Cortázar: Literatura Argentina y realidad política*. Buenos Aires: Siglo Veinte, 1971.

Virgillo, Carmelo, and Naomi Lindstrom, eds. *Woman as Myth and Metaphor in Latin American Literature*. Columbia: University of Missouri Press, 1985.

Volek, Emil. *Cuatro claves para la modernidad*. Madrid: Gredos, 1984.

Williams, Raymond L. *Una década de la novela colombiana: La experiencia de los setenta*. Bogotá: Plaza & Janés, 1981.

Williams, ed. *Ensayos de literatura colombiana*. Bogotá: Plaza & Janés, 1985.

Yates, Donald A., ed. *Otros mundos otros fuegos: Fantasía y realismo mágico en Iberoamérica*. East Lansing: Michigan State University, 1975.

Contributors

Steven Boldy	*Emmanuel College, Cambridge*
Alicia Borinsky	*Boston University*
Sara Castro-Klarén	*Johns Hopkins University*
Bobby J. Chamberlain	*University of Pittsburgh*
Antonio Cornejo-Polar	*University of Pittsburgh*
Earl E. Fitz	*Pennsylvania State University*
Zunilda Gertel	*University of California, Davis*
Aníbal González	*Michigan State University*
Roberto González-Echevarría	*Yale University*
Ricardo Gutiérrez Mouat	*Emory University*
Lanin A. Gyurko	*University of Arizona*
Lucille Kerr	*University of Southern California*
Julia A. Kushigian	*Connecticut College*
María-Inés Lagos	*Washington University in St. Louis*
Luis Leal	*University of California, Santa Barbara*
Suzanne Jill Levine	*University of California, Santa Barbara*
Fábio Lucas	*Universidade de Brasilia*
Jorge Marbán	*College of Charleston*
Diane E. Marting	*Columbia University*
Willy O. Muñoz	*Kent State University*
Ardis L. Nelson	*Florida State University*
María Rosa Olivera-Williams	*University of Notre Dame*
Antonio Olliz Boyd	*Temple University*
Alberto Julián Pérez	*Dartmouth College*
Sara Poot-Herrera	*University of California, Santa Barbara*
Randolph D. Pope	*Washington University in St. Louis*
Leticia Reyes-Tatinclaux	*Community College of Vermont*
J. C. Ulloa	*Virginia Tech*
L. A. de Ulloa	*Radford University*
Jon S. Vincent	*University of Kansas*
Raymond Leslie Williams	*University of Colorado*

Cumulative Index

Dictionary of Literary Biography, Volumes 1-113
Dictionary of Literary Biography Yearbook, 1980-1990
Dictionary of Literary Biography Documentary Series, Volumes 1-9

Cumulative Index

DLB before number: *Dictionary of Literary Biography,* Volumes 1-113
Y before number: *Dictionary of Literary Biography Yearbook,* 1980-1990
DS before number: *Dictionary of Literary Biography Documentary Series,* Volumes 1-9

A

Abbey Press DLB-49
The Abbey Theatre and Irish Drama, 1900-1945 ....DLB-10
Abbot, Willis J. 1863-1934 ....DLB-29
Abbott, Jacob 1803-1879 ....DLB-1
Abbott, Lyman 1835-1922 ....DLB-79
Abbott, Robert S. 1868-1940 ....DLB-29, 91
Abelard-Schuman DLB-46
Abell, Arunah S. 1806-1888 ....DLB-43
Abercrombie, Lascelles 1881-1938 ....DLB-19
Aberdeen University Press Limited DLB-106
Abrams, M. H. 1912- DLB-67
Abse, Dannie 1923- DLB-27
Academy Chicago Publishers DLB-46
Ace Books DLB-46
Acorn, Milton 1923-1986 ....DLB-53
Acosta, Oscar Zeta 1935?- DLB-82
Actors Theatre of Louisville DLB-7
Adair, James 1709?-1783? DLB-30
Adam, Graeme Mercer 1839-1912 ....DLB-99
Adame, Leonard 1947- DLB-82
Adamic, Louis 1898-1951 ....DLB-9
Adams, Alice 1926- Y-86
Adams, Brooks 1848-1927 ....DLB-47
Adams, Charles Francis, Jr. 1835-1915 ....DLB-47
Adams, Douglas 1952- Y-83
Adams, Franklin P. 1881-1960 ....DLB-29
Adams, Henry 1838-1918 ....DLB-12, 47
Adams, Herbert Baxter 1850-1901 ....DLB-47
Adams, J. S. and C. [publishing house] DLB-49
Adams, James Truslow 1878-1949 ....DLB-17
Adams, John 1735-1826 ....DLB-31
Adams, John Quincy 1767-1848 ....DLB-37
Adams, Léonie 1899-1988 ....DLB-48

Adams, Levi 1802-1832 ....DLB-99
Adams, Samuel 1722-1803 ....DLB-31, 43
Adams, William Taylor 1822-1897 ....DLB-42
Adamson, Sir John 1867-1950 ....DLB-98
Adcock, Betty 1938- DLB-105
Adcock, Betty, Certain Gifts DLB-105
Adcock, Fleur 1934- DLB-40
Addison, Joseph 1672-1719 ....DLB-101
Ade, George 1866-1944 ....DLB-11, 25
Adeler, Max (see Clark, Charles Heber)
Advance Publishing Company DLB-49
AE 1867-1935 ....DLB-19
Aesthetic Poetry (1873), by Walter Pater DLB-35
Afro-American Literary Critics: An Introduction DLB-33
Agassiz, Jean Louis Rodolphe 1807-1873 ....DLB-1
Agee, James 1909-1955 ....DLB-2, 26
The Agee Legacy: A Conference at the University of Tennessee at Knoxville Y-89
Aichinger, Ilse 1921- DLB-85
Aiken, Conrad 1889-1973 ....DLB-9, 45, 102
Ainsworth, William Harrison 1805-1882 ....DLB-21
Aitken, Robert [publishing house] DLB-49
Akenside, Mark 1721-1770 ....DLB-109
Akins, Zoë 1886-1958 ....DLB-26
Alain-Fournier 1886-1914 ....DLB-65
Alba, Nanina 1915-1968 ....DLB-41
Albee, Edward 1928- DLB-7
Alberti, Rafael 1902- DLB-108
Alcott, Amos Bronson 1799-1888 ....DLB-1
Alcott, Louisa May 1832-1888 ....DLB-1, 42, 79
Alcott, William Andrus 1798-1859 ....DLB-1
Alden, Henry Mills 1836-1919 ....DLB-79
Alden, Isabella 1841-1930 ....DLB-42
Alden, John B. [publishing house] DLB-49

Alden, Beardsley and Company	DLB-49
Aldington, Richard 1892-1962	DLB-20, 36, 100
Aldis, Dorothy 1896-1966	DLB-22
Aldiss, Brian W. 1925-	DLB-14
Aldrich, Thomas Bailey 1836-1907	DLB-42, 71, 74, 79
Alegría, Ciro 1909-1967	DLB-113
Aleixandre, Vicente 1898-1984	DLB-108
Alexander, Charles 1868-1923	DLB-91
Alexander, Charles Wesley [publishing house]	DLB-49
Alexander, James 1691-1756	DLB-24
Alexander, Lloyd 1924-	DLB-52
Alger, Horatio, Jr. 1832-1899	DLB-42
Algonquin Books of Chapel Hill	DLB-46
Algren, Nelson 1909-1981	DLB-9; Y-81, 82
Allan, Andrew 1907-1974	DLB-88
Allan, Ted 1916-	DLB-68
Allbeury, Ted 1917-	DLB-87
Alldritt, Keith 1935-	DLB-14
Allen, Ethan 1738-1789	DLB-31
Allen, Gay Wilson 1903-	DLB-103
Allen, George 1808-1876	DLB-59
Allen, George [publishing house]	DLB-106
Allen, George, and Unwin Limited	DLB-112
Allen, Grant 1848-1899	DLB-70, 92
Allen, Henry W. 1912-	Y-85
Allen, Hervey 1889-1949	DLB-9, 45
Allen, James 1739-1808	DLB-31
Allen, James Lane 1849-1925	DLB-71
Allen, Jay Presson 1922-	DLB-26
Allen, John, and Company	DLB-49
Allen, Samuel W. 1917-	DLB-41
Allen, Woody 1935-	DLB-44
Alline, Henry 1748-1784	DLB-99
Allingham, Margery 1904-1966	DLB-77
Allingham, William 1824-1889	DLB-35
Allison, W. L. [publishing house]	DLB-49
Allott, Kenneth 1912-1973	DLB-20
Allston, Washington 1779-1843	DLB-1
Alonzo, Dámaso 1898-1990	DLB-108
Alsop, George 1636-post 1673	DLB-24
Alsop, Richard 1761-1815	DLB-37
Altemus, Henry, and Company	DLB-49
Altenberg, Peter 1885-1919	DLB-81
Altolaguirre, Manuel 1905-1959	DLB-108
Alurista 1947-	DLB-82
Alvarez, A. 1929-	DLB-14, 40
Amado, Jorge 1912-	DLB-113
Ambler, Eric 1909-	DLB-77
America: or, a Poem on the Settlement of the British Colonies (1780?), by Timothy Dwight	DLB-37
American Conservatory Theatre	DLB-7
American Fiction and the 1930s	DLB-9
American Humor: A Historical Survey East and Northeast South and Southwest Midwest West	DLB-11
American News Company	DLB-49
The American Poets' Corner: The First Three Years (1983-1986)	Y-86
American Publishing Company	DLB-49
American Stationers' Company	DLB-49
American Sunday-School Union	DLB-49
American Temperance Union	DLB-49
American Tract Society	DLB-49
The American Writers Congress (9-12 October 1981)	Y-81
The American Writers Congress: A Report on Continuing Business	Y-81
Ames, Fisher 1758-1808	DLB-37
Ames, Mary Clemmer 1831-1884	DLB-23
Amini, Johari M. 1935-	DLB-41
Amis, Kingsley 1922-	DLB-15, 27, 100
Amis, Martin 1949-	DLB-14
Ammons, A. R. 1926-	DLB-5
Amory, Thomas 1691?-1788	DLB-39
Anaya, Rudolfo A. 1937-	DLB-82
Andersch, Alfred 1914-1980	DLB-69
Anderson, Margaret 1886-1973	DLB-4, 91
Anderson, Maxwell 1888-1959	DLB-7
Anderson, Patrick 1915-1979	DLB-68
Anderson, Paul Y. 1893-1938	DLB-29
Anderson, Poul 1926-	DLB-8
Anderson, Robert 1917-	DLB-7
Anderson, Sherwood 1876-1941	DLB-4, 9, 86; DS-1
Andreas-Salomé, Lou 1861-1937	DLB-66
Andres, Stefan 1906-1970	DLB-69

Andrews, Charles M. 1863-1943	DLB-17
Andrews, Miles Peter ?-1814	DLB-89
Andrieux, Louis (see Aragon, Louis)	
Andrian, Leopold von 1875-1951	DLB-81
Andrus, Silas, and Son	DLB-49
Angell, James Burrill 1829-1916	DLB-64
Angelou, Maya 1928-	DLB-38
Angers, Félicité (see Conan, Laure)	
The "Angry Young Men"	DLB-15
Angus and Robertson (UK) Limited	DLB-112
Anhalt, Edward 1914-	DLB-26
Anners, Henry F. [publishing house]	DLB-49
Anthony, Piers 1934-	DLB-8
Anthony Burgess's *99 Novels*: An Opinion Poll	Y-84
Antin, Mary 1881-1949	Y-84
Antschel, Paul (see Celan, Paul)	
Apodaca, Rudy S. 1939-	DLB-82
Appleton, D., and Company	DLB-49
Appleton-Century-Crofts	DLB-46
Applewhite, James 1935-	DLB-105
Apple-wood Books	DLB-46
Aquin, Hubert 1929-1977	DLB-53
Aragon, Louis 1897-1982	DLB-72
Arbor House Publishing Company	DLB-46
Arbuthnot, John 1667-1735	DLB-101
Arcadia House	DLB-46
Arce, Julio G. (see Ulica, Jorge)	
Archer, William 1856-1924	DLB-10
Arden, John 1930-	DLB-13
Arden of Faversham	DLB-62
Ardis Publishers	Y-89
The Arena Publishing Company	DLB-49
Arena Stage	DLB-7
Arensberg, Ann 1937-	Y-82
Arguedas, José María 1911-1969	DLB-113
Arias, Ron 1941-	DLB-82
Arland, Marcel 1899-1986	DLB-72
Arlen, Michael 1895-1956	DLB-36, 77
Armed Services Editions	DLB-46
Arndt, Ernst Moritz 1769-1860	DLB-90
Arnim, Achim von 1781-1831	DLB-90
Arnim, Bettina von 1785-1859	DLB-90
Arno Press	DLB-46

Arnold, Edwin 1832-1904	DLB-35
Arnold, Matthew 1822-1888	DLB-32, 57
Arnold, Thomas 1795-1842	DLB-55
Arnold, Edward [publishing house]	DLB-112
Arnow, Harriette Simpson 1908-1986	DLB-6
Arp, Bill (see Smith, Charles Henry)	
Arreola, Juan José 1918-	DLB-113
Arrowsmith, J. W. [publishing house]	DLB-106
Arthur, Timothy Shay 1809-1885	DLB-3, 42, 79
Artmann, H. C. 1921-	DLB-85
Arvin, Newton 1900-1963	DLB-103
As I See It, by Carolyn Cassady	DLB-16
Asch, Nathan 1902-1964	DLB-4, 28
Ash, John 1948-	DLB-40
Ashbery, John 1927-	DLB-5; Y-81
Ashendene Press	DLB-112
Asher, Sandy 1942-	Y-83
Ashton, Winifred (see Dane, Clemence)	
Asimov, Isaac 1920-	DLB-8
Asselin, Olivar 1874-1937	DLB-92
Asturias, Miguel Angel 1899-1974	DLB-113
Atheneum Publishers	DLB-46
Atherton, Gertrude 1857-1948	DLB-9, 78
Athlone Press	DLB-112
Atkins, Josiah circa 1755-1781	DLB-31
Atkins, Russell 1926-	DLB-41
The Atlantic Monthly Press	DLB-46
Attaway, William 1911-1986	DLB-76
Atwood, Margaret 1939-	DLB-53
Aubert, Alvin 1930-	DLB-41
Aubert de Gaspé, Phillipe-Ignace-François 1814-1841	DLB-99
Aubert de Gaspé, Phillipe-Joseph 1786-1871	DLB-99
Aubin, Napoléon 1812-1890	DLB-99
Aubin, Penelope 1685-circa 1731	DLB-39
Aubrey-Fletcher, Henry Lancelot (see Wade, Henry)	
Auchincloss, Louis 1917-	DLB-2; Y-80
Auden, W. H. 1907-1973	DLB-10, 20
Audio Art in America: A Personal Memoir	Y-85
Auernheimer, Raoul 1876-1948	DLB-81
Austin, Alfred 1835-1913	DLB-35
Austin, Mary 1868-1934	DLB-9, 78

Austin, William 1778-1841.................................DLB-74

The Author's Apology for His Book
    (1684), by John Bunyan.............................DLB-39

An Author's Response, by Ronald Sukenick Y-82

Authors and Newspapers Association...................DLB-46

Authors' Publishing Company...........................DLB-49

Avalon Books DLB-46

Avendaño, Fausto 1941- DLB-82

Avison, Margaret 1918- DLB-53

Avon Books DLB-46

Ayckbourn, Alan 1939- DLB-13

Aymé, Marcel 1902-1967...................................DLB-72

Aytoun, William Edmondstoune 1813-1865 ....DLB-32

B

Babbitt, Irving 1865-1933...................................DLB-63

Babbitt, Natalie 1932- DLB-52

Babcock, John [publishing house].......................DLB-49

Bache, Benjamin Franklin 1769-1798 ....DLB-43

Bachmann, Ingeborg 1926-1973.........................DLB-85

Bacon, Delia 1811-1859.....................................DLB-1

Bacon, Thomas circa 1700-1768.........................DLB-31

Badger, Richard G., and Company......................DLB-49

Bage, Robert 1728-1801 ....DLB-39

Bagehot, Walter 1826-1877 ....DLB-55

Bagley, Desmond 1923-1983..............................DLB-87

Bagnold, Enid 1889-1981..................................DLB-13

Bahr, Hermann 1863-1934.................................DLB-81

Bailey, Alfred Goldsworthy 1905- DLB-68

Bailey, Francis [publishing house].......................DLB-49

Bailey, H. C. 1878-1961 ....DLB-77

Bailey, Jacob 1731-1808....................................DLB-99

Bailey, Paul 1937- DLB-14

Bailey, Philip James 1816-1902..........................DLB-32

Baillargeon, Pierre 1916-1967............................DLB-88

Baillie, Hugh 1890-1966...................................DLB-29

Baillie, Joanna 1762-1851.................................DLB-93

Bailyn, Bernard 1922- DLB-17

Bainbridge, Beryl 1933- DLB-14

Baird, Irene 1901-1981 ....DLB-68

The Baker and Taylor Company DLB-49

Baker, Carlos 1909-1987 ....DLB-103

Baker, Herschel C. 1914-1990 ....DLB-111

Baker, Houston A., Jr. 1943- DLB-67

Baker, Walter H., Company
    ("Baker's Plays")....................................DLB-49

Bald, Wambly 1902- DLB-4

Balderston, John 1889-1954..............................DLB-26

Baldwin, James 1924-1987.........................DLB-2, 7, 33; Y-87

Baldwin, Joseph Glover 1815-1864.....................DLB-3, 11

Ballantine Books DLB-46

Ballard, J. G. 1930- DLB-14

Ballou, Maturin Murray 1820-1895....................DLB-79

Ballou, Robert O. [publishing house]..................DLB-46

Bambara, Toni Cade 1939- DLB-38

Bancroft, A. L., and Company...........................DLB-49

Bancroft, George 1800-1891...............................DLB-1, 30, 59

Bancroft, Hubert Howe 1832-1918 ....DLB-47

Bangs, John Kendrick 1862-1922 ....DLB-11, 79

Banks, John circa 1653-1706.............................DLB-80

Bantam Books DLB-46

Banville, John 1945- DLB-14

Baraka, Amiri 1934- DLB-5, 7, 16, 38; DS-8

Barbauld, Anna Laetitia 1743-1825....................DLB-107, 109

Barbeau, Marius 1883-1969...............................DLB-92

Barber, John Warner 1798-1885........................DLB-30

Barbour, Ralph Henry 1870-1944 ....DLB-22

Barbusse, Henri 1873-1935................................DLB-65

Barclay, E. E., and Company DLB-49

Bardeen, C. W. [publishing house]......................DLB-49

Baring, Maurice 1874-1945................................DLB-34

Barker, A. L. 1918- DLB-14

Barker, George 1913- DLB-20

Barker, Harley Granville 1877-1946....................DLB-10

Barker, Howard 1946- DLB-13

Barker, James Nelson 1784-1858........................DLB-37

Barker, Jane 1652-1727?..................................DLB-39

Barker, Arthur, Limited DLB-112

Barks, Coleman 1937- DLB-5

Barlach, Ernst 1870-1938.................................DLB-56

Barlow, Joel 1754-1812....................................DLB-37

Barnard, John 1681-1770..................................DLB-24

Barnes, A. S., and Company DLB-49

Barnes, Djuna 1892-1982..................................DLB-4, 9, 45

Barnes, Margaret Ayer 1886-1967......................DLB-9

Barnes, Peter 1931- DLB-13

Barnes, William 1801-1886 ....DLB-32

Barnes and Noble Books	DLB-46
Barney, Natalie 1876-1972	DLB-4
Baron, Richard W., Publishing Company	DLB-46
Barr, Robert 1850-1912	DLB-70, 92
Barrax, Gerald William 1933-	DLB-41
Barrie, James M. 1860-1937	DLB-10
Barrie and Jenkins	DLB-112
Barrio, Raymond 1921-	DLB-82
Barry, Philip 1896-1949	DLB-7
Barry, Robertine (see Françoise)	
Barse and Hopkins	DLB-46
Barstow, Stan 1928-	DLB-14
Barth, John 1930-	DLB-2
Barthelme, Donald 1931-1989	DLB-2; Y-80, 89
Barthelme, Frederick 1943-	Y-85
Bartlett, John 1820-1905	DLB-1
Bartol, Cyrus Augustus 1813-1900	DLB-1
Barton, Bernard 1784-1849	DLB-96
Bartram, John 1699-1777	DLB-31
Bartram, William 1739-1823	DLB-37
Basic Books	DLB-46
Bass, T. J. 1932-	Y-81
Bassett, John Spencer 1867-1928	DLB-17
Bassler, Thomas Joseph (see Bass, T. J.)	
Bate, Walter Jackson 1918-	DLB-67, 103
Bates, Katharine Lee 1859-1929	DLB-71
Batsford, B. T. [publishing house]	DLB-106
Baum, L. Frank 1856-1919	DLB-22
Baum, Vicki 1888-1960	DLB-85
Baumbach, Jonathan 1933-	Y-80
Bawden, Nina 1925-	DLB-14
Bax, Clifford 1886-1962	DLB-10, 100
Bayer, Eleanor (see Perry, Eleanor)	
Bayer, Konrad 1932-1964	DLB-85
Bazin, Hervé 1911-	DLB-83
Beach, Sylvia 1887-1962	DLB-4
Beacon Press	DLB-49
Beadle and Adams	DLB-49
Beagle, Peter S. 1939-	Y-80
Beal, M. F. 1937-	Y-81
Beale, Howard K. 1899-1959	DLB-17
Beard, Charles A. 1874-1948	DLB-17
A Beat Chronology: The First Twenty-five Years, 1944-1969	DLB-16
Beattie, Ann 1947-	Y-82
Beattie, James 1735-1803	DLB-109
Beauchemin, Nérée 1850-1931	DLB-92
Beauchemin, Yves 1941-	DLB-60
Beaugrand, Honoré 1848-1906	DLB-99
Beaulieu, Victor-Lévy 1945-	DLB-53
Beaumont, Francis circa 1584-1616 and Fletcher, John 1579-1625	DLB-58
Beauvoir, Simone de 1908-1986	DLB-72; Y-86
Becher, Ulrich 1910-	DLB-69
Becker, Carl 1873-1945	DLB-17
Becker, Jurek 1937-	DLB-75
Becker, Jürgen 1932-	DLB-75
Beckett, Samuel 1906-1989	DLB-13, 15, Y-90
Beckford, William 1760-1844	DLB-39
Beckham, Barry 1944-	DLB-33
Beddoes, Thomas Lovell 1803-1849	DLB-96
Beecher, Catharine Esther 1800-1878	DLB-1
Beecher, Henry Ward 1813-1887	DLB-3, 43
Beer, George L. 1872-1920	DLB-47
Beer, Patricia 1919-	DLB-40
Beerbohm, Max 1872-1956	DLB-34, 100
Beer-Hofmann, Richard 1866-1945	DLB-81
Beers, Henry A. 1847-1926	DLB-71
Beeton, S. O. [publishing house]	DLB-106
Bégon, Elisabeth 1696-1755	DLB-99
Behan, Brendan 1923-1964	DLB-13
Behn, Aphra 1640?-1689	DLB-39, 80
Behn, Harry 1898-1973	DLB-61
Behrman, S. N. 1893-1973	DLB-7, 44
Belaney, Archibald Stansfeld (see Grey Owl)	
Belasco, David 1853-1931	DLB-7
Belford, Clarke and Company	DLB-49
Belitt, Ben 1911-	DLB-5
Belknap, Jeremy 1744-1798	DLB-30, 37
Bell, James Madison 1826-1902	DLB-50
Bell, Marvin 1937-	DLB-5
Bell, Millicent 1919-	DLB-111
Bell, George, and Sons	DLB-106
Bell, Robert [publishing house]	DLB-49
Bellamy, Edward 1850-1898	DLB-12
Bellamy, Joseph 1719-1790	DLB-31
La Belle Assemblée 1806-1837	DLB-110
Belloc, Hilaire 1870-1953	DLB-19, 100

Bellow, Saul 1915- DLB-2, 28; Y-82; DS-3	Bernanos, Georges 1888-1948.......................................DLB-72
Belmont Productions DLB-46	Bernard, Harry 1898-1979...DLB-92
Bemelmans, Ludwig 1898-1962 ....DLB-22	Bernard, John 1756-1828..DLB-37
Bemis, Samuel Flagg 1891-1973 ....DLB-17	Bernhard, Thomas 1931-1989 ....DLB-85
Bemrose, William [publishing house] DLB-106	Berrigan, Daniel 1921- DLB-5
Benchley, Robert 1889-1945 ....DLB-11	Berrigan, Ted 1934-1983 ....DLB-5
Benedetti, Mario 1920- DLB-113	Berry, Wendell 1934- DLB-5, 6
Benedictus, David 1938- DLB-14	Berryman, John 1914-1972 ....DLB-48
Benedikt, Michael 1935- DLB-5	Bersianik, Louky 1930- DLB-60
Benét, Stephen Vincent 1898-1943 ....DLB-4, 48, 102	Berton, Pierre 1920- DLB-68
Benét, William Rose 1886-1950 ....DLB-45	Bessette, Gerard 1920- DLB-53
Benford, Gregory 1941- Y-82	Bessie, Alvah 1904-1985 ....DLB-26
Benjamin, Park 1809-1864............................DLB-3, 59, 73	Bester, Alfred 1913- DLB-8
Benn, Gottfried 1886-1956...DLB-56	The Bestseller Lists: An Assessment...............................Y-84
Benn Brothers Limited DLB-106	Betjeman, John 1906-1984 ....DLB-20; Y-84
Bennett, Arnold 1867-1931 ....DLB-10, 34, 98	Betts, Doris 1932- Y-82
Bennett, Charles 1899- DLB-44	Beveridge, Albert J. 1862-1927......................................DLB-17
Bennett, Gwendolyn 1902- DLB-51	Beverley, Robert circa 1673-1722 ....DLB-24, 30
Bennett, Hal 1930- DLB-33	Bibaud, Adèle 1854-1941 ....DLB-92
Bennett, James Gordon 1795-1872...............................DLB-43	Bibaud, Michel 1782-1857...DLB-99
Bennett, James Gordon, Jr. 1841-1918 ....DLB-23	Bibliographical and Textual Scholarship
Bennett, John 1865-1956...DLB-42	Since World War II Y-89
Benoit, Jacques 1941- DLB-60	The Bicentennial of James Fenimore Cooper:
Benson, A. C. 1862-1925...DLB-98	An International Celebration Y-89
Benson, Jackson J. 1930- DLB-111	Bichsel, Peter 1935- DLB-75
Benson, Stella 1892-1933 ....DLB-36	Bickerstaff, Isaac John 1733-circa 1808.......................DLB-89
Bentham, Jeremy 1748-1832...DLB-107	Biddle, Drexel [publishing house]................................DLB-49
Bentley, E. C. 1875-1956...DLB-70	Bidwell, Walter Hilliard 1798-1881 ....DLB-79
Bentley, Richard [publishing house] DLB-106	Bienek, Horst 1930- DLB-75
Benton, Robert 1932- and Newman, David 1937- DLB-44	Bierbaum, Otto Julius 1865-1910 ....DLB-66
Benziger Brothers DLB-49	Bierce, Ambrose 1842-1914?..............DLB-11, 12, 23, 71, 74
Beresford, Anne 1929- DLB-40	Bigelow, William F. 1879-1966 ....DLB-91
Beresford-Howe, Constance 1922- DLB-88	Biggle, Lloyd, Jr. 1923- DLB-8
Berford, R. G., Company DLB-49	Biglow, Hosea (see Lowell, James Russell)
Berg, Stephen 1934- DLB-5	Billings, Josh (see Shaw, Henry Wheeler)
Bergengruen, Werner 1892-1964 ....DLB-56	Binding, Rudolf G. 1867-1938......................................DLB-66
Berger, John 1926- DLB-14	Bingham, Caleb 1757-1817..DLB-42
Berger, Meyer 1898-1959 ....DLB-29	Binyon, Laurence 1869-1943 ....DLB-19
Berger, Thomas 1924- DLB-2; Y-80	Biographical Documents I Y-84
Berkeley, Anthony 1893-1971 ....DLB-77	Biographical Documents II Y-85
Berkeley, George 1685-1753 ....DLB-31, 101	Bioren, John [publishing house] DLB-49
The Berkley Publishing Corporation...........................DLB-46	Bioy Casares, Adolfo 1914- DLB-113
Bernal, Vicente J. 1888-1915 ....DLB-82	Bird, William 1888-1963 ....DLB-4
	Birney, Earle 1904- DLB-88

Birrell, Augustine 1850-1933	DLB-98
Bishop, Elizabeth 1911-1979	DLB-5
Bishop, John Peale 1892-1944	DLB-4, 9, 45
Bissett, Bill 1939-	DLB-53
Black, David (D. M.) 1941-	DLB-40
Black, Walter J. [publishing house]	DLB-46
Black, Winifred 1863-1936	DLB-25
The Black Aesthetic: Background	DS-8
The Black Arts Movement, by Larry Neal	DLB-38
Black Theaters and Theater Organizations in America, 1961-1982: A Research List	DLB-38
Black Theatre: A Forum [excerpts]	DLB-38
Blackamore, Arthur 1679-?	DLB-24, 39
Blackburn, Alexander L. 1929-	Y-85
Blackburn, Paul 1926-1971	DLB-16; Y-81
Blackburn, Thomas 1916-1977	DLB-27
Blackmore, R. D. 1825-1900	DLB-18
Blackmur, R. P. 1904-1965	DLB-63
Blackwell, Basil, Publisher	DLB-106
Blackwood, Caroline 1931-	DLB-14
Blackwood's Edinburgh Magazine 1817-1980	DLB-110
Blair, Eric Arthur (see Orwell, George)	
Blair, Francis Preston 1791-1876	DLB-43
Blair, James circa 1655-1743	DLB-24
Blair, John Durburrow 1759-1823	DLB-37
Blais, Marie-Claire 1939-	DLB-53
Blaise, Clark 1940-	DLB-53
Blake, Nicholas 1904-1972 (see Day Lewis, C.)	DLB-77
Blake, William 1757-1827	DLB-93
The Blakiston Company	DLB-49
Blanchot, Maurice 1907-	DLB-72
Blanckenburg, Christian Friedrich von 1744-1796	DLB-94
Bledsoe, Albert Taylor 1809-1877	DLB-3, 79
Blelock and Company	DLB-49
Blennerhassett, Margaret Agnew 1773-1842	DLB-99
Bles, Geoffrey [publishing house]	DLB-112
Blish, James 1921-1975	DLB-8
Bliss, E., and E. White [publishing house]	DLB-49
Bloch, Robert 1917-	DLB-44
Block, Rudolph (see Lessing, Bruno)	
Blondal, Patricia 1926-1959	DLB-88
Bloom, Harold 1930-	DLB-67
Bloomer, Amelia 1818-1894	DLB-79
Bloomfield, Robert 1766-1823	DLB-93
Blotner, Joseph 1923-	DLB-111
Blume, Judy 1938-	DLB-52
Blunck, Hans Friedrich 1888-1961	DLB-66
Blunden, Edmund 1896-1974	DLB-20, 100
Blunt, Wilfrid Scawen 1840-1922	DLB-19
Bly, Nellie (see Cochrane, Elizabeth)	
Bly, Robert 1926-	DLB-5
Boaden, James 1762-1839	DLB-89
The Bobbs-Merrill Archive at the Lilly Library, Indiana University	Y-90
The Bobbs-Merrill Company	DLB-46
Bobrowski, Johannes 1917-1965	DLB-75
Bodenheim, Maxwell 1892-1954	DLB-9, 45
Bodkin, M. McDonnell 1850-1933	DLB-70
Bodley Head	DLB-112
Bodmer, Johann Jakob 1698-1783	DLB-97
Bodmershof, Imma von 1895-1982	DLB-85
Bodsworth, Fred 1918-	DLB-68
Boehm, Sydney 1908-	DLB-44
Boer, Charles 1939-	DLB-5
Bogan, Louise 1897-1970	DLB-45
Bogarde, Dirk 1921-	DLB-14
Bogue, David [publishing house]	DLB-106
Bohn, H. G. [publishing house]	DLB-106
Boie, Heinrich Christian 1744-1806	DLB-94
Bok, Edward W. 1863-1930	DLB-91
Boland, Eavan 1944-	DLB-40
Bolingbroke, Henry St. John, Viscount 1678-1751	DLB-101
Böll, Heinrich 1917-1985	Y-85, DLB-69
Bolling, Robert 1738-1775	DLB-31
Bolt, Carol 1941-	DLB-60
Bolt, Robert 1924-	DLB-13
Bolton, Herbert E. 1870-1953	DLB-17
Bonaventura	DLB-89
Bond, Edward 1934-	DLB-13
Boni, Albert and Charles [publishing house]	DLB-46
Boni and Liveright	DLB-46
Robert Bonner's Sons	DLB-49
Bontemps, Arna 1902-1973	DLB-48, 51
The Book League of America	DLB-46
Book Reviewing in America: I	Y-87

Book Reviewing in America: II	Y-88
Book Reviewing in America: III	Y-89
Book Reviewing in America: IV	Y-90
Book Supply Company	DLB-49
The Booker Prize Address by Anthony Thwaite, Chairman of the Booker Prize Judges Comments from Former Booker Prize Winners	Y-86
Boorstin, Daniel J. 1914-	DLB-17
Booth, Mary L. 1831-1889	DLB-79
Booth, Philip 1925-	Y-82
Booth, Wayne C. 1921-	DLB-67
Borchardt, Rudolf 1877-1945	DLB-66
Borchert, Wolfgang 1921-1947	DLB-69
Borges, Jorge Luis 1899-1986	DLB-113; Y-86
Börne, Ludwig 1786-1837	DLB-90
Borrow, George 1803-1881	DLB-21, 55
Bosco, Henri 1888-1976	DLB-72
Bosco, Monique 1927-	DLB-53
Boswell, James 1740-1795	DLB-104
Botta, Anne C. Lynch 1815-1891	DLB-3
Bottomley, Gordon 1874-1948	DLB-10
Bottoms, David 1949-	Y-83
Bottrall, Ronald 1906-	DLB-20
Boucher, Anthony 1911-1968	DLB-8
Boucher, Jonathan 1738-1804	DLB-31
Boucher de Boucherville, George 1814-1894	DLB-99
Boudreau, Daniel (see Coste, Donat)	
Bourassa, Napoléon 1827-1916	DLB-99
Bourinot, John George 1837-1902	DLB-99
Bourjaily, Vance Nye 1922-	DLB-2
Bourne, Edward Gaylord 1860-1908	DLB-47
Bourne, Randolph 1886-1918	DLB-63
Bousoño, Carlos 1923-	DLB-108
Bousquet, Joë 1897-1950	DLB-72
Bova, Ben 1932-	Y-81
Bove, Emmanuel 1898-1945	DLB-72
Bovard, Oliver K. 1872-1945	DLB-25
Bowen, Elizabeth 1899-1973	DLB-15
Bowen, Francis 1811-1890	DLB-1, 59
Bowen, John 1924-	DLB-13
Bowen-Merrill Company	DLB-49
Bowering, George 1935-	DLB-53
Bowers, Claude G. 1878-1958	DLB-17
Bowers, Edgar 1924-	DLB-5
Bowles, Paul 1910-	DLB-5, 6
Bowles, Samuel III 1826-1878	DLB-43
Bowles, William Lisles 1762-1850	DLB-93
Bowman, Louise Morey 1882-1944	DLB-68
Boyd, James 1888-1944	DLB-9
Boyd, John 1919-	DLB-8
Boyd, Thomas 1898-1935	DLB-9
Boyesen, Hjalmar Hjorth 1848-1895	DLB-12, 71
Boyle, Kay 1902-	DLB-4, 9, 48, 86
Boyle, Roger, Earl of Orrery 1621-1679	DLB-80
Boyle, T. Coraghessan 1948-	Y-86
Brackenbury, Alison 1953-	DLB-40
Brackenridge, Hugh Henry 1748-1816	DLB-11, 37
Brackett, Charles 1892-1969	DLB-26
Brackett, Leigh 1915-1978	DLB-8, 26
Bradburn, John [publishing house]	DLB-49
Bradbury, Malcolm 1932-	DLB-14
Bradbury, Ray 1920-	DLB-2, 8
Bradbury and Evans	DLB-106
Braddon, Mary Elizabeth 1835-1915	DLB-18, 70
Bradford, Andrew 1686-1742	DLB-43, 73
Bradford, Gamaliel 1863-1932	DLB-17
Bradford, John 1749-1830	DLB-43
Bradford, Roark 1896-1948	DLB-86
Bradford, William 1590-1657	DLB-24, 30
Bradford, William III 1719-1791	DLB-43, 73
Bradlaugh, Charles 1833-1891	DLB-57
Bradley, David 1950-	DLB-33
Bradley, Ira, and Company	DLB-49
Bradley, J. W., and Company	DLB-49
Bradley, Marion Zimmer 1930-	DLB-8
Bradley, William Aspenwall 1878-1939	DLB-4
Bradstreet, Anne 1612 or 1613-1672	DLB-24
Brady, Frank 1924-1986	DLB-111
Brady, Frederic A. [publishing house]	DLB-49
Bragg, Melvyn 1939-	DLB-14
Brainard, Charles H. [publishing house]	DLB-49
Braine, John 1922-1986	DLB-15; Y-86
Braithwaite, William Stanley 1878-1962	DLB-50, 54
Bräker, Ulrich 1735-1798	DLB-94
Bramah, Ernest 1868-1942	DLB-70

Branagan, Thomas 1774-1843	DLB-37
Branch, William Blackwell 1927-	DLB-76
Branden Press	DLB-46
Brault, Jacques 1933-	DLB-53
Braun, Volker 1939-	DLB-75
Brautigan, Richard 1935-1984	DLB-2, 5; Y-80, 84
Braxton, Joanne M. 1950-	DLB-41
Bray, Thomas 1656-1730	DLB-24
Braziller, George [publishing house]	DLB-46
The Bread Loaf Writers' Conference 1983	Y-84
The Break-Up of the Novel (1922), by John Middleton Murry	DLB-36
Breasted, James Henry 1865-1935	DLB-47
Brecht, Bertolt 1898-1956	DLB-56
Bredel, Willi 1901-1964	DLB-56
Breitinger, Johann Jakob 1701-1776	DLB-97
Bremser, Bonnie 1939-	DLB-16
Bremser, Ray 1934-	DLB-16
Brentano, Bernard von 1901-1964	DLB-56
Brentano, Clemens 1778-1842	DLB-90
Brentano's	DLB-49
Brenton, Howard 1942-	DLB-13
Breton, André 1896-1966	DLB-65
Brewer, Warren and Putnam	DLB-46
Brewster, Elizabeth 1922-	DLB-60
Bridgers, Sue Ellen 1942-	DLB-52
Bridges, Robert 1844-1930	DLB-19, 98
Bridie, James 1888-1951	DLB-10
Briggs, Charles Frederick 1804-1877	DLB-3
Brighouse, Harold 1882-1958	DLB-10
Brimmer, B. J., Company	DLB-46
Brinnin, John Malcolm 1916-	DLB-48
Brisbane, Albert 1809-1890	DLB-3
British Academy	DLB-112
Brisbane, Arthur 1864-1936	DLB-25
The British Critic 1793-1843	DLB-110
The British Review and London Critical Journal 1811-1825	DLB-110
Broadway Publishing Company	DLB-46
Broch, Hermann 1886-1951	DLB-85
Brochu, André 1942-	DLB-53
Brock, Edwin 1927-	DLB-40
Brod, Max 1884-1968	DLB-81
Brodhead, John R. 1814-1873	DLB-30
Brome, Richard circa 1590-1652	DLB-58
Bromfield, Louis 1896-1956	DLB-4, 9, 86
Broner, E. M. 1930-	DLB-28
Brontë, Anne 1820-1849	DLB-21
Brontë, Charlotte 1816-1855	DLB-21
Brontë, Emily 1818-1848	DLB-21, 32
Brooke, Frances 1724-1789	DLB-39, 99
Brooke, Henry 1703?-1783	DLB-39
Brooke, Rupert 1887-1915	DLB-19
Brooker, Bertram 1888-1955	DLB-88
Brooke-Rose, Christine 1926-	DLB-14
Brookner, Anita 1928-	Y-87
Brooks, Charles Timothy 1813-1883	DLB-1
Brooks, Cleanth 1906-	DLB-63
Brooks, Gwendolyn 1917-	DLB-5, 76
Brooks, Jeremy 1926-	DLB-14
Brooks, Mel 1926-	DLB-26
Brooks, Noah 1830-1903	DLB-42
Brooks, Richard 1912-	DLB-44
Brooks, Van Wyck 1886-1963	DLB-45, 63, 103
Brophy, Brigid 1929-	DLB-14
Brossard, Chandler 1922-	DLB-16
Brossard, Nicole 1943-	DLB-53
Brother Antoninus (see Everson, William)	
Brougham and Vaux, Henry Peter Brougham, Baron 1778-1868	DLB-110
Brougham, John 1810-1880	DLB-11
Broughton, James 1913-	DLB-5
Broughton, Rhoda 1840-1920	DLB-18
Broun, Heywood 1888-1939	DLB-29
Brown, Alice 1856-1948	DLB-78
Brown, Bob 1886-1959	DLB-4, 45
Brown, Cecil 1943-	DLB-33
Brown, Charles Brockden 1771-1810	DLB-37, 59, 73
Brown, Christy 1932-1981	DLB-14
Brown, Dee 1908-	Y-80
Browne, Francis Fisher 1843-1913	DLB-79
Brown, Frank London 1927-1962	DLB-76
Brown, Fredric 1906-1972	DLB-8
Brown, George Mackay 1921-	DLB-14, 27
Brown, Harry 1917-1986	DLB-26
Brown, Marcia 1918-	DLB-61
Brown, Margaret Wise 1910-1952	DLB-22
Brown, Morna Doris (see Ferrars, Elizabeth)	

Brown, Oliver Madox 1855-1874	DLB-21
Brown, Sterling 1901-1989	DLB-48, 51, 63
Brown, T. E. 1830-1897	DLB-35
Brown, William Hill 1765-1793	DLB-37
Brown, William Wells 1814-1884	DLB-3, 50
Browne, Charles Farrar 1834-1867	DLB-11
Browne, Michael Dennis 1940-	DLB-40
Browne, Wynyard 1911-1964	DLB-13
Browne and Nolan	DLB-106
Brownell, W. C. 1851-1928	DLB-71
Browning, Elizabeth Barrett 1806-1861	DLB-32
Browning, Robert 1812-1889	DLB-32
Brownjohn, Allan 1931-	DLB-40
Brownson, Orestes Augustus 1803-1876	DLB-1, 59, 73
Bruccoli, Matthew J. 1931-	DLB-103
Bruce, Charles 1906-1971	DLB-68
Bruce, Leo 1903-1979	DLB-77
Bruce, Philip Alexander 1856-1933	DLB-47
Bruce Humphries [publishing house]	DLB-46
Bruce-Novoa, Juan 1944-	DLB-82
Bruckman, Clyde 1894-1955	DLB-26
Brundage, John Herbert (see Herbert, John)	
Bryant, William Cullen 1794-1878	DLB-3, 43, 59
Brydges, Sir Samuel Egerton 1762-1837	DLB-107
Buchan, John 1875-1940	DLB-34, 70
Buchanan, Robert 1841-1901	DLB-18, 35
Buchman, Sidney 1902-1975	DLB-26
Buck, Pearl S. 1892-1973	DLB-9, 102
Bucke, Charles 1781-1846	DLB-110
Bucke, Richard Maurice 1837-1902	DLB-99
Buckingham, Joseph Tinker 1779-1861 and Buckingham, Edwin 1810-1833	DLB-73
Buckler, Ernest 1908-1984	DLB-68
Buckley, William F., Jr. 1925-	Y-80
Buckminster, Joseph Stevens 1784-1812	DLB-37
Buckner, Robert 1906-	DLB-26
Budd, Thomas ?-1698	DLB-24
Budrys, A. J. 1931-	DLB-8
Buechner, Frederick 1926-	Y-80
Buell, John 1927-	DLB-53
Buffum, Job [publishing house]	DLB-49
Bugnet, Georges 1879-1981	DLB-92
Buies, Arthur 1840-1901	DLB-99
Bukowski, Charles 1920-	DLB-5
Bullins, Ed 1935-	DLB-7, 38
Bulwer-Lytton, Edward (also Edward Bulwer) 1803-1873	DLB-21
Bumpus, Jerry 1937-	Y-81
Bunce and Brother	DLB-49
Bunner, H. C. 1855-1896	DLB-78, 79
Bunting, Basil 1900-1985	DLB-20
Bunyan, John 1628-1688	DLB-39
Burch, Robert 1925-	DLB-52
Burciaga, José Antonio 1940-	DLB-82
Bürger, Gottfried August 1747-1794	DLB-94
Burgess, Anthony 1917-	DLB-14
Burgess, Gelett 1866-1951	DLB-11
Burgess, John W. 1844-1931	DLB-47
Burgess, Thornton W. 1874-1965	DLB-22
Burgess, Stringer and Company	DLB-49
Burk, John Daly circa 1772-1808	DLB-37
Burke, Edmund 1729?-1797	DLB-104
Burke, Kenneth 1897-	DLB-45, 63
Burlingame, Edward Livermore 1848-1922	DLB-79
Burnet, Gilbert 1643-1715	DLB-101
Burnett, Frances Hodgson 1849-1924	DLB-42
Burnett, W. R. 1899-1982	DLB-9
Burney, Fanny 1752-1840	DLB-39
Burns, Alan 1929-	DLB-14
Burns, John Horne 1916-1953	Y-85
Burns, Robert 1759-1796	DLB-109
Burns and Oates	DLB-106
Burnshaw, Stanley 1906-	DLB-48
Burr, C. Chauncey 1815?-1883	DLB-79
Burroughs, Edgar Rice 1875-1950	DLB-8
Burroughs, John 1837-1921	DLB-64
Burroughs, Margaret T. G. 1917-	DLB-41
Burroughs, William S., Jr. 1947-1981	DLB-16
Burroughs, William Seward 1914-	DLB-2, 8, 16; Y-81
Burroway, Janet 1936-	DLB-6
Burt, A. L., and Company	DLB-49
Burt, Maxwell S. 1882-1954	DLB-86
Burton, Miles (see Rhode, John)	
Burton, Richard F. 1821-1890	DLB-55
Burton, Virginia Lee 1909-1968	DLB-22
Burton, William Evans 1804-1860	DLB-73

Burwell, Adam Hood 1790-1849	DLB-99
Busch, Frederick 1941-	DLB-6
Busch, Niven 1903-	DLB-44
Bussières, Arthur de 1877-1913	DLB-92
Butler, E. H., and Company	DLB-49
Butler, Juan 1942-1981	DLB-53
Butler, Octavia E. 1947-	DLB-33
Butler, Samuel 1613-1680	DLB-101
Butler, Samuel 1835-1902	DLB-18, 57
Butor, Michel 1926-	DLB-83
Butterworth, Hezekiah 1839-1905	DLB-42
B. V. (see Thomson, James)	
Byars, Betsy 1928-	DLB-52
Byatt, A. S. 1936-	DLB-14
Byles, Mather 1707-1788	DLB-24
Bynner, Witter 1881-1968	DLB-54
Byrd, William II 1674-1744	DLB-24
Byrne, John Keyes (see Leonard, Hugh)	
Byron, George Gordon, Lord 1788-1824	DLB-96, 110

C

Caballero Bonald, José Manuel 1926-	DLB-108
Cabell, James Branch 1879-1958	DLB-9, 78
Cable, George Washington 1844-1925	DLB-12, 74
Cabrera Infante, Guillermo 1929-	DLB-113
Cady, Edwin H. 1917-	DLB-103
Cahan, Abraham 1860-1951	DLB-9, 25, 28
Cain, George 1943-	DLB-33
Calder, John (Publishers), Limited	DLB-112
Caldwell, Ben 1937-	DLB-38
Caldwell, Erskine 1903-1987	DLB-9, 86
Caldwell, H. M., Company	DLB-49
Calhoun, John C. 1782-1850	DLB-3
Calisher, Hortense 1911-	DLB-2
Callaghan, Morley 1903-1990	DLB-68
Callaloo	Y-87
A Call to Letters and an Invitation to the Electric Chair, by Siegfried Mandel	DLB-75
Calmer, Edgar 1907-	DLB-4
Calverley, C. S. 1831-1884	DLB-35
Calvert, George Henry 1803-1889	DLB-1, 64
Cambridge Press	DLB-49

Cameron, Eleanor 1912-	DLB-52
Cameron, George Frederick 1854-1885	DLB-99
Cameron, William Bleasdell 1862-1951	DLB-99
Camm, John 1718-1778	DLB-31
Campbell, Gabrielle Margaret Vere (see Shearing, Joseph)	
Campbell, James Edwin 1867-1896	DLB-50
Campbell, John 1653-1728	DLB-43
Campbell, John W., Jr. 1910-1971	DLB-8
Campbell, Thomas 1777-1844	DLB-93
Campbell, William Wilfred 1858-1918	DLB-92
Campbell, Roy 1901-1957	DLB-20
Campion, Thomas 1567-1620	DLB-58
Camus, Albert 1913-1960	DLB-72
Canby, Henry Seidel 1878-1961	DLB-91
Candelaria, Cordelia 1943-	DLB-82
Candelaria, Nash 1928-	DLB-82
Candour in English Fiction (1890), by Thomas Hardy	DLB-18
Canetti, Elias 1905-	DLB-85
Cannan, Gilbert 1884-1955	DLB-10
Cannell, Kathleen 1891-1974	DLB-4
Cannell, Skipwith 1887-1957	DLB-45
Cantwell, Robert 1908-1978	DLB-9
Cape, Jonathan, and Harrison Smith [publishing house]	DLB-46
Cape, Jonathan, Limited	DLB-112
Capen, Joseph 1658-1725	DLB-24
Capote, Truman 1924-1984	DLB-2; Y-80, 84
Cardinal, Marie 1929-	DLB-83
Carey, Henry circa 1687-1689-1743	DLB-84
Carey, M., and Company	DLB-49
Carey, Mathew 1760-1839	DLB-37, 73
Carey and Hart	DLB-49
Carlell, Lodowick 1602-1675	DLB-58
Carleton, G. W. [publishing house]	DLB-49
Carlile, Richard 1790-1843	DLB-110
Carlyle, Jane Welsh 1801-1866	DLB-55
Carlyle, Thomas 1795-1881	DLB-55
Carman, Bliss 1861-1929	DLB-92
Carnero, Guillermo 1947-	DLB-108
Carossa, Hans 1878-1956	DLB-66

Carpenter, Stephen Cullen ?-1820?	DLB-73
Carpentier, Alejo 1904-1980	DLB-113
Carr, Emily 1871-1945	DLB-68
Carr, Virginia Spencer 1929-	DLB-111
Carrier, Roch 1937-	DLB-53
Carroll, Gladys Hasty 1904-	DLB-9
Carroll, John 1735-1815	DLB-37
Carroll, John 1809-1884	DLB-99
Carroll, Lewis 1832-1898	DLB-18
Carroll, Paul 1927-	DLB-16
Carroll, Paul Vincent 1900-1968	DLB-10
Carroll and Graf Publishers	DLB-46
Carruth, Hayden 1921-	DLB-5
Carryl, Charles E. 1841-1920	DLB-42
Carswell, Catherine 1879-1946	DLB-36
Carter, Angela 1940-	DLB-14
Carter, Elizabeth 1717-1806	DLB-109
Carter, Henry (see Leslie, Frank)	
Carter, Landon 1710-1778	DLB-31
Carter, Lin 1930-	Y-81
Carter, Robert, and Brothers	DLB-49
Carter and Hendee	DLB-49
Caruthers, William Alexander 1802-1846	DLB-3
Carver, Jonathan 1710-1780	DLB-31
Carver, Raymond 1938-1988	Y-84, 88
Cary, Joyce 1888-1957	DLB-15, 100
Casey, Juanita 1925-	DLB-14
Casey, Michael 1947-	DLB-5
Cassady, Carolyn 1923-	DLB-16
Cassady, Neal 1926-1968	DLB-16
Cassell and Company	DLB-106
Cassell Publishing Company	DLB-49
Cassill, R. V. 1919-	DLB-6
Cassity, Turner 1929-	DLB-105
Castellanos, Rosario 1925-1974	DLB-113
Castlemon, Harry (see Fosdick, Charles Austin)	
Caswall, Edward 1814-1878	DLB-32
Cather, Willa 1873-1947	DLB-9, 54, 78; DS-1
Catherwood, Mary Hartwell 1847-1902	DLB-78
Catton, Bruce 1899-1978	DLB-17
Causley, Charles 1917-	DLB-27
Caute, David 1936-	DLB-14
Cawein, Madison 1865-1914	DLB-54
The Caxton Printers, Limited	DLB-46
Cayrol, Jean 1911-	DLB-83
Celan, Paul 1920-1970	DLB-69
Celaya, Gabriel 1911-1991	DLB-108
Céline, Louis-Ferdinand 1894-1961	DLB-72
Center for the Book Research	Y-84
Centlivre, Susanna 1669?-1723	DLB-84
The Century Company	DLB-49
Cervantes, Lorna Dee 1954-	DLB-82
Chacón, Eusebio 1869-1948	DLB-82
Chacón, Felipe Maximiliano 1873-?	DLB-82
Challans, Eileen Mary (see Renault, Mary)	
Chalmers, George 1742-1825	DLB-30
Chamberlain, Samuel S. 1851-1916	DLB-25
Chamberland, Paul 1939-	DLB-60
Chamberlin, William Henry 1897-1969	DLB-29
Chambers, Charles Haddon 1860-1921	DLB-10
Chambers, W. and R. [publishing house]	DLB-106
Chamisso, Albert von 1781-1838	DLB-90
Chandler, Harry 1864-1944	DLB-29
Chandler, Raymond 1888-1959	DS-6
Channing, Edward 1856-1931	DLB-17
Channing, Edward Tyrrell 1790-1856	DLB-1, 59
Channing, William Ellery 1780-1842	DLB-1, 59
Channing, William Ellery II 1817-1901	DLB-1
Channing, William Henry 1810-1884	DLB-1, 59
Chaplin, Charlie 1889-1977	DLB-44
Chapman, George 1559 or 1560-1634	DLB-62
Chapman, John	DLB-106
Chapman, William 1850-1917	DLB-99
Chapman and Hall	DLB-106
Chappell, Fred 1936-	DLB-6, 105
Chappell, Fred, A Detail in a Poem	DLB-105
Charbonneau, Jean 1875-1960	DLB-92
Charbonneau, Robert 1911-1967	DLB-68
Charles, Gerda 1914-	DLB-14
Charles, William [publishing house]	DLB-49
The Charles Wood Affair: A Playwright Revived	Y-83
Charlotte Forten: Pages from her Diary	DLB-50
Charteris, Leslie 1907-	DLB-77
Charyn, Jerome 1937-	Y-83
Chase, Borden 1900-1971	DLB-26
Chase, Edna Woolman 1877-1957	DLB-91

Chase-Riboud, Barbara 1936- DLB-33

Chatterton, Thomas 1752-1770 ....DLB-109

Chatto and Windus.................................DLB-106

Chauncy, Charles 1705-1787........................DLB-24

Chauveau, Pierre-Joseph-Olivier
  1820-1890......................................DLB-99

Chávez, Fray Angélico 1910- DLB-82

Chayefsky, Paddy 1923-1981 ....DLB-7, 44; Y-81

Cheever, Ezekiel 1615-1708 ....DLB-24

Cheever, George Barrell 1807-1890 ....DLB-59

Cheever, John 1912-1982 ....DLB-2, 102; Y-80, 82

Cheever, Susan 1943- Y-82

Chelsea House DLB-46

Cheney, Ednah Dow (Littlehale) 1824-1904 ....DLB-1

Cheney, Harriet Vaughn 1796-1889 ....DLB-99

Cherry, Kelly 1940- Y-83

Cherryh, C. J. 1942- Y-80

Chesnutt, Charles Waddell 1858-1932 ....DLB-12, 50, 78

Chester, George Randolph 1869-1924 ....DLB-78

Chesterfield, Philip Dormer Stanhope,
  Fourth Earl of 1694-1773 ....DLB-104

Chesterton, G. K. 1874-1936 ....DLB-10, 19, 34, 70, 98

Cheyney, Edward P. 1861-1947 ....DLB-47

Chicano History DLB-82

Chicano Language DLB-82

Child, Francis James 1825-1896 ....DLB-1, 64

Child, Lydia Maria 1802-1880 ....DLB-1, 74

Child, Philip 1898-1978 ....DLB-68

Childers, Erskine 1870-1922 ....DLB-70

Children's Book Awards and Prizes DLB-61

Childress, Alice 1920- DLB-7, 38

Childs, George W. 1829-1894 ....DLB-23

Chilton Book Company DLB-46

Chittenden, Hiram Martin 1858-1917 ....DLB-47

Chivers, Thomas Holley 1809-1858 ....DLB-3

Chopin, Kate 1850-1904 ....DLB-12, 78

Chopin, Rene 1885-1953 ....DLB-92

Choquette, Adrienne 1915-1973 ....DLB-68

Choquette, Robert 1905- DLB-68

The Christian Publishing Company DLB-49

Christie, Agatha 1890-1976 ....DLB-13, 77

Church, Benjamin 1734-1778 ....DLB-31

Church, Francis Pharcellus 1839-1906 ....DLB-79

Church, William Conant 1836-1917 ....DLB-79

Churchill, Caryl 1938- DLB-13

Churchill, Charles 1731-1764......................DLB-109

Churchill, Sir Winston 1874-1965.................DLB-100

Churton, E., and Company DLB-106

Chute, Marchette 1909- DLB-103

Ciardi, John 1916-1986 ....DLB-5; Y-86

Cibber, Colley 1671-1757 ....DLB-84

City Lights Books................................DLB-46

Cixous, Hélène 1937- DLB-83

Clampitt, Amy 1920- DLB-105

Clapper, Raymond 1892-1944 ....DLB-29

Clare, John 1793-1864............................DLB-55, 96

Clarendon, Edward Hyde, Earl of
  1609-1674......................................DLB-101

Clark, Alfred Alexander Gordon (see Hare, Cyril)

Clark, Ann Nolan 1896- DLB-52

Clark, C. M., Publishing Company DLB-46

Clark, Catherine Anthony 1892-1977 ....DLB-68

Clark, Charles Heber 1841-1915 ....DLB-11

Clark, Davis Wasgatt 1812-1871....................DLB-79

Clark, Eleanor 1913- DLB-6

Clark, Lewis Gaylord 1808-1873 ....DLB-3, 64, 73

Clark, Walter Van Tilburg 1909-1971 ....DLB-9

Clarke, Austin 1896-1974..........................DLB-10, 20

Clarke, Austin C. 1934- DLB-53

Clarke, Gillian 1937- DLB-40

Clarke, James Freeman 1810-1888 ....DLB-1, 59

Clarke, Rebecca Sophia 1833-1906 ....DLB-42

Clarke, Robert, and Company DLB-49

Claudius, Matthias 1740-1815 ....DLB-97

Clausen, Andy 1943- DLB-16

Claxton, Remsen and Haffelfinger DLB-49

Clay, Cassius Marcellus 1810-1903.................DLB-43

Cleary, Beverly 1916- DLB-52

Cleaver, Vera 1919-   and
  Cleaver, Bill 1920-1981 ....DLB-52

Cleland, John 1710-1789 ....DLB-39

Clemens, Samuel Langhorne
  1835-1910 ....DLB-11, 12, 23, 64, 74

Clement, Hal 1922- DLB-8

Clemo, Jack 1916- DLB-27

Clifford, James L. 1901-1978 ....DLB-103

Clifton, Lucille 1936- DLB-5, 41

Clode, Edward J. [publishing house] DLB-46

Cumulative Index

Clough, Arthur Hugh 1819-1861 ....DLB-32

Cloutier, Cécile 1930- DLB-60

Clutton-Brock, Arthur 1868-1924..............................DLB-98

Coates, Robert M. 1897-1973 ....DLB-4, 9, 102

Coatsworth, Elizabeth 1893- DLB-22

Cobb, Jr., Charles E. 1943- DLB-41

Cobb, Frank I. 1869-1923 ....DLB-25

Cobb, Irvin S. 1876-1944 ....DLB-11, 25, 86

Cobbett, William 1763-1835..............................DLB-43, 107

Cochran, Thomas C. 1902- DLB-17

Cochrane, Elizabeth 1867-1922..............................DLB-25

Cockerill, John A. 1845-1896..............................DLB-23

Cocteau, Jean 1889-1963..............................DLB-65

Coderre, Emile (see Jean Narrache)

Coffee, Lenore J. 1900?-1984 ....DLB-44

Coffin, Robert P. Tristram 1892-1955..............................DLB-45

Cogswell, Fred 1917- DLB-60

Cogswell, Mason Fitch 1761-1830..............................DLB-37

Cohen, Arthur A. 1928-1986 ....DLB-28

Cohen, Leonard 1934- DLB-53

Cohen, Matt 1942- DLB-53

Colden, Cadwallader 1688-1776..............................DLB-24, 30

Cole, Barry 1936- DLB-14

Colegate, Isabel 1931- DLB-14

Coleman, Emily Holmes 1899-1974..............................DLB-4

Coleridge, Hartley 1796-1849..............................DLB-96

Coleridge, Mary 1861-1907..............................DLB-19, 98

Coleridge, Samuel Taylor 1772-1834..............................DLB-93, 107

Colette 1873-1954..............................DLB-65

Colette, Sidonie Gabrielle (see Colette)

Collier, John 1901-1980..............................DLB-77

Collier, Mary 1690-1762..............................DLB-95

Collier, P. F. [publishing house]..............................DLB-49

Collier, Robert J. 1876-1918 ....DLB-91

Collin and Small DLB-49

Collins, Isaac [publishing house]..............................DLB-49

Collins, Mortimer 1827-1876 ....DLB-21, 35

Collins, Wilkie 1824-1889 ....DLB-18, 70

Collins, William 1721-1759 ....DLB-109

Collyer, Mary 1716?-1763? DLB-39

Colman, Benjamin 1673-1747 ....DLB-24

Colman, George, the Elder 1732-1794..............................DLB-89

Colman, George, the Younger 1762-1836..............................DLB-89

Colman, S. [publishing house]..............................DLB-49

Colombo, John Robert 1936- DLB-53

Colter, Cyrus 1910- DLB-33

Colum, Padraic 1881-1972 ....DLB-19

Colwin, Laurie 1944- Y-80

Comden, Betty 1919- and Green, Adolph 1918- DLB-44

The Comic Tradition Continued [in the British Novel]..............................DLB-15

Commager, Henry Steele 1902- DLB-17

The Commercialization of the Image of Revolt, by Kenneth Rexroth..............................DLB-16

Community and Commentators: Black Theatre and Its Critics DLB-38

Compton-Burnett, Ivy 1884?-1969 ....DLB-36

Conan, Laure 1845-1924 ....DLB-99

Conde, Carmen 1901- DLB-108

Conference on Modern Biography Y-85

Congreve, William 1670-1729..............................DLB-39, 84

Conkey, W. B., Company DLB-49

Connell, Evan S., Jr. 1924- DLB-2; Y-81

Connelly, Marc 1890-1980 ....DLB-7; Y-80

Connolly, Cyril 1903-1974..............................DLB-98

Connolly, James B. 1868-1957..............................DLB-78

Connor, Ralph 1860-1937 ....DLB-92

Connor, Tony 1930- DLB-40

Conquest, Robert 1917- DLB-27

Conrad, John, and Company DLB-49

Conrad, Joseph 1857-1924..............................DLB-10, 34, 98

Conroy, Jack 1899-1990..............................Y-81

Conroy, Pat 1945- DLB-6

The Consolidation of Opinion: Critical Responses to the Modernists..............................DLB-36

Constable and Company Limited..............................DLB-112

Constantin-Weyer, Maurice 1881-1964..............................DLB-92

Constantine, David 1944- DLB-40

Contempo Caravan: Kites in a Windstorm..............................Y-85

A Contemporary Flourescence of Chicano Literature..............................Y-84

The Continental Publishing Company..............................DLB-49

A Conversation with Chaim Potok..............................Y-84

Conversations with Publishers I: An Interview with Patrick O'Connor..............................Y-84

Conversations with Rare Book Dealers I: An Interview with Glenn Horowitz	Y-90
The Conversion of an Unpolitical Man, by W. H. Bruford	DLB-66
Conway, Moncure Daniel 1832-1907	DLB-1
Cook, David C., Publishing Company	DLB-49
Cook, Ebenezer circa 1667-circa 1732	DLB-24
Cook, Michael 1933-	DLB-53
Cooke, George Willis 1848-1923	DLB-71
Cooke, Increase, and Company	DLB-49
Cooke, John Esten 1830-1886	DLB-3
Cooke, Philip Pendleton 1816-1850	DLB-3, 59
Cooke, Rose Terry 1827-1892	DLB-12, 74
Coolbrith, Ina 1841-1928	DLB-54
Cooley, Peter 1940-	DLB-105
Cooley, Peter, Into the Mirror	DLB-105
Coolidge, George [publishing house]	DLB-49
Coolidge, Susan (see Woolsey, Sarah Chauncy)	
Cooper, Giles 1918-1966	DLB-13
Cooper, James Fenimore 1789-1851	DLB-3
Cooper, Kent 1880-1965	DLB-29
Coover, Robert 1932-	DLB-2; Y-81
Copeland and Day	DLB-49
Coppel, Alfred 1921-	Y-83
Coppola, Francis Ford 1939-	DLB-44
Corcoran, Barbara 1911-	DLB-52
Corelli, Marie 1855-1924	DLB-34
Corle, Edwin 1906-1956	Y-85
Corman, Cid 1924-	DLB-5
Cormier, Robert 1925-	DLB-52
Corn, Alfred 1943-	Y-80
Cornish, Sam 1935-	DLB-41
Cornwall, Barry (see Procter, Bryan Waller)	
Cornwell, David John Moore (see le Carré, John)	
Corpi, Lucha 1945-	DLB-82
Corrington, John William 1932-	DLB-6
Corrothers, James D. 1869-1917	DLB-50
Corso, Gregory 1930-	DLB-5, 16
Cortázar, Julio 1914-1984	DLB-113
Cortez, Jayne 1936-	DLB-41
Corvo, Baron (see Rolfe, Frederick William)	
Cory, William Johnson 1823-1892	DLB-35
Cosmopolitan Book Corporation	DLB-46
Costain, Thomas B. 1885-1965	DLB-9
Coste, Donat 1912-1957	DLB-88
Cotter, Joseph Seamon, Sr. 1861-1949	DLB-50
Cotter, Joseph Seamon, Jr. 1895-1919	DLB-50
Cotton, John 1584-1652	DLB-24
Coulter, John 1888-1980	DLB-68
Cournos, John 1881-1966	DLB-54
Coventry, Francis 1725-1754	DLB-39
Coverly, N. [publishing house]	DLB-49
Covici-Friede	DLB-46
Coward, Noel 1899-1973	DLB-10
Coward, McCann and Geoghegan	DLB-46
Cowles, Gardner 1861-1946	DLB-29
Cowley, Hannah 1743-1809	DLB-89
Cowley, Malcolm 1898-1989	DLB-4, 48; Y-81, 89
Cowper, William 1731-1800	DLB-104, 109
Cox, A. B. (see Berkeley, Anthony)	
Cox, Palmer 1840-1924	DLB-42
Coxe, Louis 1918-	DLB-5
Coxe, Tench 1755-1824	DLB-37
Cozzens, James Gould 1903-1978	DLB-9; Y-84; DS-2
Crabbe, George 1754-1832	DLB-93
Craddock, Charles Egbert (see Murfree, Mary N.)	
Cradock, Thomas 1718-1770	DLB-31
Craig, Daniel H. 1811-1895	DLB-43
Craik, Dinah Maria 1826-1887	DLB-35
Cranch, Christopher Pearse 1813-1892	DLB-1, 42
Crane, Hart 1899-1932	DLB-4, 48
Crane, R. S. 1886-1967	DLB-63
Crane, Stephen 1871-1900	DLB-12, 54, 78
Crapsey, Adelaide 1878-1914	DLB-54
Craven, Avery 1885-1980	DLB-17
Crawford, Charles 1752-circa 1815	DLB-31
Crawford, F. Marion 1854-1909	DLB-71
Crawford, Isabel Valancy 1850-1887	DLB-92
Crawley, Alan 1887-1975	DLB-68
Crayon, Geoffrey (see Irving, Washington)	
Creasey, John 1908-1973	DLB-77
Creative Age Press	DLB-46
Creel, George 1876-1953	DLB-25
Creeley, Robert 1926-	DLB-5, 16
Creelman, James 1859-1915	DLB-23
Cregan, David 1931-	DLB-13
Creighton, Donald Grant 1902-1979	DLB-88
Cremazie, Octave 1827-1879	DLB-99

Cumulative Index

Crémer, Victoriano 1909?- DLB-108

Cresset Press..DLB-112

Crèvecoeur, Michel Guillaume Jean de
  1735-1813..DLB-37

Crews, Harry 1935- DLB-6

Crichton, Michael 1942- Y-81

A Crisis of Culture: The Changing Role
  of Religion in the New Republic...........................DLB-37

Crispin, Edmund 1921-1978..DLB-87

Cristofer, Michael 1946- DLB-7

"The Critic as Artist" (1891), by Oscar Wilde...............DLB-57

Criticism In Relation To Novels (1863),
  by G. H. Lewes...DLB-21

Crockett, David (Davy) 1786-1836...........................DLB-3, 11

Croft-Cooke, Rupert (see Bruce, Leo)

Crofts, Freeman Wills 1879-1957 ....DLB-77

Croker, John Wilson 1780-1857...................................DLB-110

Croly, Herbert 1869-1930 ....DLB-91

Croly, Jane Cunningham 1829-1901..............................DLB-23

Crosby, Caresse 1892-1970...DLB-48

Crosby, Caresse 1892-1970 and Crosby,
  Harry 1898-1929...DLB-4

Crosby, Harry 1898-1929 ....DLB-48

Crossley-Holland, Kevin 1941- DLB-40

Crothers, Rachel 1878-1958 ....DLB-7

Crowell, Thomas Y., Company DLB-49

Crowley, John 1942- Y-82

Crowley, Mart 1935- DLB-7

Crown Publishers DLB-46

Crowne, John 1641-1712..DLB-80

Crowninshield, Frank 1872-1947 ....DLB-91

Croy, Homer 1883-1965...DLB-4

Crumley, James 1939- Y-84

Cruz, Victor Hernández 1949- DLB-41

Csokor, Franz Theodor 1885-1969.................................DLB-81

Cuala Press DLB-112

Cullen, Countee 1903-1946 ....DLB-4, 48, 51

Culler, Jonathan D. 1944- DLB-67

The Cult of Biography
  Excerpts from the Second Folio Debate:
  "Biographies are generally a disease of
  English Literature"–Germaine Greer,
  Victoria Glendinning, Auberon Waugh,
  and Richard Holmes Y-86

Cumberland, Richard 1732-1811....................................DLB-89

Cummings, E. E. 1894-1962.......................................DLB-4, 48

Cummings, Ray 1887-1957..DLB-8

Cummings and Hilliard..DLB-49

Cummins, Maria Susanna 1827-1866 ....DLB-42

Cundall, Joseph [publishing house]..............................DLB-106

Cuney, Waring 1906-1976..DLB-51

Cuney-Hare, Maude 1874-1936......................................DLB-52

Cunningham, J. V. 1911- DLB-5

Cunningham, Peter F. [publishing house]....................DLB-49

Cuomo, George 1929- Y-80

Cupples and Leon...DLB-46

Cupples, Upham and Company.....................................DLB-49

Cuppy, Will 1884-1949...DLB-11

Currie, Mary Montgomerie Lamb Singleton,
  Lady Currie (see Fane, Violet)

Curti, Merle E. 1897- DLB-17

Curtis, Cyrus H. K. 1850-1933..DLB-91

Curtis, George William 1824-1892 ....DLB-1, 43

Curzon, Sarah Anne 1833-1898......................................DLB-99

D

D. M. Thomas: The Plagiarism Controversy....................Y-82

Dabit, Eugène 1898-1936 ....DLB-65

Daborne, Robert circa 1580-1628 ....DLB-58

Dacey, Philip 1939- DLB-105

Dacey, Philip, Eyes Across Centuries:
  Contemporary Poetry and "That
  Vision Thing"..DLB-105

Daggett, Rollin M. 1831-1901 ....DLB-79

Dahlberg, Edward 1900-1977 ....DLB-48

Dale, Peter 1938- DLB-40

Dall, Caroline Wells (Healey) 1822-1912 ....DLB-1

Dallas, E. S. 1828-1879..DLB-55

The Dallas Theater Center DLB-7

D'Alton, Louis 1900-1951..DLB-10

Daly, T. A. 1871-1948...DLB-11

Damon, S. Foster 1893-1971..DLB-45

Damrell, William S. [publishing house]........................DLB-49

Dana, Charles A. 1819-1897 ....DLB-3, 23

Dana, Richard Henry, Jr. 1815-1882................................DLB-1

Dandridge, Ray Garfield DLB-51

Dane, Clemence 1887-1965...DLB-10

Danforth, John 1660-1730 ....DLB-24

Danforth, Samuel I 1626-1674..DLB-24

Danforth, Samuel II 1666-1727	DLB-24
Dangerous Years: London Theater, 1939-1945	DLB-10
Daniel, John M. 1825-1865	DLB-43
Daniel, Samuel 1562 or 1563-1619	DLB-62
Daniel Press	DLB-106
Daniells, Roy 1902-1979	DLB-68
Daniels, Josephus 1862-1948	DLB-29
Danner, Margaret Esse 1915-	DLB-41
Dantin, Louis 1865-1945	DLB-92
Darley, George 1795-1846	DLB-96
Darwin, Charles 1809-1882	DLB-57
Darwin, Erasmus 1731-1802	DLB-93
Daryush, Elizabeth 1887-1977	DLB-20
Dashwood, Edmée Elizabeth Monica de la Pasture (see Delafield, E. M.)	
d'Aulaire, Edgar Parin 1898- and d'Aulaire, Ingri 1904-	DLB-22
Davenant, Sir William 1606-1668	DLB-58
Davenport, Robert ?-?	DLB-58
Daves, Delmer 1904-1977	DLB-26
Davey, Frank 1940-	DLB-53
Davies, Peter, Limited	DLB-112
Davidson, Avram 1923-	DLB-8
Davidson, Donald 1893-1968	DLB-45
Davidson, John 1857-1909	DLB-19
Davidson, Lionel 1922-	DLB-14
Davie, Donald 1922-	DLB-27
Davies, Robertson 1913-	DLB-68
Davies, Samuel 1723-1761	DLB-31
Davies, W. H. 1871-1940	DLB-19
Daviot, Gordon 1896?-1952 (see also Tey, Josephine)	DLB-10
Davis, Charles A. 1795-1867	DLB-11
Davis, Clyde Brion 1894-1962	DLB-9
Davis, Dick 1945-	DLB-40
Davis, Frank Marshall 1905-?	DLB-51
Davis, H. L. 1894-1960	DLB-9
Davis, John 1774-1854	DLB-37
Davis, Margaret Thomson 1926-	DLB-14
Davis, Ossie 1917-	DLB-7, 38
Davis, Rebecca Harding 1831-1910	DLB-74
Davis, Richard Harding 1864-1916	DLB-12, 23, 78, 79
Davis, Samuel Cole 1764-1809	DLB-37
Davison, Peter 1928-	DLB-5
Davys, Mary 1674-1732	DLB-39
DAW Books	DLB-46
Dawson, William 1704-1752	DLB-31
Day, Benjamin Henry 1810-1889	DLB-43
Day, Clarence 1874-1935	DLB-11
Day, Dorothy 1897-1980	DLB-29
Day, Frank Parker 1881-1950	DLB-92
Day, John circa 1574-circa 1640	DLB-62
Day, The John, Company	DLB-46
Day Lewis, C. 1904-1972 (see also Blake, Nicholas)	DLB-15, 20
Day, Mahlon [publishing house]	DLB-49
Day, Thomas 1748-1789	DLB-39
Deacon, William Arthur 1890-1977	DLB-68
Deal, Borden 1922-1985	DLB-6
de Angeli, Marguerite 1889-1987	DLB-22
De Bow, James Dunwoody Brownson 1820-1867	DLB-3, 79
de Bruyn, Günter 1926-	DLB-75
de Camp, L. Sprague 1907-	DLB-8
The Decay of Lying (1889), by Oscar Wilde [excerpt]	DLB-18
Dedication, *Ferdinand Count Fathom* (1753), by Tobias Smollett	DLB-39
Dedication, *Lasselia* (1723), by Eliza Haywood [excerpt]	DLB-39
Dedication, *The History of Pompey the Little* (1751), by Francis Coventry	DLB-39
Dedication, *The Wanderer* (1814), by Fanny Burney	DLB-39
Defense of *Amelia* (1752), by Henry Fielding	DLB-39
Defoe, Daniel 1660-1731	DLB-39, 95, 101
de Fontaine, Felix Gregory 1834-1896	DLB-43
De Forest, John William 1826-1906	DLB-12
DeFrees, Madeline 1919-	DLB-105
DeFrees, Madeline, The Poet's Kaleidoscope: The Element of Surprise in the Making of the Poem	DLB-105
de Graff, Robert 1895-1981	Y-81
Deighton, Len 1929-	DLB-87
DeJong, Meindert 1906-	DLB-52
Dekker, Thomas circa 1572-1632	DLB-62
Delacorte, Jr., George T. 1894-	DLB-91
Delafield, E. M. 1890-1943	DLB-34
Delahaye, Guy 1888-1969	DLB-92

de la Mare, Walter 1873-1956 ....DLB-19

Deland, Margaret 1857-1945...DLB-78

Delaney, Shelagh 1939- DLB-13

Delany, Martin Robinson 1812-1885 ....DLB-50

Delany, Samuel R. 1942- DLB-8, 33

de la Roche, Mazo 1879-1961...DLB-68

Delbanco, Nicholas 1942- DLB-6

De León, Nephtalí 1945- DLB-82

Delgado, Abelardo Barrientos 1931- DLB-82

DeLillo, Don 1936- DLB-6

Dell, Floyd 1887-1969...DLB-9

Dell Publishing Company..DLB-46

delle Grazie, Marie Eugene 1864-1931........................DLB-81

del Rey, Lester 1915- DLB-8

Del Vecchio, John M. 1947- DS-9

de Man, Paul 1919-1983..DLB-67

Demby, William 1922- DLB-33

Deming, Philander 1829-1915......................................DLB-74

Demorest, William Jennings 1822-1895....................DLB-79

Denham, Sir John 1615-1669...DLB-58

Denison, Merrill 1893-1975...DLB-92

Denison, T. S., and Company DLB-49

Dennie, Joseph 1768-1812.........................DLB-37, 43, 59, 73

Dennis, John 1658-1734 ....DLB-101

Dennis, Nigel 1912-1989 ....DLB-13, 15

Dent, Tom 1932- DLB-38

Dent, J. M., and Sons...DLB-112

Denton, Daniel circa 1626-1703 ....DLB-24

DePaola, Tomie 1934- DLB-61

De Quincey, Thomas 1785-1859...............................DLB-110

Derby, George Horatio 1823-1861.............................DLB-11

Derby, J. C., and Company DLB-49

Derby and Miller DLB-49

Derleth, August 1909-1971 ....DLB-9

The Derrydale Press DLB-46

Desaulniers, Gonsalve 1863-1934................................DLB-92

Desbiens, Jean-Paul 1927- DLB-53

des Forêts, Louis-René 1918- DLB-83

DesRochers, Alfred 1901-1978 ....DLB-68

Desrosiers, Léo-Paul 1896-1967 ....DLB-68

Destouches, Louis-Ferdinand (see Céline,
    Louis-Ferdinand)

De Tabley, Lord 1835-1895..DLB-35

Deutsch, Babette 1895-1982...DLB-45

Deutsch, André, Limited DLB-112

Deveaux, Alexis 1948- DLB-38

The Development of Lighting in the Staging
    of Drama, 1900-1945 [in Great Britain] DLB-10

de Vere, Aubrey 1814-1902...DLB-35

The Devin-Adair Company DLB-46

De Voto, Bernard 1897-1955 ....DLB-9

De Vries, Peter 1910- DLB-6; Y-82

Dewdney, Christopher 1951- DLB-60

Dewdney, Selwyn 1909-1979...DLB-68

DeWitt, Robert M., Publisher.......................................DLB-49

DeWolfe, Fiske and Company DLB-49

Dexter, Colin 1930- DLB-87

de Young, M. H. 1849-1925..DLB-25

The Dial Press..DLB-46

Diamond, I. A. L. 1920-1988 ....DLB-26

Di Cicco, Pier Giorgio 1949- DLB-60

Dick, Philip K. 1928- DLB-8

Dick and Fitzgerald...DLB-49

Dickens, Charles 1812-1870 ....DLB-21, 55, 70

Dickey, James 1923- DLB-5; Y-82; DS-7

Dickey, William 1928- DLB-5

Dickinson, Emily 1830-1886..DLB-1

Dickinson, John 1732-1808 ....DLB-31

Dickinson, Jonathan 1688-1747 ....DLB-24

Dickinson, Patric 1914- DLB-27

Dickinson, Peter 1927- DLB-87

Dicks, John [publishing house]...................................DLB-106

Dickson, Gordon R. 1923- DLB-8

Didion, Joan 1934- DLB-2; Y-81, 86

Di Donato, Pietro 1911- DLB-9

Dillard, Annie 1945- Y-80

Dillard, R. H. W. 1937- DLB-5

Dillingham, Charles T., Company DLB-49

The G. W. Dillingham Company DLB-49

Dintenfass, Mark 1941- Y-84

Diogenes, Jr. (see Brougham, John)

DiPrima, Diane 1934- DLB-5, 16

Disch, Thomas M. 1940- DLB-8

Disney, Walt 1901-1966 ....DLB-22

Disraeli, Benjamin 1804-1881 ....DLB-21, 55

D'Israeli, Isaac 1766-1848...DLB-107

Ditzen, Rudolf (see Fallada, Hans)

Dix, Dorothea Lynde 1802-1887....................................DLB-1

Dix, Dorothy (see Gilmer, Elizabeth Meriwether)

Dix, Edwards and Company DLB-49

Dixon, Paige (see Corcoran, Barbara)

Dixon, Richard Watson 1833-1900 .... DLB-19

Dobell, Sydney 1824-1874 .... DLB-32

Döblin, Alfred 1878-1957 .... DLB-66

Dobson, Austin 1840-1921 .... DLB-35

Doctorow, E. L. 1931- DLB-2, 28; Y-80

Dodd, William E. 1869-1940 .... DLB-17

Dodd, Mead and Company DLB-49

Doderer, Heimito von 1896-1968 .... DLB-85

Dodge, B. W., and Company DLB-46

Dodge, Mary Mapes 1831?-1905 .... DLB-42, 79

Dodge Publishing Company DLB-49

Dodgson, Charles Lutwidge (see Carroll, Lewis)

Dodsley, Robert 1703-1764 .... DLB-95

Dodson, Owen 1914-1983 .... DLB-76

Doesticks, Q. K. Philander, P. B. (see Thomson, Mortimer)

Donahoe, Patrick [publishing house] DLB-49

Donald, David H. 1920- DLB-17

Donaldson, Scott 1928- DLB-111

Donleavy, J. P. 1926- DLB-6

Donnadieu, Marguerite (see Duras, Marguerite)

Donnelley, R. R., and Sons Company DLB-49

Donnelly, Ignatius 1831-1901 .... DLB-12

Donohue and Henneberry DLB-49

Donoso, José 1924- DLB-113

Doolady, M. [publishing house] DLB-49

Dooley, Ebon (see Ebon)

Doolittle, Hilda 1886-1961 .... DLB-4, 45

Dor, Milo 1923- DLB-85

Doran, George H., Company DLB-46

Dorgelès, Roland 1886-1973 .... DLB-65

Dorn, Edward 1929- DLB-5

Dorr, Rheta Childe 1866-1948 .... DLB-25

Dorst, Tankred 1925- DLB-75

Dos Passos, John 1896-1970 .... DLB-4, 9; DS-1

Doubleday and Company DLB-49

Dougall, Lily 1858-1923 .... DLB-92

Doughty, Charles M. 1843-1926 .... DLB-19, 57

Douglas, Keith 1920-1944 .... DLB-27

Douglas, Norman 1868-1952 .... DLB-34

Douglass, Frederick 1817?-1895 .... DLB-1, 43, 50, 79

Douglass, William circa 1691-1752 .... DLB-24

Dover Publications DLB-46

Doves Press DLB-112

Dowden, Edward 1843-1913 .... DLB-35

Downes, Gwladys 1915- DLB-88

Downing, J., Major (see Davis, Charles A.)

Downing, Major Jack (see Smith, Seba)

Dowson, Ernest 1867-1900 .... DLB-19

Doxey, William [publishing house] DLB-49

Doyle, Sir Arthur Conan 1859-1930 .... DLB-18, 70

Doyle, Kirby 1932- DLB-16

Drabble, Margaret 1939- DLB-14

Drach, Albert 1902- DLB-85

The Dramatic Publishing Company DLB-49

Dramatists Play Service DLB-46

Draper, John W. 1811-1882 .... DLB-30

Draper, Lyman C. 1815-1891 .... DLB-30

Dreiser, Theodore 1871-1945 .... DLB-9, 12, 102; DS-1

Drewitz, Ingeborg 1923-1986 .... DLB-75

Drieu La Rochelle, Pierre 1893-1945 .... DLB-72

Drinkwater, John 1882-1937 .... DLB-10, 19

The Drue Heinz Literature Prize
Excerpt from "Excerpts from a Report of the Commission," in David Bosworth's *The Death of Descartes* An Interview with David Bosworth Y-82

Drummond, William Henry 1854-1907 .... DLB-92

Dryden, John 1631-1700 .... DLB-80, 101

Duane, William 1760-1835 .... DLB-43

Dubé, Marcel 1930- DLB-53

Dubé, Rodolphe (see Hertel, François)

Du Bois, W. E. B. 1868-1963 .... DLB-47, 50, 91

Du Bois, William Pène 1916- DLB-61

Ducharme, Réjean 1941- DLB-60

Duck, Stephen 1705?-1756 .... DLB-95

Duckworth, Gerald, and Company Limited DLB-112

Dudek, Louis 1918- DLB-88

Duell, Sloan and Pearce DLB-46

Duffield and Green DLB-46

Duffy, Maureen 1933- DLB-14

Dugan, Alan 1923- DLB-5

Dugas, Marcel 1883-1947 .... DLB-92

Dugdale, William [publishing house] DLB-106

Duhamel, Georges 1884-1966 .... DLB-65

Dukes, Ashley 1885-1959 ....DLB-10

Dumas, Henry 1934-1968..................................DLB-41

Dunbar, Paul Laurence 1872-1906..............DLB-50, 54, 78

Duncan, Norman 1871-1916................................DLB-92

Duncan, Robert 1919-1988 ....DLB-5, 16

Duncan, Ronald 1914-1982................................DLB-13

Duncan, Sara Jeannette 1861-1922.......................DLB-92

Dunigan, Edward, and Brother............................DLB-49

Dunlap, John 1747-1812 ....DLB-43

Dunlap, William 1766-1839..................DLB-30, 37, 59

Dunn, Douglas 1942- DLB-40

Dunn, Stephen 1939- DLB-105

Dunn, Stephen,
  The Good, The Not So Good..............................DLB-105

Dunne, Finley Peter 1867-1936.......................DLB-11, 23

Dunne, John Gregory 1932- Y-80

Dunne, Philip 1908- DLB-26

Dunning, Ralph Cheever 1878-1930 ....DLB-4

Dunning, William A. 1857-1922 ....DLB-17

Plunkett, Edward John Moreton Drax,
  Lord Dunsany 1878-1957...............................DLB-10, 77

Durand, Lucile (see Bersianik, Louky)

Duranty, Walter 1884-1957 ....DLB-29

Duras, Marguerite 1914- DLB-83

Durfey, Thomas 1653-1723..................................DLB-80

Durrell, Lawrence 1912-1990 ....DLB-15, 27; Y-90

Durrell, William [publishing house] DLB-49

Dürrenmatt, Friedrich 1921- DLB-69

Dutton, E. P., and Company DLB-49

Duvoisin, Roger 1904-1980 ....DLB-61

Duyckinck, Evert Augustus 1816-1878..................DLB-3, 64

Duyckinck, George L. 1823-1863...........................DLB-3

Duyckinck and Company DLB-49

Dwight, John Sullivan 1813-1893 ....DLB-1

Dwight, Timothy 1752-1817................................DLB-37

Dyer, Charles 1928- DLB-13

Dyer, George 1755-1841 ....DLB-93

Dyer, John 1699-1757.....................................DLB-95

Dylan, Bob 1941- DLB-16

E

Eager, Edward 1911-1964 ....DLB-22

Earle, James H., and Company.............................DLB-49

Early American Book Illustration,
  by Sinclair Hamilton...................................DLB-49

Eastlake, William 1917- DLB-6

Eastman, Carol ?- DLB-44

Eastman, Max 1883-1969 ....DLB-91

Eberhart, Richard 1904- DLB-48

Ebner, Jeannie 1918- DLB-85

Ebner-Eschenbach, Marie von
  1830-1916..DLB-81

Ebon 1942- DLB-41

Ecco Press..DLB-46

The Eclectic Review 1805-1868..........................DLB-110

Edel, Leon 1907- DLB-103

Edes, Benjamin 1732-1803.................................DLB-43

Edgar, David 1948- DLB-13

The Edinburgh Review 1802-1929........................DLB-110

Edinburgh University Press..............................DLB-112

The Editor Publishing Company DLB-49

Edmonds, Randolph 1900- DLB-51

Edmonds, Walter D. 1903- DLB-9

Edschmid, Kasimir 1890-1966..............................DLB-56

Edwards, Jonathan 1703-1758 ....DLB-24

Edwards, Jonathan, Jr. 1745-1801 ....DLB-37

Edwards, Junius 1929- DLB-33

Edwards, Richard 1524-1566 ....DLB-62

Effinger, George Alec 1947- DLB-8

Eggleston, Edward 1837-1902..............................DLB-12

Eggleston, Wilfred 1901-1986 ....DLB-92

Ehrenstein, Albert 1886-1950 ....DLB-81

Ehrhart, W. D. 1948- DS-9

Eich, Günter 1907-1972...................................DLB-69

Eichendorff, Joseph Freiherr von
  1788-1857..DLB-90

1873 Publishers' Catalogues DLB-49

Eighteenth-Century Aesthetic Theories....................DLB-31

Eighteenth-Century Philosophical
  Background...DLB-31

Eigner, Larry 1927- DLB-5

Eisenreich, Herbert 1925-1986 ....DLB-85

Eisner, Kurt 1867-1919 ....DLB-66

Eklund, Gordon 1945- Y-83

Elder, Lonne III 1931- DLB-7, 38, 44

Elder, Paul, and Company DLB-49

Elements of Rhetoric (1828; revised, 1846),
  by Richard Whately [excerpt].........................DLB-57

Elie, Robert 1915-1973 ....DLB-88
Eliot, George 1819-1880 ....DLB-21, 35, 55
Eliot, John 1604-1690 ....DLB-24
Eliot, T. S. 1888-1965 ....DLB-7, 10, 45, 63
Elizondo, Sergio 1930- DLB-82
Elkin, Stanley 1930- DLB-2, 28; Y-80
Elles, Dora Amy (see Wentworth, Patricia)
Ellet, Elizabeth F. 1818?-1877 ....DLB-30
Elliot, Ebenezer 1781-1849 ....DLB-96
Elliott, George 1923- DLB-68
Elliott, Janice 1931- DLB-14
Elliott, William 1788-1863 ....DLB-3
Elliott, Thomes and Talbot DLB-49
Ellis, Edward S. 1840-1916 ....DLB-42
Ellis, Frederick Staridge [publishing house] DLB-106
The George H. Ellis Company DLB-49
Ellison, Harlan 1934- DLB-8
Ellison, Ralph 1914- DLB-2, 76
Ellmann, Richard 1918-1987 ....DLB-103; Y-87
The Elmer Holmes Bobst Awards
   in Arts and Letters Y-87
Emanuel, James Andrew 1921- DLB-41
The Emergence of Black Women Writers DS-8
Emerson, Ralph Waldo 1803-1882 ....DLB-1, 59, 73
Emerson, William 1769-1811 ....DLB-37
Empson, William 1906-1984 ....DLB-20
The End of English Stage Censorship,
   1945-1968 ....DLB-13
Ende, Michael 1929- DLB-75
Engel, Marian 1933-1985 ....DLB-53
Engle, Paul 1908- DLB-48
English Composition and Rhetoric (1866),
   by Alexander Bain [excerpt] DLB-57
The English Renaissance of Art (1908),
   by Oscar Wilde..DLB-35
Enright, D. J. 1920- DLB-27
Enright, Elizabeth 1909-1968 ....DLB-22
L'Envoi (1882), by Oscar Wilde DLB-35
Epps, Bernard 1936- DLB-53
Epstein, Julius 1909- and
   Epstein, Philip 1909-1952 ....DLB-26
Equiano, Olaudah circa 1745-1797 ....DLB-37, 50
Eragny Press DLB-112
Erichsen-Brown, Gwethalyn Graham
   (see Graham, Gwethalyn)

Ernst, Paul 1866-1933 ....DLB-66
Erskine, John 1879-1951 ....DLB-9, 102
Ervine, St. John Greer 1883-1971 ....DLB-10
Eschenburg, Johann Joachim 1743-1820 ....DLB-97
Eshleman, Clayton 1935- DLB-5
Ess Ess Publishing Company DLB-49
Essay on Chatterton (1842),
   by Robert Browning.....................................DLB-32
Essex House Press..DLB-112
Estes, Eleanor 1906-1988 ....DLB-22
Estes and Lauriat DLB-49
Etherege, George 1636-circa 1692 ....DLB-80
Ets, Marie Hall 1893- DLB-22
Etter, David 1928- DLB-105
Eudora Welty: Eye of the Storyteller Y-87
Eugene O'Neill Memorial Theater Center DLB-7
Eugene O'Neill's Letters: A Review Y-88
Evans, Donald 1884-1921 ....DLB-54
Evans, George Henry 1805-1856 ....DLB-43
Evans, Hubert 1892-1986 ....DLB-92
Evans, M., and Company DLB-46
Evans, Mari 1923- DLB-41
Evans, Mary Ann (see Eliot, George)
Evans, Nathaniel 1742-1767 ....DLB-31
Evans, Sebastian 1830-1909 ....DLB-35
Everett, Alexander Hill 1790-1847 ....DLB-59
Everett, Edward 1794-1865 ....DLB-1, 59
Everson, R. G. 1903- DLB-88
Everson, William 1912- DLB-5, 16
Every Man His Own Poet; or, The
   Inspired Singer's Recipe Book (1877),
   by W. H. Mallock......................................DLB-35
Ewart, Gavin 1916- DLB-40
Ewing, Juliana Horatia 1841-1885 ....DLB-21
The Examiner 1808-1881 ....DLB-110
Exley, Frederick 1929- Y-81
Experiment in the Novel (1929),
   by John D. Beresford DLB-36
Eyre and Spottiswoode DLB-106

F

"F. Scott Fitzgerald: St. Paul's Native Son
   and Distinguished American Writer":
   University of Minnesota Conference,
   29-31 October 1982 ....Y-82

Cumulative Index

Faber, Frederick William 1814-1863 ....DLB-32

Faber and Faber Limited DLB-112

Fair, Ronald L. 1932- DLB-33

Fairfax, Beatrice (see Manning, Marie)

Fairlie, Gerard 1899-1983 ....DLB-77

Fallada, Hans 1893-1947 ....DLB-56

Fancher, Betsy 1928- Y-83

Fane, Violet 1843-1905 ....DLB-35

Fanfrolico Press DLB-112

Fantasy Press Publishers DLB-46

Fante, John 1909-1983 ....Y-83

Farber, Norma 1909-1984 ....DLB-61

Farigoule, Louis (see Romains, Jules)

Farley, Walter 1920-1989 ....DLB-22

Farmer, Philip José 1918- DLB-8

Farquhar, George circa 1677-1707 ....DLB-84

Farquharson, Martha (see Finley, Martha)

Farrar and Rinehart DLB-46

Farrar, Straus and Giroux DLB-46

Farrell, James T. 1904-1979 ....DLB-4, 9, 86; DS-2

Farrell, J. G. 1935-1979 ....DLB-14

Fast, Howard 1914- DLB-9

Faulkner, William 1897-1962
..............................DLB-9, 11, 44, 102; DS-2; Y-86

Fauset, Jessie Redmon 1882-1961 ....DLB-51

Faust, Irvin 1924- DLB-2, 28; Y-80

Fawcett Books DLB-46

Fearing, Kenneth 1902-1961 ....DLB-9

Federal Writers' Project DLB-46

Federman, Raymond 1928- Y-80

Feiffer, Jules 1929- DLB-7, 44

Feinberg, Charles E. 1899-1988 ....Y-88

Feinstein, Elaine 1930- DLB-14, 40

Felipe, León 1884-1968 ....DLB-108

Fell, Frederick, Publishers DLB-46

Fels, Ludwig 1946- DLB-75

Felton, Cornelius Conway 1807-1862 ....DLB-1

Fennario, David 1947- DLB-60

Fenno, John 1751-1798 ....DLB-43

Fenno, R. F., and Company DLB-49

Fenton, James 1949- DLB-40

Ferber, Edna 1885-1968 ....DLB-9, 28, 86

Ferdinand, Vallery III (see Salaam, Kalamu ya)

Ferguson, Sir Samuel 1810-1886 ....DLB-32

Ferguson, William Scott 1875-1954 ....DLB-47

Fergusson, Robert 1750-1774 ....DLB-109

Ferland, Albert 1872-1943 ....DLB-92

Ferlinghetti, Lawrence 1919- DLB-5, 16

Fern, Fanny (see Parton, Sara Payson Willis)

Ferrars, Elizabeth 1907- DLB-87

Ferret, E., and Company DLB-49

Ferrini, Vincent 1913- DLB-48

Ferron, Jacques 1921-1985 ....DLB-60

Ferron, Madeleine 1922- DLB-53

Fetridge and Company DLB-49

Feuchtwanger, Lion 1884-1958 ....DLB-66

Fichte, Johann Gottlieb 1762-1814 ....DLB-90

Ficke, Arthur Davison 1883-1945 ....DLB-54

Fiction Best-Sellers, 1910-1945 ....DLB-9

Fiction into Film, 1928-1975: A List of Movies
Based on the Works of Authors in
British Novelists, 1930-1959 ....DLB-15

Fiedler, Leslie A. 1917- DLB-28, 67

Field, Edward 1924- DLB-105

Field, Edward, The Poetry File DLB-105

Field, Eugene 1850-1895 ....DLB-23, 42

Field, Nathan 1587-1619 or 1620 ....DLB-58

Field, Rachel 1894-1942 ....DLB-9, 22

A Field Guide to Recent Schools of
American Poetry Y-86

Fielding, Henry 1707-1754 ....DLB-39, 84, 101

Fielding, Sarah 1710-1768 ....DLB-39

Fields, James Thomas 1817-1881 ....DLB-1

Fields, Julia 1938- DLB-41

Fields, W. C. 1880-1946 ....DLB-44

Fields, Osgood and Company DLB-49

Fifty Penguin Years Y-85

Figes, Eva 1932- DLB-14

Figuera, Angela 1902-1984 ....DLB-108

Filson, John circa 1753-1788 ....DLB-37

Finch, Anne, Countess of Winchilsea
1661-1720 ....DLB-95

Finch, Robert 1900- DLB-88

Findley, Timothy 1930- DLB-53

Finlay, Ian Hamilton 1925- DLB-40

Finley, Martha 1828-1909 ....DLB-42

Finney, Jack 1911- DLB-8

Finney, Walter Braden (see Finney, Jack)

Firbank, Ronald 1886-1926	DLB-36
Firmin, Giles 1615-1697	DLB-24
First Strauss "Livings" Awarded to Cynthia Ozick and Raymond Carver An Interview with Cynthia Ozick An Interview with Raymond Carver	Y-83
Fischer, Karoline Auguste Fernandine 1764-1842	DLB-94
Fish, Stanley 1938-	DLB-67
Fisher, Clay (see Allen, Henry W.)	
Fisher, Dorothy Canfield 1879-1958	DLB-9, 102
Fisher, Leonard Everett 1924-	DLB-61
Fisher, Roy 1930-	DLB-40
Fisher, Rudolph 1897-1934	DLB-51, 102
Fisher, Sydney George 1856-1927	DLB-47
Fisher, Vardis 1895-1968	DLB-9
Fiske, John 1608-1677	DLB-24
Fiske, John 1842-1901	DLB-47, 64
Fitch, Thomas circa 1700-1774	DLB-31
Fitch, William Clyde 1865-1909	DLB-7
FitzGerald, Edward 1809-1883	DLB-32
Fitzgerald, F. Scott 1896-1940	DLB-4, 9, 86; Y-81; DS-1
Fitzgerald, Penelope 1916-	DLB-14
Fitzgerald, Robert 1910-1985	Y-80
Fitzgerald, Thomas 1819-1891	DLB-23
Fitzgerald, Zelda Sayre 1900-1948	Y-84
Fitzhugh, Louise 1928-1974	DLB-52
Fitzhugh, William circa 1651-1701	DLB-24
Flanagan, Thomas 1923-	Y-80
Flanner, Hildegarde 1899-1987	DLB-48
Flanner, Janet 1892-1978	DLB-4
Flavin, Martin 1883-1967	DLB-9
Flecker, James Elroy 1884-1915	DLB-10, 19
Fleeson, Doris 1901-1970	DLB-29
Fleidser, Marieluise 1901-1974	DLB-56
Fleming, Ian 1908-1964	DLB-87
The Fleshly School of Poetry and Other Phenomena of the Day (1872), by Robert Buchanan	DLB-35
The Fleshly School of Poetry: Mr. D. G. Rossetti (1871), by Thomas Maitland (Robert Buchanan)	DLB-35
Fletcher, J. S. 1863-1935	DLB-70
Fletcher, John (see Beaumont, Francis)	
Fletcher, John Gould 1886-1950	DLB-4, 45

Flieg, Helmut (see Heym, Stefan)	
Flint, F. S. 1885-1960	DLB-19
Flint, Timothy 1780-1840	DLB-734
Folio Society	DLB-112
Follen, Eliza Lee (Cabot) 1787-1860	DLB-1
Follett, Ken 1949-	Y-81, DLB-87
Follett Publishing Company	DLB-46
Folsom, John West [publishing house]	DLB-49
Foote, Horton 1916-	DLB-26
Foote, Samuel 1721-1777	DLB-89
Foote, Shelby 1916-	DLB-2, 17
Forbes, Calvin 1945-	DLB-41
Forbes, Ester 1891-1967	DLB-22
Forbes and Company	DLB-49
Force, Peter 1790-1868	DLB-30
Forché, Carolyn 1950-	DLB-5
Ford, Charles Henri 1913-	DLB-4, 48
Ford, Corey 1902-1969	DLB-11
Ford, Ford Madox 1873-1939	DLB-34, 98
Ford, J. B., and Company	DLB-49
Ford, Jesse Hill 1928-	DLB-6
Ford, John 1586-?	DLB-58
Ford, R. A. D. 1915-	DLB-88
Ford, Worthington C. 1858-1941	DLB-47
Fords, Howard, and Hulbert	DLB-49
Foreman, Carl 1914-1984	DLB-26
Forester, Frank (see Herbert, Henry William)	
Fornés, María Irene 1930-	DLB-7
Forrest, Leon 1937-	DLB-33
Forster, E. M. 1879-1970	DLB-34, 98
Forster, Georg 1754-1794	DLB-94
Forsyth, Frederick 1938-	DLB-87
Forten, Charlotte L. 1837-1914	DLB-50
Fortune, T. Thomas 1856-1928	DLB-23
Fosdick, Charles Austin 1842-1915	DLB-42
Foster, Genevieve 1893-1979	DLB-61
Foster, Hannah Webster 1758-1840	DLB-37
Foster, John 1648-1681	DLB-24
Foster, Michael 1904-1956	DLB-9
Fouqué, Caroline de la Motte 1774-1831	DLB-90
Fouqué, Friedrich de la Motte 1777-1843	DLB-90
Four Essays on the Beat Generation, by John Clellon Holmes	DLB-16
Four Seas Company	DLB-46

Four Winds Press	DLB-46
Fournier, Henri Alban (see Alain-Fournier)	
Fowler and Wells Company	DLB-49
Fowles, John 1926-	DLB-14
Fox, John, Jr. 1862 or 1863-1919	DLB-9
Fox, Paula 1923-	DLB-52
Fox, Richard K. [publishing house]	DLB-49
Fox, Richard Kyle 1846-1922	DLB-79
Fox, William Price 1926-	DLB-2; Y-81
Fraenkel, Michael 1896-1957	DLB-4
France, Richard 1938-	DLB-7
Francis, C. S. [publishing house]	DLB-49
Francis, Convers 1795-1863	DLB-1
Francis, Dick 1920-	DLB-87
Francis, Jeffrey, Lord 1773-1850	DLB-107
François 1863-1910	DLB-92
Francke, Kuno 1855-1930	DLB-71
Frank, Leonhard 1882-1961	DLB-56
Frank, Melvin (see Panama, Norman)	
Frank, Waldo 1889-1967	DLB-9, 63
Franken, Rose 1895?-1988	Y-84
Franklin, Benjamin 1706-1790	DLB-24, 43, 73
Franklin, James 1697-1735	DLB-43
Franklin Library	DLB-46
Frantz, Ralph Jules 1902-1979	DLB-4
Fraser, G. S. 1915-1980	DLB-27
Frayn, Michael 1933-	DLB-13, 14
Frederic, Harold 1856-1898	DLB-12, 23
Freeling, Nicolas 1927-	DLB-87
Freeman, Douglas Southall 1886-1953	DLB-17
Freeman, Legh Richmond 1842-1915	DLB-23
Freeman, Mary E. Wilkins 1852-1930	DLB-12, 78
Freeman, R. Austin 1862-1943	DLB-70
French, Alice 1850-1934	DLB-74
French, David 1939-	DLB-53
French, James [publishing house]	DLB-49
French, Samuel [publishing house]	DLB-49
Samuel French, Limited	DLB-106
Freneau, Philip 1752-1832	DLB-37, 43
Fried, Erich 1921-1988	DLB-85
Friedman, Bruce Jay 1930-	DLB-2, 28
Friel, Brian 1929-	DLB-13
Friend, Krebs 1895?-1967?	DLB-4
Fries, Fritz Rudolf 1935-	DLB-75
Fringe and Alternative Theater in Great Britain	DLB-13
Frisch, Max 1911-	DLB-69
Frischmuth, Barbara 1941-	DLB-85
Fritz, Jean 1915-	DLB-52
Frost, Robert 1874-1963	DLB-54; DS-7
Frothingham, Octavius Brooks 1822-1895	DLB-1
Froude, James Anthony 1818-1894	DLB-18, 57
Fry, Christopher 1907-	DLB-13
Frye, Northrop 1912-1991	DLB-67, 68
Fuchs, Daniel 1909-	DLB-9, 26, 28
Fuentes, Carlos 1928-	DLB-113
Fuertas, Gloria 1918-	DLB-108
The Fugitives and the Agrarians: The First Exhibition	Y-85
Fuller, Charles H., Jr. 1939-	DLB-38
Fuller, Henry Blake 1857-1929	DLB-12
Fuller, John 1937-	DLB-40
Fuller, Roy 1912-	DLB-15, 20
Fuller, Samuel 1912-	DLB-26
Fuller, Sarah Margaret, Marchesa D'Ossoli 1810-1850	DLB-1, 59, 73
Fulton, Len 1934-	Y-86
Fulton, Robin 1937-	DLB-40
Furman, Laura 1945-	Y-86
Furness, Horace Howard 1833-1912	DLB-64
Furness, William Henry 1802-1896	DLB-1
Furthman, Jules 1888-1966	DLB-26
The Future of the Novel (1899), by Henry James	DLB-18

G

The G. Ross Roy Scottish Poetry Collection at the University of South Carolina	Y-89
Gaddis, William 1922-	DLB-2
Gág, Wanda 1893-1946	DLB-22
Gagnon, Madeleine 1938-	DLB-60
Gaine, Hugh 1726-1807	DLB-43
Gaine, Hugh [publishing house]	DLB-49
Gaines, Ernest J. 1933-	DLB-2, 33; Y-80
Gaiser, Gerd 1908-1976	DLB-69
Galaxy Science Fiction Novels	DLB-46

Gale, Zona 1874-1938	DLB-9, 78
Gallagher, William Davis 1808-1894	DLB-73
Gallant, Mavis 1922-	DLB-53
Gallico, Paul 1897-1976	DLB-9
Galsworthy, John 1867-1933	DLB-10, 34, 98
Galt, John 1779-1839	DLB-99
Galvin, Brendan 1938-	DLB-5
Gambit	DLB-46
Gammer Gurton's Needle	DLB-62
Gannett, Frank E. 1876-1957	DLB-29
García, Lionel G. 1935-	DLB-82
García Lorca, Federico 1898-1936	DLB-108
García Marquez, Gabriel 1928-	DLB-113
Gardam, Jane 1928-	DLB-14
Garden, Alexander circa 1685-1756	DLB-31
Gardner, John 1933-1982	DLB-2; Y-82
Garis, Howard R. 1873-1962	DLB-22
Garland, Hamlin 1860-1940	DLB-12, 71, 78
Garneau, Francis-Xavier 1809-1866	DLB-99
Garneau, Hector de Saint-Denys 1912-1943	DLB-88
Garneau, Michel 1939-	DLB-53
Garner, Hugh 1913-1979	DLB-68
Garnett, David 1892-1981	DLB-34
Garraty, John A. 1920-	DLB-17
Garrett, George 1929-	DLB-2, 5; Y-83
Garrick, David 1717-1779	DLB-84
Garrison, William Lloyd 1805-1879	DLB-1, 43
Garth, Samuel 1661-1719	DLB-95
Garve, Andrew 1908-	DLB-87
Gary, Romain 1914-1980	DLB-83
Gascoyne, David 1916-	DLB-20
Gaskell, Elizabeth Cleghorn 1810-1865	DLB-21
Gass, William Howard 1924-	DLB-2
Gates, Doris 1901-	DLB-22
Gates, Henry Louis, Jr. 1950-	DLB-67
Gates, Lewis E. 1860-1924	DLB-71
Gauvreau, Claude 1925-1971	DLB-88
Gay, Ebenezer 1696-1787	DLB-24
Gay, John 1685-1732	DLB-84, 95
The Gay Science (1866), by E. S. Dallas [excerpt]	DLB-21
Gayarré, Charles E. A. 1805-1895	DLB-30
Gaylord, Charles [publishing house]	DLB-49
Geddes, Gary 1940-	DLB-60
Geddes, Virgil 1897-	DLB-4
Geis, Bernard, Associates	DLB-46
Geisel, Theodor Seuss 1904-	DLB-61
Gelb, Arthur 1924-	DLB-103
Gelb, Barbara 1926-	DLB-103
Gelber, Jack 1932-	DLB-7
Gélinas, Gratien 1909-	DLB-88
Gellert, Christian Füerchtegott 1715-1769	DLB-97
Gellhorn, Martha 1908-	Y-82
Gems, Pam 1925-	DLB-13
A General Idea of the College of Mirania (1753), by William Smith [excerpts]	DLB-31
Genet, Jean 1910-1986	Y-86, DLB-72
Genevoix, Maurice 1890-1980	DLB-65
Genovese, Eugene D. 1930-	DLB-17
Gent, Peter 1942-	Y-82
George, Henry 1839-1897	DLB-23
George, Jean Craighead 1919-	DLB-52
Gerhardie, William 1895-1977	DLB-36
Gérin-Lajoie, Antoine 1824-1882	DLB-99
German Transformation from the Baroque to the Enlightenment, The	DLB-97
Germanophilism, by Hans Kohn	DLB-66
Gernsback, Hugo 1884-1967	DLB-8
Gerould, Katharine Fullerton 1879-1944	DLB-78
Gerrish, Samuel [publishing house]	DLB-49
Gerrold, David 1944-	DLB-8
Gerstenberg, Heinrich Wilhelm von 1737-1823	DLB-97
Geßner, Salomon 1730-1788	DLB-97
Geston, Mark S. 1946-	DLB-8
Gibbon, Edward 1737-1794	DLB-104
Gibbon, John Murray 1875-1952	DLB-92
Gibbon, Lewis Grassic (see Mitchell, James Leslie)	
Gibbons, Floyd 1887-1939	DLB-25
Gibbons, William ?-?	DLB-73
Gibson, Graeme 1934-	DLB-53
Gibson, Wilfrid 1878-1962	DLB-19
Gibson, William 1914-	DLB-7
Gide, André 1869-1951	DLB-65
Giguère, Diane 1937-	DLB-53
Giguère, Roland 1929-	DLB-60
Gil de Biedma, Jaime 1929-1990	DLB-108

Gilbert, Anthony 1899-1973..................................DLB-77
Gilbert, Michael 1912- DLB-87
Gilder, Jeannette L. 1849-1916..............................DLB-79
Gilder, Richard Watson 1844-1909.................DLB-64, 79
Gildersleeve, Basil 1831-1924.................................DLB-71
Giles, Henry 1809-1882...DLB-64
Gill, Eric 1882-1940..DLB-98
Gill, William F., Company......................................DLB-49
Gillespie, A. Lincoln, Jr. 1895-1950.........................DLB-4
Gilliam, Florence ?-?..DLB-4
Gilliatt, Penelope 1932- DLB-14
Gillott, Jacky 1939-1980..DLB-14
Gilman, Caroline H. 1794-1888........................DLB-3, 73
Gilman, W. and J. [publishing house]....................DLB-49
Gilmer, Elizabeth Meriwether 1861-1951............DLB-29
Gilmer, Francis Walker 1790-1826........................DLB-37
Gilroy, Frank D. 1925- DLB-7
Ginsberg, Allen 1926- DLB-5, 16
Ginzkey, Franz Karl 1871-1963..............................DLB-81
Giono, Jean 1895-1970..DLB-72
Giovanni, Nikki 1943- DLB-5, 41
Gipson, Lawrence Henry 1880-1971....................DLB-17
Girard, Rodolphe 1879-1956.................................DLB-92
Giraudoux, Jean 1882-1944 ....DLB-65
Gissing, George 1857-1903.....................................DLB-18
Gladstone, William Ewart 1809-1898...................DLB-57
Glaeser, Ernst 1902-1963..DLB-69
Glanville, Brian 1931- DLB-15
Glapthorne, Henry 1610-1643?..............................DLB-58
Glasgow, Ellen 1873-1945..................................DLB-9, 12
Glaspell, Susan 1876-1948.............................DLB-7, 9, 78
Glass, Montague 1877-1934...................................DLB-11
Glassco, John 1909-1981...DLB-68
Glauser, Friedrich 1896-1938.................................DLB-56
F. Gleason's Publishing Hall...................................DLB-49
Gleim, Johann Wilhelm Ludwig
  1719-1803..DLB-97
Glover, Richard 1712-1785.....................................DLB-95
Glück, Louise 1943- DLB-5
Godbout, Jacques 1933- DLB-53
Goddard, Morrill 1865-1937..................................DLB-25
Goddard, William 1740-1817.................................DLB-43
Godey, Louis A. 1804-1878.....................................DLB-73
Godey and McMichael...DLB-49

Godfrey, Dave 1938- DLB-60
Godfrey, Thomas 1736-1763..................................DLB-31
Godine, David R., Publisher...................................DLB-46
Godkin, E. L. 1831-1902...DLB-79
Godwin, Gail 1937- DLB-6
Godwin, Parke 1816-1904..................................DLB-3, 64
Godwin, William 1756-1836............................DLB-39, 104
Goes, Albrecht 1908- DLB-69
Goethe, Johann Wolfgang von 1749-1832...........DLB-94
Goffe, Thomas circa 1592-1629.............................DLB-58
Goffstein, M. B. 1940- DLB-61
Gogarty, Oliver St. John 1878-1957.................DLB-15, 19
Goines, Donald 1937-1974......................................DLB-33
Gold, Herbert 1924- DLB-2; Y-81
Gold, Michael 1893-1967....................................DLB-9, 28
Goldberg, Dick 1947- DLB-7
Golden Cockerel Press..DLB-112
Golding, William 1911- DLB-15, 100
Goldman, William 1931- DLB-44
Goldsmith, Oliver
  1730 or 1731-1774................................DLB-39, 89, 104
Goldsmith, Oliver 1794-1861.................................DLB-99
Goldsmith Publishing Company.............................DLB-46
Gollancz, Victor, Limited......................................DLB-112
Gomme, Laurence James
  [publishing house]...DLB-46
González-T., César A. 1931- DLB-82
González, Angel 1925- DLB-108
The Goodman Theatre..DLB-7
Goodrich, Frances 1891-1984 and
  Hackett, Albert 1900- DLB-26
Goodrich, S. G. [publishing house].......................DLB-49
Goodrich, Samuel Griswold 1793-1860.........DLB-1, 42, 73
Goodspeed, C. E., and Company............................DLB-49
Goodwin, Stephen 1943- Y-82
Gookin, Daniel 1612-1687......................................DLB-24
Gordon, Caroline 1895-1981................DLB-4, 9, 102; Y-81
Gordon, Giles 1940- DLB-14
Gordon, Mary 1949- DLB-6; Y-81
Gordone, Charles 1925- DLB-7
Gorey, Edward 1925- DLB-61
Görres, Joseph 1776-1848......................................DLB-90
Gosse, Edmund 1849-1928.....................................DLB-57
Gotlieb, Phyllis 1926- DLB-88

Gottsched, Johann Christoph 1700-1766.......................DLB-97

Götz, Johann Nikolaus 1721-1781.............................DLB-97

Gould, Wallace 1882-1940....................................DLB-54

Goyen, William 1915-1983..........................DLB-2; Y-83

Gracq, Julien 1910- DLB-83

Grady, Henry W. 1850-1889..................................DLB-23

Graf, Oskar Maria 1894-1967.................................DLB-56

Graham, George Rex 1813-1894................................DLB-73

Graham, Gwethalyn 1913-1965.................................DLB-88

Graham, Lorenz 1902-1989....................................DLB-76

Graham, R. B. Cunninghame 1852-1936.........................DLB-98

Graham, Shirley 1896-1977...................................DLB-76

Graham, W. S. 1918- DLB-20

Graham, William H. [publishing house].......................DLB-49

Graham, Winston 1910- DLB-77

Grahame, Kenneth 1859-1932..................................DLB-34

Grainger, Martin Allerdale 1874-1941........................DLB-92

Gramatky, Hardie 1907-1979..................................DLB-22

Grandbois, Alain 1900-1975..................................DLB-92

Granich, Irwin (see Gold, Michael)

Grant, George 1918-1988.....................................DLB-88

Grant, George Monro 1835-1902...............................DLB-99

Grant, Harry J. 1881-1963...................................DLB-29

Grant, James Edward 1905-1966...............................DLB-26

Grass, Günter 1927- DLB-75

Grasty, Charles H. 1863-1924................................DLB-25

Grau, Shirley Ann 1929- DLB-2

Graves, John 1920- Y-83

Graves, Richard 1715-1804...................................DLB-39

Graves, Robert 1895-1985..................DLB-20, 100; Y-85

Gray, Asa 1810-1888...DLB-1

Gray, David 1838-1861.......................................DLB-32

Gray, Simon 1936- DLB-13

Gray, Thomas 1716-1771.....................................DLB-109

Grayson, William J. 1788-1863..........................DLB-3, 64

The Great War and the Theater, 1914-1918
  [Great Britain]...DLB-10

Greeley, Horace 1811-1872..............................DLB-3, 43

Green, Adolph (see Comden, Betty)

Green, Duff 1791-1875.......................................DLB-43

Green, Gerald 1922- DLB-28

Green, Henry 1905-1973......................................DLB-15

Green, Jonas 1712-1767......................................DLB-31

Green, Joseph 1706-1780.....................................DLB-31

Green, Julien 1900- DLB-4, 72

Green, Paul 1894-1981..........................DLB-7, 9; Y-81

Green, T. and S. [publishing house].........................DLB-49

Green, Timothy [publishing house]...........................DLB-49

Greenberg: Publisher..DLB-46

Green Tiger Press...DLB-46

Greene, Asa 1789-1838.......................................DLB-11

Greene, Benjamin H. [publishing house]......................DLB-49

Greene, Graham 1904-1991 ....DLB-13, 15, 77, 100; Y-85

Greene, Robert 1558-1592....................................DLB-62

Greenhow, Robert 1800-1854..................................DLB-30

Greenough, Horatio 1805-1852.................................DLB-1

Greenwell, Dora 1821-1882...................................DLB-35

Greenwillow Books...DLB-46

Greenwood, Grace (see Lippincott, Sara Jane Clarke)

Greenwood, Walter 1903-1974.................................DLB-10

Greer, Ben 1948- DLB-6

Greg, W. R. 1809-1881.......................................DLB-55

Gregg Press...DLB-46

Gregory, Isabella Augusta
  Persse, Lady 1852-1932....................................DLB-10

Gregory, Horace 1898-1982...................................DLB-48

Gregynog Press...DLB-112

Grenfell, Wilfred Thomason 1865-1940........................DLB-92

Greve, Felix Paul (see Grove, Frederick Philip)

Greville, Fulke, First Lord Brooke
  1554-1628...DLB-62

Grey, Zane 1872-1939...DLB-9

Grey Owl 1888-1938..DLB-92

Grey Walls Press...DLB-112

Grier, Eldon 1917- DLB-88

Grieve, C. M. (see MacDiarmid, Hugh)

Griffith, Elizabeth 1727?-1793.........................DLB-39, 89

Griffiths, Trevor 1935- DLB-13

Griggs, S. C., and Company..................................DLB-49

Griggs, Sutton Elbert 1872-1930.............................DLB-50

Grignon, Claude-Henri 1894-1976.............................DLB-68

Grigson, Geoffrey 1905- DLB-27

Grimké, Angelina Weld 1880-1958........................DLB-50, 54

Grimm, Hans 1875-1959.......................................DLB-66

Grimm, Jacob 1785-1863......................................DLB-90

Grimm, Wilhelm 1786-1859....................................DLB-90

Griswold, Rufus Wilmot 1815-1857.......................DLB-3, 59

Gross, Milt 1895-1953.......................................DLB-11

Grosset and Dunlap DLB-49

Grossman Publishers DLB-46

Grosvenor, Gilbert H. 1875-1966 .... DLB-91

Groulx, Lionel 1878-1967 .... DLB-68

Grove, Frederick Philip 1879-1949 .... DLB-92

Grove Press DLB-46

Grubb, Davis 1919-1980 .... DLB-6

Gruelle, Johnny 1880-1938 .... DLB-22

Guare, John 1938- DLB-7

Guest, Barbara 1920- DLB-5

Guèvremont, Germaine 1893-1968 .... DLB-68

Guillén, Jorge 1893-1984 .... DLB-108

Guilloux, Louis 1899-1980 .... DLB-72

Guiney, Louise Imogen 1861-1920 .... DLB-54

Guiterman, Arthur 1871-1943 .... DLB-11

Günderrode, Caroline von 1780-1806 .... DLB-90

Gunn, Bill 1934-1989 .... DLB-38

Gunn, James E. 1923- DLB-8

Gunn, Neil M. 1891-1973 .... DLB-15

Gunn, Thom 1929- DLB-27

Gunnars, Kristjana 1948- DLB-60

Gurik, Robert 1932- DLB-60

Gustafson, Ralph 1909- DLB-88

Gütersloh, Albert Paris 1887-1973 .... DLB-81

Guthrie, A. B., Jr. 1901- DLB-6

Guthrie, Ramon 1896-1973 .... DLB-4

The Guthrie Theater DLB-7

Guy, Ray 1939- DLB-60

Guy, Rosa 1925- DLB-33

Gwynne, Erskine 1898-1948 .... DLB-4

Gyles, John 1680-1755 .... DLB-99

Gysin, Brion 1916- DLB-16

H

H. D. (see Doolittle, Hilda)

Hackett, Albert (see Goodrich, Frances)

Hadden, Briton 1898-1929 .... DLB-91

Hagelstange, Rudolf 1912-1984 .... DLB-69

Haggard, H. Rider 1856-1925 .... DLB-70

Haig-Brown, Roderick 1908-1976 .... DLB-88

Haight, Gordon S. 1901-1985 .... DLB-103

Hailey, Arthur 1920- DLB-88; Y-82

Haines, John 1924- DLB-5

Hake, Thomas Gordon 1809-1895 .... DLB-32

Haldeman, Joe 1943- DLB-8

Haldeman-Julius Company DLB-46

Hale, E. J., and Son DLB-49

Hale, Edward Everett 1822-1909 .... DLB-1, 42, 74

Hale, Leo Thomas (see Ebon)

Hale, Lucretia Peabody 1820-1900 .... DLB-42

Hale, Nancy 1908-1988 .... DLB-86; Y-80, 88

Hale, Sarah Josepha (Buell) 1788-1879 .... DLB-1, 42, 73

Haley, Alex 1921- DLB-38

Haliburton, Thomas Chandler 1796-1865 .... DLB-11, 99

Hall, Donald 1928- DLB-5

Hall, James 1793-1868 .... DLB-73, 74

Hall, Samuel [publishing house] DLB-49

Hallam, Arthur Henry 1811-1833 .... DLB-32

Halleck, Fitz-Greene 1790-1867 .... DLB-3

Hallmark Editions DLB-46

Halper, Albert 1904-1984 .... DLB-9

Halperin, John William 1941- DLB-111

Halstead, Murat 1829-1908 .... DLB-23

Hamann, Johann Georg 1730-1788 .... DLB-97

Hamburger, Michael 1924- DLB-27

Hamilton, Alexander 1712-1756 .... DLB-31

Hamilton, Alexander 1755?-1804 .... DLB-37

Hamilton, Cicely 1872-1952 .... DLB-10

Hamilton, Edmond 1904-1977 .... DLB-8

Hamilton, Gail (see Corcoran, Barbara)

Hamilton, Ian 1938- DLB-40

Hamilton, Patrick 1904-1962 .... DLB-10

Hamilton, Virginia 1936- DLB-33, 52

Hamilton, Hamish, Limited DLB-112

Hammett, Dashiell 1894-1961 .... DS-6

Hammon, Jupiter 1711-died between
    1790 and 1806 .... DLB-31, 50

Hammond, John ?-1663 .... DLB-24

Hamner, Earl 1923- DLB-6

Hampton, Christopher 1946- DLB-13

Handel-Mazzetti, Enrica von 1871-1955 .... DLB-81

Handke, Peter 1942- DLB-85

Handlin, Oscar 1915- DLB-17

Hankin, St. John 1869-1909 .... DLB-10

Hanley, Clifford 1922- DLB-14

Hannah, Barry 1942- DLB-6

Hannay, James 1827-1873	DLB-21
Hansberry, Lorraine 1930-1965	DLB-7, 38
Hapgood, Norman 1868-1937	DLB-91
Harcourt Brace Jovanovich	DLB-46
Hardenberg, Friedrich von (see Novalis)	
Harding, Walter 1917-	DLB-111
Hardwick, Elizabeth 1916-	DLB-6
Hardy, Thomas 1840-1928	DLB-18, 19
Hare, Cyril 1900-1958	DLB-77
Hare, David 1947-	DLB-13
Hargrove, Marion 1919-	DLB-11
Harlow, Robert 1923-	DLB-60
Harness, Charles L. 1915-	DLB-8
Harper, Fletcher 1806-1877	DLB-79
Harper, Frances Ellen Watkins 1825-1911	DLB-50
Harper, Michael S. 1938-	DLB-41
Harper and Brothers	DLB-49
Harrap, George G., and Company Limited	DLB-112
Harris, Benjamin ?-circa 1720	DLB-42, 43
Harris, Christie 1907-	DLB-88
Harris, George Washington 1814-1869	DLB-3, 11
Harris, Joel Chandler 1848-1908	DLB-11, 23, 42, 78, 91
Harris, Mark 1922-	DLB-2; Y-80
Harrison, Charles Yale 1898-1954	DLB-68
Harrison, Frederic 1831-1923	DLB-57
Harrison, Harry 1925-	DLB-8
Harrison, James P., Company	DLB-49
Harrison, Jim 1937-	Y-82
Harrison, Paul Carter 1936-	DLB-38
Harrison, Susan Frances 1859-1935	DLB-99
Harrison, Tony 1937-	DLB-40
Harrisse, Henry 1829-1910	DLB-47
Harsent, David 1942-	DLB-40
Hart, Albert Bushnell 1854-1943	DLB-17
Hart, Julia Catherine 1796-1867	DLB-99
Hart, Moss 1904-1961	DLB-7
Hart, Oliver 1723-1795	DLB-31
Hart-Davis, Rupert, Limited	DLB-112
Harte, Bret 1836-1902	DLB-12, 64, 74, 79
Hartlaub, Felix 1913-1945	DLB-56
Hartley, L. P. 1895-1972	DLB-15
Hartley, Marsden 1877-1943	DLB-54
Härtling, Peter 1933-	DLB-75
Hartman, Geoffrey H. 1929-	DLB-67
Hartmann, Sadakichi 1867-1944	DLB-54
Harvey, Jean-Charles 1891-1967	DLB-88
Harvill Press Limited	DLB-112
Harwood, Lee 1939-	DLB-40
Harwood, Ronald 1934-	DLB-13
Haskins, Charles Homer 1870-1937	DLB-47
Hass, Robert 1941-	DLB-105
The Hatch-Billops Collection	DLB-76
Hauff, Wilhelm 1802-1827	DLB-90
A Haughty and Proud Generation (1922), by Ford Madox Hueffer	DLB-36
Hauptmann, Carl 1858-1921	DLB-66
Hauptmann, Gerhart 1862-1946	DLB-66
Hauser, Marianne 1910-	Y-83
Hawker, Robert Stephen 1803-1875	DLB-32
Hawkes, John 1925-	DLB-2, 7; Y-80
Hawkins, Sir John 1719 or 1721-1789	DLB-104
Hawkins, Walter Everette 1883-?	DLB-50
Hawthorne, Nathaniel 1804-1864	DLB-1, 74
Hay, John 1838-1905	DLB-12, 47
Hayden, Robert 1913-1980	DLB-5, 76
Haydon, Benjamin Robert 1786-1846	DLB-110
Hayes, John Michael 1919-	DLB-26
Hayley, William 1745-1820	DLB-93
Hayman, Robert 1575-1629	DLB-99
Hayne, Paul Hamilton 1830-1886	DLB-3, 64, 79
Haywood, Eliza 1693?-1756	DLB-39
Hazard, Willis P. [publishing house]	DLB-49
Hazlitt, William 1778-1830	DLB-110
Hazzard, Shirley 1931-	Y-82
Headley, Joel T. 1813-1897	DLB-30
Heaney, Seamus 1939-	DLB-40
Heard, Nathan C. 1936-	DLB-33
Hearn, Lafcadio 1850-1904	DLB-12, 78
Hearne, Samuel 1745-1792	DLB-99
Hearst, William Randolph 1863-1951	DLB-25
Heath, Catherine 1924-	DLB-14
Heath-Stubbs, John 1918-	DLB-27
Heavysege, Charles 1816-1876	DLB-99
Hebel, Johann Peter 1760-1826	DLB-90
Hébert, Anne 1916-	DLB-68
Hébert, Jacques 1923-	DLB-53

Hecht, Anthony 1923- DLB-5

Hecht, Ben 1894-1964 ....DLB-7, 9, 25, 26, 28, 86

Hecker, Isaac Thomas 1819-1888 ....DLB-1

Hedge, Frederic Henry 1805-1890 ....DLB-1, 59

Hegel, Georg Wilhelm Friedrich 1770-1831 ....DLB-90

Heidish, Marcy 1947- Y-82

Heidsenbüttel 1921- DLB-75

Heine, Heinrich 1797-1856 ....DLB-90

Heinemann, Larry 1944- DS-9

Heinemann, William, Limited DLB-112

Heinlein, Robert A. 1907- DLB-8

Heinrich, Willi 1920- DLB-75

Heinse, Wilhelm 1746-1803 ....DLB-94

Heller, Joseph 1923- DLB-2, 28; Y-80

Hellman, Lillian 1906-1984 ....DLB-7; Y-84

Helprin, Mark 1947- Y-85

Helwig, David 1938- DLB-60

Hemans, Felicia 1793-1835 ....DLB-96

Hemingway, Ernest 1899-1961
...................................DLB-4, 9, 102; Y-81, 87; DS-1

Hemingway: Twenty-Five Years Later...............................Y-85

Hémon, Louis 1880-1913 ....DLB-92

Hemphill, Paul 1936- Y-87

Hénault, Gilles 1920- DLB-88

Henchman, Daniel 1689-1761 ....DLB-24

Henderson, Alice Corbin 1881-1949 ....DLB-54

Henderson, Archibald 1877-1963 ....DLB-103

Henderson, David 1942- DLB-41

Henderson, George Wylie 1904- DLB-51

Henderson, Zenna 1917- DLB-8

Henisch, Peter 1943- DLB-85

Henley, Beth 1952- Y-86

Henley, William Ernest 1849-1903 ....DLB-19

Henry, Alexander 1739-1824 ....DLB-99

Henry, Buck 1930- DLB-26

Henry, Marguerite 1902- DLB-22

Henry, Robert Selph 1889-1970 ....DLB-17

Henry, Will (see Allen, Henry W.)

Henschke, Alfred (see Klabund)

Hensley, Sophie Almon 1866-1946...........................DLB-99

Henty, G. A. 1832-1902 ....DLB-18

Hentz, Caroline Lee 1800-1856 ....DLB-3

Herbert, Alan Patrick 1890-1971 ....DLB-10

Herbert, Frank 1920-1986 ....DLB-8

Herbert, Henry William 1807-1858 ....DLB-3, 73

Herbert, John 1926- DLB-53

Herbst, Josephine 1892-1969 ....DLB-9

Herburger, Günter 1932- DLB-75

Hercules, Frank E. M. 1917- DLB-33

Herder, B., Book Company DLB-49

Herder, Johann Gottfried 1744-1803 ....DLB-97

Hergesheimer, Joseph 1880-1954 ....DLB-9, 102

Heritage Press DLB-46

Hermes, Johann Timotheus 1738-1821 ....DLB-97

Hermlin, Stephan 1915- DLB-69

Hernton, Calvin C. 1932- DLB-38

"The Hero as Man of Letters: Johnson,
Rousseau, Burns" (1841), by Thomas
Carlyle [excerpt]..DLB-57

The Hero as Poet. Dante; Shakspeare (1841),
by Thomas Carlyle...DLB-32

Herrick, E. R., and Company DLB-49

Herrick, Robert 1868-1938 ....DLB-9, 12, 78

Herrick, William 1915- Y-83

Herrmann, John 1900-1959 ....DLB-4

Hersey, John 1914- DLB-6

Hertel, François 1905-1985 ....DLB-68

Hervé Bazin, Jean Pierre Marie (see Bazin, Hervé)

Hervey, John, Lord 1696-1743 ....DLB-101

Herzog, Emile Salomon Wilhelm (see Maurois, André)

Hesse, Hermann 1877-1962 ....DLB-66

Hewat, Alexander circa 1743-circa 1824 ....DLB-30

Hewitt, John 1907- DLB-27

Hewlett, Maurice 1861-1923 ....DLB-34

Heyen, William 1940- DLB-5

Heyer, Georgette 1902-1974 ....DLB-77

Heym, Stefan 1913- DLB-69

Heyward, Dorothy 1890-1961 and
Heyward, DuBose 1885-1940 ....DLB-7

Heyward, DuBose 1885-1940 ....DLB-7, 9, 45

Heywood, Thomas 1573 or 1574-1641 ....DLB-62

Hickman, William Albert 1877-1957 ....DLB-92

Hidalgo, José Luis 1919-1947 ....DLB-108

Hiebert, Paul 1892-1987 ....DLB-68

Hierro, José 1922- DLB-108

Higgins, Aidan 1927- DLB-14

Higgins, Colin 1941-1988 ....DLB-26

Higgins, George V. 1939- DLB-2; Y-81

Higginson, Thomas Wentworth 1823-1911	DLB-1, 64
Highwater, Jamake 1942?-	DLB-52; Y-85
Hildesheimer, Wolfgang 1916-	DLB-69
Hildreth, Richard 1807-1865	DLB-1, 30, 59
Hill, Aaron 1685-1750	DLB-84
Hill, Geoffrey 1932-	DLB-40
Hill, George M., Company	DLB-49
Hill, "Sir" John 1714?-1775	DLB-39
Hill, Lawrence, and Company, Publishers	DLB-46
Hill, Leslie 1880-1960	DLB-51
Hill, Susan 1942-	DLB-14
Hill, Walter 1942-	DLB-44
Hill and Wang	DLB-46
Hilliard, Gray and Company	DLB-49
Hillyer, Robert 1895-1961	DLB-54
Hilton, James 1900-1954	DLB-34, 77
Hilton and Company	DLB-49
Himes, Chester 1909-1984	DLB-2, 76
Hine, Daryl 1936-	DLB-60
Hinojosa-Smith, Rolando 1929-	DLB-82
Hippel, Theodor Gottlieb von 1741-1796	DLB-97
The History of the Adventures of Joseph Andrews (1742), by Henry Fielding [excerpt]	DLB-39
Hirsch, E. D., Jr. 1928-	DLB-67
Hoagland, Edward 1932-	DLB-6
Hoagland, Everett H. III 1942-	DLB-41
Hoban, Russell 1925-	DLB-52
Hobsbaum, Philip 1932-	DLB-40
Hobson, Laura Z. 1900-	DLB-28
Hochman, Sandra 1936-	DLB-5
Hodder and Stoughton, Limited	DLB-106
Hodgins, Jack 1938-	DLB-60
Hodgman, Helen 1945-	DLB-14
Hodgson, Ralph 1871-1962	DLB-19
Hodgson, William Hope 1877-1918	DLB-70
Hoffenstein, Samuel 1890-1947	DLB-11
Hoffman, Charles Fenno 1806-1884	DLB-3
Hoffman, Daniel 1923-	DLB-5
Hoffmann, E. T. A. 1776-1822	DLB-90
Hofmann, Michael 1957-	DLB-40
Hofmannsthal, Hugo von 1874-1929	DLB-81
Hofstadter, Richard 1916-1970	DLB-17
Hogan, Desmond 1950-	DLB-14
Hogan and Thompson	DLB-49
Hogarth Press	DLB-112
Hogg, James 1770-1835	DLB-93
Hohl, Ludwig 1904-1980	DLB-56
Holbrook, David 1923-	DLB-14, 40
Holcroft, Thomas 1745-1809	DLB-39, 89
Holden, Jonathan 1941-	DLB-105
Holden, Jonathan, Contemporary Verse Story-telling	DLB-105
Holden, Molly 1927-1981	DLB-40
Hölderlin, Friedrich 1770-1843	DLB-90
Holiday House	DLB-46
Holland, Norman N. 1927-	DLB-67
Hollander, John 1929-	DLB-5
Holley, Marietta 1836-1926	DLB-11
Hollingsworth, Margaret 1940-	DLB-60
Hollo, Anselm 1934-	DLB-40
Holloway, Emory 1885-1977	DLB-103
Holloway, John 1920-	DLB-27
Holloway House Publishing Company	DLB-46
Holme, Constance 1880-1955	DLB-34
Holmes, Abraham S. 1821?-1908	DLB-99
Holmes, Oliver Wendell 1809-1894	DLB-1
Holmes, John Clellon 1926-1988	DLB-16
Holst, Hermann E. von 1841-1904	DLB-47
Holt, Henry, and Company	DLB-49
Holt, John 1721-1784	DLB-43
Holt, Rinehart and Winston	DLB-46
Holthusen, Hans Egon 1913-	DLB-69
Hölty, Ludwig Christoph Heinrich 1748-1776	DLB-94
Home, Henry, Lord Kames (see Kames, Henry Home, Lord)	
Home, John 1722-1808	DLB-84
Home Publishing Company	DLB-49
Home, William Douglas 1912-	DLB-13
Homes, Geoffrey (see Mainwaring, Daniel)	
Honan, Park 1928-	DLB-111
Hone, William 1780-1842	DLB-110
Honig, Edwin 1919-	DLB-5
Hood, Hugh 1928-	DLB-53
Hood, Thomas 1799-1845	DLB-96
Hooker, Jeremy 1941-	DLB-40
Hooker, Thomas 1586-1647	DLB-24
Hooper, Johnson Jones 1815-1862	DLB-3, 11

Hopkins, Gerard Manley 1844-1889	DLB-35, 57
Hopkins, John H., and Son	DLB-46
Hopkins, Lemuel 1750-1801	DLB-37
Hopkins, Pauline Elizabeth 1859-1930	DLB-50
Hopkins, Samuel 1721-1803	DLB-31
Hopkinson, Francis 1737-1791	DLB-31
Horgan, Paul 1903-	DLB-102; Y-85
Horizon Press	DLB-46
Horne, Frank 1899-1974	DLB-51
Horne, Richard Henry (Hengist) 1802 or 1803-1884	DLB-32
Hornung, E. W. 1866-1921	DLB-70
Horovitz, Israel 1939-	DLB-7
Horton, George Moses 1797?-1883?	DLB-50
Horváth, Ödön von 1901-1938	DLB-85
Horwood, Harold 1923-	DLB-60
Hosford, E. and E. [publishing house]	DLB-49
Hotchkiss and Company	DLB-49
Hough, Emerson 1857-1923	DLB-9
Houghton Mifflin Company	DLB-49
Houghton, Stanley 1881-1913	DLB-10
Household, Geoffrey 1900-1988	DLB-87
Housman, A. E. 1859-1936	DLB-19
Housman, Laurence 1865-1959	DLB-10
Houwald, Ernst von 1778-1845	DLB-90
Hovey, Richard 1864-1900	DLB-54
Howard, Donald R. 1927-1987	DLB-111
Howard, Maureen 1930-	Y-83
Howard, Richard 1929-	DLB-5
Howard, Roy W. 1883-1964	DLB-29
Howard, Sidney 1891-1939	DLB-7, 26
Howe, E. W. 1853-1937	DLB-12, 25
Howe, Henry 1816-1893	DLB-30
Howe, Irving 1920-	DLB-67
Howe, Joseph 1804-1873	DLB-99
Howe, Julia Ward 1819-1910	DLB-1
Howell, Clark, Sr. 1863-1936	DLB-25
Howell, Evan P. 1839-1905	DLB-23
Howell, Soskin and Company	DLB-46
Howells, William Dean 1837-1920	DLB-12, 64, 74, 79
Howitt, William 1792-1879 and Howitt, Mary 1799-1888	DLB-110
Hoyem, Andrew 1935-	DLB-5
de Hoyos, Angela 1940-	DLB-82
Hoyt, Henry [publishing house]	DLB-49
Hubbard, Elbert 1856-1915	DLB-91
Hubbard, Kin 1868-1930	DLB-11
Hubbard, William circa 1621-1704	DLB-24
Huber, Therese 1764-1829	DLB-90
Huch, Friedrich 1873-1913	DLB-66
Huch, Ricarda 1864-1947	DLB-66
Huck at 100: How Old Is *Huckleberry Finn*?	Y-85
Hudson, Henry Norman 1814-1886	DLB-64
Hudson, W. H. 1841-1922	DLB-98
Hudson and Goodwin	DLB-49
Huebsch, B. W. [publishing house]	DLB-46
Hughes, David 1930-	DLB-14
Hughes, John 1677-1720	DLB-84
Hughes, Langston 1902-1967	DLB-4, 7, 48, 51, 86
Hughes, Richard 1900-1976	DLB-15
Hughes, Ted 1930-	DLB-40
Hughes, Thomas 1822-1896	DLB-18
Hugo, Richard 1923-1982	DLB-5
Hugo Awards and Nebula Awards	DLB-8
Hull, Richard 1896-1973	DLB-77
Hulme, T. E. 1883-1917	DLB-19
Humboldt, Alexander von 1769-1859	DLB-90
Humboldt, Wilhelm von 1767-1835	DLB-90
Hume, David 1711-1776	DLB-104
Hume, Fergus 1859-1932	DLB-70
Humorous Book Illustration	DLB-11
Humphrey, William 1924-	DLB-6
Humphreys, David 1752-1818	DLB-37
Humphreys, Emyr 1919-	DLB-15
Huncke, Herbert 1915-	DLB-16
Huneker, James Gibbons 1857-1921	DLB-71
Hunt, Irene 1907-	DLB-52
Hunt, Leigh 1784-1859	DLB-96, 110
Hunt, William Gibbes 1791-1833	DLB-73
Hunter, Evan 1926-	Y-82
Hunter, Jim 1939-	DLB-14
Hunter, Kristin 1931-	DLB-33
Hunter, N. C. 1908-1971	DLB-10
Hunter-Duvar, John 1821-1899	DLB-99
Hurd and Houghton	DLB-49
Hurst, Fannie 1889-1968	DLB-86
Hurst and Blackett	DLB-106

Hurst and Company DLB-49

Hurston, Zora Neale 1901?-1960 ....DLB-51, 86

Huston, John 1906- DLB-26

Hutcheson, Francis 1694-1746 ....DLB-31

Hutchinson, Thomas 1711-1780 ....DLB-30, 31

Hutchinson and Company (Publishers) Limited
....DLB-112

Hutton, Richard Holt 1826-1897 ....DLB-57

Huxley, Aldous 1894-1963 ....DLB-36, 100

Huxley, Elspeth Josceline 1907- DLB-77

Huxley, T. H. 1825-1895 ....DLB-57

Huyghue, Douglas Smith 1816-1891 ....DLB-99

Hyman, Trina Schart 1939- DLB-61

I

The Iconography of Science-Fiction Art DLB-8

Iffland, August Wilhelm 1759-1814 ....DLB-94

Ignatow, David 1914- DLB-5

Iles, Francis (see Berkeley, Anthony)

Imbs, Bravig 1904-1946 ....DLB-4

Inchbald, Elizabeth 1753-1821 ....DLB-39, 89

Inge, William 1913-1973 ....DLB-7

Ingelow, Jean 1820-1897 ....DLB-35

The Ingersoll Prizes Y-84

Ingraham, Joseph Holt 1809-1860 ....DLB-3

Inman, John 1805-1850 ....DLB-73

Innerhofer, Franz 1944- DLB-85

Innis, Harold Adams 1894-1952 ....DLB-88

Innis, Mary Quayle 1899-1972 ....DLB-88

International Publishers Company DLB-46

An Interview with Peter S. Prescott Y-86

An Interview with Tom Jenks Y-86

An Interview with Russell Hoban Y-90

Introduction to Paul Laurence Dunbar,
Lyrics of Lowly Life (1896),
by William Dean Howells DLB-50

Introductory Essay: *Letters of Percy Bysshe
Shelley* (1852), by Robert Browning DLB-32

Introductory Letters from the Second Edition
of *Pamela* (1741), by Samuel Richardson DLB-39

Irving, John 1942- DLB-6; Y-82

Irving, Washington
1783-1859 ....DLB-3, 11, 30, 59, 73, 74

Irwin, Grace 1907- DLB-68

Irwin, Will 1873-1948 ....DLB-25

Isherwood, Christopher 1904-1986 ....DLB-15; Y-86

The Island Trees Case: A Symposium on School
Library Censorship
An Interview with Judith Krug
An Interview with Phyllis Schlafly
An Interview with Edward B. Jenkinson
An Interview with Lamarr Mooneyham
An Interview with Harriet Bernstein Y-82

Ivers, M. J., and Company DLB-49

J

Jackmon, Marvin E. (see Marvin X)

Jackson, Angela 1951- DLB-41

Jackson, Helen Hunt 1830-1885 ....DLB-42, 47

Jackson, Holbrook 1874-1948 ....DLB-98

Jackson, Laura Riding 1901- DLB-48

Jackson, Shirley 1919-1965 ....DLB-6

Jacob, Piers Anthony Dillingham (see Anthony, Piers)

Jacobi, Friedrich Heinrich 1743-1819 ....DLB-94

Jacobi, Johann Georg 1740-1841 ....DLB-97

Jacobs, George W., and Company DLB-49

Jacobson, Dan 1929- DLB-14

Jahnn, Hans Henny 1894-1959 ....DLB-56

Jakes, John 1932- Y-83

James, Henry 1843-1916 ....DLB-12, 71, 74

James, John circa 1633-1729 ....DLB-24

James Joyce Centenary: Dublin, 1982 ....Y-82

James Joyce Conference Y-85

James, P. D. 1920- DLB-87

James, U. P. [publishing house] DLB-49

Jameson, Anna 1794-1860 ....DLB-99

Jameson, Fredric 1934- DLB-67

Jameson, J. Franklin 1859-1937 ....DLB-17

Jameson, Storm 1891-1986 ....DLB-36

Jarrell, Randall 1914-1965 ....DLB-48, 52

Jarrold and Sons DLB-106

Jasmin, Claude 1930- DLB-60

Jay, John 1745-1829 ....DLB-31

Jefferies, Richard 1848-1887 ....DLB-98

Jeffers, Lance 1919-1985 ....DLB-41

Jeffers, Robinson 1887-1962 ....DLB-45

Jefferson, Thomas 1743-1826 ....DLB-31

Jelinek, Elfriede 1946- DLB-85

Jellicoe, Ann 1927-	DLB-13
Jenkins, Robin 1912-	DLB-14
Jenkins, William Fitzgerald (see Leinster, Murray)	
Jenkins, Herbert, Limited	DLB-112
Jennings, Elizabeth 1926-	DLB-27
Jens, Walter 1923-	DLB-69
Jensen, Merrill 1905-1980	DLB-17
Jephson, Robert 1736-1803	DLB-89
Jerome, Jerome K. 1859-1927	DLB-10, 34
Jerome, Judson 1927-	DLB-105
Jerome, Judson, Reflections: After a Tornado	DLB-105
Jesse, F. Tennyson 1888-1958	DLB-77
Jewett, John P., and Company	DLB-49
Jewett, Sarah Orne 1849-1909	DLB-12, 74
The Jewish Publication Society	DLB-49
Jewitt, John Rodgers 1783-1821	DLB-99
Jewsbury, Geraldine 1812-1880	DLB-21
Joans, Ted 1928-	DLB-16, 41
John Edward Bruce: Three Documents	DLB-50
John O'Hara's Pottsville Journalism	Y-88
John Steinbeck Research Center	Y-85
John Webster: The Melbourne Manuscript	Y-86
Johnson, B. S. 1933-1973	DLB-14, 40
Johnson, Benjamin [publishing house]	DLB-49
Johnson, Benjamin, Jacob, and Robert [publishing house]	DLB-49
Johnson, Charles 1679-1748	DLB-84
Johnson, Charles R. 1948-	DLB-33
Johnson, Charles S. 1893-1956	DLB-51, 91
Johnson, Diane 1934-	Y-80
Johnson, Edgar 1901-	DLB-103
Johnson, Edward 1598-1672	DLB-24
Johnson, Fenton 1888-1958	DLB-45, 50
Johnson, Georgia Douglas 1886-1966	DLB-51
Johnson, Gerald W. 1890-1980	DLB-29
Johnson, Helene 1907-	DLB-51
Johnson, Jacob, and Company	DLB-49
Johnson, James Weldon 1871-1938	DLB-51
Johnson, Lionel 1867-1902	DLB-19
Johnson, Nunnally 1897-1977	DLB-26
Johnson, Owen 1878-1952	Y-87
Johnson, Pamela Hansford 1912-	DLB-15
Johnson, Pauline 1861-1913	DLB-92
Johnson, Samuel 1696-1772	DLB-24
Johnson, Samuel 1709-1784	DLB-39, 95, 104
Johnson, Samuel 1822-1882	DLB-1
Johnson, Uwe 1934-1984	DLB-75
Johnston, Annie Fellows 1863-1931	DLB-42
Johnston, Basil H. 1929-	DLB-60
Johnston, Denis 1901-1984	DLB-10
Johnston, George 1913-	DLB-88
Johnston, Jennifer 1930-	DLB-14
Johnston, Mary 1870-1936	DLB-9
Johnston, Richard Malcolm 1822-1898	DLB-74
Johnstone, Charles 1719?-1800?	DLB-39
Jolas, Eugene 1894-1952	DLB-4, 45
Jones, Alice C. 1853-1933	DLB-92
Jones, Charles C., Jr. 1831-1893	DLB-30
Jones, D. G. 1929-	DLB-53
Jones, David 1895-1974	DLB-20, 100
Jones, Ebenezer 1820-1860	DLB-32
Jones, Ernest 1819-1868	DLB-32
Jones, Gayl 1949-	DLB-33
Jones, Glyn 1905-	DLB-15
Jones, Gwyn 1907-	DLB-15
Jones, Henry Arthur 1851-1929	DLB-10
Jones, Hugh circa 1692-1760	DLB-24
Jones, James 1921-1977	DLB-2
Jones, LeRoi (see Baraka, Amiri)	
Jones, Lewis 1897-1939	DLB-15
Jones, Major Joseph (see Thompson, William Tappan)	
Jones, Preston 1936-1979	DLB-7
Jones, Sir William 1746-1794	DLB-109
Jones, William Alfred 1817-1900	DLB-59
Jones's Publishing House	DLB-49
Jong, Erica 1942-	DLB-2, 5, 28
Jonke, Gert F. 1946-	DLB-85
Jonson, Ben 1572?-1637	DLB-62
Jordan, June 1936-	DLB-38
Joseph, Jenny 1932-	DLB-40
Joseph, Michael, Limited	DLB-112
Josephson, Matthew 1899-1978	DLB-4
Josiah Allen's Wife (see Holley, Marietta)	
Josipovici, Gabriel 1940-	DLB-14
Josselyn, John ?-1675	DLB-24
Joudry, Patricia 1921-	DLB-88

Joyaux, Philippe (see Sollers, Philippe)

Joyce, Adrien (see Eastman, Carol)

Joyce, James 1882-1941 ....DLB-10, 19, 36

Judd, Orange, Publishing Company DLB-49

Judd, Sylvester 1813-1853 ....DLB-1

June, Jennie (see Croly, Jane Cunningham)

Jünger, Ernst 1895- DLB-56

Jung-Stilling, Johann Heinrich
    1740-1817 ....DLB-94

Justice, Donald 1925- Y-83

K

Kacew, Romain (see Gary, Romain)

Kafka, Franz 1883-1924 ....DLB-81

Kalechofsky, Roberta 1931- DLB-28

Kaler, James Otis 1848-1912 ....DLB-12

Kames, Henry Home, Lord 1696-1782 ....DLB-31, 104

Kandel, Lenore 1932- DLB-16

Kanin, Garson 1912- DLB-7

Kant, Hermann 1926- DLB-75

Kant, Immanuel 1724-1804 ....DLB-94

Kantor, Mackinlay 1904-1977 ....DLB-9, 102

Kaplan, Fred 1937- DLB-111

Kaplan, Johanna 1942- DLB-28

Kaplan, Justin 1925- DLB-111

Karsch, Anna Louisa 1722-1791 ....DLB-97

Kasack, Hermann 1896-1966 ....DLB-69

Kaschnitz, Marie Luise 1901-1974 ....DLB-69

Kästner, Erich 1899-1974 ....DLB-56

Kattan, Naim 1928- DLB-53

Katz, Steve 1935- Y-83

Kauffman, Janet 1945- Y-86

Kaufman, Bob 1925- DLB-16, 41

Kaufman, George S. 1889-1961 ....DLB-7

Kavanagh, Patrick 1904-1967 ....DLB-15, 20

Kavanagh, P. J. 1931- DLB-40

Kaye-Smith, Sheila 1887-1956 ....DLB-36

Kazin, Alfred 1915- DLB-67

Keane, John B. 1928- DLB-13

Keating, H. R. F. 1926- DLB-87

Keats, Ezra Jack 1916-1983 ....DLB-61

Keats, John 1795-1821 ....DLB-96, 110

Keble, John 1792-1866 ....DLB-32, 55

Keeble, John 1944- Y-83

Keeffe, Barrie 1945- DLB-13

Keeley, James 1867-1934 ....DLB-25

W. B. Keen, Cooke and Company DLB-49

Keillor, Garrison 1942- Y-87

Keith, Marian 1874?-1961 ....DLB-92

Keller, Gary D. 1943- DLB-82

Kelley, Edith Summers 1884-1956 ....DLB-9

Kelley, William Melvin 1937- DLB-33

Kellogg, Ansel Nash 1832-1886 ....DLB-23

Kellogg, Steven 1941- DLB-61

Kelly, George 1887-1974 ....DLB-7

Kelly, Hugh 1739-1777 ....DLB-89

Kelly, Piet and Company DLB-49

Kelly, Robert 1935- DLB-5

Kelmscott Press DLB-112

Kemble, Fanny 1809-1893 ....DLB-32

Kemelman, Harry 1908- DLB-28

Kempowski, Walter 1929- DLB-75

Kendall, Claude [publishing company] DLB-46

Kendell, George 1809-1867 ....DLB-43

Kenedy, P. J., and Sons DLB-49

Kennedy, Adrienne 1931- DLB-38

Kennedy, John Pendleton 1795-1870 ....DLB-3

Kennedy, Leo 1907- DLB-88

Kennedy, Margaret 1896-1967 ....DLB-36

Kennedy, Richard S. 1920- DLB-111

Kennedy, William 1928- Y-85

Kennedy, X. J. 1929- DLB-5

Kennelly, Brendan 1936- DLB-40

Kenner, Hugh 1923- DLB-67

Kennerley, Mitchell [publishing house] DLB-46

Kent, Frank R. 1877-1958 ....DLB-29

Keppler and Schwartzmann DLB-49

Kerner, Justinus 1776-1862 ....DLB-90

Kerouac, Jack 1922-1969 ....DLB-2, 16; DS-3

Kerouac, Jan 1952- DLB-16

Kerr, Charles H., and Company DLB-49

Kerr, Orpheus C. (see Newell, Robert Henry)

Kesey, Ken 1935- DLB-2, 16

Kessel, Joseph 1898-1979 ....DLB-72

Kessel, Martin 1901- DLB-56

Kesten, Hermann 1900- DLB-56

Keun, Irmgard 1905-1982	DLB-69
Key and Biddle	DLB-49
Keyserling, Eduard von 1855-1918	DLB-66
Kidd, Adam 1802?-1831	DLB-99
Kidd, William [publishing house]	DLB-106
Kiely, Benedict 1919-	DLB-15
Kiggins and Kellogg	DLB-49
Kiley, Jed 1889-1962	DLB-4
Killens, John Oliver 1916-	DLB-33
Killigrew, Thomas 1612-1683	DLB-58
Kilmer, Joyce 1886-1918	DLB-45
King, Clarence 1842-1901	DLB-12
King, Florence 1936-	Y-85
King, Francis 1923-	DLB-15
King, Grace 1852-1932	DLB-12, 78
King, Solomon [publishing house]	DLB-49
King, Stephen 1947-	Y-80
King, Woodie, Jr. 1937-	DLB-38
Kinglake, Alexander William 1809-1891	DLB-55
Kingsley, Charles 1819-1875	DLB-21, 32
Kingsley, Henry 1830-1876	DLB-21
Kingsley, Sidney 1906-	DLB-7
Kingston, Maxine Hong 1940-	Y-80
Kinnell, Galway 1927-	DLB-5; Y-87
Kinsella, Thomas 1928-	DLB-27
Kipling, Rudyard 1865-1936	DLB-19, 34
Kirby, William 1817-1906	DLB-99
Kirk, John Foster 1824-1904	DLB-79
Kirkconnell, Watson 1895-1977	DLB-68
Kirkland, Caroline M. 1801-1864	DLB-3, 73, 74
Kirkland, Joseph 1830-1893	DLB-12
Kirkup, James 1918-	DLB-27
Kirouac, Conrad (see Marie-Victorin, Frère)	
Kirsch, Sarah 1935-	DLB-75
Kirst, Hans Hellmut 1914-1989	DLB-69
Kitchin, C. H. B. 1895-1967	DLB-77
Kizer, Carolyn 1925-	DLB-5
Klabund 1890-1928	DLB-66
Klappert, Peter 1942-	DLB-5
Klass, Philip (see Tenn, William)	
Klein, A. M. 1909-1972	DLB-68
Kleist, Ewald von 1715-1759	DLB-97
Kleist, Heinrich von 1777-1811	DLB-90
Klinger, Friedrich Maximilian 1752-1831	DLB-94
Klopstock, Friedrich Gottlieb 1724-1803	DLB-97
Klopstock, Meta 1728-1758	DLB-97
Kluge, Alexander 1932-	DLB-75
Knapp, Joseph Palmer 1864-1951	DLB-91
Knapp, Samuel Lorenzo 1783-1838	DLB-59
Knickerbocker, Diedrich (see Irving, Washington)	
Knigge, Adolph Franz Friedrich Ludwig, Freiherr von 1752-1796	DLB-94
Knight, Damon 1922-	DLB-8
Knight, Etheridge 1931-	DLB-41
Knight, John S. 1894-1981	DLB-29
Knight, Sarah Kemble 1666-1727	DLB-24
Knight, Charles, and Company	DLB-106
Knister, Raymond 1899-1932	DLB-68
Knoblock, Edward 1874-1945	DLB-10
Knopf, Alfred A. 1892-1984	Y-84
Knopf, Alfred A. [publishing house]	DLB-46
Knowles, John 1926-	DLB-6
Knox, Frank 1874-1944	DLB-29
Knox, John Armoy 1850-1906	DLB-23
Knox, Ronald Arbuthnott 1888-1957	DLB-77
Kober, Arthur 1900-1975	DLB-11
Koch, Howard 1902-	DLB-26
Koch, Kenneth 1925-	DLB-5
Koenigsberg, Moses 1879-1945	DLB-25
Koeppen, Wolfgang 1906-	DLB-69
Koertge, Ronald 1940-	DLB-105
Koestler, Arthur 1905-1983	Y-83
Kolb, Annette 1870-1967	DLB-66
Kolbenheyer, Erwin Guido 1878-1962	DLB-66
Kolleritsch, Alfred 1931-	DLB-85
Kolodny, Annette 1941-	DLB-67
Komroff, Manuel 1890-1974	DLB-4
Konigsburg, E. L. 1930-	DLB-52
Kooser, Ted 1939-	DLB-105
Kopit, Arthur 1937-	DLB-7
Kops, Bernard 1926?-	DLB-13
Kornbluth, C. M. 1923-1958	DLB-8
Körner, Theodor 1791-1813	DLB-90
Kosinski, Jerzy 1933-	DLB-2; Y-82
Kotzebue, August von 1761-1819	DLB-94
Kraf, Elaine 1946-	Y-81

Krasna, Norman 1909-1984 ....DLB-26
Krauss, Ruth 1911- DLB-52
Kreisel, Henry 1922- DLB-88
Kreuder, Ernst 1903-1972 ....DLB-69
Kreymborg, Alfred 1883-1966 ....DLB-4, 54
Krieger, Murray 1923- DLB-67
Krim, Seymour 1922-1989 ....DLB-16
Krock, Arthur 1886-1974 ....DLB-29
Kroetsch, Robert 1927- DLB-53
Krutch, Joseph Wood 1893-1970 ....DLB-63
Kubin, Alfred 1877-1959 ....DLB-81
Kubrick, Stanley 1928- DLB-26
Kumin, Maxine 1925- DLB-5
Kunnert, Günter 1929- DLB-75
Kunitz, Stanley 1905- DLB-48
Kunjufu, Johari M. (see Amini, Johari M.)
Kunze, Reiner 1933- DLB-75
Kupferberg, Tuli 1923- DLB-16
Kurz, Isolde 1853-1944 ....DLB-66
Kusenberg, Kurt 1904-1983 ....DLB-69
Kuttner, Henry 1915-1958 ....DLB-8
Kyd, Thomas 1558-1594 ....DLB-62
Kyger, Joanne 1934- DLB-16
Kyne, Peter B. 1880-1957 ....DLB-78

L

L. E. L. (see Landon, Letitia Elizabeth)
Laberge, Albert 1871-1960 ....DLB-68
Laberge, Marie 1950- DLB-60
Lacombe, Patrice (see Trullier-Lacombe, Joseph Patrice)
Lacretelle, Jacques de 1888-1985 ....DLB-65
Ladd, Joseph Brown 1764-1786 ....DLB-37
La Farge, Oliver 1901-1963 ....DLB-9
Lafferty, R. A. 1914- DLB-8
Lahaise, Guillaume (see Delahaye, Guy)
Lahontan, Louis-Armand de Lom d'Arce, Baron de 1666-1715? DLB-99
Laird, Caroberth 1895- Y-82
Laird and Lee DLB-49
Lalonde, Michèle 1937- DLB-60
Lamantia, Philip 1927- DLB-16

Lamb, Charles 1775-1834 ....DLB-93, 107
Lambert, Betty 1933-1983 ....DLB-60
L'Amour, Louis 1908?- Y-80
Lampman, Archibald 1861-1899 ....DLB-92
Lamson, Wolffe and Company DLB-49
Lancer Books DLB-46
Landesman, Jay 1919- and
    Landesman, Fran 1927- DLB-16
Landon, Letitia Elizabeth 1802-1838 ....DLB-96
Landor, William Savage 1775-1864 ....DLB-93, 107
Landry, Napoléon-P. 1884-1956 ....DLB-92
Lane, Charles 1800-1870 ....DLB-1
The John Lane Company DLB-49
Lane, Laurence W. 1890-1967 ....DLB-91
Lane, M. Travis 1934- DLB-60
Lane, Patrick 1939- DLB-53
Lane, Pinkie Gordon 1923- DLB-41
Laney, Al 1896- DLB-4
Lang, Andrew 1844-1912 ....DLB-98
Langevin, André 1927- DLB-60
Langgässer, Elisabeth 1899-1950 ....DLB-69
Langhorne, John 1735-1779 ....DLB-109
Langton, Anna 1804-1893 ....DLB-99
Lanham, Edwin 1904-1979 ....DLB-4
Lanier, Sidney 1842-1881 ....DLB-64
Lapointe, Gatien 1931-1983 ....DLB-88
Lapointe, Paul-Marie 1929- DLB-88
Lardner, Ring 1885-1933 ....DLB-11, 25, 86
Lardner, Ring, Jr. 1915- DLB-26
Lardner 100: Ring Lardner
    Centennial Symposium Y-85
Larkin, Philip 1922-1985 ....DLB-27
La Roche, Sophie von 1730-1807 ....DLB-94
La Rocque, Gilbert 1943-1984 ....DLB-60
Laroque de Roquebrune, Robert
    (see Roquebrune, Robert de)
Larrick, Nancy 1910- DLB-61
Larsen, Nella 1893-1964 ....DLB-51
Lasker-Schüler, Else 1869-1945 ....DLB-66
Lasnier, Rina 1915- DLB-88
Lathrop, Dorothy P. 1891-1980 ....DLB-22
Lathrop, George Parsons 1851-1898 ....DLB-71
Lathrop, John, Jr. 1772-1820 ....DLB-37
Latimore, Jewel Christine McLawler (see Amini, Johari M.)

Laughlin, James 1914-	DLB-48
Laumer, Keith 1925-	DLB-8
Laurence, Margaret 1926-1987	DLB-53
Laurents, Arthur 1918-	DLB-26
Laurie, Annie (see Black, Winifred)	
Laut, Agnes Christiana 1871-1936	DLB-92
Lavater, Johann Kaspar 1741-1801	DLB-97
Lavin, Mary 1912-	DLB-15
Lawless, Anthony (see MacDonald, Philip)	
Lawrence, David 1888-1973	DLB-29
Lawrence, D. H. 1885-1930	DLB-10, 19, 36, 98
Lawson, John ?-1711	DLB-24
Lawson, Robert 1892-1957	DLB-22
Lawson, Victor F. 1850-1925	DLB-25
Layton, Irving 1912-	DLB-88
Lea, Henry Charles 1825-1909	DLB-47
Lea, Tom 1907-	DLB-6
Leacock, John 1729-1802	DLB-31
Leacock, Stephen 1869-1944	DLB-92
Leadenhall Press	DLB-106
Leapor, Mary 1722-1746	DLB-109
Lear, Edward 1812-1888	DLB-32
Leary, Timothy 1920-	DLB-16
Leary, W. A., and Company	DLB-49
Léautaud, Paul 1872-1956	DLB-65
Leavitt and Allen	DLB-49
le Carré, John 1931-	DLB-87
Lécavelé, Roland (see Dorgelès, Roland)	
Lechlitner, Ruth 1901-	DLB-48
Leclerc, Félix 1914-	DLB-60
Le Clézio, J. M. G. 1940-	DLB-83
Lectures on Rhetoric and Belles Lettres (1783), by Hugh Blair [excerpts]	DLB-31
Leder, Rudolf (see Hermlin, Stephan)	
Lederer, Charles 1910-1976	DLB-26
Ledwidge, Francis 1887-1917	DLB-20
Lee, Dennis 1939-	DLB-53
Lee, Don L. (see Madhubuti, Haki R.)	
Lee, George W. 1894-1976	DLB-51
Lee, Harper 1926-	DLB-6
Lee, Harriet (1757-1851) and Lee, Sophia (1750-1824)	DLB-39
Lee, Laurie 1914-	DLB-27
Lee, Nathaniel circa 1645 - 1692	DLB-80
Lee, Vernon 1856-1935	DLB-57
Lee and Shepard	DLB-49
Le Fanu, Joseph Sheridan 1814-1873	DLB-21, 70
Leffland, Ella 1931-	Y-84
le Fort, Gertrud von 1876-1971	DLB-66
Le Gallienne, Richard 1866-1947	DLB-4
Legaré, Hugh Swinton 1797-1843	DLB-3, 59, 73
Legaré, James M. 1823-1859	DLB-3
Léger, Antoine-J. 1880-1950	DLB-88
Le Guin, Ursula K. 1929-	DLB-8, 52
Lehman, Ernest 1920-	DLB-44
Lehmann, John 1907-	DLB-27, 100
Lehmann, John, Limited	DLB-112
Lehmann, Rosamond 1901-1990	DLB-15
Lehmann, Wilhelm 1882-1968	DLB-56
Leiber, Fritz 1910-	DLB-8
Leicester University Press	DLB-112
Leinster, Murray 1896-1975	DLB-8
Leisewitz, Johann Anton 1752-1806	DLB-94
Leitch, Maurice 1933-	DLB-14
Leland, Charles G. 1824-1903	DLB-11
Lemay, Pamphile 1837-1918	DLB-99
Lemelin, Roger 1919-	DLB-88
Le Moine, James MacPherson 1825-1912	DLB-99
Le Moyne, Jean 1913-	DLB-88
L'Engle, Madeleine 1918-	DLB-52
Lennart, Isobel 1915-1971	DLB-44
Lennox, Charlotte 1729 or 1730-1804	DLB-39
Lenski, Lois 1893-1974	DLB-22
Lenz, Hermann 1913-	DLB-69
Lenz, J. M. R. 1751-1792	DLB-94
Lenz, Siegfried 1926-	DLB-75
Leonard, Hugh 1926-	DLB-13
Leonard, William Ellery 1876-1944	DLB-54
Leonowens, Anna 1834-1914	DLB-99
LePan, Douglas 1914-	DLB-88
Leprohon, Rosanna Eleanor 1829-1879	DLB-99
Le Queux, William 1864-1927	DLB-70
Lerner, Max 1902-	DLB-29
Lernet-Holenia, Alexander 1897-1976	DLB-85
Le Rossignol, James 1866-1969	DLB-92
Lescarbot, Marc circa 1570-1642	DLB-99

LeSieg, Theo. (see Geisel, Theodor Seuss)	
Leslie, Frank 1821-1880	DLB-43, 79
The Frank Leslie Publishing House	DLB-49
Lesperance, John 1835?-1891	DLB-99
Lessing, Bruno 1870-1940	DLB-28
Lessing, Doris 1919-	DLB-15; Y-85
Lessing, Gotthold Ephraim 1729-1781	DLB-97
LeSeur, William Dawson 1840-1917	DLB-92
Lettau, Reinhard 1929-	DLB-75
Letter to [Samuel] Richardson on *Clarissa* (1748), by Henry Fielding	DLB-39
Lever, Charles 1806-1872	DLB-21
Levertov, Denise 1923-	DLB-5
Levi, Peter 1931-	DLB-40
Levien, Sonya 1888-1960	DLB-44
Levin, Meyer 1905-1981	DLB-9, 28; Y-81
Levine, Norman 1923-	DLB-88
Levine, Philip 1928-	DLB-5
Levy, Benn Wolfe 1900-1973	DLB-13; Y-81
Lewes, George Henry 1817-1878	DLB-55
Lewis, Alfred H. 1857-1914	DLB-25
Lewis, Alun 1915-1944	DLB-20
Lewis, C. Day (see Day Lewis, C.)	
Lewis, Charles B. 1842-1924	DLB-11
Lewis, C. S. 1898-1963	DLB-15, 100
Lewis, Henry Clay 1825-1850	DLB-3
Lewis, Janet 1899-	Y-87
Lewis, Matthew Gregory 1775-1818	DLB-39
Lewis, R. W. B. 1917-	DLB-111
Lewis, Richard circa 1700-1734	DLB-24
Lewis, Sinclair 1885-1951	DLB-9, 102; DS-1
Lewis, Wyndham 1882-1957	DLB-15
Lewisohn, Ludwig 1882-1955	DLB-4, 9, 28, 102
Lezama Lima, José 1910-1976	DLB-113
The Library of America	DLB-46
The Licensing Act of 1737	DLB-84
Lichtenberg, Georg Christoph 1742-1799	DLB-94
Liebling, A. J. 1904-1963	DLB-4
Lieutenant Murray (see Ballou, Maturin Murray)	
Lighthall, William Douw 1857-1954	DLB-92
Lilar, Françoise (see Mallet-Joris, Françoise)	
Lillo, George 1691-1739	DLB-84
Lilly, Wait and Company	DLB-49
Limited Editions Club	DLB-46
Lincoln and Edmands	DLB-49
Lindsay, Jack 1900-	Y-84
Lindsay, Vachel 1879-1931	DLB-54
Linebarger, Paul Myron Anthony (see Smith, Cordwainer)	
Link, Arthur S. 1920-	DLB-17
Linn, John Blair 1777-1804	DLB-37
Linton, Eliza Lynn 1822-1898	DLB-18
Linton, William James 1812-1897	DLB-32
Lion Books	DLB-46
Lionni, Leo 1910-	DLB-61
Lippincott, J. B., Company	DLB-49
Lippincott, Sara Jane Clarke 1823-1904	DLB-43
Lippmann, Walter 1889-1974	DLB-29
Lipton, Lawrence 1898-1975	DLB-16
Liscow, Christian Ludwig 1701-1760	DLB-97
Lispector, Clarice 1925-1977	DLB-113
The Literary Chronicle and Weekly Review 1819-1828	DLB-110
Literary Documents: William Faulkner and the People-to-People Program	Y-86
Literary Documents II: *Library Journal*– Statements and Questionnaires from First Novelists	Y-87
Literary Effects of World War II [British novel]	DLB-15
Literary Prizes [British]	DLB-15
Literary Research Archives: The Humanities Research Center, University of Texas	Y-82
Literary Research Archives II: Berg Collection of English and American Literature of the New York Public Library	Y-83
Literary Research Archives III: The Lilly Library	Y-84
Literary Research Archives IV: The John Carter Brown Library	Y-85
Literary Research Archives V: Kent State Special Collections	Y-86
Literary Research Archives VI: The Modern Literary Manuscripts Collection in the Special Collections of the Washington University Libraries	Y-87
"Literary Style" (1857), by William Forsyth [excerpt]	DLB-57
Literatura Chicanesca: The View From Without	DLB-82
Literature at Nurse, or Circulating Morals (1885), by George Moore	DLB-18

Littell, Eliakim 1797-1870	DLB-79
Littell, Robert S. 1831-1896	DLB-79
Little, Brown and Company	DLB-49
Littlewood, Joan 1914-	DLB-13
Lively, Penelope 1933-	DLB-14
Liverpool University Press	DLB-112
Livesay, Dorothy 1909-	DLB-68
Livesay, Florence Randal 1874-1953	DLB-92
Livings, Henry 1929-	DLB-13
Livingston, Anne Howe 1763-1841	DLB-37
Livingston, Myra Cohn 1926-	DLB-61
Livingston, William 1723-1790	DLB-31
Lizárraga, Sylvia S. 1925-	DLB-82
Llewellyn, Richard 1906-1983	DLB-15
Lloyd, Edward [publishing house]	DLB-106
Lobel, Arnold 1933-	DLB-61
Lochridge, Betsy Hopkins (see Fancher, Betsy)	
Locke, David Ross 1833-1888	DLB-11, 23
Locke, John 1632-1704	DLB-31, 101
Locke, Richard Adams 1800-1871	DLB-43
Locker-Lampson, Frederick 1821-1895	DLB-35
Lockhart, John Gibson 1794-1854	DLB-110
Lockridge, Ross, Jr. 1914-1948	Y-80
Locrine and *Selimus*	DLB-62
Lodge, David 1935-	DLB-14
Lodge, George Cabot 1873-1909	DLB-54
Lodge, Henry Cabot 1850-1924	DLB-47
Loeb, Harold 1891-1974	DLB-4
Logan, James 1674-1751	DLB-24
Logan, John 1923-	DLB-5
Logue, Christopher 1926-	DLB-27
London, Jack 1876-1916	DLB-8, 12, 78
The London Magazine 1820-1829	DLB-110
Long, H., and Brother	DLB-49
Long, Haniel 1888-1956	DLB-45
Longfellow, Henry Wadsworth 1807-1882	DLB-1, 59
Longfellow, Samuel 1819-1892	DLB-1
Longley, Michael 1939-	DLB-40
Longmans, Green and Company	DLB-49
Longmore, George 1793?-1867	DLB-99
Longstreet, Augustus Baldwin 1790-1870	DLB-3, 11, 74
Longworth, D. [publishing house]	DLB-49
Lonsdale, Frederick 1881-1954	DLB-10
A Look at the Contemporary Black Theatre Movement	DLB-38
Loos, Anita 1893-1981	DLB-11, 26; Y-81
Lopate, Phillip 1943-	Y-80
López, Diana (see Isabella, Ríos)	
Loranger, Jean-Aubert 1896-1942	DLB-92
Lorca, Federico García 1898-1936	DLB-108
The Lord Chamberlain's Office and Stage Censorship in England	DLB-10
Lord, John Keast 1818-1872	DLB-99
Lorde, Audre 1934-	DLB-41
Lorimer, George Horace 1867-1939	DLB-91
Loring, A. K. [publishing house]	DLB-49
Loring and Mussey	DLB-46
Lossing, Benson J. 1813-1891	DLB-30
Lothar, Ernst 1890-1974	DLB-81
Lothrop, D., and Company	DLB-49
Lothrop, Harriet M. 1844-1924	DLB-42
The Lounger, no. 20 (1785), by Henry Mackenzie	DLB-39
Lounsbury, Thomas R. 1838-1915	DLB-71
Lovell, John W., Company	DLB-49
Lovell, Coryell and Company	DLB-49
Lovesey, Peter 1936-	DLB-87
Lovingood, Sut (see Harris, George Washington)	
Low, Samuel 1765-?	DLB-37
Lowell, Amy 1874-1925	DLB-54
Lowell, James Russell 1819-1891	DLB-1, 11, 64, 79
Lowell, Robert 1917-1977	DLB-5
Lowenfels, Walter 1897-1976	DLB-4
Lowndes, Marie Belloc 1868-1947	DLB-70
Lowry, Lois 1937-	DLB-52
Lowry, Malcolm 1909-1957	DLB-15
Lowther, Pat 1935-1975	DLB-53
Loy, Mina 1882-1966	DLB-4, 54
Lozeau, Albert 1878-1924	DLB-92
Lucas, E. V. 1868-1938	DLB-98
Lucas, Fielding, Jr. [publishing house]	DLB-49
Luce, Henry R. 1898-1967	DLB-91
Luce, John W., and Company	DLB-46
Lucie-Smith, Edward 1933-	DLB-40
Ludlum, Robert 1927-	Y-82
Ludwig, Jack 1922-	DLB-60
Luke, Peter 1919-	DLB-13

The F. M. Lupton Publishing Company.........................DLB-49

Lurie, Alison 1926- DLB-2

Lyall, Gavin 1932- DLB-87

Lyly, John circa 1554-1606..............................DLB-62

Lynd, Robert 1879-1949..................................DLB-98

Lyon, Matthew 1749-1822.................................DLB-43

Lytle, Andrew 1902- DLB-6

Lytton, Edward (see Bulwer-Lytton, Edward)

Lytton, Edward Robert Bulwer 1831-1891..................DLB-32

M

Maass, Joachim 1901-1972 ....DLB-69

Mabie, Hamilton Wright 1845-1916........................DLB-71

Mac A'Ghobhainn, Iain (see Smith, Iain Crichton)

MacArthur, Charles 1895-1956 ....DLB-7, 25, 44

Macaulay, Catherine 1731-1791 ....DLB-104

Macaulay, David 1945- DLB-61

Macaulay, Rose 1881-1958 ....DLB-36

Macaulay, Thomas Babington 1800-1859................DLB-32, 55

Macaulay Company..DLB-46

MacBeth, George 1932- DLB-40

Macbeth, Madge 1880-1965 ....DLB-92

MacCaig, Norman 1910- DLB-27

MacDiarmid, Hugh 1892-1978..............................DLB-20

MacDonald, Cynthia 1928- DLB-105

MacDonald, George 1824-1905.............................DLB-18

MacDonald, John D. 1916-1986......................DLB-8; Y-86

MacDonald, Philip 1899?-1980 ....DLB-77

Macdonald, Ross (see Millar, Kenneth)

MacDonald, Wilson 1880-1967 ....DLB-92

Macdonald and Company (Publishers) DLB-112

MacEwen, Gwendolyn 1941- DLB-53

Macfadden, Bernarr 1868-1955......................DLB-25, 91

MacGregor, Mary Esther (see Keith, Marian)

Machado, Antonio 1875-1939.............................DLB-108

Machado, Manuel 1874-1947..............................DLB-108

Machar, Agnes Maule 1837-1927 ....DLB-92

Machen, Arthur Llewelyn Jones 1863-1947 ....DLB-36

MacInnes, Colin 1914-1976...............................DLB-14

MacInnes, Helen 1907-1985...............................DLB-87

Mack, Maynard 1909- DLB-111

MacKaye, Percy 1875-1956................................DLB-54

Macken, Walter 1915-1967................................DLB-13

Mackenzie, Alexander 1763-1820 ....DLB-99

Mackenzie, Compton 1883-1972.......................DLB-34, 100

Mackenzie, Henry 1745-1831..............................DLB-39

Mackey, William Wellington 1937- DLB-38

Mackintosh, Elizabeth (see Tey, Josephine)

Macklin, Charles 1699-1797 ....DLB-89

MacLean, Katherine Anne 1925- DLB-8

MacLeish, Archibald 1892-1982 ....DLB-4, 7, 45; Y-82

MacLennan, Hugh 1907-1990...............................DLB-68

MacLeod, Alistair 1936- DLB-60

Macleod, Norman 1906- DLB-4

Macmillan and Company..................................DLB-106

The Macmillan Company...................................DLB-49

MacNamara, Brinsley 1890-1963 ....DLB-10

MacNeice, Louis 1907-1963 ....DLB-10, 20

MacPhail, Andrew 1864-1938 ....DLB-92

Macpherson, James 1736-1796............................DLB-109

Macpherson, Jay 1931- DLB-53

Macpherson, Jeanie 1884-1946 ....DLB-44

Macrae Smith Company DLB-46

Macrone, John [publishing house] DLB-106

MacShane, Frank 1927- DLB-111

Macy-Masius..DLB-46

Madden, David 1933- DLB-6

Maddow, Ben 1909- DLB-44

Madgett, Naomi Long 1923- DLB-76

Madhubuti, Haki R. 1942- DLB-5, 41; DS-8

Madison, James 1751-1836................................DLB-37

Maginn, William 1794-1842..............................DLB-110

Mahan, Alfred Thayer 1840-1914 ....DLB-47

Maheux-Forcier, Louise 1929- DLB-60

Mahin, John Lee 1902-1984...............................DLB-44

Mahon, Derek 1941- DLB-40

Mailer, Norman 1923- DLB-2, 16, 28; Y-80, 83; DS-3

Maillet, Adrienne 1885-1963.............................DLB-68

Maillet, Antonine 1929- DLB-60

Main Selections of the Book-of-the-Month Club,
1926-1945..DLB-9

Main Trends in Twentieth-Century
Book Clubs...DLB-46

Mainwaring, Daniel 1902-1977 ....DLB-44

Mair, Charles 1838-1927 ....DLB-99

Major, André 1942- DLB-60

Major, Clarence 1936-	DLB-33
Major, Kevin 1949-	DLB-60
Major Books	DLB-46
Makemie, Francis circa 1658-1708	DLB-24
The Making of a People, by J. M. Ritchie	DLB-66
Malamud, Bernard 1914-1986	DLB-2, 28; Y-80, 86
Malleson, Lucy Beatrice (see Gilbert, Anthony)	
Mallet-Joris, Françoise 1930-	DLB-83
Mallock, W. H. 1849-1923	DLB-18, 57
Malone, Dumas 1892-1986	DLB-17
Malraux, André 1901-1976	DLB-72
Malthus, Thomas Robert 1766-1834	DLB-107
Maltz, Albert 1908-1985	DLB-102
Malzberg, Barry N. 1939-	DLB-8
Mamet, David 1947-	DLB-7
Manchester University Press	DLB-112
Mandel, Eli 1922-	DLB-53
Mandeville, Bernard 1670-1733	DLB-101
Mandiargues, André Pieyre de 1909-	DLB-83
Manfred, Frederick 1912-	DLB-6
Mangan, Sherry 1904-1961	DLB-4
Mankiewicz, Herman 1897-1953	DLB-26
Mankiewicz, Joseph L. 1909-	DLB-44
Mankowitz, Wolf 1924-	DLB-15
Manley, Delarivière 1672?-1724	DLB-39, 80
Mann, Abby 1927-	DLB-44
Mann, Heinrich 1871-1950	DLB-66
Mann, Horace 1796-1859	DLB-1
Mann, Klaus 1906-1949	DLB-56
Mann, Thomas 1875-1955	DLB-66
Manning, Marie 1873?-1945	DLB-29
Manning and Loring	DLB-49
Mano, D. Keith 1942-	DLB-6
Manor Books	DLB-46
March, William 1893-1954	DLB-9, 86
Marchand, Leslie A. 1900-	DLB-103
Marchessault, Jovette 1938-	DLB-60
Marcus, Frank 1928-	DLB-13
Marek, Richard, Books	DLB-46
Mariani, Paul 1940-	DLB-111
Marie-Victorin, Frère 1885-1944	DLB-92
Marion, Frances 1886-1973	DLB-44
Marius, Richard C. 1933-	Y-85
The Mark Taper Forum	DLB-7
Markfield, Wallace 1926-	DLB-2, 28
Markham, Edwin 1852-1940	DLB-54
Markle, Fletcher 1921-	DLB-68
Marlatt, Daphne 1942-	DLB-60
Marlowe, Christopher 1564-1593	DLB-62
Marlyn, John 1912-	DLB-88
Marmion, Shakerley 1603-1639	DLB-58
Marquand, John P. 1893-1960	DLB-9, 102
Marqués, René 1919-1979	DLB-113
Marquis, Don 1878-1937	DLB-11, 25
Marriott, Anne 1913-	DLB-68
Marryat, Frederick 1792-1848	DLB-21
Marsh, George Perkins 1801-1882	DLB-1, 64
Marsh, James 1794-1842	DLB-1, 59
Marsh, Capen, Lyon and Webb	DLB-49
Marsh, Ngaio 1899-1982	DLB-77
Marshall, Edison 1894-1967	DLB-102
Marshall, Edward 1932-	DLB-16
Marshall, James 1942-	DLB-61
Marshall, Joyce 1913-	DLB-88
Marshall, Paule 1929-	DLB-33
Marshall, Tom 1938-	DLB-60
Marston, John 1576-1634	DLB-58
Marston, Philip Bourke 1850-1887	DLB-35
Martens, Kurt 1870-1945	DLB-66
Martien, William S. [publishing house]	DLB-49
Martin, Abe (see Hubbard, Kin)	
Martin, Claire 1914-	DLB-60
Martin, Jay 1935-	DLB-111
Martin du Gard, Roger 1881-1958	DLB-65
Martineau, Harriet 1802-1876	DLB-21, 55
Martínez, Max 1943-	DLB-82
Martyn, Edward 1859-1923	DLB-10
Marvin X 1944-	DLB-38
Marzials, Theo 1850-1920	DLB-35
Masefield, John 1878-1967	DLB-10, 19
Mason, A. E. W. 1865-1948	DLB-70
Mason, Bobbie Ann 1940-	Y-87
Mason Brothers	DLB-49
Massey, Gerald 1828-1907	DLB-32
Massinger, Philip 1583-1640	DLB-58
Masters, Edgar Lee 1868-1950	DLB-54

Mather, Cotton 1663-1728	DLB-24, 30
Mather, Increase 1639-1723	DLB-24
Mather, Richard 1596-1669	DLB-24
Matheson, Richard 1926-	DLB-8, 44
Matheus, John F. 1887-	DLB-51
Mathews, Cornelius 1817?-1889	DLB-3, 64
Mathews, Elkin [publishing house]	DLB-112
Mathias, Roland 1915-	DLB-27
Mathis, June 1892-1927	DLB-44
Mathis, Sharon Bell 1937-	DLB-33
Matthews, Brander 1852-1929	DLB-71, 78
Matthews, Jack 1925-	DLB-6
Matthews, William 1942-	DLB-5
Matthiessen, F. O. 1902-1950	DLB-63
Matthiessen, Peter 1927-	DLB-6
Maugham, W. Somerset 1874-1965	DLB-10, 36, 77, 100
Mauriac, Claude 1914-	DLB-83
Mauriac, François 1885-1970	DLB-65
Maurice, Frederick Denison 1805-1872	DLB-55
Maurois, André 1885-1967	DLB-65
Maury, James 1718-1769	DLB-31
Mavor, Elizabeth 1927-	DLB-14
Mavor, Osborne Henry (see Bridie, James)	
Maxwell, H. [publishing house]	DLB-49
Maxwell, John [publishing house]	DLB-106
Maxwell, William 1908-	Y-80
May, Elaine 1932-	DLB-44
May, Thomas 1595 or 1596-1650	DLB-58
Mayer, Mercer 1943-	DLB-61
Mayer, O. B. 1818-1891	DLB-3
Mayes, Wendell 1919-	DLB-26
Mayfield, Julian 1928-1984	DLB-33; Y-84
Mayhew, Henry 1812-1887	DLB-18, 55
Mayhew, Jonathan 1720-1766	DLB-31
Mayne, Seymour 1944-	DLB-60
Mayor, Flora Macdonald 1872-1932	DLB-36
Mayröcker, Friederike 1924-	DLB-85
Mazursky, Paul 1930-	DLB-44
McAlmon, Robert 1896-1956	DLB-4, 45
McArthur, Peter 1866-1924	DLB-92
McBride, Robert M., and Company	DLB-46
McCaffrey, Anne 1926-	DLB-8
McCarthy, Cormac 1933-	DLB-6
McCarthy, Mary 1912-1989	DLB-2; Y-81
McCay, Winsor 1871-1934	DLB-22
McClatchy, C. K. 1858-1936	DLB-25
McClellan, George Marion 1860-1934	DLB-50
McCloskey, Robert 1914-	DLB-22
McClung, Nellie Letitia 1873-1951	DLB-92
McClure, Joanna 1930-	DLB-16
McClure, Michael 1932-	DLB-16
McClure, Phillips and Company	DLB-46
McClure, S. S. 1857-1949	DLB-91
McClurg, A. C., and Company	DLB-49
McCluskey, John A., Jr. 1944-	DLB-33
McCollum, Michael A. 1946	Y-87
McConnell, William C. 1917-	DLB-88
McCord, David 1897-	DLB-61
McCorkle, Jill 1958-	Y-87
McCorkle, Samuel Eusebius 1746-1811	DLB-37
McCormick, Anne O'Hare 1880-1954	DLB-29
McCormick, Robert R. 1880-1955	DLB-29
McCourt, Edward 1907-1972	DLB-88
McCoy, Horace 1897-1955	DLB-9
McCrae, John 1872-1918	DLB-92
McCullagh, Joseph B. 1842-1896	DLB-23
McCullers, Carson 1917-1967	DLB-2, 7
McCulloch, Thomas 1776-1843	DLB-99
McDonald, Forrest 1927-	DLB-17
McDonald, Walter 1934-	DLB-105, DS-9
McDonald, Walter, Getting Started: Accepting the Regions You Own— or Which Own You	DLB-105
McDougall, Colin 1917-1984	DLB-68
McDowell, Obolensky	DLB-46
McEwan, Ian 1948-	DLB-14
McFadden, David 1940-	DLB-60
McFarlane, Leslie 1902-1977	DLB-88
McGahern, John 1934-	DLB-14
McGee, Thomas D'Arcy 1825-1868	DLB-99
McGeehan, W. O. 1879-1933	DLB-25
McGill, Ralph 1898-1969	DLB-29
McGinley, Phyllis 1905-1978	DLB-11, 48
McGirt, James E. 1874-1930	DLB-50
McGlashan and Gill	DLB-106
McGough, Roger 1937-	DLB-40
McGraw-Hill	DLB-46

Cumulative Index

McGuane, Thomas 1939- DLB-2; Y-80
McGuckian, Medbh 1950- DLB-40
McGuffey, William Holmes 1800-1873......................DLB-42
McIlvanney, William 1936- DLB-14
McIlwraith, Jean Newton 1859-1938 ....DLB-92
McIntyre, James 1827-1906.....................................DLB-99
McIntyre, O. O. 1884-1938 ....DLB-25
McKay, Claude 1889-1948 ....DLB-4, 45, 51
The David McKay Company DLB-49
McKean, William V. 1820-1903 ....DLB-23
McKinley, Robin 1952- DLB-52
McLachlan, Alexander 1818-1896 ....DLB-99
McLaren, Floris Clark 1904-1978 ....DLB-68
McLaverty, Michael 1907- DLB-15
McLean, John R. 1848-1916....................................DLB-23
McLean, William L. 1852-1931 ....DLB-25
McLennan, William 1856-1904 ....DLB-92
McLoughlin Brothers..DLB-49
McLuhan, Marshall 1911-1980 ....DLB-88
McMaster, John Bach 1852-1932 ....DLB-47
McMurtry, Larry 1936- DLB-2; Y-80, 87
McNally, Terrence 1939- DLB-7
McNeil, Florence 1937- DLB-60
McNeile, Herman Cyril 1888-1937.........................DLB-77
McPherson, James Alan 1943- DLB-38
McPherson, Sandra 1943- Y-86
McWhirter, George 1939- DLB-60
Mead, Matthew 1924- DLB-40
Mead, Taylor ?- DLB-16
Medill, Joseph 1823-1899..DLB-43
Medoff, Mark 1940- DLB-7
Meek, Alexander Beaufort 1814-1865......................DLB-3
Meinke, Peter 1932- DLB-5
Mejia Vallejo, Manuel 1923- DLB-113
Melançon, Robert 1947- DLB-60
Mell, Max 1882-1971..DLB-81
Mellow, James R. 1926- DLB-111
Meltzer, David 1937- DLB-16
Meltzer, Milton 1915- DLB-61
Melville, Herman 1819-1891..............................DLB-3, 74
Memoirs of Life and Literature (1920),
 by W. H. Mallock [excerpt] DLB-57
Mencken, H. L. 1880-1956 ....DLB-11, 29, 63
Mendelssohn, Moses 1729-1786 ....DLB-97

Méndez M., Miguel 1930- DLB-82
Mercer, Cecil William (see Yates, Dornford)
Mercer, David 1928-1980 ....DLB-13
Mercer, John 1704-1768...DLB-31
Meredith, George 1828-1909............................DLB-18, 35, 57
Meredith, Owen (see Lytton, Edward Robert Bulwer)
Meredith, William 1919- DLB-5
Merivale, John Herman 1779-1844 ....DLB-96
Meriwether, Louise 1923- DLB-33
Merlin Press...DLB-112
Merriam, Eve 1916- DLB-61
The Merriam Company..DLB-49
Merrill, James 1926- DLB-5; Y-85
Merrill and Baker DLB-49
The Mershon Company..DLB-49
Merton, Thomas 1915-1968...........................DLB-48; Y-81
Merwin, W. S. 1927- DLB-5
Messner, Julian [publishing house].........................DLB-46
Metcalf, J. [publishing house]..................................DLB-49
Metcalf, John 1938- DLB-60
The Methodist Book Concern..................................DLB-49
Methuen and Company DLB-112
Mew, Charlotte 1869-1928 ....DLB-19
Mewshaw, Michael 1943- Y-80
Meyer, E. Y. 1946- DLB-75
Meyer, Eugene 1875-1959..DLB-29
Meyers, Jeffrey 1939- DLB-111
Meynell, Alice 1847-1922.................................DLB-19, 98
Meyrink, Gustav 1868-1932....................................DLB-81
Micheaux, Oscar 1884-1951 ....DLB-50
Micheline, Jack 1929- DLB-16
Michener, James A. 1907?- DLB-6
Micklejohn, George circa 1717-1818 ....DLB-31
Middle Hill Press DLB-106
Middleton, Christopher 1926- DLB-40
Middleton, Stanley 1919- DLB-14
Middleton, Thomas 1580-1627 ....DLB-58
Miegel, Agnes 1879-1964 ....DLB-56
Miles, Josephine 1911-1985....................................DLB-48
Milius, John 1944- DLB-44
Mill, James 1773-1836 ....DLB-107
Mill, John Stuart 1806-1873 ....DLB-55
Millar, Kenneth 1915-1983.....................DLB-2; Y-83; DS-6

Millay, Edna St. Vincent 1892-1950	DLB-45
Miller, Arthur 1915-	DLB-7
Miller, Caroline 1903-	DLB-9
Miller, Eugene Ethelbert 1950-	DLB-41
Miller, Henry 1891-1980	DLB-4, 9; Y-80
Miller, J. Hillis 1928-	DLB-67
Miller, James [publishing house]	DLB-49
Miller, Jason 1939-	DLB-7
Miller, May 1899-	DLB-41
Miller, Perry 1905-1963	DLB-17, 63
Miller, Walter M., Jr. 1923-	DLB-8
Miller, Webb 1892-1940	DLB-29
Millhauser, Steven 1943-	DLB-2
Millican, Arthenia J. Bates 1920-	DLB-38
Mills and Boon	DLB-112
Milman, Henry Hart 1796-1868	DLB-96
Milne, A. A. 1882-1956	DLB-10, 77, 100
Milner, Ron 1938-	DLB-38
Milner, William [publishing house]	DLB-106
Milnes, Richard Monckton (Lord Houghton) 1809-1885	DLB-32
Minton, Balch and Company	DLB-46
Miron, Gaston 1928-	DLB-60
Mitchel, Jonathan 1624-1668	DLB-24
Mitchell, Adrian 1932-	DLB-40
Mitchell, Donald Grant 1822-1908	DLB-1
Mitchell, Gladys 1901-1983	DLB-77
Mitchell, James Leslie 1901-1935	DLB-15
Mitchell, John (see Slater, Patrick)	
Mitchell, John Ames 1845-1918	DLB-79
Mitchell, Julian 1935-	DLB-14
Mitchell, Ken 1940-	DLB-60
Mitchell, Langdon 1862-1935	DLB-7
Mitchell, Loften 1919-	DLB-38
Mitchell, Margaret 1900-1949	DLB-9
Mitchell, W. O. 1914-	DLB-88
Mitford, Mary Russell 1787-1855	DLB-110
Mitterer, Erika 1906-	DLB-85
Mizener, Arthur 1907-1988	DLB-103
Modern Age Books	DLB-46
"Modern English Prose" (1876), by George Saintsbury	DLB-57
The Modern Language Association of America Celebrates Its Centennial	Y-84
The Modern Library	DLB-46
Modern Novelists–Great and Small (1855), by Margaret Oliphant	DLB-21
"Modern Style" (1857), by Cockburn Thomson [excerpt]	DLB-57
The Modernists (1932), by Joseph Warren Beach	DLB-36
Modiano, Patrick 1945-	DLB-83
Moffat, Yard and Company	DLB-46
Monkhouse, Allan 1858-1936	DLB-10
Monro, Harold 1879-1932	DLB-19
Monroe, Harriet 1860-1936	DLB-54, 91
Monsarrat, Nicholas 1910-1979	DLB-15
Montagu, Lady Mary Wortley 1689-1762	DLB-95, 101
Montague, John 1929-	DLB-40
Montgomery, James 1771-1854	DLB-93
Montgomery, John 1919-	DLB-16
Montgomery, Lucy Maud 1874-1942	DLB-92
Montgomery, Marion 1925-	DLB-6
Montgomery, Robert Bruce (see Crispin, Edmund)	
Montherlant, Henry de 1896-1972	DLB-72
The Monthly Review 1749-1844	DLB-110
Montigny, Louvigny de 1876-1955	DLB-92
Moodie, John Wedderburn Dunbar 1797-1869	DLB-99
Moodie, Susanna 1803-1885	DLB-99
Moody, Joshua circa 1633-1697	DLB-24
Moody, William Vaughn 1869-1910	DLB-7, 54
Moorcock, Michael 1939-	DLB-14
Moore, Catherine L. 1911-	DLB-8
Moore, Clement Clarke 1779-1863	DLB-42
Moore, Dora Mavor 1888-1979	DLB-92
Moore, George 1852-1933	DLB-10, 18, 57
Moore, Marianne 1887-1972	DLB-45; DS-7
Moore, Mavor 1919-	DLB-88
Moore, Richard 1927-	DLB-105
Moore, Richard, The No Self, the Little Self, and the Poets	DLB-105
Moore, T. Sturge 1870-1944	DLB-19
Moore, Thomas 1779-1852	DLB-96
Moore, Ward 1903-1978	DLB-8
Moore, Wilstach, Keys and Company	DLB-49
The Moorland-Spingarn Research Center	DLB-76

Moraga, Cherríe 1952-	DLB-82
Morales, Alejandro 1944-	DLB-82
Morales, Rafael 1919-	DLB-108
More, Hannah 1745-1833	DLB-107, 109
Morency, Pierre 1942-	DLB-60
Morgan, Berry 1919-	DLB-6
Morgan, Charles 1894-1958	DLB-34, 100
Morgan, Edmund S. 1916-	DLB-17
Morgan, Edwin 1920-	DLB-27
Morgner, Irmtraud 1933-	DLB-75
Morin, Paul 1889-1963	DLB-92
Morison, Samuel Eliot 1887-1976	DLB-17
Moritz, Karl Philipp 1756-1793	DLB-94
Morley, Christopher 1890-1957	DLB-9
Morley, John 1838-1923	DLB-57
Morris, George Pope 1802-1864	DLB-73
Morris, Lewis 1833-1907	DLB-35
Morris, Richard B. 1904-1989	DLB-17
Morris, William 1834-1896	DLB-18, 35, 57
Morris, Willie 1934-	Y-80
Morris, Wright 1910-	DLB-2; Y-81
Morrison, Arthur 1863-1945	DLB-70
Morrison, Charles Clayton 1874-1966	DLB-91
Morrison, Toni 1931-	DLB-6, 33; Y-81
Morrow, William, and Company	DLB-46
Morse, James Herbert 1841-1923	DLB-71
Morse, Jedidiah 1761-1826	DLB-37
Morse, John T., Jr. 1840-1937	DLB-47
Mortimer, John 1923-	DLB-13
Morton, John P., and Company	DLB-49
Morton, Nathaniel 1613-1685	DLB-24
Morton, Sarah Wentworth 1759-1846	DLB-37
Morton, Thomas circa 1579-circa 1647	DLB-24
Möser, Justus 1720-1794	DLB-97
Mosley, Nicholas 1923-	DLB-14
Moss, Arthur 1889-1969	DLB-4
Moss, Howard 1922-	DLB-5
The Most Powerful Book Review in America [*New York Times Book Review*]	Y-82
Motion, Andrew 1952-	DLB-40
Motley, John Lothrop 1814-1877	DLB-1, 30, 59
Motley, Willard 1909-1965	DLB-76
Motteux, Peter Anthony 1663-1718	DLB-80
Mottram, R. H. 1883-1971	DLB-36
Mouré, Erin 1955-	DLB-60
Movies from Books, 1920-1974	DLB-9
Mowat, Farley 1921-	DLB-68
Mowbray, A. R., and Company, Limited	DLB-106
Mowrer, Edgar Ansel 1892-1977	DLB-29
Mowrer, Paul Scott 1887-1971	DLB-29
Moxon, Edward [publishing house]	DLB-106
Mucedorus	DLB-62
Mueller, Lisel 1924-	DLB-105
Muhajir, El (see Marvin X)	
Muhajir, Nazzam Al Fitnah (see Marvin X)	
Muir, Edwin 1887-1959	DLB-20, 100
Muir, Helen 1937-	DLB-14
Mukherjee, Bharati 1940-	DLB-60
Muldoon, Paul 1951-	DLB-40
Müller, Friedrich (see Müller, Maler)	
Müller, Maler 1749-1825	DLB-94
Müller, Wilhelm 1794-1827	DLB-90
Mumford, Lewis 1895-1990	DLB-63
Munby, Arthur Joseph 1828-1910	DLB-35
Munday, Anthony 1560-1633	DLB-62
Munford, Robert circa 1737-1783	DLB-31
Munro, Alice 1931-	DLB-53
Munro, George [publishing house]	DLB-49
Munro, H. H. 1870-1916	DLB-34
Munro, Norman L. [publishing house]	DLB-49
Munroe, James, and Company	DLB-49
Munroe, Kirk 1850-1930	DLB-42
Munroe and Francis	DLB-49
Munsell, Joel [publishing house]	DLB-49
Munsey, Frank A. 1854-1925	DLB-25, 91
Munsey, Frank A., and Company	DLB-49
Murdoch, Iris 1919-	DLB-14
Murfree, Mary N. 1850-1922	DLB-12, 74
Muro, Amado 1915-1971	DLB-82
Murphy, Arthur 1727-1805	DLB-89
Murphy, Beatrice M. 1908-	DLB-76
Murphy, Emily 1868-1933	DLB-99
Murphy, John, and Company	DLB-49
Murphy, Richard 1927-	DLB-40
Murray, Albert L. 1916-	DLB-38
Murray, Gilbert 1866-1957	DLB-10
Murray, Judith Sargent 1751-1820	DLB-37

Murray, Pauli 1910-1985 ....DLB-41

Musäus, Johann Karl August 1735-1787 ....DLB-97

Muschg, Adolf 1934- DLB-75

Musil, Robert 1880-1942 ....DLB-81

Mussey, Benjamin B., and Company DLB-49

Myers, Gustavus 1872-1942 ....DLB-47

Myers, L. H. 1881-1944 ....DLB-15

Myers, Walter Dean 1937- DLB-33

N

Nabbes, Thomas circa 1605-1641 ....DLB-58

Nabl, Franz 1883-1974 ....DLB-81

Nabokov, Vladimir 1899-1977 ....DLB-2; Y-80; DS-3

Nabokov Festival at Cornell Y-83

Nafis and Cornish DLB-49

Naipaul, Shiva 1945-1985 ....Y-85

Naipaul, V. S. 1932- Y-85

Nancrede, Joseph [publishing house] DLB-49

Narrache, Jean 1893-1970 ....DLB-92

Nasby, Petroleum Vesuvius (see Locke, David Ross)

Nash, Ogden 1902-1971 ....DLB-11

Nash, Eveleigh [publishing house] DLB-112

Nast, Condé 1873-1942 ....DLB-91

Nathan, Robert 1894-1985 ....DLB-9

The National Jewish Book Awards Y-85

The National Theatre and the Royal Shakespeare
  Company: The National Companies DLB-13

Naughton, Bill 1910- DLB-13

Neagoe, Peter 1881-1960 ....DLB-4

Neal, John 1793-1876 ....DLB-1, 59

Neal, Joseph C. 1807-1847 ....DLB-11

Neal, Larry 1937-1981 ....DLB-38

The Neale Publishing Company DLB-49

Neely, F. Tennyson [publishing house] DLB-49

"The Negro as a Writer," by
  G. M. McClellan DLB-50

"Negro Poets and Their Poetry," by
  Wallace Thurman DLB-50

Neihardt, John G. 1881-1973 ....DLB-9, 54

Nelligan, Emile 1879-1941 ....DLB-92

Nelson, Alice Moore Dunbar 1875-1935 ....DLB-50

Nelson, Thomas, and Sons [U.S.] DLB-49

Nelson, Thomas, and Sons [U.K.] DLB-106

Nelson, William 1908-1978 ....DLB-103

Nelson, William Rockhill 1841-1915 ....DLB-23

Nemerov, Howard 1920-1991 ....DLB-5, 6; Y-83

Ness, Evaline 1911-1986 ....DLB-61

Neugeboren, Jay 1938- DLB-28

Neumann, Alfred 1895-1952 ....DLB-56

Nevins, Allan 1890-1971 ....DLB-17

The New American Library DLB-46

New Approaches to Biography: Challenges
  from Critical Theory, USC Conference
  on Literary Studies, 1990 ....Y-90

New Directions Publishing Corporation DLB-46

A New Edition of *Huck Finn* Y-85

New Forces at Work in the American Theatre:
  1915-1925 ....DLB-7

New Literary Periodicals: A Report
  for 1987 ....Y-87

New Literary Periodicals: A Report
  for 1988 ....Y-88

New Literary Periodicals: A Report
  for 1989 ....Y-89

New Literary Periodicals: A Report
  for 1990 ....Y-90

The New Monthly Magazine 1814-1884 ....DLB-110

The New *Ulysses* Y-84

The New Variorum Shakespeare Y-85

A New Voice: The Center for the Book's First
  Five Years Y-83

The New Wave [Science Fiction] DLB-8

Newbolt, Henry 1862-1938 ....DLB-19

Newbound, Bernard Slade (see Slade, Bernard)

Newby, P. H. 1918- DLB-15

Newby, Thomas Cautley [publishing house] DLB-106

Newcomb, Charles King 1820-1894 ....DLB-1

Newell, Peter 1862-1924 ....DLB-42

Newell, Robert Henry 1836-1901 ....DLB-11

Newman, David (see Benton, Robert)

Newman, Frances 1883-1928 ....Y-80

Newman, John Henry 1801-1890 ....DLB-18, 32, 55

Newman, Mark [publishing house] DLB-49

Newnes, George, Limited DLB-112

Newsome, Effie Lee 1885-1979 ....DLB-76

Newspaper Syndication of American Humor DLB-11

Nichol, B. P. 1944- DLB-53

Nichols, Dudley 1895-1960 ....DLB-26

Nichols, John 1940- Y-82

Nichols, Mary Sargeant (Neal) Gove
  1810-1884..DLB-1

Nichols, Peter 1927- DLB-13

Nichols, Roy F. 1896-1973..................................DLB-17

Nichols, Ruth 1948- DLB-60

Nicolson, Harold 1886-1968.............................DLB-100

Nicholson, Norman 1914- DLB-27

Ní Chuilleanáin, Eiléan 1942- DLB-40

Nicol, Eric 1919- DLB-68

Nicolai, Friedrich 1733-1811...............................DLB-97

Nicolay, John G. 1832-1901 and
  Hay, John 1838-1905..DLB-47

Niebuhr, Reinhold 1892-1971.............................DLB-17

Niedecker, Lorine 1903-1970..............................DLB-48

Nieman, Lucius W. 1857-1935.............................DLB-25

Niggli, Josefina 1910- Y-80

Niles, Hezekiah 1777-1839..................................DLB-43

Nims, John Frederick 1913- DLB-5

Nin, Anaïs 1903-1977..DLB-2, 4

1985: The Year of the Mystery:
  A Symposium..Y-85

Nissenson, Hugh 1933- DLB-28

Niven, Frederick John 1878-1944......................DLB-92

Niven, Larry 1938- DLB-8

Nizan, Paul 1905-1940...DLB-72

Nobel Peace Prize
  The 1986 Nobel Peace Prize
    Nobel Lecture 1986: Hope, Despair
      and Memory
    Tributes from Abraham Bernstein,
      Norman Lamm, and John R. Silber.................Y-86

The Nobel Prize and Literary
  Politics..Y-88

Nobel Prize in Literature
  The 1982 Nobel Prize in Literature
    Announcement by the Swedish Academy
      of the Nobel Prize
    Nobel Lecture 1982: The Solitude of Latin
      America
    Excerpt from *One Hundred Years
      of Solitude*
    The Magical World of Macondo
    A Tribute to Gabriel García Márquez..................Y-82
  The 1983 Nobel Prize in Literature
    Announcement by the Swedish
      Academy
    Nobel Lecture 1983
      The Stature of William Golding.......................Y-83
  The 1984 Nobel Prize in Literature

    Announcement by the Swedish
      Academy
    Jaroslav Seifert Through the Eyes of the
      English-Speaking Reader
    Three Poems by Jaroslav Seifert.......................Y-84
  The 1985 Nobel Prize in Literature
    Announcement by the Swedish
      Academy
    Nobel Lecture 1985..Y-85
  The 1986 Nobel Prize in Literature
    Nobel Lecture 1986: This Past Must
      Address Its Present...Y-86
  The 1987 Nobel Prize in Literature
    Nobel Lecture 1987..Y-87
  The 1988 Nobel Prize in Literature
    Nobel Lecture 1988..Y-88
  The 1989 Nobel Prize in Literature
    Nobel Lecture 1989..Y-89
  The 1990 Nobel Prize in Literature
    Nobel Lecture 1990..Y-90

Noel, Roden 1834-1894..DLB-35

Nolan, William F. 1928- DLB-8

Noland, C. F. M. 1810?-1858..............................DLB-11

Nonesuch Press..DLB-112

Noonday Press...DLB-46

Noone, John 1936- DLB-14

Nordhoff, Charles 1887-1947...............................DLB-9

Norman, Charles 1904- DLB-111

Norman, Marsha 1947- Y-84

Norris, Charles G. 1881-1945................................DLB-9

Norris, Frank 1870-1902.....................................DLB-12

Norris, Leslie 1921- DLB-27

Norse, Harold 1916- DLB-16

North Point Press..DLB-46

Norton, Alice Mary (see Norton, Andre)

Norton, Andre 1912- DLB-8, 52

Norton, Andrews 1786-1853..................................DLB-1

Norton, Caroline 1808-1877...............................DLB-21

Norton, Charles Eliot 1827-1908....................DLB-1, 64

Norton, John 1606-1663......................................DLB-24

Norton, Thomas (see Sackville, Thomas)

Norton, W. W., and Company............................DLB-46

Norwood, Robert 1874-1932...............................DLB-92

Nossack, Hans Erich 1901-1977..........................DLB-69

A Note on Technique (1926), by Elizabeth
  A. Drew [excerpts]...DLB-36

Nourse, Alan E. 1928- DLB-8

Novalis 1772-1801...DLB-90

The Novel in [Robert Browning's] "The Ring
    and the Book" (1912), by Henry James DLB-32
The Novel of Impressionism,
    by Jethro Bithell DLB-66
Novel-Reading: *The Works of Charles Dickens*,
    The Works of W. Makepeace Thackeray (1879),
    by Anthony Trollope DLB-21
The Novels of Dorothy Richardson (1918), by
    May Sinclair DLB-36
Novels with a Purpose (1864),
    by Justin M'Carthy DLB-21
Nowlan, Alden 1933-1983 .... DLB-53
Noyes, Alfred 1880-1958 .... DLB-20
Noyes, Crosby S. 1825-1908 .... DLB-23
Noyes, Nicholas 1647-1717 .... DLB-24
Noyes, Theodore W. 1858-1946 .... DLB-29
Nugent, Frank 1908-1965 .... DLB-44
Nutt, David [publishing house] DLB-106
Nye, Edgar Wilson (Bill) 1850-1896 .... DLB-11, 23
Nye, Robert 1939- DLB-14

O

Oakes, Urian circa 1631-1681 .... DLB-24
Oates, Joyce Carol 1938- DLB-2, 5; Y-81
Oberholtzer, Ellis Paxson 1868-1936 .... DLB-47
O'Brien, Edna 1932- DLB-14
O'Brien, Fitz-James 1828-1862 .... DLB-74
O'Brien, Kate 1897-1974 .... DLB-15
O'Brien, Tim 1946- Y-80, DS-9
O'Casey, Sean 1880-1964 .... DLB-10
Ochs, Adolph S. 1858-1935 .... DLB-25
O'Connor, Flannery 1925-1964 .... DLB-2; Y-80
Octopus Publishing Group DLB-112
Odell, Jonathan 1737-1818 .... DLB-31, 99
O'Dell, Scott 1903-1989 .... DLB-52
Odets, Clifford 1906-1963 .... DLB-7, 26
Odhams Press Limited DLB-112
O'Donnell, Peter 1920- DLB-87
O'Faolain, Julia 1932- DLB-14
O'Faolain, Sean 1900- DLB-15
Off Broadway and Off-Off-Broadway DLB-7
Off-Loop Theatres DLB-7
Offord, Carl Ruthven 1910- DLB-76
O'Flaherty, Liam 1896-1984 .... DLB-36; Y-84

Ogilvie, J. S., and Company DLB-49
O'Grady, Desmond 1935- DLB-40
O'Hagan, Howard 1902-1982 .... DLB-68
O'Hara, Frank 1926-1966 .... DLB-5, 16
O'Hara, John 1905-1970 .... DLB-9, 86; DS-2
O. Henry (see Porter, William Sydney)
O'Keeffe, John 1747-1833 .... DLB-89
Old Franklin Publishing House DLB-49
Older, Fremont 1856-1935 .... DLB-25
Oliphant, Laurence 1829?-1888 .... DLB-18
Oliphant, Margaret 1828-1897 .... DLB-18
Oliver, Chad 1928- DLB-8
Oliver, Mary 1935- DLB-5
Ollier, Claude 1922- DLB-83
Olsen, Tillie 1913?- DLB-28; Y-80
Olson, Charles 1910-1970 .... DLB-5, 16
Olson, Elder 1909- DLB-48, 63
On Art in Fiction (1838), by
    Edward Bulwer DLB-21
On Learning to Write Y-88
On Some of the Characteristics of Modern
    Poetry and On the Lyrical Poems of Alfred
    Tennyson (1831), by Arthur Henry
    Hallam DLB-32
"On Style in English Prose" (1898), by Frederic
    Harrison DLB-57
"On Style in Literature: Its Technical Elements"
    (1885), by Robert Louis Stevenson DLB-57
"On the Writing of Essays" (1862),
    by Alexander Smith DLB-57
Ondaatje, Michael 1943- DLB-60
O'Neill, Eugene 1888-1953 .... DLB-7
Onetti, Juan Carlos 1909- DLB-113
Oppen, George 1908-1984 .... DLB-5
Oppenheim, E. Phillips 1866-1946 .... DLB-70
Oppenheim, James 1882-1932 .... DLB-28
Oppenheimer, Joel 1930- DLB-5
Optic, Oliver (see Adams, William Taylor)
Orczy, Emma, Baroness 1865-1947 .... DLB-70
Orlovitz, Gil 1918-1973 .... DLB-2, 5
Orlovsky, Peter 1933- DLB-16
Ormond, John 1923- DLB-27
Ornitz, Samuel 1890-1957 .... DLB-28, 44
Orton, Joe 1933-1967 .... DLB-13
Orwell, George 1903-1950 .... DLB-15, 98

Cumulative Index

The Orwell Year Y-84

Osbon, B. S. 1827-1912 .... DLB-43

Osborne, John 1929- DLB-13

Osgood, Herbert L. 1855-1918 .... DLB-47

Osgood, James R., and Company DLB-49

Osgood, McIlvaine and Company DLB-112

O'Shaughnessy, Arthur 1844-1881 .... DLB-35

O'Shea, Patrick [publishing house] DLB-49

Oswald, Eleazer 1755-1795 .... DLB-43

Ostenso, Martha 1900-1963 .... DLB-92

Otero, Miguel Antonio 1859-1944 .... DLB-82

Otis, James (see Kaler, James Otis)

Otis, James, Jr. 1725-1783 .... DLB-31

Otis, Broaders and Company DLB-49

Ottendorfer, Oswald 1826-1900 .... DLB-23

Otway, Thomas 1652-1685 .... DLB-80

Ouellette, Fernand 1930- DLB-60

Ouida 1839-1908 .... DLB-18

Outing Publishing Company DLB-46

Outlaw Days, by Joyce Johnson DLB-16

The Overlook Press DLB-46

Overview of U.S. Book Publishing, 1910-1945 .... DLB-9

Owen, Guy 1925- DLB-5

Owen, John [publishing house] DLB-49

Owen, Robert 1771-1858 .... DLB-107

Owen, Wilfred 1893-1918 .... DLB-20

Owen, Peter, Limited DLB-112

Owsley, Frank L. 1890-1956 .... DLB-17

Ozick, Cynthia 1928- DLB-28; Y-82

P

Pacey, Desmond 1917-1975 .... DLB-88

Pack, Robert 1929- DLB-5

Packaging Papa: *The Garden of Eden* Y-86

Padell Publishing Company DLB-46

Padgett, Ron 1942- DLB-5

Page, L. C., and Company DLB-49

Page, P. K. 1916- DLB-68

Page, Thomas Nelson 1853-1922 .... DLB-12, 78

Page, Walter Hines 1855-1918 .... DLB-71, 91

Paget, Violet (see Lee, Vernon)

Pain, Philip ?-circa 1666 .... DLB-24

Paine, Robert Treat, Jr. 1773-1811 .... DLB-37

Paine, Thomas 1737-1809 .... DLB-31, 43, 73

Paley, Grace 1922- DLB-28

Palfrey, John Gorham 1796-1881 .... DLB-1, 30

Palgrave, Francis Turner 1824-1897 .... DLB-35

Paltock, Robert 1697-1767 .... DLB-39

Pan Books Limited DLB-112

Panamaa, Norman 1914- and
 Frank, Melvin 1913-1988 .... DLB-26

Panero, Leopoldo 1909-1962 .... DLB-108

Pangborn, Edgar 1909-1976 .... DLB-8

"Panic Among the Philistines": A Postscript,
 An Interview with Bryan Griffin Y-81

Panneton, Philippe (see Ringuet)

Panshin, Alexei 1940- DLB-8

Pansy (see Alden, Isabella)

Pantheon Books DLB-46

Paperback Library DLB-46

Paperback Science Fiction DLB-8

Paquet, Alfons 1881-1944 .... DLB-66

Paradis, Suzanne 1936- DLB-53

Parents' Magazine Press DLB-46

Parisian Theater, Fall 1984: Toward
 A New Baroque Y-85

Parizeau, Alice 1930- DLB-60

Parke, John 1754-1789 .... DLB-31

Parker, Dorothy 1893-1967 .... DLB-11, 45, 86

Parker, Gilbert 1860-1932 .... DLB-99

Parker, James 1714-1770 .... DLB-43

Parker, Theodore 1810-1860 .... DLB-1

Parker, William Riley 1906-1968 .... DLB-103

Parker, J. H. [publishing house] DLB-106

Parker, John [publishing house] DLB-106

Parkman, Francis, Jr. 1823-1893 .... DLB-1, 30

Parks, Gordon 1912- DLB-33

Parks, William 1698-1750 .... DLB-43

Parks, William [publishing house] DLB-49

Parley, Peter (see Goodrich, Samuel Griswold)

Parnell, Thomas 1679-1718 .... DLB-95

Parrington, Vernon L. 1871-1929 .... DLB-17, 63

Partridge, S. W., and Company DLB-106

Parton, James 1822-1891 .... DLB-30

Parton, Sara Payson Willis 1811-1872 .... DLB-43, 74

Pastan, Linda 1932- DLB-5

Pastorius, Francis Daniel 1651-circa 1720	DLB-24
Patchen, Kenneth 1911-1972	DLB-16, 48
Pater, Walter 1839-1894	DLB-57
Paterson, Katherine 1932-	DLB-52
Patmore, Coventry 1823-1896	DLB-35, 98
Paton, Joseph Noel 1821-1901	DLB-35
Patrick, John 1906-	DLB-7
Pattee, Fred Lewis 1863-1950	DLB-71
Pattern and Paradigm: History as Design, by Judith Ryan	DLB-75
Patterson, Eleanor Medill 1881-1948	DLB-29
Patterson, Joseph Medill 1879-1946	DLB-29
Pattillo, Henry 1726-1801	DLB-37
Paul, Elliot 1891-1958	DLB-4
Paul, Jean (see Richter, Johann Paul Friedrich)	
Paul, Kegan, Trench, Trübner and Company Limited	DLB-106
Paul, Peter, Book Company	DLB-49
Paul, Stanley, and Company Limited	DLB-112
Paulding, James Kirke 1778-1860	DLB-3, 59, 74
Paulin, Tom 1949-	DLB-40
Pauper, Peter, Press	DLB-46
Paxton, John 1911-1985	DLB-44
Payn, James 1830-1898	DLB-18
Payne, John 1842-1916	DLB-35
Payne, John Howard 1791-1852	DLB-37
Payson and Clarke	DLB-46
Peabody, Elizabeth Palmer 1804-1894	DLB-1
Peabody, Elizabeth Palmer [publishing house]	DLB-49
Peabody, Oliver William Bourn 1799-1848	DLB-59
Peachtree Publishers, Limited	DLB-46
Peacock, Thomas Love 1785-1866	DLB-96
Pead, Deuel ?-1727	DLB-24
Peake, Mervyn 1911-1968	DLB-15
Pear Tree Press	DLB-112
Pearson, H. B. [publishing house]	DLB-49
Peck, George W. 1840-1916	DLB-23, 42
Peck, H. C., and Theo. Bliss [publishing house]	DLB-49
Peck, Harry Thurston 1856-1914	DLB-71, 91
Peele, George 1556-1596	DLB-62
Pellegrini and Cudahy	DLB-46
Pelletier, Aimé (see Vac, Bertrand)	
Pemberton, Sir Max 1863-1950	DLB-70
Penguin Books [U.S.]	DLB-46
Penguin Books [U.K.]	DLB-112
Penn Publishing Company	DLB-49
Penn, William 1644-1718	DLB-24
Penner, Jonathan 1940-	Y-83
Pennington, Lee 1939-	Y-82
Pepys, Samuel 1633-1703	DLB-101
Percy, Thomas 1729-1811	DLB-104
Percy, Walker 1916-1990	DLB-2; Y-80, 90
Perec, Georges 1936-1982	DLB-83
Perelman, S. J. 1904-1979	DLB-11, 44
Periodicals of the Beat Generation	DLB-16
Perkins, Eugene 1932-	DLB-41
Perkoff, Stuart Z. 1930-1974	DLB-16
Perley, Moses Henry 1804-1862	DLB-99
Permabooks	DLB-46
Perry, Bliss 1860-1954	DLB-71
Perry, Eleanor 1915-1981	DLB-44
"Personal Style" (1890), by John Addington Symonds	DLB-57
Perutz, Leo 1882-1957	DLB-81
Pestalozzi, Johann Heinrich 1746-1827	DLB-94
Peter, Laurence J. 1919-1990	DLB-53
Peterkin, Julia 1880-1961	DLB-9
Peters, Robert 1924-	DLB-105
Peters, Robert, Foreword to *Ludwig of Bavaria*	DLB-105
Petersham, Maud 1889-1971 and Petersham, Miska 1888-1960	DLB-22
Peterson, Charles Jacobs 1819-1887	DLB-79
Peterson, Len 1917-	DLB-88
Peterson, Louis 1922-	DLB-76
Peterson, T. B., and Brothers	DLB-49
Petitclair, Pierre 1813-1860	DLB-99
Petry, Ann 1908-	DLB-76
Phaidon Press Limited	DLB-112
Pharr, Robert Deane 1916-1989	DLB-33
Phelps, Elizabeth Stuart 1844-1911	DLB-74
Philippe, Charles-Louis 1874-1909	DLB-65
Philips, John 1676-1708	DLB-95
Phillips, David Graham 1867-1911	DLB-9, 12
Phillips, Jayne Anne 1952-	Y-80
Phillips, Robert 1938-	DLB-105

Phillips, Robert, Finding, Losing, Reclaiming: A Note on My Poems	DLB-105
Phillips, Stephen 1864-1915	DLB-10
Phillips, Ulrich B. 1877-1934	DLB-17
Phillips, Willard 1784-1873	DLB-59
Phillips, Sampson and Company	DLB-49
Phillpotts, Eden 1862-1960	DLB-10, 70
Philosophical Library	DLB-46
"The Philosophy of Style" (1852), by Herbert Spencer	DLB-57
Phinney, Elihu [publishing house]	DLB-49
Phoenix, John (see Derby, George Horatio)	
PHYLON (Fourth Quarter, 1950), The Negro in Literature: The Current Scene	DLB-76
Pickard, Tom 1946-	DLB-40
Pickering, William [publishing house]	DLB-106
Pickthall, Marjorie 1883-1922	DLB-92
Pictorial Printing Company	DLB-49
Pike, Albert 1809-1891	DLB-74
Pilon, Jean-Guy 1930-	DLB-60
Pinckney, Josephine 1895-1957	DLB-6
Pindar, Peter (see Wolcot, John)	
Pinero, Arthur Wing 1855-1934	DLB-10
Pinget, Robert 1919-	DLB-83
Pinnacle Books	DLB-46
Pinsky, Robert 1940-	Y-82
Pinter, Harold 1930-	DLB-13
Piontek, Heinz 1925-	DLB-75
Piozzi, Hester Lynch [Thrale] 1741-1821	DLB-104
Piper, H. Beam 1904-1964	DLB-8
Piper, Watty	DLB-22
Pisar, Samuel 1929-	Y-83
Pitkin, Timothy 1766-1847	DLB-30
The Pitt Poetry Series: Poetry Publishing Today	Y-85
Pitter, Ruth 1897-	DLB-20
Pix, Mary 1666-1709	DLB-80
The Place of Realism in Fiction (1895), by George Gissing	DLB-18
Plante, David 1940-	Y-83
Platen, August von 1796-1835	DLB-90
Plath, Sylvia 1932-1963	DLB-5, 6
Platt and Munk Company	DLB-46
Playboy Press	DLB-46
Plays, Playwrights, and Playgoers	DLB-84
Playwrights and Professors, by Tom Stoppard	DLB-13
Playwrights on the Theater	DLB-80
Plenzdorf, Ulrich 1934-	DLB-75
Plessen, Elizabeth 1944-	DLB-75
Plievier, Theodor 1892-1955	DLB-69
Plomer, William 1903-1973	DLB-20
Plumly, Stanley 1939-	DLB-5
Plumpp, Sterling D. 1940-	DLB-41
Plunkett, James 1920-	DLB-14
Plymell, Charles 1935-	DLB-16
Pocket Books	DLB-46
Poe, Edgar Allan 1809-1849	DLB-3, 59, 73, 74
Poe, James 1921-1980	DLB-44
The Poet Laureate of the United States Statements from Former Consultants in Poetry	Y-86
Pohl, Frederik 1919-	DLB-8
Poirier, Louis (see Gracq, Julien)	
Polanyi, Michael 1891-1976	DLB-100
Poliakoff, Stephen 1952-	DLB-13
Polite, Carlene Hatcher 1932-	DLB-33
Pollard, Edward A. 1832-1872	DLB-30
Pollard, Percival 1869-1911	DLB-71
Pollard and Moss	DLB-49
Pollock, Sharon 1936-	DLB-60
Polonsky, Abraham 1910-	DLB-26
Poniatowski, Elena 1933-	DLB-113
Poole, Ernest 1880-1950	DLB-9
Poore, Benjamin Perley 1820-1887	DLB-23
Pope, Alexander 1688-1744	DLB-95, 101
Popular Library	DLB-46
Porlock, Martin (see MacDonald, Philip)	
Porpoise Press	DLB-112
Porter, Eleanor H. 1868-1920	DLB-9
Porter, Henry ?-?	DLB-62
Porter, Katherine Anne 1890-1980	DLB-4, 9, 102; Y-80
Porter, Peter 1929-	DLB-40
Porter, William Sydney 1862-1910	DLB-12, 78, 79
Porter, William T. 1809-1858	DLB-3, 43
Porter and Coates	DLB-49
Portis, Charles 1933-	DLB-6

Poston, Ted 1906-1974 ....DLB-51

Postscript to [the Third Edition of] *Clarissa* (1751), by Samuel Richardson.............................DLB-39

Potok, Chaim 1929- DLB-28; Y-84

Potter, David M. 1910-1971................................DLB-17

Potter, John E., and Company DLB-49

Pottle, Frederick A. 1897-1987 ....DLB-103; Y-87

Poulin, Jacques 1937- DLB-60

Pound, Ezra 1885-1972 ....DLB-4, 45, 63

Powell, Anthony 1905- DLB-15

Pownall, David 1938- DLB-14

Powys, John Cowper 1872-1963.....................DLB-15

Powys, Llewelyn 1884-1939 ....DLB-98

Powys, T. F. 1875-1953 ....DLB-36

The Practice of Biography: An Interview with Stanley Weintraub Y-82

The Practice of Biography II: An Interview with B. L. Reid Y-83

The Practice of Biography III: An Interview with Humphrey Carpenter Y-84

The Practice of Biography IV: An Interview with William Manchester Y-85

The Practice of Biography V: An Interview with Justin Kaplan Y-86

The Practice of Biography VI: An Interview with David Herbert Donald Y-87

Praed, Winthrop Mackworth 1802-1839 ....DLB-96

Praeger Publishers DLB-46

Pratt, E. J. 1882-1964 ....DLB-92

Pratt, Samuel Jackson 1749-1814....................DLB-39

Preface to *Alwyn* (1780), by Thomas Holcroft DLB-39

Preface to *Colonel Jack* (1722), by Daniel Defoe DLB-39

Preface to *Evelina* (1778), by Fanny Burney DLB-39

Preface to *Ferdinand Count Fathom* (1753), by Tobias Smollett...DLB-39

Preface to *Incognita* (1692), by William Congreve DLB-39

Preface to *Joseph Andrews* (1742), by Henry Fielding DLB-39

Preface to *Moll Flanders* (1722), by Daniel Defoe DLB-39

Preface to *Poems* (1853), by Matthew Arnold DLB-32

Preface to *Robinson Crusoe* (1719), by Daniel Defoe DLB-39

Preface to *Roderick Random* (1748), by Tobias Smollett DLB-39

Preface to *Roxana* (1724), by Daniel Defoe DLB-39

Preface to *St. Leon* (1799), by William Godwin...................................DLB-39

Preface to Sarah Fielding's *Familiar Letters* (1747), by Henry Fielding [excerpt] DLB-39

Preface to Sarah Fielding's *The Adventures of David Simple* (1744), by Henry Fielding..................DLB-39

Preface to *The Cry* (1754), by Sarah Fielding................DLB-39

Preface to *The Delicate Distress* (1769), by Elizabeth Griffin DLB-39

Preface to *The Disguis'd Prince* (1733), by Eliza Haywood [excerpt]...................................DLB-39

Preface to *The Farther Adventures of Robinson Crusoe* (1719), by Daniel Defoe DLB-39

Preface to the First Edition of *Pamela* (1740), by Samuel Richardson DLB-39

Preface to the First Edition of *The Castle of Otranto* (1764), by Horace Walpole DLB-39

Preface to *The History of Romances* (1715), by Pierre Daniel Huet [excerpts] DLB-39

Preface to *The Life of Charlotta du Pont* (1723), by Penelope Aubin....................................DLB-39

Preface to *The Old English Baron* (1778), by Clara Reeve DLB-39

Preface to the Second Edition of *The Castle of Otranto* (1765), by Horace Walpole DLB-39

Preface to *The Secret History, of Queen Zarah, and the Zarazians* (1705), by Delarivière Manley...DLB-39

Preface to the Third Edition of *Clarissa* (1751), by Samuel Richardson [excerpt] DLB-39

Preface to *The Works of Mrs. Davys* (1725), by Mary Davys DLB-39

Preface to Volume 1 of *Clarissa* (1747), by Samuel Richardson DLB-39

Preface to Volume 3 of *Clarissa* (1748), by Samuel Richardson DLB-39

Préfontaine, Yves 1937- DLB-53

Prelutsky, Jack 1940- DLB-61

Premisses, by Michael Hamburger................DLB-66

Prentice, George D. 1802-1870 ....DLB-43

Prentice-Hall DLB-46

Prescott, William Hickling 1796-1859 ....DLB-1, 30, 59

The Present State of the English Novel (1892), by George Saintsbury.............................DLB-18

Preston, Thomas 1537-1598............................DLB-62

Price, Reynolds 1933- DLB-2

Price, Richard 1949- Y-81

Priest, Christopher 1943- DLB-14

Priestley, J. B. 1894-1984................DLB-10, 34, 77, 100; Y-84

Prime, Benjamin Young 1733-1791 ....DLB-31

Prince, F. T. 1912- DLB-20

Prince, Thomas 1687-1758..DLB-24

The Principles of Success in Literature (1865), by
    George Henry Lewes [excerpt]..............................DLB-57

Prior, Matthew 1664-1721 ....DLB-95

Pritchard, William H. 1932- DLB-111

Pritchett, V. S. 1900- DLB-15

Procter, Adelaide Anne 1825-1864..............................DLB-32

Procter, Bryan Waller 1787-1874................................DLB-96

The Profession of Authorship:
    Scribblers for Bread..Y-89

The Progress of Romance (1785), by Clara Reeve
    [excerpt] DLB-39

Prokosch, Frederic 1906-1989....................................DLB-48

The Proletarian Novel DLB-9

Propper, Dan 1937- DLB-16

The Prospect of Peace (1778), by Joel Barlow.................DLB-37

Proud, Robert 1728-1813..DLB-30

Proust, Marcel 1871-1922..DLB-65

Prynne, J. H. 1936- DLB-40

Przybyszewski, Stanislaw 1868-1927.............................DLB-66

The Public Lending Right in America
    Statement by Sen. Charles McC. Mathias, Jr.
    PLR and the Meaning of Literary Property
    Statements on PLR by American Writers....................Y-83

The Public Lending Right in the United Kingdom
    Public Lending Right: The First Year in the
    United Kingdom..Y-83

The Publication of English Renaissance
    Plays..DLB-62

Publications and Social Movements
    [Transcendentalism]..DLB-1

Publishers and Agents: The Columbia
    Connection Y-87

Publishing Fiction at LSU Press Y-87

Pugin, A. Welby 1812-1852 ....DLB-55

Puig, Manuel 1932-1990..DLB-113

Pulitzer, Joseph 1847-1911..DLB-23

Pulitzer, Joseph, Jr. 1885-1955...................................DLB-29

Pulitzer Prizes for the Novel, 1917-1945.........................DLB-9

Purdy, Al 1918- DLB-88

Purdy, James 1923- DLB-2

Pusey, Edward Bouverie 1800-1882 ....DLB-55

Putnam, George Palmer 1814-1872.........................DLB-3, 79

Putnam, Samuel 1892-1950...DLB-4

G. P. Putnam's Sons [U.S.] DLB-49

G. P. Putnam's Sons [U.K.] DLB-106

Puzo, Mario 1920- DLB-6

Pyle, Ernie 1900-1945..DLB-29

Pyle, Howard 1853-1911 ....DLB-42

Pym, Barbara 1913-1980.................................DLB-14; Y-87

Pynchon, Thomas 1937- DLB-2

Pyramid Books..DLB-46

Pyrnelle, Louise-Clarke 1850-1907 ....DLB-42

Q

Quad, M. (see Lewis, Charles B.)

The Quarterly Review 1809-1967 ....DLB-110

The Queen City Publishing House DLB-49

Queneau, Raymond 1903-1976...................................DLB-72

Quesnel, Joseph 1746-1809...DLB-99

The Question of American Copyright
    in the Nineteenth Century
        Headnote
        Preface, by George Haven Putnam
        The Evolution of Copyright, by Brander
            Matthews
        Summary of Copyright Legislation in the
            United States, by R. R. Bowker
        Analysis of the Provisions of the Copyright
            Law of 1891, by George Haven Putnam
        The Contest for International Copyright,
            by George Haven Putnam
        Cheap Books and Good Books,
            by Brander Matthews...........................DLB-49

Quin, Ann 1936-1973..DLB-14

Quincy, Samuel, of Georgia ?-?..................................DLB-31

Quincy, Samuel, of Massachusetts 1734-1789...............DLB-31

Quintana, Leroy V. 1944- DLB-82

Quist, Harlin, Books..DLB-46

Quoirez, Françoise (see Sagan, Françoise)

R

Rabe, David 1940- DLB-7

Radcliffe, Ann 1764-1823..DLB-39

Raddall, Thomas 1903- DLB-68

Radiguet, Raymond 1903-1923...................................DLB-65

Radványi, Netty Reiling (see Seghers, Anna)	
Raimund, Ferdinand Jakob 1790-1836	DLB-90
Raine, Craig 1944-	DLB-40
Raine, Kathleen 1908-	DLB-20
Ralph, Julian 1853-1903	DLB-23
Ralph Waldo Emerson in 1982	Y-82
Rambler, no. 4 (1750), by Samuel Johnson [excerpt]	DLB-39
Ramée, Marie Louise de la (see Ouida)	
Ramler, Karl Wilhelm 1725-1798	DLB-97
Rampersad, Arnold 1941-	DLB-111
Ramsay, Allan 1684 or 1685-1758	DLB-95
Ramsay, David 1749-1815	DLB-30
Rand, Avery and Company	DLB-49
Rand McNally and Company	DLB-49
Randall, Dudley 1914-	DLB-41
Randall, Henry S. 1811-1876	DLB-30
Randall, James G. 1881-1953	DLB-17
The Randall Jarrell Symposium: A Small Collection of Randall Jarrells Excerpts From Papers Delivered at the Randall Jarrell Symposium	Y-86
Randolph, A. Philip 1889-1979	DLB-91
Randolph, Anson D. F. [publishing house]	DLB-49
Randolph, Thomas 1605-1635	DLB-58
Random House	DLB-46
Ranlet, Henry [publishing house]	DLB-49
Ransom, John Crowe 1888-1974	DLB-45, 63
Raphael, Frederic 1931-	DLB-14
Raphaelson, Samson 1896-1983	DLB-44
Raskin, Ellen 1928-1984	DLB-52
Rattigan, Terence 1911-1977	DLB-13
Rawlings, Marjorie Kinnan 1896-1953	DLB-9, 22, 102
Raworth, Tom 1938-	DLB-40
Ray, David 1932-	DLB-5
Ray, Gordon N. 1915-1986	DLB-103
Ray, Henrietta Cordelia 1849-1916	DLB-50
Raymond, Henry J. 1820-1869	DLB-43, 79
Raymond Chandler Centenary Tributes from Michael Avallone, James Elroy, Joe Gores, and William F. Nolan	Y-88
Reach, Angus 1821-1856	DLB-70
Read, Herbert 1893-1968	DLB-20
Read, Opie 1852-1939	DLB-23
Read, Piers Paul 1941-	DLB-14
Reade, Charles 1814-1884	DLB-21
Reader's Digest Condensed Books	DLB-46
Reading, Peter 1946-	DLB-40
Reaney, James 1926-	DLB-68
Rechy, John 1934-	Y-82
Redding, J. Saunders 1906-1988	DLB-63, 76
Redfield, J. S. [publishing house]	DLB-49
Redgrove, Peter 1932-	DLB-40
Redmon, Anne 1943-	Y-86
Redmond, Eugene B. 1937-	DLB-41
Redpath, James [publishing house]	DLB-49
Reed, Henry 1808-1854	DLB-59
Reed, Henry 1914-	DLB-27
Reed, Ishmael 1938-	DLB-2, 5, 33; DS-8
Reed, Sampson 1800-1880	DLB-1
Reedy, William Marion 1862-1920	DLB-91
Reese, Lizette Woodworth 1856-1935	DLB-54
Reese, Thomas 1742-1796	DLB-37
Reeve, Clara 1729-1807	DLB-39
Reeves, John 1926-	DLB-88
Regnery, Henry, Company	DLB-46
Reid, Alastair 1926-	DLB-27
Reid, B. L. 1918-1990	DLB-111
Reid, Christopher 1949-	DLB-40
Reid, Helen Rogers 1882-1970	DLB-29
Reid, James ?-?	DLB-31
Reid, Mayne 1818-1883	DLB-21
Reid, Thomas 1710-1796	DLB-31
Reid, Whitelaw 1837-1912	DLB-23
Reilly and Lee Publishing Company	DLB-46
Reimann, Brigitte 1933-1973	DLB-75
Reisch, Walter 1903-1983	DLB-44
Remarque, Erich Maria 1898-1970	DLB-56
"Re-meeting of Old Friends": The Jack Kerouac Conference	Y-82
Remington, Frederic 1861-1909	DLB-12
Renaud, Jacques 1943-	DLB-60
Renault, Mary 1905-1983	Y-83
Rendell, Ruth 1930-	DLB-87
Representative Men and Women: A Historical Perspective on the British Novel, 1930-1960	DLB-15
(Re-)Publishing Orwell	Y-86

Reuter, Gabriele 1859-1941	DLB-66
Revell, Fleming H., Company	DLB-49
Reventlow, Franziska Gräfin zu 1871-1918	DLB-66
Review of Reviews Office	DLB-112
Review of [Samuel Richardson's] *Clarissa* (1748), by Henry Fielding	DLB-39
The Revolt (1937), by Mary Colum [excerpts]	DLB-36
Rexroth, Kenneth 1905-1982	DLB-16, 48; Y-82
Rey, H. A. 1898-1977	DLB-22
Reynal and Hitchcock	DLB-46
Reynolds, G. W. M. 1814-1879	DLB-21
Reynolds, John Hamilton 1794-1852	DLB-96
Reynolds, Mack 1917-	DLB-8
Reynolds, Sir Joshua 1723-1792	DLB-104
Reznikoff, Charles 1894-1976	DLB-28, 45
"Rhetoric" (1828; revised, 1859), by Thomas de Quincey [excerpt]	DLB-57
Rhett, Robert Barnwell 1800-1876	DLB-43
Rhode, John 1884-1964	DLB-77
Rhodes, James Ford 1848-1927	DLB-47
Rhys, Jean 1890-1979	DLB-36
Ricardo, David 1772-1823	DLB-107
Ricardou, Jean 1932-	DLB-83
Rice, Elmer 1892-1967	DLB-4, 7
Rice, Grantland 1880-1954	DLB-29
Rich, Adrienne 1929-	DLB-5, 67
Richards, David Adams 1950-	DLB-53
Richards, George circa 1760-1814	DLB-37
Richards, I. A. 1893-1979	DLB-27
Richards, Laura E. 1850-1943	DLB-42
Richards, William Carey 1818-1892	DLB-73
Richards, Grant [publishing house]	DLB-112
Richardson, Charles F. 1851-1913	DLB-71
Richardson, Dorothy M. 1873-1957	DLB-36
Richardson, Jack 1935-	DLB-7
Richardson, John 1796-1852	DLB-99
Richardson, Samuel 1689-1761	DLB-39
Richardson, Willis 1889-1977	DLB-51
Richler, Mordecai 1931-	DLB-53
Richter, Conrad 1890-1968	DLB-9
Richter, Hans Werner 1908-	DLB-69
Richter, Johann Paul Friedrich 1763-1825	DLB-94
Rickerby, Joseph [publishing house]	DLB-106
Rickword, Edgell 1898-1982	DLB-20
Riddell, John (see Ford, Corey)	
Ridge, Lola 1873-1941	DLB-54
Riding, Laura (see Jackson, Laura Riding)	
Ridler, Anne 1912-	DLB-27
Ridruego, Dionisio 1912-1975	DLB-108
Riel, Louis 1844-1885	DLB-99
Riffaterre, Michael 1924-	DLB-67
Riis, Jacob 1849-1914	DLB-23
Riker, John C. [publishing house]	DLB-49
Riley, John 1938-1978	DLB-40
Rilke, Rainer Maria 1875-1926	DLB-81
Rinehart and Company	DLB-46
Ringuet 1895-1960	DLB-68
Ringwood, Gwen Pharis 1910-1984	DLB-88
Rinser, Luise 1911-	DLB-69
Ríos, Isabella 1948-	DLB-82
Ripley, Arthur 1895-1961	DLB-44
Ripley, George 1802-1880	DLB-1, 64, 73
The Rising Glory of America: Three Poems	DLB-37
The Rising Glory of America: Written in 1771 (1786), by Hugh Henry Brackenridge and Philip Freneau	DLB-37
Riskin, Robert 1897-1955	DLB-26
Risse, Heinz 1898-	DLB-69
Ritchie, Anna Mowatt 1819-1870	DLB-3
Ritchie, Anne Thackeray 1837-1919	DLB-18
Ritchie, Thomas 1778-1854	DLB-43
Rites of Passage [on William Saroyan]	Y-83
The Ritz Paris Hemingway Award	Y-85
Rivard, Adjutor 1868-1945	DLB-92
Rivera, Tomás 1935-1984	DLB-82
Rivers, Conrad Kent 1933-1968	DLB-41
Riverside Press	DLB-49
Rivington, James circa 1724-1802	DLB-43
Rivkin, Allen 1903-1990	DLB-26
Roa Bastos, Augusto 1917-	DLB-113
Robbe-Grillet, Alain 1922-	DLB-83
Robbins, Tom 1936-	Y-80
Roberts, Charles G. D. 1860-1943	DLB-92
Roberts, Dorothy 1906-	DLB-88
Roberts, Elizabeth Madox 1881-1941	DLB-9, 54, 102
Roberts, Kenneth 1885-1957	DLB-9

Roberts Brothers	DLB-49
Robertson, A. M., and Company	DLB-49
Robertson, William 1721-1793	DLB-104
Robinson, Casey 1903-1979	DLB-44
Robinson, Edwin Arlington 1869-1935	DLB-54
Robinson, Henry Crabb 1775-1867	DLB-107
Robinson, James Harvey 1863-1936	DLB-47
Robinson, Lennox 1886-1958	DLB-10
Robinson, Mabel Louise 1874-1962	DLB-22
Robinson, Therese 1797-1870	DLB-59
Roblès, Emmanuel 1914-	DLB-83
Rodgers, Carolyn M. 1945-	DLB-41
Rodgers, W. R. 1909-1969	DLB-20
Rodriguez, Richard 1944-	DLB-82
Roethke, Theodore 1908-1963	DLB-5
Rogers, Pattiann 1940-	DLB-105
Rogers, Samuel 1763-1855	DLB-93
Rogers, Will 1879-1935	DLB-11
Rohmer, Sax 1883-1959	DLB-70
Roiphe, Anne 1935-	Y-80
Rojas, Arnold R. 1896-1988	DLB-82
Rolfe, Frederick William 1860-1913	DLB-34
Rolland, Romain 1866-1944	DLB-65
Rolvaag, O. E. 1876-1931	DLB-9
Romains, Jules 1885-1972	DLB-65
Roman, A., and Company	DLB-49
Romero, Orlando 1945-	DLB-82
Roosevelt, Theodore 1858-1919	DLB-47
Root, Waverley 1903-1982	DLB-4
Roquebrune, Robert de 1889-1978	DLB-68
Rosa, João Guimarães 1908-1967	DLB-113
Rose, Reginald 1920-	DLB-26
Rosei, Peter 1946-	DLB-85
Rosen, Norma 1925-	DLB-28
Rosenberg, Isaac 1890-1918	DLB-20
Rosenfeld, Isaac 1918-1956	DLB-28
Rosenthal, M. L. 1917-	DLB-5
Ross, Leonard Q. (see Rosten, Leo)	
Ross, Sinclair 1908-	DLB-88
Ross, W. W. E. 1894-1966	DLB-88
Rossen, Robert 1908-1966	DLB-26
Rossetti, Christina 1830-1894	DLB-35
Rossetti, Dante Gabriel 1828-1882	DLB-35
Rossner, Judith 1935-	DLB-6
Rosten, Leo 1908-	DLB-11
Roth, Gerhard 1942-	DLB-85
Roth, Henry 1906?-	DLB-28
Roth, Joseph 1894-1939	DLB-85
Roth, Philip 1933-	DLB-2, 28; Y-82
Rothenberg, Jerome 1931-	DLB-5
Routhier, Adolphe-Basile 1839-1920	DLB-99
Routier, Simone 1901-1987	DLB-88
Routledge, George, and Sons	DLB-106
Rowe, Elizabeth Singer 1674-1737	DLB-39, 95
Rowe, Nicholas 1674-1718	DLB-84
Rowlandson, Mary circa 1635-circa 1678	DLB-24
Rowley, William circa 1585-1626	DLB-58
Rowson, Susanna Haswell circa 1762-1824	DLB-37
Roy, Camille 1870-1943	DLB-92
Roy, Gabrielle 1909-1983	DLB-68
Roy, Jules 1907-	DLB-83
The Royal Court Theatre and the English Stage Company	DLB-13
The Royal Court Theatre and the New Drama	DLB-10
The Royal Shakespeare Company at the Swan	Y-88
Royall, Anne 1769-1854	DLB-43
The Roycroft Printing Shop	DLB-49
Rubens, Bernice 1928-	DLB-14
Rudd and Carleton	DLB-49
Rudkin, David 1936-	DLB-13
Ruffin, Josephine St. Pierre 1842-1924	DLB-79
Ruggles, Henry Joseph 1813-1906	DLB-64
Rukeyser, Muriel 1913-1980	DLB-48
Rule, Jane 1931-	DLB-60
Rulfo, Juan 1918-1986	DLB-113
Rumaker, Michael 1932-	DLB-16
Rumens, Carol 1944-	DLB-40
Runyon, Damon 1880-1946	DLB-11, 86
Rush, Benjamin 1746-1813	DLB-37
Rusk, Ralph L. 1888-1962	DLB-103
Ruskin, John 1819-1900	DLB-55
Russ, Joanna 1937-	DLB-8
Russell, B. B., and Company	DLB-49
Russell, Benjamin 1761-1845	DLB-43
Russell, Bertrand 1872-1970	DLB-100

Russell, Charles Edward 1860-1941.................................DLB-25

Russell, George William (see AE)

Russell, R. H., and Son..DLB-49

Rutherford, Mark 1831-1913...DLB-18

Ryan, Michael 1946-..Y-82

Ryan, Oscar 1904-..DLB-68

Ryga, George 1932-..DLB-60

Rymer, Thomas 1643?-1713...DLB-101

Ryskind, Morrie 1895-1985..DLB-26

S

The Saalfield Publishing Company.................................DLB-46

Saberhagen, Fred 1930-..DLB-8

Sackler, Howard 1929-1982..DLB-7

Sackville, Thomas 1536-1608
 and Norton, Thomas 1532-1584..................................DLB-62

Sackville-West, V. 1892-1962..DLB-34

Sadlier, D. and J., and Company....................................DLB-49

Sadlier, Mary Anne 1820-1903.......................................DLB-99

Saffin, John circa 1626-1710..DLB-24

Sagan, Françoise 1935-...DLB-83

Sage, Robert 1899-1962..DLB-4

Sagel, Jim 1947-..DLB-82

Sahagún, Carlos 1938-..DLB-108

Sahkomaapii, Piitai (see Highwater, Jamake)

Sahl, Hans 1902-...DLB-69

Said, Edward W. 1935-...DLB-67

Saiko, George 1892-1962..DLB-85

St. Dominic's Press...DLB-112

St. Johns, Adela Rogers 1894-1988................................DLB-29

St. Martin's Press..DLB-46

Saint-Exupéry, Antoine de 1900-1944............................DLB-72

Saint Pierre, Michel de 1916-1987.................................DLB-83

Saintsbury, George 1845-1933.......................................DLB-57

Saki (see Munro, H. H.)

Salaam, Kalamu ya 1947-..DLB-38

Salas, Floyd 1931-..DLB-82

Salemson, Harold J. 1910-1988.....................................DLB-4

Salinas, Luis Omar 1937-...DLB-82

Salinger, J. D. 1919-...DLB-2, 102

Salt, Waldo 1914-...DLB-44

Salverson, Laura Goodman 1890-1970.........................DLB-92

Sampson, Richard Henry (see Hull, Richard)

Samuels, Ernest 1903-..DLB-111

Sanborn, Franklin Benjamin 1831-1917.......................DLB-1

Sánchez, Ricardo 1941-..DLB-82

Sanchez, Sonia 1934-..DLB-41; DS-8

Sandburg, Carl 1878-1967...DLB-17, 54

Sanders, Ed 1939-...DLB-16

Sandoz, Mari 1896-1966..DLB-9

Sandwell, B. K. 1876-1954...DLB-92

Sandys, George 1578-1644...DLB-24

Sangster, Charles 1822-1893..DLB-99

Santayana, George 1863-1952.......................................DLB-54, 71

Santmyer, Helen Hooven 1895-1986............................Y-84

Sapir, Edward 1884-1939...DLB-92

Sapper (see McNeile, Herman Cyril)

Sarduy, Severo 1937-..DLB-113

Sargent, Pamela 1948-..DLB-8

Saroyan, William 1908-1981...DLB-7, 9, 86; Y-81

Sarraute, Nathalie 1900-..DLB-83

Sarrazin, Albertine 1937-1967.......................................DLB-83

Sarton, May 1912-..DLB-48; Y-81

Sartre, Jean-Paul 1905-1980..DLB-72

Sassoon, Siegfried 1886-1967...DLB-20

Saturday Review Press..DLB-46

Saunders, James 1925-...DLB-13

Saunders, John Monk 1897-1940..................................DLB-26

Saunders, Margaret Marshall
 1861-1947...DLB-92

Saunders and Otley..DLB-106

Savage, James 1784-1873...DLB-30

Savage, Marmion W. 1803?-1872..................................DLB-21

Savage, Richard 1697?-1743..DLB-95

Savard, Félix-Antoine 1896-1982..................................DLB-68

Sawyer, Ruth 1880-1970..DLB-22

Sayers, Dorothy L. 1893-1957.......................................DLB-10, 36, 77, 100

Sayles, John Thomas 1950-..DLB-44

Scannell, Vernon 1922-..DLB-27

Scarry, Richard 1919-...DLB-61

Schaeffer, Albrecht 1885-1950.......................................DLB-66

Schaeffer, Susan Fromberg 1941-..................................DLB-28

Schaper, Edzard 1908-1984...DLB-69

Scharf, J. Thomas 1843-1898..DLB-47

Schelling, Friedrich Wilhelm Joseph von
 1775-1854..DLB-90

Schickele, René 1883-1940..DLB-66

Schiller, Friedrich 1759-1805 ....DLB-94

Schlegel, August Wilhelm 1767-1845 ....DLB-94

Schlegel, Dorothea 1763-1839 ....DLB-90

Schlegel, Friedrich 1772-1829 ....DLB-90

Schleiermacher, Friedrich 1768-1834 ....DLB-90

Schlesinger, Arthur M., Jr. 1917- DLB-17

Schlumberger, Jean 1877-1968 ....DLB-65

Schmid, Eduard Hermann Wilhelm
 (see Edschmid, Kasimir)

Schmidt, Arno 1914-1979 ....DLB-69

Schmidt, Michael 1947- DLB-40

Schmitz, James H. 1911- DLB-8

Schnitzler, Arthur 1862-1931 ....DLB-81

Schnurre, Wolfdietrich 1920- DLB-69

Schocken Books DLB-46

Scholartis Press DLB-112

The Schomburg Center for Research
 in Black Culture DLB-76

Schopenhauer, Arthur 1788-1860 ....DLB-90

Schopenhauer, Johanna 1766-1838 ....DLB-90

Schorer, Mark 1908-1977 ....DLB-103

Schouler, James 1839-1920 ....DLB-47

Schrader, Paul 1946- DLB-44

Schreiner, Olive 1855-1920 ....DLB-18

Schroeder, Andreas 1946- DLB-53

Schubart, Christian Friedrich Daniel
 1739-1791 ....DLB-97

Schubert, Gotthilf Heinrich 1780-1860 ....DLB-90

Schulberg, Budd 1914- DLB-6, 26, 28; Y-81

Schulte, F. J., and Company DLB-49

Schurz, Carl 1829-1906 ....DLB-23

Schuyler, George S. 1895-1977 ....DLB-29, 51

Schuyler, James 1923- DLB-5

Schwartz, Delmore 1913-1966 ....DLB-28, 48

Schwartz, Jonathan 1938- Y-82

Science Fantasy DLB-8

Science-Fiction Fandom and Conventions DLB-8

Science-Fiction Fanzines: The Time Binders DLB-8

Science-Fiction Films DLB-8

Science Fiction Writers of America and the
 Nebula Awards DLB-8

Scott, Dixon 1881-1915 ....DLB-98

Scott, Duncan Campbell 1862-1947 ....DLB-92

Scott, Evelyn 1893-1963 ....DLB-9, 48

Scott, F. R. 1899-1985 ....DLB-88

Scott, Frederick George
 1861-1944 ....DLB-92

Scott, Harvey W. 1838-1910 ....DLB-23

Scott, Paul 1920-1978 ....DLB-14

Scott, Sarah 1723-1795 ....DLB-39

Scott, Tom 1918- DLB-27

Scott, Sir Walter 1771-1832 ....DLB-93, 107

Scott, William Bell 1811-1890 ....DLB-32

Scott, Walter, Publishing Company Limited DLB-112

Scott, William R. [publishing house] DLB-46

Scott-Heron, Gil 1949- DLB-41

Charles Scribner's Sons DLB-49

Scripps, E. W. 1854-1926 ....DLB-25

Scudder, Horace Elisha 1838-1902 ....DLB-42, 71

Scudder, Vida Dutton 1861-1954 ....DLB-71

Scupham, Peter 1933- DLB-40

Seabrook, William 1886-1945 ....DLB-4

Seabury, Samuel 1729-1796 ....DLB-31

Sears, Edward I. 1819?-1876 ....DLB-79

Sears Publishing Company DLB-46

Seaton, George 1911-1979 ....DLB-44

Seaton, William Winston 1785-1866 ....DLB-43

Secker, Martin, and Warburg Limited DLB-112

Secker, Martin [publishing house] DLB-112

Sedgwick, Arthur George 1844-1915 ....DLB-64

Sedgwick, Catharine Maria 1789-1867 ....DLB-1, 74

Sedgwick, Ellery 1872-1930 ....DLB-91

Seeger, Alan 1888-1916 ....DLB-45

Seers, Eugene (see Dantin, Louis)

Segal, Erich 1937- Y-86

Seghers, Anna 1900-1983 ....DLB-69

Seid, Ruth (see Sinclair, Jo)

Seidel, Frederick Lewis 1936- Y-84

Seidel, Ina 1885-1974 ....DLB-56

Seizin Press DLB-112

Séjour, Victor 1817-1874 ....DLB-50

Séjour Marcou et Ferrand,
 Juan Victor (see Séjour, Victor)

Selby, Hubert, Jr. 1928- DLB-2

Selden, George 1929-1989 ....DLB-52

Selected English-Language Little Magazines and
 Newspapers [France, 1920-1939] DLB-4

Selected Humorous Magazines (1820-1950) DLB-11

Selected Science-Fiction Magazines and Anthologies DLB-8

Seligman, Edwin R. A. 1861-1939 ....DLB-47

Seltzer, Chester E. (see Muro, Amado)

Seltzer, Thomas [publishing house] DLB-46

Sendak, Maurice 1928- DLB-61

Senécal, Eva 1905- DLB-92

Sensation Novels (1863), by H. L. Manse DLB-21

Seredy, Kate 1899-1975 ....DLB-22

Serling, Rod 1924-1975 ....DLB-26

Service, Robert 1874-1958 ....DLB-92

Seton, Ernest Thompson 1860-1942 ....DLB-92

Settle, Mary Lee 1918- DLB-6

Seume, Johann Gottfried 1763-1810 ....DLB-94

Seuss, Dr. (see Geisel, Theodor Seuss)

Sewall, Joseph 1688-1769 ....DLB-24

Sewall, Richard B. 1908- DLB-111

Sewell, Samuel 1652-1730 ....DLB-24

Sex, Class, Politics, and Religion [in the British Novel, 1930-1959] DLB-15

Sexton, Anne 1928-1974 ....DLB-5

Shaara, Michael 1929-1988 ....Y-83

Shadwell, Thomas 1641?-1692 ....DLB-80

Shaffer, Anthony 1926- DLB-13

Shaffer, Peter 1926- DLB-13

Shaftesbury, Anthony Ashley Cooper, Third Earl of 1671-1713 ....DLB-101

Shairp, Mordaunt 1887-1939 ....DLB-10

Shakespeare, William 1564-1616 ....DLB-62

Shakespeare Head Press DLB-112

Shange, Ntozake 1948- DLB-38

Shapiro, Karl 1913- DLB-48

Sharon Publications DLB-46

Sharpe, Tom 1928- DLB-14

Shaw, Albert 1857-1947 ....DLB-91

Shaw, Bernard 1856-1950 ....DLB-10, 57

Shaw, Henry Wheeler 1818-1885 ....DLB-11

Shaw, Irwin 1913-1984 ....DLB-6, 102; Y-84

Shaw, Robert 1927-1978 ....DLB-13, 14

Shay, Frank [publishing house] DLB-46

Shea, John Gilmary 1824-1892 ....DLB-30

Sheaffer, Louis 1912- DLB-103

Shearing, Joseph 1886-1952 ....DLB-70

Shebbeare, John 1709-1788 ....DLB-39

Sheckley, Robert 1928- DLB-8

Shedd, William G. T. 1820-1894 ....DLB-64

Sheed, Wilfred 1930- DLB-6

Sheed and Ward [U.S.] DLB-46

Sheed and Ward Limited [U.K.] DLB-112

Sheldon, Alice B. (see Tiptree, James, Jr.)

Sheldon, Edward 1886-1946 ....DLB-7

Sheldon and Company DLB-49

Shelley, Mary Wollstonecraft 1797-1851 ....DLB-110

Shelley, Percy Bysshe 1792-1822 ....DLB-96, 110

Shenstone, William 1714-1763 ....DLB-95

Shepard, Sam 1943- DLB-7

Shepard, Thomas I 1604 or 1605-1649 ....DLB-24

Shepard, Thomas II 1635-1677 ....DLB-24

Shepard, Clark and Brown DLB-49

Sheridan, Frances 1724-1766 ....DLB-39, 84

Sheridan, Richard Brinsley 1751-1816 ....DLB-89

Sherman, Francis 1871-1926 ....DLB-92

Sherriff, R. C. 1896-1975 ....DLB-10

Sherwood, Robert 1896-1955 ....DLB-7, 26

Shiels, George 1886-1949 ....DLB-10

Shillaber, B.[enjamin] P.[enhallow] 1814-1890 ....DLB-1, 11

Shine, Ted 1931- DLB-38

Ship, Reuben 1915-1975 ....DLB-88

Shirer, William L. 1904- DLB-4

Shirley, James 1596-1666 ....DLB-58

Shockley, Ann Allen 1927- DLB-33

Shorthouse, Joseph Henry 1834-1903 ....DLB-18

Showalter, Elaine 1941- DLB-67

Shulevitz, Uri 1935- DLB-61

Shulman, Max 1919-1988 ....DLB-11

Shute, Henry A. 1856-1943 ....DLB-9

Shuttle, Penelope 1947- DLB-14, 40

Sidgwick and Jackson Limited DLB-112

Sidney, Margaret (see Lothrop, Harriet M.)

Sidney's Press DLB-49

Siegfried Loraine Sassoon: A Centenary Essay Tributes from Vivien F. Clarke and Michael Thorpe Y-86

Sierra Club Books DLB-49

Sigourney, Lydia Howard (Huntley) 1791-1865 ....DLB-1, 42, 73

Silkin, Jon 1930- DLB-27

Silliphant, Stirling 1918-	DLB-26
Sillitoe, Alan 1928-	DLB-14
Silman, Roberta 1934-	DLB-28
Silverberg, Robert 1935-	DLB-8
Silverman, Kenneth 1936-	DLB-111
Simak, Clifford D. 1904-1988	DLB-8
Simcoe, Elizabeth 1762-1850	DLB-99
Simcox, George Augustus 1841-1905	DLB-35
Sime, Jessie Georgina 1868-1958	DLB-92
Simenon, Georges 1903-1989	DLB-72; Y-89
Simic, Charles 1938-	DLB-105
Simic, Charles, Images and "Images"	DLB-105
Simmel, Johannes Mario 1924-	DLB-69
Simmons, Ernest J. 1903-1972	DLB-103
Simmons, Herbert Alfred 1930-	DLB-33
Simmons, James 1933-	DLB-40
Simms, William Gilmore 1806-1870	DLB-3, 30, 59, 73
Simms and M'Intyre	DLB-106
Simon, Claude 1913-	DLB-83
Simon, Neil 1927-	DLB-7
Simon and Schuster	DLB-46
Simons, Katherine Drayton Mayrant 1890-1969	Y-83
Simpson, Helen 1897-1940	DLB-77
Simpson, Louis 1923-	DLB-5
Simpson, N. F. 1919-	DLB-13
Sims, George 1923-	DLB-87
Sims, George R. 1847-1922	DLB-35, 70
Sinclair, Andrew 1935-	DLB-14
Sinclair, Bertrand William 1881-1972	DLB-92
Sinclair, Jo 1913-	DLB-28
Sinclair Lewis Centennial Conference	Y-85
Sinclair, Lister 1921-	DLB-88
Sinclair, May 1863-1946	DLB-36
Sinclair, Upton 1878-1968	DLB-9
Sinclair, Upton [publishing house]	DLB-46
Singer, Isaac Bashevis 1904-1991	DLB-6, 28, 52
Singmaster, Elsie 1879-1958	DLB-9
Siodmak, Curt 1902-	DLB-44
Sissman, L. E. 1928-1976	DLB-5
Sisson, C. H. 1914-	DLB-27
Sitwell, Edith 1887-1964	DLB-20
Sitwell, Osbert 1892-1969	DLB-100
Skeffington, William [publishing house]	DLB-106
Skelton, Robin 1925-	DLB-27, 53
Skinner, Constance Lindsay 1877-1939	DLB-92
Skinner, John Stuart 1788-1851	DLB-73
Skipsey, Joseph 1832-1903	DLB-35
Slade, Bernard 1930-	DLB-53
Slater, Patrick 1880-1951	DLB-68
Slavitt, David 1935-	DLB-5, 6
Sleigh, Burrows Willcocks Arthur 1821-1869	DLB-99
A Slender Thread of Hope: The Kennedy Center Black Theatre Project	DLB-38
Slesinger, Tess 1905-1945	DLB-102
Slick, Sam (see Haliburton, Thomas Chandler)	
Sloane, William, Associates	DLB-46
Small, Maynard and Company	DLB-49
Small Presses in Great Britain and Ireland, 1960-1985	DLB-40
Small Presses I: Jargon Society	Y-84
Small Presses II: The Spirit That Moves Us Press	Y-85
Small Presses III: Pushcart Press	Y-87
Smart, Christopher 1722-1771	DLB-109
Smart, Elizabeth 1913-1986	DLB-88
Smiles, Samuel 1812-1904	DLB-55
Smith, A. J. M. 1902-1980	DLB-88
Smith, Adam 1723-1790	DLB-104
Smith, Alexander 1829-1867	DLB-32, 55
Smith, Betty 1896-1972	Y-82
Smith, Carol Sturm 1938-	Y-81
Smith, Charles Henry 1826-1903	DLB-11
Smith, Charlotte 1749-1806	DLB-39, 109
Smith, Cordwainer 1913-1966	DLB-8
Smith, Dave 1942-	DLB-5
Smith, Dodie 1896-	DLB-10
Smith, Doris Buchanan 1934-	DLB-52
Smith, E. E. 1890-1965	DLB-8
Smith, Elihu Hubbard 1771-1798	DLB-37
Smith, Elizabeth Oakes (Prince) 1806-1893	DLB-1
Smith, George O. 1911-1981	DLB-8
Smith, Goldwin 1823-1910	DLB-99
Smith, H. Allen 1907-1976	DLB-11, 29
Smith, Harrison, and Robert Haas [publishing house]	DLB-46

Smith, Horatio (Horace) 1779-1849 and
    James Smith 1775-1839 .... DLB-96

Smith, Iain Chrichton 1928- DLB-40

Smith, J. Allen 1860-1924 .... DLB-47

Smith, J. Stilman, and Company DLB-49

Smith, John 1580-1631 .... DLB-24, 30

Smith, Josiah 1704-1781 .... DLB-24

Smith, Ken 1938- DLB-40

Smith, Lee 1944- Y-83

Smith, Logan Pearsall 1865-1946 .... DLB-98

Smith, Mark 1935- Y-82

Smith, Michael 1698-circa 1771 .... DLB-31

Smith, Red 1905-1982 .... DLB-29

Smith, Roswell 1829-1892 .... DLB-79

Smith, Samuel Harrison 1772-1845 .... DLB-43

Smith, Samuel Stanhope 1751-1819 .... DLB-37

Smith, Seba 1792-1868 .... DLB-1, 11

Smith, Stevie 1902-1971 .... DLB-20

Smith, Sydney 1771-1845 .... DLB-107

Smith, Sydney Goodsir 1915-1975 .... DLB-27

Smith, W. B., and Company DLB-49

Smith, W. H., and Son DLB-106

Smith, William 1727-1803 .... DLB-31

Smith, William 1728-1793 .... DLB-30

Smith, William Gardner 1927-1974 .... DLB-76

Smith, William Jay 1918- DLB-5

Smithers, Leonard [publishing house] DLB-112

Smollett, Tobias 1721-1771 .... DLB-39, 104

Snellings, Rolland (see Touré, Askia Muhammad)

Snodgrass, W. D. 1926- DLB-5

Snow, C. P. 1905-1980 .... DLB-15, 77

Snyder, Gary 1930- DLB-5, 16

Sobiloff, Hy 1912-1970 .... DLB-48

The Society for Textual Scholarship
    and TEXT Y-87

Solano, Solita 1888-1975 .... DLB-4

Sollers, Philippe 1936- DLB-83

Solomon, Carl 1928- DLB-16

Solway, David 1941- DLB-53

Solzhenitsyn and America Y-85

Sontag, Susan 1933- DLB-2, 67

Sorrentino, Gilbert 1929- DLB-5; Y-80

Sotheby, William 1757-1833 .... DLB-93

Soto, Gary 1952- DLB-82

Sources for the Study of Tudor
    and Stuart Drama DLB-62

Souster, Raymond 1921- DLB-88

Southerland, Ellease 1943- DLB-33

Southern, Terry 1924- DLB-2

Southern Writers Between the Wars DLB-9

Southerne, Thomas 1659-1746 .... DLB-80

Southey, Robert 1774-1843 .... DLB-93, 107

Spacks, Barry 1931- DLB-105

Spark, Muriel 1918- DLB-15

Sparks, Jared 1789-1866 .... DLB-1, 30

Sparshott, Francis 1926- DLB-60

Späth, Gerold 1939- DLB-75

The Spectator 1828- DLB-110

Spellman, A. B. 1935- DLB-41

Spencer, Anne 1882-1975 .... DLB-51, 54

Spencer, Elizabeth 1921- DLB-6

Spencer, Herbert 1820-1903 .... DLB-57

Spencer, Scott 1945- Y-86

Spender, J. A. 1862-1942 .... DLB-98

Spender, Stephen 1909- DLB-20

Spicer, Jack 1925-1965 .... DLB-5, 16

Spielberg, Peter 1929- Y-81

Spier, Peter 1927- DLB-61

Spinrad, Norman 1940- DLB-8

Spofford, Harriet Prescott 1835-1921 .... DLB-74

Squibob (see Derby, George Horatio)

Stafford, Jean 1915-1979 .... DLB-2

Stafford, William 1914- DLB-5

Stage Censorship: "The Rejected Statement"
    (1911), by Bernard Shaw [excerpts] DLB-10

Stallings, Laurence 1894-1968 .... DLB-7, 44

Stallworthy, Jon 1935- DLB-40

Stampp, Kenneth M. 1912- DLB-17

Stanford, Ann 1916- DLB-5

Stanton, Elizabeth Cady 1815-1902 .... DLB-79

Stanton, Frank L. 1857-1927 .... DLB-25

Stapledon, Olaf 1886-1950 .... DLB-15

Star Spangled Banner Office DLB-49

Starkweather, David 1935- DLB-7

Statements on the Art of Poetry DLB-54

Stead, Robert J. C. 1880-1959 .... DLB-92

Steadman, Mark 1930- DLB-6

The Stealthy School of Criticism (1871), by
 Dante Gabriel Rossetti DLB-35

Stearns, Harold E. 1891-1943 .... DLB-4

Stedman, Edmund Clarence 1833-1908 .... DLB-64

Steegmuller, Francis 1906- DLB-111

Steele, Max 1922- Y-80

Steele, Richard 1672-1729 .... DLB-84, 101

Steele, Wilbur Daniel 1886-1970 .... DLB-86

Steere, Richard circa 1643-1721 .... DLB-24

Stegner, Wallace 1909- DLB-9

Stehr, Hermann 1864-1940 .... DLB-66

Steig, William 1907- DLB-61

Stein, Gertrude 1874-1946 .... DLB-4, 54, 86

Stein, Leo 1872-1947 .... DLB-4

Stein and Day Publishers DLB-46

Steinbeck, John 1902-1968 .... DLB-7, 9; DS-2

Steiner, George 1929- DLB-67

Stephen Crane: A Revaluation Virginia
 Tech Conference, 1989 .... Y-89

Stephen, Leslie 1832-1904 .... DLB-57

Stephens, Alexander H. 1812-1883 .... DLB-47

Stephens, Ann 1810-1886 .... DLB-3, 73

Stephens, Charles Asbury 1844?-1931 .... DLB-42

Stephens, James 1882?-1950 .... DLB-19

Sterling, George 1869-1926 .... DLB-54

Sterling, James 1701-1763 .... DLB-24

Stern, Gerald 1925- DLB-105

Stern, Madeleine B. 1912- DLB-111

Stern, Gerald, Living in Ruin DLB-105

Stern, Richard 1928- Y-87

Stern, Stewart 1922- DLB-26

Sterne, Laurence 1713-1768 .... DLB-39

Sternheim, Carl 1878-1942 .... DLB-56

Stevens, Wallace 1879-1955 .... DLB-54

Stevenson, Anne 1933- DLB-40

Stevenson, Robert Louis 1850-1894 .... DLB-18, 57

Stewart, Donald Ogden 1894-1980 .... DLB-4, 11, 26

Stewart, Dugald 1753-1828 .... DLB-31

Stewart, George, Jr. 1848-1906 .... DLB-99

Stewart, George R. 1895-1980 .... DLB-8

Stewart and Kidd Company DLB-46

Stewart, Randall 1896-1964 .... DLB-103

Stickney, Trumbull 1874-1904 .... DLB-54

Stiles, Ezra 1727-1795 .... DLB-31

Still, James 1906- DLB-9

Stith, William 1707-1755 .... DLB-31

Stock, Elliot [publishing house] DLB-106

Stockton, Frank R. 1834-1902 .... DLB-42, 74

Stoddard, Ashbel [publishing house] DLB-49

Stoddard, Richard Henry 1825-1903 .... DLB-3, 64

Stoddard, Solomon 1643-1729 .... DLB-24

Stoker, Bram 1847-1912 .... DLB-36, 70

Stokes, Frederick A., Company DLB-49

Stokes, Thomas L. 1898-1958 .... DLB-29

Stolberg, Christian Graf zu 1748-1821 .... DLB-94

Stolberg, Friedrich Leopold Graf zu
 1750-1819 .... DLB-94

Stone, Herbert S., and Company DLB-49

Stone, Lucy 1818-1893 .... DLB-79

Stone, Melville 1848-1929 .... DLB-25

Stone, Ruth 1915- DLB-105

Stone, Samuel 1602-1663 .... DLB-24

Stone and Kimball DLB-49

Stoppard, Tom 1937- DLB-13; Y-85

Storey, Anthony 1928- DLB-14

Storey, David 1933- DLB-13, 14

Story, Thomas circa 1670-1742 .... DLB-31

Story, William Wetmore 1819-1895 .... DLB-1

Storytelling: A Contemporary Renaissance Y-84

Stoughton, William 1631-1701 .... DLB-24

Stowe, Harriet Beecher 1811-1896 .... DLB-1, 12, 42, 74

Stowe, Leland 1899- DLB-29

Strand, Mark 1934- DLB-5

Strahan and Company DLB-106

Stratemeyer, Edward 1862-1930 .... DLB-42

Stratton and Barnard DLB-49

Straub, Peter 1943- Y-84

Street, Cecil John Charles (see Rhode, John)

Street and Smith DLB-49

Streeter, Edward 1891-1976 .... DLB-11

Stribling, T. S. 1881-1965 .... DLB-9

Strickland, Samuel 1804-1867 .... DLB-99

Stringer and Townsend DLB-49

Stringer, Arthur 1874-1950 .... DLB-92

Strittmatter, Erwin 1912- DLB-69

Strother, David Hunter 1816-1888 .... DLB-3

Strouse, Jean 1945- DLB-111

Stuart, Dabney 1937- DLB-105

Stuart, Dabney, Knots into Webs:
   Some Autobiographical Sources DLB-105

Stuart, Jesse 1906-1984 ....DLB-9, 48, 102; Y-84

Stuart, Lyle [publishing house] DLB-46

Stubbs, Harry Clement (see Clement, Hal)

Studio DLB-112

The Study of Poetry (1880), by Matthew
   Arnold DLB-35

Sturgeon, Theodore 1918-1985 ....DLB-8; Y-85

Sturges, Preston 1898-1959 ....DLB-26

"Style" (1840; revised, 1859), by Thomas
   de Quincey [excerpt] DLB-57

"Style" (1888), by Walter Pater DLB-57

Style (1897), by Walter Raleigh [excerpt] DLB-57

"Style" (1877), by T. H. Wright [excerpt] DLB-57

"Le Style c'est l'homme" (1892),
   by W. H. Mallock DLB-57

Styron, William 1925- DLB-2; Y-80

Suárez, Mario 1925- DLB-82

Such, Peter 1939- DLB-60

Suckling, Sir John 1609-1642 ....DLB-58

Suckow, Ruth 1892-1960 ....DLB-9, 102

Suggs, Simon (see Hooper, Johnson Jones)

Sukenick, Ronald 1932- ....Y 81

Suknaski, Andrew 1942- DLB-53

Sullivan, Alan 1868-1947 ....DLB-92

Sullivan, C. Gardner 1886-1965 ....DLB-26

Sullivan, Frank 1892-1976 ....DLB-11

Sulte, Benjamin 1841-1923 ....DLB-99

Sulzer, Johann Georg 1720-1779 ....DLB-97

Summers, Hollis 1916- DLB-6

Sumner, Henry A. [publishing house] DLB-49

Surtees, Robert Smith 1803-1864 ....DLB-21

A Survey of Poetry
   Anthologies, 1879-1960 ....DLB-54

Surveys of the Year's Biography
   A Transit of Poets and Others: American
      Biography in 1982 ....Y-82
   The Year in Literary Biography Y-83
   The Year in Literary Biography Y-84
   The Year in Literary Biography Y-85
   The Year in Literary Biography Y-86
   The Year in Literary Biography Y-87
   The Year in Literary Biography Y-88
   The Year in Literary Biography Y-89

Surveys of the Year's Book Publishing
   The Year in Book Publishing Y-86

Surveys of the Year's Drama
   The Year in Drama Y-82
   The Year in Drama Y-83
   The Year in Drama Y-84
   The Year in Drama Y-85
   The Year in Drama Y-87
   The Year in Drama Y-88
   The Year in Drama Y-89

Surveys of the Year's Fiction
   The Year's Work in Fiction: A Survey Y-82
   The Year in Fiction: A Biased View Y-83
   The Year in Fiction Y-84
   The Year in Fiction Y-85
   The Year in Fiction Y-86
   The Year in the Novel Y-87
   The Year in Short Stories Y-87
   The Year in the Novel Y-88
   The Year in Short Stories Y-88
   The Year in Fiction Y-89

Surveys of the Year's Poetry
   The Year's Work in American Poetry Y-82
   The Year in Poetry Y-83
   The Year in Poetry Y-84
   The Year in Poetry Y-85
   The Year in Poetry Y-86
   The Year in Poetry Y-87
   The Year in Poetry Y-88
   The Year in Poetry Y-89

Sutherland, John 1919-1956 ....DLB-68

Sutro, Alfred 1863-1933 ....DLB-10

Swados, Harvey 1920-1972 ....DLB-2

Swain, Charles 1801-1874 ....DLB-32

Swallow Press DLB-46

Swan Sonnenschein Limited DLB-106

Swanberg, W. A. 1907- DLB-103

Swenson, May 1919-1989 ....DLB-5

Swerling, Jo 1897- DLB-44

Swift, Jonathan 1667-1745 ....DLB-39, 95, 101

Swinburne, A. C. 1837-1909 ....DLB-35, 57

Swinnerton, Frank 1884-1982 ....DLB-34

Swisshelm, Jane Grey 1815-1884 ....DLB-43

Swope, Herbert Bayard 1882-1958 ....DLB-25

Swords, T. and J., and Company DLB-49

Swords, Thomas 1763-1843 and
   Swords, James ?-1844 ....DLB-73

Symonds, John Addington 1840-1893 ....DLB-57

Symons, Arthur 1865-1945 ....DLB-19, 57

Symons, Julian 1912- DLB-87

Symons, Scott 1933- DLB-53

Synge, John Millington 1871-1909 ....DLB-10, 19

T

Taché, Joseph-Charles 1820-1894 ....DLB-99

Tafolla, Carmen 1951- DLB-82

Taggard, Genevieve 1894-1948 ....DLB-45

Tait, J. Selwin, and Sons DLB-49

Tait's Edinburgh Magazine 1832-1861 ....DLB-110

Talvj or Talvi (see Robinson, Therese)

Taradash, Daniel 1913- DLB-44

Tarbell, Ida M. 1857-1944 ....DLB-47

Tardivel, Jules-Paul 1851-1905 ....DLB-99

Tarkington, Booth 1869-1946 ....DLB-9, 102

Tashlin, Frank 1913-1972 ....DLB-44

Tate, Allen 1899-1979 ....DLB-4, 45, 63

Tate, James 1943- DLB-5

Tate, Nahum circa 1652-1715 ....DLB-80

Taylor, Bayard 1825-1878 ....DLB-3

Taylor, Bert Leston 1866-1921 ....DLB-25

Taylor, Charles H. 1846-1921 ....DLB-25

Taylor, Edward circa 1642-1729 ....DLB-24

Taylor, Henry 1942- DLB-5

Taylor, Sir Henry 1800-1886 ....DLB-32

Taylor, Mildred D. ?- DLB-52

Taylor, Peter 1917- Y-81

Taylor, William, and Company DLB-49

Taylor-Made Shakespeare? Or Is
  "Shall I Die?" the Long-Lost Text
  of Bottom's Dream? Y-85

Teasdale, Sara 1884-1933 ....DLB-45

The Tea-Table (1725), by Eliza Haywood
  [excerpt] DLB-39

Telles, Lygia Fagundes 1924- DLB-113

Temple, Sir William 1628-1699 ....DLB-101

Tenn, William 1919- DLB-8

Tennant, Emma 1937- DLB-14

Tenney, Tabitha Gilman 1762-1837 ....DLB-37

Tennyson, Alfred 1809-1892 ....DLB-32

Tennyson, Frederick 1807-1898 ....DLB-32

Terhune, Albert Payson 1872-1942 ....DLB-9

Terry, Megan 1932- DLB-7

Terson, Peter 1932- DLB-13

Tesich, Steve 1943- Y-83

Tey, Josephine 1896?-1952 ....DLB-77

Thacher, James 1754-1844 ....DLB-37

Thackeray, William Makepeace
  1811-1863 ....DLB-21, 55

Thames and Hudson Limited DLB-112

Thanet, Octave (see French, Alice)

The Theater in Shakespeare's Time DLB-62

The Theatre Guild DLB-7

Thelwall, John 1764-1834 ....DLB-93

Theriault, Yves 1915-1983 ....DLB-88

Thério, Adrien 1925- DLB-53

Theroux, Paul 1941- DLB-2

Thibaudeau, Colleen 1925- DLB-88

Thielen, Benedict 1903-1965 ....DLB-102

Thoma, Ludwig 1867-1921 ....DLB-66

Thoma, Richard 1902- DLB-4

Thomas, Audrey 1935- DLB-60

Thomas, D. M. 1935- DLB-40

Thomas, Dylan 1914-1953 ....DLB-13, 20

Thomas, Edward 1878-1917 ....DLB-19, 98

Thomas, Gwyn 1913-1981 ....DLB-15

Thomas, Isaiah 1750-1831 ....DLB-43, 73

Thomas, Isaiah [publishing house] DLB-49

Thomas, John 1900-1932 ....DLB-4

Thomas, Joyce Carol 1938- DLB-33

Thomas, Lorenzo 1944- DLB-41

Thomas, R. S. 1915- DLB-27

Thompson, David 1770-1857 ....DLB-99

Thompson, Dorothy 1893-1961 ....DLB-29

Thompson, Francis 1859-1907 ....DLB-19

Thompson, George Selden (see Selden, George)

Thompson, John 1938-1976 ....DLB-60

Thompson, John R. 1823-1873 ....DLB-3, 73

Thompson, Lawrance 1906-1973 ....DLB-103

Thompson, Maurice 1844-1901 ....DLB-71, 74

Thompson, Ruth Plumly 1891-1976 ....DLB-22

Thompson, Thomas Phillips 1843-1933 ....DLB-99

Thompson, William Tappan 1812-1882 ....DLB-3, 11

Thomson, Edward William
  1849-1924 ....DLB-92

Thomson, James 1700-1748 ....DLB-95

Thomson, James 1834-1882 ....DLB-35

Thomson, Mortimer 1831-1875 ....DLB-11

Thoreau, Henry David 1817-1862 ....DLB-1

Thorpe, Thomas Bangs 1815-1878 ....DLB-3, 11

Thoughts on Poetry and Its Varieties (1833),
  by John Stuart Mill DLB-32

Thrale, Hester Lynch (see Piozzi,
  Hester Lynch [Thrale])

Thümmel, Moritz August von
  1738-1817 .... DLB-97

Thurber, James 1894-1961 .... DLB-4, 11, 22, 102

Thurman, Wallace 1902-1934 .... DLB-51

Thwaite, Anthony 1930- DLB-40

Thwaites, Reuben Gold 1853-1913 .... DLB-47

Ticknor, George 1791-1871 .... DLB-1, 59

Ticknor and Fields DLB-49

Ticknor and Fields (revived) DLB-46

Tieck, Ludwig 1773-1853 .... DLB-90

Tietjens, Eunice 1884-1944 .... DLB-54

Tilt, Charles [publishing house] DLB-106

Tilton, J. E., and Company DLB-49

Time and Western Man (1927), by Wyndham
  Lewis [excerpts] DLB-36

Time-Life Books DLB-46

Times Books DLB-46

Timothy, Peter circa 1725-1782 .... DLB-43

Timrod, Henry 1828-1867 .... DLB-3

Tinsley Brothers DLB-106

Tiptree, James, Jr. 1915- DLB-8

Titus, Edward William 1870-1952 .... DLB-4

Toklas, Alice B. 1877-1967 .... DLB-4

Tolkien, J. R. R. 1892-1973 .... DLB-15

Tollet, Elizabeth 1694-1754 .... DLB-95

Tolson, Melvin B. 1898-1966 .... DLB-48, 76

Tom Jones (1749), by Henry
  Fielding [excerpt] DLB-39

Tomlinson, Charles 1927- DLB-40

Tomlinson, H. M. 1873-1958 .... DLB-36, 100

Tompkins, Abel [publishing house] DLB-49

Tompson, Benjamin 1642-1714 .... DLB-24

Tonks, Rosemary 1932- DLB-14

Toole, John Kennedy 1937-1969 .... Y-81

Toomer, Jean 1894-1967 .... DLB-45, 51

Tor Books DLB-46

Torberg, Friedrich 1908-1979 .... DLB-85

Torrence, Ridgely 1874-1950 .... DLB-54

Toth, Susan Allen 1940- Y-86

Tough-Guy Literature DLB-9

Touré, Askia Muhammad 1938- DLB-41

Tourgée, Albion W. 1838-1905 .... DLB-79

Tourneur, Cyril circa 1580-1626 .... DLB-58

Tournier, Michel 1924- DLB-83

Tousey, Frank [publishing house] DLB-49

Tower Publications DLB-46

Towne, Benjamin circa 1740-1793 .... DLB-43

Towne, Robert 1936- DLB-44

Tracy, Honor 1913- DLB-15

Traill, Catharine Parr 1802-1899 .... DLB-99

Train, Arthur 1875-1945 .... DLB-86

The Transatlantic Publishing Company DLB-49

Transcendentalists, American DS-5

Traven, B. 1882? or 1890?-1969? DLB-9, 56

Travers, Ben 1886-1980 .... DLB-10

Trelawny, Edward John 1792-1881 .... DLB-110

Tremain, Rose 1943- DLB-14

Tremblay, Michel 1942- DLB-60

Trends in Twentieth-Century
  Mass Market Publishing DLB-46

Trent, William P. 1862-1939 .... DLB-47

Trescot, William Henry 1822-1898 .... DLB-30

Trevor, William 1928- DLB-14

Trilling, Lionel 1905-1975 .... DLB-28, 63

Triolet, Elsa 1896-1970 .... DLB-72

Tripp, John 1927- DLB-40

Trocchi, Alexander 1925- DLB-15

Trollope, Anthony 1815-1882 .... DLB-21, 57

Trollope, Frances 1779-1863 .... DLB-21

Troop, Elizabeth 1931- DLB-14

Trotter, Catharine 1679-1749 .... DLB-84

Trotti, Lamar 1898-1952 .... DLB-44

Trottier, Pierre 1925- DLB-60

Troupe, Quincy Thomas, Jr. 1943- DLB-41

Trow, John F., and Company DLB-49

Truillier-Lacombe, Joseph-Patrice
  1807-1863 .... DLB-99

Trumbo, Dalton 1905-1976 .... DLB-26

Trumbull, Benjamin 1735-1820 .... DLB-30

Trumbull, John 1750-1831 .... DLB-31

T. S. Eliot Centennial Y-88

Tucholsky, Kurt 1890-1935 .... DLB-56

Tucker, George 1775-1861 .... DLB-3, 30

Tucker, Nathaniel Beverley 1784-1851 .... DLB-3

Tucker, St. George 1752-1827 .... DLB-37

Tuckerman, Henry Theodore 1813-1871 ....DLB-64
Tunis, John R. 1889-1975 ....DLB-22
Tuohy, Frank 1925- DLB-14
Tupper, Martin F. 1810-1889 ....DLB-32
Turbyfill, Mark 1896- DLB-45
Turco, Lewis 1934- Y-84
Turnbull, Andrew 1921-1970 ....DLB-103
Turnbull, Gael 1928- DLB-40
Turner, Arlin 1909-1980 ....DLB-103
Turner, Charles (Tennyson) 1808-1879 ....DLB-32
Turner, Frederick 1943- DLB-40
Turner, Frederick Jackson 1861-1932 ....DLB-17
Turner, Joseph Addison 1826-1868 ....DLB-79
Turpin, Waters Edward 1910-1968 ....DLB-51
Twain, Mark (see Clemens, Samuel Langhorne)
The 'Twenties and Berlin,
    by Alex Natan DLB-66
Tyler, Anne 1941- DLB-6; Y-82
Tyler, Moses Coit 1835-1900 ....DLB-47, 64
Tyler, Royall 1757-1826 ....DLB-37
Tylor, Edward Burnett 1832-1917 ....DLB-57

U

Udall, Nicholas 1504-1556 ....DLB-62
Uhland, Ludwig 1787-1862 ....DLB-90
Uhse, Bodo 1904-1963 ....DLB-69
Ulibarrí, Sabine R. 1919- DLB-82
Ulica, Jorge 1870-1926 ....DLB-82
Unamuno, Miguel de 1864-1936 ....DLB-108
Under the Microscope (1872), by A. C.
    Swinburne DLB-35
Unger, Friederike Helene 1741-1813 ....DLB-94
United States Book Company DLB-49
Universal Publishing and Distributing
    Corporation DLB-46
The University of Iowa Writers'
    Workshop Golden Jubilee Y-86
University of Wales Press DLB-112
"The Unknown Public" (1858), by
    Wilkie Collins [excerpt] DLB-57
Unruh, Fritz von 1885-1970 ....DLB-56
Unwin, T. Fisher [publishing house] DLB-106
Upchurch, Boyd B. (see Boyd, John)
Updike, John 1932- DLB-2, 5; Y-80, 82; DS-3

Upton, Charles 1948- DLB-16
Upward, Allen 1863-1926 ....DLB-36
Urista, Alberto Baltazar (see Alurista)
Urzidil, Johannes 1896-1976 ....DLB-85
The Uses of Facsimile Y-90
Uslar Pietri, Arturo 1906- DLB-113
Ustinov, Peter 1921- DLB-13
Uz, Johann Peter 1720-1796 ....DLB-97

V

Vac, Bertrand 1914- DLB-88
Vail, Laurence 1891-1968 ....DLB-4
Vailland, Roger 1907-1965 ....DLB-83
Vajda, Ernest 1887-1954 ....DLB-44
Valente, José Angel 1929- DLB-108
Valenzuela, Luisa 1938- DLB-113
Valgardson, W. D. 1939- DLB-60
Valverde, José María 1926- DLB-108
Van Allsburg, Chris 1949- DLB-61
Van Anda, Carr 1864-1945 ....DLB-25
Vanbrugh, Sir John 1664-1726 ....DLB-80
Vance, Jack 1916?- DLB-8
Van Doren, Mark 1894-1972 ....DLB-45
van Druten, John 1901-1957 ....DLB-10
Van Duyn, Mona 1921- DLB-5
Van Dyke, Henry 1852-1933 ....DLB-71
Van Dyke, Henry 1928- DLB-33
Vane, Sutton 1888-1963 ....DLB-10
Vanguard Press DLB-46
van Itallie, Jean-Claude 1936- DLB-7
Vann, Robert L. 1879-1940 ....DLB-29
Van Rensselaer, Mariana Griswold
    1851-1934 ....DLB-47
Van Rensselaer, Mrs. Schuyler (see Van
    Rensselaer, Mariana Griswold)
Van Vechten, Carl 1880-1964 ....DLB-4, 9
van Vogt, A. E. 1912- DLB-8
Varley, John 1947- Y-81
Varnhagen von Ense, Karl August
    1785-1858 ....DLB-90
Varnhagen von Ense, Rahel
    1771-1833 ....DLB-90
Vassa, Gustavus (see Equiano, Olaudah)

Cumulative Index

Vega, Janine Pommy 1942- DLB-16
Veiller, Anthony 1903-1965 ....DLB-44
Venegas, Daniel ?-? DLB-82
Verplanck, Gulian C. 1786-1870 ....DLB-59
Very, Jones 1813-1880 ....DLB-1
Vian, Boris 1920-1959 ....DLB-72
Vickers, Roy 1888?-1965 ....DLB-77
Victoria 1819-1901...DLB-55
Victoria Press..DLB-106
Vidal, Gore 1925- DLB-6
Viebig, Clara 1860-1952 ....DLB-66
Viereck, George Sylvester 1884-1962 ....DLB-54
Viereck, Peter 1916- DLB-5
Viets, Roger 1738-1811 ....DLB-99
Viewpoint: Politics and Performance, by David
    Edgar..DLB-13
Vigneault, Gilles 1928- DLB-60
The Viking Press..DLB-46
Villanueva, Tino 1941- DLB-82
Villard, Henry 1835-1900 ....DLB-23
Villard, Oswald Garrison 1872-1949 ....DLB-25, 91
Villarreal, José Antonio 1924- DLB-82
Villemaire, Yolande 1949- DLB-60
Villiers, George, Second Duke
    of Buckingham 1628-1687 ....DLB-80
Vine Press...DLB-112
Viorst, Judith ?- DLB-52
Vivanco, Luis Felipe 1907-1975 ....DLB-108
Vizetelly and Company..DLB-106
Voaden, Herman 1903- DLB-88
Volkoff, Vladimir 1932- DLB-83
Volland, P. F., Company..DLB-46
von der Grün, Max 1926- DLB-75
Vonnegut, Kurt 1922- DLB-2, 8; Y-80; DS-3
Voß, Johann Heinrich 1751-1826 ....DLB-90
Vroman, Mary Elizabeth circa 1924-1967 ....DLB-33

W

Wackenroder, Wilhelm Heinrich
    1773-1798..DLB-90
Waddington, Miriam 1917- DLB-68
Wade, Henry 1887-1969..DLB-77
Wagenknecht, Edward 1900- DLB-103

Wagner, Heinrich Leopold 1747-1779 ....DLB-94
Wagoner, David 1926- DLB-5
Wah, Fred 1939- DLB-60
Waiblinger, Wilhelm 1804-1830............................DLB-90
Wain, John 1925- DLB-15, 27
Wainwright, Jeffrey 1944- DLB-40
Waite, Peirce and Company..................................DLB-49
Wakoski, Diane 1937- DLB-5
Walck, Henry Z..DLB-46
Walcott, Derek 1930- Y-81
Waldman, Anne 1945- DLB-16
Walker, Alice 1944- DLB-6, 33
Walker, George F. 1947- DLB-60
Walker, Joseph A. 1935- DLB-38
Walker, Margaret 1915- DLB-76
Walker, Ted 1934- DLB-40
Walker and Company DLB-49
Walker, Evans and Cogswell Company................DLB-49
Walker, John Brisben 1847-1931...........................DLB-79
Wallace, Edgar 1875-1932.....................................DLB-70
Wallant, Edward Lewis 1926-1962...................DLB-2, 28
Walpole, Horace 1717-1797 ....DLB-39, 104
Walpole, Hugh 1884-1941 ....DLB-34
Walrond, Eric 1898-1966.......................................DLB-51
Walser, Martin 1927- DLB-75
Walser, Robert 1878-1956 ....DLB-66
Walsh, Ernest 1895-1926 ....DLB-4, 45
Walsh, Robert 1784-1859 ....DLB-59
Wambaugh, Joseph 1937- DLB-6; Y-83
Warburton, William 1698-1779............................DLB-104
Ward, Aileen 1919- DLB-111
Ward, Artemus (see Browne, Charles Farrar)
Ward, Arthur Henry Sarsfield
    (see Rohmer, Sax)
Ward, Douglas Turner 1930- DLB-7, 38
Ward, Lynd 1905-1985...DLB-22
Ward, Lock and Company DLB-106
Ward, Mrs. Humphry 1851-1920..........................DLB-18
Ward, Nathaniel circa 1578-1652..........................DLB-24
Ward, Theodore 1902-1983 ....DLB-76
Wardle, Ralph 1909-1988....................................DLB-103
Ware, William 1797-1852 ....DLB-1
Warne, Frederick, and Company [U.S.] DLB-49
Warne, Frederick, and Company [U.K.]..............DLB-106

Warner, Charles Dudley 1829-1900	DLB-64
Warner, Rex 1905-	DLB-15
Warner, Susan Bogert 1819-1885	DLB-3, 42
Warner, Sylvia Townsend 1893-1978	DLB-34
Warner Books	DLB-46
Warr, Bertram 1917-1943	DLB-88
Warren, John Byrne Leicester (see De Tabley, Lord)	
Warren, Lella 1899-1982	Y-83
Warren, Mercy Otis 1728-1814	DLB-31
Warren, Robert Penn 1905-1989	DLB-2, 48; Y-80, 89
Warton, Joseph 1722-1800	DLB-104, 109
Warton, Thomas 1728-1790	DLB-104, 109
Washington, George 1732-1799	DLB-31
Wassermann, Jakob 1873-1934	DLB-66
Wasson, David Atwood 1823-1887	DLB-1
Waterhouse, Keith 1929-	DLB-13, 15
Waterman, Andrew 1940-	DLB-40
Waters, Frank 1902-	Y-86
Watkins, Tobias 1780-1855	DLB-73
Watkins, Vernon 1906-1967	DLB-20
Watmough, David 1926-	DLB-53
Watson, James Wreford (see Wreford, James)	
Watson, Sheila 1909-	DLB-60
Watson, Wilfred 1911-	DLB-60
Watt, W. J., and Company	DLB-46
Watterson, Henry 1840-1921	DLB-25
Watts, Alan 1915-1973	DLB-16
Watts, Franklin [publishing house]	DLB-46
Watts, Isaac 1674-1748	DLB-95
Waugh, Auberon 1939-	DLB-14
Waugh, Evelyn 1903-1966	DLB-15
Way and Williams	DLB-49
Wayman, Tom 1945-	DLB-53
Weatherly, Tom 1942-	DLB-41
Weaver, Robert 1921-	DLB-88
Webb, Frank J. ?-?	DLB-50
Webb, James Watson 1802-1884	DLB-43
Webb, Mary 1881-1927	DLB-34
Webb, Phyllis 1927-	DLB-53
Webb, Walter Prescott 1888-1963	DLB-17
Webster, Augusta 1837-1894	DLB-35
Webster, Charles L., and Company	DLB-49
Webster, John 1579 or 1580-1634?	DLB-58
Webster, Noah 1758-1843	DLB-1, 37, 42, 43, 73
Weems, Mason Locke 1759-1825	DLB-30, 37, 42
Weidenfeld and Nicolson	DLB-112
Weidman, Jerome 1913-	DLB-28
Weinbaum, Stanley Grauman 1902-1935	DLB-8
Weintraub, Stanley 1929-	DLB-111
Weisenborn, Günther 1902-1969	DLB-69
Weiß, Ernst 1882-1940	DLB-81
Weiss, John 1818-1879	DLB-1
Weiss, Peter 1916-1982	DLB-69
Weiss, Theodore 1916-	DLB-5
Weisse, Christian Felix 1726-1804	DLB-97
Welch, Lew 1926-1971?	DLB-16
Weldon, Fay 1931-	DLB-14
Wellek, René 1903-	DLB-63
Wells, Carolyn 1862-1942	DLB-11
Wells, Charles Jeremiah circa 1800-1879	DLB-32
Wells, H. G. 1866-1946	DLB-34, 70
Wells, Robert 1947-	DLB-40
Wells-Barnett, Ida B. 1862-1931	DLB-23
Welty, Eudora 1909-	DLB-2, 102; Y-87
Wendell, Barrett 1855-1921	DLB-71
Wentworth, Patricia 1878-1961	DLB-77
Werfel, Franz 1890-1945	DLB-81
The Werner Company	DLB-49
Werner, Zacharias 1768-1823	DLB-94
Wersba, Barbara 1932-	DLB-52
Wescott, Glenway 1901-	DLB-4, 9, 102
Wesker, Arnold 1932-	DLB-13
Wesley, Charles 1707-1788	DLB-95
Wesley, John 1703-1791	DLB-104
Wesley, Richard 1945-	DLB-38
Wessels, A., and Company	DLB-46
West, Anthony 1914-1988	DLB-15
West, Dorothy 1907-	DLB-76
West, Jessamyn 1902-1984	DLB-6; Y-84
West, Mae 1892-1980	DLB-44
West, Nathanael 1903-1940	DLB-4, 9, 28
West, Paul 1930-	DLB-14
West, Rebecca 1892-1983	DLB-36; Y-83
West and Johnson	DLB-49
Western Publishing Company	DLB-46
The Westminster Review 1824-1914	DLB-110

Wetherald, Agnes Ethelwyn 1857-1940	DLB-99
Wetherell, Elizabeth (see Warner, Susan Bogert)	
Wetzel, Friedrich Gottlob 1779-1819	DLB-90
Wezel, Johann Karl 1747-1819	DLB-94
Whalen, Philip 1923-	DLB-16
Whalley, George 1915-1983	DLB-88
Wharton, Edith 1862-1937	DLB-4, 9, 12, 78
Wharton, William 1920s?-	Y-80
What's Really Wrong With Bestseller Lists	Y-84
Wheatley, Dennis Yates 1897-1977	DLB-77
Wheatley, Phillis circa 1754-1784	DLB-31, 50
Wheeler, Charles Stearns 1816-1843	DLB-1
Wheeler, Monroe 1900-1988	DLB-4
Wheelock, John Hall 1886-1978	DLB-45
Wheelwright, John circa 1592-1679	DLB-24
Wheelwright, J. B. 1897-1940	DLB-45
Whetstone, Colonel Pete (see Noland, C. F. M.)	
Whicher, Stephen E. 1915-1961	DLB-111
Whipple, Edwin Percy 1819-1886	DLB-1, 64
Whitaker, Alexander 1585-1617	DLB-24
Whitaker, Daniel K. 1801-1881	DLB-73
Whitcher, Frances Miriam 1814-1852	DLB-11
White, Andrew 1579-1656	DLB-24
White, Andrew Dickson 1832-1918	DLB-47
White, E. B. 1899-1985	DLB-11, 22
White, Edgar B. 1947-	DLB-38
White, Ethel Lina 1887-1944	DLB-77
White, Henry Kirke 1785-1806	DLB-96
White, Horace 1834-1916	DLB-23
White, Phyllis Dorothy James (see James, P. D.)	
White, Richard Grant 1821-1885	DLB-64
White, Walter 1893-1955	DLB-51
White, William, and Company	DLB-49
White, William Allen 1868-1944	DLB-9, 25
White, William Anthony Parker (see Boucher, Anthony)	
White, William Hale (see Rutherford, Mark)	
Whitechurch, Victor L. 1868-1933	DLB-70
Whitehead, Alfred North 1861-1947	DLB-100
Whitehead, James 1936-	Y-81
Whitehead, William 1715-1785	DLB-84, 109
Whitfield, James Monroe 1822-1871	DLB-50
Whiting, John 1917-1963	DLB-13
Whiting, Samuel 1597-1679	DLB-24
Whitlock, Brand 1869-1934	DLB-12
Whitman, Albert, and Company	DLB-46
Whitman, Albery Allson 1851-1901	DLB-50
Whitman, Sarah Helen (Power) 1803-1878	DLB-1
Whitman, Walt 1819-1892	DLB-3, 64
Whitman Publishing Company	DLB-46
Whittemore, Reed 1919-	DLB-5
Whittier, John Greenleaf 1807-1892	DLB-1
Whittlesey House	DLB-46
Wideman, John Edgar 1941-	DLB-33
Wiebe, Rudy 1934-	DLB-60
Wiechert, Ernst 1887-1950	DLB-56
Wied, Martina 1882-1957	DLB-85
Wieland, Christoph Martin 1733-1813	DLB-97
Wieners, John 1934-	DLB-16
Wier, Ester 1910-	DLB-52
Wiesel, Elie 1928-	DLB-83; Y-87
Wiggin, Kate Douglas 1856-1923	DLB-42
Wigglesworth, Michael 1631-1705	DLB-24
Wilbur, Richard 1921-	DLB-5
Wild, Peter 1940-	DLB-5
Wilde, Oscar 1854-1900	DLB-10, 19, 34, 57
Wilde, Richard Henry 1789-1847	DLB-3, 59
Wilde, W. A., Company	DLB-49
Wilder, Billy 1906-	DLB-26
Wilder, Laura Ingalls 1867-1957	DLB-22
Wilder, Thornton 1897-1975	DLB-4, 7, 9
Wiley, Bell Irvin 1906-1980	DLB-17
Wiley, John, and Sons	DLB-49
Wilhelm, Kate 1928-	DLB-8
Wilkes, George 1817-1885	DLB-79
Wilkinson, Anne 1910-1961	DLB-88
Wilkinson, Sylvia 1940-	Y-86
Wilkinson, William Cleaver 1833-1920	DLB-71
Willard, L. [publishing house]	DLB-49
Willard, Nancy 1936-	DLB-5, 52
Willard, Samuel 1640-1707	DLB-24
Williams, A., and Company	DLB-49
Williams, Ben Ames 1889-1953	DLB-102
Williams, C. K. 1936-	DLB-5
Williams, Chancellor 1905-	DLB-76
Williams, Charles 1886-1945	DLB-100

Williams, Emlyn 1905-	DLB-10, 77
Williams, Garth 1912-	DLB-22
Williams, George Washington 1849-1891	DLB-47
Williams, Heathcote 1941-	DLB-13
Williams, Hugo 1942-	DLB-40
Williams, Isaac 1802-1865	DLB-32
Williams, Joan 1928-	DLB-6
Williams, John A. 1925-	DLB-2, 33
Williams, John E. 1922-	DLB-6
Williams, Jonathan 1929-	DLB-5
Williams, Miller 1930-	DLB-105
Williams, Raymond 1921-	DLB-14
Williams, Roger circa 1603-1683	DLB-24
Williams, Samm-Art 1946-	DLB-38
Williams, Sherley Anne 1944-	DLB-41
Williams, T. Harry 1909-1979	DLB-17
Williams, Tennessee 1911-1983	DLB-7; Y-83; DS-4
Williams, Valentine 1883-1946	DLB-77
Williams, William Appleman 1921-	DLB-17
Williams, William Carlos 1883-1963	DLB-4, 16, 54, 86
Williams, Wirt 1921-	DLB-6
Williams Brothers	DLB-49
Williamson, Jack 1908-	DLB-8
Willingham, Calder Baynard, Jr. 1922-	DLB-2, 44
Willis, Nathaniel Parker 1806-1867	DLB-3, 59, 73, 74
Wilmer, Clive 1945-	DLB-40
Wilson, A. N. 1950-	DLB-14
Wilson, Angus 1913-	DLB-15
Wilson, Arthur 1595-1652	DLB-58
Wilson, Augusta Jane Evans 1835-1909	DLB-42
Wilson, Colin 1931-	DLB-14
Wilson, Edmund 1895-1972	DLB-63
Wilson, Ethel 1888-1980	DLB-68
Wilson, Harriet E. Adams 1828?-1863?	DLB-50
Wilson, Harry Leon 1867-1939	DLB-9
Wilson, John 1588-1667	DLB-24
Wilson, John 1785-1854	DLB-110
Wilson, Lanford 1937-	DLB-7
Wilson, Margaret 1882-1973	DLB-9
Wilson, Michael 1914-1978	DLB-44
Wilson, Woodrow 1856-1924	DLB-47
Wimsatt, William K., Jr. 1907-1975	DLB-63
Winchell, Walter 1897-1972	DLB-29
Winchester, J. [publishing house]	DLB-49
Winckelmann, Johann Joachim 1717-1768	DLB-97
Windham, Donald 1920-	DLB-6
Wingate, Allan [publishing house]	DLB-112
Winsor, Justin 1831-1897	DLB-47
John C. Winston Company	DLB-49
Winters, Yvor 1900-1968	DLB-48
Winthrop, John 1588-1649	DLB-24, 30
Winthrop, John, Jr. 1606-1676	DLB-24
Wirt, William 1772-1834	DLB-37
Wise, John 1652-1725	DLB-24
Wiseman, Adele 1928-	DLB-88
Wishart and Company	DLB-112
Wisner, George 1812-1849	DLB-43
Wister, Owen 1860-1938	DLB-9, 78
Witherspoon, John 1723-1794	DLB-31
Withrow, William Henry 1839-1908	DLB-99
Wittig, Monique 1935-	DLB-83
Wodehouse, P. G. 1881-1975	DLB-34
Wohmann, Gabriele 1932-	DLB-75
Woiwode, Larry 1941-	DLB-6
Wolcot, John 1738-1819	DLB-109
Wolcott, Roger 1679-1767	DLB-24
Wolf, Christa 1929-	DLB-75
Wolfe, Gene 1931-	DLB-8
Wolfe, Thomas 1900-1938	DLB-9, 102; Y-85; DS-2
Wollstonecraft, Mary 1759-1797	DLB-39, 104
Wondratschek, Wolf 1943-	DLB-75
Wood, Benjamin 1820-1900	DLB-23
Wood, Charles 1932-	DLB-13
Wood, Mrs. Henry 1814-1887	DLB-18
Wood, Joanna E. 1867-1927	DLB-92
Wood, Samuel [publishing house]	DLB-49
Wood, William ?-?	DLB-24
Woodberry, George Edward 1855-1930	DLB-71, 103
Woodbridge, Benjamin 1622-1684	DLB-24
Woodcock, George 1912-	DLB-88
Woodhull, Victoria C. 1838-1927	DLB-79
Woodmason, Charles circa 1720-?	DLB-31
Woodress, Jr., James Leslie 1916-	DLB-111
Woodson, Carter G. 1875-1950	DLB-17
Woodward, C. Vann 1908-	DLB-17
Woolf, David (see Maddow, Ben)	

Woolf, Leonard 1880-1969 .... DLB-100

Woolf, Virginia 1882-1941 .... DLB-36, 100

Woollcott, Alexander 1887-1943 .... DLB-29

Woolman, John 1720-1772 .... DLB-31

Woolner, Thomas 1825-1892 .... DLB-35

Woolsey, Sarah Chauncy 1835-1905 .... DLB-42

Woolson, Constance Fenimore 1840-1894 .... DLB-12, 74

Worcester, Joseph Emerson 1784-1865 .... DLB-1

Wordsworth, Dorothy 1771-1855 .... DLB-107

Wordsworth, Elizabeth 1840-1932 .... DLB-98

Wordsworth, William 1770-1850 .... DLB-93, 107

The Works of the Rev. John Witherspoon
  (1800-1801) [excerpts] DLB-31

A World Chronology of Important Science
  Fiction Works (1818-1979) DLB-8

World Publishing Company DLB-46

Worthington, R., and Company DLB-49

Wouk, Herman 1915- Y-82

Wreford, James 1915- DLB-88

Wright, Charles 1935- Y-82

Wright, Charles Stevenson 1932- DLB-33

Wright, Frances 1795-1852 .... DLB-73

Wright, Harold Bell 1872-1944 .... DLB-9

Wright, James 1927-1980 .... DLB-5

Wright, Jay 1935- DLB-41

Wright, Louis B. 1899-1984 .... DLB-17

Wright, Richard 1908-1960 .... DLB-76, 102; DS-2

Wright, Richard B. 1937- DLB-53

Wright, Sarah Elizabeth 1928- DLB-33

Writers and Politics: 1871-1918,
  by Ronald Gray DLB-66

Writers' Forum Y-85

Writing for the Theatre, by Harold Pinter DLB-13

Wycherley, William 1641-1715 .... DLB-80

Wylie, Elinor 1885-1928 .... DLB-9, 45

Wylie, Philip 1902-1971 .... DLB-9

Y

Yates, Dornford 1885-1960 .... DLB-77

Yates, J. Michael 1938- DLB-60

Yates, Richard 1926- DLB-2; Y-81

Yearsley, Ann 1753-1806 .... DLB-109

Yeats, William Butler 1865-1939 .... DLB-10, 19, 98

Yep, Laurence 1948- DLB-52

Yerby, Frank 1916- DLB-76

Yezierska, Anzia 1885-1970 .... DLB-28

Yolen, Jane 1939- DLB-52

Yonge, Charlotte Mary 1823-1901 .... DLB-18

A Yorkshire Tragedy DLB-58

Yoseloff, Thomas [publishing house] DLB-46

Young, Al 1939- DLB-33

Young, Edward 1683-1765 .... DLB-95

Young, Stark 1881-1963 .... DLB-9, 102

Young, Waldeman 1880-1938 .... DLB-26

Young, William [publishing house] DLB-49

Yourcenar, Marguerite 1903-1987 .... DLB-72; Y-88

"You've Never Had It So Good," Gusted by
  "Winds of Change": British Fiction in the
  1950s, 1960s, and After DLB-14

Z

Zachariä, Friedrich Wilhelm 1726-1777 .... DLB-97

Zamora, Bernice 1938- DLB-82

Zand, Herbert 1923-1970 .... DLB-85

Zangwill, Israel 1864-1926 .... DLB-10

Zapata Olivella, Manuel 1920- DLB-113

Zebra Books DLB-46

Zebrowski, George 1945- DLB-8

Zech, Paul 1881-1946 .... DLB-56

Zelazny, Roger 1937- DLB-8

Zenger, John Peter 1697-1746 .... DLB-24, 43

Zieber, G. B., and Company DLB-49

Zieroth, Dale 1946- DLB-60

Zimmer, Paul 1934- DLB-5

Zindel, Paul 1936- DLB-7, 52

Zolotow, Charlotte 1915- DLB-52

Zschokke, Heinrich 1771-1848 .... DLB-94

Zubly, John Joachim 1724-1781 .... DLB-31

Zu-Bolton II, Ahmos 1936- DLB-41

Zuckmayer, Carl 1896-1977 .... DLB-56

Zukofsky, Louis 1904-1978 .... DLB-5

zur Mühlen, Hermynia 1883-1951 .... DLB-56

Zweig, Arnold 1887-1968 .... DLB-66

Zweig, Stefan 1881-1942 .... DLB-81